Lecture Notes in Computer Science 4663

Commenced Publication in 1973
Founding and Former Series Editors:
Gerhard Goos, Juris Hartmanis, and Jan van Leeuwen

Cécilia Baranauskas
Philippe Palanque   Julio Abascal
Simone Diniz Junqueira Barbosa (Eds.)

Human-Computer Interaction – INTERACT 2007

11th IFIP TC 13 International Conference
Rio de Janeiro, Brazil, September 10-14, 2007
Proceedings, Part II

 Springer

Volume Editors

Cécilia Baranauskas
UNICAMP, State University of Campinas, SP, Brazil
E-mail: cecilia@ic.unicamp.br

Philippe Palanque
LIIHS – IRIT, Université Paul Sabatier
31062 Toulouse, France
E-mail: palanque@irit.fr

Julio Abascal
University of the Basque Country
Laboratory of Human Computer
20018 Donostia, Spain
E-mail: julio@si.ehu.es

Simone Diniz Junqueira Barbosa
PUC-Rio, Departamento de Informática
22453-900 Rio de Janeiro, RJ, Brazil
E-mail: simone@inf.puc-rio.br

Library of Congress Control Number: 2007934538

CR Subject Classification (1998): H.5.2, H.5.3, H.3-5, I.2.10, D.2, K.3, K.4, K.8

LNCS Sublibrary: SL 3 – Information Systems and Application, incl. Internet/Web
and HCI

ISSN   0302-9743
ISBN-10   3-540-74799-0 Springer Berlin Heidelberg New York
ISBN-13   978-3-540-74799-4 Springer Berlin Heidelberg New York

Springer is a part of Springer Science+Business Media

springer.com

©IFIP International Federation for Information Processing 2007
Printed in Germany

Typesetting: Camera-ready by author, data conversion by Scientific Publishing Services, Chennai, India
Printed on acid-free paper   SPIN: 12119202   06/3180   5 4 3 2 1 0

Foreword

INTERACT 2007 was the 11th of a series of INTERACT international conferences supported by the IFIP Technical Committee 13 on Huma – Computer Interaction. This year, INTERACT was held in Rio de Janeiro (Brazil), organized by the Informatics Department at the Pontifcia Universidade Catlica do Rio de Janeiro, with the support of PETROBRAS, CGI.BR (Comit Gestor da Internet no Brasil), and Microsoft.

Like its predecessors, INTERACT 2007 highlighted, to both the academic and industrial world, the importance of the human – computer interaction (HCI) area and its most recent breakthroughs on current applications. Both experienced HCI researchers and professionals, as well as newcomers to the HCI field, interested in designing or evaluating interactive software, developing new interaction technologies, or investigating overarching theories of HCI, found in INTERACT 2007 a great forum to communicate with people with similar interests, to encourage collaboration, and to learn.

INTERACT 2007 had "socially responsible interaction as its special theme. Human beings have evolved for many millennia; during most of that time, our major social contacts were within small, tightly knit groups who shared a common language culture and physical context. In the last historical eyeblink, we rather suddenly find ourselves part of a global community. We have very different cultures, languages, perspectives, and physical contexts. Moreover, as a species, we face the possibility of bringing about our own extinction if we cannot solve some exceedingly challenging problems. Our individual brainpower has not increased significantly in the last 100,000 years. Computing and communication technologies offer some potential, however, to increase greatly our collective intelligence and creativity. With the proper attention to both the human and technological aspects of HCI, we have the possibility to make a crucial difference in a variety of issues. For example, it is now possible as never before to design technology to support universal usability and accessibility. We desperately need new thinking for our political, social, economic, and ecological problems. We can now build tools to support creativity, discovery, and innovation. Recently, we have begun to understand more about how to use technology to help integrate how we work as a team or in groups and communities. Medical informatics and personal medical devices offer new opportunities to reduce skyrocketing health care costs in the developed world and offer new hope to eradicate disease in developing countries.

Being the first edition in Latin America, INTERACT 2007 served as a window to new purposes, focuses, and cultural approaches. If one of the main aims of the International Federation for Information Processing is to balance the development of computer technology internationally and to assist in the sharing of the knowledge in this area among all the countries, then the HCI field is of vital importance so to facilitate the access to technology by all kinds of users. We hope that INTERACT 2007 will be remembered as a milestone in the progress towards a world able to share and balance the benefits of computer technologies.

Septemper 2007   Simone D.J. Barbosa
                                                              Julio Abascal

IFIP TC13

Established in 1989, the International Federation for Information Processing Technical Committee on Human – Computer Interaction (IFIP TC13) is an international committee of 29-member national societies and 5 working groups, representing specialists in human factors, ergonomics, cognitive science, computer science, design and related disciplines. INTERACT is its flagship conference, staged biennially in different countries.

IFIP TC13 aims to develop the science and technology of human – computer interaction (HCI) by encouraging empirical research, promoting the use of knowledge and methods from the human sciences in design and evaluation of computer systems; promoting better understanding of the relation between formal design methods and system usability and acceptability; developing guidelines, models and methods by which designers may provide better human-oriented computer systems; and, cooperating with other groups, inside and outside IFIP, to promote user-orientation and humanization in system design. Thus, TC13 seeks to improve interactions between people and computers, encourage the growth of HCI research and disseminate these benefits world-wide.

The main orientation is towards users, especially non-computer professional users, and how to improve human – computer relations. Areas of study include: the problems people have with computers; the impact on people in individual and organizational contexts; the determinants of utility, usability and acceptability; the appropriate allocation of tasks between computers and users; modeling the user to aid better system design; and harmonizing the computer to user characteristics and needs.

While the scope is thus set wide, with a tendency towards general principles rather than particular systems, it is recognized that progress will only be achieved through both general studies to advance theoretical understanding and specific studies on practical issues (e.g., interface design standards, software system consistency, documentation, appropriateness of alternative communication media, human factor guidelines for dialogue design, the problems of integrating multimedia systems to match system needs and organizational practices, etc.).

IFIP TC13 stimulates working events and activities through its working groups (WGs). WGs consist of HCI experts from many countries, who seek to expand knowledge and find solutions to HCI issues and concerns within their domains, as outlined below.

In 1999, TC13 initiated a special IFIP Award, the Brian Shackel Award, for the most outstanding contribution in the form of a refereed paper submitted to and delivered at each INTERACT event. The award draws attention to the need for a comprehensive human-centred approach in the design and use of information technology in which the human and social implications have been taken into account. Since the process to decide the award takes place after papers are submitted for publication, the award is not identified in the proceedings.

WG13.1 (Education in HCI and HCI Curricula) aims to improve HCI education at all levels of higher education, coordinate and unite efforts to develop HCI curricula and promote HCI teaching.

WG13.2 (Methodology for User-Centred System Design) aims to foster research, dissemination of information and good practice in the methodical application of HCI to software engineering.

WG13.3 (HCI and Disability) aims to make HCI designers aware of the needs of people with disabilities and encourage development of information systems and tools permitting adaptation of interfaces to specific users.

WG13.4 (also WG2.7) (User Interface Engineering) investigates the nature, concepts and construction of user interfaces for software systems, using a framework for reasoning about interactive systems and an engineering model for developing user interfaces.

WG13.5 (Human Error, Safety and System Development) seeks a framework for studying human factors relating to systems failure, develops leading-edge techniques in hazard analysis and safety engineering of computer-based systems, and guides international accreditation activities for safety-critical systems.

WG13.6 (Human-Work Interaction Design) aims at establishing relationships between extensive empirical work-domain studies and HCI design. It will promote the use of knowledge, concepts, methods and techniques that enables user studies to procure a better apprehension of the complex interplay between individual, social and organizational contexts and thereby a better understanding of how and why people work in the ways that they do.

New Working Groups are formed as areas of significance to HCI arise. Further information is available at the IFIP TC13 Web site: http://www.ifip-hci.org/

IFIP TC13 Members

Australia
Judy Hammond
Australian Computer Society

Austria
Horst Hörtner
Austrian Computer Society

Belgium
Monique Noirhomme-Fraiture
Federation des Associations Informatiques de Belgique

Brazil
Cecilia Baranauskas
Brazilian Computer Society (SBC)

Canada
Gitte Lindgaard (Secretary)
Canadian Information Processing Society

China
Zhenquing Zong
Chinese Computer Society

Czech Republic
Vaclav Matousek
Czech Society for Cybernetics and Informatics

Denmark
Annelise Mark Pejtersen (Chair)
Danish Federation for Information Processing

Finland
Kari-Jouko Räihä
Finnish Information Processing Association

France
Philippe Palanque
Association Francaise des Sciences et Technologies de l'Information et des Systemes (AFCET)

Germany
Horst Oberquelle
Gesellschaft fur Informatik

Greece
John Darzentas
Greek Computer Society

India
Anirudha Joshi
Computer Society of India

Ireland
Liam J. Bannon
Irish Computer Society

Italy
Fabio Paternò
Associazione Italiana per l'Informatica ed il Calcolo Automatico

Japan
Masaaki Kurosu
Information Processing Society of Japan

Netherlands
Gerrit C. van der Veer
Nederlands Genootschap voor Informatica

New Zealand
Mark Apperley
*New Zealand Computer Society
(NZCS)*

Nigeria
Chris C. Nwannenna
Nigeria Computer Society

Norway
Svein A. Arnesen
Norwegian Computer Society

Poland
J.L. Kulikowski
Poland Academy of Sciences

Portugal
Joaquim A. Jorge
Associacao Portuguesa de Informatica

Singapore
Kee Yong Lim
Singabore Computer Society

South Africa
Janet L. Wesson (Vice chair)
The Computer Society of South Africa

Spain
Julio Abascal
*Federacion Espanola de Sociedades de
Informatica*

Sweden
Lars Oestreicher
*Swedish Federation for Information
Processing*

Switzerland
Ute Klotz
*Swiss Federation for Information
Processing*

UK
Phil Gray
British Computer Society

USA
John Karat
Federation on Computing US (FoCUS)
Nahum Gershon
IEEE

Working Group Chairpersons

WG13.1 (Education in HCI and HCI Curricula)
Paula Kotzé, *South Africa*
WG13.2 (Methodology for User-Centered System Design)
Peter Forbrig, *Germany*
WG13.3 (HCI and Disability)
Monique Noirhomme-Fraiture, *Belgium*
WG13.4 (also 2.7) (User Interface Engineering)
Nick Graham - *Queens University, Canada*
WG13.5 (Human Error, Safety, and System Development)
Philippe Palanque, *France*
WG13.6 (Human-Work Interaction Design)
Annelise Mark Pejtersen, *Denmark*

INTERACT 2007 Technical Committee

Conference Committee

General Co-chairs

Julio Abascal - *Universidad del País Vasco, Spain*
Simone Diniz Junqueira Barbosa - *PUC-Rio, Brazil*

Technical Program Co-chairs

Cecília Baranauskas, *Unicamp, Brazil*
Philippe Palanque, *University Paul Sabatier, Toulouse III, France*

Socially Responsible Interaction

Special Theme Co-chairs

John C. Thomas, *IBM, USA*
Zhengjie Liu, *School of Computer Science & Technology of Dalian Maritime University, China*

Technical Program

Doctoral Consortium Co-chairs

Mary Czerwinski - *Microsoft Research, USA*
Marcelo Pimenta - *UFRGS, Brazil*

Full-Paper Co-chairs

Cecília Baranauskas, *Unicamp, Brazil*
Philippe Palanque, *University Paul Sabatier, Toulouse III, France*

HCI Societies Worldwide Co-chairs

Carla Freitas - *UFRGS, Brazil*
Fabio Paternò - *ISTI/CNR Pisa, Italy*

Interactive Experience Co-chairs

Tom Gross - *Bauhaus University Weimar, Germany*
Carlos Scolari - *Universitat de Vic, Spain*

Interactive Poster Co-chairs

Júnia Coutinho Anacleto - *UFSCar, Brazil*
Monique Noirhomme-Fraiture - *Facultés Universitaires Notre-Dame de la Paix, Belgium*

Keynote Speaker Co-chairs

Nahum Gershon - *MITRE, USA*
Matthias Rauterberg - *Technical University Eindhoven, The Netherlands*

Organization Overview Co-chairs

Lucia Filgueiras - *Poli-USP, Brazil*
Laurence Nigay - *University Joseph Fourier Grenoble 1, France*

Panel Co-chairs

Stefano Levialdi - *La Sapienza, Università degli Studi di Roma, Italy*
Clarisse Sieckenius de Souza - *PUC-Rio, Brazil*

Short-Paper Co-chairs

Andy Cockburn - *University of Canterbury, New Zealand*
Manuel A. Pérez-Quiñones - *Virginia Tech, USA*

Special Interest Groups (SIGs) Co-chairs

Paula Kotzé - *University of South Africa, South Africa*
Jonathan Lazar - *Towson University, USA*

Student Poster Co-chairs

Regina Bernhaupt - *University of Salzburg, Austria*
Juliana Salles - *Microsoft Corporation, USA*

Tutorial Co-chairs

Jan Gulliksen - *Uppsala University, Sweden*
Raquel Prates - *UFMG, Brazil*

Video Paper Co-chairs

Nick Graham - *Queens University, Canada*
John Zimmerman - *Carnegie Mellon University, USA*

Workshop Co-chairs

Oscar Mayora Ibarra - *CREATE-NET, Italy*
Jean Vanderdonckt - *Université Catholique de Louvain, Belgium*

Organization

Proceedings Publication Co-chairs

Vaclav Matousek - *University of West Bohemia, Czech Republic*
Marco Winckler - *University Toulouse 3, France*

Sponsoring Co-chairs

Ana Cristina Bicharra Garcia - *UFF, Brazil*
Gerrit van der Veer - *Open Universiteit, The Netherlands*

Student Volunteer Co-chairs

Effie Law - *ETH Zurich, Switzerland*
Kristijan Mihalic - *ICT-S, University of Salzburg, Austria*
Luciana Nedel - *UFRGS, Brazil*

Program Committee Members

Abascal, Julio - *Spain*
Abowd, Gregory - *USA*
Apperley, Mark - *New Zealand*
Avouris, Nikolaos - *Greece*
Bannon, Liam - *Ireland*
Baranauskas, Cecilia - *Brazil*
Barbosa, Simone - *Brazil*
Bass, Len - *USA*
Baudisch, Patrick - *USA*
Baudouin-Lafon, Michel - *France*
Bernhaupt, Regina - *Austria*
Blandford, Ann - *UK*
Blignaut, Pieter - *South Africa*
Bonacin, Rodrigo - *Brazil*
Bottoni, Paolo - *Italy*
Braendle, Alexander - *UK*
Brewster, Stephen - *UK*
Buono, Paolo - *Italy*
Campos, José C. - *Portugal*
Catarci, Tiziana - *Italy*
Celentano, Augusto - *Italy*
Chittaro, Luca - *Italy*
Cockton, Gilbert - *UK*
Coninx, Karin - *Belgium*
Correia, Nuno - *Portugal*
Costabile, Maria Francesca - *Italy*

Coutaz, Joëlle - *France*
Crowley, James - *France*
Cunha, João - *Portugal*
da Silva, Sergio Roberto - *Brazil*
Davies, Nigel - *UK*
De Angeli, Antonella - *UK*
De Carolis, Berardina - *Italy*
de Ruyter, Boris - *The Netherlands*
de Souza, Clarisse - *Brazil*
Del bimbo, Alberto - *Italy*
Dewan, Prasun - *USA*
Di Nocera, Francesco - *Italy*
Doherty, Gavin - *Ireland*
Faconti, Giorgio - *Italy*
Felix, Daniel - *Switzerland*
Ferre, Xavier - *Spain*
Filgueiras, Lucia - *Brazil*
Forbrig, Peter - *Germany*
Francisco Borges, Marcos Augusto - *Brazil*
Furtado, Elizabeth - *Brazil*
Garcia, Laura Sanchez - *Brazil*
Gea, Miguel - *Spain*
Glavinic, Vlado - *Croatia*
Graham, Nicholas - *Canada*
Granollers, Toni - *Spain*

Gray, Phil - *UK*
Gross, Tom - *Germany*
Grudin, Jonathan - *USA*
Grundy, John - *New Zealand*
Gulliksen, Jan - *Sweden*
Hammond, Judy - *Australia*
Harning, Morten Borup - *Denmark*
Harrison, Michael - *UK*
Hayes, Gillian - *USA*
Herczeg, Michael - *Germany*
Holzinger, Andreas - *Austria*
Hosking, John - *New Zealand*
Hvannberg, Ebba - *Iceland*
Jacko, Julie - *USA*
Johnson, Chris - *UK*
Jones, Matt - *UK*
Jorge, Joaquim - *Portugal*
Karat, John - *USA*
Kazman, Rick - *USA*
Kotzé, Paula - *South Africa*
Kulikowski, Juiliusz *Poland*
Law, Effie Lai-Chong - *Switzerland*
Leclercq, Pierre - *Belgium*
Lecolinet, Eric - *France*
Leporini, Barbara - *Italy*
Levialdi, Stefano - *Italy*
Lieberman, Henry - *USA*
Lindgaard, Gitte - *Canada*
Liu, Zhengjie - *China*
Mäntyjärvi, Jani - *Filand*
Martens, Jean-Bernard -
   The Netherlands
Matousek, Vaclav - *Czech Republic*
McCrickard, Scott - *Czech Republic*
Mihalic, Kristijan - *Austria*
Moher, Tom - *USA*
Moriyon, Roberto - *Spain*
Navarre, David - *France*
Nicolle, Colette - *UK*
Nigay, Laurence - *France*
Noirhomme, Monique - *Belgium*
Noldus, Lucas - *The Netherlands*
Nunes, Nuno - *Portugal*

Oberquelle, Horst - *Germany*
Oestreicher, Lars - *Sweden*
Oppermann, Reinhard - *Germany*
Palanque, Philippe - *France*
Paris, Cecile - *Australia*
Paternò, Fabio - *Italy*
Pederson, Thomas - *Sweden*
Pejtersen, Annelise - *Denmark*
Piccinno, Antonio - *Italy*
Pleuss, Andreas - *Germany*
Pribeanu, Costin - *Romania*
Puerta, Angel - *USA*
Räihä, Kari-Jouko - *Finland*
Rauterberg, Matthias -
   The Netherlands
Rist, Thomas - *Germany*
Rosa, Lanzilotti - *Italy*
Salles, Juliana - *USA*
Santoro, Carmen - *Italy*
Sauer, Stefan - *Germany*
Savidis, Anthony - *Greece*
Scapin, Dominique - *France*
Schmidt, Albrecht - *Germany*
Schwabe, Gerhard - *Switzerland*
Shneiderman, Ben - *USA*
Springett, Mark - *UK*
Stolze, Markus - *Switzerland*
Stuerzlinger, Wolfgang - *Canada*
Sukaviriya, Noi - *USA*
Sutcliffe, Alistair - *UK*
Thalmann, Nadia - *Switzerland*
Thapliyal, Mathura - *India*
Truong, Khai - *Canada*
Tscheligi, Manfred - *Autria*
van der Veer, Gerrit -
   The Netherlands
Vanderdonckt, Jean - *Belgium*
Vertegaal, Roel - *Canada*
Wesson, Janet - *South Africa*
Winckler, Marco - *France*
Wulf, Volker - *USA*
Ziegler, Jürgen - *Germany*

Additional Reviewers

Al Mahmud, Abdullah -
  The Netherlands
Alexander, Jason - *New Zealand*
Almas, Almir - *Brazil*
Almeida, Rodrigo - *France*
Aquino Junior, Plinio Thomaz - *Brazil*
Ardito, Carmelo - *Italy*
Bellucci, Andrea - *Italy*
Bhamidipaty, Anuradha - *India*
Block, Florian - *UK*
Bowman Doug - *USA*
Braz, Christina - *Canada*
Buchmann, Volkert - *New Zealand*
Camelo Pinto, Vladimir - *Brazil*
Capra, R. - *USA*
Cassens, Jörg - *Norway*
Coutinho Anacleto, Júnia - *Brazil*
Champion, Erik - *Singapore*
Clemmensen,Torkil - *Denmark*
Cockburn, Andy - *New Zealand*
Coyle, Cheryl - *USA*
de Oliveira Neto, João Soares - *Brazil*
de Oliveira, Rodrigo - *Brazil*
Deepak P - IBM Research, *India*
Diniz, Nancy - *UK*
Eng, Kynan - *Switzerland*
Farooq Ali, Mir - *USA*
Farrell, Stephen - *USA*
Foglia, Efrain - *Spain*
Freeman, Isaac - *New Zealand*
Freitas, Carla M.D.S. - *Brazil*
Fujisawa, Kumiko - *Japan*
Gonçalves, Daniel - *Portugal*
Gonzalez,Victor - *UK*
Graniæ, Andrina - *Croatia*
Grasset, Raphael - *New Zealand*
Gundelsweiler, Fredrik - *Germany*
Hauber, Joerg - *New Zealand*
Hazlewood, William - *USA*
Hoggan, Eve - *UK*
Howarth, Jonathan - *USA*
Hüsken, Peter - *Germany*

Ibanez Martinez, Jesus - *Spain*
Kanis, Marije - *UK*
Khalil, Ashraf - *USA*
Lazar, Jonathan - *USA*
Light, Ann - *UK*
Lima, Fernanda - *Brazil*
Looser, Julian - *New Zealand*
Maciel, Cristiano - *Brazil*
Makri, Stephann - *UK*
Mayora-Ibarra, Oscar - *Italy*
Melo, Cassio - *Brazil*
Melo, Paulo - *Brazil*
Morris, Meredith - *USA*
Mueller, Hendrik - *USA*
Nacenta, Miguel - *Canada*
Nadine, Vigouroux - *France*
Nagamatsu, Takashi - *Japan*
Nagasaki, Hitoshi - *Japan*
Neris, Vania - *Brazil*
Otjacques, Benoit - *Luxembourg*
Paterman,Ilana - UERJ - *Brazil*
Pérez-Quiñones, Manuel - *USA*
Pimenta, Marcelo - *Brazil*
Ponsa, Pere - *Spain*
Prates, Raquel - *Brazil*
Riche, Yann - *France*
Salminen, Mikko - *Finland*
Scolari, Carlos - *Spain*
Shi, Qingxin - *Denmark*
Silva, Elton - *Brazil*
Singh, Shawren - *South Africa*
Stach, Tadeusz - *Canada*
Sugimoto, Masanori - *Japan*
Suh, Sunah - *USA*
Takeda, Tatsuya - *Japan*
Taneva, Svetlena - *Switzerland*
Tripathi, Sanjay - *India*
Tungare, Manas - *USA*
Turner, Scott - *USA*
Yin, Jibin - *Japan*
Zimmerman, Thomas - *USA*

Sponsors and Supporters

Platinum

Gold

Bronze

Promotion

Organization

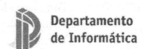

Table of Contents – Part II

User and Usability Studies

Focus + Context Visualization Techniques, and Tagging

Visualizing Social Information

Online Communities and e-Learning

Children, Games, and the Elderly

Usability Studies on Collaborative Systems

Interaction for Selection

Software Engineering and HCI

Part Three: Doctoral Consortium

Part Four: HCI Societies Worldwide

Part Five: Interactive Experience

Part Six: Interactive Posters and Student Posters

Part Seven: Organizational Overviews

Part Eight: Panels

Part Nine: Special Interest Groups (SIGs)

Part Ten: Tutorials

Part Eleven: Video Papers

Interfacing Video Capture, Editing and Publication in a Tangible Environment

Cati Vaucelle and Hiroshi Ishii

MIT Media Laboratory, Tangible Media Group
20, Ames Street, Cambridge MA 02139, USA
{cati, ishii}@media.mit.edu

Abstract. The paper presents a novel approach to collecting, editing and performing visual and sound clips in real time. The cumbersome process of capturing and editing becomes fluid in the improvisation of a story, and accessible as a way to create a final movie. It is shown how a graphical interface created for video production informs the design of a tangible environment that provides a spontaneous and collaborative approach to video creation, selection and sequencing. Iterative design process, participatory design sessions and workshop observations with 10-12 year old users from Sweden and Ireland are discussed. The limitations of interfacing video capture, editing and publication in a self-contained platform are addressed.

Keywords: Tangible User Interface, Video, Authorship, Mobile Technology, Digital Media, Video Jockey, Learning, Children, Collaboration.

1 Introduction

Enriching a digital interface with the natural language of physical objects offers an aesthetic experience that is exciting for users to share with one another. This paper presents a framework for designing a tangible platform based on a graphical user interface that we implement for video production. We explore the design of tangible interfaces for supporting inter-personal production of digital media. We synthesize performance and editing to facilitate a flow between improvisation and post-production of a movie. Our multi-user system is targeted for 10-12 year olds. It integrates different layers of complexity, from digitizing the media and performing a movie, to storyboarding a more complex narrative.

Our research departs from *Textable Movie*, a graphical user interface we created for video production [41]. Textable Movie reduces the technical difficulties of creating a publishable movie by coupling the performative act of telling a story to editing a final movie. Users create a personal mode of interaction with the system by mapping their own keywords to videos and incorporating new video clips and sound samples to their database. A real time engine responds to the user vocal or written keywords by projecting the corresponding movie clips. A set of parameters affects the movie in real time such as zoom, speed, colors, and loop. The same process is used to assemble final movies. In the framework of computational storytelling, Textable Movie promotes the idea of maker-controlled media and can be contrasted to automatic

C. Baranauskas et al. (Eds.): INTERACT 2007, LNCS 4663, Part II, pp. 1–14, 2007.
© IFIP International Federation for Information Processing 2007

presentation systems. By improvising movie-stories created from their personal video database and by suddenly being projected into someone else's video database during the same story, users can be surprised as they visualize video elements corresponding to a story that they would not have expected. Users make their own inference about the visual discoveries rather than being passive to an artificial system that usually makes the inference for them.

The complexity, power and flexibility of Textable Movie can be seen in how novel projects present themselves through its use. The children's immediate response towards the system made it comparable to a video game. Considering this, we created *Textable Game*, a variation that more directly extends the concepts of Textable Movie to the realm of video games. With Textable Game, teenagers design their action games, exploration games, and mystery games, using their personal video and audio media. They create their own game strategies, rules and scenarios, and become their own video game producers.

During the course of observations, it became apparent that more fusion between capturing, editing and publishing was necessary. This could allow children to focus their attention on content creation. We started exploring the realm of tangible interfaces. For a revisit of Textable Movie, we coupled mobile technologies to a platform that materializes ideas and retrieves them seamlessly. We explored the concept of tangibility of digital data as a way for children to gather and capture data around the city for later retrieval. In this case, tangible objects become metaphors of the captured elements. We created the *Moving Pictures* device using mobile technology coupled with tangible objects as metaphors [40].

2 Prior Work

2.1 Tangible User Interaction with Video

We implement a tangible user interface [33], inspired by the tangible bits concept [17] that combines physical objects to digital data. Digital data covers physical objects in a display space [27]. Previous tangible systems move digital media clips around, arrange digital information physically [19], create multimedia stories [22], offer a token-based access to digital information [16, 38], and explore a direct physical organization of digital video clips using multiple handheld computers [42]. A smaller set of displays can be physically manipulated as a group to interact with digital information and media [23].

Moving Pictures builds upon and contributes to previous research on tangible tools for children [12, 25]. Much of our research centered around the design of a tangible movie-making machine for children thus complementing previous work on supporting children's fantasy and storytelling [5]. Coupling tangible to video is shown to support collaborative exploration of a video collection [34]. A modified camera can also capture both the child and the video of the child [20].

2.2 Tangible User Interface for Collaboration

Tangible User Interfaces are designed to encourage collaboration between children [2, 30]. Tangible mixing tables enable a performance-oriented approach to media construction [21]. In StoryMat, a childhood map invites collaboration between children by telling and acting out stories using props, and listening back to stories of others [5]. With ClearBoard, users draw together digitally while talking to each other [18]. In I/O Brush, children use a paintbrush to gather picturesque information from their surroundings and share them with their peers digitally [31].

Moving Pictures contributes to recent attempts in supporting human-human collaboration with ubiquitous computing [32], especially with research on ubiquitous computing devices for sharing pictures at a distance [37].

2.3 Tangible User Interface for Authorship

A broad range of interactive table-tops have been conceived for collaboration. The DiamondTouch table [7] invites multiple users to collaborate at the same time. Yumiko Tanaka's Plable is a traditional looking table with which children build an imaginary world [36]. Designers developed a new concept for movie editing to help children understand the process of editing. It consists of printed movie cards that can be re-arranged in any order. Their bar code is used to identify them on a digital screen [24]. Offering authorship though the interaction with tangible interfaces is rare. It is probably because it requires a flexible interface and a software architecture that takes care of data management. Authorship allows children to become active participants instead of simply observers. Our work builds upon research on physical metaphors of recorded personal stories and points of view [39]. In Flights of Fantasy [6] everyday visitors in a gallery move blocks around a tangible table-top to edit sequences based on icons that represent story elements. Philips Design developed a system that replays visual sequences using tangible objects with a stationary computer for capturing and associating media to objects [28]. While these systems invite for capturing and editing movie segments, none of them propose to edit, perform, publish, or share final edited movies with peers. Moving Pictures contains a videojockey mode for children to perform edited movies and to invite them to revisit their effect on an audience.

2.4 Tangible User Interface for VideoJockeying

Derived from disc jockey (DJ), the term VJ was used for the first time at the end of the '70s. A disc jockey performs pre-sampled sounds in real-time, a video jockey is a live performer of visuals. The mechanism of video jockeying is similar to the mechanism employed by silent film directors in constructing a narrative using visual elements, and later in accompanying these visuals with live music [10]. Robots are also videojockeys when they perform and edit movies in real time. The Filmmaking Robot of Douglas Bagnall edits short films by selecting video footages and taking aesthetic decisions [3].

In Moving Pictures, tangible media containers are integrated into mobile technology. Later, the media containers are assembled on an interactive table for performance. The contribution of Moving Pictures resides in three main functions: 1- video capture with tangible media containers 2- Video editing on an interactive table using the tangible media containers and a storyboard ring 3- Video and sound performance on the interactive table.

3 The Design of Moving Pictures

We combine form, interaction and function throughout our design process informed by research on rich user interfaces [13]. Our design decisions are coupled with user participation. The users are children age 10-12. Our design methodology is based on evaluation results with Textable Movie. We created a series of low fidelity prototypes expressing our evaluation results from Textable Movie. We explored the needs and preferences of 10-12 year old children regarding group interaction, attitudes and trends that potentially influence their choice of products. We applied a participatory design approach to implement a functional prototype of Moving Pictures [8, 9]. Our first design decisions for a tangible revision of Textable Movie were used as a starting point for the children in our participatory design sessions.

Several moderators from Ireland and Sweden organized design sessions with children as co-partners over a period of 8 months. Four structured groups of children were involved. Group 1, involved in participatory design sessions, evaluated the concept throughout the entire project. Group 2 started participating later on, when a first functional prototype was developed. Groups 3 and 4, located in Sweden and Ireland respectively, were involved in a final evaluation. The final evaluation, with groups 3 and 4, is based on a cross-cultural workshop with users from a local school in Umeå, Sweden, and participants from a workshop on video making in Dublin, Ireland. Children in groups 1, 2 and 3 attended the same school in Sweden. All sessions with group 1 were carried out at the school's after-school club and the children participated voluntarily. Sessions with group 2 were planned within school hours and in agreement with teachers.

During initial sessions we learned about the children's use of video-related hardware and software. This led us to observe the complexity of existing products and notice their effects on children's creativity and group interaction. The Textable Movie system was used as a departure point. Low fidelity prototypes were shown to convey the concept of collaboratively mixing media using tangible tokens on an interactive table. The moderators progressively introduced the movie making process as well as electronic components that are used to create an interactive movie-making device.

Together with the research team, users explored different types of input tools and tested a series of design ideas. Children were introduced to a number of cinematic concepts, such as space, time, continuity, point of view and action-reaction sequences. We developed solutions for a spatial, tangible interface that enables a flexible approach to these expressions. Based on our design sessions with the children as participants, we concluded on a variety of prototypes, including the camera (see Figure 1) and the final editing, mixing and performing table (see Figure 2). Besides the structured participant groups, a number of Swedish children from several local schools tested iterations of the prototype during one-day events. Swedish and Irish children from different communities created movie-stories with their own footage.

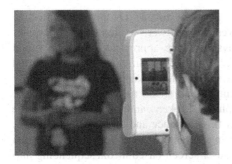

Fig. 1. Camera first prototype vs camera final prototype

Fig. 2. First prototype of the table vs its final prototype

3.1   System and Method for Media Editing Using Tangible Media Tokens

Moving Pictures is a table top with three Radio Frequency Identification (RFID) readers, a laptop computer, a set of speakers, a display, two cameras built into PDAs with RFID capabilities, and a collection of RFID tokens (see Figure 3). Recorded media is associated with digital ID and physical token. Software written for the PDA

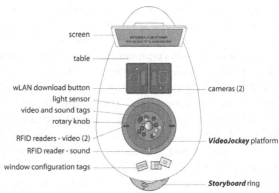

Fig. 3. Moving Pictures

wirelessly sends the mapped information between token ID and media to the computer as well as the media files themselves. The software written for the computer instantly retrieves the information and plays back the appropriate video or sound segment on a display screen. More specifically, a token with a digital ID is inserted into a PDA that has a camera built into it, so that the token's ID is permanently associated with the temporal sequence of image and sound as it is recorded by the camera. Once removed from the PDA, the physical token can be used to retrieve the sequence of images from memory, to display this sequence and to place this sequence within a longer media sequence. By offering a tangible representation of media elements, Moving Pictures transforms single-user screen-based media sequencing into multi-user physical interaction, adding a collaborative dimension. Moving Pictures incorporates three modes of interaction:

1- Video Capture: Users insert a token in the camera to record a shot.

2- Video Jockeying: Once removed from the camera, the tokens are used as a composition element on the interactive table. Users place the camera on the table and the material collected is transferred to the computer. Users improvise video compositions using the tokens while witnessing at the same time the clips instantaneously being played on the display screen.

3- Video and Sound Editing: Five tokens can be inserted at a time in a personally tailored ring. The rotation of the ring on the table triggers a graphical interface on which the video clips are played instantaneously and sequentially. When the sequence of five video clips, or less, seems satisfying, the children export their final movie on green tokens. These green tokens can themselves be assembled altogether to construct a longer movie. From small clips to longer sequences, children can build up a long and meaningful movie. Sound effects can be applied at any time. In this version of Moving Pictures, sound effects are not edited, but only applied to movie sequences, at a selected point in time. Several aesthetic decisions were made to resemble the DJ's scratching tables. Sounds can overlap with one another, or be individually scratched. Furthermore, the soundtrack is recorded as it is performed.

3.2 Results from Our Design Process

Designing a computational object means designing for people. It demands reflecting on the object's critical and aesthetic roles. To this end, researchers propose that designers develop sensitivity to and control of aesthetics, for instance by designing purposeful constraints on communications media [14]. It is within this context that we revisited Textable Movie with specific constraints.

With the use of digital cameras, the technical barriers of producing a final still or moving picture are minimized. The possibility to take risks and experiment is encouraged enabling more expression though the use of visual media. For a majority of the population who do not master the conventions of visual media, some scaffolding, context and constraints may be necessary. Intentionally, in Moving Pictures the user is limited in the length of the captured movie. The tangible metaphor of a token symbolizing a single shot had to be consistent with common motion pictures language. During our evaluation, young adults adopted the physical metaphor accordingly. They were careful with the length of the captured clips. It enabled them to practice limited rules in standard video editing without being too conscious of them. Our technical simplification aims to not break the creative flow. We also integrated spatial components in the video cameras to potentially take two points of view on the same scene at the same time. This conveys a sense of space such as close-up and large view on a scene. Users establish an exchange using visuals and sound where capturing and editing is made seamless. The technology is voluntarily not the users' main focus, because we mainly support creative activities generated from organized narratives, visual and spatial movie content. Each object is designed with an individual digital function. For example, the physical storyboard ring controls a graphical storyboard. This ring contains physical tokens and acts as a rotating device to feed the digital storyboard on a computer screen.

To discuss the design of Moving Pictures, we refer to data obtained through participant observations and interviews involving children from groups 1 and 2 as co-designers. Group 1 includes seven 12 year-old girls and group 2 consists of five 11 year-old boys and six 11 year-old girls. The following synthesizes the children's interaction with Moving Pictures [11].

General interaction: Half of the children understood it without instruction.

Confidence in the system: The lack of explanation on what to do with Moving Pictures made the children exchange ideas and explore the system with each other.

The use of the tokens: The children actively used the tokens for data retrieval.

The level of complexity of the interaction: Half of the children retrieved data created by others and the other half mixed their own footage with sound effects.

Our customized cameras versus professional cameras: Children found easy to remember how to interact with them and easy to use. Some children mentioned preferring to use a smaller camera that they can carry in the pocket.

Round shape of the table: Children manifested their preference for a round shaped table to interact with simultaneously as well as to move around. According to the children, a square table would have meant a four user table.

Table size: Children suggested that the table should be smaller if used in a home. However, the table was too small to accommodate more than eight users at a time.

Group Size: In group 2 (22 participants, divided in 2 working sub-groups) some children expressed that the group was too large. Not all participants got a chance to interact during the process of previewing and arranging movies and sounds.

Effectiveness of Group Work: Children recommended the working groups to be smaller, but they also expressed that it was more *fun* to work in a large group, even though the work was not very *effective*. In contrast, some children expressed that working in a group made the work easier and more effective, because participants helped each other in generating ideas for movie making.

Agreement vs disagreement: Children pointed out that it could be difficult to work with each other if participants disagree. Many children considered disagreement as being a negative factor in their creative work. They explained how they made efforts in achieving a consensus. They also realized that it was not always possible to keep track of everyone's ideas.

4 Evaluation

We originally created a methodology for international workshops on creative media making and sharing for the Textable Movie project. The workshop engage teenagers from around the world in digital media making using the Textable Movie tool set. The workshop features a design cycle that begins with concept development and continues onto storyboarding, video production, editing and publication on a public display; as it is realized, participants test and evaluate their video-stories using Textable Movie. The workshop global strategy focuses on fostering intercultural visual communication and play. One goal of the international program is to generate a cross-cultural study focused on the creative construction of media by teenagers. The same methodology was used for Moving Pictures, however we included more experts in the language of motion pictures to help us guide and moderate the workshop.

4.1 Roles Assumed by the Children While Designing and Using Moving Pictures

In all sessions, children were free to choose their role in the film-making activity. Driven by their personal interests, they chose to be film script-writers, director, actors, camera-men, or scenographers. Children and moderators discussed and clarified the tasks for each role during the sessions. Most children chose the same role repeatedly. When asked if they thought there should be a leader in the group, children had different opinions. Some appreciated not having a leader and being able to have equal participation. Others said they thought it would be better to have a child taking the leading role.

Several children thought that group members had different skills and this could allow them to learn from each other. During the sessions it was obvious the children influenced and learned from each other. For example children sometimes helped each other by explaining and showing one another how to perform different tasks. Piaget describes how children influence one another in different ways and how when it happens is of great importance for a child [4]. The children often changed opinions during the sessions, influenced by their friends. This might be a sign of a close collaboration. Prior research shows that when working on film-making, children learned a great deal from each other [9].

As time passed, children became more accustomed to the technologies used in the design sessions and behaved more spontaneously and independently around them. Some children chose to spend much time arranging video clips and adding corresponding sounds to them, eventually becoming "experts" at this task. Others "specialized" in their acting skills or in camera techniques.

4.2 Creativity and Learning

Observing the creativity process of the children working on digital media with Moving Pictures, we reflected on the four aspects of student *Understanding of the Arts* proposed by Ross [29] and reintroduced by Somers [35]: *Conventionalisation* – an awareness and ability to use the conventions of the art form, *Appropriation* – embracing, for personal use, the available expressive forms, *Transformation* – in which the student searches for knowledge and meaning through the expression of 'feeling impulses', and *Publication* – the placing of the result in the public domain. Using Moving Pictures, children understood the process of making a movie using a series of traditional shots symbolized by physical tokens. They made a movie respecting the collaborative storyboard they created. They contributed to a multinational visual database by expressing their visual narratives for children living in another country.

4.3   Results from the Process of Capturing a Movie to Projecting it

Through the course of the evaluation, Irish children created a series of movies. Children chose and selected the different themes. The choices varied from: journalistic interviews that were limited to five shots, explorations in the city using more than ten shots, five individual shots of the children acting in front of their favorite city place, a more sophisticated five-shot criminal story with a beginning, a middle, and an end, and a theater play using ten shots. The most popular edited movies are the individual shots of the children and the sophisticated criminal story. We analyzed the two most popular movies to understand how the interfacing of video capture, editing and publication were optimally taken advantage of in our tangible environment (see the Table bellow).

	Individual shots	**The story**
Paper storyboard / planning	No storyboard. The children had in mind their favorite place they wanted to be videotaped in front of.	Children spent an hour planning their story, storyboarding and looking for the right spot.
Video Capture / process of revisiting/erasing shots	One child revisited the way to jump from one side to the other side of the frame to create continuity within the final movie. His peers were part of his exploration and repeated the same idea.	The shots were constantly revisited, erased and accumulated. Children labeled the token to have the choice of different shots for the same segment of the story.
Visualizing briefly the shots	All of the shots were pre-visualized and organized.	All of them were visualized and organized.
Editing using the storyboard ring on the table	No editing of the sequences seemed necessary. Children used their appearance order when they started shooting.	Children enjoyed different outcomes using the same shots. They end up selecting three final movies.
Editing a soundtrack using the respective yellow tokens	One specific sound per location. Children did not choose to perform complex sound mix, but carefully chose their sounds.	Children performed a complex sound mix, overlapping sounds and creating continuity within the soundtrack.
Publication as performance	Children did not try various movies out of the shots, only performed a final movie.	Children kept three favorite movies for videojockeying.

The students did not want to edit the other country's final movies. Instead, they were excited to watch the variations in the movies and to continue them. This shows potential for cultural exchange through video making.

4.4 Discussion

The tangible integration of a video production process allows anyone to revisit the footage. It presents benefits in improvising and performing movies collaboratively. The shape of the table specifically invites children to collaborate with each other. Videojockeying is a spontaneous way to perform final pieces and to integrate selected sounds. Children were engaged and attentive in the production of all the video-stories they created. They considerably focused on the content and were comfortable with the technology. They preferred two of their creations: the individual shots movie - consisting of sequences of children jumping in different parts of a city - and the sophisticated criminal story in the center of Dublin. We noticed that the most complex features of Moving Pictures were used while editing the sophisticated story.

Reducing the complexity in personal production of digital media and interfacing the process of capturing, editing and performing allows children to experiment effectively with movie sequences.

Even though the system is not empirically compared with commercialized video editing tools, we did prior user testing with iMovie. We chose iMovie as we found it an easy tool to edit movies. In this study, the children were from the same community as the students who participated in the workshop presented in this paper. Almost all the children were impatiently waiting for their movies to be digitalized in iMovie. Some gave up on their original objectives. Other children kept capturing with the professional video camera not wanting to edit anything. When editing, children wanted a final movie almost instantly and were confused when they had to erase parts of their movies. For this reason Moving pictures uses raw data captured in small clips. This functionality in our system seemed to work better for the children. Having the digital data represented by a physical object helped them understand the construction of their movies. At no time they were bored or overwhelmed. One main complaint was that the number of the shots possible to take at one time was too small. They also asked for the ability to incorporate their own sound effects. As it is, Moving Pictures only offers the recording of sounds with the video. With iMovie, children never experimented using different endings with their video footages. In our evaluation with Moving Pictures, children captured and revisited their video story elements, edited and experimented with various positions of their shots within the story and this even if the number of shots was only five for the story. With Moving Pictures, children created a soundtrack using sound mixed together.

In early sessions, children asked each other and test leaders for help as soon as they did not understand the instructions. The lack of instructions seemed to be a way to get to know each other better. Research shows that students at various performance levels, working together toward a common goal, can enhance each other's analysis, synthesis, and evaluation of the concepts they are exploring [15]. However, Ackermann [1] explains that changing perspectives and switching roles requires the difficult balance between being simultaneously immersed and disengaged. We studied how people engage in relationships where they exchange their perspectives and transfer a sense of space through play, collaboration, and storytelling using dynamic media containers and tangible media interfaces. During our observations, we found that even though generally children in the same group age have a similar cognitive development, it is important to design systems that are flexible enough to accommodate individual characteristics.

5 Limitations

Based on our evaluations with children, we found that Moving Pictures suffers from several limitations related to the problem of how to best digitally support meaningful interactions in the physical space and interfacing video capture, editing and publication in a tangible environment. First the scalability of such a system at a networked and international level is flawed. We need to redesign the software technology to centralize the linked data and distribute the nodes of contained data in an organized fashion. To have the technology better assist how an individual moves about the physical space while capturing content, their platform needs to be mediated by a centralized software architecture.

Second, system centralization implies new communication technology to mediate the video platforms and allow them to communicate with one another. The RFID technology in the wireless cameras could be redesigned into a pattern based technology using the video camera of any device.

Lastly, we would like to escape the hardware limitations of commercial video cameras. Users could use any phone, any camera or text based device to exchange material. The system should be designed to generalize despite different input modalities. All of these modifications shift the emphasis of the system from a simple, transparent, video platform, and into an architecture for supporting content generation that reflects the physical environment of the user through multiple information platforms.

6 Conclusion and Future Work

In a world in which media is everywhere, individual and collaborative media creation can provide a means of exploring our environment. Technology can bring people together, even if they have never met before. Our research trajectory is to understand interfaces that empower people in expressing and sharing ideas about their social environment, actively "constructing" personal content. Constructionists suggest that users benefit from systems that support self-expression rather than systems that create content for the user. Papert proposes that systems for children can relate to their 'real-world' experiences to learn specific skills such as mathematics [26].

Movie editing systems support personal creations and offer the opportunity for one to reflect on 'real world' experiences. Authorship is enhanced if the assembly of the movie is made out of elements in a story that can be explored and combined in real time. *"Children build, make or manipulate objects or artifacts and in doing so are confronted with the results of their actions, learning as they go"* [26]. In Moving Pictures, the children create the content of their stories that can be used for performance and editing, and they also learn the process of making a movie "as they go".

The ultimate goal of this research is to interface video capture, video editing and video publication in a self-contained platform. In addition to identifying limitations, we have also shown the changes that need to take place for the improvement of this, and similar systems. During the design and evaluation sessions, we noticed that Moving Pictures helps to engage smaller groups of children in one task - movie-making. Even though it allows users to participate in different activities, the level of participation depends on individual initiative. It would therefore be interesting to use multi-user systems in a learning environment, for instance within the school's curriculum. With Moving Pictures anyone could test movie scenarios by capturing quickly a few shots and assembling a quick movie draft. Future work will include improvisational theatre sessions organized using the wireless video camera as an expressive tool and the video jockey table as an instant review display of the improvisation to assemble a collaborative video. Throughout the workshops with the children we collected valuable data for future iterations. At times, we observed how children interact with the system in unexpected ways, which has inspired us to explore new functionality and to improve existing features. The empirical evaluation of children's analysis of their personal work as well as children's analysis of the work of other students in remote locations must be left for future work.

Acknowledgments. We would like to thank the Media Lab Europe for supporting the implementation of Textable Movie and Moving Pictures. Glorianna Davenport for advising this research from 2002-2005. Diana Africano and Oskar Fjellström for our collaborative research on Moving Pictures in 2004 at the Umeå Institute of Design in Sweden, Joakim Sällberg for the model making of Moving Pictures and Jenny Fredriksson for co-observing the participatory design sessions in Sweden. Michael John Gorman, Leo Mc Kenna, the Ark in Dublin, Vincent Le Bail, Eoghan Kidney, the School of Ostermalm who participated in our evaluations. Diana Africano, Adam Boulanger and the conference reviewers for their feedback on the paper. The tangible media group - past and present members - for their valuable input and The MIT Media Lab community.

References

1. Ackermann, E.K.: A learning zone of one's own: Sharing representations and flow in collaborative learning environments. In: Tokoro, M., Steels, L. (eds.), Amsterdam, Berlin, Oxford, Tokyo, Washington, DC, Part 1. Ch. 2, pp. 15–37. IOS Press, Amsterdam (2004)
2. Africano, D., Berg, S., Lindbergh, K., Lundholm, P., Nilbrink, F., Persson, A.: Designing tangible interfaces for children's collaboration. In: CHI '04 Extended Abstracts on Human Factors in Computing Systems, pp. 853–868. ACM Press, New York (2004)
3. Bagnall, D.: The Filmmaking Robot (2006), http://www.halo.gen.nz/robot/
4. Bukowski, W.M., Newcomb, A.F., Hartup, W.W.: The company they keep: Friendship in childhood and adolescence. Cambridge University Press, New York (1996)
5. Cassell, J., Ryokai, K.: Making Space for Voice: Technologies to Support Children's Fantasy and Storytellin. Personal Technologies 5(3), 203–224 (2001)
6. Davenport, G.: Flights of Fantasy (2001), http://www.decordova.org/decordova/exhibit/flights.htm

7. Dietz, P., Leigh, D.: DiamondTouch: a multi-user touch technology. In: Proceedings of the 14th Annual ACM Symposium on User interface Software and Technology. UIST '01, pp. 219–226. ACM Press, New York (2001)
8. Douglas, S., Aki, N.: Participatory Design: Principles and Practices. Lawrence Erlbaum, Mahwah (1993)
9. Druin, A., Bederson, B., Boltman, A., Miura, A., Knotts-Callahan, D., Platt, M.: Children as our Technology Design Partners. In: Druin (ed.) The Design of Children's Technology, pp. 51–72. Morgan Kaufmann Publishers, San Francisco (1999)
10. Faulkner, M.: D-Fuse - VJ, Audio-visual Art and VJ Culture. Laurence King Publishing (2006)
11. Fredriksson, J.: Children's Collaboration when Interacting with a Multi-User System. Master Thesis in Cognitive Science. Umeå University (2006)
12. Frei, P., Su, V., Mikhak, B., Ishii, H.: Curlybot: designing a new class of computational toys. In: Proceedings of the SIGCHI Conference on Human Factors in Computing Systems. CHI '00, pp. 129–136. ACM Press, New York (2000)
13. Frens, J.W., Djajadiningrat, J.P., Overbeeke, C.J.: Rich Interaction: issues. Ambient Intelligence. In: Markopoulos, P., Eggen, B., Aarts, E., Crowley, J.L. (eds.) EUSAI 2004. LNCS, vol. 3295, pp. 271–278. Springer, Heidelberg (2004)
14. Gaver, B.: Provocative Awareness. Computer Supported Cooperative Work 11(3), 475–493 (2002)
15. Gokhale, A.A.: Collaborative Learning Enhances Critical Thinking. Journal of Technology Education 7(1) (1995)
16. Holmquist, L.E., Redström, J., Ljungstrand, P.: Token-Based Access to Digital Information in Lecture Notes in Computer Science, p. 234. Springer, Heidelberg (1999)
17. Ishii, H., Ullmer, B.: Tangible bits: towards seamless interfaces between people, bits and atoms. In: Pemberton, S. (ed.) CHI '97. Proceedings of the SIGCHI Conference on Human Factors in Computing Systems, pp. 234–241. ACM Press, New York (1997)
18. Ishii, H., Kobayashi, M.: ClearBoard: a seamless medium for shared drawing and conversation with eye contact. In: Bauersfeld, P., Bennett, J., Lynch, G. (eds.) Proceedings of the SIGCHI Conference on Human Factors in Computing Systems. CHI '92, pp. 525–532. ACM Press, New York (1992)
19. Jacob, R.J., Ishii, H., Pangaro, G., Patten, J.: A tangible interface for organizing information using a grid. In: Proceedings of the SIGCHI Conference on Human Factors in Computing Systems: Changing Our World, Changing Ourselves. CHI '02, pp. 339–346. ACM Press, New York (2002)
20. Labrune, J., Mackay, W.: Tangicam: exploring observation tools for children. In: Proceeding of the 2005 Conference on interaction Design and Children. IDC '05, pp. 95–102. ACM Press, New York (2005)
21. Lew, M.: Live cinema: an instrument for cinema editing as a live performance. In: Barzel, R. (ed.) ACM SIGGRAPH 2004 Sketches. SIGGRAPH '04, p. 117. ACM Press, New York (2004)
22. Mazalek, A., Davenport, G.: A tangible platform for documenting experiences and sharing multimedia stories. In: Proceedings of the 2003 ACM SIGMM Workshop on Experiential Telepresence. ETP '03, pp. 105–109. ACM Press, New York (2003)
23. Merrill, D., Kalanithi, J., Maes, P.: Siftables: towards sensor network user interfaces. In: Proceedings of the 1st international Conference on Tangible and Embedded interaction. TEI '07, pp. 75–78. ACM Press, New York (2007)
24. Miyabara, M., Sugimoto, T.: Movie Cards (2006), http://www.videologue.com/

14   C. Vaucelle and H. Ishii

25. Montemayor, J., Druin, A., Chipman, G., Farber, A., Guha, M.: Storyrooms and playsets: Tools for children to create physical interactive storyrooms. Computers in Entertainment 2(1) (2004)
26. Papert, S., Harel, I.: Constructionism. Ablex Publishing Corporation, NJ (1991)
27. Patten, J., Ishii, H., Hines, J., Pangaro, G.: Sensetable: a wireless object tracking platform for tangible user interfaces. In: Proceedings of the SIGCHI Conference on Human Factors in Computing Systems. CHI '01, pp. 253–260. ACM Press, New York (2001)
28. Rizzo, A., Marti, P., Decortis, F., Rutgers, J., Thursfield, P.: Building narratives experiences for children through real time media manipulation: POGOworld. In: Blythe, M.A., Monk, A.F., Overbeeke, K., Wright, P.C. (eds.) Funology: from usability to enjoyment (1-12), Kluwer Academic Publisher, Amsterdam (2003)
29. Ross, M., Radnor, H., Mitchell, S., Bierton, C.: Assessing Achievement in the Arts. Open Univ. Press, Stony Stratford, England (1993)
30. Ryokai, K., Vaucelle, C., Cassell, J.: Virtual Peers as Partners in Storytelling and Literacy Learning. Journal of Computer Assisted Learning 19(2), 195–208 (2003)
31. Ryokai, K., Marti, S., Ishii, H.: I/O brush: drawing with everyday objects as ink. In: Proceedings of the SIGCHI Conference on Human Factors in Computing Systems. CHI '04, pp. 303–310. ACM Press, New York (2004)
32. Salvador, T., Barile, S., Sherry, J.: Ubiquitous computing design principles: supporting human-human and human-computer transactions. In: CHI '04 Extended Abstracts on Human Factors in Computing Systems. CHI '04, pp. 1497–1500. ACM Press, New York (2004)
33. Sharlin, E., Watson, B., Kitamura, Y., Kishino, F., Itoh, Y.: On tangible user interfaces, humans and spatiality. Personal and Ubiquitous Computing 8(5) (2004)
34. Sokoler, T., Edeholt, H.: Physically embodied video snippets supporting collaborative exploration of video material during design sessions. In: Proceedings of the Second Nordic Conference on Human-Computer interaction. NordiCHI '02, vol. 31, pp. 139–148. ACM Press, New York (2002)
35. Somers, J.: Measuring the shadow or knowing the bird. Evaluation and assessment of drama in education. In: Sefton-Green, J., Sinker, R. (eds.) Evaluating creativity. Making and Learning by Young People, pp. 107–128. Routledge, London (2000)
36. Tanaka, Y.: Plable (2006), http://yumikotanaka.net/
37. Truong, K.N., Richter, H., Hayes, G.R., Abowd, G.D.: Devices for sharing thoughts and affection at a distance. In: CHI '04 Extended Abstracts on Human Factors in Computing Systems. CHI '04, pp. 1203–1206. ACM Press, New York (2004)
38. Ullmer, B., Ishii, H.: Emerging frameworks for tangible user interfaces. IBM Journal (2000)
39. Vaucelle, C., Jehan, T.: Dolltalk: a computational toy to enhance children's creativity. In: CHI '02 Extended Abstracts on Human Factors in Computing Systems. CHI '02, pp. 776–777. ACM Press, New York (2002)
40. Vaucelle, C., Africano, D., Davenport, G., Wiberg, M., Fjellstrom, O.: Moving pictures: looking out/looking in. In: Beckmann-Wells, P. (ed.) ACM SIGGRAPH 2005 Educators Program. SIGGRAPH '05, pp. 27–34. ACM Press, New York (2005)
41. Vaucelle, C., Davenport, G.: A System to Compose Movies for Cross-Cultural Storytelling: Textable Movie. In: Göbel, S., Spierling, U., Hoffmann, A., Iurgel, I., Schneider, O., Dechau, J., Feix, A. (eds.) TIDSE 2004. LNCS, vol. 3105, pp. 126–131. Springer, Heidelberg (2004)
42. Zigelbaum, J., Horn, M.S., Shaer, O., Jacob, R.J.: The tangible video editor: collaborative video editing with active tokens. In: Proceedings of the 1st international Conference on Tangible and Embedded interaction. TEI '07, pp. 43–46. ACM Press, New York (2007)

PaperCP: Exploring the Integration of Physical and Digital Affordances for Active Learning

Chunyuan Liao[1], François Guimbretière[1], Richard Anderson[2], Natalie Linnell[2], Craig Prince[2], and Valentin Razmov[2]

[1] Dept. of Computer Science, Univ. of Maryland, College Park, U.S.A
[2] Dept. of Computer Science & Engineering, Univ. of Washington, Seattle, U.S.A
{liaomay, francois}@cs.umd.edu;
{anderson, linnell, cmprince, valentin}@cs.washington.edu

Abstract. Active Learning in the classroom domain presents an interesting case for integrating physical and digital affordances. Traditional physical handouts and transparencies are giving way to new digital slides and PCs, but the fully digital systems still lag behind the physical artifacts in many aspects such as readability and tangibility. To better understand the interplay between physical and digital affordances in this domain, we developed PaperCP, a paper-based interface for a Tablet PC-based classroom interaction system (Classroom Presenter), and deployed it in an actual university course. This paper reports on an exploratory experiment studying the use of the system in a real-world scenario. The experiment confirms the feasibility of the paper interface in supporting student-instructor communication for Active Learning. We also discuss the challenges associated with creating a physical interface such as print layout, the use of pen gestures, and logistical issues.

Keywords: Active Learning, Affordances, Paper-based Interface, Physical Interface, Tablet PC.

1 Introduction

Active Learning refers to augmenting the traditional lecture with student-participation activities such as brainstorming, quizzing, and polling. Also vital to Active Learning is sharing (e.g., displaying) student responses as part of a lecture. Because of this two-way instructor-student communication, Active Learning increases student engagement, helps with the construction of knowledge, and improves the level of understanding of students, as well as the instructors' awareness of it [25].

Designing a system to support Active Learning is challenging because of the tension between traditional physical interfaces and newer electronic ones. For example, traditional printouts and transparencies are easy to read and write on, convenient to navigate, and easy to manipulate by hand. But the manual distribution, collection, summarization, and display of the physical artifacts is often inefficient and distracting. To address this issue, fully digital systems have been developed [3, 10, 24, 29]. For instance, Classroom Presenter (CP) [3], a digital Active Learning system, allows the instructor to deliver slides and gather student responses wirelessly via networked

C. Baranauskas et al. (Eds.): INTERACT 2007, LNCS 4663, Part II, pp. 15–28, 2007.

pen-based Tablet PCs. Despite the digital solutions' advantages in data transfer and archiving, some drawbacks are associated with these systems: a degraded reading and writing experience due to limited screen size and screen resolution, the cost of the devices, and the limitations imposed by battery life. To ease the tension

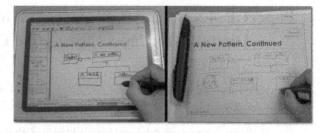

Fig. 1. (Left) The original Tablet PC interface of a digital Active Learning infrastructure. (Right) The new equivalent interface, PaperCP, based on Anoto technology, which consists of Bluetooth digital pens and printouts.

between physical and digital affordances, a natural solution is to integrate them to create a better overall user experience.

In this paper, we investigate how to combine the advantages of physical artifacts like paper with the convenience of an electronic communication and archiving infrastructure. Specifically, based on a communication model for Active Learning, we propose a new Anoto [5]-based paper interface, PaperCP (Paper Classroom Presenter) (Figure 1), for Classroom Presenter, aimed at addressing the interaction and cost-benefit problems of the fully digital system. Our physical interface allows students to use Anoto-enabled slide printouts as an input interface, so that users can still enjoy the inherent advantages of paper. Using a digital pen, students can write directly on the handouts and can electronically submit their handwritten notes to the instructor, thereby maintaining two-way communication with the instructor. Furthermore, the compatibility of paper and digital interfaces allows multiple heterogeneous interfaces (i.e., paper and Tablet PC) to be simultaneously deployed with our system, so that users can choose which system to use for a given Active Learning activity.

To evaluate this system, we deployed it during four regular class sessions of an actual Software Engineering course at the University of Washington. Using qualitative in-class observations in addition to quantitative results from questionnaires and user logs, our study confirmed the feasibility of implementing and deploying PaperCP in a real-use scenario. The study also revealed that the choice of a print layout and digital pen configuration has a large impact on the perceived tangibility advantage of the physical interface. Finally, our experiences provide insight into designing new interfaces that combine paper and digital affordances.

2 Related Work

2.1 Computer-Supported Teaching and Learning

Technological support for teaching has been informed by the educational literature on the difficulties of engaging students with traditional university-style lectures [7, 9]. Active Learning [16] was proposed to address such issues by promoting in-class student involvement through activities, e.g., in Classtalk [10], and actively seeking feedback on the level of student learning [4].

The idea behind much of the work in classroom technology has been to enhance or offload certain activities, so that students and instructors can be more effective in the classroom. Opportunities for this include capturing the classroom experience to reduce note taking demands in Classroom 2000 [1], creating new communication channels for student-student in-class interaction in LiveNotes [17] and student-instructor communication in Classtalk [10], ActiveClass [24], and Classroom Presenter [3].

Specifically, Classroom Presenter (CP) supports sharing ink-based artifacts between students and the instructor in real-time by using networked Tablet PCs. Other similar systems include Debbie (now DyKnow) [11] and Ubiquitous Presenter [29]. Classroom Response Systems (also known as clickers) [10, 21] take a different approach, aggregating student information, as opposed to providing rich individual responses. Our system is built on top of the CP infrastructure, supporting the same real time student-instructor communication with a new paper interface.

The communication in Active Learning could also be non-real-time, e.g. without a fixed time relation between the actions of students and the instructor. For instance, ActiveClass [24] allows students to use PDAs to deliver asynchronous feedback to the instructor via web pages; Classroom Feedback Systems [2] are similar.

2.2 Paper-Computer Integration

There are many systems in the literature detailing paper-computer integration. Among them are DigitalDesk [28], A-Book [20] and PaperWindows [15], all of which use augmenting devices, such as overhead projectors, graphics tablets, and cameras to overlap digital and paper display content. Despite their high display fidelity and powerful digital functions, the augmenting devices' lack of portability limits these systems' paper affordances.

New Anoto technology [5] allows handwriting capture on paper with highly portable digital pens. Based on this, PADD [13] supports mapping handwriting from printouts to the corresponding digital pages. Using the PADD infrastructure, Papier-Craft [18] proposes a paper command system by using paper documents as a proxy to their digital copies, and mapping pen gesture commands on paper to corresponding digital manipulations. ButterflyNet [30] employs PapierCraft gestures to help field biologists organize and collect multimedia data centered on paper. The work presented in this paper borrows the idea of a "paper proxy", but targets the real-time student-instructor communication in Active Learning.

In the literature, similar real-time paper-digital interaction applications include PaperPoint [27]. Based also on Anoto technology, PaperPoint helps a presenter to annotate and select digital slides to show via printouts. In contrast, PaperCP focuses on instructor-student communication during in-class activities. Designed specifically for presentation practices, Palette [22] uses paper index cards to organize and choose digital slides to display, but it does not support digital editing on paper and is less general than PaperPoint.

3   A Communication Model of Active Learning

Active Learning involves students performing activities in the classroom and communicating with other students and the instructor. Here we focus on the student-instructor interactions, which can be characterized by the following communication model.

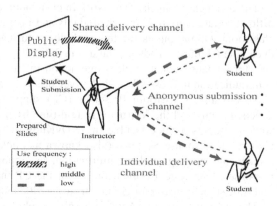

As illustrated in Fig. 2, there are two parties in the model, the instructor and the students. The instructor navigates through slides, presenting prepared lecture material or showing student artifacts, perhaps adding on-the-fly comments or sketches according to the students' understanding level. Each student follows the

Fig. 2. A communication model of Active Learning. It consists of three channels denoted by dashed lines, whose thickness corresponds to the amount of data transmitted over each specific channel.

presentation; navigating and annotating his/her own copy of the lecture materials, as well as taking notes.

Active Learning is achieved by the two parties via three main communication channels (Figure 2): First, the instructor uses the *individual delivery channel* to distribute activities and lecture materials to individual students, e.g., traditional paper handouts, transparencies, or digital PowerPoint slides. These materials are relatively static through the course of the class and are intended for the students' personal use. The distribution typically occurs just once, at the beginning of a lecture. The channel's digital implementation is highly efficient. In comparison, delivering physical handouts before class is a burden, but will not severely affect what happens during the class time.

At certain points during the lecture, the instructor announces prepared activities to involve students in thinking and presenting ideas, such as drawing workflow diagrams, ranking key factors, selecting a multiple choice answer, or writing snippets of source code. Then, students use the *anonymous submission* channel to anonymously submit to the instructor answers or artifacts that they dynamically create during class. This channel is often accessed several times during a class session. Compared to handing in physical artifacts, electronic submission is much more efficient. It is important to note that the amount of data (e.g., brief comments, ranking, polls, as well as rich responses like graphs or drawings) traveling from the students to the instructor is usually smaller than in the reverse direction. This makes it possible to use a simple student interface with only inking functions to support Active Learning. The support for anonymous artifact submission is important for encouraging shyer students to take part in classroom activities too.

After collecting student submissions, the instructor uses the *shared delivery* channel, usually a public display, for showing selected student-submitted artifacts. She may comment on the student answers, lead discussion on the open questions, and elicit further activities. Thus, the students not only receive feedback about their level of understanding, but are also encouraged to think more deeply about the lecture material. This channel is the dominant channel for class-wide presentation and is the focus of classroom discussions. The implementation of this channel increasingly employs digital projectors, which take the place of traditional overhead projectors or whiteboards, and accordingly student submissions need to have some electronic form to be displayed and discussed on the digital projectors.

4 Classroom Presenter: A System Supporting the Model

The PaperCP system is an extension of the Classroom Presenter system (Fig. 3), which employs wirelessly connected Tablet PCs for the two-way instructor-student communication. The instructor Tablet PC acts as a server, while the student Tablet PCs are clients. The *individual delivery* channel is implemented with IP multicast, through which all slides of a lecture can be efficiently delivered from the server to each student device at the beginning of the class. When the instructor reaches a slide with a prepared question, each student writes a response directly on their Tablet PC and digitally submits it via point-to-point connections to the instructor station. This is the *anonymous submission* channel. In addition, a public display conwwwnected to the instructor station is used as the *shared delivery* channel, which the instructor uses to display selected student submissions and offer her comments.

Classroom Presenter highlights the advantages of digital affordances:

- Efficiency: It makes instructor-student communication less distracting.
- Flexibility: Instructors can edit slides or student-submissions on-the-fly.
- Compatibility with existing practices using a data projector and digital slides.

However, there are drawbacks of the Tablet PC interface in terms of the interaction experience and the cost-benefit alignment:

- Tablet PCs are still relatively inferior to paper in terms of readability, writability, tangibility, and social acceptance.
- Computers can be distracting, as students may be tempted to use other unrelated applications (e.g., instant messaging or email) in class.
- Taking notes on a Tablet PC may be incompatible with some students' existing paper-based note taking styles.
- The cost of a Tablet PC may be too high for some students to own one.

In contrast to the Tablet PC interface, traditional physical printouts and transparencies are easy to read and write on, flexible in spatial layout, readily manipulated by hand, and relatively cheap. We explore how to integrate these advantages of physical interfaces into the highly efficient communication infrastructure of Classroom Presenter, in order to achieve a better balance between physical and digital affordances.

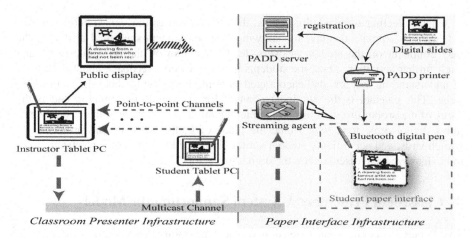

Fig. 3. Architecture of PaperCP system: an integration of the Classroom Presenter Infrastructure (left area) and the Paper Interface Infrastructure (right area). The three communication channels are denoted by dashed arrowed lines. The system supports the concurrent use of the student Tablet PC interface and the paper interface.

5 Designing a Paper-Based Interface for Classroom Presenter

The following principles guided our design:

- *Paper affordances.* Constraints on paper-based note-taking or annotating should be minimized since the paper affordances are the key to overcoming the limitations of the digital interface.
- *Efficient communication.* The paper interface should support efficient student submissions, a key enabling aspect of Active Learning communication.
- *Compatibility.* The paper-based interface should be deployable alongside a Tablet PC interface for flexibility in choosing and comparing interfaces.
- *Realistic deployment.* The implementation should be suitable for real classroom deployment, so that realistic user experiences can be observed.

Based on these principles, we first examined the Active Learning communication media according to the characteristics of relevant interactions.

For instructor interactions, the purely digital interface is believed to work best. First, the instructor needs an interface that allows her to review and selectively display digital student submissions that are dynamically created in class, which is impossible with a purely paper interface like PaperPoint [27]. Although an additional computer interface could be used for this task, frequent switching between paper and computer interfaces may be inconvenient and distracting to the instructor.

For student interactions, however, a paper-based interface is preferred because of its better trade-off between physical and digital affordances. First, paper possesses good interaction advantages as discussed above and a digital pen is much cheaper than a Tablet PC. Second, as used in PaperPoint [27], the new Bluetooth digital pens make it possible to capture and submit students' handwriting on paper in real time. Thus, a paper interface for digital submission is technically possible.

As a result, we devised an architecture that mixes paper and computer components (Fig. 3). The instructor interface remains unchanged, but the student interface can be implemented either on paper (the part in the dashed box in the middle of Fig. 3) or on a Tablet PC. Both implementations share the same underlying Classroom Presenter infrastructure. The paper interface consists of only Bluetooth digital pens and slides printed on Anoto paper Fig. 4). Using digital pens, students can annotate the handouts or take notes as if using a normal pen and paper, and, more importantly, they can issue commands to delete or submit specific notes on paper via the underlying electronic communication channels.

5.1 Student Note-taking and Submission

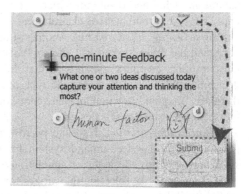

The use of digital pens and printed slides is fully compatible with existing pen-and-paper note-taking practices. Students' writing on the printout is automatically captured by the digital pen. However, due to the static nature of printed content, we need special mechanisms to implement student sub-mission, equivalent to that of the Tablet PC interface.

In the simplest case, the instructor uses a dedicated slide to solicit a sub-mission from students, and the written artifacts on the slide are expected to be submitted. In such a case, students can submit their writing by simply ticking

Fig. 4. A paper interface. (a) printed button "deselect". (b) printed button "submit". The inset illustrates a button ticking mark. (c) lasso selection to submit. (d) personal doodling, not for submission. Further, the area within the frame is "public" and the rest is "private".

(i.e., drawing a check mark as illustrated in Fig. 4) the printed button labeled "submit" on the handouts. All digital notes captured from the slide are immediately sent to the instructor's computer. Our experiments show that such button clicking is very robust and easy to use.

However, when personal notes and activity answers occur in the same slide, we need to distinguish the public notes, which the student is willing to show to the class, from the private ones, which are for the student's private use (e.g., personal comments or doodles like (d) in Fig. 4). Similar privacy issues are discussed in systems such as Stitching [14], which supports varying cross-Tablet PC interaction patterns according to the collaboration levels of co-located users. PaperCP focuses on sharing notes with all class members via the public display, and thus presents as small a cognitive foot-print as possible.

5.2 Advanced Features

While the Tablet PC interface provides dynamic visual feedback for distinguishing notes, e.g., by changing color of selected strokes, it is impossible for a paper-only interface to take the same approach. Instead, we examined three different methods for public-private note selection, namely spatial differentiation, pen-switching differentiation, and gesture differentiation. The adopted strategy was to combine spatial and gesture differentiation.

Spatial differentiation. The idea was borrowed from systems like SharedNotes [12] in which a specific region within a slide is defined as a "public" area and the rest of the slide is a "private" area. In our case, only notes within the public area (the area within the frame, see Fig. 4) may be shown on the public display. This design is intuitive and robust, but it prevents users from writing personal comments near pertinent information in the public area. Furthermore, users must determine a priori what to submit and what not to submit, which is not compatible with the typical user experience. Thus we turn to pen-based strategies.

Pen-switching differentiation. Another strategy is to use two pens: one for "public" notes and the other for "private" notes. Although this method can overcome the spatial constraint, our pilot test showed that this method also suffered from the a priori decision problem, and changing the type of a written stroke is often awkward. Furthermore, frequently switching pens turns out to be a non-trivial extra burden for users. So, we excluded this design.

Gesture differentiation. Here we borrow the ink/gesture approach of PapierCraft [18], a gesture-based command system for paper interfaces. In this approach, *ink strokes* are used to add notes or annotations at any location, and *gestures strokes* to issue commands like selecting ink strokes for submission. This method provides good spatial flexibility and avoids the a priori decision problem.

For distinguishing between ink and gesture strokes, our interface takes an explicit mode-based approach similar to PapierCraft's. Due to the lack of a convenient mode-switch button on the digital pen, we decided to use two pens, one for ink strokes and the other for gesture strokes. This two-pen configuration is far less problematic than that of the *pen-switching differentiation* due to the lower frequency of changing pens: users can first write free-form notes with the ink pen then select a subset of the content for submission with the gesture pen. Note that at this point the users can change their minds about any previously written strokes.

For easiness-flexibility tradeoff, we opted to combine the *spatial* and *gesture differentiation* methods as follows. If there is no selection gesture in the "public" area, all strokes in public area are sent, otherwise only the selected strokes are submitted. To further reduce the burden of switching pens, we allow submission with either pen. Thus, if a student uses only the simple *spatial differentiation*, she can keep using the ink pen for both writing and ticking the submission button.

Deleting unwanted content is another important issue. In many cases, simply crossing out unwanted strokes may be enough, but sometimes students want to remove certain writing from the digital record for neatness or privacy. To this end, PaperCP supports two deleting gestures, a zigzag, which removes strokes crossed by the gesture, and a lasso with zigzag inside, which deletes strokes inside the lasso. Of course, without physical erasing, the digitally deleted strokes will still remain on the printout. For the sake of simplicity, we have not implemented "undo" for stroke deletion.

5.3 System Implementation

Fig. 3 illustrates the system architecture, in which the Streaming Agent plays a vital role in bridging the gap between the paper interface and the digital infrastructure. The agent receives handwriting captured by the digital pen via a Bluetooth connection, and contacts the PADD server for physical-to-digital mapping information, which was registered when the printouts were generated (refer to [13] for details). With the mapping information, the agent translates the strokes from physical page coordinates into a digital counterpart and then processes the data in the digital domain. Much like a standard student CP client, the agent communicates with the instructor CP station to receive broadcast slides and submit student input over a point-to-point channel. Thus, the new system scales similarly as the original Classroom Presenter [3] system, which can usually handle a classroom of about 30 student tablets.

The streaming agent implements the exactly same communication protocols as the original student CP, so the paper-based interface is completely transparent to the rest of the CP infrastructure. One agent is needed for each paper interface user, and we use one PC near a user to run only one agent for simplicity. For larger classes and to minimize deployment costs, it is desirable to employ a Bluetooth infrastructure with multiple access points [8] distributed in the classroom, so that all digital pens are within Bluetooth signal range and multiple agents can share computing resources on one host computer.

6   Exploratory User Study

To examine the feasibility of our new paper interface and to explore possible design issues, we conducted an exploratory user study using PaperCP alongside the original Tablet PC-based system. Specifically, we focused on the following aspects of the system:

- **Student-instructor communication**: whether or not PaperCP can effectively support student-instructor communication for Active Learning.
- **Interface integration**: whether or not the paper interface can be naturally and efficiently integrated into Active Learning with little disruption.
- **Gesture commands**: whether or not the gesture operations on the paper interface can achieve the designed functionality.

6.1 Experiment Setting

The general goal of the experiment was to get a real sense about how a paper-interface works. We ran the experiment in a real-life scenario, instead of a lab setting, for a more realistic evaluation. During our evaluation, we changed as little as possible the instructor's lecture material, teaching style, and schedule, and did not force students to do any special actions. Finally, experiment data logging was done in the background without interference with participants and strictly kept anonymous.

We deployed the system in an undergraduate Software Engineering class at the University of Washington. A 20-minute training session was first conducted to allow all students to try out the new paper interface and to answer questions. Students were asked to write their answers on handouts and submit them to the instructor, who then showed the submissions on a public display. Subsequently, we conducted four formal experimental sessions (each lasting 60 minutes) in regular classes on four days within a period of two weeks. During the sessions, the instructor used the Classroom Presenter infrastructure to present slides, collect student submission, and conduct in-class discussion as is usual for the course. The students, our participants, used either the Tablet PC interface or the paper counterpart for the Active Learning interactions.

To limit the variance introduced by different subjects and lecture topics in each class session, half of the students used the paper interface and the other half used the computer interface. Each student alternated between the two interfaces across sessions. At the end of each session, every student was asked to fill out a very brief questionnaire about the interface that he/she used during that session. After the final (fourth) session, they were asked to answer an overall comparison questionnaire.

For qualitative measurements, we used Likert-scale questionnaires about the users' perceived difficulty level of specific actions with an interface, such as note-taking, submission, and erasing. For quantitative measurements, we instrumented the two interfaces, and logged important events such as pen property changes, strokes, gestures, slide navigation, and submission.

6.2 Apparatus and Participants

During an experiment session, each participant was given a PaperCP interface or a Tablet PC running Classroom Presenter. In the current PaperCP implementation, we used a Tablet PC to run the Bluetooth data processing program (see section 5.3) for each participant, but it was placed several feet away from the participant, to minimize distraction. To reduce the user experience variance caused by the different size and layout of slides on the different interfaces, we intentionally printed one slide on one letter-sized sheet of paper, and made it roughly the size of its digital counterpart on a Tablet PC. For better navigation flexibility, we did not staple the handout pages.

All eight registered students for the class participated in the user study without pay. According to the background survey, two of the participants use laptops and another participant uses a Tablet PC to take notes occasionally. Seven participants frequently use normal pen and paper for notes. None of them had ever used a digital pen, but all of them had had experience with Classroom Presenter in previous courses.

6.3 Experiment Results and Discussion

We report the user experiences and lessons learned from the experiment with respect to our axes of evaluation: Student-instructor communication, Interface integration, and Gesture commands. Due to the small number of participants and high variability in the data, we focus here on qualitative rather than statistical analysis of the collected data.

6.3.1 Student-Instructor Communication

There were 11 class activities in total during the four experimental sessions, or about 3 per session. The 11 class activities covered a wide range of question types, including drawing diagrams, ranking items, brainstorming answers to open-ended questions, commenting source code, drawing curves, and so on.

Fig. 5 illustrates such a digital student submission from the paper interface, in which the instructor added the comments in green during the public discussion.

Generally, all 11 activities went smoothly without any show-stopping technical problems. The paper interface was well-received by the students. In

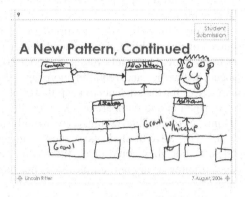

Fig. 5. An example of a student submission from the paper interface. The green strokes are the instructor's comments.

terms of the workflow, both interfaces successfully sent student submissions in real time. The paper interface was used by students as actively as the Tablet PC interface. According to our log data, the instructor received 33 submissions from paper interfaces and 29 from Tablet PCs during the experiment, and all participants had submissions via both interfaces. This suggests a high level of robustness for the paper interface. As a result, both instructor and students were able to focus on the Active Learning process, and not be distracted by issues with the technology.

We also found that the unfamiliar paper interface may have caused usability problems. For example, participant P1 complained "the pen didn't send what you wrote exactly". The log shows P1 mistook the "deselect" button for "deleting", and his personal doodling had been submitted accidentally, which may have led to his negative impression. To avoid such issues, more user training and/or stronger real time feedback are needed for the new paper interface.

Note that the number of activities was limited by the available time, as each activity involved a series of actions including question announcement, student thinking, answer collection, submission comments and discussion. Plus, given the small class size, the instructor commented on almost every student submission to encourage student participation.

6.3.2 Interface Integration

Here we consider the interface integration in terms of interface compatibility, user interaction and workflow. First, the paper interface is confirmed to be compatible with the original Tablet PC interface, because in the experiment both interfaces worked concurrently without interference. This is important to supporting heterogeneous device deployment as well as varying user preferences and needs.

Second, students could easily integrate paper interaction with the learning activities. They spread out and browsed the handouts on their desks, wrote answers with pens and submitted results on their paper. Participant P2 preferred the paper interface because of the high degree of control over the handouts, noting "Sometimes, we can not control slides using Tablet PC". However, two other participants, P3 and P4 complained of "too much paper to flip through", indicating unexpected inconveniences of the new interface.

Looking further into the questionnaire comments and logs, we identify two main sources of this problem: 1) the one-slide-per-page layout forces students to flip paper for every slide. Given an average of about 30 slides per session, manual flipping was indeed distracting and required more user effort. 2) Unstapled paper slides require more effort for the students to keep things organized; the original intent was for flexible navigation and comparison. As a result, such negative effects counteract paper's advantages of quick browsing, convenient bi-manual manipulation and flexible spatial layout [26]. Several students suggested using paper slides only for the submission slides, so that they could enjoy the writing experience of paper but avoid annoying paper flipping. Printing multiple slides per page is another way to reduce the interference.

Finally, for the workflow, it is revealed that PaperCP has a potential drawback in out-of-class logistics: because the printing takes time, the instructor usually has to finalize the slides the day before classes at the latest. This may prevent lecturers from doing "last-minute" work, a flexibility which some like. Moreover, once the slides are printed out, it becomes hard to change or even add slides. These workflow problems could be solved by an optimized printing facility for Anoto-enabled handouts.

6.3.3 Gesture Commands

Here, we examine the effectiveness of gesture commands for the selective submission and deletion functions. In general, students seldom used the lasso to select partial notes for submission on either the paper or Tablet PC interfaces. The two interfaces each had only one user of the lasso selection. This phenomenon can be attributed to the design of the presentation slides: the submission slides are usually dedicated to the activity, so almost all user writing on those slides were answers for class activities; thus few lasso gestures were required to distinguish public notes from private ones.

The deletion gesture also suffered from infrequent use. This could be attributed to the weak feedback of the paper interface, which the users were not used to. The inconvenience of pen-switching is another possible reason. This suggests the importance of stronger feedback and single-pen operations.

7 Future Work

Our preliminary experiment has effectively proven the feasibility of the paper interface and its compatibility with existing practices. It has also revealed challenges in the design of the paper interface. In response, we will investigate appropriate layouts of printed slides. Specifically, we will consider factors such as the number of sheets of paper, the space for pen input, and the content of slides, as well as students' note-taking styles. This will help us to better understand the previously revealed problems and to validate proposed solutions.

Moreover, as the experiment analysis suggests, real-time feedback is the key for complex interactions on paper. It could be useful to enhance the current system with a pen-top feedback mechanism compatible with standard pen-and-paper interaction. For instance, the multimodal feedback pen [19] proposed by Liao et al. can provide real-time feedback information via built-in LEDs, vibration motors, and speech. Furthermore, considering users' high likelihood of working in a computer-rich environment, it will be interesting to combine the electronic and paper interfaces, e.g., providing digital visual feedback on a handheld device for paper interaction and incorporating multimedia data into student submissions. Similar methods are used in systems like Paper++ [23] and PaperLink [6], which employ a separate display or PDA to render dynamic content associated with specific regions in paper documents.

8 Conclusion

This paper examined the interplay between physical and digital affordances via a case study of an Active Learning support system. We identify key usability issues with the full digital system and present a paper-based interface which combines paper flexibility with the digital editing and communication. By deploying the system in a real classroom and conducting experiments in comparison with the Tablet PC interface, we have confirmed the feasibility of such a paper interface within a digital infrastructure. Our experiment also suggests that print layout, pen configuration, and sufficient user training are crucial aspects for paper interfaces to retain the tangibility advantage of the physical interface.

Acknowledgements

This work was supported by Microsoft Research (as part of the Microsoft Center for Interaction Design and Visualization at the University of Maryland) and NSF under Grant IIS-0414699 and IIS-00447730. We would like to thank all volunteer participants and appreciate Anoto for their support with streaming pattern space, Logitech for streaming software, and HP for hardware donations.

References

1. Abowd, G.D.: Classroom 2000: an experiment with the instrumentation of a living educational environment. IBM Syst. J. 38(4), 508–530 (1999)
2. Anderson, R., VanDeGrift, T., Wolfman, S.A., Yasuhara, K., Anderson, R.: Interaction patterns with a classroom feedback system: making time for feedback. In: Proceedings of CHI '03 extended abstracts, pp. 880–881 (2003)
3. Anderson, R., Anderson, R., Simon, B., Wolfman, S.A., VanDe Grift, T., Yasuhara, K.: Experiences with a tablet PC based lecture presentation system in computer science courses. In: Proceedings of the 35th SIGCSE technical symposium on computer science education, pp. 56–60
4. Angelo, T.A., Cross, K.P.: Classroom Assessment Techniques: A Handbook for College Teachers. Jossey-Bass Publishers, San Francisco (1993)
5. Anoto, Development Guide for Service Enabled by Anoto Functionality. Anoto (2002)
6. Arai, T., Aust, D., Hudson, S.E.: PaperLink: a technique for hyperlinking from real paper to electronic content. In: Proceedings of CHI'97, pp. 327–334 (1997)
7. Bligh, D.A.: What's the Use of Lectures? Jossey-Bass Publishers, San Francisco (2000)

8. Bluegiga, Bluetooth Access Server, http://www.bluegiga.com/
9. Bransford, J.D., Brown, A.L., Cocking, R.R.e.: How People Learn: Brain, Mind, Experience, and School (Expanded Edition). National Academy Press, Washington (2000)
10. Dufresne, R., Gerace, W., Leonard, W., Mestre, J., Wenk, L.: Classtalk: A Classroom Communication System for Active Learning. Journal of Computing in Higher Education 7, 3–47 (1996)
11. DyKnow (2006), http://www.dyknow.com/
12. Greenberg, S., Boyle, M., LaBerge, J.: PDAs and shared public displays: Making personal information public, and public information personal. Personal Technologies 3(1) (1999)
13. Guimbretiere, F.: Paper Augmented Digital Documents. In: Proceedings of UIST'03, pp. 51–60 (2003)
14. Hinckley, K., Ramos, G., Guimbretiere, F., Baudisch, P., Smith, M.: Stitching: Pen Gestures that Span Multiple Displays. In: Proceedings of AVI'04, pp. 23–31 (2004)
15. Holman, D., Vertegaal, R., Altosaar, M., Troje, N., Johns, D.: Paper windows: interaction techniques for digital paper. In: Proceedings of CHI'05, pp. 591–599 (2005)
16. Johnson, D., Johnson, R., Smith, K.: Active Learning: Cooperation in the College Classroom. Interaction Book Company, Minnesota (1998)
17. Kam, M., Wang, J., Iles, A., Tse, E., Chiu, J., Glaser, D., Tarshish, O., Canny, J.: Livenotes: a system for cooperative and augmented note-taking in lectures. In: Proceedings of CHI'05, pp. 531–540 (2005)
18. Liao, C., Guimbretière, F., Hinckley, K.: PapierCraft: a command system for interactive paper. In: Proceedings of UIST05, pp. 241–244 (2005)
19. Liao, C., Guimbretière, F., Loeckenhoff, C.E.: Pentop feedback for paper-based interfaces. In: Proceedings of UIST'06, pp. 211–220 (2006)
20. Mackay, W.E., Pothier, G., Letondal, C., Bøegh, K., Sørensen, H.E.: The missing link: augmenting biology laboratory notebooks. In: Proceedings of UIST'02, pp. 41–50 (2002)
21. Mazur, E.: Peer Instruction: A User's Manual. Prentice Hall, New Jersey (1997)
22. Nelson, L., Ichimura, S., Pedersen, E.R., Adams, L.: Palette: a paper interface for giving presentations. In: Proceedings of CHI'99, pp. 354–361 (1999)
23. Norrie, M.C.,Signer, B.: Switching Over to Paper: A New Web Channel. In: Proceedings of Web Information Systems Engineering'03, pp. 209–218 (2003)
24. Ratto, M., Shapiro, R.B., Truong, T.M., Griswold, W.G.: The ActiveClass Project: Experiments in Encouraging Classroom Participation. In: Proceedings of CSCL'03, pp. 477–486 (2003)
25. Razmov, V.,, Anderson, R.: Pedagogical techniques supported by the use of student devices in teaching software engineering. In: Proceedings of SIGCSE'06, pp. 344–348 (2006)
26. Sellen, A.J., Harper, R.H.R.: The Myth of the Paperless Office, 1st edn. MIT press, Cambridge (2001)
27. Signer, B.: Fundamental Concepts for Interactive Paper and Cross-Media Information Spaces (ETH No. 16218), PhD thesis, Swiss Federal Institute of Technology, Zurich(2005)
28. Wellner, P.: Interacting with paper on the DigitalDesk. Communications of the ACM 36(7), 87–96 (1993)
29. Wilkerson, M., Griswold, W.G., Simon, B.: Ubiquitous presenter: increasing student access and control in a digital lecturing environment. In: Proceedings of SIGCSE'05, pp. 116–120 (2005)
30. Yeh, R.B., Liao, C., Klemmer, S.R., Guimbretière, F., Lee, B., Kakaradov, B., Stamberger, J., Paepcke, A.: ButterflyNet: A Mobile Capture and Access System for Field Biology Research. In: Proceedings of CHI'06, pp. 571–580 (2006)

Seeing More: Visualizing Audio Cues

Tony Bergstrom and Karrie Karahalios

Department of Computer Science
University of Illinois Urbana-Champaign
Urbana, IL 61801
{abergst2, kkarahal}@cs.uiuc.edu

Abstract. Using audio visualization, we seek to demonstrate how natural interaction is augmented with the addition of interaction history. Our *Conversation Clock* visualization captures and represents audio in a persistent and meaningful representation to provide social cues not available in an otherwise ephemeral conversation. In this paper we present user study evaluation of the *Conversation Clock* as utilized by familiar groups and demonstrate how individuals use the salient cues to evaluate their own interaction.

1 Introduction

Having spent thousands of years of socializing, communication and speech are natural interactions for most people. It is a skill so honed that most people do not consider how complicated communication is. More than just speaking, face to face communication can be broken into 7% words, 38% tone of voice and 55% body language [1]. These social cues are sensed and utilized as necessary during conversation; however, details of interaction are promptly forgotten [2][3] or the cue is interpreted and reciprocated unconsciously [4].

Social interaction contains observable aspects of conversational dominance, interruption, length of turns, turn taking, interruption, overlapping of speech, the rhythm and flow of conversation, etc. These aspects can be detected by reviewing or recording interaction, but are difficult to utilize as cues during a conversation. With the *Conversation Clock*, we use these aspects to visually augment collocated conversation with new conversational cues.

The *Conversation Clock* makes salient aspects of conversation that would be otherwise unnoticed. In this paper, we demonstrate the effects of augmenting collocated conversation to gauge how people percieve themselves and others. As results of our user study have shown, participants in conversation become more aware of their own and other participants' interaction and react to cues differently creating a more balanced conversation.

2 Related Work

The bulk of our work is situated in audio visualization. Before discussing our own project, we will briefly present previous work in visualizing sound and conversation.

C. Baranauskas et al. (Eds.): INTERACT 2007, LNCS 4663, Part II, pp. 29–42, 2007.

DiMicco et al. describe groups of four and how their participation might be affected by a shared display[5][6]. The display was projected onto two walls facing each other. Participants in this system must significantly divert their gaze to view and interpret the displayed information. The visualization consisted of a labeled histogram, each bar depicting the corresponding participant's contribution to discussion. Though the contribution represented aggregated interaction data, participants could not directly examine the conversation history. Based on the measured contribution, the histogram explicitly labeled participants as "over-participating," "participating" and "under-participating" on the shared screen. The goal of this system was to aid group decision making by balancing interaction during discussion. During a study of group problem solving situations, DiMicco measured the change of participation levels. Observational and experimental data indicated that the over-participators were more likely to back off than the under-participators were to speak up.

In later work, DiMicco compiled and examined Second Messenger, a suite of visualizations, for asynchronous review of a meeting [5][7]. Having shown that live displays influence group participation, the suite explored more expressive visualizations. These visualizations are examined post-meeting, at times when participants have opportunity to contemplate and interpret the meaning of the visuals. Each visualization focused on different aspects of interaction including relative participation, turn-taking, overlapping speech, and history.

Previous work with Visiphone examined the effect of visualizing audio in remotely mediated conversation between two locations[8][9]. Visiphone presented a domed projection surface, allowing participants to gather around and focus their gaze on the device while talking. A spiraling and cascading stream of circles on the surface continuously show speech and aural activity between the two spaces. The visualization conveyed the degree of aural contribution by adjusting the diameter of the circles as they spiraled down the sides. Simultaneous activity on both ends of the Visiphone connection presents overlapping circles allowing the device to reveal patterns of conversational dominance, turn taking, and interruption. The visualization allows you to "see things you know, but do not realize you know." Visiphone directly influenced the interaction between two parties without explicitly providing direction. Participants in the local spaces adjusted the volume of their own speech to visually match the volume of the remote speakers rather than by ear. Additionally, conversational dominance became obvious as the dome's color becomes visually dominated by a single hue. Due to the salience of balance in communication, Visiphone was recommended for use in areas such as marriage counseling. We extend this investigation to explore how this interaction changes when there are no remote individuals and whether visualization provides the same influence when participants are in the same space.

As a museum installation, Vigas presented Artifacts of the Presence Era to demonstrate history of a space over time [10]. This visualization used a geological metaphor to aggregate time. Pictures of the space were regularly taken, portions of which were layered on the already existing history. Audio input was sampled to determine the shape of the next layer. The audio samples, based on volume, revealed a larger portion of the image during periods of activity. Older layers were compressed as the new images were added to facilitate a geological metaphor. The result is a visualization of the installation space that highlights the change of activity and gives a sense of a space's history.

A work by Karahalios, Telemurals, connected two remote spaces by abstractly rendering and projecting video [11]. Individuals were obscured but became more visible and clear as both spaces interacted. Speech recognition provided a channel of interaction as it was displayed along with the abstract depiction of the other space. Telemurals, effectively increased conversation to at least five times it's normal level.

Numerous artistic installations have visualized live conversation and sound [12][13]. Work by Levin and Lieberman included *Hidden Worlds*, a visualization of speech as three dimensional bubbles that float over the table as participants wear special glasses to see these bubbles. Another piece, *RE:MARK* creates shapes symbolic of spoken phonemes that escape from the head of a person's shadow. Many other installations were also on display. These installations have been successful at encouraging both individual and group interaction by allowing users to manipulate a visual depiction of their aural input.

Another branch of audio visualization is music visualization. Most computer based music players utilize visualizations such as G-Force, Geiss, Advanced Visual Studio (AVS), or something similar [14][15][16]. To generate visuals, these visualizations incorporate physical characteristics of audio input such as amplitude, frequency analysis, beat detection, etc. Used for performance and entertainment, these visualizations focus on the physical characteristics of sound and not the interaction between multiple sound sources.

Aside from audio visualization, text-based chat systems have been augmented to include additional visual cues for remote participants. Systems like Babble and Chat Circles have sought to create a new interaction environments to show conversational activity, history and status [17][18].

In the following sections, we describe our own work with audio and visualization in order to provide social mirrors to collocated groups. We present a user study and demonstrate how the *Conversation Clock* makes interaction patterns more salient to participants.

3   Conversation Clock

As we describe in our previous work [19][20], the *Conversation Clock* visualizes the interaction visualizes the interaction patterns of up to four individual and provides participants with a communal social mirror. Representing each participant with an associated color, the *Conversation Clock* builds a visual history of ephemeral audio (Figure 1). Using a circular structure to represent the passage

Fig. 1. Participants are seated around the *Conversation Clock* table (*left*). Lapel microphones monitor conversation while the visualization of history is projected in the center. The *Conversation Clock* provides a visual history of interaction and communication (*right*). Each contribution displays bars colored to indicate the speakers' identities. The lengths of these bars indicate the degree of participation, measured by volume. As a conversation progresses, a history is built with concentric rings reminiscent of the rings on a tree.

Fig. 2. Above we see a close up of aural contribution represented in the *Conversation Clock*. The length of individual bars correspond to the aural activity of speakers; longer bars indicate louder speech. Individual speech is seen as solid colored bars while layered bars demonstrate simultaneous speech. The dots at the right indicate no aural contribution. As time progresses clockwise (left to right in this image), we see the changing dynamics of conversation contribution.

of time, the *Conversation Clock* emphasizes recent interaction in the outer ring while showing past interaction in the interior.

Aural contribution is gauged by sampling audio from a microphone assigned to each participant. We chose to use a calibrated amplitude as the main measure of determining speakers and contribution. Individual samples are translated into discrete marks on the table; the amplitude of the sample proportionally determines the length of the projected mark (Figure 2). These marks can be examined for current speaker, shown as the longest mark on the table; and multiple speakers, shown with overlapping marks.

The *Conversation Clock* displays a wide variety of conversational cues during interaction: turn taking, interruption, conversational dominance, silence, agreement, aural back-channels, mimicry, time spans, rhythm and flow. The cues persist on the table allowing participants to view the visualization when convenient.

4   Conversational Context

The *Conversation Clock* does not explicitly represent the context of a conversation. Rather than telling people how to interpret their conversation, we allow participants at the table to imbue meaning into the visualization and visual cues provided by the mirror. In this section we explain the intricacy of context in conversation and how it has influenced our design.

Conversation and language are flexible. Understanding spoken words is not the equivalent of understanding meaning. Similarly, observing characteristics of interaction is not the same as understanding their significance. It is easy to note occurrences of overlapping speech, changes in speaker, and periods of silence; examining recordings and sensor data reveals these events. Showing interruptions as opposed to a change of turn requires context.

Overlapping speech is a prime example where context must be used to understand its meaning. In the course of normal conversation, speech overlaps more often than people perceive [2]. Overlapping speech might be a hostile interruption, a back channel comment, an emphasis of a point, a change of turns or a misjudged transition. Looking at patterns without context, one cannot judge the true intent of the speakers.

The context of a conversation includes location, time, speaker, topic, word choice, inflection, etc. These are relevant to interpreting the meaning of the conversation. To understand interaction, one must examine cultural expectations, relationships of participants, gender, conversational style, etc. Altering the context of an individual significantly affects conversational patterns and style [21].

Context determines how interaction should be interpreted. Consider the simple case of remaining silent in response to a question. The silence could be an indication the questioned doubts his or her response, doesn't like to speak, or wasn't paying attention. When both parties are fully aware of the question, the questioner might prolong the silence, in order to apply pressure for a response. In another context, silence might be used to build curiosity by playfully choosing not to respond and building curiosity. Additionally, some people think silently when asked a question. These are all hypothetical situations; there are many more that can be arrived at by altering the context of the situation. Knowing that context is important to the interpretation of silence [2].

To be able to correctly characterize interactions such as interruptions, overpowering, conflict, and agreement we must first detect context. Our system is not sophisticated enough to analyze and interpret interaction adequately. To cope with context, we chose to provide no explicit interpretation in our visuals. Participants are presented with a visualization of their interactions over time, a social mirror of their conversation. Interpreting the context is left to the participants, making the Conversation Clock a meaningful and personal object to each group and conversation.

5   User Study

In order to gauge the influence of the *Conversation Clock* a user study was conducted over the course of a month. Participants were asked to commit to multiple sessions during that month under different experimental conditions. From these multiple sessions we gain better insight into how the *Conversation Clock* influences both groups and individuals.

5.1   Configuration

The user study took place in the HCI/Graphics lab in the UIUC Computer Science building. Four lapel microphones were wired to the bottom of our table. Tags on each individual microphone indicated the color associated with that microphone. Participants were informed that this color visualizes their activity in the *Conversation Clock*. A DV-camcorder monitored interaction from a nearby tripod during all sessions. During conversation, this video recorded gestures and physical references for later analysis.

5.2   Scenario

Participants were solicited as groups. Each member was expected to be familiar with all other members of the group and have a predefined purpose for meeting. We chose to use familiar groups in order to ensure a more comfortable and natural interaction environment. We felt that using random groups over the course of three separate sessions would alter interaction patterns as individuals became more familiar with the other participants in their group. We were also wary of mixing groups as each set of individuals would likely have different group dynamics due to the makeup of the group [21]. The focus of group conversation ranged from weekly meetings for a class project to casual conversation about movies and music.

Prior to each meeting, groups were asked to plan for a 30 minute session. However, groups were allowed to finish early as this would capture the natural break up of a session and would not force interaction and conversation.

5.3   Sessions

Each group met for three sessions. Groups first met in a session with no visualization present. Their interaction was observed and recorded. This session offered a baseline for later comparisons. In the second session, we introduced participants to the *Conversation Clock*. The final session was a repeat of the conditions in first session, allowing us to capture the natural variation inherent in different conversations amongst the same group.

In all sessions, participants wore microphones and underwent a calibration process. The *Conversation Clock* was generated for each session, though only projected for the second session. The purpose of running the visualization was to generate comparable data between the two conditions for analysis. The *Conversation Clock* stores a log of data that can be used to count turns taken and measure the amount spoken during the sessions.

When the visualization was first projected onto the table, participants were reminded of the color associated with their microphone. Speaking was encouraged to better understand how the visualization worked. This period allowed participants to become familiar with the visualization before the session began.

Within the visualization condition, two settings were examined. Each group would use the *Conversation Clock* with a visualization history of 5 minutes and a history of 20 minutes. To account for possible ordering effects, half of the groups were randomly chosen to receive the short history first. Participants were informed that they would be interrupted after 10 or 20 minutes (appropriately). A brief survey was administered and the *Conversation Clock* was cleared and set to use the remaining history setting before proceeding.

6 Study Results

During the second session, participants completed a brief questionnaire and survey. The surveys followed both the 10-minute condition and the 20-minute condition. In both cases participants reported their interaction to have been moderately altered by the table. Additionally, using a Wilcoxon Signed Rank Test, we found that the 20-minute session with the longer history had a significantly greater perceived effect upon participants (Table 1).

Table 1. Results of the Likert Scale surveys in the *Conversation Clock* User study. Using a Wilcoxon Signed Rank Test, we show that the longer history was perceived to have a greater effect on participation than the short history.

Measurement	10-minute	20-minute	Wilcoxon Z	Significance
Distracting	2.56	2.80	-1.364	$p < .2$
Helpful	2.46	2.36	-.966	$p < .4$
Altered You	2.48	3.00	-2.871	$p < .004$
Altered Others	2.65	3.02	-2.066	$p < .04$
Satisfaction	3.24	3.04	-1.475	$p < .2$

Level of satisfaction with the *Conversation Clock* varied greatly (ranging from 1 to 5) depending on the individual, group, and task. In the end, participants were neither particularly satisfied nor greatly dissatisfied. Participants reported the *Conversation Clock* to be somewhat distracting and somewhat helpful.

In addition to self-reported measures of interaction, coded video and audio recordings provided additional measures. The two sources of data we utilized were the audio logs and video.

Video coding and a repeated measures ANOVA revealed participants significantly changing their gaze patterns ($F(3,3)=15.56$ $p=0.03$) by averting their eyes more often from the conversation and to the *Conversation Clock* (Figure 3).

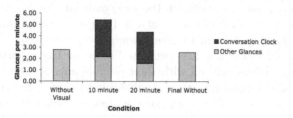

Fig. 3. The *Conversation Clock* contributed significantly to the increase of gaze movement on top of the gaze movement already present

A notable change in the table gestures was observed, though our sample could not show significance (F(3,3)=5.98 p=0.09).

Further examining the change in gaze patterns induced by the *Conversation Clock*, the 10-minute and 20-minute sessions were compared via paired t-test (t(6)=0.94 p=0.38). No significant change was observed, indicating gaze patterns were not affected by the length of visualized history.

Examining the audio data, we split participants into two categories. Based upon the initial non-visualization session, participants were categorized as above average and below average participants. As shown in Dimicco's earlier work, we expected the different categorizations of individuals to alter their participation differently [6]. This categorization is made strictly for analysis; participants were never informed of their categorization.

Running a repeated measures ANOVA, we found significant alteration in some areas (Table 2). Specifically, we noted reductions in turn length of the above average participants, and the increase in the number of turns taken by below average speakers. Having seen significance overall, we investigated the two visualization conditions. Once again, we found no indication of notable differences between the short and long history.

The *Conversation Clock's* observed data was also sorted to examine how interaction changed over time. As no significant differences were observed between

Table 2. Audio data, automatically logged and analyzed, was available for each participant. Expecting different changes to occur in each, participants were categorized as above average or below average participants based upon the initial session. We ran a repeated measures ANOVA and found above average participants change the length of there turns while below average participants changed the number of turns.

Participation	Metric	F value	Significance
	Leading	$F(3, 10) = 1.29$	$p = 0.3$
Above Average	Turns	$F(3, 8) = 1.19$	$p = 0.4$
	Length	$\mathbf{F(3, 5) = 9.22}$	$\mathbf{p = 0.02}$
	Leading	$F(3, 7) = 0.52$	$p = 0.7$
Below Average	Turns	$\mathbf{F(3, 9) = 3.89}$	$\mathbf{p = 0.05}$
	Length	$F(3, 12) = 3.32$	$p = 0.06$

Table 3. Re-sorting to indicate the first condition seen and the second condition seen, it becomes apparent there were learning or novelty effects. Participants in both the above and below average participation categories significantly altered the amount of time spent leading. Examining the other notable statistics, the above average category seems to have altered the length of their turns while the below average participants seemed to change the number of turns to accomplish this feat.

Participation	Metric	N	Condition 1	Condition 2	Paired t	Significance
	Leading	15	20.24	16.85	$t(14) = 2.66$	$p < 0.02$
Above Average	Turns	12	1.79	1.67	$t(11) = 0.839$	$p = 0.4$
	Length	11	14.87	12.21	$t(10) = 2.16,$	$p = 0.06$
	Leading	8	6.86	11.20	$t(7) = -3.56$	$p < 0.01$
Below Average	Turns	11	0.98	1.19	$t(10) = -2.06$	$p = .07$
	Length	12	7.69	9.30	$t(11) = -1.13$	$p = .3$

the 10 and 20 minute sessions, we became interested in how interaction changed with continued exposure. We see in Table 3, the most affected audio feature was the amount of time spent leading the conversation. This is true for both the above average and below average categorizations.

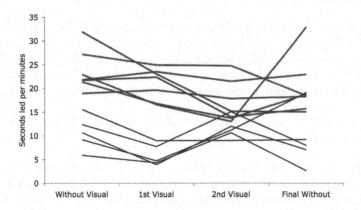

Fig. 4. Filtering participants based on their survey responses, we chose the individuals who reported a 4 or 5 when asked if their interaction was altered. Viewed chronologically, we see the same pattern in the individuals, below average participants (upper lines) lead more while above average (lower lines) lead less in the second visualization session.

Limiting our scope to the people reporting to be most affected, reporting a 4 or 5 on the written survey, we see a similarly striking pattern (Figure 4). After an initial break in period, the participants' conversation converges and reduces variance between speakers.

Data coded from the video is also emphasized by a chronological examination. Both the gaze patterns (**$F(3,4)=24.5$ p$=0.005$**) and gestures to the table

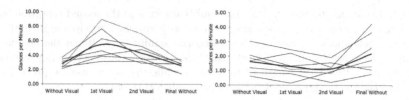

Fig. 5. When viewed chronologically, we see the first visualization session attracted a large number of glances away from conversation (left). Individual groups are indicated with black lines and the average with a thicker blue line. Overall, the *Conversation Clock* attracted looks and glances from participants in addition to other glances away from the table (Figure 3). Conversly, the *Conversation Clock* reduced the number of gestures made by participants during conversation (right).

($F(3,4)=10.20$ $p=0.02$) are significantly altered, according to a repeated measures ANOVA. Examination of the actual data shown the *Conversation Clock* still increasing the number of gazes averted from conversation and objects referenced in conversation and the decrease in the number of gestures (Figure 5).

6.1 Qualitative

The first session was perceived by most participants to be a normal interaction. As we purposely chose to use groups that were already formed and familiar, participants were in a familiar scenario. We consider the lab environment to be a small change, as many groups we studied do not meet at a regular location. A few minor comments were made when questioned, but nothing more than:

> "After a while it was [normal], once we got on topic... That and we had to sit at a table."

Observing the interaction of the groups during the sessions, we noticed that many of these initial sessions had skewed participation levels. This included three groups that had a combined four participants with less than 10% of contributed audio. Only one group reported an unbalanced conversation. Another stated it was very typical to what they had seen in past meetings.

The second session displayed our social mirror, the *Conversation Clock*. Participants seemed more aware of their own and others' participation.

> "I realized that I could monitor my speech patterns by watching the colors. It was interesting to train myself not to say 'umm' as much or pause."

> "It's easy to judge who is driving conversation."

> "I was trying to look at the circle to see whether we were balanced."

> "It's more salient, what's going on."

The awareness of conversation affected both speakers and listeners. Participants reported that when speaking they would desire to finish quickly and pass the conversation over to another; however, when listening, participants were aware of their silence and were compelled to speak.

During one group's discussion, a collaborative decision on what movies to watch at a weekly meeting, participants felt there should be a balance between themselves. However upon seeing the visualization they realized how heavily dominated the conversation was:

> *"I noticed when you're the one talking, you want to stop. But if you're mid topic you couldn't stop, because you had to finish your topic. But as soon as you finished your topic, you'd shut up."*

When the same group was asked if their interaction had been a balanced conversation the heaviest contributer (about 40% of the leads and 40% of the turns) responded, *"Not after looking at the clock."* This group also indicated an expectation of equal participation in this group, whereas a similarly 'unbalanced' viewed the contributions differently,

> *"Project managers communicate more than testers or developers, thus it is reasonable for it to be unbalanced."*

Another participant making a heavy contribution to conversation commented on the completed ring as a milestone, noting,

> *"By the time the ring had returned to the starting point I was like 'That's too much' and a stopped talking because I feel like I completed that ring. That's one unit that's mine."*

Whereas participants who had been silent for a while could be prompted or compelled to speak by the *Conversation Clock.*

> *"Based upon more of the history after a while, when I did glance at the clock and then it like reminded me to prompt [Blue] or direct questions to him."*

> *"It became all red, should green or yellow speak next?"* - Yellow

Very little conversation during the sessions directly referenced the *Conversation Clock.* Over the course of conversation a group would generally only mention the *Conversation Clock* one time if at all. During the experiment, the focus was on topic for their group. However, during the break between conditions and after the experiment was over, participants focused direct attention to the clock. Some just spoke to watch their contribution, others would yell and try to make their own color dominate, another group began to whistle. Groups reported it was *"fun"*, *"interesting"* and *"amusing"*.

The *Conversation Clock* encountered criticism in groups with a task based purpose or a more defined schedule. Groups with more structure and predefined interaction had less flexibility. One participant explained his lack of contribution,

"Due to our group roles each member was expected to talk about a certain project anyway, so I had little input on something I didn't know."

Some participants also found the visualization distracted them from the meeting at hand.

"I found it a bit distracting, I don't like things in my visual space."

Though *Conversation Clock* was not visible in the third session, participants reported thinking about it during their interaction. One participant stated:

"The first [session] I wasn't aware of it ... the second [session] I looked at the clock and tried to make it balanced. Now, I don't have a measure ... but I still tried to use the impression from last time. Because he always talked more [last time], I tried to consciously talk more [this time]."

Another participant who had been the heaviest participant in his group during session two commented:

"I think I consciously tried not to talk. Then I realized I wasn't talking at all."

7   Discussion

Our research illustrates that live social mirrors, like the *Conversation Clock*, influence the dynamics of interaction among collocated groups. By providing visual cues generated from the ephemeral audio conversation, we have created a visualization that allows participants to evaluate their own interaction and the history of conversation during that conversation. In this section we will summarize and discuss our findings.

- *People perceive a notable difference between short and long histories.* According to self reporting, longer histories are more effective at altering one's own interaction. However, no noticeable change in gaze, gestures made, time spent leading, turns taken, or length of turns ever corroborated this observation. We speculate if this perceived change does exist, it was something which we did not measure or the difference in what we did measure may be more subtle. Additionally, due to fallibility of self reporting, there may be no real difference in interaction [3].
- *The Conversation Clock encourages participants to remove their gaze from the conversation.* People looked away from the conversation more often. Glances to the *Conversation Clock* did not replace other glances that occur naturally during a conversation, and participants did not report a loss of quality interaction. As supported by the qualitative data, the social mirror led individuals to become curious of their representation. Some glances to the table are a result of inspecting one's own interaction.

- *Above average speakers alter the length of their turns while below average speakers alter the number of turns.* These observations illustrate how the common social mirror can be individually interpreted. The different interpretation could be seen in the their verbal adjustments and interview responses. Below average participants commented on domination of the entire table, noting it was mostly one color. Whereas above average participants mentioned completing rings as a milestone. This difference in observation and perception of interaction demonstrate the principle of small multiples [22]. In the larger picture made visible by history, one can see how they have contributed over the course of conversation. In the outer ring, detail is exposed for the recent past, distinctly affecting the current speaker.
- *Participants showed particular interest in their own interactions.* Qualitative feedback indicated that people were most aware of their own interaction and monitored their own contributions. They felt they were speaking too much or too little based upon what they saw. Additionally, some participants evaluated his own contribution and usage of filler words like "umm."
- *Ordering demonstrates a notable break in period for the Conversation Clock.* Many patterns of change in interaction become apparent when viewed chronologically. Nearly all our measurements indicated significant change. This strong change motivates a break-in period. Future studies are needed to investigate the continued, both regular and prolonged, use of the *Conversation Clock* to fully understand it's effect. This point is underscored by one group's comment almost 30 minutes into their second session when the realized, *"This IS useful."*

8   Conclusion

Audio visualization provides an informative medium to convey social, interactive, and meaningful cues. We have used varied lengths of audio history to show that live visualization of audio through social mirrors can provide influential cues for individual participation in conversation. Participants alter themselves in order to equalize the contribution of individuals.

References

1. Mehrabian, A.: Silent messages. Wadsworth, Belmont, California (1971)
2. Tannen, D.: Gender and Discourse. Oxford University Press, Oxford (1994)
3. Bernard, H.R., Killworth, P., Kronenfeld, D., Sailer, L.: The problem of informant accuracy: The validity of retrospective data. Annual Reviews Anthropology 13 (1984)
4. Whyte, W.H.: The Social Life of Small Urban Spaces. Municipal Art Society of New York (1988)
5. DiMicco, J.M.: Changing Small Group Interaction through Visual Reflections of Social Behavior. PhD thesis, Massachusetts Institute of Technology (2005)
6. DiMicco, J.M., Pandolfo, A., Bender, W.: Influencing group participation with a shared display. In: CSCW '04. Proceedings of the 2004 ACM conference on Computer supported cooperative work, pp. 614–623. ACM Press, New York (2004)

7. DiMicco, J.M., Hollenbach, K.J., Bender, W.: Using visualizations to review a group's interaction dynamics. In: CHI '06 extended abstracts on Human factors in computing systems, New York, USA, pp. 706–711. ACM Press, New York (2006)
8. Donath, J., Karahalios, K., Viégas, F.: Visualizing conversation. Journal of Computer Mediated Communication 4(4) (1999)
9. Donath, J., Karahalios, K., Viégas, F.: Visiphone. In: ICAD 2000: International Conference on Auditory Display (2000)
10. Viégas, F.B., Perry, E., Howe, E., Donath, J.: Artifacts of the presence era: Using information visualization to create an evocative souvenir. In: INFOVIS '04. Proceedings of the IEEE Symposium on Information Visualization (INFOVIS'04), Washington, DC, USA, pp. 105–111. IEEE Computer Society Press, Los Alamitos (2004)
11. Karahalios, K., Donath, J.: Telemurals: linking remote spaces with social catalysts. In: CHI '04: Proceedings of the SIGCHI conference on Human factors in computing systems, pp. 615–622. ACM Press, New York (2004)
12. Levin, G., Lieberman, Z.: Messa di Voce. Audiovisual Performance and Installation (2003)
13. Levin, G., Lieberman, Z.: In-situ speech visualization in real-time interactive installation and performance. In: NPAR '04: Proceedings of the 3rd international symposium on Non-photorealistic animation and rendering, pp. 7–14. ACM Press, New York (2004)
14. Geiss, R.: Geiss, http://www.geisswerks.com/geiss/index.html
15. Frankel, J.: Advanced visualization studio. (Nullsoft)
16. O'Meara, A.: G-force. http://www.soundspectrum.com/g-force/
17. Erickson, T., Smith, D.N., Kellogg, W.A., Laff, M., Richards, J.T., Bradner, E.: Socially translucent systems: social proxies, persistent conversation, and the design of 'babble'. In: CHI '99: Proceedings of the SIGCHI conference on Human factors in computing systems, New York, NY, USA, pp. 72–79. ACM Press, New York (1999)
18. Donath, J., Viégas, F.B.: The chat circles series: explorations in designing abstract graphical communication interfaces. In: DIS '02. Proceedings of the conference on Designing interactive systems, pp. 359–369. ACM Press, New York (2002)
19. Bergstrom, T., Karahalios, K.: Visualizing audio patterns in co-located groups. In: HICSS '07: Proceedings of the Fourtieth Annual Hawaii International Conference on System Sciences (2007)
20. Karahalios, K., Bergstrom, T.: Visualizing audio in group table conversation. In: TABLETOP '06: Proceedings of the First IEEE International Workshop on Horizontal Interactive Human-Computer Systems, Washington, DC, USA, pp. 131–134. IEEE Computer Society Press, Los Alamitos (2006)
21. Tannen, D.: Teachers classroom strategies should recognize that men and women use language differently. The Chronicle of Higher Education (1991)
22. Tufte, E.R.: The Visual Display of Quantitative Information. Graphics Press (1983)

CubeExplorer: An Evaluation of Interaction Techniques in Architectural Education

Hyunyoung Song[1], François Guimbretière[1], Michael A.Ambrose[2], and Carl Lostritto[2]

[1] Human-Computer Interaction Lab, Department of Computer Science,
[2] Architecture Program, School of Architecture, Planning and Preservation
University of Maryland, College Park, MD 20742, U.S.A
{hsong, francois}@cs.umd.edu, {ambrosem, carllos}@umd.edu

Abstract. During the early stages of architectural training, tangibility plays an important role in developing spatial awareness. In such contexts, tangible user interfaces are believed to provide a significant advantage as they combine the affordances of both the physical and the digital world. We introduce CubeExplorer, a hybrid 3D conceptual aid that combines physical interaction and digital modeling in an effort to complement conventional architectural space-training tools (such as physical materials and digital CAD programs). Using a digital pen as an input mechanism, CubeExplorer lets users perform subtractive 3D geometric operations on a simple paper based cube model while observing the resulting model on a display. The tangibility of the model simplifies navigation and command execution, while the digital interface makes it easy for users to explore multiple alternative designs. To evaluate the potential of such an approach, we conducted a user study in a normal classroom environment where students were provided with physical (wooden block), hybrid (CubeExplorer), and virtual (FormZ) interfaces to complete the same assignment. Our evaluation showed that CubeExplorer combined the advantages of both digital and tangible media. The advantages of CubeExplorer over digital media were substantiated in a follow-up study comparing CubeExplorer and SketchUp in a similar building task.

Keywords: Education, 3D modeling, pen-based interface, tangible user interface.

1 Introduction

One of the challenges in introductory architectural education is to develop the conceptual understanding of form and space in abstract ways [18]. Points, lines, and planes are used in increasingly sophisticated ways to describe geometric volumes of solids and voids. To do so, modern curricula are mixing physical media such as wood blocks, and digital media such as CAD programs, to help students discover these basic concepts in introductory classes. Unfortunately, both approaches come with advantages and disadvantages. Wood blocks offer a simplified format palette that they are easy to use, which helps students to focus on concepts. Yet, their physical restrictions might limit the scope of the students' composition. For example, gravity

C. Baranauskas et al. (Eds.): INTERACT 2007, LNCS 4663, Part II, pp. 43–56, 2007.
© IFIP International Federation for Information Processing 2007

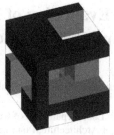

Fig. 1. Teaching students how to develop negative figural voids "The Cube Project", a class project in the Department of Architecture at our university, employed wooden blocks as physical tools (First), FormZ as a virtual tool (Second), and CubeExplorer as a hybrid tool (Last).

forces students to use a bottom up design, requiring students to focus on constructability. CAD tools such as AutoCAD [1], SketchUp [3], or FormZ [2], although not limited by physical constraints, are often complicated to learn and, as a result, limit exploration by novice users. In both cases, users have to adjust their intent to the capabilities and requirements of the tool, which prevents the student from quickly acquiring spatial concepts.

To address this problem, several tangible interfaces [4, 15-17] have been proposed to mitigate the limitations imposed by both physical and virtual tools. For example, digital cube systems [4, 17] allow users to build digital models using tangible cubes. This interaction via direct manipulation [13] makes the basic operations more transparent and reduces the learning curve. However, special equipment is required and only defined sets of operations are allowed.

In this paper, we explore an alternative tangible interface that has a lightweight infrastructure and is well-adapted to the exploration of the concepts of form and space. Using our system, CubeExplorer, students can explore the concepts of void and space by drawing subtractive operations directly on the surface of a paper cube with a digital pen. Commands are transmitted in real-time to a nearby computer which executes them and displays the resulting digital model. A simple, paper-based interface allows students to explore the resulting model, change the visualization style and delete unwanted operations. CubeExplorer offers a transparent means of communication between the designer and the 3D CAD program because the pen input is in the same order that designers conceptualize basic geometry; points, lines, shapes, and objects .

To evaluate the potential of this approach, we conducted a comparative study in an introductory course in the Department of Architecture at our university. We asked students to explore the concept of overlapping voids using three different tools: a set of wooden blocks, CubeExplorer and FormZ, a CAD package used extensively in the architecture curriculum at our university (see Figure 1). Students rated our system as just as easy to use as the wooden blocks, while offering the flexibility of digital modeling when it comes to exploring complex shapes. To explore the role of our choice of FormZ as a possible confounding factor, we conducted a follow-up study to evaluate CubeExplorer in relation to SketchUp [3], a schematic digital modeler designed for rapid design exploration. In this study, participants with limited experience in CAD systems were asked to reproduce 3D models using both techniques. CubeExplorer proved to be significantly faster than SketchUp for this simple task, validating our results of our first experiment.

2 Related Work

Cube-based tangible user interfaces bring unique affordances to 3D modeling. In these approaches, basic building blocks such as cubes [4, 7, 17, 21] or triangles [19] are augmented with a set of sensors and a communication network which allows the system to automatically infer the spatial relationship between the different blocks. With ActiveCube [17], a user can assemble multimodal cube components, and the system will automatically construct the physical model on a display. This approach makes it possible to automatically transform the appearance of the model to reflect the task at hand [4]. This approach has proven quite successful. Sharlin et al. [12] used the ActiveCube system to assess the 3D spatial and constructional ability of people and showed that the tangible cube system increased participants' spatial awareness. In comparison, CubeExplorer explores the potential of tangible interfaces when performing subtractive modeling, letting users draw directly on the surface of the model to create voids. We believe that both approaches are complementary as both the additive and subtractive processes are important in developing and understanding space.

An alternative approach to simplifying access to digital modeling is to alter sketching practice. Although hand drawn sketches can express every possible blueprint of a conceptual model and are efficient to produce, translating different type of stroke and mapping it to corresponding CAD operation is a tedious process. Several intelligent sketch systems such as TEDDY, 3D Journal and SKETCH [9, 10, 20] have been proposed to bridge the gap between hand sketching and computer-based modeling. Whereas these intelligent sketch systems interpret a two-dimensional drawing as the projection of an intended shape, CubeExplorer, like ModelCraft [14] captures and interprets strokes directly from the model's surface using a digital pen and Anoto pattern paper [5]. This approach offers a more direct mapping between the students' objectives and the actions to be performed on the model, by reducing the navigation burden. Although CubeExplorer was inspired by ModelCraft, the two systems are different. In particular, CubeExplorer explores how the ModelCraft command system can be extended to real-time settings in which commands are reflected on a nearby computer. Also, to adapt to the constraints of a teaching environment, CubeExplorer does not offer the full set of ModelCraft commands.

Because interaction with physical artifacts is essential for architects, several tangible workbenches for manipulating digital representations have been proposed. Luminous Planning Table [16] simulates the shadows and reflections on top of physical architectural models while users modify the position of the model on a table surface. Illuminating Clay [11] allows user to alter the topography of a clay landscape model using traditional techniques. The system automatically captures the resulting surface and projects the results of the analysis back onto the clay landscape. The focus of these interfaces is more on collaborative work where interactions are mediated through physical proxies. CubeExplorer, in contrast, is focused on the representation of basic geometry and 3D operations in architectural education. However, the two approaches could be easily integrated.

3 "The Cube Project" in a Classroom

Teaching students how to think in three dimensions is an essential part of introductory architecture curricula. One component of this type of spatial thinking is the ability to understand different types of space: solid (interior of a frame), void (subtraction of a frame), and overlapping (intersection of two frames). "The Cube Project" is a classroom activity for introductory architecture students that aims to give insight into the understanding of space. The activity was designed to train students to configure different types of *figural voids* (Fig. 2) in a single cube and understand the composition of the interior, specifically overlapping spaces.

The project fulfills several goals: First, it lets students explore the implications of 2D manipulations (such as orthographic projection) on a 3D design, and observe how different manipulations might interact. Second, it introduces students to the role of abstraction and representation in different media by using 3D planning tools to create different figural solids/voids. For example, void space, which is an abstraction of a physical or virtual cut, can be configured by removing individual cubes from a block of cubes (physical media), or using constructive solid geometry (CSG) operations in a CAD program (digital media). Third, it helps students develop conceptual clarity by performing these operations in different environments.

To fulfill the requirements of the project, several approaches have been used in the past. One approach was to use physical wooden blocks. This solution is appealing for its simplicity, but unfortunately, physical tools have a ground plane constrained by gravity which limits the range of figures that can be constructed and explored. Furthermore, wooden blocks do not encourage students to explore the relationship between 2D and 3D manipulation. Another approach is to use CAD programs, which are more flexible and will be used extensively later in the curriculum. Yet current CAD programs are often difficult to learn because their conceptual model requires understanding advanced concepts.. Without a thorough understanding of these concepts, CAD programs are often difficult to use. This fundamentally limits their use in introductory curricula because the complexity of their interfaces (in particular the navigation interface) can be distracting to students.

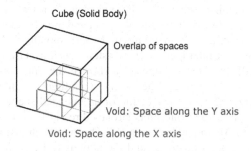

Cube (Solid Body)

Overlap of spaces

Void: Space along the Y axis

Void: Space along the X axis

Fig. 2. Figural Solid, Void, and Overlap

The design objective of CubeExplorer was to create an interface combining the positive features of both tangible and digital approaches. To do so, CubeExplorer captures input on tangible models (in this case, paper cubes) and displays the electronic results on a display where user can take full advantage of the digital representation (such as the ease of undoing one's work). A unique feature of CubeExplorer is that it encourages users to understand the spatial implications of a sketch drawn on the surface of a cube. This fosters the conceptual understanding of overlap among voids expressed in the reference frames of each of the six faces, with different implications in each frame.

3.1 CubeExplorer Interface

The CubeExplorer interface consists of three main elements:

- A paper cube whose faces are covered with Anoto pattern [5] paper that can be recognized by a Logitech io2 pen. The pen transmits the strokes drawn on the surface of the cube directly to a computer through a Bluetooth link.
- A paper tool palette, also covered with Anoto paper. The palette is used to control the orientation of the cube on the screen, and to perform operations such as changing the display style or undoing operations.
- A computer which receives input from the pen display and executes the results. The computer runs SolidWorks as the underlying CAD software. The specific CAD package is not important here as users do not need to interact directly with SolidWorks while using the system.

Using this configuration, users can complete the Cube Project using only the Logitech io2 digital pen and the paper cubes as input devices.

Shape	Depth	Pigtail

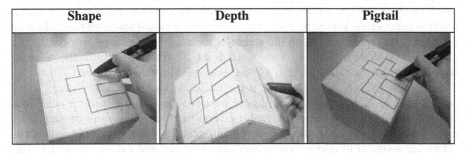

Fig. 3. Operation Syntax for the Cube Explorer system The Syntax for the cut feature consists of shape, depth, and pigtail. The result of the operation is shown in Figure 1.

To create a void, users simply draw the shape of the volume to cut on a side of the cube. This sketch becomes the basis for the subtractive operation. Then, users draw the depth of the cut on any perpendicular surface, and mark the area to cut using a simple pigtail gesture (Fig. 3). If no specific depth is provided, the system cuts though the entire solid. This syntax was inspired by the ModelCraft system [14] from which our system is derived. As in ModelCraft, the last pigtail lets users indicate whether the inner or outer part of the shape should be used for the cut operation.

When the user starts marking, the model on the display automatically rotates so that the face being drawn upon is shown. As users draw the shape to be cut, the system provides immediate feedback via ink on the surface of the 3D model on the screen. The ink is accumulated until the system detects a closed shape. At this point, the system beeps and replaces the ink on the screen with the final shape to be cut. Operations are executed as soon as a pigtail is detected. Different tones of beeps are used for each command element (shape, depth, and pigtail). This makes it possible to use the interface without looking at the screen.

The paper-based tool palette is composed of two main areas. On top is a navigation pad. Pen input in this area is used to rotate the model on the screen. At the bottom of the palette we implemented a series of paper buttons (similar to Anoto's pidgets[5]) to help users during their work. The "View mode" button let users toggle between shaded and wire frame views. Users can select cuts in one of two ways: either by drawing a pigtail inside of the drawing which generated the cut, or by using the "Up" and "Down" buttons to move through the list of cuts presented on the left of the screen. The "Delete" button lets users delete the currently selected cut. The interface also provides a "Reset" button to reset the internal state of the command system if needed.

3.2 Implementation

The system was implemented as a plug-in for the SolidWorks CAD program. One of the major challenges we encountered was to ensure that the free form input provided by users could be interpreted correctly by the system. Human sketches are ambiguous in nature, whereas CAD requires precise parameters [8]. The Cube Project's requirement that all cuts be performed on a grid simplified the amount of processing of input required before calling the SolidWorks API functions. We simply determined which edges in the grid matrix were closest to the pen strokes and used them as the function parameters. When the user finishes drawing a closed shape on the surface of the model, the free-form ink on the screen is replaced with a shape snapped to the grid. For a system with a more relaxed set of drawing constraints, a more complicated approach such as Arvo's Fluid sketches [6] would be required.

Since CubeExplorer uses a simple paper model without a tracking system, users are required to align physical and digital models separately. Because a cube is a symmetrical object with respect to each face and the four orientations of each face, users may easily become disoriented. To differentiate among the faces, different colors are assigned to corresponding faces in the paper and the screen model. The orientation within each face is indicated by a cross symbol at the lower right. When a user starts drawing on the desired color face, the cube on the screen automatically orients to the corresponding face and direction. When the user writes on a different surface, such as creating a depth mark, the cube rotates automatically to render both faces on the screen.

4 Evaluation

To evaluate the potential of CubeExplorer to complement conventional architectural education tools, we conducted two experiments. In our first experiment, we compared CubeExplorer to the use of wooden cubes and FormZ, a CAD program, used extensively later in the curriculum. As our findings may depend heavily on the choice of the CAD program used, we complemented our evaluation with a second experiment, comparing the CubeExplorer system to SketchUp, a CAD program specifically designed for quick spatial exploration.

4.1 Experiment I

The goal of this experiment was to evaluate how students benefit from three different 3D tools (wooden blocks, CubeExplorer, and FormZ) when performing the Cube Project. Our hypothesis was that CubeExplorer would offer a synthesis of the advantages of the tangible solution (ease of navigation, ease of parameter specification, limited indirection) and the fully digital solution (relaxed physical constraints, ability to undo or save a snapshot of one's work). As a second hypothesis, we predicted that the unique reference system of CubeExplorer would encourage further exploration by facilitating the spatial cognition process in 3D.

4.1.1 Task and Apparatus
Students were instructed to start with a 6" solid cube and to remove parts of it either in physically setting, virtual setting, or hybrid setting until finalizing their design. The design goals were as follows:

1) Modify the cube using a subtractive process.
2) Create three figural voids that overlap each other within the cubic volume.
3) Demonstrate a strategy of spatial organization that conceptually connects the figural voids of the cube.

To compare the three experimental settings, each task involved a 6" cube which was either decomposed in 1'' increments (physical model) or had a grid system with snap intervals of 1" (hybrid and virtual models). Thus, every operation performed on the solid body had the resolution of 1"; the atomic unit of any construction was a 1" cube. We considered 3 conditions:

- *Physical Model Method:* Wooden blocks were used to demonstrate properties of physical media. We considered several possible options for this condition including foam cubes connected by Velcro or dowels, Lego bricks, Duplo, K'nex and wooden blocks taped together. Foam cubes were too light and are difficult to connect. Many plastic bricks such as Lego enforce a privileged construction direction and are sometimes difficult to disassemble. We finally settled on wooden cubes as they are the most practical. Tangible digital cube systems [15, 17, 21] would have been interesting interface to deploy for this task, but they suffer similar from problems as the plastic brick approach.

    A full 6" cube composed of 216 (6x6x6) 1" cubes was provided for students to remove parts of the cube to create voids inside. The students were instructed to attach different parts such as overhanging cubes with tape. They could also use pre-assembled blocks of 2"x1"x1", 2"x2"x1", and 2"x2"x2". Students could orient themselves around the model to navigate or visualize a cut.
- *Virtual Model Method:* There is a wide variety of CAD modelers that would have been appropriate in this setting. In the end, FormZ [2] was chosen because it allows users to perform subtractive operations without requiring significant understanding of multiple parameters or operations. We also considered using SketchUp [3], a system with a much simpler interface, but found that SketchUp is

a surface modeler as opposed to a solid modeler, and was not well-adapted to this task. We explored the possible influence of this choice in our second experiment.

Each student was given a FormZ template file with a rendering of a 6'' cube. Settings such as the view and the selection mode were optimized for a subtractive modeling process. Creating a cut involved three basic steps. First, students created 6-sided orthogonal 3D extrusions from the ground reference plane defined by the system to make the "cutting" object. Second, they used the "move" tool to position the cutting object in the desired position. Finally, students issued subtractive geometry operations to cut the "cutting" object from the "original" object.

• *Hybrid Model Method:* Each student received a 6" cubic box covered in Anoto paper, along with a digital pen and the navigation palette described above. Spare boxes, pens, navigation palettes were provided upon request. Using these tools, students created figural voids inside the cube on the screen by drawing on the surfaces of the physical model. Students had to hold the pen against the surface of the paper model at a right angle that maximized the pen's capture area. The digital paper palette was used to interact with the digital model shown on a nearby display (Fig. 2).

4.1.2 Protocol, Measures and Participants

At the beginning of the class in which the experiment was conducted, the construction process of LeCorbusier's Domino House was used to demonstrate different space concepts inside a solid form. After signing the consent form, participants used each techniques of the three. Before using a given technique, participants were shown how to create a void using that technique: taking apart the wooden blocks; making a cutting shape and using it as a template for a cut in FormZ; and sketching a command on the paper model surface using the CubeExplorer system. For each of the three techniques participants were given 40 minutes to complete the task .

We used two measures to compare the different techniques. First, after they finished the project, each participant was asked to fill out a questionnaire, providing a subjective evaluation of the three systems. The questionnaire covered topics such as ease of learning, ease of use, perceived efficiency while using the tool, as well as a self evaluation of how the tool helped participants to conduct the exercise. The questionnaire asked participants to rank the techniques side by side on each of these dimensions using a 1-7 Likert scale. The questionnaire took 10 minutes to complete.

We also asked two faculty in the department of architecture to rate the models produced during the experiment (in a unified file format and using randomized numerical identifiers). The criteria for evaluation were based on the three design goals described above (Section 0).

A total of nine students were divided into three groups of three participants with all members of a group using one technique at the same time (individually). We used a Latin square to counterbalance for skill transfer. Five of the participants had commercial CAD experience (AutoCAD LC, SketchUp, Maya, etc.). Only one student had experience with digital pens, such as tablet PC styli. The experiment lasted 2.5 hours.

4.1.3 Results

One-way RM ANOVAs using the techniques as the independent variable were conducted to analyze questionnaire results. Bonferroni corrections were used for multiple comparisons and Greenhouse-Geisser corrections were used when sphericity could not be assumed. For the purpose of the analyses, data were recoded such that greater numbers are better. To account for experiment-wise alpha inflation, effects with significance levels above .003 (.05/17) should be interpreted with caution.

- *Ease of use:* We first examined the questions relating to general ease of use. For ease of getting started, we found a significant effect ($F(2,16) = 14.43$, $p < .001$, partial $\eta^2 = .64$) suggesting that it was more difficult to get started with FormZ than with both wooden blocks and CubeExplorer ($p = .013$ and $p = .002$ respectively). A similar pattern was observed regarding the time spent learning ($F(2,16) = 28.32$, partial, $p < .001$, $\eta^2 = .78$) with FormZ requiring more time than the other two techniques ($p = .002$ and $p < .001$ respectively). With respect to perceived mental load, we found a significant effect ($F(2,16) = 20.8$, $p < .001$, partial $\eta^2 = .72$) suggesting that wooden block and CubeExplorer were significantly easier to use than FormZ ($p = .002$, and $p < .001$ respectively). In each of these analyses, the differences between CubeExplorer and wooden blocks were not significant. Finally, participants perceived CubeExplorer as faster and more efficient than both FormZ and wooden blocks ($F(2,16) = 8.52$, $p = .003$, partial $\eta^2 = .52$, post hoc test $p = .026$ and $p = .004$ respectively). These results were consistent with informal observations during the experiment: It took a longer time for students to reach the level of comfort necessary to start their exploration in the FormZ condition as compared to the other two conditions.
- *Ease of Navigation:* From our observations, it seemed that it was quite difficult for participants to navigate with the wooden block technique because the cube assembly was difficult to move. However, self ratings showed no significant differences between the techniques. Also, there were no significant differences in the ease of observing the model as a whole or in visualizing the cut. It is interesting to note that while CubeExplorer requires users to manually align the 3D object with the virtual representation, this did not seem to influence the perceived ease of navigation. One reason suggested by students' comments was that CubeExplorer provides many views of the model – wire frame view, shaded view, and projection views of cutting objects on the paper surface. This could have offset the manual aligning burden.
- *Tool expertise*: We also asked participants how confident they were about their control of the tool. We found a weak but significant effect with regard to the ease of performing a simple cut ($F(1.17, 9.34) = 5.52$, $p = .039$, partial $\eta^2 = .41$), with CubeExplorer being significantly better than FormZ ($p = .007$), but only marginally better than wooden blocks ($p = .062$). Interestingly, we did not observe a significant effect with regard to the ease of creating spatial overlap. Finally, we found a significant effect with respect to the ease of correcting simple errors ($F(2,16) = 7.43$, $p = .005$, partial $\eta^2 = .48$) with CubeExplorer being rated as significantly easier than wooden blocks ($p = .014$). With respect to the ease of making changes, CubeExplorer was significantly better than wooden blocks ($F(2,16) = 7.38$, $p = 005$, partial $\eta^2 = .48$, $p = .014$), but only marginally better than FormZ ($p = .078$).

- *Learning spatial concepts*: With respect to how well the tool supported the task, there were no significant effects observed from the questionnaire regarding the understanding of abstract space, how well the tool helped users convey their ideas, or whether the tool supported spatial thinking.

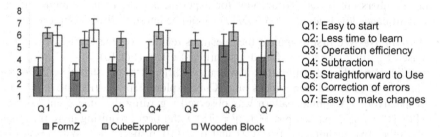

Fig. 4. Experiment I, Questionnaire Results Users rated each technique in 17 dimensions using Likert scale. 7 items showed significance. Higher values indicate higher satisfaction. Confidence levels (α=.05) are shown in error bars. CubeExplorer was easier to start, learn, and operate than FormZ. In terms of making modifications, it was more flexible than wooden blocks.

In terms of time allocation, the wooden block technique required a disproportionate amount of time to stack the component cubes, since the speed of an operation for wooden blocks is proportional to the total number of parts which have to be manipulated. The other techniques, in contrast, have constant times across operations. Hence, the total number of operations was likely lower in the wooden blocks setting. For the same reason, error correction was more difficult in the wooden block setting since it required repeated disassembly and reassembly. For CubeExplorer, adjusting the physical cubes to be aligned with the virtual cube on the screen was the most time consuming operation. For FormZ, as a consequence of the wide selection of operations, students had difficulty remembering the command set, increasing the time required.

Overall, the questionnaire findings – suggesting that CubeExplorer was rated as easy to start, quick to learn, efficient to operate, straightforward in subtraction, and efficient in correcting errors/making changes - confirm our first hypothesis that CubeExplorer combines the advantages of a tangible tool with the advantages of a digital tool. Interestingly, we didn't see any support for our second hypothesis that CubeExplorer is better than conventional tools at helping students develop conceptual clarity in spatial awareness. For the three design criteria described in section 0, the models generated with different techniques received almost identical ratings by faculty members. This is consistent with the lack of technique effects in the questionnaire responses regarding the "learning of spatial concepts" (see above).

4.2 Experiment II

In the first experiment, we used FormZ since it was well adapted to the task and also part of the curriculum at our university. However, it is clear that the interface of the CAD system could have influenced on the outcome of our experiment. For one, FormZ is a solid modeler, and different results could be obtained with a surface modeler such as SketchUp [3], which provides an intuitive interface to create the outline of a shape that users can elevate or depress to make a void. To identify the possible impact of this aspect, we conducted a follow-up study comparing the performance of CubeExplorer and SketchUp when used by novice users in a target matching task.

4.2.1 Task and Apparatus

Each participant was given two wooden block models (see sample in Figure 1, left) and was asked to replicate them in a digital form using CubeExplorer and SketchUp. To allow for a fair comparison, users were allowed to use either an additive or a subtractive design approach. Assuming that most users would choose the additive approach for SketchUp and the subtractive approach for CubeExplorer, we selected one target model that was easy to replicate with subtraction and one that favored additive operations. Each participant built one model with each of the tools. The pairing between tool and model was counterbalanced across participants (i.e., half of the participants used SketchUp for the additive model and CubeExplorer for the subtractive model and vice versa). Also, half of the participants started with CubeExplorer and the other half with SketchUp.

In the SketchUp setting, each user was given a template file with preset grids and views. Users first defined a 2D sketch using either a rectangle tool or a line tool. Then, users subtracted or added volume using the "push/pull tool" controlled by the mouse. To simulate a 6"x6" grid system, the minimal snapping unit was set to one inch. Also, users were given a template file and a set of instructional guidelines to work with. The same version of CubeExplorer as in Experiment I was used.

4.2.2 Protocol, Measures and Participants

After informed consent, participants received a 5 minute overview of the general task. Before using each of the tools to replicate the target models, participants were trained for 20 minutes in the respective tool setting. During training, all possible strategies to shorten the task were fully disclosed. For SketchUp, we demonstrated how to use shortcuts and how to deal with a surface modeler's generic problems. For CubeExplorer, participants were trained to orient the sample and paper models efficiently. After the training, participants were asked to replicate the sample model as fast as possible.

The proficiency regarding each tool was assessed by the time users spent on replicating each model. Also, each participant filled out a subset of the questionnaire used for the previous experiment (i.e., the questions related to perceived expertise in using the tool).

Three architecture students and nine students without architecture training were recruited. No student had more than two days of SketchUp experience and none of the participants had any experience with CubeExplorer. The total experiment took about 90 minutes with the last 10 minutes spent on evaluation.

4.2.3 Results

We conducted a one-way RM ANOVA using technique as the independent variable and completion time as the dependent variable. There was a significant effect of technique (F(1,10) = 8.6, p = .015, partial η^2 = .462) with CubeExplorer (M = 5.5 min, SD = 2.2 min) being faster than SketchUp (M = 8.0 min, SD = 3.9 min) .

This result may be explained by one of two aspects. First, there were frequent context switches among rotation, sketch, and push or pull using SketchUp. Second, as discussed above, SketchUp is a surface modeler. When users made two cuts that intersected in the middle, the definition of the inside/outside of the face frequently became inverted. Since the users of SketchUp had to manually fix the inverted and missing faces, this may have resulted in slower performance. If the SketchUp interface was implemented on top of a solid modeler, the result of the target matching experiment might have been very different. In addition, users adopted successful strategies to overcome the main drawback of CubeExplorer: The need to synchronize the paper cube with the virtual screen image. In this study, users focused on synchronizing the paper cube with the sample model instead of the virtual model on the screen. Thus, they spent less time trying to orient the electronic cube to align with the physical cube and this made operation very efficient.

On the questionnaire, the only significant effect was found for ease of learning (F(1,11) = 12.91, p = .004, partial η^2 = .54), suggesting that CubeExplorer was perceived as easier to learn (M = 5.41, SD = 1.1) than SketchUp (M = 3.91, SD = 1.4). None of the other differences reached significance.

In interpreting these findings, one needs to remember that this experiment focused on novice users working on a simple task. As a result, the external validity of the results might be limited and findings cannot be extended to expert users. Thus, findings are inconclusive regarding the relative performance of ModelCraft (i.e., the "expert" version of CubeExplorer) versus the full SketchUp program.

5 Discussion

Based on our observations as well as interviews with the students, we conclude that three key elements of CubeExplorer are beneficial in introductory architecture classes.

First, the *directness of interaction* supported by CubeExplorer was beneficial for students performing the Cube Project. In comparison to the digital modeler, use of a physical model and a digital pen brought the editing metaphors in the electronic model to the tangible world, making the students perceive the interface as "easy to use." In comparison to the physical model, although physical blocks are very intuitive to operate, users have to consider stability issues when stacking and removing component blocks one by one to try out different compositions. Additionally, the operations in a physical model are not performed in the order in which students conceptualize projection and this is a key element in learning 3D spatial concepts. In contrast, the interactions in CubeExplorer allow users to sketch points, lines, depth marks, and 2D shapes in the correct conceptual order. This allows the user to attend to one attribute of a geometric component at a time [8]. More importantly, the operations in CubeExplorer were simple enough that the system configuration interfered minimally with the purpose of training students in the concepts of composition of void space.

Second, the *unique self-referential system* of CubeExplorer allowed the system to receive high satisfaction rates in navigation and visualization. In comparison, when using wooden blocks, gravity limited the exploration pattern because it implicitly created a "ground" plane. Users of FormZ, in turn, were constrained by the Cartesian system that is deeply coupled with most of the functions of CAD systems. For example, users are asked to abide by the reference system of the internal XYZ axes to assign input parameters for certain operations, although they can view the object from an arbitrary vantage point. In contrast, CubeExplorer allows users to use the natural reference of their cuts, i.e. the face they are drawing on.

Third, as a hybrid interface, CubeExplorer *combines the advantages of physical and digital media*: Like physical tools, the interface is easy to use; like digital tools, modifications and undo operations are simple to execute. The hybrid visualization, consisting of the physical cube and the representation on screen, provides a direct spatial view and a variety of geometric views in digital form. Our second experiment reinforces the benefits of CubeExplorer in comparison to digital modelers by demonstrating that students can produce designs as comfortably with CubeExplorer as with purely-digital tools such as SketchUp.

However, we also observed several technical problems with CubeExplorer during the user studies. The ink that was laid on top of the paper face while executing an operation was useful at the time of the execution. However, after using the paper palette to delete a previously created feature, the residual ink confused the users. In addition, since every face was symmetric, users frequently had to reorient either the paper model in accordance to the digital model on the screen or vice versa. In short, CubeExplorer had several sources of inconsistency between the tangible model and the digital model. In future versions, this synchronization issue could be resolved by utilizing camera tracking to detect the position and rotation of the paper model and send it to the digital modeler.

6 Conclusion

In this paper, we present CubeExplorer, a tangible user interface for an introductory architecture class. CubeExplorer is designed to let students explore components of 3D spaces such as projection, overlap, and void. Users can draw on the surface of physical models to trigger operations in a CAD program running on a nearby computer and this minimizes the level of indirection between the intended operation and the manipulation tool. To evaluate the potential of CubeExplorer, we conducted two experiments comparing it to a purely physical system as well as two digital applications (FormZ and SketchUp). Our results show that the key elements of the CubeExplorer interface - directness of interaction, a unique referential system, and simultaneous advantages of physical and virtual modeling tools – cannot be obtained from conventional tools in architecture. We believe that the concepts explored in CubeExplorer could be applied to a wide variety of tangible interfaces both in teaching and professional contexts.

Acknowledgements

This work was supported by NSF Grant IIS-0447703 and Microsoft Research. We would like to thank Anoto for their support with streaming pattern space and Logitech for their support with streaming software. We would like to thank Adam Bender, Corinna Löckenhoff for providing many useful comments.

References

1. AutoCAD AutoDesk, www.autodesk.com
2. FormZ. Auto-des-sys (2005), www.formz.com
3. @Last Software, SketchUp (2005)
4. Anderson, D., Yedidia, J.S., Frankel, J.L., Marks, J., Agarwala, A., Beardsley, P., Leigh, J.H.D., Ryall, K., Sullivan, E.: Tangible interaction + graphical interpretation: a new approach to 3D modeling. In: Proceedings of SigGraph'00, pp. 393–402.
5. Anoto, Development Guide for Service Enabled by Anoto Functionality. Anoto (2002)
6. Arvo, J., Novins, K.: Fluid sketches: continuous recognition and morphing of simple hand-drawn shapes. In: Proceedings of UIST'00, pp. 73–80.
7. Frazer, J.: An Evolutionary Architecture. Themes, vol. 7. Architectural Association, London (1995)
8. Goel, V.: Sketches of Thought. MIT Press, Cambridge (1995)
9. Igarashi, T., Matsuoka, S., Tanaka, H.: Teddy: a sketching interface for 3D freeform design. In: Proceedings of SigGraph'99, pp. 409–416 (1999)
10. Masry, M., Kang, D., Lipson, H.: A Pen-Based Freehand Sketching Interface for Progressive Construction of 3D Objects. Computer & Graphics 29, 563–575 (2005)
11. Piper, B., Ratti, C., Ishii, H.: Illuminating clay: a 3-D tangible interface for landscape analysis. In: Proceedings of CHI'02, pp. 355–362 (2002)
12. Sharlin, E., Itoh, Y., Watson, B., Kitamura, Y., Sutphen, S., Liu, L.: Cognitive cubes: a tangible user interface for cognitive assessment. In: Proceedings of SIGCHI'02, pp. 347–354 (2002)
13. Shneiderman, B., Plaisant, C.: Designing the User Interface: Strategies for Effective Human-Computer Interaction, 4th edn. Addison Wesley, Reading (2004)
14. Song, H., Guimbretière, F., Lipson, H., Hu, C.: ModelCraft: capturing freehand annotations and edits on physical 3D models. In: Proceedings of UIST'06, pp. 13–22 (2006)
15. Suzuki, H., Kato, H.: Interaction-Level Support for Collaborative Learning: AlgoBlock. In: Proceedings of An Open Programming Language. Proceedings of CSCL, pp. 349–355
16. Underkoffler, J., Ishii, H.: Urp: a luminous-tangible workbench for urban planning and design. In: Proceedings of CHI'99, pp. 386–393 (1999)
17. Watanabe, R., Itoh, Y., Asai, M., Kitamura, Y., Kishino, F., Kikuchi, H.: The soul of ActiveCube: implementing a flexible, multimodal, three-dimensional spatial tangible interface. In: Proceedings of ACE'04, pp. 173–180 (2004)
18. White, J.F., Sadek, G., Hejduk, J., Shaw, E.: Education of an Architect. The Cooper Union for the Advancement of Science and Art (1971)
19. Wisneski, C., Ishii, H., Dahley, A., Gorbet, M., Brave, S., Ullmer, B., Yarin, P.: Ambient Displays: turning architectural space into an interface between people and digital information, in Cooperative Buildings. In: Streitz, N.A., Konomi, S., Burkhardt, H.-J. (eds.) CoBuild 1998. LNCS, vol. 1370, pp. 22–32. Springer, Heidelberg (1998)
20. Zeleznik, R.C., Herndon, K.P., Herndon, K.P.: SKETCH: an interface for sketching 3D scenes. In: Proceedings of SigGraph'96, pp. 163–170 (1996)
21. Zuckerman, O., Arida, S., Resnick, M.: Extending tangible interfaces for education: digital montessori-inspired manipulatives. In: Proceedings of SIGCHI'05, pp. 859–868 (2005)

InterCUBE: A Study into Merging Action and Interaction Spaces

Benjamin Salem[1] and Harold Peeters[2]

[1] Department of Industrial Design, Eindhoven University of Technology, The Netherlands &
School of Science and Technology, Kwansei Gakuin University, Japan
[2] Philips Medical Systems, The Netherlands
mail@bsalem.info, [2]haroldpeeters@gmail.com

Abstract. We describe the development of a novel tangible interface we call the InterCUBE, a cube-shaped device with no external buttons or widgets. We study the implications of such a shape in terms of interactions, notably the degrees of freedom available and the manipulations possible. We also explain and investigate the merging of the action, perception and interaction spaces, and we design the InterCUBE interaction accordingly. To investigate the system we have implemented a demonstration application: a shopping menu, in which users can navigate through a menu simply by turning the cube in either one of the four possible directions. We have evaluated the InterCUBE in comparison to an equivalent mouse based interface and discuss the results.

Keywords. Tangible User Interface, Usability, action and interaction spaces.

1 Introduction

We have developed the InterCUBE, a cube-shaped TUI (Tangible User Interface) with inherent added value. We have also integrated the action space with the interaction space. Whereby the InterCUBE is both the input and the output device. IN doing so we hope that the user attention focus will be kept consistent during the interaction. We advocate that while acting on the device, reacting to the device and interacting with an application, the user focus should be kept as much as possible onto one single point. This is a different approach to other cube-shaped THUI. In comparison computer graphics projection systems such as ToolStone [1] are different because there is a distinction between the TUI as input device and the output device that is a separate display. So are other cube-based systems such as the Cognitive Cubes [2], in this instance they do not allow for output channels. Although at this stage of development, the only output we have implemented on the InterCUBE is an LED on each face of the cube that indicates which side is up (and currently active). Intended developments include addition of displays on each side of the cube to visualise a menu.

1.1 Tangible Computing

Tangible computing generally refers to computing systems that use physical artifacts as representations and controls for digital information [3]. In other words, tangible

C. Baranauskas et al. (Eds.): INTERACT 2007, LNCS 4663, Part II, pp. 57–70, 2007.

computing is about having devices that represent some information by ways of their colour, behaviour, sound or other properties. In the spectrum of interaction from digital to physical tangible computing lies at the physical end. At one extreme are virtual reality and Graphical User Interfaces. Their main focus is the interaction within the digital context (e.g. Virtual Environment). Then come ubiquitous computing, augmented reality (also known as mixed reality) and ambient intelligence. They include interactions that are physically contextualized, e.g. attached to some physical objects. At the other end of the spectrum, tangible computing is mainly concerned with physically embodied interaction. Tangible devices can offer the benefits of strongly integrated physical representations of digital information. This is because the hands and the brain have a particularly strong partnership [4]. We have undertaken the development of a device that complies with this TUI vision but is also a relevant object as well. An object with intrinsic aesthetic value and intuitive to use.

2 Action, Perception and Interaction Spaces

In terms of the immediately surrounding physical world, we rely on our hands for exploring, manipulating and reshaping it. From cognition perspective the hand has two main purposes: (1) the manipulation (i.e. action) and (2) the experience (i.e. perception) of objects. When manipulating objects in the real world, action (hands and fingers) and perception (the object in the real world) coincide in time and space [5]. The merger of action and perception spaces is intrinsic to TUI. Users have to grasp and manipulate (actions) the TUI and experience haptics (touch and weight) and motor experience (perception) of the device.

It also has been proven that offering task-relevant information in the same space as where actions take place leads to increased performance [6]. This suggests a merging of the user interface (task relevant information) and the device (where action take place). In other words a merging of (1) the action, (2) the perception and (3) the interaction spaces. This merger would ensure that the user attention is at the same time on what s/he is doing , where feedback will be experienced and where the application interface is displayed to her/him. All these happen to be on the same point. In comparison, with a screen-keyboard-mouse user interface, there is a separation between these spaces, given by the physical separation of input and output devices.

2.1 Affordance

The affordance of a form can be described as action priming activated by the appearance of an object. Although mostly visual the InterCUBE, other appearances are also relevant, such as weight and texture. The appearance of an object is triggering the user into anticipating and planning possible actions towards that object. These actions are related to the manipulation and perception of the object, for example a grasping action on a small object. At the initiation of such a grasping action people pre-shape their hands in order to match hand and object shapes [8]. We have, thus, facilitated such a pre-shaping by using a known basic form and by ensuring that the dimensions of the cube match those of the hand palm of an adult user. These ideas stem from the concept of affordance, first suggested by [9] and later applied to design by [10]. Designing a cube shaped TUI has therefore two advantages: (1) the cognitive load related to the manipulation of the TUI is kept to a minimum thanks to the clear affordance of the cube; and (2) the pre-shaping of the hand is facilitated thanks to the familiarity users have with the cube form. We find it important and relevant that interactive products clearly indicate the kind of interaction they are meant to support, this can be achieved thanks to the clear affordance of their form.

When an object affordance has been recognised, an attention grabbing effect occurs [7]. Thus if we have reinforce the affordance and simplify the manipulation planning of a TUI, we would facilitate the attention grabbing effect. To ensure the most efficient attention grabbing, such grabbing would have to be short and to the point. Short in time duration and to the point in term of relevance of the manipulation afforded. With an efficient attention grabbing, the TUI should leave more time for the user to perform other cognitive tasks. Liberate the user from having to think too long about how to grasp, manipulate and use the TUI presented. In the current implementation of the InterCUBE we have tried to address the issue of action and perception spaces merger. We have developed a device where there is no pre-requisite in terms of hand positions or handling. The simple affordance and the straightforward manipulations available, reduce greatly the complexity of interaction at the level of the device. This helps the user to focus on the menu interaction currently displayed on a monitor, instead of first paying attention to the manipulation of the InterCUBE and then observing the effects of his actions on the menu. The user focus is kept on to the same point, i.e. the GUI, and subject to a minimum of change.

3   Designing the InterCUBE

From a product design point of view our approach was about coming up with shapes that delivered simple and easy to use objects. Hence the development of our TUIs based on the exploration of pure aesthetic forms. We have investigated various physical forms that could be suitable for a TUI and have focused on basic ones, such as cube, sphere, and pyramid. Such forms are familiar to everyone. With a basic form it is possible to avoid any distraction due to the exploration of the form if it were complex or novel. Furthermore, having selected the form to be used, the implementation of a TUI was based on the understanding of what affordance such a form would have and how to implement them in an interface. This approach has led in the first instance to the development of the InterCUBE a cube shaped device, as the implementation of these principles.

3.2   Cube Based TUIs

While designing a cube shaped device, we were inspired by the early work on multidimensional icons, developed as a cubic shape in replacement of the widely used 2D icons [11]. Since then, there has been a substantial developments in cubic shaped TUIs. Solutions spanned from single [12] to modular devices [2], and from rigid [13] to deformable shape [14]. The interaction principles used were covering a wide spectrum of possibilities, from manipulation to composition. Manipulations were generally about rotating and positioning the TUIs. An early example is Bricks, as physical handles to manipulate digital objects [15]. The bricks were lying on a horizontal screen and the rotation and displacement on that horizontal plan were translated into an interaction. Within the same principle, ToolStone was developed with further investigation of the manipulations allowed [1]. ToolStone could be rotated, flipped over, tilted and moved in 3D. A Playful interface for home entertainment system based on a cube is another example of such TUI [16]. In this instance it is the rotation of the cube that is implemented in the interface. This aspect is similar to our development of the InterCUBE.

At the other end of the spectrum compositions are about assembling various TUIs into a functional grouping. This approach was adopted with ActiveCube, for instance it is the 3D arrangement of cubes that allow the construction and interaction with a 3D environment [17]. Navigation Blocks is another implementation. It is a system based on several blocks that orientation, movement and relative position correspond to various database queries [13]. Other examples ones include cognitive cubes [2] and mediaBlocks [18]. In comparison, to these TUIs, the InterCUBE is a stand-alone device.

Most of the TUIs based on the manipulation principle are projects involving a cube shaped TUI as a replacement for some functions of the mouse as an input device, like the cubic mouse. It is used to orient graphic models, joysticks on each of the cube faces are used for operation on each of the x, y, and z axis [12]). Another instance of such TUI is the Cubik, developed for the creation and manipulation of 3D models. It is based on push and pull widgets [19]. However, it is not necessary to rely on a rigid device like the InterCUBE. Indeed, a deformable cube was developed as a direct input device for the deformation and thus manipulation of a 3D shape [20].

Table 1. Various Cube based Devices

Device	Type	DoF	Interaction principle	Ref.
Cubic Mouse	Device	6	Manipulate Joysticks and buttons on each face of cube	[12]
Toolstone	Token	6	Rotations and Translations but must keep contact with base	[16]
Brick	Tokens	4	Rotations and Translations	[15]
Cubik	Device	3	Push and Pull of the cube (decrease and increase of size)	[19]
Tangible Cube	Device	3	Rotations	[16]
ActiveCube	Modules	3	Arrangement of cubes together, yielding different structures	[17]
Cognitive Cube	Modules	m3	Same as ActiveCube	[2]
Navigational Blocks	Token	3	Arrangement of cubes together	[13]
Mouse	Device	3	Translation on a horizontal plan (2 DoF) and a scroll wheel (1 DoF).	
InterCUBE	**Device**	**2**	**Rotations**	
MediaBlocks	Tokens	n/a	Insertion or removal of blocks from a console	[18]
DO-IT	Device	n/a	Deformation of the cube.	[20]

It is noticeable that few projects go as far as developing the TUI as a physical representation of some digital information. An exception is ActiveCube with an LED array display that represents some information from the application [21]. This is the closest to the concept we are thinking of when advocating the merger of the action and the interaction spaces (as described in section 4.1).

It is also remarkable that no comparison between the various devices proposed and the mouse has been included in the above papers. One would have hoped that if any of the devices was to become as widely used as the mouse for an application or an interface, there should be some comparison made. In table 1 (next) we list the cube-based interfaces and compare their DoF (Degree of Freedom), we also include the mouse.

As comparison, in the case of the InterCUBE we have ensured that there are no buttons, widgets or other features that could invite manipulations. The only possible manipulations remain holding, moving and rotating the cube.

4 Interaction Design

The InterCUBE is an unconstrained token that is hand held. It can be rotated and moved freely with no physical constraints. As such it is a device can have up to 6DoF. This is a substantial extension of possibilities compared to cube shaped token combined with a device (e.g. MediaBlocks). Such token system falls under the Token+Constraint classification [22]. In this classification the TUI is based on a token and a reference device (such as an active surface) that reduce the available DoF of the token. From this perspective.

Within the current implementation, we have limited the DoF implemented as part of the interface to : rotations forth/back and rotations right/left. During these rotations, the very nature of the cube shape yields a device with two states, discreet and transitional. The discreet states correspond to one of the face facing upwards towards the user and the transitional states correspond to the rotation from one orientation/face to another (in other words from one discreet state to another). The current state is then used as a departure point for the selection of the next option. Before reaching the desired option the device goes through a transitional state when the cube is being rotated, and no face is fully upwards. There is a threshold at midway between two discreet states when the interface is shifted from the previous state/option to the next. By design, this happens at around 45degrees of the rotation. In the current version, where the device is used for menu navigation, at the 45 degrees angle the user can see that the menu changes to the next options.

4.1 User Actions and User Interaction

The only actions necessary to interact with the cube are picking it up and turning it either up, down, right or left. There are many implications from the user interface (UI) point of view. The InterCUBE could be used for object manipulations or menu navigation. If the device is to be used for 2D or 3D objects manipulations, there could be a direct mapping between the user actions on the InterCUBE and their translation into manipulations of an object. Such a mapping could be done in two ways. The

InterCUBE being a discreet device, the mapping could be either (1) discreet to discreet or (2) discreet to continuous. For the object manipulation interface to work the rotation of the InterCUBE could be (1) a rotational step the object should follow, of which the ration device/object rotations could be controlled or (2) an indication of which direction the object should rotate towards, and the rotational speed could be specified by the angle of rotation of the device.

In the case of menu interaction, the InterCUBE can be mapped to a menu structure that takes into account the 4 possible choices available at each step (corresponding to the 4 possible faces that can be turned up). This a series of discreet states, for the interface to work, we need a discreet to discreet mapping and a one to one mapping between rotation and menu steps. The menu structure will hence be made of a series of decision tress with 4 branches at each node.

Within the developed system we have implemented a shopping application. We have selected this application as it fits well with the requirements of a menu structure. Users can browse through some clothes shopping categories (starting at Women, Kids and Men) and down to clothing items such as trousers, ties, pyjamas… At each step of the interaction the user is faced with a maximum of 4 possible options.

5 Comparing the InterCUBE and the Mouse

In our opinion this is relevant and important to compare the InterCUBE to the mouse as we are hopping our device could emerge as replacement or as complement to the mouse in some specific applications. In particular applications where efficiency is not that relevant compared to for example the experience. In its current implementation the cube is designed for menu based interactions. It therefore could be compared with an equivalent setting where the mouse is used. Even though there is a difference in DoF and handling principles between the two devices. Bearing in mind that computer users are by now all familiar with the mouse, it puts the InterCUBE in an unfavorable starting position. Nevertheless, in the next parts of this paper we present and discuss some comparative experiments, between the InterCUBE and the Mouse.

Fig. 1. The InterCUBE

5.1 Tests to Evaluate the InterCUBE

The comparison tests were set up whereby users had to perform the same tasks using one and then the other device. The users had to complete all the tasks using one device before moving onto using the other device. The one condition changed was the system configuration: Mouse or InterCUBE based. The device order was randomly chosen with half participants starting with the InterCUBE and half with the mouse. This would eliminate the possible effects of mutual influence of devices. We ran a series of assessments: (1) subjective assessment and, (2) objective assessments. In the subjective assessment, we would like to evaluate how intuitive the InterCUBE, a novel input device is. Would the test subjects be able to use the InterCUBE at all? . We also assessed the perceived usability of the InterCUBE when judged directly and the perceived usability of each device when compared one against another. This was done through a questionnaire. In the objective assessment the InterCUBE efficiency was compared to the mouse. In this assessment equivalent time measurements were compared between the two devices for a series of tasks.

In our tests the independent variables were the Menu and GUI, Device used and the dependent variables were the tasks performance.

5.2 Participants

Students of the Department of Industrial Design were the test participants. All of our students have significant computer and Internet experience. Most of the students were in the age group 18 -25 years. As they are ID students they will be more open in using alternative technological systems in performing a task. At least 20 (N22) individuals took part in the test.

5.3 Methods and Scenarios

We have run a series of comparative studies between the InterCUBE interface and a mouse interface. Participants were given a list of tasks to perform arranged in three major parts for each device (as described in table 2). Our aim is to establish a comparative study between the mouse and the InterCUBE based on the performance of a series of tasks of increasing complexity, thus increasing the cognitive load on the user: (1) single manipulation tasks without a Graphical User Interface (GUI), (2) sequence of manipulations without GUI and finally (3) full realistic shopping tasks with GUI. So we could compare the resulting time measurements between single manipulations, then between sequences of manipulations and finally between a fully fledge GUI setting. Furthermore we also investigate the ratios of time duration between manipulation sequences without and with a GUI (i.e. equivalent tasks with increased cognitive load on the user).

We perform a measurement of the time duration of each task for quantitative analysis (see table 2 for description of tasks), as well as a post-test questionnaire for qualitative analysis. All tests were recorded with a video camera and the subjects knew this. This was to ensure we captured detailed information in case we noticed some unusual data or comments from the participants.

Table 2. List of tasks. The performed tasks were in random order within one part, however the parts order was not randomised as it relate to a cognitive load build-up. The order of which device to use was also random. In the case of the mouse the users were not required to bring the mouse back to the initial position after each movement. Tasks of part 2 and 3 are identical but without and with the Graphical User Interface.

InterCUBE	Mouse
On both columns the tasks are identical but translated into InterCUBE or mouse actions **Part 1 : Single step manipulation**	
Turn the cube right	Move the mouse right
Turn the cube left	Move the mouse left
Turn the cube forwards/up	Move the mouse forwards/up
Turn the cube backwards/down	Move the mouse backwards/down
Part 2 : Manipulation without Graphical User Interface	
Turn the cube:	Move the mouse:
down-down-down-left-down-down-any side	down-down-down-left-down-down-any direction
Turn the cube:	
down-left-left-left-down-down-any side	Move the mouse:
Turn the cube:	down-left-left-left-down-down-any direction
down-right-right-right-down-down-down-	Move the mouse:
any side	down-right-right-right-down-down-down-any direction
Part 3 : realistic shopping tasks with menu	
Buy the "Kids pyjama 1" Buy the "Women shirt 1" Buy the "Men tie 2"	

An experiment pack was distributed to all the participants. It included a questionnaire and some introductions and short explanations about the experiment and the devices used. Subjects were asked to fill a questionnaire consisting of four parts: (1) Participant background, to know and understand the type of user and the relevance of her/his comments (this part filled before the tests); (2) Assessment of the InterCUBE setting, to find out the perceived usability of the InterCUBE within the setting of the experiment; (3) Assessment of the Mouse setting, to find out the perceived usability of the mouse within the setting of the experiment; (2 and 3 were swapped in case of different device order); (4) Relative ranking by the user of the InterCUBE Vs the mouse devices, to discover the user perceived preference.

5.4 Experiment Setting

The experiment was set-up using two different computer systems one based on the InterCUBE and the other on the mouse. However both systems run the same application (i.e. a shopping menu) and user interface as far as possible (i.e. layout, levels and options etc). Both settings were in an office environment and using common arrangements as much as possible. That is the displays are on a desktop, the devices are positioned in front of the displays and the users are required to sit right in front of one of these arrangements at a time. One key difference however, is that for the InterCUBE system the display is actually on a horizontal plane, parallel to the top surface of the cube. This is to simulate the intended display on the topside of the InterCUBE. As for the mouse system we kept to the common settings of a desktop PC.

While the InterCUBE selection is done by rotating the device the mouse selection is done by moving the device over the selected option and clicking the mouse left button. To allow for a fair comparison, we have set the distance between the options in the mouse system to be such that the time for mouse displacement should be approximately the same than an average rotation of the InterCUBE. Within the menu structure, options have consistent and identical positions on the display. The option at the top of the display is always used to go back, and the option at the bottom, when applicable, is used as a confirmation of choice. Left and Right options are used for choices, and when not available are simply not displayed. Both menus are identical and have a maximum of four options located at the top, bottom, right and left of the display.

6 Evaluation Results

6.1 Subjective Study

The participants were required to subjectively assess both the InterCUBE and the Mouse. This was done using a satisfaction questionnaire, the System Usability Scale (SUS) (Brooke, 1986). This is a bipolar rated questionnaire. The users have answered that for both they feel positive (SUS scores above 50%) without significant difference between the two devices. There is no significant difference between the perceived usability scoring of the InterCUBE (mean 77.8, std 2.3, N 22) and of the mouse (mean 79.9, std 3.5, N 22), (ANOVA, df=1, F=0.167, p = 0.687). Within the context of evaluation and application, the InterCUBE was therefore assessed as being as good, in perceived usability, as the mouse.

As part of the subjective study, users were asked four questions about the two devices. When asked the three questions next, there was no significant advantage for either the mouse or the InterCUBE (bipolar aggregate scoring with 1 for mouse and 22 for InterCUBE a score of 66 would be neutral): (1) I felt more in control using the mouse or the InterCUBE (mean 2.86, N 22). (2) I felt more exhausted after using the mouse or the InterCUBE and (mean 3.04, N 22). (3) Performing the tasks was easier while using the mouse or the InterCUBE. (mean 3.31, N 22). However there was a significant advantage for the InterCUBE with the following fourth question: I prefer the interface together with the mouse or the InterCUBE (mean 3.90, N 22). These results indicate that there is no overwhelming difference between the two devices, however there is a subjective preference for the InterCUBE. Even though none of the participants had prior experience with the device.

6.2 Objective Study (Time Measurements)

While performing the tasks described in table 4, the time duration of the InterCUBE and the mouse interaction were measured in seconds. Figure 7 shows the results of these measurements.

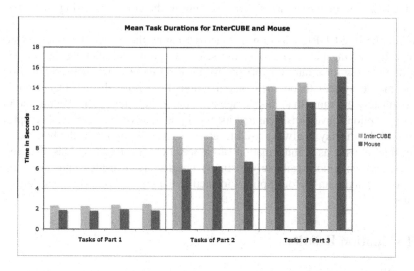

Fig. 2. Tasks duration as measured in seconds for both the InterCUBE and the mouse. There is a significant difference between the two sets of measurements. The mouse is significant faster for all the individual tasks with a mean difference of ~2sec. Note that the perceived increase trend between tasks is to be ignored as the data represent different tasks of increased cognitive load. Part 1: single step manipulation, part 2: manipulations without GUI, part 3: manipulations with GUI.

The mouse yields significantly faster results than the InterCUBE, for all the tasks performed. The mean difference is approximately 2 seconds. Furthermore, we have also investigated the comparison of time duration of parts 2 and 3 of the test (i.e. without and with a GUI). Such a comparison for both the InterCUBE and the mouse gives interesting results. The ratio for both sets of data is calculated by dividing the duration of task performance with GUI by the time duration of task performance without GUI. We compare the ratio of the InterCUBE with the ratio of the Mouse and we have discovered that it is significantly smaller (Sig. 0.004) for the InterCUBE data than it is for the mouse data. In other words, the addition of an interface yields a relative larger increase of the duration of a mouse based task compared to an InterCUBE based task. This implies that within the current context of evaluation and application, the cognitive load of the GUI is smaller with the InterCUBE than it is with the Mouse. Indeed the impact of the interface is a third longer with the mouse than with the InterCUBE (1.33 average ratio, see figure 4). This indicates that if the action space and the perception space are merged, there is significantly less of a cognitive load on the user than if the two spaces are separated. In the case of the InterCUBE, the user manipulates the device and gets haptics and motor feedbacks from it. The user attention can focus on the display and the menu interface. In the case of the mouse, the user manipulates the device but obtain feedback on the separate display, where s/he needs to check that he is moving the mouse pointer onto the desired option.

In our experiment, the Mouse performs better than the InterCUBE. However, it would be useful to investigate if this implies that further training would result in the InterCUBE being significantly better than the mouse within the context of specific applications. In particular with the planned integration of displays on the device that will result in a device with merged action, perception and interaction spaces.

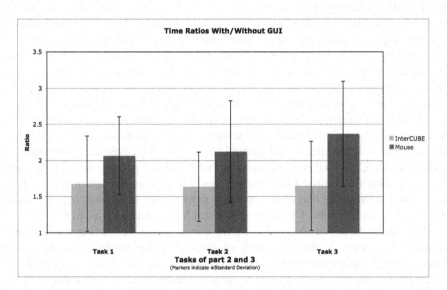

Fig. 4 . The time ratio for both devices according the three tasks performed. The InterCUBE ratio is significantly smaller that the mouse one.

6.3 Further Results

During the experiment, it appeared that 45% of users have suggested a smaller size for the InterCUBE. Users made such a comment in the hope that the device could be easily manipulated by one hand only. Interestingly enough, this was a fact that was overseen during the development of the InterCUBE. The device was designed to fit on one hand but must have been oversized. Another clear request from the users (77%) is for the removal of the umbilical cord used for power supplied and signal transmission. This should be addressed in the next developments.

7 Conclusion

Through this paper we have presented the current developments of the InterCUBE as a device for menu navigation. We have selected a shopping menu application for demonstration and evaluation. Rather than just investigate the device we have compared its performances with those of a mouse in an equivalent setting. With hindsight, we realise that the training and familiarity users have with the mouse make it a formidable challenger. However our tests have shown that the InterCUBE when used for the first time is still an acceptable contender. The different tests seem to be enough training to let the user handle the InterCUBE sufficiently well to finish all the tasks. Significant training on the InterCUBE would probably yields more balanced results. Our results show that a novel, unknown interaction device could be used as a replacement to the mouse within specific context. In such a context, the InterCUBE was favoured due to it being perceived as easier to use than the mouse. Even in a case like ours where users have no prior training. The single manipulation and the sequence manipulation without interface were expected to be sufficient training, but probably not to balance out the effects of five years experience with the mouse. It would be interesting to run similar tests with users unfamiliar with either device. Summary explanations given in the experiment packs to users and the part 1 of the experiments are enough for them to figure out how to use the InterCUBE. This has opened a promising perspective, one of the development of a series of novel TUI based on our interest with basic pure forms and common action space, perception and interaction space like in old fashion tools. Our objectives are two folds: (1) render the InterCUBE a device that does merge the action, perception and interaction spaces, beyond the limited LED currently used to display the active face and (2) deliver a stand-alone device with processing units, power supply and application all integrated within the cube. Our future plans call for the integration of LCD displays on each side of the device. As well as for the integration of the running application in an on-board circuit. Additionally such stand-alone device would avoid movement hampering and cable entanglement due to the current umbilical cord. We would like to test the system with users who have no mouse experience or with reduced motor skills (young children, elderly). We are also interested in other applications such as gaming.

Acknowledgments. The InterCUBE was initially developed by the first author while at Polywork Ltd. The original idea of the InterCUBE comes from a cooperation with Alex Watkins, an artist interested in boxes. We also wish to thank the following people for their help and advices : Ben Patterson, Rob Yates, Lorenzo Cervera and Matthias Rauterberg .

References

1. Rekimoto, J., Sciammarella, E.: ToolStone: Effective Use of the Physical Manipulation Vocabularies of Input Devices. In: Proceedings of UIST 2000, pp. 109–117. ACM, New York (2000)
2. Sharlin, E., Itoh, Y., Watson, B., Kitamura, Y., Sutphen, S., Liu, L.: Cognitive Cubes: A Tangible User Interface for Cognitive Assessment. In: Proceedings of CHI 2002, New York, NY, USA, pp. 347–354. ACM, New York (2002)

3. Dourish, P.: Where the action is: The foundation of embodied interaction. MIT-Press, Cambridge, Massachusetts (2001)
4. Flanagan, J.R., Johansson, R.S.: Hand Movements. In: Encyclopaedia of the Human Brain, vol. 2, Elsevier Science, Amsterdam (2002)
5. Rauterberg, M.: Ueber die Quantifizierung software-ergonomischer Richtlinien, PhD Thesis. University of Zurich. Refered in Fjeld, M., Bichsel, M., Rauterberg, M.: BUILD-IT: a brick-based tool for direct interaction. In: Harris, D.(ed.) Engineering, Psychology and Cognitive Ergonomics, vol. 4, pp. 205–212, Ashgate, Hampshire (1995)
6. Hacker, W., Clauss, A.: Kognitive Operationen, inneres Modell und Leistung bei einer Motagetatigkeit. Deutscher Verlag des Wissenschaften, Berlin, Germany. Refered in Fjeld, M., Bichsel, M., Rauterberg, M.: BUILD-IT: a brick-based tool for direct interaction. In: Harris, D. (ed.) Engineering, Psychology and Cognitive Ergonomics, vol. 4, pp. 205–212, Ashgate, Hampshire (1999) (1976)
7. Handy, T.C., Grafton, S.T., Shroff, N.M., Ketay, S., Gazzaniga, M.S.: Graspable object grab attention when the potential for action is recognised. Nature Neuroscience 6(4), 421–427 (2003)
8. Schettino, L.F., Adamovich, S.V., Poizner, H.: Effects of object shape and visual feedback on hand configuration during grasping. Experimental Brain Research 151, 158–166 (2003)
9. Gibson, J.J.: The ecological approach to visual perception. Lawrence Erlbaum, London, England (1986)
10. Norman, D.A.: The Design of Everyday Things. MIT Press, London, England (2001)
11. Henry, T.R., Hudson, S.E.: Multidimensional Icons. ACM Transactions on Graphics 9(1), 133–137 (1990)
12. Frohlich, B., Plate, J.: The Cubic Mouse: A New Device for Three-Dimensional Input. In: Turner, T., Szwillus, G., Czerwinski, M., Paterno, F. (eds.) Proceedings of CHI2000, pp. 526–531. ACM, New York (2000)
13. Camatara, K., Do, E.Y.-L., Johnson, B.R., Gross, M.D.: Navigational Blocks: Navigating Information Space with Tangible Media. In: Gil, Y., Leake, D.B. (eds.) Proceedings of UIU-02, International Conference on Intelligent User Interfaces, pp. 31–38. ACM, New York (2002)
14. Murakami, T., Hayashi, K., Oikawa, K., Nakajima, N.: DO-IT: Deformable Objects as Input Tools. In: Proceedings of CHI95, pp. 87–88. ACM, New York (1995)
15. Fitzmaurice, G.W., Ishii, H., Buxton, W.A.S.: Bricks: Laying the foundations for graspable user interfaces. In: Proceedings of SIGCHI '95, pp. 442–449. ACM, New York (1995)
16. Block, F., Schmidt, A., Villar, N., Gellersen, H.W.: Towards a Playful User Interface for Home Entertainment Systems. In: Markopoulos, P., Eggen, B., Aarts, E., Crowley, J.L. (eds.) EUSAI 2004. LNCS, vol. 3295, pp. 207–217. Springer, Heidelberg (2004)
17. Kitamura, Y., Itoh, Y., Kishino, F.: Real-time 3D Interaction with ActiveCube. In: Jacko, J.A., Sears, A., Beudouin-Lafon, M., Jacob, R.J.K. (eds.) Proceedings of CHI2001, pp. 355–356. ACM, New York (2001)
18. Ullmer, B., Ishii, H.: MediaBlocks: Physical Containers, Transports, and Controls for Online Media. In: Proceedings of SIGGRAPH 98, pp. 379–386. ACM, New York (1998)
19. Lertsithichai, S., Seegmiller, M.: CUBIK: A Bi-Directional Tangible Modeling Interface. In: Proceedings of SIGCHI 2002, pp. 756–757. ACM, New York (2002)
20. Murakami, T., Nakajima, N.: Direct and Intuitive Input Device for 3-D Shape Deformation. In: Adelson, B., Dumais, S., Olson, J. (eds.) Proceedings of CHI'94, pp. 465–470. ACM, New York (1994)

21. Watanabe, R., Itoh, Y., Asai, M., Kitamura, Y., Kishino, F., Kikuchi, H.: The Soul of ActiveCube – Implementing a Flexible, Multimodal, Three-Dimensional Spatial Tangible Interface. ACM Computers in Entertainment 2(4), 1–13 (2004)
22. Ullmer, B.: Tangible interface for manipulating aggregates if digital information, doctoral dissertation, MA, USA. MIT, Cambridge (2002), available at http://alumni.media.mit.edu/ullmer/dissertation/

EMA-Tactons: Vibrotactile External Memory Aids in an Auditory Display

Johan Kildal and Stephen A. Brewster

Glasgow Interactive Systems Group, Department of Computing Science
University of Glasgow. Glasgow, G12 8QQ, UK
{johank, stephen}@dcs.gla.ac.uk - www.multivis.org

Abstract. Exploring any new data set always starts with gathering overview information. When this process is done non-visually, interactive sonification techniques have proved to be effective and efficient ways of getting overview information, particularly for users who are blind or visually impaired. Under certain conditions, however, the process of data analysis cannot be completed due to saturation of the user's working memory. This paper introduces EMA-Tactons, vibrotactile external memory aids that are intended to support working memory during the process of data analysis, combining vibrotactile and audio stimuli in a multimodal interface. An iterative process led to a design that significantly improves the performance (in terms of effectiveness) of users solving complex data explorations. The results provide information about the convenience of using EMA-Tactons with other auditory displays, and the iterative design process illustrates the challenges of designing multimodal interaction techniques.

Keywords: vibrotactile, external memory aid, overview, visual impairment, high-density sonification.

1 Motivation and Description of the Problem

Data explorations are performed at many different levels of detail, in a continuum that ranges from very general overview information (including size and structure of the data set, nature and meaning of the data), through global description of the relations in the data set (general trends in the data), to more detailed descriptions in particular areas of interest or even to the retrieval of each piece of information in full detail. Every data exploration should start by obtaining overview information, as Shneiderman expresses in his visual information-seeking mantra, "overview first, zoom and filter, then details on demand" [1], which was later extended to non-visual modalities [2].

Previous work by the authors focused on the problem of obtaining overview information non-visually, concentrating in particular on users who are blind or visual impaired (VI), who generally suffer great difficulties retrieving overview information using current accessibility tools. For the common problem of exploring complex tabular numerical data sets (spreadsheets are a typical example), the authors developed TableVis, an interface intended to explore numerical data tables by generating sonifications of the data interactively, with particular focus on obtaining overview information at the beginning of the exploration of a data set [3]. In brief, TableVis uses a

C. Baranauskas et al. (Eds.): INTERACT 2007, LNCS 4663, Part II, pp. 71–84, 2007.
© Springer-Verlag Berlin Heidelberg 2007

pen-based tangible input device (a graphics tablet) onto which a data table is scaled to fill the complete active area (Figure 1, left), providing a number of invariants for the user to rely on during the exploration. The first invariant is that the complete data set is always on display, and the tangible borders of the tablet correspond to the boundaries of the data set (Figure 1, right). The second invariant is that all of the data are directly accessible by pointing at a particular location on the tablet, which is a constant location. The third invariant is that the active area on the tablet has a fixed size. These invariants provide enough context information for users to explore data tables in search for overview information at various levels of detail. Using a sonification strategy widely tested in creating auditory graphs [4], information is transformed into sound, mapping each numerical value to a particular pitch of sound within a predefined range, in such a way that the lowest value in the data set corresponds to the lowest pitch and the highest value corresponds to the highest pitch, with all of the intermediate numerical values being mapped proportionally to pitches in that range. By default, a continuum pitch-space approximately ranging 60-2600Hz is used to map all the values in any table. Information can be accessed by listening to one cell at a time (*cells* mode) or by listening to all the cells in a complete row or column (*rows* and *columns* modes) in a single sound event. The latter modes are particularly appropriate to obtain overview information. In them, a complete row or column is sonified by playing each one of the cells in that row or column in so fast an arpeggio that it is perceived as a chord. Thus, a single complex sound (a combination of all the frequencies to which the values in that row or column map) is heard for each row or column, with a particular perceived overall pitch. This sonification technique is called *High-Density Sonification* (HDS). Comparing the relative perceived pitches of adjacent rows and columns is a very fast and effective way of scanning a large table in only a few seconds and obtaining a good overview representation of the whole data table [5].

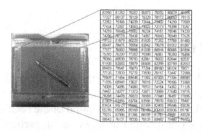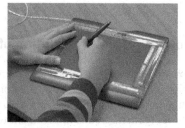

Fig. 1. The data table to be explored is presented on the active area of the tablet, scaled to fill it completely (left).A user explores a data table creating an interactive sonification with the pen, while the left hand feels the boundaries of the data set to provide contextual information (right).

Kwasnik [6] proposed the following components of browsing: orientation, place marking, identification, resolution of anomalies, comparison and transitions. TableVis was designed to provide support for these functional components by maintaining permanently a focus+context metaphor while chunking information with HDS to minimise the number of comparisons that have to be performed. During experimental evaluation studies conducted with blind and sighted blindfolded participants, it was observed that, under certain conditions, the working memory of some users reached saturation. While the actual circumstances in which this happened will be described in detail later, they involved performing large numbers of comparisons between specific areas in a data table as intermediate steps towards the completion of an exploratory task. Qualitative data from those studies revealed that some form of external memory aid could support performing those intermediate steps, preventing saturation.

This paper introduces EMA-Tactons, vibrotactile external memory aids (EMA's) that are combined with interactive sonification techniques for the exploration of data. EMA's are used to mark interesting areas in a data set where the user may want to go back to. By explicitly marking them, the user's working memory can be freed, preventing saturation of this kind of memory before an exploratory task is completed. An iterative design process is described in detail for the illustrative case of TableVis.

2 Requirements Capture and the First Design Iteration

During experimental evaluations of TableVis, some participants had difficulties to complete certain exploratory tasks that required performing multiple comparisons as intermediate steps, due to working memory saturation. Those tasks involved exploring numerical data tables with 7 rows and 24 columns finding overview information in terms of the meaning of the data in those tables (see [5] for a detailed description of the study). The task was completed exploring the data using HDS, comparing the 7-note chords corresponding to all 24 columns and then choosing the column with the pitch that was perceived to be the highest among the 24. This process required comparing all the chords against each other, and remembering both pitches and spatial locations. These problems arouse mainly with data sets in which there were no apparent patterns and where peaks in the data were randomly located, without smooth variations that led towards them. From those observations, the characteristics of the tasks and data sets that lead to such situations were derived:

- Data tables with a moderately large number of rows and/or columns (it was observed that 24 was big enough);
- Data sets that do not contain smooth patterns. In other words, data sets where data are distributed (apparently) randomly;
- Tasks that require obtaining information with an intermediate level of detail.

Those characteristics in task and data set require a user to perform large numbers of comparisons and to remember a lot of intermediate information temporarily. In the studies described above, users had to remember where the columns with the largest numbers were (spatial memory) and what each one of them did sound like (pitch memory). A list of columns candidate to producing the highest overall perceived pitch was constructed by comparing all the columns against each other and adding them to that list or rejecting them. All that temporary information had to be held in the very limited storage capacity of working memory [7]. In situations like those, some kind of EMA could significantly improve the chances to complete the task by preventing working memory saturation. Some of the participants tried to mark the exact locations of the isolated peaks with their fingers, so that once all the candidate columns were marked they could go back to those positions on the tablet and compare them, choosing the highest one. This technique posed several difficulties. Firstly, marking positions on the tablet with a finger was quite inaccurate. Fingers moved accidentally and references were often lost. Additionally, it was often very difficult to mark three or more positions distributed across the tablet. Rearranging the fingers to mark an additional position often resulted in accidentally losing all the references. Finally, the non-dominant hand could not assist the dominant hand that held the pen by providing good references to known positions on the data set (corners, middle points of sides etc), used in maintaining the focus+context metaphor through proprioception.

2.1 Design

A list of characteristics for EMA marks (using an analogy with marks often created with pencil on printed documents) was derived from the observations above:

- Marks should be easily added and removed;
- They should not be limited in number;
- Each mark must remain in the same position, unless explicitly moved by the user;
- Marks must be easy to find;
- Adding a mark must not alter the information in the data set;
- A mark should not obstruct the access to the information in that position;
- Marking should combine with other techniques and tools for data exploration and analysis available in the interface, to support the process of information seeking.

Using the fingers from one hand clearly does not comply with some of the characteristics in the list. An initial solution that we considered was using tangible physical objects that could be placed on the tablet. One example was to utilise reusable putty-like adhesive material (commercially available products like BluTack, Pritt-tack or others). This design would comply with most of the characteristics in the list, in addition to having many other advantages such as being cheap and disposable. There was, however, an important limitation, as the markers have to be recognised and supported by a computer in order to also comply with the last point in the list. In a realistic exploratory task with TableVis, a user needs to be able to explore complementary views of the same data set (using *rows* and *columns* modes) that, when combined, help to build an understanding of the whole data set. Changing the exploratory modality should present the marks corresponding to the new modality only, and all the marks corresponding to other views of the data would be stored and preserved. In the case of other interfaces for interactive data sonification, EMA's should combine with the functionality available in those interfaces to support information seeking, which in many cases will require that EMA's are recognised and managed by a computer.

2.1.1 Computer-Supported EMA's

In TableVis, the auditory channel is used intensively to maximise the transmission of information to the user. Designing EMA's in the form of non-speech sounds, although appropriate in principle, would have increased the amount of auditory information transmitted through this channel, potentially creating problems of masking and overloading. On the contrary, information is less intensively transmitted through the somatic senses in most interactive sonification interfaces. In the case of TableVis, proprioception and kinesthesis are used to maintain the context of the information that is in focus, but very little information is perceived cutaneously apart from feeling the tangible borders of the exploration area with the non-dominant hand. Wall and Brewster [8] used force-feedback to provide EMA's in similar situations. Incorporating force-feedback devices to TableVis would have meant removing one of the dominant criteria for its design, which was to make use of inexpensive off-the-shelf technology that resulted in affordable systems, easily scaleable and where components could be replaced flexibly. Vibrotactile actuators are much more common devices, which are already used in multiple applications (the most popular of them being vibration in mobile phones), and they can be very small and even wireless. These actuators can generate vibrotactile messages that are easy to control, and that can be perceived subtly on the skin. Vibrotactile stimuli can be used to generate Tactons, which are structured, abstract tactile messages that can communicate complex concepts to users non-visually [9]. Using Tactons as EMA's (thus, EMA-Tactons), the potential to transmit information to users via cutaneous stimulation can transcend a mere binary indication of whether certain piece of data has been marked or not. The information conveyed could be richer, potentially including the type of the annotation (a marked cell, or complete row or column in the case of a data table) and ranking the information according to its importance in a particular search. Ideally, this richness of information would approximate that of simple annotations that sighted users make while exploring a data set presented in the visual medium.

2.2 Implementation

A Tactaid VBW32 transducer (Figure 2, left) was selected to generate the vibrotactile stimuli (www.tactaid.com). The nominal vibration frequency of a Tactaid (where amplitude of frequency is highest) is 250Hz. A Tactaid transducer was mounted laterally on the rear end of the tablet's electronic pen (Figure 2, right), using adhesive tape that ensured hard contact between the transducer and the pen. First tests showed that it was important that this contact was not loose otherwise the external shell of the transducer rattled against the surface of the pen, which could be heard by the user. Lee *et al.* [10] mounted a solenoid axially on their Haptic Pen, to accurately simulate a physical event. EMA-Tactons are abstract information with no physical tangible equivalent. Thus, the lateral mounting was used instead, for ease and reliability. The user does not touch the transducer directly during the exploration; the vibration is transmitted and felt on the surface of the pen while holding it normally (Figure 2, right). The pen+transducer assembly was informally tested to observe the frequency at which the whole combined item vibrated with the highest amplitude, which would provide a good transmission of vibration to the skin without causing movement on the pen that could affect accuracy of pointing. It was observed that the vibration was most noticeable at 270Hz. Therefore, a sine wave with frequency 270Hz was chosen to generate vibrotactile stimuli. Fine-tuning the intensity of the vibration was left to the discretion of the user, for reasons of comfort.

During the exploration of a data table, a user could mark any position that the pen was pointing at by pressing a button. Depending on the selected navigation mode, only the cell or the complete row or column being pointed at would be marked. The vibration would be felt as long as the pen remained on the selected cell, row or

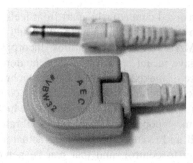

Fig. 2. Tactaid VBW32 transducer (left). Tactaid mounted on the pen of the tablet (right).

column. The vibration would be felt every time the pen re-entered a selected area during the exploration. An EMA-Tacton could be removed by pressing the same button while the pen was on the marked area. Adding or removing a mark was confirmed by a different, easily distinguishable, percussion sound. Data could be marked in different navigation modes, and switching between modes would not delete any marks, but make them selectively accessible (e.g. in *columns* mode, only marks affecting complete columns would be accessible). This model could easily be extended to selecting a cell by intersection of a selected row and a selected column. In this study, EMA-Tactons convey only binary information, i.e. whether data has been marked or not.

2.3 Pilot Evaluation

Five participants took part in the pilot evaluation of EMA-Tactons in TableVis, with the implementation described in the previous section. All participants were visually impaired and used screen reading software to access information in computers. The structure of the evaluation session was as follows: introduction to the interface and to the concepts involved in exploring data through interactive sonification; set several tasks for data exploration and observe the participant perform the task, encouraging think-aloud explorations; finish with a semi-structured interview. Only the *columns* navigation mode was used, where complete columns were compared by using HDS in TableVis.

The data sets used for the evaluation were tables with 7 rows and 24 columns, the same size as some of the tables used in earlier evaluations of TableVis and with which working memory saturation problems had been observed [5]. When navigating by columns, one such table is sonified into an array of 24 chords (with 7 piano notes each) arranged side-by-side horizontally on the tablet. Participants could access the chords by moving the electronic pen from one column to another. Tapping repeatedly on the same column would replay the chord representing that column. The data presented in the tables were such that each set of 7 values in each column had a different arithmetic mean (all means were approximately equidistant from the nearest higher and lower ones) and all the 24 columns had approximately the same standard deviation. In each data table, columns were placed in random order, so that means did not follow any discernible progression. The task set was to find the column with the highest perceived overall pitch.

For the first two participants, the task of finding the highest single column happened to be simple enough to allow them to complete it without the need for EMA-Tactons. While both participants agreed that EMA-Tactons offered help to complete the task, they completed it making little or no use of them. One of the participants explained that a first scan of all the columns showed where the highest few columns where. Then, this participant claimed to be able to remember one of those pitches and compare it against every other pitch until the highest was found. Only the pitch and position of the current highest sound had to be remembered, and after finding a higher one the previous pitch and position were replaced with the new ones, never overloading working memory. This participant was consistently correct. The authors concluded that, while the task was probably challenging enough for some users, it did not always saturate working memory and cause interaction problems. It is interesting to observe that Wall and Brewster reached a similar conclusion in their study [8].

To further challenge working memory, the task set to the remaining three participants required that the 5 columns with the highest pitched sounds were selected, instead of the single absolute highest. The number of comparisons was much larger, as was the number of intermediate results to be temporarily remembered (positions, pitches associated to those positions and number of positions selected). The procedure to be followed was to explore the data with the pen and when one of those five sounds was identified to select it by pressing a push-button, while the pen was still on the position of that column. Columns could be selected and deselected by pressing the same button. Two experimental conditions were defined: i) selecting a column would add an EMA-Tacton to that location, which would be felt when going over it with the pen; ii) selecting a column would not add an EMA-Tacton, although the selection/deselection confirmation sounds would still be heard (which would alert about trying to select the same column twice, as the user would know from the confirmation sound that a mark had been removed from an already selected column). Thus, the only difference between both conditions was that in the second one the user would not be able to find marked areas easily, having to rely on his/her memory more heavily. In the first condition, he user would not have to consciously decide to use the EMA-Tactons, as they would simply appear when columns were selected. Then, participants would be able to keep track of the number of columns that had already been selected (by counting the number of vibrating columns) and they would also be able to check more easily if each one of the selected columns did actually belong to the group of the 5 columns with the highest pitch, resulting in a better performance at solving the task.

The new task was observed to overload the participants' working memory very quickly during the pilot study, and participants reported that it was easier to complete the task when the EMA-Tactons were available. In addition to providing qualitative feedback, two of the participants completed the exploration of the 12 data sets (which were described earlier). The 12 data sets were presented in random order in each condition, and the order of the conditions was counterbalanced. Participants had up to 120 seconds to perform an exploration and select the columns. The subjective workload experience was assessed after each condition using NASA-TLX [11] questionnaires, followed by a semi-structured interview. The quantitative results from this experimental test are presented in the next section, together with quantitative data from the same experiment that was run with a bigger group of sighted blindfolded participants, and both are compared. From a qualitative point of view, it was concluded from the pilot study that the EMA-Tactons had good acceptance once the task was challenging enough.

In the studies presented here, data ordering was randomised to maximise the chances of users' working memory getting saturated. This was a major difference to the setup used in previous evaluations of TableVis, where data always followed more or less smoothly-changing patterns. Exploring random data sets using HDS has limitations. This technique is appropriate for obtaining overview information (general description of trends and patterns) and for finding areas in the data set with high or low values when data change smoothly (leading towards them), or if extremes are obviously high or low. In the case of very random data, like in this study, HDS can help pick and group areas by ranges of values (as in the task where the five highest sounds have to be identified), but there is no guarantee that the absolute highest pitch can be singled out reliably, or that the sixth highest sound will be thought to have a lower pitch than the fifth highest. To compensate for any confounding effects introduced by this limitation in the data discrimination technique used, the final version of the design is also evaluated using single tones instead of chords, which, although further from the scenario being replicated, provides an unequivocal criterion to judge the correctness of the answers. A parallel line of research from the authors is investigating how relative pitch is perceived in complex dissonant chords

3   Experimental Evaluation of the First Design Iteration

A group of 8 sighted persons was recruited to take part in the experiment designed during the pilot study (due to our limited supply of visually-impaired people we often have to test with sighted blindfolded participants. The approach we take is to scope out the problem with our target users and then test sighted participants to gain more data. The performance of the two groups is commonly very similar). The setup, data sets and procedure were exactly the same as those described in the previous section and used in the pilot study. To asses quantitatively the effectiveness of the EMA-Tactons, the correctness of the results at solving the task was divided in two parts, each providing a metric of effectiveness. A third metric was obtained considering the task as a whole:

- *Sub-task 1 (number of selections).* Correctness in selecting exactly 5 positions on the tablet. 100% correct obtained only when exactly 5 positions are selected. This metric is calculated with the formula:

$$\text{Correctness sub-task 1 (\%)} = 100 \cdot (1 - |Ss - 5| / 5) . \qquad (1)$$

- *Sub-task 2 (pitch of the selected sounds).* Correctness in having selected the positions with the highest pitch sounds. 100% correct obtained only if all the positions selected correspond to the group of the same number of sounds with the highest pitch. For example, if 7 positions are selected and they are the 7 sounds with the highest pitch in the whole set of 24 sounds then sub-task 2 is 100% correct.

$$\text{Correctness sub-task 2 (\%)} = 100 \cdot (Sc / Ss) . \qquad (2)$$

- *Overall task (Combination of sub-tasks 1 and 2).* Metric to asses the correctness of the overall task, as the product of both sub-tasks. 100% correctness is only obtained if exactly 5 positions were selected *and* they correspond to the 5 highest pitch sounds in the set. This metric is calculated with the following formula:

$$\text{Overall correctness (\%)} = 100 \cdot (1 - |Ss - 5| / 5) \cdot Sc / Ss . \qquad (3)$$

In all formulae, Ss is the number of sounds selected and Sc is the number of sounds from the selection that are in the group of the Ss sounds with the highest pitch.

Results from the evaluation with sighted blindfolded participants (Figure 3, left) show that the effect of using EMA-Tactons is small, differences not being significant for any of the metrics, according to two-tailed t-tests (paired two sample for means): sub-task 1 ($T_7=1.609$; P=0.152); sub-task 2 ($T_7=-0.378$; P=0.717); overall task (T7=1.27; P=0.245). The results by the two VI participants (Figure 3, centre and right) are approximately within the ranges obtained in the experiment with the group of sighted blindfolded participants (although performance in sub-task 2 was slightly lower for the first VI participant).

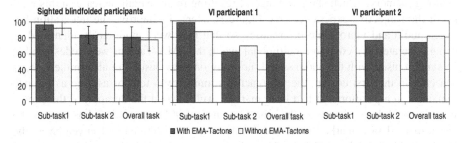

Fig. 3. Left: results (percentage of task completion) from experimental evaluation of the first design iteration (unsynchronised sound and vibration). Centre and right: results from the pilot study, by participants with visual impairments. Error-bars represent 95% confidence interval.

The hypothesis that effectiveness would be higher with EMA-Tactons could not be proved, according to these results. Among the qualitative feedback provided by the participants, many of them agreed in saying that the vibrotactile information could both help and interfere in the process of solving the task. EMA-Tactons were helpful to keep count of how many locations had already been selected (thus the slight improvements in sub-task 1). Several participants, however, reported that sometimes the vibration on the pen could be distracting, stating that it could even get in the way when the user was trying to listen to the sounds. Others said that they found EMA-Tactons helpful in general but that it was very difficult to get information simultaneously from sound and from vibration and that they concentrated on the source of information they needed at each time, ignoring the other. One participant also reported that vibration and sound sometimes seemed to be two unrelated events.

An explanation for these results and comments can be found in the differences between endogenous and exogenous spatial attention, and in aspects of crossmodal spatial attention. When a participant wanted to count how many sounds were already selected, attention was endogenously (voluntarily) diverted to the hand holding the pen, monitoring for vibrotactile cues. If, on the contrary the user was trying to listen to the sounds and unexpectedly a vibration was produced in the pen, attention got diverted to the hand exogenously (involuntarily, stimulus driven), thus potentially interfering with the listening. Multiple sensory inputs are processed selectively, and some stimuli get processed more thoroughly than others, which can be ignored more easily. There are very complex interactions between crossmodal attention and multisensory integration and much research is being carried out in that field that will inform the designers of multimodal interfaces (see chapters 8, 9 and 11 in Spence and Driver [12]).

4 Second Design Iteration and Experimental Evaluations

Results from the first design iteration suggested that presenting a vibrotactile cue simultaneously with the onset of the sound did not bind them enough to create a single multimodal event, where users could perceive both sensory cues to be related to a common event. A conscious binding of both events was required, what could increase the subjective overall mental workload despite the support that was being provided to working memory, which should reduce it, resulting in an overall increase in this metric of the subjective experience (see Figure 6, later). To improve the integration between audio and vibrotactile information so that they were more easily identified as being generated at a common multimodal event, the EMA-Tactons were redesigned to be synchronised with the audio signal, not only on their onset, but also in their decay and end. In the first design, the vibrotactile stimulus was felt for as long as the pen remained on a position that had been marked, well beyond the duration of the sound. In the second design iteration, the vibration, instead of being produced as long as the pen remained in a marked area, had similar duration (200ms) and envelope as the sound. A sharp attack was followed by a 120ms sustain period (so that the presence of the vibration was clearly perceived), and then the amplitude of the vibration decayed during the last 80ms. As an extension of sound-grouping principles from auditory scene analysis, which suggest that sounds that are likely to have originated in the same event in the physical world are grouped together [13], the authors hypothesised that two stimuli in different sensory modalities that were synchronised and equally shaped could be more easily perceived as having been generated at the same event (as when in the physical world some mechanical action generates decaying vibration and sound that are perfectly synchronised throughout).

Having made this change, the same experimental evaluation setup was conducted with another 12 sighted blindfolded participants. As it was effectiveness and not efficiency the aspect that was being targeted with this study, up to 180 seconds were allowed in this case to explore each data set in order to permit extended, thorough data explorations. The results are shown in Figure 4. Performance in sub-task 1 (accuracy in the number of selections) was statistically significantly better with EMA-Tactons ($T_{11}=3.008$; $P=0.012$). The improvement in performance for sub-task 2 (selecting the highest-pitched sounds) was still not significant ($T_{11}=1.379$; $P=0.195$). The performance with EMA-Tactons for the overall task showed a statistically significant improvement ($T_{11}=2.89$; $P=0.015$).

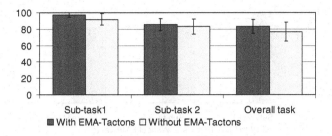

Fig. 4. Results (percentage of task completion) from first experimental evaluation (chords) with the second design iteration (synchronised sound and vibration). Error-bars represent 95% confidence interval.

The possible existence of two confounding factors was identified in this study. Many participants started their exploration taking a quick overview of all the data, looking for the areas on the tablet with the highest-pitched chords, and then they tried to concentrate their search in those areas. In every data set, the five highest-pitched chords were in a similar range of frequencies. It was therefore possible that there was a learning process during which target frequencies were learnt, reducing the initial scan to identifying those pitches only and ignoring any other sounds from the beginning. Relying on pitch memory in this way would reduce the number of comparisons that had to be performed, increasing performance in both conditions and reducing the potential benefit EMA-Tactons could offer. Another possible confounding factor was comparing the perceived overall pitches of two similar chords, as it has been discussed in 2.4, earlier. These two possible factors were addressed by creating new data sets in which sounds were single piano notes instead of chords. Each data set was a succession of 24 notes in a chromatic scale (one semitone distance between any two consecutive notes), arranged in random order. It was expected that any possible ambiguity in the judgement of relative pitches would disappear for the majority of participants. To prevent participants from remembering target pitches between data sets, each one of the 12 data sets would cover a different range of 23 consecutive semitones. Since data sets were presented in random order, it was not possible to predict what the highest-pitched sounds in a new data set would be like before every position had been examined, thus preserving the need to perform a full set of comparisons.

Having created new data sets in the way that has just been described, a new group of 12 participants was recruited to test again the effect of EMA-Tactons in their second design iteration (with audio and vibrotactile stimuli synchronised). In this case (Figure 5), the improvement in performance for sub-task 1 (number of selections) was not significant ($T_{11}=1.892$; P=0.085). In contrast, the performance in sub-task 2 (selecting highest pitches) improved significantly with EMA-Tactons ($T_{11}=2.216$; P=0.049). The performance considering the overall task saw, again, a significant improvement when EMA-Tactons were used ($T_{11}=2.490$; P=0.030).

The increase in significance for sub-task 2 (selecting the highest pitches) could well be due to having removed both confounding factors. In particular, it is believed that participants could have been obtaining benefit from pitch memory in the previous setup, hence facing less working memory saturation problems and obtaining less

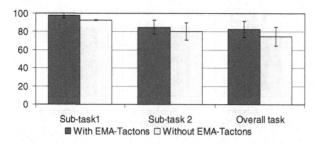

Fig. 5. Results (percentage of task completion) from the second experimental evaluation (single tones) with the second design iteration (synchronised sound and vibration). Error-bars: 95% confidence interval.

benefit from EMA-Tactons. Other results presented in the next section support this idea. The reasons for the loss of significance for sub-task 1 need to be investigated further, but there is no reason to think that it is due to using tones instead of chords.

5 Other Results

In all three experiments conducted, the time to complete the task (an aspect not targeted by this research work) was in average longer when EMA-Tactons were used than when they were not. This was also true for the two visually-impaired participants, who required on average 90.9 and 75.9 seconds respectively to complete the task with EMA-Tactons, while it took only 67.3 and 57.8 seconds respectively to complete it without them. Based on qualitative feedback, this is attributed to the fact that with EMA-Tactons, participants could be more thorough in their search without reaching saturation of working memory, resulting in more focused, and thus longer, data explorations. The difference in time to complete task was only significant in the second design (synchronised sound and vibration) with chords (T_{11}=2.789; P=0.018). It is interesting to observe that, comparing the conditions without EMA-Tactons from both experiments in the second design (synchronised sound and vibration), the average time to complete the task was longer in the second experiment (single tones) than in the first one (chords). This supports the hypothesis that pitch memory was being used in the first case to simplify the task.

The overall subjective workload (derived from the NASA-TLX ratings) was perceived to be significantly lower when EMA-Tactons in their second design iteration (synchronised sound and vibration) were used (T_{11}=-2.970; P=0.012 for chords and T_{11}=-3.546; P=0.005 for single notes). Again, the difference was bigger in the last experiment, when saturation of working memory was higher and with more room for improvement. With the first design of EMA-Tactons, the difference was not significant (T_{7}=0.558; P=0.594). The task was exactly the same in both cases, as it was the amount of information provided by both prototypes of EMA-Tactons. Therefore, the fact that the overall subjective workload using EMA-Tactons was significantly lower with the second design while showing no significant difference with the first design must be attributed to the actual design, suggesting that synchronising sound and vibration to integrate sensory channels was the correct approach.

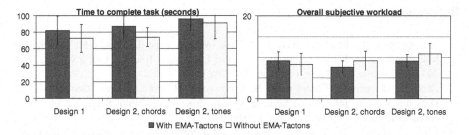

Fig. 6. Time to complete task, in seconds (left) and overall subjective workload, derived from NASA-TLX ratings (right). Error-bars represent 95% confidence interval.

6 Conclusions

This paper has introduced EMA-Tactons as a way of enhancing interactive data soni-fication interfaces with vibrotactile external memory aids, to tackle common problems of working memory saturation in non-visual environments. An iterative design proc-ess produced two prototype designs that were tested quantitatively and qualitatively. This process showed that designing multimodal interfaces for good integration of sen-sory channels is difficult and complex. Subtle changes can make a big difference in perceiving a single multimodal event instead of unrelated events in different sensory channels. EMA-Tactons were tested in TableVis, an interactive data sonification interface designed to explore tabular numerical data non-visually. In the first design iteration, enhancing the interaction with external memory aids in the form of vibrotac-tile stimuli to avoid saturation of the users' working memory did not produce any significant improvements in the performance in terms of accuracy of retrieved infor-mation. Careful redesign of the vibrotactile stimuli following principles of ecological perception produced a better integration of multisensory information, which led to significant improvements in performance. Consistently saturating the participants' working memory in order to test the prototypes also proved to be difficult. Even with very demanding tasks, resourceful participants were believed to have used pitch memory to simplify those tasks, so that the need for any external memory aids was reduced at the expense of very small loss in accuracy. This illustrates the difficulty of replicating scenarios where working memory saturation problems had been observed, and which would produce the same effect on the whole population of participants in a study. Despite the human resourcefulness observed, the second prototype of EMA-Tactons produced significant improvements in effective task completion. In future de-sign iterations, using more than one bit of information from the EMA-Tactons can permit adding richer annotations. Additionally, the combination of rich annotations in different exploratory modalities (*rows*, *columns* and *cells*) has the potential to offer support for complex exploratory tasks that today can only be done visually.

Acknowledgements

We want to acknowledge the contribution of all the participants in this study, and in particular the committed support received from the RNC in Hereford. This research is funded by EPSRC grant GR/S86150/01.

References

1. Shneiderman, B.: The Eyes Have It: A Task by Data Type Taxonomy for Information Visualizations. In: IEEE Symposium on Visual Languages, Boulder, CO, USA, pp. 336–343. IEEE Comp. Soc. Press, Los Alamitos (1996)
2. Zhao, H., Plaisant, C., Shneiderman, B., Duraiswami, R.: Sonification of Geo-Referenced Data for Auditory Information Seeking: Design Principle and Pilot Study. In: Int. Conf. Auditory Display, Sydney, Australia (2004)
3. Kildal, J., Brewster, S.: Exploratory Strategies and Procedures to Obtain Non-Visual Overviews Using Tablevis. Int. J. Disabil. Human Dev. 5(3), 285–294 (2006)
4. Flowers, J.H.: Thirteen Years of Reflection on Auditory Graphing: Promises, Pitfalls, and Potential New Directions. In: Int. Symposium Auditory Graphs. Int. Conf. Auditory Display, Limerick, Ireland (2005)
5. Kildal, J., Brewster, S.: Providing a Size-Independent Overview of Non-Visual Tables. In: Int. Conf. Auditory Display, Queen Mary, University of London, pp. 8–15 (2006)
6. Kwasnik, B.H.: A Descriptive Study of the Functional Components of Browsing. In: Ifip Tc2/Wg2.7 Working Conference on Engineering for Human-Computer Interaction, pp. 191–203. North-Holland, Amsterdam (1992)
7. Miller, G.A.: The Magical Number Seven Plus or Minus Two: Some Limits on Our Capacity for Processing Information. The Psychological Review 63, 81–97 (1956)
8. Wall, S., Brewster, S.: Providing External Memory Aids in Haptic Visualisations for Blind Computer Users. Int. J. Disabil. Human Dev. 4(3), 285–294 (2006)
9. Brewster, S., Brown, L.: Tactons: Structured Tactile Messages for Non-Visual Information Display. In: Australasian User Interface Conf., pp. 15–23. Australian Comp. Soc., Dunedin, New Zealand (2004)
10. Lee, J.C., Dietz, P.H., Leigh, D., Yerazunis, W.S., Hudson, S.E.: Haptic Pen: A Tactile Feedback Stylus for Touch Screens. In: Annual ACM Symposium on User Interface Software and Technology, pp. 291–294. ACM Press, New York (2004)
11. Hart, S., Wickens, C.: Workload Assessment and Prediction. Manprint, an Approach to Systems Integration. In: Booher, H.R.(ed.) Van Nostrand Reinhold, pp. 257–296 (1990)
12. Spence, C., Driver, J.: Crossmodal Space and Crossmodal Attention. Oxford University Press, Oxford (2004)
13. Bregman, A.: Auditory Scene Analysis: The Perceptual Organization of Sound. The MIT Press, Cambridge (1994)

Institutionalizing HCI in Asia

Andy Smith[1], Anirudha Joshi[2], Zhengjie Liu[3], Liam Bannon[4],
Jan Gulliksen[5], and Christina Li[1]

[1] Thames Valley University United Kingdom
andy.smith@tvu.ac.uk
[2] Industrial Design Centre, IIT Bombay, Mumbai, India
anirudha@iitb.ac.in
[3] Sino-European Usability Center, Dalian Maritime University
liuzhj@dlmu.edu.cn
[4] Interaction Design Centre, University of Limerick, Ireland
liam.bannon@ul.ie
[5] Uppsala University, Sweden
jan.gulliksen@it.uu.se

Abstract. In this paper we investigate the problems and potential solutions to the effective establishment of HCI and usability in India and China. Our discussion is motivated by five years of collaboration with relevant bodies in both countries through EU-funded projects encouraging the development of a usability culture in academic and industrial sectors. In order to contribute to socially-responsible interaction in these countries the 'institutionalization' of HCI is necessary. For us, this involves three elements: firstly an appropriation of HCI concepts and methods to suit the local country / culture, secondly the forming of a national organization around the reshaped discipline that can actively promote HCI in industry and academia and establish links with local national organizations, and thirdly the roll-out of effective usability practice in industry. Some efforts made in this regard are briefly outlined.

Keywords: cross-cultural usability, India, China, institutionalization.

1 Introduction

With a combined population accounting for nearly two-fifths of humanity, the neighbouring Asian countries of India and China, are two of the world's fastest-growing economies. These countries have embarked on radical, liberalising economic reforms that are resulting in improved living standards for many, though not all, its peoples. At the same time, there are huge problems in terms of providing for adequate housing, sanitation, education and welfare for all the population. In India more than half of women and 30 per cent of men remain illiterate. In China the economic inequalities between Western (mainly agricultural and Eastern (highly industrialised) China is resulting in migration from poverty-stricken rural areas to the fastly developing cities.

Nowhere is the so-called "digital divide" – in terms of those who have, or have not, access to computing and communication services and infrastructure - more

C. Baranauskas et al. (Eds.): INTERACT 2007, LNCS 4663, Part II, pp. 85–99, 2007.
© IFIP International Federation for Information Processing 2007

pronounced than in some Asian countries. Internet penetration ranges from below 1% in countries like Bangladesh, Cambodia and Laos, to above 65% in South Korea. Furthermore, both India and China have their own internal digital divides. Whilst regions such as Shanghai and Bangalore have almost the same level of Internet and mobile phone connections as Western nations there are rural areas across India and in Western China which are at the other end of the spectrum.

Both India and China have fast developing IT industries supporting both local and off-shoring software development. However, again, the internal divides within the Indian and Chinese economies are evident. In India whilst at US$30bn the IT industry contributed 4.1 per cent of GDP in 2005 it employed only 0.25% of the entire workforce. Similarly, although China is the world's fourth-richest economy, it has a per capita GDP of only US$17,000 compared to the OECD average of US$30,000. These facts are evident in the Economist's 'e-readiness rankings' [1] where in 2006 India and China ranked 53rd and 57th out of 58 countries.

There are signs of a new world economic and political order, where countries like India, Brazil and China are emerging key players. There are signs of an awareness of their increased economic and political "muscle", especially as they begin to develop bilateral and multilateral agreements among themselves, increasing their strategic importance on the world stage. India and China could push globalization in a new direction, ending 600 years of Western dominance [2]. Significantly as part of an agreed programme the countries have called for the combination of Indian software technology with Chinese hardware technology to achieve world leadership in the global information technology industry.

It is against these generic economic and specific ICT backgrounds that we seek to explore the role that a human-centred approach to the development and use of ICT could play in the socially-responsible development of the Indian and Chinese information societies. The human-centred approach that we refer to here is of key importance in major segments of the ICT industry, in software applications for business and industry, in consumer markets, and in areas of health and defence.[1] Successful growth of the ICT sectors in these countries, focusing on both internal and external markets, will be dependent on paying increased attention to human, social and cultural factors.

Given that the disciplines of HCI and usability can be traced back over two decades or more in certain Western countries, both India and China are at a relatively early stage of development in this regard, having paid very little attention to the discipline of human-computer interaction in Universities, nor to a formal implementation of usability principles as understood internationally in industrial practice. The reasons for this are diverse, but are rooted in both countries highly skilled, yet technically oriented, approach to computing as a subject and software development as a practice, and in the "backstage" software maintenance work originally being outsourced. In addition, the HCI area in China has been slow to develop due to a socio-political perspective, that had been suspicious of disciplines

---

[1] In what follows we will use the generic term HCI (Human-Computer Interaction) for this human-centred approach, encompassing a range of human-technology interactions - usability, interaction design, user-centred design, participative design, collaborative working, etc.

such as psychology and sociology – disciplines that underpin much of the HCI approach.

According to Rogers [4] the first two of five stages in the diffusion of innovation are *knowledge* (learning about the existence and function of the innovation) and *persuasion* (becoming convinced of the value of the innovation). Through European Union funded projects we have attempted to assist in developing knowledge about HCI and encouraging individuals and organisations to implement such knowledge. The Indo European Systems Usability Partnership (IESUP) [5] and the Sino European Systems Usability Network (SESUN) [www.sesun-usability.org] have enabled collaboration between academics and practitioners in India and China with their counterparts in Europe and globally. We have worked in six major cities across India and eight cities in China with the aim of raising the profile of HCI at institutional levels in both academia and industry. This paper reports on some of our experiences on these projects. Specifically, in the next sections, we discuss

- the state of play of HCI and usability in India and China,
- differences in HCI in the these countries compared to the West,
- a model for the institutionalization of HCI.

2   Usability Practice in Indian and Chinese industry

Before exploring the development of HCI and usability it will be useful to provide a framework for analysis. The Usability Maturity Model (UMM) [6] provides us one possible measure of the progress of HCI capabilities in industry. This describes the maturity of the company in terms of various levels and gives indicators for each level. Table 1 summarizes the levels of the UMM and their indicators.

Table 1. Levels of usability maturity and their indicators

Level	Indicators
Unrecognized	(no indicators)
Recognised	Problem recognition, performed processes
Considered	Quality in use awareness, user focus
Implemented	User involvement, human factors technology, human factors skills
Integrated	Integration, improvement, iteration
Institutionalized	Human-centred leadership, organizational human-centeredness

The darker lines under Unrecognized and Implemented indicate current barriers in industry.

A company is considered in the *unrecognized* level if most people in the company believe that there are no usability problems in its products and investments and developing HCI skills are not warranted. A progression to the *recognized* level is typically unsystematic. This level is marked with possibly sincere, but haphazard attempts to resolve the usability issues of the problem cases. A company moves to the *considered* level when it starts making systematic financial investments. This happens either in terms of hiring HCI consultants on specific projects or by inviting professionals to conduct training. A company moves to the *implemented* level when it realizes that it needs to use HCI skills on an on-going basis and sets up a specialized HCI group. At this level, the company has the capability of producing usable products, but it does not use this capability consistently in all projects. A company becomes *integrated* when its HCI activity becomes mainstream and routine for all projects, not just for critical projects. A company would be considered *institutionalized* when it starts considering itself as a human-centred solutions company rather than a technology company.

2.1 India

The emergence of HCI in India occurred in the early 1990s [3]. However by the mid nineties the only Indian software companies that were employing professional user interface designers were multimedia content developers which could not be considered to be in the 'mainstream' of software development. A few large software services companies offered a course on graphical user interfaces in their training schedule, but the quality of these courses was often poor. HCI was rarely taken seriously or applied in projects.

The dot-com boom attracted a few talented and largely self-taught professionals into the HCI fold. In the second half of the nineties, many of the early multimedia companies had evolved into mature web and e-learning operations with active interface design and information architecture groups. Some of these would have been at the *implemented* level of UMM, while others at the *considered* level. Around this time, international companies set up software development centres in India. Some of these also set up usability groups, consistent with their organizational structures elsewhere. Many of these companies would be at the *implemented* level of UMM.

The dot-com bust towards the end of the nineties brought many young, creative professionals into the software service industry. Also a few medium-sized software service companies in India began making investments in HCI. They recognized that the web was increasingly becoming an important medium of software delivery, and delivery needed significant design inputs. For an estimated 10% of Indian software companies, this was the transition from *recognized* to *considered*. But most of the Indian software industry was at the *unrecognized* level till the end of the nineties.

The first seven years of the new millennium has seen a significant transition in terms of acceptability of HCI in India in industry, community and academia. The few software services companies that started out early are today 'on the verge' of the *integrated* level of the UMM. The HCI practice within these organizations is rapidly becoming mainstream and some process improvement is already visible. Also in this period, we have witnessed a couple of international companies offering services in HCI through their Indian operations. Meanwhile, a few of the larger software services companies have moved from *unrecognized* level to the *considered* and *implemented* levels.

2.2 China

HCI and usability emerged in China even later than it did in India, really only establishing itself as a field after 2000 and especially more significantly since 2003. The reasons for this late development are as a result of a variety of social, economic and cultural reasons. Firstly historic levels of Chinese economic and industrial development have not been conducive to HCI. From the 1950s to 1980s, China had a planned economy. At this time disciplines like psychology and sociology suffered from various restrictions before and during the Cultural Revolution. There has long been a preference for technology-related disciplines rather than humanities-related disciplines in Chinese society.

However with the rapid growth of the Chinese economy and the process of globalization in recent years, Chinese enterprises realized that they had to strengthen their competitive edge to be able to survive and compete in the future. At the same time, more and more multinational companies have entered the Chinese market. These two factors have brought about a rapid increase in demand for usability. Indeed usability practice in China started from activities conducted by multinational companies, some setting up usability groups. Stiff international competition and the desire for development have also made user experience an important issue for many leading Chinese companies. Some maintain usability groups of over twenty people and have integrated user-centered design (UCD) into their processes.

In order to better understand the current situation of usability in China, an organizational human-centeredness assessment at Chinese IT enterprises was undertaken [7] using the usability maturity model. Although the study was based on a small sample the assessment results showed that the usability maturity level for all enterprises was only at the *recognized* level. Because the enterprises represent the advanced level in the Chinese IT sector, this evaluation actually reflected the current maturity level of most leading enterprises in the sector. As part of the current Sino-European Systems Usability Network project further usability maturity studies are currently being undertaken.

Although the number of people in China dedicated full-time to usability practice is still small, maybe around 400, many product designers and developers are interested in usability. They are young, full of enthusiasm, and eager to learn. Of the people who are most interested in usability, quite a few are from design backgrounds, probably because many companies employ design-trained people for user-interface design jobs.

At the first Sino-European Usability Seminar Tour held in Beijing, Shanghai, and Shenzhen, in 2005 more than 200 people attended, with eighty percent from industry. Several companies sent more than ten of their employees to the event. A survey we conducted during the tour revealed that most of these companies have set up usability-related positions and departments. The respondents said they believed that usability would become more important in their organizations and that the major challenges at the moment are to master usability practices and skills and then to get their work recognized by their bosses and product-line units. Therefore, they wanted to attend training courses and learn from case studies so as to be able to start practicing usability in their daily work quickly.

2.3 The Problems of Off-Shoring

In both India and China (but most particularly in India) in the past two decades, the IT industry has relied on providing quality software services in a cost-effective manner. It has effectively leveraged the huge difference between the labour costs of equivalent skills in India and the developed part of the world. IT companies have developed excellent software engineering processes to manage such projects effectively. For example, the largest number of 'CMM level 5' companies is in India [8].

In the early days, much of the requirements and the initial design specifications were all done in the West, and then "shipped" overseas for the actual development and implementation. From the perspective of designing human-computer interaction, this had significant negative consequences. This effectively transfers many HCI and usability issues in the first part of the project to the client. At the end of the development life cycle products are evaluated for quality against requirements and sent back for 'acceptance testing' to the client. Formal usability evaluations were rarely done until recently. Informal usability evaluations, if at all, were usually carried out as part of acceptance tests and were managed as 'upgrades' or 'change requests' as they were deviations from the original requirements. Having high CMM levels did not help as such certifications are largely based on software engineering literature. Traditional software engineering process literature does not integrate HCI activities well into the software engineering processes [9].

In effect the prevalence of this kind of off-shoring project has led to the marginalization of HCI skills in India and China in the early days of out-sourcing. This led to the image that India and China are mainly destinations of off-shoring 'low-end', implementation oriented software work. More recently, though, these very skills are being considered as important means by the IT companies to move up the 'value chain' and provide complete, full-lifecycle solutions. Usability groups in some large IT services companies are currently flooded with work and scaling up rapidly from 10-20 people a few years ago to 100-300 people now, though 'full-lifecycle' projects are still relatively few.

3 Building Education, Research and Development

Education in HCI has begun only recently in India. Before 2000 the Industrial Design Centre of the Indian Institute of Technology, Bombay started two formal courses related to interaction design, but it was, to our knowledge, the only university in India doing so at that time. Since 2000 some other universities (National Institute of Design, and Department of Design, IIT Guwahati) have become active in this field, but the overall coverage is still poor. Interestingly, the interest in HCI is present in the design schools in India, rather than in the computing or technology sections of the more well-known Indian Institutes of Technology, or in psychology or human sciences.

The HCI community of practitioners in India has, however, become active in the last five years. A mailing list of Indian HCI professionals was formed in the year 2001 [http://groups.yahoo.com/group/hciidc/]. The membership of this group has since grown from about 200 at its inception to over 1100 today. Other special interest mailing lists and city-level groups have since been formed. The South India chapter of the Association for Computing Machinery – Special Interest Group on Computer Human Interaction (ACM SIGCHI) was formed in 2001. Since the year 2001, the chapter organizes Easy – the first annual conference related to HCI in India.

The last few years have seen new activities emerge. Our Indo-European Systems Usability Partnership allowed for the organization of a series of seminars and culminated in the first peer-reviewed conference on HCI in India - the all-India Conference on HCI (IHCI 2004) held in Bangalore. There are currently plans to form additional ACM SIGCHI chapters, a chapter of the Usability Professionals Association (UPA) and possibly a national body of professionals.

Regarding China, although some interest in HCI can be traced back in certain universities to the 1990s, as with India, it is only in the last few years that it has begun to take root. Today there are about twenty institutions working in HCI, including computer science, industrial engineering, and psychology departments in universities, research institutes, and industrial R+D departments. Although there are over a thousand computer-science departments in Chinese universities, only ten offer HCI courses to undergraduate students. Where they do exist the majority of HCI people come from either computer science or design backgrounds rather than psychology or other disciplines. Reflecting the historical technological expertise in China, HCI research in computing / IT centres is still largely concentrated on HCI technologies like multimodal interfaces using speech and pen, and emotion-based interaction while paying less attention to industry's needs in relation to user-centred design.

However there has been significant growth in the usability field in China, and interest groups have become involved in the formation of professional organizations. Founded in 2003 ChinaUI [http://www.chinaui.com] is China's most popular user interface design and usability website with some 85,000 registered members nationwide. Founded in 2004, ACM SIGCHI China [http://www.hci.org.cn] sponsors an annual national conference. UPA China [http://www.upachna.org] was set up in 2004 in Shanghai and organizes the User Friendly conference every year. The large HCI International Conference for 2007 is taking place in China this year.

4 Cultural Differences

It is clear from the analysis to date that the development of usability and HCI in India and China would appear to have much in common. Both countries are experiencing rapid growth from a very low base of only five or ten years ago. The progress of the disciplines is of great interest to Western experts, particularly so given the clear cultural and business environment differences both between these countries and Western ones.

Significant cultural differences also exist within each country. China's population consists of 56 officially recognized nationalities, with the Han nationality (94%) most numerous. Although there are many different local dialects and accents, Chinese writing is uniform throughout the country, owing to the government's long-standing efforts to unify the people through a uniform language. Although India is bound as a nation as a result of its common history, the differing regions, 28 states and 7 union territories have their own distinct cultural identities. In contrast to China, India has 18 official languages and about 300 dialects. Although English is widely spoken, it is not an official language.

The global HCI community's understanding of the practical relevance of cultural issues in HCI has mirrored the timescale of the development of the subjects in India and China. In the last ten years HCI practitioners have changed their approach significantly to embrace cross-cultural development. When defining culture, researchers often refer to patterns of values, attitudes, and behaviours which are shared by two or more people. They further point out that culture is socially acquired, and that relationships with other people, relationships with the environment, and assumptions in term of space and language (for example) affect and shape culture, and are themselves affected by the culture [10]. Culture remains difficult to study, alone and certainly in relation to HCI practices. It is in particularly difficult to identify meanings, attitudes and expectations, not to mention the deeply embedded values and beliefs behind people's thoughts, behaviours and actions. People's behaviours might be influenced by other factors (e.g., environmental conditions) rather than by their cultural traits, and the reasons for, and meaning of, an action can seldom be observed wholly and directly. We would also note that we must be careful in ascribing people's specific behaviours as being due to national "cultural" differences, as nation states themselves are, in a sense, recent fabrications, and thus their citizens are not homogeneous, and stereotyping of people from different countries can often result, without a proper scientific foundation.

Studies in cross-cultural HCI have often embraced some consideration of cultural cognitive models. Cultural models are based on the assumption that cultural differences are the result of social learning and are of very long duration. These cultural models serve as a point of departure as described by Hoft [11] for example Edward Hall [12], Trompenaars [13], Victor [14], and Hofstede [15]. The model of national culture proposed by Hofstede has been frequently involved in the intercultural study of the use of systems [16]. However being based on a study of IBM employees in the 1970s there are significant gaps for the developing world, not to mention the fact that there is increasing critique of both the methods used by Hofstede and the fundamental cultural "dimensions" he has put forward [17].

Most Western software developers would support the principles of user-centred design [18] but underlying concepts and assumptions are derived from USA / Northern European cultures. It is inevitable that those tools and techniques which involve users the most would be those very techniques which were most sensitive to cultural issues. Up to now, both non-native and native personnel have practiced usability in India and China. However, with the growth of local usability expertise, the "localization" of usability practice is a necessary and inevitable trend.

5   Institutionalizing HCI

In both India and China the number of usability professional is growing significantly. Through a wide range of engagements with usability practitioners it is clear that there is a considerable appetite to learn about Western HCI case studies in the expectation that these can be implemented locally. However there are two problems to overcome:

a) Firstly a richer, more nuanced, understanding of HCI is necessary in order for the most effective tools or techniques to be successfully selected and implemented – this implies a much broader 'education in HCI' rather than just 'training in tools'. We need to be able to judge the appropriateness of particular tools for particular tasks, and this requires HCI education, not simply training in techniques.

b) Secondly the cultural and organisational differences between countries means that HCI tools and techniques that have been developed in Western countries may not be effective in developing countries. What is required is the localisation of methods to meet local requirements.

We seek therefore to support the institutionalisation of HCI in the two separate countries, as one key way to ensure that HCI is properly developed and implemented. Institutionalisation needs to exist both in academia (so that effective teaching and research can be supported) and industry (so that software engineers can understand and implement the principles and practices of HCI).

We see this institutionalisation to have three elements; firstly the re-conceptualization / redefinition of HCI in the local country or culture, secondly the embedding of HCI concerns and its importance in local national organizations and finally the rollout of usability training and best practice into industry. We recognize that in practice these elements will occur in parallel (and indeed all have started) but the critical issue is to ensure sufficient feedback between the elements.

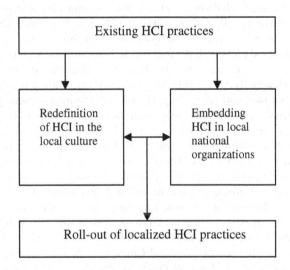

Fig. 1. Elements in the institutionalization of HCI in India and China

6   Redefining HCI in the Local Setting

For HCI and usability to be useful and acceptable in India and China they need to adapt to the needs of the local societies, both to individuals who interact with the artefacts that are produced, and with the development communities who produce them. Of course this redefinition does not need to start from scratch, but neither is it appropriate to apply methods that may have been successful elsewhere without local testing for suitability. In order to achieve this redefinition both indigenous and global approaches are required, critically involving collaboration between them.

6.1 Localizing Established HCI Methods

In the process of developing local expertise, it is, of course, necessary for local experts to learn from the experiences accumulated over the past twenty years in the West. Nevertheless, there has long been a discussion as to whether the usability methods developed in the West can be suitably used in other cultures.

User based testing / evaluation techniques are often based upon the concepts of cooperative evaluation or contextual inquiry [19] and are embodied in a variety of methods such as thinking-aloud protocols. The methods aim to gain meaningful information about the user's work by empowering the users in direct conversation with the designer on equal terms. These 'traditional' methods of testing are difficult and costly to operate across cultures and remote geographical locations [20]. As an illustration Murphy [21] describes the problems that can arise in international usability testing. Usability professionals trying to undertake such techniques in Asian cultures often find that users have particular difficulty [22]. Users vary in their ability and willingness to articulate their thoughts to the evaluator depending on both their individual personality and cultural background. Recognizing that in many Asian countries that the main challenge with usability testing is that it is impolite to tell someone they have a bad design, Chavan [24] has developed the "Bollywood" method (which inherits from the Bollywood film genre, which typically involves 'emotionally involved plots with great dramatic flourish) to reduce user inhibitions.

Based on our experiences, the fundamental principles of HCI and usability engineering undoubtedly work well, however, the operational details, for example, participant recruitment and scheduling, the use of informed consent agreements, and manners and behavior when interacting with participants, need to be adjusted for the local culture. In our own studies within IESUP we have found evidence that Indian users have significant difficulty in engaging in role-playing situations as is required in think-aloud usability methods. Furthermore we have found some evidence that Indian users do not adapt readily to sequential task-based testing. This is in accordance with India's supposed polycronic culture as defined in cultural models [12] in which multiple tasks are handled at the same time, and time is subordinate to interpersonal relations. However more work is required to recommend any generalisable guidelines.

Even so, these issues require us to consider the degree in which the replication of Western approaches to HCI in India and China is to be encouraged. The problem is particularly acute as our evidence in practical projects in India and China is that the developing local usability communities are probably too keen to implement 'best practice'; from the West before fully testing its relevance in the local culture.

6.2 Building HCI into Off-Shoring Development

Current techniques in user-centred design extensively rely on close and continuous contact of the design team with the users. In the context of the model of global software development discussed earlier, the business model of many software companies relies on distributed development, with the bulk of the work being done off-shore. The people involved in the on-site components of projects typically are involved in marketing or project management activities and are often disinclined to do HCI related tasks.

Whilst the dominance of off-shoring / outsourcing have significantly constrained the development of HCI in India, and to a lesser extent in China, it does lead to a significant research and development issue. How do we integrate sound user-centred systems design (UCSD) principles into an outsourcing development approach where the end-user is remote from the development team? Asian software companies are very process driven in their software engineering processes. However, current HCI techniques have not been well-integrated in software engineering [9]. There are both old and new proposals to integrate HCI in traditional software engineering process models such as the waterfall model, but these are nascent proposals that have not yet been widely verified and accepted. Also there are several other process models such as the Rational Unified Process or the wide variety of agile process models where more such work is necessary. There have been a few experiments at training business analysts in HCI techniques or hiring local usability resources. More experimentation and experience sharing is required, particularly in the area of integration between HCI, software engineering and business analysis.

As part of the re-definition of HCI, localized methods for 'remote UCSD' could enhance both the range and quality of off-shoring IT services. Specifically researchers in India and China need to collaborate with colleagues in the West to address the following issues:

- How to develop systems with an active user focus when the users are thousands of miles away?
- How best to organize and distribute usability expertise between the range of personnel involved?
- How can cultural differences between users and developers be best handled?

7   Embedding HCI in Local National Organizations

The institutionalisation of HCI includes developing institutional structures for the ownership, indigenous development and promotion of the discipline. We believe it is critical for developing countries to take local ownership of the discipline. However helpful international groups such as CHI chapters can be, we believe that national organisations are critical to ensure effective HCI development in promoting the localisation of methods, supporting the growth of HCI teaching (and research) in universities and disseminating best practice within industry (most notably in organisations where HCI and usability has yet to take root).

IESUP has enabled collaboration with the Computer Society of India (CSI) and SESUN is currently establishing active collaboration with the CSIP (Chinese Ministry of Information Industry - Software and Integrated Circuit Promotion Centre). This has helped spread awareness, but it is important that independent national organizations with linkages to established organizations be formed (on the lines of the British HCI Group a Specialist Group of the British Computer Society). In India few HCI practitioners are members of the Computer Society of India in the first place, and even if all of them were to enrol, they are most likely to be lost in a larger organization. Through current contact and future activities we hope to be able to provide whatever support we can to these organisations (and others) to guide the socially responsible development of HCI in their respective countries.

Formal education, or the lack of it, is an important reason why there is so little mainstream awareness about HCI. Even today, very few undergraduate students have the option of taking HCI courses. More courses and programmes along with the 'pull' from the industry are needed to make a difference in the area of education. The field of HCI has widely adapted many techniques from several disciplines. There are techniques for understanding users and analyzing their needs, as well as techniques for design and iterative usability evaluation. HCI skills need to be learned systematically before they can be used reliably and confidently. Estimates of the number of HCI professionals needed in India vary from a modest 40,000 to a high of 400,000 within the next few years. But even the smaller figure is much higher than the currently estimated community strength of about 2,200 professionals in the country.

8 Roll Out of Localized Usability Practice

HCI activities will become sustainable only if industry is able to convert the skills into profitable revenue. Arguably, if HCI skills could push industry up the value chain, currently projected levels of IT growth could potentially be greater. But this potential does not get realized in the bottom line unless entrepreneurship can harness it well.

Training a sufficient number of well qualified HCI and usability personnel could well be the biggest challenge and the hardest to achieve. There is a need to increase the number of trained people as well as the need to develop new, integrated techniques that work well with few HCI professionals and much support from other disciplines. Usability engineering needs a multidisciplinary team, especially personnel with psychology and HCI design backgrounds. There is a severe lack of such personnel in both Indian and Chinese industry; almost all the employees in the development departments are trained in computer science or related technology oriented specialties.

Training courses for user interface design and usability as well as corresponding certifications should be provided to show the value to the profession and to encourage enterprises to set up specific job positions for usability experts. This effort would foster the accumulation and development of related expertise in the industry.

Pilot projects need to be carefully selected and conducted to provide successful cases for convincing more enterprises to adopt UCD approaches. Emphasis of the pilot should be placed on the localization of the UCD methods (especially their suitability for technology-oriented staff), cost-benefit analysis, as well as development of guidelines for the methods, training materials, case studies, and tools.

International or industrial standards, like ISO 9000, CMM etc., have been well respected in both the Indian and Chinese IT sector. Evaluations and certifications for product usability and process usability maturity might be a potential factor that can substantially drive the acceptance of usability engineering in industry.

In the path to usability maturity, and given the current context in both India and China, two changes in usability maturity model levels will be the hardest to achieve:

From Unrecognized to Recognized: Firstly moving from the unrecognized level to the *recognized* level represents a major cultural change for a technology company. In the past, technology has been a major strength of the company and was always sufficient to deliver what a client asked for. However, the very success of technology and its wide-spread use has changed the world. This change is not necessarily obvious to an 'industry-insider'. It is important to consciously recognize that success of the past is the very reason why the future needs to be different.

From Implemented to Integrated: Once a company recognizes that they have a problem, they can usually figure out how to solve it. It makes investments (on training or consultants) and moves to *considered*. If it can see the value, it sets us a specialized HCI group and moves to *implemented*. This is where they run into the next major barrier. Moving to from *implemented* to *integrated* requires a dual challenge. Firstly, it is a significant change of scale - it is not the relatively simple matter of hiring a small group of people any more. HCI skills need to be a part of each project. Estimates of the amount of HCI effort required in a mature operation vary from 5% to 15%. That can be quite a task for a company with 5,000+ people and 500+ projects annually. Secondly, being integrated means investments into ongoing process improvement, something which will strain already limited HCI workforce

9 The Future

Whichever way one looks at it, it seems that HCI will have a more significant role to play in the next few years in the Indian and Chinese software industries. Even the Chinese government in the recently published National Science and Technology Plan for 2006-2020 for the first time uses phrases like *human-centered* and *ease of use*.

The impact of HCI on industry itself could be dramatic. The Indian software services industry in particular has already moved on from the perception of being 'cheap, outsourcing destination of largely low-end work' to being 'providers of solutions and services in a highly process-driven, professional environment'. HCI inputs can help the industry move ahead in this course as 'providers of innovative, proactive, full-lifecycle, integrated solutions'.

Supported by enhanced HCI and usability practices the sustained growth of the IT sector in both India and China will contribute to overall economic growth. This in turn has the potential to feedback into economic development across both nations thereby reducing the gap between the urban rich and the rural poor. The speed and the extent to which this occurs will be determined by national governments and is outside the scope of this paper, but at least a well formed, globally integrated, indigenous HCI community will be able to enhance the quality of ICT systems that are accessible to the socially excluded. This must be the desire of all engaged in socially responsible IT development.

References

1. Economist Intelligence Unit: The 2006 e-readiness Rankings. (Retrieved January 9th 2007) (2006), from http://www.eiu.com/site_info.asp?info_name=eiu_2006_e_readiness_ rankings
2. Prestowitz, C.: China-India Entente Shifts Global Balance. Yale Global Online. (Retrieved January 9th 2007) (2005), from http://yaleglobal.yale.edu/display.article?id=5578
3. Joshi, A.: Institutionalizing HCI - the Challenges in India. CSI Communications 29(3) (2005)
4. Rogers, E.M.: Diffusion of Innovation. Free Press, New York (1962)
5. Smith, A., Gulliksen, J., Bannon, L.: Building Usability in India: Reflections from the Indo European Systems Usability Partnership. In: McEwan, T., Gulliksen, J., Benyon, D. (eds.) People and Computers XIX - The Bigger Picture: Proceedings of HCI 2005, Springer, Heidelberg (2005)
6. Earthy, J.: Usability Maturity Model: Human Centeredness Scale. Lloyd's Register (1998)
7. Liu, Z., Zhang, L., Zhang, H.: An Organisational Human-centeredness Assessment at Chinese Software Enterprises. In: Proceedings of APCHI2002, pp. 251–259. Academic Press, London (2002)
8. NASSCOM: Why India? National Association of Software and Service Companies, (Retrieved January 9th 2007), from
   http://www.nasscom.in/Nasscom/templates/NormalPage.aspx?id=6316
9. Joshi, A.: HCI in SE Process Literature. Indo-Dan HCI Research Symposium, Guwahati (2006)
10. Smith, A., Yetim, F.: Global Human-computer Systems: Cultural Determinants of Usability. Special Issue Editorial. Interacting with Computers 16(1), 1–5 (2004)
11. Hoft, N.: Developing a Cultural Model. In: del Galdo, E., Nielsen, J. (eds.) International User Interfaces, pp. 41–73. Wiley Computer Publishing, New York (1996)
12. Hall, E.T.: Beyond Culture, Doubleday. Garden City, New York (1976)
13. Trompenaars, F.: Managing Across Cultures. Business Books. Random House Books, London (1993)
14. Victor, D.A.: International Business Communication. HarperCollins, New York (1992)
15. Hofstede, G.: Cultures and Organizations: Software of the Mind. Mc Graw-Hill, Berkshire, UK (1991)
16. Smith, A., Dunckley, L.: Using the LUCID Method to Optimize the Acceptability of Shared Interfaces. Interacting with Computers 9(3), 333–345 (1998)
17. McSweeney, B.: Hofstede's Model of National Cultural Differences and Consequences: a Triumph of Faith - a Failure of Analysis. Human Relations 55(1), 89–118 (2002)
18. Gulliksen, J., Göransson, B., Boivie, I., Persson, J., Blomkvist, S., Cajander, A., Cajander, A: Key principles for user centred systems design. Behaviour and Information Technology 22(6), 397–409 (2003)
19. Beyer, H., Holtzblatt, K.: Contextual Design: Defining Customer-centred Systems. Morgan Kaufmann, San Francisco (1998)
20. Dray, S.: Usable for the World: A Practical Guide to International User Studies. In: Day, D., Dunckley, L. (eds.) Designing for Global Markets 3. Proceedings of IWIPS 2001, IWIPS, pp. 153–154 (2001)
21. Murphy, J.: Modelling, Designer-tester-Subject Relationships in International Usability Testing. In: Day, D., Dunckley, L. (eds.) Designing for Global Markets 3. IWIPS 2001, IWIPS 2001, Milton Keynes, UK, pp. 33–44 (2001)

22. Yeo, A.: Usability Evaluation in Malaysia. In: Proceedings of 4th Asia Pacific Computer Human Interaction Conference: APCHI 2000, pp. 275–280. Elsevier, Amsterdam (2000)
23. Yeo, A.: Global Software Development Lifecycle: an Exploratory Study. In: Jacko, J., Sears, A., Beaudouin-Lafon, M., Jacob, R. (eds.) CHI 2001: Conference on Human Factors in Computing Systems, pp. 104–111. ACM Press, New York (2001)
24. Chavan, A.: The Bollywood Method. In: Schaffer, E. (ed.) Institutionalization of Usability; a Step-by-step Guide, pp. 129–130. Adisson Wesley, New York (2004)

Cultural Mobilities:
Diversity and Agency in Urban Computing

Paul Dourish[1], Ken Anderson[2], and Dawn Nafus[2]

[1] Donald Bren School of Information and Computer Sciences
University of California, Irvine
Irvine, CA 92697-3440, USA
jpd@ics.uci.edu
[2] People and Practices Research
Intel Corporation
20270 NW AmberGlen Court
Beaverton, OR 97006, USA
ken.anderson@intel.com, dawn.nafus@intel.com

Abstract. The rise of wireless networks and portable computing devices has been accompanied by an increasing interest in technology and mobility, and in the urban environment as a site of interaction. However, most investigations have taken a relatively narrow view of urban mobility. In consequence, design practice runs the risk of privileging particular viewpoints, forms of mobility, and social groups. We are interested in a view of mobility that reaches beyond traditional assumptions about the who, when, why, and what of mobility. Based on analytic perspectives from the social sciences and on empirical fieldwork in a range of settings, we outline an alternative view of technology and mobility with both analytic and design implications.

1 Introduction

Computing is on the move. Mobile telephony, wireless networking, embedded computing and ubiquitous digital environments are manifestations of a broader pattern in which mobility plays an increasingly significant role in the computational experience. In turn, this mobilization of information technology has turned research attention towards the domains in which technology might now operate. One site of research attention has been "urban computing," investigating the ways in which information technologies shape, are shaped by, and mediate our experience of urban space. While this focus on urban settings runs the risk of furthering the traditional dominance of urban experience over the interests of suburban, exurban and rural settings, it reflects both the contemporary reality of the city as a nexus of computational infrastructures [28] and recent scholarly discussions of urbanism and information technologies, e.g. [22]. Interest in "urban computing" has appeared in papers in major conferences such as CHI and Ubicomp, and also been a topic for a number of recent journal special issues.

To date, though, while mobile devices have radically transformed and widely proliferated in recent years, mobile computing in the city has been construed quite

C. Baranauskas et al. (Eds.): INTERACT 2007, LNCS 4663, Part II, pp. 100–113, 2007.
© IFIP International Federation for Information Processing 2007

narrowly. This narrowness concerns both the applications that urban computing explores and the ways in which it construes its users. On the application side, many systems design efforts focus on the city as a site of consumption and an inherently problematic environment, one to be tamed by the introduction of technology. On the user side, many systems design efforts focus their attention on young, affluent city residents, with both disposable income and discretionary mobility.

The narrowness of both the site and "the users," we will argue, has meant that mobile and urban computing have been driven by two primary considerations. The first is how to "mobilize" static applications, allowing people to get access to information and carry out traditional desktop tasks while "on the move," the anytime/anywhere approach as manifested in PDA applications that attempt to produce mobile versions of desktop applications or connect people wirelessly to remote infrastructures "back home" (e.g. email on the RIM Blackberry.) The second is how to provide people with access to resources in unfamiliar spaces, the "where am I?" approach, as manifested in context-aware applications that attempt to help people navigate space in terms of resource such as devices (e.g. the nearest printer), services (e.g. recommending stores), or people (e.g. finding friends via Dodgeball). While these applications clearly meet needs, they fail to take the urban environment on its own terms; they are based on the idea that urban life is inherently problematic, something to be overcome, in comparison to the conventional desktop computing scenario. Further, they fail to acknowledge the lived practice of urban life, and in particular its diversity and the different urban experiences of different groups. In focusing on abstracted rather than concrete behaviors, on individual consumption rather than collective sociality, and on the pairing between discretionary mobility and urban consumption, this approach paints a very partial view of urban living that leaves many people out of the picture.

Rather than simply attempting to move existing application scenarios to mobile platforms, our approach is to take a step back and begin by thinking about mobility more broadly, particularly in connection to urban space. To do so, we turn to research in social science that seeks to understand the relationship between meaning, identity, movement, and space, drawing particularly on work in anthropology and cultural geography. Based on theoretical and empirical work from social science, we are developing a new approach to the relationship between mobility and technology.

Our work is oriented around three interrelated principles:

Mobilities, not mobility: mobility takes many forms. Not only are there different kinds of journeys (commuting to work on public transit, flying to a vacation spot, moving house), but the same journeys can be undertaken under very different auspices (taking a train from home to the town center in order to go to work, in order to go out for the evening, in order to seek medical treatment, or because you're driving the train.) An understanding of the relationship between mobility and technology requires that we take a heterogeneous view of mobility, rather than focusing only on selected social groups and patterns of urban life.

Finding more than your way: movement is not purely a way to get from A to B. It extends beyond the purely instrumental and efficacious. Routes may have symbolic significance (pilgrimages, ritual exclusions to do with gender or caste, traditions and routes of historical importance), choices may be influenced by a personal aesthetics (the pleasure of a craftily-executed maneuver on the freeway, a response to the presence and absence of particular others on public transit, or an aimless stroll through the streets of an unfamiliar city), and patterns of movement may enact social and cultural meanings (undertaking the hajj, or participating in an Orange March in Northern Ireland.) Understanding mobility in its cultural settings requires that we pay attention to the symbolic and aesthetic aspects of technological urbanism as well as the purely instrumental.

Mobility as collective: the patterns and experience of movement are collective rather than individual experiences. Mobility is experienced through social and cultural lenses that give it meaning in historical, religious, ethnic, and other terms. We move individually but collectively we produce flows of people, capital, and activities that serve to structure and organize space. In seeing urban mobility as a social phenomenon, we want to look at the ways in which new technologies provide a site for creating new forms of collective practice and meaning.

Taken together, these principles open up the design space for urban computing, by seeing mobility in urban spaces not simply as problematic alternative to static activity, but rather as a culturally meaningful and productive phenomenon in its own right. Starting with the concept of mobility, rather than starting with technology, we can achieve a better link between people and technology. From this perspective, we start to see urban and mobile technologies less as tools for problem-solving and more as sites at which social and cultural practice are produced. In turn, this raises a new and different set of questions for the design, development, and deployment of socially responsible mobile technologies.

In what follows, we explore the basis of this alternative account of urban computing and its consequences, with a particular focus on the questions of socially responsible design. We begin by exploring the theoretical background, drawing on social science accounts of mobility and spatiality to support a perspective on mobile and urban computing that stresses diversity and agency. Next, we draw on ethnographic fieldwork to present accounts of urban living that illustrate our principles in real settings. Finally, we consider how this alternative account of mobility poses new challenges for interactive system design.

2 Mobile Technologies and Urban Problems

The current interest in urban computing springs not least from research conducted for over a decade into mobile computing and its applications. We identify four broad areas of research into mobility and mobile computing applications.

The first area comprises systems that frame mobility as a *disconnection* from stable working situations, and overcome this either by providing mobile, remote access to static information resources or by attempting to reproduce static application contexts. The classic application scenario here would involve a mobile worker such as a person on a business trip who needs information from the office back home. The Satchel system, for example, sought to provide people with easy access to electronic documents, including the ability to share and exchange them, by developing mobile digital tokens that could be used to manipulate documents stored centrally [27]. The resources to which a mobile person might need connected also include other people. For example, Hubbub [25] explores means to link mobile users into traditional messaging applications; and a series of studies at the University of Glasgow have investigated forms of "co-visiting" in which static and mobile participants interact around the same physical resources [10, 11]. In this category, we also place attempts to replicate in mobile settings the sorts of applications that people might use in static or desktop settings.

Our second category of applications also sees mobility as problematic, but addresses its problems in different ways. These are applications that attempt to address the problem of *dislocation* by focusing on wayfinding and resource location. GPS navigation systems, either hand-held or installed in cars, are one obvious example, as are guides that attempt to help people find their way through an unfamiliar environment, including: tourist sites, e.g. [14]; academic conferences, e.g. [17]; museums, e.g. [23]; and university campuses, e.g. [13].

The third category focuses not on the problems of disconnection or dislocation but rather on the problems of *disruption*. Disruption problems are the ways in which a mobile technology might behave in ways inappropriate to the settings into which it is moved. Systems of this sort attempt to be sensitive to context or location so as to provide a customized service. For instance, the idea that a mobile telephone might set itself automatically to vibrate mode when in a theater, or might filter out low importance calls when in a meeting, are simple examples of context-sensitivity [2]. Other examples include health monitors that attempt to time their requests so as to minimize interruptions [24], and public displays that respond to the patterns of movement in spaces, e.g. [43]. We describe these systems as focused on disruption because they respond to a sense of rupture between the technology and the setting in which it is deployed.

Our fourth and final category is the most recent to emerge, and the most diverse. The applications that we label as "locative media" (a term coined by Vancouver-based artist Karlis Kalnins) see mobility not as a problem to be overcome but as offering certain interactional opportunities. These applications, which often emerge in artistic or entertainment contexts, seek to create interactive experiences that rely upon or exploit movement and space. For instance, the Equator project, an interdisciplinary university research consortium in the UK, has produced a series of mobile games that blend physical and virtual worlds in order to create new experiences of space and movement. Can You See Me Now [8], a game played on the streets of Sheffield, created a novel hybrid space in which participants "virtually" present would interact with those physically in the urban space; Treasure [3] encourages players to explore the "seams" in digital infrastructures as they are mapped into physical spaces (e.g. wireless network coverage) and to incorporate them into game play, while Yoshi [7] exploits similar mappings between physical and virtual, but on an urban scale. Reminiscent of studies of the urban soundscape [20], projects such as Sonic City [21] or tuna [5] explore the ways in which movement through space can create personal or collective audio experiences, giving a new (aural) form to movement. PDPal (www.pdpal.com), a project by Scott Patterson, Marina Zurkow, Julian Bleecker, and Adam Chapman, and originally co-commissioned by the Walker Art Center and the University of Minnesota Design Institute, encourages people to create and browse emotional maps of urban spaces, combining "objective" cartographic forms with more personal and intimate interpretations of the lived city.

Often, these projects have a strong critical component, and indeed the theoretical positioning of much locative media practice appeal to Michel Foucault's [19] concept of "heterotopia" (an analysis of the relationship between space, power, and cultural practice), and on the Situationist movement in 1960's artistic *avant garde*. The Situationist perspective is related in two ways. First, their critique of the "society of the spectacle" [46] motivates a form of active engagement with the everyday life and its structures, and, second, Guy Debord's [16] theory of "the dérive" (essentially, a journey with no destination) as a means to re-encounter and re-appropriate urban spaces. So, projects such as "Riot! 1831" [42] or GPSdrawing (www.gpsdrawing.com), which uses GPS traces of movements through space to literally "draw" images on maps or photographs, build upon a range of location-based technologies to provoke new ways to think about movement and spatial practice in technology-mediated contexts.

The work under the "locative media" category is particularly intriguing because it opens up a new set of intellectual conversations around mobility and technology, and a new area of the design space. What we find particularly compelling about this fourth category of work is the way in which it frames mobility not as a problem but as both an everyday fact and a new opportunity. In addition, this critical component of some of this work forms part of a broader movement to explore new hybrid disciplinary practices that have tremendous value for the development of interactive media and applications, and this plays a role in the research that we plan to conduct. Where we want to extend this work is by situating it not only in artistic considerations but also in contemporary social science of space and movement.

What we have noted in these four approaches, then, is a transition from "mobility as problem" (the first three categories) to "mobility as opportunity" (the final category.) In making this transition, the developers of mobile and urban applications have begun to incorporate lessons from social science and, in particular, from contemporary work on human geography that looks at the ways in which people produce spatial experience. If urban computing is fundamentally a technology of space, then it seems appropriate to turn to those areas of research in which spatiality plays a central role. In order to deepen this connection between technology and geographical thinking, we turn next to the research literature that approaches the nexus of technology and urban spatiality form the spatial perspective rather than the technical.

3   Social and Cultural Accounts of Mobility and Technology

Increasingly, information technology plays a significant role in both spatial research and spatial practice, and geographers and social scientists have begun to incorporate accounts of information technology into their models of spatiality and spatial practice.

Graham [22] uses the term "software-sorted geographies" to point to the ways in which software systems increasingly act as the lenses through which we encounter the world, and, in turn, their logics become inscribed into those spaces. He organizes his account around three primary examples. The first is the role of information systems in organizing and regulating mobility, drawing from studies of air travel and intelligent transportation systems, where software systems regulate flows of people and goods through space at a variety of scales. The second is the use of geographical information systems and geodemographic systems as ways in which spaces and people are categorized, stratified, and understood, and incorporated into systems of planning and provision of services. The third is the use of CCTV and face-recognition software as a means of monitoring and controlling public spaces. In each case, the use of software systems as means of spatial ordering raises important questions of the ownership, control, and visibility of the software systems, as well as the representational categories and biases built into the systems (such as cultural assumptions encoded in face recognition software, or expectations about "normal" patterns of freeway or air travel.)

These kinds of representational schemes – the mechanisms by which people, places, and activities can be categorized, counted, and regulated – are, of course the traditional tools of state governance, and indeed the development of computers as administrative tools has long been associated with the systems of local and national governance [1]. Graham is concerned, then, with the spatial politics of software systems. Thrift and French [45] explore a similar set of concerns, although with a somewhat different emphasis. Like Graham, they are motivated by the ways in which spatial settings are increasingly ordered by software systems; but they are especially concerned with the metaphors that underlie those software systems, and the ways in which, through approaches to software design and production such as neural networks, adaptive architectures, and open source development methods, software systems model themselves on corporeal and social systems.

While Thrift and French acknowledge the ways in which software systems not only reflect institutional power dynamics but provide the opportunity to rescript them, they nonetheless focus their attention primarily on the production of software. So, for instance, they acknowledge the fact that the governmentality of software systems is perhaps more the "rhizomal," horizontal governmentality of Deleuze than the hierarchical governmentality of Foucault; the ways in which the development of spreadsheet software created new opportunities and new models for organizational decision-making and alignment; and the ways in which new media artists can produce software systems that challenge conventional models of interaction.

What is missing from this picture is an account of the ways in which software is not just produced, but put to use. Graham, Thrift, and French are right to point to the ways in which software is a tool for imposing an external regulative order upon space and movement, but we would argue that it is also a means by which new spatial experiences are produced. Indeed, software systems are sites of resistance as well as control, and aspects of how new spatial experiences are produced.

4 An Alternative Framework

What this provides is a very different way to think about the relationship between information technology and spatial experience, with implications both for analysis and design of mobile technologies. It looks at information technologies not simply as things that move between different places, but as means in which spatial structures are produced. Paying attention to these power structures, and in particular to what Massey [30] (discussed below) refers to as "power-geometries", highlights the diversity of mobile experience. While young, affluent city residents with a penchant for gadgets, disposable income and discretionary mobility have one sort of urban experience – one reflected in much of contemporary urban computing, one focused largely on the city as a site of consumption – others may be positioned very differently with respect to the circuits of urban movement and habitation. The geographical studies point to the important role of *diversity* in understanding the urban experience.

At the same time, as we have noted, we feel that one failing of some of these studies is the primacy that they give to technology as a tool of regulation and surveillance, in contrast to a site for creative engagement with space. Famously, De Certeau [15] describes two modes of spatializing, what he calls the strategic and the tactical. If the strategic mode is the mode of design and regulation, then the tactical mode is the mode of use and resistance. The people who enact spatial practice are not simply the designers, architects, planners, and regulative authorities; they are people who, through their everyday movements through urban space, give that space life and meaning. So, alongside the concert with diversity, we would like to place an equal emphasis on individual and collective *agency*.

This perspective suggests three important starting points for a study of technology and mobility.

4.1 Mobilities, Not Mobility

Contemporary interest in mobility as an aspect of life and work often gloss the diverse and specific forms that mobility may take. One might question whether a term that encompasses phenomena as diverse as transnational diasporas, daily commutes, and religious pilgrimages is doing useful conceptual work at all. Even within constrained settings, the notion of "mobility" may obscure as much as it reveals.

In a brief ethnographic study of riding public transit in Orange County [9], this diversity was very much in evidence. In place of a conventional image of working commutes, we found a much richer picture of movement and mobility at work. We encountered people who rode the bus for work and for pleasure, whose journeys were dead time to be endured or spiritual moments, who were on the bus to see people or to escape from them, whose goal was to get to hospital or pick up women, and who found themselves riders of public transit due to financial, family, health, or legal causes.

While the notion of mobility and technology conjures up the image of a jet-setting businessman armed with a laptop or a smart phone, able to carry out his work "any-time, any-where." The easy, discretionary mobility of the professional stands in marked contrast to the enforced movement of the homeless, for whom movement from place to place is the only way to avoid detention [44], or some transnationals who leave their children behind in a desperate search of economic opportunity, moving to cities that they must often navigate through and around as if they are invisible. Different again is the form of urban movement forced on the South African AIDS sufferers documented by le Marcis [29]. The "suffering body" of AIDS patients, on the other hand, must move – despite difficulties presented by ill health – in an ever expanding network of clinics, hospitals, support groups and hospices, coming to rest finally in the graveyard. Both the necessity of and ability to travel are mediated by local political factors; the remnants of apartheid are reflected by the location and quality of hospitals, and the monthly disability check received by many AIDS sufferers exactly equals the cost of a month's worth of AZT. Due to the stigma still attached to the disease, people travel several hours to meet with HIV support groups because they would be recognized attending one in their own neighborhood.

If "mobility" encapsulates such heterogeneity, what of "mobile computing"? Designing "for mobility" must be, in fact, design for a host of different potential mobilities. Mobility is far from uniform, and the needs, problems, and opportunities that attend mobile computing are similarly diverse.

4.2 Finding More Than Your Way

In his study of identity issues in a Northern Irish town, William Kelleher [26] describes the ways in which sectarian identity is enmeshed into the spatial organization of the city. Residents describe the historical patterns of settlement and migration by which the contemporary urban social landscape was formed. Invisible fault lines criss-cross the city creating structures that give meaning to patterns of presence and movement. The sectarian organization of everyday life manifests itself in everything from forms of dress and speech to where one parks when in the town center. Navigation through urban space, then, enacts aspects of cultural identity. On a broader scale, Duruz's study of shopping streets in London and Sydney and the "culinary journeys" involved in shopping, eating, and living there point to the ways in which local spatial arrangements are products of broad historical patterns of movement and migration [18]. As Massey provocatively writes regarding her local high street, "It is (or ought to be) impossible even to begin thinking about Kilburn High Road without bringing into play half the world and a considerable amount of British imperialist history." [30:65]

We make sense of the spaces through which we move not simply in terms of their local geometries, but their positions in larger frames – be those historical frames as in the case invoked by Massey, mythological frames as in the case of Aboriginal landscapes described by Nancy Munn [40], moral frames as in the ties between moral lessons and the landscape for native Americans as described by Keith Basso [4], or sometimes all of these at once, as in Kelleher's Ballybogoin.

Wayfinding – either following a route or finding resources in an unfamiliar environment – has long been a domain of application for mobile technologies (e.g. [14, 17]). However, a purely instrumental reading of space – as something to be navigated efficiently and exploited effectively – neglects these other social, cultural, moral, political and historical aspects of spatial and mobile experience. When people move through space, they must find their way, but they also find more than their way.

4.3 Mobility as Collective

Running through these principles is a third view of mobility as a collective rather than an individual phenomenon. We are concerned not so much with how specific people move from A to B, but rather with collective phenomena in two senses. The first is how repeated patterns of movement create larger spatial structures, and the second is how those structures then serve to make sense of particular mobilities.

This is very much a relational view of mobility. When an individual undertakes a pilgrimage to a sacred site, the journey makes sense not purely in terms of an individual experience or in terms of the historical pattern of previous journeys, but in the relationship between the two; the journey's meaning lies very much in 'following in the footsteps' of others. Similarly, in Myerhoff's classic account of the peyote hunt in north central Mexico, the hunt draws its meaning both from the fact that it is collectively experienced by a group of people (not all copresent), and by the ways in which it is enmeshed in a larger cultural pattern [41].

Our concern here with collective experience can be contrasted with two common views in the information technology literature, the individual and the collaborative. The individual view, in HCI and elsewhere, focuses on the actions and experiences of people as solitary actors and as independent decision-makers. The collaborative view, in CSCW and elsewhere, pays attention to the ways in which the coordinated activities of multiple individuals produce larger-scale effects. However, this collaborative view of the social – as a multiplicity of individuals – often neglects a sense of the collective as a whole. Thinking of collective experience in terms of a multiplicity of individuals fails to see the forest for the trees. We want, instead, to be able to talk about collective experience; intersubjectively negotiated, individually incorporated, only more or less shared, and yet a common lens through which everyday experience can be made sense of. Within the CSCW literature, the notion of "community of practice" perhaps best approaches this, by placing the locus attention outside of the individuals but yet making this shared understanding foundational to meaning and interaction.

5 Spatiality in Practice

A recent research project that might shed some light on these directions was one that focused on cosmopolitans and their social practices The study of cosmopolitans took over a year and a half. We studied 54 people between the ages of 22 and 35 in London, Tokyo, LA, Belo Horizonte and Tallinn. We chose to look at young professionals, many in fairly freelance or autonomous employment situations. As is common in ethnographic work, we selected participants for theoretical interest and for trust relationships with the researchers rather than to serve as a statistical sample. We expected (and found) this group to be "tech savvy," mobile, and confronted with novel challenges as they adapted to a new life stage. We studied them as they went about their lives in the city. The common characteristic of the participants was a sense of cosmopolitanism. Cosmopolitanism was a reflection upon globalization from an aesthetic and moral perspective. We also sought, with some skepticism, to assess the notion that major urban areas, like London or Tokyo actually formed a coherent category – that they were essentially a single, distributed place, despite the apparent differences between urban areas. In particular, we paid close attention to objects people used to create their home space and what people carried with them to structure encounters in the urban environment. We examined how, when, and why things were used, and how it reflected who they were and wanted to be, as well as how it reflected the character, realities, and potential of the encompassing urban area. We observed the environments through which our participants traveled, shopped, worked, and recreated, and analyzed our participants' attitudes toward them, whether of fear, trust, engagement, disengagement, resignation, delight, or some combination. Our goal was to understand in detail how some residents of each of the urban areas practiced space making in the loose sense. We will highlight just a couple of participants as examples.

Jen was born in Australia, studied film in Cuba, worked for a major studio in LA and was a commercial and independent filmmaker when we caught up with her in London. Her flat in London was filled with a combination of IKEA and Italian designed furniture. She often commutes on her Vespa, listening to music on her iPod. She had acquired playlists from friends around London but also from friends in Adelaide, Sydney, and LA but also friends in Barcelona, NYC, Miami and Singapore. She often stops for food at an Italian deli for food on her way home. She frequents three coffee shops for her morning coffee, one by her home, one by her office and a Portuguese coffee shop not far from her house (usually the weekend coffeeshop). She drinks cappuccinos in the morning and either espressos or Americanos in the afternoon. She has made friends with the two coffeeshop owners; one of whom came from Australia and the other a boyfriend of a friend in the film school. Each of the coffeeshops provides a place for her to connect to the Internet via WiFi. She reads news from Sydney and works through her e-mail. She is able to move through the city with relative ease, bumping into friends and colleagues from advertising and media businesses. During our month long study with her, she traveled to Spain, Greece, and Morocco. On one 4-day trip to Madrid she gladly told us how she only took the clothes on her back and the bag she carries with her. She was able to stay in a French film friend's flat in Fez that was "just like home." Like most participants, she planned on being in the same life but different city in five years. She easily moves from place to place among friends and colleagues who suggest or offer places to stay, and guide her to the places with "good" food.

Angela was born outside Belo Horizonte. She studied design in Sao Paulo, then London. Her first job was in Barcelona. She later started up a design firm back in Belo. She had renovated her flat in a modern design with a combination of (ultra-) modern furniture. She routinely carried her mobile phone, iPod and wallet with her. Unlike others we studied, she had a laptop at work and one at home but didn't carry them between places. She has a coffee shop she goes to in the morning near home; she likes a coffee-milk for breakfast. She has felt at home where ever she goes. She seeks out places that are like all the other places she has been, regardless of where they are.

Mark lives in Tokyo. He has a 3500sq foot house in Roppongi that is supplied by the financial investment firm he works for. He has two other roommates at the house. The house is decorated just like the flats he had in London and Singapore. He goes to the ATM and withdraws his Yen using English. He has his coffee at a Starbucks, where he continuously monitors markets in London and NY on his smart phone. He meets up with other American investment bankers on Friday for drinks. On his way anywhere around town, you can see him on the train with a National Geographic and listens to his iPod. He travels with other advisors from around Asia down to Thailand to buy his clothes and take a little time off.

What we can see in these three examples, which are really representative of our other participants, was the way of taking a very local urban area and making it a particular kind of space. The cosmopolitans individually act and collective enact a particular spatial meaning through practice. Further, the examples point a number of mobilities in place. Though these have been stories of privileged technological mobility, it is clear that there are many not incorporated into the technologies. Just one example would be the lack of ATMs in Tokyo that offer Portuguese language interfaces for the many migrants who work there. While Angela can choose to visit any of the upscale Italian restaurants in the city or connect to the Internet at one of her cafes within walking distance of her house, her maid rides a bus for an hour to get to work with only other riders or an occasional newspaper as an information source. Angela, Mark and Jen are offered choices by our technologies, they are given agency and are accommodated by the technologies. The people who surround them, however, often are not. The processes of making space a place through practice are the same, while an advantage to the defining the place are given over to those with more technologies designed to meet their needs.

6 Challenging Technical Practice

Our goal, here, is not to provide detailed guidelines for the design of specific urban computing technologies. Rather, we have tried to set out an alternative perspective on what urban computing can do and can be. This perspective is deeply consequential for design practice, although its consequences lie largely in the kinds of questions that might motivate design, in the analytic perspectives that support pre-design exploration, and in the topics that might be thought of as relevant to design practice.

In line with the conference theme, we are particularly concerned with socially responsible design, and so with an approach to design that is both inclusive and progressive. To that end, our criticisms of much (certainly not all) of conventional urban applications of ubiquitous computing are that, first, they construe the city as a site for consumption, organizing it in terms of available resources; second, that they reflect only very narrowly the breadth of urban experience, focusing on particular social groups (generally young and affluent); third, that they focus on individual experience and interaction, rather than helping people connect and respond to the larger cultural patterns and urban flows within which they are enmeshed.

We see considerable opportunity for an elaboration of the urban computing agenda that takes these considerations seriously, and our goal here has been to provide a framework with which designers can begin to engage with the issues of diversity and agency in urban experience, that is an approach that is based in cultural mobilities.

For instance, *undersound* [5] goes beyond instrumental accounts of urban space to create an experience designed to reveal both the texture of urban life (as reflected by the links between urban space and musical genres) and the patterns of movement that characterize city living. Using the London Underground as an example, *undersound* creates an infrastructure in which music moves around the city through the public transportation system. Its design is based on the idea, first, that regions of the city have their own characters depending on local population groupings that can in turn shape locally-produced music; for instance, the music that emerges in one part of the city may reflect the ethnic origins of the local population. However, these must be encountered through the flows of people through the city, and the ways in which those intertwine. The system is designed to provide people with an alternative "window" onto urban life, and uses music as a means to reflect the diversity of urban living and its continual reconfigurations.

More broadly, the themes of *diversity* – a recognition and manifestation of the many different experiences of the city available to groups of different ages, economic conditions, ethnic identities, etc. – and *agency* – the active production of urban living rather than consumption and constraint – offer opportunities to reconsider the goals and methods of urban computing.

7 Conclusion

Mobility is firmly in view for HCI researchers these days, with a particular emphasis on urban environments. However, the interpretation of mobility on offer is a limited one. Mobility is considered simply as translation in a fixed spatial manifold, and the problems of a mobile subject. We have argued here for a cultural view of mobility (or mobilities). In this cultural view, we pay attention to the meaning of forms of mobility and how space and movement act as a site for the production of social and cultural meaning. To the extent that technology is always involved in the production of spatial realities, then technology is also involved in these cultural patterns, making them important for designers and analysts. At the same time, this also turns our attention back towards the social responsibilities of designers and HCI practitioners. As we have shown, the cultural perspective emphasizes that there is no one, simple mobility. There are many mobilities, and many collectives, whose view of mobility is shaped by more than simply an instrumental account of movement from A to B. A cultural view requires that we acknowledge and grapple with this diversity. In turn, this opens our eyes to a range of otherwise underrepresented groups within design.

We have suggested that we need to take diversity and agency as central aspects of a socially-responsible approach to mobile computing. This approach can also help connect current research in HCI and ubiquitous computing to contemporary work in human and social geography, providing a new foundation for design.

Acknowledgements

Johanna Brewer, Eric Kabisch, Amanda Williams, and our colleagues in Intel's People and Practices Research group made significant contributions to our work, as did those people who kindly gave of their time and insight in our fieldwork. This work was support in part by the National Science Foundation under awards 0133749, 0205724, 0326105, 0527729, and 0524033

References

1. Agar, J.: The Government Machine: A Revolutionary History of the Computer. MIT Press, Cambridge (2003)
2. Agre, P.: Changing Places: Contexts of Awareness in Computing. Human-Computer Interaction 16(2-4), 177–192 (2001)

3. Barkhuus, L., Chalmers, M., Tennent, P., Hall, M., Bell, M., Sherwood, S., Brown, B.: Picking Pockets on the Lawn: The Development of Tactics and Strategies in a Mobile Game. In: Proc. Intl. Conf. Ubiquitous Computing Ubicomp 2005 (Tokyo, Japan), Springer, Heidelberg (2005)
4. Basso, K.: Wisdom Sits in Places: Landscape and Language Among the Western Apache. University of New Mexico Press, Albuquerque, NM (1996)
5. Bassoli, A., Moore, J., Agamanolis, S.: TunA: Socialising Music Sharing on the Move. In: O'Hara, Brown (eds.) Consuming Music Together: Social and Collaborative Aspects of Music Consumption Technologies, Springer, Heidelberg (2006)
6. Bassoli, A., Brewer, J., Martin, K., Dourish, P., Mainwaring, S.: Underground Aesthetics: Rethinking Urban Computing.Technical Report LUCI-2007-002, Laboratory for Ubiquitous Computing and Interaction, University of California, Irvine, CA (2007)
7. Bell, M., Chalmers, M., Barkhuus, L., Hall, M., Sherwood, S., Tennent, P., Brown, B., Rowland, D., Benford, S., Capra, M., Hampshire, A.: Interweaving Mobile Games with Everyday Life. In: Proc. ACM Conf. Human Factors in Computing Systems CHI 2006, Montreal, CA, ACM, New York (2006)
8. Benford, S., Crabtree, A., Flintham, M., Drozd, A., Anastasi, R., Paxton, M., Tandavanitj, N., Adams, M., Row-Farr, J.: Can you see me now? ACM Trans. Comput.-Hum. Interact. 13(1), 100–133 (2006)
9. Brewer, J., Nguyen, D.: Who Rides the Bus? Alternative Mobility in Orange County. University of California, Irvine (2006)
10. Brown, B., Chalmers, M., Bell, M., MacColl, I., Hall, M., Rudman, P.: Sharing the Square. In: Proc. European Conf. Computer-Supported Cooperative Work ECSCW 2005, Paris, France, Springer, Heidelberg (2005)
11. Brown, B., MacColl, I., Chalmers, M., Galani, A., Randall, C., Steed, A.: Lessons from the Lighthouse: Collaboration in a Shared Mixed Reality System. In: Proc. ACM Conf. Human Factors in Computing Systems CHI 2003, Ft Lauderdale, FL, pp. 577–585. ACM, New York (2003)
12. Burrell, J., Gay, G., Kubo, K., Farina, N.: Context-Aware Computing: A Test Case. In: Borriello, G., Holmquist, L.E. (eds.) UbiComp 2002. LNCS, vol. 2498, Springer, Heidelberg (2002)
13. Cheverst, K., Davies, N., Mitchell, K., Friday, A.: Experiences of Developing and Deploying a Context-aware Tourist Guide. In: Proc. ACM Conf. Mobile Computing and Networking Mobicom 2000, Boston, MA, pp. 20–31. ACM, New York (2000)
14. De Certeau, M.: The Practice of Everyday Life. University of California Press (1984)
15. Debord, G.: The Society of the Spectacle (1967)
16. Dey, A., Salber, D., Abowd, G., Futakawa, M.: The Conference Assistant: Combining Context-awareness with Wearable Computing. In: Proc. Third Intl. Symposium on Wearable Computing, San Francisco, CA, pp. 21–28 (1999)
17. Duruz, J.: Eating at the Borders: Culinary Journeys. Environment and Planning D: Society and Space 23, 51–69 (2005)
18. Foucault, M.: Of Other Spaces. Diacritics 16, 22–27 (1986)
19. Garrioch, D.: Sounds of the City: The Soundscape of Early Modern European Towns. Urban History 30(1), 5–25 (2003)
20. Gaye, L., Mazé, R., Holmquist, L.E.: Sonic City: the urban environment as a musical interface. In: Proceedings of the 2003 Conference on New interfaces For Musical Expression (Montreal, Quebec, Canada, May 22 - 24, 2003) New Interfaces For Musical Expression, pp. 109–115. National University of Singapore, Singapore (2003)

21. Graham, S.: Software-Sorted Geographies. Progress in Human Geography 29, 562–580 (2005)
22. Grinter, R., Aoki, P., Hurst, A., Szymanski, M., Thornton, J., Woodruff, A.: Revisiting the Visit: Understanding How Technology Can Shape the Museum Visit. In: Proc. ACM Conf. on Computer Supported Cooperative Work (New Orleans, LA), pp. 146–155. ACM, New York (2002)
23. Ho, J., Intille, S.: Using Context-aware Computing to Reduce the Perceived Burden of Interruptions from Mobile Devices. In: Proc. ACM Conf. Human Factors in Computing Systems CHI 2005 (Portland, OR), pp. 909–918. ACM, New York (2005)
24. Isaacs, E., Walendowski, A., Ranganthan, D.: Hubbub: A Sound-enhanced Mobile Instant Messenger that Supports Awareness and Opportunistic Interactions. In: Proc. ACM Conf. Human Factors in Computing Systems CHI 2001 (Minneapolis, MN), pp. 179–186. ACM, New York (2002)
25. Kelleher, W.: The Troubles in Ballybogoin: Memory and Identity in Northern Ireland. University of Michigan Press, Ann Arbor, MI (2003)
26. Lamming, M., Eldridge, M., Flynn, M., Jones, C., Pendlebury, D.: Satchel: Providing Access to Any Document, Any Time, Anywhere. ACM Trans. Computer-Human Interaction 7(3), 322–352 (2000)
27. McCullough, M.: On Digital Ground: Architecture, Pervasive Computing, and Environmental Knowing. MIT Press, Cambridge (2003)
28. le Marcis, F.: The Suffering Body of the City. Public Culture 16(3), 453–477 (2004)
29. Massey, D.: Power-geometry and a Progressive Sense of Place. In: Bird, Curtis, Putnam, Robertson, Tickner (eds.) Mapping the Futures: Local Cultures, Global Change, Routledge, London (1993)
30. Munn, N.: Excluded Spaces: The Figure in the Australian Aboriginal Landscape. Critical Inquiry 22(3), 446–465 (1996)
31. Myerhoff, B.: Peyote Hunt: The Sacred Journey of the Huichol Indians. Cornell, Ithaca, NY (1976)
32. Reid, J., Hull, K., Cater, K., Fleuriot, C.: Magic Moments in Situated Mediascapes. In: Proc. ACM SIGCHI International Conference on Advances in Computer Entertainment Technology ACE 2005 (2005)
33. Russell, D.M., Gossweiler, R.: On the Design of Personal & Communal Large Information Scale Appliances. In: Abowd, G.D., Brumitt, B., Shafer, S. (eds.) Ubicomp 2001. LNCS, vol. 2201, pp. 354–361. Springer, Heidelberg (2001)
34. Spradley, J.: You Owe Yourself a Drunk: An Ethnography of Urban Nomads. Waveland Press, Prospect Heights, IL (1970)
35. Thrift, N., French, S.: The Automatic Production of Space. Trans. Institute of British Geographers 27(3), 309–335 (2002)
36. Vaneigem, R.: The Revolution of Everyday Life. Paris: Gallimand (1967)

Designing a Trade-Off Between Usability and Security: A Metrics Based-Model

Christina Braz[1], Ahmed Seffah[2], and David M'Raihi[3]

[1] Department of Computer Science, University of Quebec at Montreal, 201, President-Kennedy Avenue, room PK-4918, Montreal, QC H2X 3Y7 Canada
braz.christina@courrier.uqam.ca
[2] Department of Computer Science and Software Engineering, Concordia University, 1515, St. Catherine West, Montreal, QC H3G 1M8 Canada
seffah@cs.concordia.ca
[3] Innovation Group, VeriSign Inc.,
685, East Middlefield Road, Mountain View, CA 94043 United States
dmraihi@verisign.com

Abstract. The design of usable yet secure systems raises crucial questions when it comes to balancing properly security and usability. Finding the right tradeoff between these two quality attributes is not an easy endeavor. In this paper, we introduce an original design model based on a novel usability inspection method. This new method, named Security Usability Symmetry (SUS), exploits automata machines theory and introduces the concept of an advanced Multifunction Teller Machine (MTM). We demonstrate, via case study, how to use this model during the design of secure, usable interactive systems.

Keywords: Usability, Security, User-Centered Design, Critical Systems, Automata Machines, Metrics.

1 Introduction

Security has always been an important quality factor in many types of interactive systems including banking software such as Multifunction Teller Machines (MTM). Usability also is required in such systems. However, there is also a common (but false) belief that security is only related to the software systems functionality and that it can be designed independently from usability which only relates to the UI component. In fact, the term UI and the way usability is defined are perhaps major underlying obstacles that explain such erroneous conceptions. Indeed, it gives the impression that the UI is a thin layer sitting on top of the "real" system and that usability can be conceived independently from the other quality factors.

Usability has been defined differently in several standards [1], [2], [3]. Each of these standards emphasizes somewhat different sets of usability factors, such as effectiveness, efficiency, learnability, or user satisfaction. Thus, a more comprehensive model of usability should include both process-related and product-related usability characteristics such as effectiveness, efficiency, satisfaction, security, and learnability. Moreover, Usability is a generally relative measure of whether a software product enables a particular set of users to achieve specified goals in a specified context of use [4].

C. Baranauskas et al. (Eds.): INTERACT 2007, LNCS 4663, Part II, pp. 114–126, 2007.
© IFIP International Federation for Information Processing 2007

On the other hand, "Security Usability" according to [5] deals with how security information should be handled in the UI. Both usability and security can vary depending on the context of use that includes user profiles (i.e., who are the users), task characteristics, hardware (including network equipment), software, and physical or organizational environments [6]. Usability is imperative from the user's perspective (e.g., complete a task correctly without errors that could result in a security problem), from the developer's perspective (e.g., success or breakdown of a system), and from management's perspective (e.g., software with weak security support can be a major constraint to the usability of the system).

A limited amount of work has been done on the usability of security systems and in particular on the intimate relationship that exists between usability and security. The design of usable yet secure systems raises crucial questions concerning how to solve conflicts between security and usability goals. The fundamental question is therefore how to ensure usability without compromising security and vice-versa. Building an acceptable tradeoff is not an easy endeavor. We propose a novel design model named Security Usability Symmetry (SUS) inspection method and the utilization of the Quality in Use Integrated Measurement Model (QUIM) [6] as a model for usability measurement and classification of our advanced MTMs for dealing with this issue in the automata machines domain. We also show, via a case study, how to apply this model during design.

2 Usability and Security: How to Design a Trade-Off?

Some researchers, as well as other standards organizations, have identified other viewpoints on usability, and have included another usability characteristic, *security* (Table 1). Table 1 lists some of the standards where security is included within their

Table 1. Security as a usability characteristic

Tasks	Usability	Security
ITSEC: Information Technology *Security* Evaluation Criteria.	IEC 300 [7]	It presents software as *security*-critical.
International Standards Organization (ISO)	ISO 13407 [8]	It describes human-centered design as a multidisciplinary activity incorporating human factors and ergonomic and technical knowledge with the objective of raising efficiency and effectiveness, improving human working conditions, and opposing possible unfavorable effects of use on human health, *security* and performance.
	ISO/IEC 9126 [2]	It defines *security,* which is a sub-characteristic, as a set of software attributes which relates to its ability to prevent unauthorized access, whether accidental or deliberate, to programs and data.
Federal Aviation Administration (FAA) [9]	FAA, 1998	*Security* is a characteristic of the CHI, which is particularly important in an industrial context.

usability model. These standards consider that good usability is a significant condition for human security in critical systems, such as medical apparatus or nuclear power stations [4]. Within our model, we adopted this perception of security.

What exactly usability specialists and software designers have to bear in mind when designing usability for secure systems? Figure 1 models the relationship between usability and security. The key characteristics of the usability problem – represented via a usability scenario – related to security are briefly described next:

i) It is important to make sure that the users understand what they should do well enough to avoid making potentially high risk mistakes; this is especially important for security mechanisms, since if a secret is left unprotected, even for a short moment, there is no way to ensure it has not been compromised;

ii) Security is a secondary goal for many users, a necessary step on the way of achieving their primary goals such as checking their account balance or their email; therefore developers should not optimistically assume that users are motivated to read manuals or look for security rules and regulations;

iii) Security concepts might seem self evident to the security developer but are very unintuitive to many users; developers therefore need to put extra effort into understanding the users' mental models and be sure to use concepts the users are familiar with;

iv) Feed-back is often used to prevent users from making mistakes, but this is difficult in security since the state of a security mechanism is often very complex and hard to explain to the user;

v) Security is only as strong as its weakest component. Therefore users need guidance to attend all security aspects in their usage of the mechanism [10].

vi) Attackers can abuse a system that it is "too" usable but not very secure. For example, European Commission (EC) regulations were fundamentally different from usual banking practices. They forbade fees when converting national currencies to euros (fees would otherwise deter users from adopting the euro); this created a unique fraud context where money could be made by taking advantage of the EC's official rounding rules. A method to protect against such attacks is detailed in [11].

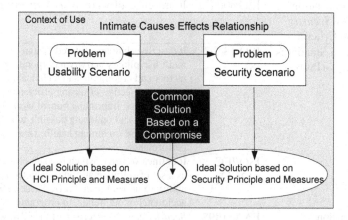

Fig. 1. Usability and Security trade-off: A common solution based on a compromise.

3 Automata Machines as a Tool for Modeling the Relationship

The banking industry pioneered the first wide-scale deployment of self-service automata machines or the Automated Teller Machines (ATMs). A Traditional Automated Teller Machine (ATM) is a device employed by mostly bank users to carry out financial transactions. Usually, a user inserts into the ATM a special plastic card that is encoded with information on a magnetic strip. The magnetic stripe contains an identification code that is transmitted to the bank's central computer by modem. To prevent unauthorized transactions, a personal identification number (PIN) must also be entered by the user using a keypad. The computer then permits the ATM to complete the transaction; most machines can perform limited transactions including for example receiving cash, making deposits, checking account balances, printing checks, printing statements, and other functions: dispense cash, accept deposits, transfer funds, and provide information on account balances. ATMs usually include one or more internal processors which carry out software instructions and enable operation of the machine. Presently most ATM software is proprietary to the particular machine manufacturer. As a result the software which causes one manufacturer's automated teller machine to operate will not operate another manufacturer's automated teller machine. Recently organizations have begun to develop standards related to devices commonly found in ATMs. These standards provide a generally uniform set of instructions for operating each particular type of device which is likely to be found in an ATM (e.g., WOSA-XFS or XFS standard).

As the technology has continued to evolve, a new generation of self service automata has emerged, known as a Multifunction Teller Machines (MTMs), which consists of the best-of-breed of traditional ATMs and the most advanced financial and purchase transactions offered at remote terminals and over the Internet. Where ATMs are really in disadvantage concerning key design factors in relation to MTM's? First, MTMs are conceived to optimize the perceptual and physical needs of the consumer for example features like smaller footprint and graphically enjoyable UIs capitalize on the appeal and adoption of MTMs. Second, time-saving efficiencies and high tech designs can make MTM's a fashionable option for consumers and deployers as well. And finally, the integration of the self-service with human service if needed in a way that optimizes both transactional efficiencies and the user experience.

The good old ATM cannot defeat the new Multifunction Teller Machine (MTM) in several aspects especially in the "transaction" factor. Being capable to perform up to 150 kinds of transactions ranging from straightforward cash withdrawals and deposits, to fund transfer to trading in stocks to purchasing mutual funds or to cash a check using check imaging to something as ordinary as processing the payment of electricity bills, booking air-tickets, purchasing concert tickets and making hotel reservations. A MTM is in effect the next generation of the old ATM, fully integrated cross-bank MTM network (e.g.: Multibanco in Portugal) providing numerous functionalities which are not straightforwardly associated to the management of one's own bank account, such as loading monetary value into pre-paid cards (e.g., cell phones, tolls, service and shopping payments, etc.). In short, it is really all about survival in the marketplace. Any bank or organization that does not provide intelligent self-service choices to their users will be at a competitive disadvantage in its industry, from a cost structure and a user stickiness and loyalty standpoint [12]. A MTM endows users with the capability to control their end-user experience pretty much in terms of the pace and outcome of this experience. ATMs transactions on the contrary are fundamentally static and linear. MTMs on the other hand dynamically reconfigure transactions "on the fly" to coordinate the actions of users, applications, and devices in real-time.

4   A Case Study: The Credit's Lyonnais French Bank

Within a Credit Lyonnais, French bank branch located at the neighboring of Paris 6 in France, the counter clerk who greeted the local clients have disappeared three years ago. The clerk was replaced by an automaton machine able to carry out 70% of current banking transactions such as money withdrawing, income statements, funds transfers, bill payments, cards orders, profile updating, automaton machine's access with mobile phone, check deposit without envelopes, and other advanced features. From now on, the clients themselves perform their banking operations on the machine.

4.1   Usability and Security Scenarios: What Scenarios Are All About?

Although the HCI literature contains plenty definitions of what a task and usability scenarios are, we would like to refine it and also introduce a new definition for a Security scenario according to below (See also Figure 1):

o   **Task Scenario.** A task scenario refers to a description of the task at hand including its context of use. According to [1], the Context of Use (CoU) analysis refers to a broad technique to determine the characteristics of the User, Tasks, and their Environments. The application of the CoU analysis mostly is used as a support to data gather requirements to build the basic components at the early development stages of the application, and also to establish if the end results which consist of effectiveness, efficiency and satisfaction.

o   **Usability Scenario.** A usability scenario details a user problem when doing a task in a certain context. Therefore a usability scenario is a problem related to a task scenario, but it should be well known meaning defined in a usability model, standard or evaluation method.

o   **Security Scenario.** A security scenario refers to a description of a task scenario which includes the use of a particular security mechanism. A Security Scenario can be tangible or intangible. A Tangible Security Scenario (TSS) includes physical infrastructure such as controlling user's access to buildings and facilities using Biometrics, or sending a silent alarm in response to a threat at a MTM, etc. An Intangible Security Scenario (ISS) includes data or other digital information, for example, a user who enter sensitive information at registration in order to purchase a concert ticket at a MTM. A Security Scenario might be (or not) a combination of TSS and ISS.

According to the Security Scenario, we classify them as indicated by the overall impact of the security risks of the security mechanisms related to the system's owner such as *High Security Impact, Moderate Security Impact, and Low Security Impact.*

A *High Security Impact* refers to the confidentiality, integrity, or availability of the security mechanisms, and it may cause severe or catastrophic loss to the owner's system (e.g., authentication credentials like private cryptographic keys, and hardware tokens); a *Moderate Security Impact* refers to the confidentiality, integrity, or availability of the security mechanisms, and it may cause a moderate loss to the owner's system (e.g., data on internal file shares for internal business use only); and finally a *Low Security Impact refers to the i*mpact on the confidentiality, integrity, or availability of the security mechanisms, and it may not cause any significant financial loss, legal or regulatory problems, operational disruptions, etc. to the owner's system (e.g., public cryptographic keys).

4.2 Tasks, Usability, and Security Scenarios for MTMs

In this section, we introduce a sample of Task, Usability and Security Scenarios related to our case study according to the table 2. A complete and detailed description of the tasks, security and usability scenarios can be viewed at the following Website: http://www.labunix.uqam.ca/~ha991381/TasksScenarios.pdf

Table 2. A sample of one of the Task, Usability and Security Scenarios: Authenticate a user to a Multifunction Teller Machine

Tasks	Usability	Security
1. Name: Authenticate yourself to a Multifunction Teller Machine (MTM). Scenario: User must authenticate her/ himself through a multipurpose contactless smart card token-based authentication (i.e., PIN) in order to have access to different systems. *Required Features:* To authenticate yourself to the following systems: • MTM: Card + card slot and card reader + PIN; • Medical Institution: card + card slot and card reader (desktop computer) + PIN; • Facility: bring card close to the card reader (physical access); • Electronic Purse: swipe the card in a card reader + PIN	*Problem: Minimal Action (User Convenience: dealing with multipurpose VS. one purpose smart cards).* *Scenario:* The card just mentioned improves user convenience since the user doesn't need to carry several cards and usually memorizing different PIN codes. However, it raises the risk if the card is lost or gets stolen, and also if the card is forgotten by the user in the reader of the MTM. Using a one purpose card is more secure, but means the user will need to carry one card for each application which is not so convenient.	*Problem: Storage of Information.* *Scenario:* A multipurpose contactless smart card however puts more sensitive information on the card (i.e., all applications in one card are clearly less secure than one card with one application), and also requires more complex organizational coordination. The risk involved if the wrong person gets access to the card, is much higher. Moreover, contactless smart cards open the door to attacks which exploit over-the-air communication channels in an unsolicited way such as eavesdropping, interruption of operations, covert transactions, and denial of service [13].

5   A Usability and Security Design Model for MTM

We propose the use of the Quality in Use Integrated Measurement (QUIM) [6] as a model for usability measurement and classification of MTMs. QUIM brings the best of breed of existing usability standards and models for evaluating usability in a single consolidated, hierarchical model of usability measurement. QUIM is hierarchical model in that it decomposes usability into *factors*, then into *criteria*, and finally into specific *metrics*. In this sense, QUIM follows the IEEE 1061 (1998) standard (Software Quality Metrics Methodology), which outlines methods for establishing quality requirements as well as identifying, implementing, analyzing, and validating both process and product quality metrics [14], [15]. Also included in QUIM are some emerging usability factors, those identified only quite recently as being important considerations in some contexts. For example, the inclusion of trustfulness and accessibility as usability factors among others.

5.1   Usability Factors

The proposed model includes 9 usability factors among the 10 existing in QUIM briefly described as follows: **Efficiency.** The capability of the software product to enable users to expend appropriate amounts of resources in relation to the effectiveness achieved in a specified context of use; **Satisfaction.** The subjective response of user while using a software product (i.e., is the user satisfied?); **Productivity.** The level of effectiveness achieved in relation to the resources (i.e. time to complete tasks, user efforts, materials or financial cost of usage) consumed by the users and the system; **Learnability.** The features required for achieving particular goals can be mastered; **Safety.** Whether a software product limits the risk of harm to people or other resources, such as hardware or stored information; **Trustfulness.** The faithfulness a software product offers to its users; **Accessibility.** The capability of a software product to be used by persons with some type of disability (e.g., visual, hearing, psychomotor); **Universality.** Whether a software product accommodates a diversity of users with different cultural backgrounds (e.g., local culture is considered); and finally, **Usefulness.** Whether a software product enables users to solve real problems in an acceptable way.

5.2   Measurable Criteria

Each factor is broken down into measurable criteria (sub-factors). A criterion is directly measurable via at least one specific metric. Definitions of 7 of the 26 existing criteria in QUIM are presented below. These definitions all assume a particular context of use or stated conditions for an application feature. Minimal Action. Capability of the application to help users achieve their tasks in a minimum number of steps; Minimal Memory Load. Whether a user is required to keep minimal amount of information in mind in order to achieve a specified task [6]; Operability. Amount of effort necessary to operate and control an application; Privacy. Whether users' personal information is appropriately protected; Security. Capability of the application to protect information and data so that unauthorized persons or systems cannot read or modify them and authorized persons or systems are not denied access [16]; Load

Time. Time required for the application to load (i.e., how fast it responds to the user); and finally, Resource Safety. Whether resources (including people) are handled properly without any hazard.

The relations between the 9 usability factors and the 7 usability criteria are described in Table 3. For example, in our MTM application, the Efficiency factor is assumed to correspond to criteria such as Minimal Action, Operability, Privacy, Resource Safety, and Minimal Memory Load. That is, we hypothesize that efficiency can be measured with metrics associated with the criteria listed for this factor in the table. Looking at Table 3 from the perspective of the criteria, we hypothesize that Minimal Action, for example, is related to at six different factors, including Efficiency, Satisfaction, Learnability, and Accessibility.

Table 3. The 9 Usability Factors and Usability Criteria

Task Number	Task Scenario	Security Problem	Usability Criteria	Efficiency	Satisfaction	Productivity	Learnability	Safety	Trustfulness	Accessibility	Universality	Usefulness
1	Authenticate yourself	Storage of Information	Minimal Action	•	•		•			•		
2	Transfer funds to an intl bank account	Access Control	Operability	•	•				•	•		•
3	Buy a ticket concert	Sensitive Information	Privacy	•	•				•	•		•
			Minimal Action	•	•		•			•		
4	Access your MTM with your cell phone	Credentials across several channels	Security					•	•			•
5	Deposit your check using checking image	Encryption	Loading Time	•	•						•	•
6	Send a silent alarm	User physical safety	Minimal Memory Load	•	•		•		•		•	•
			Resource Safety					•				

5.3 Usability Metrics

A measure or metric is basically a mapping function that assigns a number or symbol to an attribute of some entity [17]. Some metrics are basically functions that are defined in terms of a formula, but others are just simple countable data. Examples of countable metrics include the percentage of a task completed, the ratio of task successes to failures, the frequency of program help usage, the time spent dealing with program errors, and the number of on-screen UI elements. Whereas calculable metrics are the results of mathematical calculations, algorithms, or heuristics based on raw observational data or countable metrics. For example, a formula by [18] for calculating task effectiveness is TE = Quantity × Quality/100 where Quantity is the proportion of the task completed and Quality is the proportion of the goal achieved. The proportions just mentioned are the countable metrics that make up the calculable TE metric. Listed in Table 4 are calculable metrics which may be used in the MTM environment. All these metrics are detailed in QUIM model [6].

Table 4. The proposed calculable metrics for a MTM environment

Task #	Task Scenario	Usability Criteria	Metrics
1	Authenticate yourself	Minimal Action	Efficiency: Monetary cost of performing the task. Layout Appropriateness LA=100xC_optimal/C_designed[1]
2	Transfer funds to an international bank account	Operability	Layout Appropriateness LA=100xC_optimal/C_designed
3	Buy a concert ticket	Privacy	Data sharing privacy: size of smallest group that share the same identifiable properties, e.g., k-anonymity; Communication Privacy: Probability of identifying correctly the participants of a communication; Pseudonymity: Probability of possibility to link pseudonym with user identity.
		Minimal Action	Same as task 1.
4	Access your MTM with your cell phone	Security	Efficiency: Time to learn; Satisfaction: rating scale for user versus technological control of task.
5	Deposit your check using checking image	Loading Time	Essential Efficiency: EE=100xS_essential/S_enacted
6	Send a silent alarm	Minimal Memory Load	Effectiveness: Workload Task Visibility $TV = 100 \times (1 / S\_total \times \Sigma\, Vi)\ \forall i$
		Resource Safety	Effectiveness: Task Concordance TC=100 x D/P Task effectiveness (TE) TE=Quantity x Quality/100

Note: For detailed information go to http://www.er.uqam.ca/nobel/d362040/quim.pdf

5.4 The Security Usability Symmetry (SUS)

We also propose a new usability and security inspection method called Security Usability Symmetry (SUS), a variant of the *Heuristic Evaluation* method [19]. It aims

---

[1] $C=\sum Pi,j \times Di,j\ \forall i \neq j$; Pi,j=Frequency of transition between visual components i and j.

to help usability specialists and security designers to design/inspect/evaluate an interactive system to identify any usability and security user problems and check for conformance with its corresponding usability criteria and security aspects mentioned previously for Multifunction Teller Machines (MTM). These usability criteria and security aspects can be used to *guide a design decision* or to *assess a design* that has already been created.

According to [19], usability specialists were much better than those without usability expertise at finding usability problems by heuristic evaluation. Moreover, usability specialists with specific expertise (e.g., security) did much better than regular usability specialists without such expertise, especially with regard to certain usability problems that were unique to that kind of interface. Thus, SUS is developed as a security usability inspection method for evaluators who have knowledge of usability AND also computer security. In SUS, a solely usability specialist can also work in pair with a solely security specialist.

The SUS can help also to develop a MTM profile that will impact whether or how usability and security aspects will be implemented in the system. A MTM profile might present the MTM profile that is used by systems designers to determine their specific characteristics and needs.

Prior to evolving into the iterative design phase whereby a product is designed, modified, and tested repeatedly, it is critical that usability specialists and security designers understands its own specific requirements and goals for the MTM. Toward that end, we have provided the SUS that will guide you to the most suitable MTM for your organization. It focuses on the following key areas: Usability and Security requirements, Interoperability, System Application, Technology, and Resources.

The output of the SUS' inspection method. A list of usability and security problems in the interface with references to those usability principles and security aspects that were violated by the design in each case in the opinion of the evaluator is provided as the main output of the method.

Rating severity of the identified usability problems. In SUS, the rating severity is based on three factors: Frequency with which the problem occurs (i.e., is it common or rare?), Consequence of the problem if it occurs (i.e., will it be easy or difficult for the users to overcome?, and finally Persistence of the problem (i.e., is it a one-time problem that users can overcome once they know about it or will users repeatedly be bothered by the problem?).

Rating severity representation. The following Minor to Major rating scale may be used to rate the severity of usability problems: Minor= Minor usability problem; fixing this should be set low priority; Intermediate=Medium usability problem; important to fix as soon as possible. Major=important usability problem; it should be set high priority.

Rating severity of the identified security problems. In SUS, the rating severity is based on six aspects: Authentication (i.e., user identity proofing and verification); Confidentiality (i.e. information is not made available or disclosed to unauthorized individuals, entities or processes); Integrity (i.e., data has not been modified or destroyed in an unauthorised manner); Non-repudiation (i.e., the author of a document cannot later claim not to be the author; the "document" may be an e-mail message, or a credit-card order, or anything that might be sent over a network); Access Control (i.e., granting access to data or performing an action; an authentication method is used to check a user login, then the access control mechanism grants and revokes privileges based on predefined rules); Availability (i.e., a computer system asset must be available to authorized parties when needed).

Rating severity representation. The following Low to High risk level rating scale may be used to rate the severity of security problems: Low=Minor security risk problem; fixing this should be set low priority; Medium=intermediate security problem; important to fix as soon as possible. High=important security risk problem; it should be set high priority.

The usability problems can greatly be eliminated or reduced through the severity rates where we are able to identify those problems that should be tackled and fixed. The ratings also aid in the allowance of resources for treating the UI problems. According to [19], severity consists a combination of three elements: frequency ranges (i.e. from common problems to unusual ones), impact (i.e., establishes the ease or difficulty with which a user gets over a problem), and persistence (i.e., ranges from just one problem that might be surmount to the problem that constantly replicate itself becoming annoying to the user).

A sample of the SUS Review Check-List is presented in Table 4. First, we specify our *Usability Criterion*; second, we define it, and then we present the *Usability Review* questions with their respective *Occurrences*; afterwards, the *Security Review* with their respective level of security *Risk*. A complete and detailed description of the SUS model can be viewed at: http://www.labunix.uqam.ca/~ha991381/SUSmodel.pdf

Table 5. A sample of the SUS review check-list for MTMs regarding the Usability Criterion: Minimal Memory Load

Security Usability Symmetry Check-List							
6. Usability Criterion: MINIMAL MEMORY LOAD							
Whether a user is required to keep minimal amount of information in mind in order to achieve a specified task.							
#	Usability Review	Occurrence			Security Review	Occurrence		
		Y	N	NA		Y	N	NA
6.1	Is the memory load on the user minimized (i.e., no memorization of long data lists, complicated procedures, or undertake complex cognitive activities)?				If the task at hand is complex, are the procedures or steps broken down into sub-steps to facilitate securely its understanding and execution?			
6.2	Are the entries short (i.e., short term memory capacity is limited[2], so the shorter the entries, the smaller errors and reading times)?				Does the system provide displayed feedback for all user actions during data entry[3]?			

Table 5. (*Continued*)

6. Usability Criterion: *MINIMAL MEMORY LOAD*								
Whether a user is required to keep minimal amount of information in mind in order to achieve a specified task.								
#	Usability Review	Y	N	NA	Security Review	Y	N	NA
6.3	Are short PINs used such as four digits or less (i.e., they are easier to memorize and fast to type)?	▦	▦	▦	Is PIN able to be used in conjunction with a hardware device (2-factor authentication) providing stronger security?	▦	▦	▦
6.4	Is a *non-user selected* PIN avoided (i.e. more difficult to memorize since it has no meaning and can not be pronounced)?	▦	▦	▦	Can a *non-user-selected* PIN be combined with a variable such as current date and time, at each login to eliminate the risk of replay?	▦	▦	▦
6.5	Is the MTM's application based on recognition of visual items for authentication (i.e., to avoid unaided recall)?	▦	▦	▦	If recognition of visual items for authentication is used, can the users also associate a phrase to an image to enhance security?	▦	▦	▦

6   A Concluding Remark

As highlighted in this paper, a very few research has been done on the intimate relationship between usability and security. To be able to build reliable, effective and usable security systems, we need specific guidelines that take into account the specific constraints of usability mechanisms and their potential consequences on security. In this paper, we proposed a design model - a novel usability inspection method - named Security Usability Symmetry (SUS) for dealing with this issue using automata machines more specifically our advanced Multifunction Teller Machine (MTM). We also showed via a case study how to apply this model during design.

References

[1] International Organization for Standardization ISO 9241-11: Ergonomic requirements for office work with visual display terminals (VDTs - Part 11: Guidance on Usability) (1998)
[2] International Organization for Standardization: ISO/IEC 9126-1:2001 Edition 1; Software product Evaluation – Quality Characteristics and Guidelines for the User, Geneva (2001)
[3] Institute of Electrical and Electronics Engineers (IEEE): 1061-1998 IEEE Standard for a Software Quality Metrics Methodology (1998)
[4] Abran, A., Khelifi, A., Suryn, W., Seffah, A.: Usability Meanings and Interpretations in ISO Standards. Software Quality Journal 11(4) (2003)
[5] Jøsang, A., Patton, M.: UI Requirements for Authentication of Communication, White Paper, Distributed Systems Technology Centre, QUT, Brisbane, Australia (2001)

[6] Seffah, A., Donyaee, M., Kline, R., Padda, H.K.: Usability Metrics: A Roadmap for a Consolidated Model. Journal of Software Quality 14(2) (2006)

[7] Commission of the European Communities: Information Technology Security Evaluation Criteria (ITSEC), Standard EIC 300 Version 1.2 (1991)

[8] International Organization for Standardization, ISO 13407: Processes for Interactive Systems, Geneva, Author (1999)

[9] Federal Aviation Administration (FAA): Standard Terminal Automation Replacement System, Human Factors Team Report of the Computer–Human Interface Re-Evaluation (1998)

[10] Cranor, L.F., Garfinkel, S.: Security and Usability: Designing Secure Systems that People Can Use.O'Reilly (2005)

[11] M'Raïhi, D., Naccache, D., Tunstall, M.: Asymmetric Currency Rounding. In: Frankel, Y. (ed.) FC 2000. LNCS, vol. 1962, pp. 192–201. Springer, Heidelberg (2001)

[12] NCR Self-Service Universe conference, Washington, D.C. , U.S.A. (2006)

[13] Handschuh, H.: Contactless Technology Security Issues. Security Technologies Department, Gemplus. Information Security Bulletin 9, 95 (2004)

[14] Schneidewind, N.F.: Methodology for validating software metrics. IEEE Software Engineering 18, 410–422 (1992)

[15] Yamada, S., Hong, J.K., Sugita, S.: Development and Evaluation of Hypermedia for Museum Education: Validation of Metrics. ACM Transactions on Computer-Human Interaction (TOCHI) 2(4), 284–307 (1995)

[16] International Organization for Standardization/International Electro echnical Commission: ISO/IEC 12207, Information Technology, Software Life Cycle Processes Geneva Author (1995)

[17] Fenton, N.E., Pfleeger, L.: Software metrics, 2nd edn. International Thompson Publishing Company (1997)

[18] Bevan, N.: Measuring usability as quality of use. Software Quality Journal 4, 115–130 (1995)

[19] Nielsen, J.: Finding Usability Problems through Heuristic Evaluation. In: the Proceedings of ACM Computer Human Interaction (CHI'92), Monterey, CA (US), May 3–7, 1992 (1992)

Recognising Erroneous and Exploratory Interactions

Jonathan Back[1], Ann Blandford[1], and Paul Curzon[2]

[1] University College London Interaction Centre
[2] Queen Mary, University of London
j.back@ucl.ac.uk, a.blandford@ucl.ac.uk, pc@dcs.qmul.ac.uk

Abstract. A better understanding of "human error" is needed to help overcome problems of people assuming they are to blame for their inability to use poorly designed technology. In order to investigate people's ability to recognize, and reflect on the causes of, particular types of errors, a problem solving environment was designed that allowed participants to verbally self-report erroneous and exploratory interactions. It was found that the pervasiveness of errors was recognizable but underlying cognitive and attentional causes of errors were not. Participants found that providing a causal account of device-specific errors during interaction was especially difficult. A striking feature of device-specific errors is that they involve actions that do not move an individual towards a goal state, but remain critical to performing a task correctly. Successfully identifying why an error has occurred requires an understanding of environmental cues and salience. Findings imply that HCI practitioners need to develop techniques to adjust the visual salience of cues, making it is possible to recognize and recover from error.

Keywords: Human error, self-report, HCI.

1 Introduction

It is now recognized that many errors in routine interactive behaviour are not the product of some stochastic process, and that causal explanations of human error can be developed [1]. However, little is known about what factors influence an individual's ability to recognize errors. Recognition that an error has been made is a prerequisite for error recovery. The focus of this paper is on this recognition process rather than the error recovery process as a whole.

Errors are sensitive to external influences. For example, forgetting to collect the original document after making photocopies is more likely if an individual is thinking about 'other things' or is interrupted. Although forgetting your original document can be inconvenient, research has shown that similar underlying causal factors can result in catastrophic social consequences (e.g., aircraft crashes and nuclear power station failures) [2]. Much of the previous work on understanding human error has relied on participants generating retrospective self-reports, often some time after the event [3], or accounts of particular incidents – for example, accident investigation reports [4]. These forms of data collection have provided a high-level understanding of error, but lack the information about timing and context needed to develop a more detailed account of error phenomena and their cognitive causes.

C. Baranauskas et al. (Eds.): INTERACT 2007, LNCS 4663, Part II, pp. 127–140, 2007.

In an attempt to develop a cognitive account some work [1, 5, 6] has been based on behavioural traces, recording user activity and classifying actions as correct or erroneous according to experimenter-defined criteria. In the work reported here, we have investigated the use of real-time self-reports to further investigate human error, based on participants' own definitions of errors.

1.1 Background

One of the first attempts at demonstrating the non-stochastic nature of errors was suggested by Rasmussen and Jensen [7]. The idea that errors can be categorized as being skill-based, rule-based, or knowledge-based allows errors to be attributed to different cognitive factors. However, whether an error is classified as skill-based, rule-based, or knowledge-based may depend more on the level of analysis rather than on its ontogeny [8]. For example Gray [5] argued that the same behavior, e.g. "taking the wrong route during rush hour", can result from lack of knowledge (not knowing about a faster route) or misapplication of a rule (knowing that one route is the fastest during rush hour and the other is fastest on the off hours but applying the 'off hours' rule). In addition, this behavior could be caused by a slip (taking the more familiar route when the intention was to take the less familiar but faster one) or be intentionally wrong (cannot get into the correct lane due to traffic).

Investigating a situation where an error has occurred outside the 'laboratory environment' requires an individual to provide a self-report, or requires the use of an error analysis framework such as CREAM [9]. Such frameworks focus on the probabilities of error types occurring; 'fine grained' explanations are unlikely to be elicited. The use of self-report when investigating human error has traditionally been post hoc and incidental. Questionnaire studies can yield interesting data with regard to individual differences in error proneness, the relatedness of various error types, and the organization of the underlying control mechanisms [2]. Responses to questionnaire items asking about the incidence of a wide variety of minor cognitive failures remain consistent over several months [3]. Broadbent, Cooper, Fitzgerald and Parks [10] showed that stress-vulnerability (or a certain style of cognitive management) is associated with cognitive failure in everyday life.

Recently there is a move towards understanding how the task environment influences working memory, attention and other cognitive functions [5]. Questionnaires and interviews cannot be used to reveal failures in specific cognitive functions that may have caused an error. Moreover, the cognitive context in which error types occur, in relation to a specific cognitive activity, cannot be established. When investigating problem solving, one method of self-report that has been found useful is the collection of concurrent verbal protocols (a commentary provided by the participant throughout an experimental trial). The question is: can this type of reporting be used successfully in understanding the factors that influence the recognition of error?

1.2 Concurrent Verbal Protocols

Previous research on verbal protocols has argued that it is essential to ensure that self-report procedures do not interfere with task behavior. If it is found that procedures do interfere with task behavior then this invalidates the approach. Generally, concurrent verbalization has been shown not to change the nature or sequence of thought processes if two conditions are adhered to: a) participant should only be instructed to verbalize thoughts that are already the focus of attention (participants should not elaborate on past events) [11]; b) training in the use of the think-aloud procedure ensures that valid representations of participants' thought processes are obtained since causal explanations should be provided in 'real-time' [12]. It seems unlikely that these conditions can be adhered to when investigating human error.

The nature of recognizing a slip error (non-knowledge based error) always requires an individual's focus of attention to be shifted to the environment. Noticing that the system is in the wrong state requires a 'salient' signal from the device or a user will continue to attempt to execute task goals. For example when setting a wake-up alarm on a digital clock, a user is often required to switch to the alarm set mode before inputting the wake-up time. If the alarm set mode is not selected then inputting the wake-up time can reset the current time. Alarm setting is a trivial example of a mode error; however, mode errors can sometimes have catastrophic social consequences. They can cause automation surprises - a phenomenon which can trigger operator confusion about the status of an automatic flight control system [2].

Training individuals to report errors as they occur is impossible since cognitive limitations often prevent instant error recognition. For example, some errors are caused by a loss of activation - when the presumed mechanism associated with the 'activation' of a goal has decayed from working memory [13]. Omission errors (forgetting to do something) are often indicative of these limitations which may delay or prevent recognition, prohibiting 'real-time' causal explanations. Thus, the use of concurrent verbal protocols where participants should not elaborate on past events and always provide 'real-time' explanations is inappropriate for studying human error.

A self-report mechanism is needed that is able to represent the way in which individuals recognize they have made an error without interfering with thought processes. Error recognition may be initiated by unexpected changes in the device state. For example, slip errors can be recognized if device feedback alerts the user of a mismatch between intentions and performance. However, if feedback from a device is not 'salient enough' to be noticed, then an individual might remain unaware of an erroneous interaction. There are situations where it is not easy to recognize an error since many problem solving strategies are likely to be automated unconscious elements of cognition [14]. However in some situations, reviewing previous interactions may force individuals to assess the suitability of strategies and thereby facilitate the recognition of errors. What is explicit is likely to be those aspects of an interaction that are not routine. Capture errors, for example, occur when there is an overlap in the sequence required for the performance of two different actions, especially if one is done more frequently than the other [15]. Reviewing actions may enable the identification of these types of incidents. Accidentally switching to the 'automatic routine' for a different goal that begins with the same set of actions is a common slip (e.g., taking the familiar route home when the intention was to take the less familiar but faster one).

1.3 Proposed Mechanisms for the Self-report of Error

Errors are one measure of the quality of human performance. For example, Miller [16] identified an important property of working memory by discovering that individuals make errors when recalling more than 7 (+/-2) elements of information. However, the everyday concept of error presupposes a goal. This can make the classification of errors difficult if an individual is interacting in an exploratory way to satisfy a learning goal, especially when a user is adopting a trial-and-error approach. A full understanding of human error is only possible if there is a way of differentiating between errors and exploratory interactions (where errors or sub-optimal moves can be an expected or even a desired outcome). Humans are not always able to describe their goals or able to recognize the extent to which a goal has been addressed.

Research has shown that exploratory interactions are used extensively during problem solving [11]. Exploratory actions are typically attempts to address a learning goal. Problematically, situations are likely to arise where learning goals cannot or will not be explicitly described, making self-reporting difficult. For example, the goal could be integrated within an automated schema; an individual may not be aware that they are acting in an exploratory way; the goal could be recognizable but the additional cognitive effort required to report the goal might push levels of cognitive load beyond available mental resources; an individual might be unwilling to report it if they believe that the goal is trivial; or they simply might not want to expend additional effort that reduces the efficiency of the problem solving process.

When an individual is able and willing to self-report an exploratory interaction, an explanation requires the lack of knowledge to be coherently described. If the task environment explicitly indicates that such knowledge is required, then an individual can simply report the feature or object that needs to be better understood. For example if an individual encounters an unknown feature or object that they believe might be pertinent to a task, they might decide to perform an exploratory interaction. Once the interaction is performed, it might then be possible to provide a self-report about whether they were able to discover an unknown property. Likewise it should be possible for an individual to self-report instances where an interaction is easily recognized as the wrong approach for the situation, prompting subsequent exploratory interactions. In this case, an individual can provide a self-report by justifying an exploratory interaction on the basis that a prior approach was erroneous.

For this work it was decided that when providing a self-report a participant should be able to differentiate exploratory interactions from erroneous ones. It was hoped that by identifying situations where differentiating errors from exploratory moves was difficult, and comparing them to situations where differentiating was easy, this would elucidate factors associated with the self-recognition of error. As previously discussed, the use of a concurrent verbal protocol is inappropriate. Instead, a participant must be given the opportunity to report an error when it is discovered. The simplest way of allowing this is to encourage participants to provide an 'Elective Report' at any time during interaction. The time that a participant chooses to make a report may reveal some contextual information that can be used to provide an insight into the process of recognizing errors. There is a strong possibility, however, that some errors may remain undetected due to the level of cognitive load imposed by the problem solving environment or due to an attentional failure. It is for this reason that a 'Debrief Reporting Mechanism' [17], which requires a participant to review a trace of their own behaviour after a task is completed, was also implemented. This type of self-report mechanism prompts an individual to review previous interactions in an attempt to identify those that can now be seen as erroneous. By comparing elective reports with debrief reports, factors that make the recognition of errors during a task possible may be better understood.

One major difference between historical and non-historical judgment is that the historical judge typically knows how things turned out. This may influence the way in which self-reports are provided. The utility of such self-reports may be compromised by hindsight bias. In an attempt to explore the influence of hindsight bias, Fischhoff [18] presented a series of descriptions of clinical or historical events for which four possible outcomes were provided. Participants were asked to rate the likelihood of occurrence. It was found that participants who were told that one of the events was true were more likely to increase its perceived probability of occurrence. Critically, Fischhoff found that participants who had outcome knowledge were largely unaware of the effect that outcome knowledge had on their perceptions. As a result, they overestimated what they would have known without outcome knowledge. It was concluded that this lack of awareness may restrict the ability to learn from the past. Within the medical domain, Flach [19] argued that error elimination strategies rely on hindsight as they involve systematically reducing causes of error so that the system is made increasingly safer. Given outcome knowledge, it has been suggested by Woods et al. [20] that reviewers will tend to simplify the problem solving situation. Woods et al. claimed that outcome knowledge blinds individuals to causal factors by biasing the uncertainties, tradeoffs, and the attentional demands. The very notion of causality may indeed be a symptom of hindsight bias. Flach suggested this is why safety management strategists prefer to focus on constraints rather than causes.

In this work we focus on better understanding the error recognition process. Although comparing elective self-reports with debrief self-reports is not a reliable method for the development of error elimination strategies, it may provide an insight into the factors that make errors unrecognizable during interaction.

2 Method

An adventure game was designed that allowed participants to interact freely within a problem solving environment. This game was developed using the 'Quest Development Tool Kit' (available at http://www.axeuk.com/quest/). The game specified a series of locations (rooms) and placed objects within rooms or within the player's inventory (possessions). The key element of the game involved problem solving. Objects such as a locked door were not designed as permanent obstacles, but merely as problems to be tackled. Solving problems frequently involved finding objects (adding them to the inventory) and then using them in the appropriate way. The game required a high level of attention to be maintained by participants as solutions to similar looking problems were not learnable. An aim of this cognitively demanding environment was to provoke a high error rate.

When commencing a new task, a participant was prompted to click on the 'objectives button' (see Figure 1). Pressing the button activated a scrolling ticker. The ticker was only capable of displaying one line of text (approximately 14 words) at any time. Task objectives were always six lines long. Ticker speed was set at 0.25 seconds per word. It took approximately 20 seconds for the ticker to display all of the task objectives, after which it was deactivated. Instructions presented to participants at the beginning suggested that they need not attempt to remember the task objectives as they can press the 'objectives button' at any time during the task. The 'objectives button' and associated ticker perform two important functions. Firstly, both the level of cognitive load imposed on an individual (remembering objectives) and amount of attentional load (monitoring the status of the ticker) is high. The status of the ticker is likely to require attention as it will not always be displaying required information. Deciding to perform another interaction while the ticker is scrolling requires a participant to predict how long they have until they have to shift their attention back to the ticker. This increased load on the individual was designed to provoke high rates of erroneous behaviour. Another reason for encouraging the regular use of the 'objectives' button is to draw attention to that particular interface panel. Maintaining the salience of this panel is important as the interface features used for the elicitation of self-reports were located there.

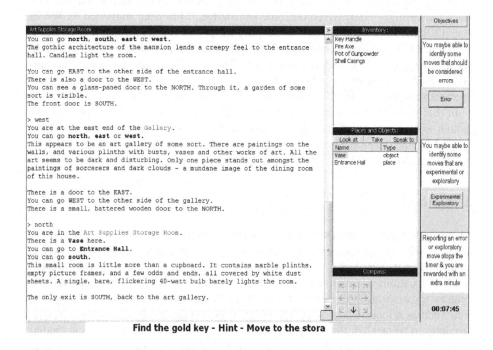

Fig. 1. The user interface, including reporting buttons (right) and ticker tape display (bottom)

Navigating around the game environment required the use of a paper-based map. Before commencing experimentation, a participant was shown their starting position relative to other rooms and floors in the house. Participants were free to refer to the map at any time. An example of the type of problem a participant was required to solve is presented below:

Task Aim: Dissolve concrete to get a golden key.
Task Objectives: Find concrete block and some acid, then make use of the sink.
Hints: Concrete block is hidden in a bedroom, you will need to find a key in the store room. Acid is hidden in dining room. Sink is in the workshop.

Possible Solution: Move to store room: the only object is a vase. Examine vase to discover that something rattles inside. Drop vase to break it and take key 001. Move to bedroom 1 (since key is labeled 001); use key to unlock door. Find concrete block in ensuite bathroom. Move to dining room. Examine drinks cabinet to activate pop-up dialog "Do you want to open cabinet doors?". Click yes and look at drinks cabinet (since doors are now open). Take bottle and examine bottle (i.e. open it) to identify that it contains acid. Move to workshop. Examine sink to activate pop-up dialog "Do you want to plug sink?". Click yes and use bottle on sink. Use concrete on sink, concrete dissolves to reveal golden key. Examine sink to activate pop-up dialog "Do you want to unplug sink?". Click yes and take golden key.

2.1 Procedure

Twenty participants were recruited for experimentation. Participants were pooled from: research staff at University College London Interaction Centre; research staff at the Department of Computer Science at Queen Mary, University of London (CSQMUL); MSci students at CSQMUL. Each participant completed three tasks in total: one training task and two test tasks. The objective of the training task was to allow participants to familiarise themselves with the interface. Participants were allowed to refer to instructions that explained interface features during training. After the training task was successfully completed these instructions were removed. The training trial did not provide opportunities to self-report.

All tasks were isomorphic, in that the same number of problem solving moves were needed to solve task objectives. Although participants were set task objectives, the nature of the game ensured participants adopted an exploratory approach. Task objectives were presented on the ticker display, as described above, but executing these objectives required exploratory iterations. Four objectives were set for each task. In order to complete an objective, at least one set of actions had to be performed that were not explicitly specified in the instructions. This requirement could only be discovered during interaction. A correct way of solving problems was not specified. Participants were able to solve problems in any order, although all problems had to be solved to complete a task.

After the training task was completed, counterbalancing was performed as shown in Table 1. Participants performed either the Elective or Debrief self-report for each task. The 'Elective Report' required participants to click either the 'error button' or the 'exploratory button' at any time during problem solving (*see* Figure 1). When either button was clicked, the participant was asked to give a brief oral description of the error or exploratory move. The 'Debrief Report' required participants to review the moves they had performed in order to identify any errors and exploratory moves. After a task was completed, a trace of the moves they had made was presented on screen.

Table 1. Allocation of participants to conditions

Task Order	Report Mechanism Order	
	Elective then Debrief	Debrief then Elective
Task 1 then Task 2	S1...S5	S11...S15
Task 2 then Task 1	S6...S10	S16...S20

Unlike the training trial, the task trials were time limited. Participants were given fifteen minutes to complete each task trial. In a pilot study, four participants took an average of nine minutes thirteen seconds to complete each task trial. The imposed time limit was designed to further increase levels of cognitive load in an attempt to increase the number of errors. Participants were informed that when they provided a self-report the clock would stop and they would be given an extra minute as an incentive to self-report. They were informed that providing a self-report that did not relate to an error or exploratory move was unacceptable. It was decided that a participant should determine themselves whether a particular move should be described as an error or exploratory (or not at all) and, if so, how it should be described. It was anticipated that analysing different error reporting styles might provide an insight into the type of error or exploratory move. Before undertaking task trials participants were presented with a second set of paper-based instructions. Instructions included an illustration of where the self-report buttons were located on the interface, and included a guideline that clarified the difference between reporting erroneous and exploratory moves. Although a guideline was provided, participants were informed that these were only suggestions. Participants were encouraged to develop their own distinctions between what should be considered erroneous or exploratory.

For the debrief report, participants were asked to use the paper based map to trace back through the navigational decisions they made. Decisions to manipulate objects could be reviewed by identifying the associated 'action label' in the move description panel (*see* Figure 1). Participants did not have access to task objectives. It was hoped that this would encourage individuals to cognitively reconstruct the original context in which they performed an action. If an erroneous or exploratory move could be identified then participants were required to click the 'Error Button' or the 'Exploratory Button' and provide a brief verbal description. If a participant was unable to recall the context of their actions, they were prompted by the experimenter. The experimenter identified the relevant task objectives that were the focus of activities and reminded the participant. If this was not possible or the participant was still unable to understand the context, the experimenter moved the reviewing processes forward through to a point in the trace that a participant was able to identify with.

3   Results and Analysis

The overall aim was to discover whether self-reports provide useful information about the recognition of error. By performing a quantitative analysis (*see* Section 3.2) on the categories that emerged from a qualitative analysis (*see* Section 3.1), the following questions were addressed: What types of errors and exploratory moves can be self-reported? When comparing elective reports to debrief reports; can factors that allow or prevent the recognition of error during interaction be identified?

3.1 Qualitative Analysis

From the 262 reports elicited 27 (10%) provided insufficient information to allow a useful insight into an individual's thought processes because they did not comprehensibly describe the nature of the error or exploratory move; these reports are omitted. 48 (18%). A qualitative analysis identified two main self-report categories: 1) reports about goal-specific actions; 2) reports about device-specific actions. Goal-specific actions move an individual towards a goal. These types of actions can be considered to be 'salient' since they are always associated with performing recognized task goals. In contrast, device-specific actions do not move an individual towards a goal state though still remain critical to performing a task correctly. The requirement to perform device-specific actions often varies from device to device (e.g., some ATMs do not require users to press enter after entering a PIN). Examples of device-specific actions include: initializing a device before using it (e.g., on a Web page form: clicking on a text entry field before entering text); switching modes so that inputs are interpreted correctly (e.g., switching to non-predictive text mode on a mobile/cellular phone); and performing an additional step after completing a task that cannot be done prior to task completion (e.g., collecting the original document after making photocopies). Both the two main categories were assigned two sub-categories: a) learning; b) attending and remembering. Reports about learning were focused on the development of problem solving strategies. Reports on attending and remembering were about executing intentions.

Learning goal-specific actions: 48 reports (18%) – 29 Erroneous, 19 Exploratory. Clicking on the task objectives button activated the ticker. Each objective required a participant to engage in problem solving. It became apparent to participants that these objectives could not be addressed without exploration of the game environment. Participants discovered that in order to address task objectives, new aspects associated with task objectives had to be learnt. These aspects were not explicitly specified by the ticker. It was found that participants were able to describe learning requirements in terms of the relationships between game objects and locations. For example when participants recognised that achieving Objective 1 using Object 1 was impossible without finding Object 2 first, they were willing to report this inferred requirement. Learning took place either by undertaking exploratory interactions, or recognising why an interaction was erroneous and thereby reducing the problem state space i.e. by adopting a trial and error approach.

Remembering and attending to goal-specific actions: 39 reports (15%) – 28 Erroneous, 11 Exploratory. Participants reported situations where they thought that they might have forgotten to perform a required objective – for example, forgetting to retrieve Object 1 from Location 1 before going to Location 2. Participants also provided self-reports that suggested that a lack of attention was to blame for forgetting – for example, when participants knew what they should be doing but were somehow caught up in a different activity.

Learning device-specific actions: 68 reports (26%) – 26 Erroneous, 42 Exploratory. Participants were able to identify situations involving a mismatch between a reportable intention and perceived performance. This mismatch was attributed to a lack of knowledge associated with how to interact with objects when a participant believed they knew what they had to do – for example, when a participant knew they had to play a video tape but did not know how to operate the VCR. Participants used exploratory interactions and drew conclusions from errors in order to develop interaction strategies. Participants were willing to disclose when these strategies, learnt from previously successful interactions, did not work.

Remembering and attending to device-specific actions: 32 reports (13%) – 24 Erroneous, 8 Exploratory. Participants reported situations where they believed that they had forgotten to perform a required interaction – for example, forgetting to examine Object 1 (to change the object state) before using it on Object 2. Reports also suggested that errors or exploratory behaviour could have been avoided if the participant had paid more attention to feedback from the system. For example, when using the paper-based map, participants 'overshot' locations when navigating around the game due to a failure in attending to feedback about where they were.

Critically, the qualitative analysis also looked at the proportion of reports that were considered to be 'reasoned'. If the objective of the interaction was clearly stated, and the description identified one or more causal factors, then a report was classified as being reasoned (*see* Table 2). Example of a reasoned report (from Participant 7, Timed Task A, Self-report 5): 'After finding where a key is hidden I must remember to take the key, add it to my inventory, and not leave it in the room. Now that I have recognized this error hopefully I will not make it again'. Example of an unreasoned report (from Participant 11, Timed Task B, Self-report 6): 'I seem to have missed out a crucial step, maybe I'm not using the right command, but I'm not sure what happened'.

3.2 Quantitative Analysis

The aim of the quantitative analysis was to determine whether differences between the elective reports and the debrief reports existed. The numbers of reports in each category for each reporting mechanism are shown in Table 2. This table also shows the proportion of each report type that was classed as reasoned (expressed as a percentage).

Results that suggest elective reports are better than the debrief reports: Significantly more exploratory reports were made using 'elective report' than 'debrief report' (Wilcoxon signed-rank test, $Z = 2.160$, $p<0.05$). This suggests that participants were better able to recognize exploratory moves during interaction. Furthermore, elective reporting enabled a significantly greater proportion of reasoned exploratory reports to be made (Wilcoxon signed-rank test, $Z = 2.040$, $p<0.05$).

Results that suggest the debrief report is better than the elective report: The number of error reports made were evenly distributed between the elective and debrief mechanisms (Wilcoxon signed-rank test, $Z = 0.360$, $p>0.05$). However, a trend towards more reasoned error reports during debrief is observable. On closer inspection it is clear that this trend is due to the difficulty participants have when reasoning about device-specific errors during interaction. The proportion of reasoned device-specific self-reports associated with the debrief mechanism is significantly higher than the elective mechanism (Wilcoxon signed-rank test, $Z = 1.940$, $p<0.05$).

Table 2. Self-report categories and frequencies

	Number of **elective** reports	Percentage of reasoned **elective** reports	Number of **debrief** reports	Percentage of reasoned **debrief** reports
Exploratory (all)	55	51%	25	31%
Erroneous (all)	53	36%	54	68%
Goal-specific errors	28	50%	29	66%
Device-specific errors	25	20%	25	72%

4 General Discussion

It was found that reporting a wide range of both erroneous and exploratory interactions was possible. A qualitative analysis revealed two main report categories: 'goal-specific' and 'device-specific'. Two sub-categories: 'learning' and 'remembering / attending' were also identified. In order to provide a 'reasoned' self-report an individual must attribute their erroneous or exploratory behavior to causal factors. Identifying these factors is dependent on how well an individual can elucidate the context in which the erroneous or exploratory move occurred. A cognitive context defines the set of all possible interactions that an individual is capable of performing at that moment. The context in which an individual makes an error is likely to be different from the context in which an individual self-reports. Therefore during interaction, an individual must be able to reconstruct the series of actions that led to an error or exploratory move. This was not an easy process: only 51% of exploratory and 36% of erroneous reports provided a causal explanation.

When comparing the elective mechanism with the debrief mechanism no significant differences were associated with the frequency of erroneous reports. However, exploratory interactions were significantly more frequently reported using the elective self-report mechanism. Woods et al. [20] argued that self-reports can be biased by hindsight which prevents them from being a useful tool for understanding interaction. Our analyses showed that the elective mechanism was able to elicit a significantly wider range of exploratory move types than the debrief mechanism. This supports the notion that outcome knowledge (knowing how things turned out) biases self-reporting processes, especially when reporting exploratory moves.

Comparing the qualities of reports elicited using both elective and debrief mechanisms provided an insight into how individuals detect erroneous interactions. Interestingly analysis revealed that during interaction, the pervasiveness of device-specific errors was recognizable but underlying cognitive and attentional causes were not. The frequency of reporting these error types was identical: 50 elective reports, 50 debrief reports. However, only 20% of elective error reports associated with device-specific actions were reasoned accounts of error. During debrief reporting, participants were more able to provide a reasoned account of device-specific error. 72% of these reports were reasoned.

Based on these findings we argue that the error recognition process is dependent on cognitive context and the availability of environmental cues. Reporting device-specific errors during interaction is harder than when performing a debrief report because different environmental cues are 'salient'. During the debriefing session participants were required to debug their task performance. Critically, participants were not reminded of task objectives. Therefore, the only way of detecting erroneous moves was to recall intentions based on the availability of environmental cues. When performing a debrief report immediately after interaction, participants were able to remember intentions and were actively looking for environmental cues that could be used to execute those intentions. In the following example, a participant remembered that they had the intention to open a door but then made a device-specific error. An example of a debrief report (from Participant 16, Timed Task A, Self-report 2) is: 'Now I can see why I tried to use the wrong key to open the door (intention). I forgot that I had to examine the key first to check that it was the right key (device-specific error). When it did not work, I wrongly assumed that the door could not be opened using any key (erroneous intention formulated)'. For this error to be reportable a participant must recognize that they formulated an erroneous intention. This is not easily recognized during interaction since attention is allocated to achieving task goals and not on the retrospective analysis of previous actions that were unsuccessful.

During interaction, participants were better able to report causal accounts of goal-specific errors (50%) compared to when reporting device-specific errors (20%) (statistically significantly better). When engaged in problem solving participants reported switching between goals. In contrast to device-specific actions, goal-specific actions are salient. When occupied by multiple goal-specific activities it is easy to forget to make an attentional check. This type of error can be reported during interaction. Example (from Participant 10, Timed Task A, Self-report 5): 'I didn't realize that the Shells were already in my inventory. I wasn't really thinking about that objective at the time. I realize that I have made an error in not checking my inventory, I did not need to go and find any more Shells.'

In summary, participants found it easier to reason about goal-specific errors during interaction when compared to device-specific errors. When activities are seen to be essential to enabling progress towards a goal state, errors associated with these activities can be better explained. This is because they are more salient than activities that are required to perform an intention but do not themselves enable progress towards a goal (*see* [21] for an extended discussion on salience).

Participants used for experimentation were HCI experts. They are likely to be practiced in evaluating their own behaviour. Therefore, their ability to recognize and reason about error is representative of the 'best case scenario'. Novice users are likely to find it even harder to discover causes of error. A better understanding of "human error" is needed to help overcome problems of people assuming they are to blame for their inability to use poorly designed technology.

5 Conclusion

While "human error" may be the immediate and direct cause of failure, other factors such as system design are instrumental in facilitating or provoking error. Laboratory research suggests device-specific actions are the hardest type of actions to perform correctly [5]. Work reported in this paper has shown that although these types of errors are recognizable, they are the hardest types of actions to provide reasoned reports about during interaction. An inability to provide reasoned reports suggests that recovering from these types of errors is unlikely since their causes cannot be easily identified. Unfortunately, designing systems where device-specific actions are not required may not always be possible. Not all device-specific actions can be made goal-specific. For example: some devices need to be initialized before running a process; some devices require modes of operation; some require a post-completion step. Therefore, error recognition and recovery needs to be better supported by system designers. During debrief, participants were able to identify device-specific errors because they remembered previously formulated intentions and found environmental cues that allowed these intentions to be executed. During interaction these cues are not salient because participants are allocating their attention to the task, and do not develop retrospective accounts of actions that do not move them towards a goal state. Therefore, designers should attempt to modify visual salience. For example: start buttons should be 'grayed out' making them less visually salient if initialization steps (before pressing "start") may be required; modes should have visually salient indicators; post-completion steps should incorporate just-in-time cues [21]. Although the cognitive salience of an action for a particular individual may not always be captured by visual salience, when an error is recognized then the visual salience of these cues may help individuals to develop a more reasoned retrospective causal account.

Acknowledgments. This work is funded by EPSRC grants GR/S67494 and GR/S67500. We are grateful to all participants in our studies.

References

1. Byrne, M., Bovair, S.: A Working Memory Model of a Common Procedural Error. Cognitive Science 21(1), 31–69 (1997)
2. Reason, J.T.: Human Error. Cambridge University Press, Cambridge, UK (1990)
3. Reason, J.T., Lucas, D.A.: Using cognitive diaries to investigate naturally occurring memory blocks. In: Harris, J., Morris, P. (eds.) Everyday Memory, Actions and Absent-Mindedness, Academic Press, London (1984)
4. Johnson, C.W.: Representing the Impact of Time on Human Error and Systems Failure. Interacting with Computers 11, 53–86 (1998)
5. Gray, W.D.: The nature and processing of errors in interactive behavior. Cognitive Science 24(2), 205–248 (2000)
6. Back, J., Cheng, W.L., Dann, R., Curzon, P., Blandford, A.: Does being motivated to avoid procedural errors influence their systematicity? People and Computers XX - Engage. In: Proceedings of HCI 2006, London, UK, vol. 1 (2006)
7. Rasmussen, J., Jensen, A.: Mental procedures in real-life tasks: A case of electronic troubleshooting. Ergonomics 17, 293–307 (1974)

8. Hollnagel, E., Mancini, G., Woods, D.: Cognitive Engineering in Complex Dynamic Worlds. Academic Press, London (1988)
9. Hollnagel, E.: Cognitive reliability and error analysis method. Elsevier, Oxford, UK (1998)
10. Broadbent, D., Cooper, P., FitzGerald, P., Parkes, K.: The Cognitive Failures Questionnaire (CFQ) and its correlates. British Journal of Clinical Psychology 21, 1–16 (1982)
11. Ericsson, K.A., Simon, H.A.: Protocol analysis: Verbal reports as data (rev. ed.). MIT Press, Cambridge, MA (1993)
12. Perkins, D.: The mind's best work. Harvard University Press, Cambridge, MA (1981)
13. Altmann, E., Trafton, J.: Memory for goals: an activation-based model. Cognitive Science 26(1), 39–83 (2002)
14. Mandler, G.: Consciousness: Respectable, useful, and probably necessary. In: Solso, R. (ed.) Information Processing and Cognition, Erlbaum, NJ (1975)
15. Norman, D.: Categorization of action slips. Psychological Review 88(1), 1–15 (1981)
16. Miller, G.: Human memory and the storage of information. IRE Transactions on Information Theory, IT-2(3), 128–137 (1956)
17. Hoc, J., Leplat, J.: Evaluation of different modalities of verbalization in a sorting task. International Journal of Man-Machine Studies 18, 283–306 (1983)
18. Fischhoff, B.: Hindsight ≠ foresight: the effect of outcome knowledge on judgement under uncertainty. Journal of Experimental Psychology: Human Perception and Performance 1, 288–299 (1975)
19. Flach, J.M.: For those condemned to live in the future. Quality and Safety in Health Care 12, 304–312 (2003)
20. Woods, D. D., Johannesen, L. J., Cook, R. I., Sarter, N. B.: Behind human error: Cognitive systems, computers, complexity and hindsight. CSERIAC, 94–101 (1994)
21. Blandford, A., Back, J., Curzon, P., Li, S., Ruksenas, R.: Reasoning about human error by modeling cognition and interaction. In: Proc. Resilience Engineering Symposium (2006)

Usability Challenges in Security and Privacy Policy-Authoring Interfaces

Robert W. Reeder[1], Clare-Marie Karat[2], John Karat[2], and Carolyn Brodie[2]

[1] Carnegie Mellon University, 5000 Forbes Ave., Pittsburgh PA 15213, USA
reeder@cs.cmu.edu,
[2] IBM T.J. Watson Research Center, 19 Skyline Dr., Hawthorne NY 10532, USA
{ckarat, jkarat, brodiec}@us.ibm.com

Abstract. Policies, sets of rules that govern permission to access resources, have long been used in computer security and online privacy management; however, the usability of authoring methods has received limited treatment from usability experts. With the rise in networked applications, distributed data storage, and pervasive computing, authoring comprehensive and accurate policies is increasingly important, and is increasingly performed by relatively novice and occasional users. Thus, the need for highly usable policy-authoring interfaces across a variety of policy domains is growing. This paper presents a definition of the security and privacy policy-authoring task in general and presents the results of a user study intended to discover some usability challenges that policy authoring presents. The user study employed SPARCLE, an enterprise privacy policy-authoring application. The usability challenges found include supporting object grouping, enforcing consistent terminology, making default policy rules clear, communicating and enforcing rule structure, and preventing rule conflicts. Implications for the design of SPARCLE and of user interfaces in other policy-authoring domains are discussed.

Keywords: Policy, policy-authoring, privacy, security, usability.

1 Introduction

Policies are fundamental to providing security and privacy in applications such as file sharing, Web browsing, Web publishing, networking, and mobile computing. Such applications demand highly accurate policies to ensure that resources remain available to authorized access but not prone to compromise. Thus, one aspect of usability, very low error rates, is of the highest importance for user interfaces for authoring these policies. Security and privacy management tasks were previously left to expert system administrators who could invest the time to learn and use complex user interfaces, but now these tasks are increasingly left to end-users. Two non-expert groups of policy authors are on the rise. First are non-technical enterprise policy authors, typically lawyers or business executives, who have the responsibility to write policies governing an enterprise's handling of personal information [1]. Second are end-users, such as those who wish to set

C. Baranauskas et al. (Eds.): INTERACT 2007, LNCS 4663, Part II, pp. 141–155, 2007.

up their own spam filters, share files with friends but protect them from unwanted access [2,3,4], or share shipping information with Web merchants while maintaining privacy [5]. These two groups of non-expert users need to complete their tasks accurately, yet cannot be counted on to gain the expertise to tolerate a poorly designed or unnecessarily complex user interface.

Despite the need for usable policy-authoring interfaces, numerous studies and incidents have shown that several widely-used policy-authoring interfaces are prone to serious errors. The "Memogate" scandal, in which staffers from one political party on the United States Senate Judiciary Committee stole confidential memos from an opposing party, was caused in part by an inexperienced system administrator's error using the Windows NT interface for setting file permissions [6]. Maxion and Reeder showed cases in which users of the Windows XP file permissions interface made errors that exposed files to unauthorized access [4]. Good and Krekelberg showed that users unwittingly shared confidential personal files due to usability problems with the KaZaA peer-to-peer file-sharing application's interface for specifying shared files [3]. This evidence suggests that designing a usable policy-authoring interface is not trivial, and that designers could benefit from a list of potential vulnerabilities of which to be aware.

This paper reports the results of a user study which had the goal of identifying common usability challenges that all policy-authoring interface designers must address. The study employed SPARCLE [7], an application designed to support enterprise privacy policy authoring. However, the study was not intended to evaluate SPARCLE itself, but rather to reveal challenges that must be addressed in policy authoring in general. SPARCLE-specific usability issues aside, the study revealed five general usability challenges that any policy-authoring system must confront if it is to be usable:

1. **Supporting object grouping;**
2. **Enforcing consistent terminology;**
3. **Making default rules clear;**
4. **Communicating and enforcing rule structure;**
5. **Preventing rule conflicts.**

These challenges are explained in detail in the discussion in Sect. 6. Although these challenges have been identified from a user study in just one policy-authoring domain, namely enterprise privacy policies, a review of related work, presented in Sect. 7, confirms that the challenges identified here have been encountered in a variety of other policy-authoring domains, including file access control, firewalls, website privacy, and pervasive computing. This work, however, is the first we are aware of to describe policy-authoring applications as a general class and present usability challenges that are common to all.

2   Policy Authoring Defined

"Policy" can mean many things in different contexts, so it is important to give a definition that is germane to the present work on security and privacy policies.

For the purposes of this work, a policy is defined as a function that maps sets of elements (tuples) onto a discrete set of results, typically the set {ALLOW, DENY} (however, other result sets are possible; for example, Lederer et al. describe a policy-based privacy system in which tuples representing requests for a person's location are mapped to the set {PRECISE, APPROXIMATE, VAGUE, UNDISCLOSED} [8]). Elements are defined as the attributes relevant to a specific policy domain; the values those attributes can take on are referred to as element values. Element values may be literal values, such as the username "jsmith", or they may be expressions, such as "if the customer has opted in." Policies are expressed through rules, which are statements of specific mappings of tuples to results. Policy authoring is the task of specifying the element values in a domain, specifying rules involving those elements, and verifying that the policy comprised by those rules matches the policy that is intended.

In the privacy policy domain, for example, a policy maps tuples of the form (<user category>, <action>, <data category>, <purpose>, <condition>) to the set {ALLOW, DENY} [9]. Here, user category, action, data category, purpose, and condition are elements. ALLOW and DENY are results. An example privacy policy rule would map the tuple ("Marketing Reps", "use", "customer address", "mailing advertisements", "the customer has opted in") to the value ALLOW, indicating that marketing representatives can use the customer address data field for the purpose of mailing advertisements if the customer has opted in. Here, "Marketing Reps", "use", "customer address", "mailing advertisements", and "the customer has opted in" are element values.

To take another example, in the file permissions domain, a policy maps tuples of the form (<principal>, <action>, <file>) to the set ALLOW, DENY. An example rule might map ("jsmith", "execute", "calculator.exe") to the value DENY, indicating that the user jsmith cannot execute the program calculator.exe.

Since the rules in a policy may not cover all possible tuples, policy-based security and privacy systems typically have a default rule. For example, the SPARCLE system has the default rule that all 5-tuples of (<user category>, <action>, <data category>, <purpose>, <condition>) map to DENY. Additional rules are specified by policy authors and all author-specified rules map a 5-tuple to ALLOW. The default rule need not necessarily be a default DENY; a default ALLOW is also possible (policies with a default ALLOW rule are often called "blacklists", because any element value listed explicitly in the policy is denied access), or the default can vary according to some values in the tuples (for instance, a default rule might state that all accesses to shared files on a computer are allowed by default to local users but denied by default to remote users). Similarly, user-specified rules need not necessarily map exclusively to ALLOW or exclusively to DENY; it is possible to allow users to specify rules that map to either ALLOW or DENY. However, policy systems that allow users to specify both types of rules introduce the potential for rule conflicts, which can be a significant source of user difficulty [10,2,4].

3   The SPARCLE Policy Workbench

In the present work, policy authoring usability was investigated through a user study in which participants used the SPARCLE Policy Workbench application. SPARCLE is a Web-based application for enterprise privacy policy management. The application includes a front-end user interface for authoring privacy policies using a combination of natural language and structured lists. While the current embodiment of SPARCLE is tailored for the privacy policy domain, the user interface was designed with an eye toward supporting policy authoring in other domains such as file access control. From a research perspective, the two inter-action paradigms supported by SPARCLE, natural language and structured list entry, can as easily be applied to privacy policy management as to file, network, system, email, or other policy management. Thus SPARCLE is a suitable tool for studying policy authoring in the general sense. Portions of the SPARCLE user interface relevant to the present study are described below; a more complete description of the SPARCLE system can be found elsewhere [1].

One way to write policy rules in SPARCLE is to use the natural language interface on the Natural Language Authoring page. The Natural Language Authoring page contains a rule guide, which is a template that reads, "[User Category(ies)] can [Action(s)] [Data Category(ies)] for the purpose(s) of [Purpose(s)] if [(optional) Condition(s)]." This template indicates what elements are expected in a valid rule. The Natural Language Authoring page further contains a large textbox for entering rule text. Policy authors can type rules, in natural language, directly into the textbox. For example, a rule might read, "Customer Service Reps, Pharmacists, and Billing Reps can collect and use customer name and date of birth to confirm identity." SPARCLE has functionality for parsing an author's rules so that it can extract rule element values automatically from the author's text. When parsing has completed, the user proceeds to the Structured Authoring page to see the structured format of the policy.

The Structured Authoring page, shown in Fig. 1, shows the results of parsing each policy rule. When SPARCLE parses each policy rule, it saves the elements (i.e., user categories, actions, data categories, purposes, and conditions) found in that rule. The elements are reconstructed into sentences and shown next to radio buttons in a list of rules. The lower half of the Structured Authoring page contains lists of element values, one list for each of the five elements of a privacy policy rule. These lists contain some pre-defined, common element values (e.g., "Billing Reps" as a user category, "collect" as an action, or "address" as a data category) as well as all element values defined by the policy author and found by the parser in rules written on the Natural Language Authoring page. Policy authors can also alter these element value lists directly by adding or deleting elements. When a rule is selected from the list of rules at the top of the Structured Authoring page, all of the element values in that rule are highlighted in the lists of element values. Policy authors can edit rules by selecting different element values from the lists. It is also possible to create rules from scratch on the Structured Authoring page.

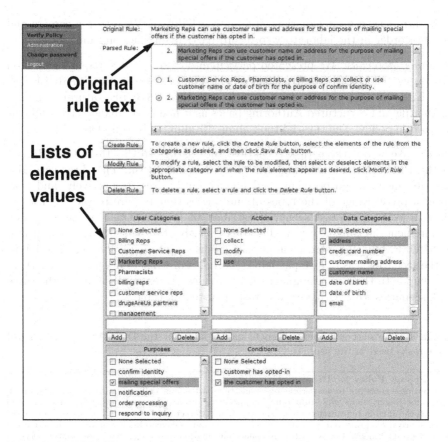

Fig. 1. SPARCLE's Structured Authoring page. Policy authors can create or edit rules on this page by selecting from the lists of element values in the lower half of the page.

4   Policy Authoring Usability Evaluation

We conducted a laboratory user study using the SPARCLE application to identify usability problems experienced by users in policy-authoring tasks.

4.1   User Study Method

Participants. We recruited twelve participants, consisting of research staff and summer interns at a corporate research facility, for the user study. Participants varied in age from 20 to 49; four were female. Since participants did not have experience authoring privacy policies or using SPARCLE, we considered them novice users for our purposes. Participants were compensated for their participation with a certificate for a free lunch.

Apparatus. Participants accessed SPARCLE through the Internet Explorer web browser on a computer running Windows XP. SPARCLE ran on a server on a local intranet, so users experienced no network delays. We set up a camera and voice recorder in the laboratory to record participants' actions and words.

Training Materials. We presented participants with a 4-page paper tutorial on how to use SPARCLE to give them a basic introduction to the SPARCLE system. The tutorial walked participants through the SPARCLE Natural Language Authoring and Structured Authoring pages as it had participants write and edit a two-rule policy. The tutorial took about 15 minutes to complete.

Tasks. We wrote three task scenarios: the "DrugsAreUs" task, the "Bureau of the Public Debt" task, and the "First Finance" task. The three scenarios describe medical, government, and finance enterprises, respectively, and thus cover a broad range of the types of enterprises that require privacy policies in the real world. Each task scenario described an enterprise and its privacy policy requirements in language that did not explicitly state rules to be written into SPARCLE, but suggested content that might go into explicit rules. The intent of the scenarios was to give participants an idea of what to do, but to have them come up with their own language for their rules. An example of one of the three task scenarios, the "DrugsAreUs" task, is listed in Table 1.

Table 1. The task statement given to participants for the DrugsAreUs task, one of three tasks used in the user study

The Privacy Policy for DrugsAreUs
Our business goals are to answer customer questions when they call in (Customer Service), fulfill orders for prescriptions while protecting against drug interactions (Pharmacists), and to provide customers valuable information about special offers (Marketing). In order to make sure our customers' privacy is protected, we make the following promises concerning the privacy of information we collect at DrugsAreUs. We will only collect information necessary to provide quality service. We will ask the customers to provide us with full name, permanent address and contact information such as telephone numbers and email addresses, and a variety of demographic and personal information such as date of birth, gender, marital status, social security number, and current medications taken. On occasions where we need to verify a customer's identity, Customer Service Reps will only use the social security number to do so. Our pharmacists will use the current medication information when processing new orders to check for drug interactions.
We will make reports for our internal use that include age and gender breakdowns for specific drug prescriptions, but will not include other identifying information in the reports and will delete them after five years. For example, our research department might access customer data to produce reports of particular drug use by various demographic groups.

Procedure. We asked participants to complete a demographic survey before beginning the user study. We then gave participants the SPARCLE tutorial and asked them to complete it. We provided help as needed as the participants worked through the tutorial. After they had completed the tutorial, we instructed participants to think aloud during the study [11]. We then presented participants with tasks. Each participant was presented with two of the three task scenarios and asked to complete them one at a time. We instructed participants to imagine they were the Chief Privacy Officer of the enterprise described in each scenario and to use SPARCLE to author the rules they thought were necessary to protect personal information held by the enterprise while still allowing the enterprise to carry out its business. We counter-balanced the selection and presentation of the scenarios across participants so that each scenario was presented to eight participants and each scenario was the first scenario presented to four participants and the second scenario presented to four other participants.

Data Collection. The data we collected included text of rules written, video of participants and the computer screen on which they worked, think-aloud audio, and results of the demographic survey.

4.2   Data Analysis Method

We performed two data analyses. In the first analysis, we looked at the rules participants wrote to find errors in rules. In the second analysis, we reviewed videos and think-aloud audio data to find any additional incidents of errors and usability problems not found in the first analysis.

First Analysis: Errors in Rules In the first analysis, we read through participants' final rules and considered their implementability. An implementable privacy rule was defined as a rule that can be unambiguously interpreted by an implementer, which is a human or machine that produces the actionable code to carry out automated enforcement of a policy's intentions. With respect to implementability, we identified seven errors. Two of these errors, undetected parser errors and unsaved rule changes, are system-specific issues to SPARCLE, and are not further discussed here, because the objective of this work was to identify errors that might occur in any interface for policy-authoring. The five non-system-specific errors we found were group ambiguities, terminology mismatches, negative rules, missing elements, and rule conflicts. We identified and counted occurrences of each type of error. The five errors, criteria used to identify each type of error, and examples of each error are below:

1. **Group ambiguity:** Composite terms, i.e., terms that represented a set of other terms, were used in the same policy as the terms they apparently represented. This was considered an error for implementation because it was often not clear exactly which terms were represented by the composite term. For example, one rule said, "DrugsAreUs can collect necessary information...," in which "necessary information" is a composite term presumably representing data referred to in other rules such as "customer mailing address," and "current medications taken." However, it is not immediately clear just what data is referred to by "necessary information." As another example, one rule contained both the terms "contact information" and "permanent address." This would imply that, contrary to common usage, "permanent address" is not part of "contact information." An implementer could easily be confused as to whether the term "contact information" used in a different rule included permanent address data or not.

2. **Terminology mismatch:** Multiple terms were used to refer to the same object within the same policy. Examples of terminology mismatches included "email address" and "email addres"; "Financial control" and "Finacial control"; "gender" and "gender information"; "properly reporting information to the IRS" and "providing required reports to the IRS."
3. **Negative rule:** A rule's action contained the word "not". Although SPAR-CLE is a default-deny policy system, implying that it is only necessary to specify what is allowed, some participants attempted to write negative rules, i.e., rules that prohibited access. These rules are unnecessary, and can lead to confusion on the part of an implementer who is expecting only positive rules. An example of a negative rule was, "Bureau of the Public Debt can not use persistent cookies...."
4. **Missing element:** A rule was missing a required element. The missing element was usually purpose. An example of a rule with no purpose was "Customer Service Reps can ask full name, permanent address, and medication taken."
5. **Rule conflict:** Two different rules applied to the same situation. Only one rule conflict was observed in our study. SPARCLE's policy semantics avoid most potential for rule conflict by taking the union of all access allowed by the rules except in the case of conditions, for which the intersection of all applicable conditions is taken. The one observed example of a rule conflict included the rules, "Customer Service Reps can access customer name for the purpose of contacting a customer **if the customer has submitted a request**," and "Customer Service Reps can access customer name for the purpose of contacting a customer **if the customer has expressed a concern**." Since the user category ("Customer Service Reps"), action ("access"), data category ("customer name"), and purpose ("contacting a customer") all match in these rules, taking the intersection of conditions would imply that "Customer Service Reps can access customer name for the purpose of contacting a customer" only when both "the customer has submitted a request" and "the customer has expressed a concern" are true. Thus, in the case that the customer has submitted a request but not expressed a concern, the first rule would seem to apply but is in conflict with the latter rule.

Second Analysis: Review of Video and Think-Aloud Data. In the second analysis, we reviewed video of user sessions and transcripts of user think-aloud data for critical incidents which indicated errors or other usability problems. We defined critical incidents in the video as incidents in which users created a rule with one of the errors indicated in the first analysis but subsequently corrected it. We defined critical incidents in the think-aloud data as incidents in which users expressed confusion, concern, or an interface-relevant suggestion. Once we had identified critical incidents, we classified them according to the error or usability problem that they indicated. While critical incidents were caused by a variety of SPARCLE-specific usability problems, only those incidents relevant to the five general policy-authoring rule errors identified in the first data analysis are reported here. There were no critical incidents that indicated general rule errors not already identified in the first data analysis; thus, the second data analysis simply served to confirm the results of the first through an independent data stream.

Below are some typical examples of user statements classified as critical incidents, followed by the error under which we classified them in parentheses:

- "I don't want to have to write out a long list of types of information without being able to find a variable that represents that information to be able to label that information. In this case the label might be personal information defined to include customer name, address, and phone number." (Group ambiguity)
- "I'm not sure how to do negations in this template." (Negative rule)
- "It says I must specify at least one purpose, and I say, 'why do I have to specify at least one purpose?' " (Missing element)

5   Results

Results from the two data analyses, combined by adding the unique error instances found in the second analysis to those already found in the first analysis, are shown in Fig. 2. The errors in Fig. 2 are listed according to total frequency of occurrence, and within each error, are broken down by the task scenario in which they occurred. Since 2 of the 3 task scenarios were presented to each of 12 participants, there were 24 total task-sessions, 8 of each of the three scenarios. Thus, for example, the "group ambiguity" bar in Fig. 2 indicates that group ambiguity errors occurred in 11 of 24 task-sessions, including 5 of 8 "DrugsAreUs" sessions, 1 of 8 "Bureau of the Public Debt" sessions, and 5 of 8 "First Finance" sessions.

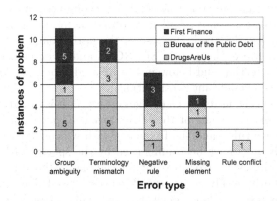

Fig. 2. Results of first and second data analyses, showing instances of five types of errors, broken down by task scenario in which they were observed. There were 24 total task-sessions, 8 sessions for each of the three tasks.

Of the five errors, group ambiguity errors were observed most frequently; a total of 11 instances of group ambiguity errors were found. The other errors, in order of frequency of occurrence, were terminology mismatches, negative rules, missing elements, and rule conflicts.

6 Discussion

The errors that participants made in this study suggest the five general policy-authoring usability challenges listed in the introduction to this paper. The challenges arise from inherent difficulties in the task of articulating policies; however, good interface design can help users overcome these difficulties. Group ambiguities suggest that users have a need for composite terms, but also need support to define these terms unambiguously. Terminology mismatches suggest the need for the interface to enforce, or at least provide some support for, consistent terminology. Negative rules are not necessary in SPARCLE's default-deny policy-based system, so users' attempts to write negative rules suggest that they did not know or did not understand the default rule. Missing elements are caused by users' failure to understand or remember the requirement for certain rule elements. Finally, rule conflicts are a known problem that a good interface can help address.

The identification of these five policy-authoring usability challenges is the primary result of this study. One of these challenges, communicating and enforcing rule structure, had already been anticipated, and SPARCLE's rule guide on the Natural Language Authoring page was designed to guide policy authors to write rules with correct structure. Rule conflicts, a well-known problem in policy-authoring domains, were also anticipated. SPARCLE, in fact, was designed to prevent rule conflicts by using a default-deny system and requiring that policy authors only write rules that mapped exclusively to ALLOW. It is only in the optional condition element that a conflict is possible in SPARCLE rules, so it was not surprising that only one rule conflict was observed in the present study. The remaining three usability challenges observed were largely unanticipated when SPARCLE was designed. Because of the fairly common failure to anticipate some of the five challenges, in SPARCLE and in other designs discussed above in the Introduction and below in the Related Work, the identification of these challenges is a significant contribution.

Before discussing the usability challenges observed, it is worth considering one methodological concern. Some of the errors revealed, particularly group ambiguities and negative rules, and the frequency with which they were observed in the present study, may have been influenced by the specific task scenarios presented to users. However, errors, except for the one instance of a rule conflict, are distributed fairly evenly across the three tasks, so it does not appear that any one task was responsible for eliciting a particular error type. Furthermore, the task scenarios were written based on experience with real enterprise policy authors and real enterprise scenarios, so the errors revealed are very likely to come up in the real world. However, the frequency values reported here should not be taken as necessarily indicative of the relative frequency of occurrence of these errors in real-world policy work.

Having identified five usability challenges for policy-authoring domains, it is worth discussing how these challenges might be addressed. Each challenge is discussed in turn below.

6.1 Supporting Object Grouping

Group ambiguities were caused by users not understanding what terms covered what other terms. Many solutions already exist to help users with tasks that involve grouped elements. Perhaps the most prominent grouping solution is the file system hierarchy browser. A hierarchy browser allows users to create groups, name groups, add objects to and remove objects from groups, and view group memberships. Hierarchy browsers may often be appropriate for policy-authoring tasks. However, hierarchical grouping may not always be sufficient. In file permissions, for instance, system users often belong to multiple, partially-overlapping groups. Any of a variety of means for visualizing sets or graphs may be useful here; also needed is a means for interacting with such a visualization to choose terms to go into policy rules. What visualizations and interaction techniques would best support grouping for policy authoring is an open problem.

6.2 Enforcing Consistent Terminology

Ambiguous terminology is nearly inevitable, but there are certainly ways to mitigate the most common causes, which, in this study, included typos and users' forgetting what term they had previously used to refer to a concept. A spell-checker could go a long way toward eliminating many typos, like "socail security number", in which "social security number" was obviously intended. A domain-specific thesaurus could help resolve abbreviations, aliases, and cases in which the same object necessarily has multiple names. For example, a thesaurus could indicate that "SSN" expands to "social security number", and that "e-mail", "email", and "email address" all represent the same thing. A display of previously used terms for an object might help users remember to reuse the same term when referring to that object again; SPARCLE's structured lists are an example of such a display. In some policy-authoring domains, the terminology problem may be resolved for the policy author by pre-defining terms. For example, in file permissions, the actions that can be performed on a file are typically pre-defined by the file system (e.g., read, write, and execute).

6.3 Making Default Rules Clear

Showing default rules may be a trivial matter of including the default rule in interface documentation or in the interface display itself. However, the concept of a default rule and why it exists may itself be confusing. One method of illustrating the default rule to users is to present a visualization showing what happens in unspecified cases [4]. SPARCLE includes such a visualization, although it is not onscreen at the same time a user is authoring rules [12].

6.4   Communicating and Enforcing Rule Structure

SPARCLE already does a fairly good job of enforcing rule structure. Participants in the present study recovered from forgotten purpose elements in 2 out of 5 cases due to SPARCLE's prominent display of the phrase "None Selected" as the purpose element when no purpose was specified; a corresponding "Missing Purpose" error dialog also helped. Other interaction techniques like wizards, in which users are prompted for each element in turn, would likely get even higher rates of correct structure. Which of these techniques or combination of techniques leads to the fewest missed elements will be the subject of future work.

6.5   Preventing Rule Conflicts

Rule conflicts were rare in this study; the one observed conflict can be attributed to a lack of awareness about the semantics of the condition element. However, rule conflicts have been shown to be a serious usability problem in past work in other policy-authoring domains [10,2,4]. Clearly, interfaces need to make users aware of conflicts, and if possible, show them how conflicts can be resolved.

Rule conflicts have been the focus of some non-interface-related theoretical work [13,14]; algorithms exist for detecting conflicts in a variety of policy contexts. This work could be leveraged by interface designers. However, the means for presenting policy conflicts to authors have yet to be evaluated. A few visualizations and interfaces have attempted to do this, such as those discussed below in the Related Work [10,2,4], but it is not clear whether they succeed at conveying conflicts, the need to resolve them, and the means to resolve them to users.

7   Related Work

Although the present study looked for usability challenges in just one policy-authoring domain, related work in other domains confirms that the usability challenges identified here are general problems encountered in a variety of policy-authoring domains. However, past work has only identified the challenges as unique to specific domains, rather than as part of the more general policy-authoring problem.

A need for supporting groups of element values has been found in several domains. Lederer et al. found a need for supporting groups of people in a user interface for setting location-disclosure policies in a pervasive computing environment so that policies could be scaled to environments with many people [15]. They present an interface for setting location-disclosure policies, but mention support for grouping as future work. The IBM P3P Policy Editor is a policy-authoring interface that uses hierarchical browsers to show users how Platform for Privacy Preferences (P3P) element values are grouped [16]. Zurko et al.'s Visual Policy Builder, an application for authoring access-control policies, allowed authors to create and label groups and to set constraints on groups to prevent conflicts due to group overlaps [17].

Finding good terminology and using it consistently has long been recognized as a problem for virtually every user interface [18]. In the policy-authoring area, Cranor et al. acknowledged the difficulty of finding comprehensible terminology in developing an interface for allowing users to specify what privacy practices they prefer in websites with which they interact [5]. Good and Krekelberg found that the use of four different terms for the same folder confused users in an interface for specifying shared folders in the KaZaA peer-to-peer file-sharing application [3].

Communicating default rules has been shown to be a problem in setting file permissions by both Maxion and Reeder [4] and Cao and Iverson[2]. Cranor et al. also discuss their efforts to come up with an appropriate default rule and communicate that rule to users [5]. Good and Krekelberg found that that KaZaA did not adequately communicate default shared files and folders to users [3].

The above-referenced independent studies of file-permissions-setting interfaces, Maxion and Reeder [4] and Cao and Iverson [2], also found that users have difficulty detecting, understanding, and correcting rule conflicts in access control systems. Zurko et al. considered the problem of conveying rule conflicts to users in their design of the Visual Policy Builder [17]. Al-Shaer and Hamed acknowledge the difficulties that rule conflicts cause for authors of firewall policies [10]. Besides human-computer interaction work, some theoretical work has acknowledged the problem of rule conflicts and found algorithms for detecting conflicts in policies [13,14].

Lederer et al. report five design pitfalls of personal privacy policy-authoring applications that do not include the same usability challenges listed here, but do raise the important question of whether configuration-like policy-authoring interfaces are needed at all [19]. They argue that in personal privacy in pervasive computing environments, desired policies are so dependent on context, that users cannot or will not specify them in advance. While their argument is undoubtedly correct for some domains, there remains a need for up-front policy authoring in many situations: the system administrator setting up a default policy for users, the policy maker in an enterprise writing a privacy policy to govern how data will be handled within the organization, and even the end-user who does not want to be bothered with constant requests for access, but prefers to specify up-front what access is allowed.

8   Conclusion

In order to be usable, policy-authoring interfaces, which are needed for a wide variety of security and privacy applications, must address the five usability challenges identified in the user study described in this paper: supporting object grouping, enforcing consistent terminology, making default policy rules clear, communicating and enforcing rule structure, and preventing rule conflicts. Some of these issues have been addressed before in domain-specific policy-authoring interfaces and elsewhere, but all might benefit from novel, general interaction techniques. As more policy authoring interfaces for users are created to fit the variety of applications that depend on accurate policies, researchers and designers would benefit from considering the five usability challenges discussed in this paper and creating innovative interaction techniques to address them.

References

1. Karat, J., Karat, C.-M., Brodie, C., Feng, J.: Privacy in information technology: Designing to enable privacy policy management in organizations. International Journal of Human-Computer Studies 63(1-2), 153–174 (2005)
2. Cao, X., Iverson, L.: Intentional access management: Making access control usable for end-users. In: Proceedings of the Second Symposium on Usable Privacy and Security (SOUPS 2006), New York, NY, pp. 20–31. ACM Press, New York (2006)
3. Good, N.S., Krekelberg, A.: Usability and privacy: a study of Kazaa P2P file-sharing. In: Proceedings of the ACM SIGCHI Conference on Human Factors in Computing Systems(CHI 2003), New York, NY, April 2003, pp. 137–144. ACM Press, New York (2003)
4. Maxion, R.A., Reeder, R.W.: Improving user-interface dependability through mitigation of human error. International Journal of Human-Computer Studies 63(1-2), 25–50 (2005)
5. Cranor, L.F., Guduru, P., Arjula, M.: User interfaces for privacy agents. ACM Transactions on Computer-Human Interaction 13(2), 135–178 (2006)
6. U.S. Senate Sergeant at Arms: Report on the investigation into improper access to the Senate Judiciary Committee's computer system (2004), available at http://judiciary.senate.gov/testimony.cfm?id=1085\&wit_id=2514
7. Karat, C.-M., Karat, J., Brodie, C., Feng, J.: Evaluating interfaces for privacy policy rule authoring. In: Proceedings of the ACM SIGCHI Conference on Human Factors in Computing Systems(CHI 2006), New York, NY, pp. 83–92. ACM Press, New York (2006)
8. Lederer, S., Mankoff, J., Dey, A.K., Beckmann, C.P.: Managing personal information disclosure in ubiquitous computing environments. Technical Report UCB-CSD-03-1257, University of California, Berkeley, Berkeley, CA (2003), available at http://www.eecs.berkeley.edu/Pubs/TechRpts/2003/CSD-03-1257.pdf
9. Ashley, P., Hada, S., Karjoth, G., Powers, C., Schunter, M.: Enterprise Privacy Architecture Language (EPAL 1.2). W3C Member Submission 10-Nov-2003 (2003), available at http:www.w3.org/Submission/EPAL
10. Al-Shaer, E.S., Hamed, H.H.: Firewall Policy Advisor for anomaly discovery and rule editing. In: Marshall, A., Agoulmine, N. (eds.) MMNS 2003. LNCS, vol. 2839, pp. 17–30. Springer, Heidelberg (2003)
11. Ericsson, K.A., Simon, H.A.: Protocol Analysis: Verbal Reports as Data. Revised edn., MIT Press, Cambridge, MA (1993)
12. Brodie, C., Karat, C.M., Karat, J.: An empirical study of natural language parsing of privacy policy rules using the SPARCLE policy workbench. In: Proceedings of the 2006 Symposium on Usable Privacy and Security (SOUPS 2006), New York, NY, July 2006, pp. 8–19. ACM Press, New York (2006)
13. Agrawal, D., Giles, J., Lee, K.-W., Lobo, J.: Policy ratification. In: Proceedings of the Sixth IEEE International Workshop on Policies for Distributed Systems and Networks (POLICY 2005), Los Alamitos, CA, June 2005, pp. 223–232. IEEE Computer Society Press, Los Alamitos (2005)

14. Fisler, K., Krishnamurthi, S., Meyerovich, L.A., Tschantz, M.C.: Verification and change-impact analysis of access-control policies. In: ICSE 2005, pp. 196–205. IEEE Computer Society Press, Los Alamitos (2005)
15. Lederer, S., Hong, J.I., Jiang, X., Dey, A.K., Landay, J.A., Mankoff, J.: Towards everyday privacy for ubiquitous computing. Technical Report UCB-CSD-03-1283, University of California, Berkeley, Berkeley, CA (2003), available at http://www.eecs.berkeley.edu/Pubs/TechRpts/2003/CSD-03-1283.pdf
16. Cranor, L.F.: Web Privacy with P3P. O'Reilly, Sebastopol, CA (2002)
17. Zurko, M.E., Simon, R., Sanfilippo, T.: A user-centered, modular authorization service built on an RBAC foundation. In: Proceedings 1999 IEEE Symposium on Security and Privacy, Los Alamitos, CA, May 1999, pp. 57–71. IEEE Computer Society Press, Los Alamitos (1999)
18. Molich, R., Nielsen, J.: Improving a human-computer dialogue. Communications of the ACM 33(3), 338–348 (1990)
19. Lederer, S., Hong, J., Dey, A.K., Landay, J.: Personal privacy through understanding and action: Five pitfalls for designers. Personal and Ubiquitous Computing 8(6), 440–454 (2004)

Understanding Compliance to Privacy Guidelines Using Text-and Video-Based Scenarios

Abdullah Al Mahmud[1], Maurits Kaptein[1], Oliver Moran[1],
Evelien van de Garde-Perik[2], and Panos Markopoulos[2]

[1] User-System Interaction Program, Eindhoven University of Technology
P.O. Box 513, 5600 MB Eindhoven, The Netherlands
{A.Al-Mahmud, M.C.Kaptein, O.P.Moran}@tm.tue.nl
[2] Department of Industrial Design, Eindhoven University of Technology
P.O. Box 513, 5600 MB Eindhoven, The Netherlands
{e.m.v.d.garde, p.markopoulos}@tue.nl

Abstract. Privacy is a major concern for the design and user acceptance of pervasive technology. Investigating privacy poses several methodological challenges. A popular approach involves surveying reactions of people to scenarios that highlight privacy issues. This paper examines the validity of this approach. It reports an experiment that compared people's ability to correctly judge compliance to privacy principles when scenarios are presented in video versus textual form. It was found that such privacy-related concepts are hard to understand, leading to a large number of erroneous judgments regardless of medium and that interpretation varied across media. Comprehension in such studies can be improved, if a text scenario is preceded by a video-based version.

1 Introduction

Developments in the related fields of ubiquitous computing, pervasive computing and ambient intelligence have been paralleled by warnings for caution against invading people's privacy [25], considered as an interpersonal need or even an individual right. A growing body of research has been pursuing the development of privacy enhancing technologies, interaction design principles, and design methods that can help ensure people's privacy. Recently researchers into privacy and ubicomp have come to recognize the methodological difficulties for researching privacy in this domain and successive workshops at international conferences were organized on this topic [22, 23].

There are several serious methodological difficulties in studying privacy. Inquiry into user preferences is not sufficient to guide design, and privacy requirements tend to vary a lot depending on the technological and societal context in which an application is used, let alone its value to the individual. A well-known issue concerns the apparent discrepancy between privacy-related attitudes and behaviors, which has been reported in several different empirical investigations of privacy preferences, e.g., [2, 5, 12]. An important reason for this, which is well known in psychological studies concerning attitudes, is that attitudes expressed outside a specific context and without taking into account the context specific difficulty of a particular privacy-related behavior are very poor predictors of actual behavior [4]. In order to make reported

C. Baranauskas et al. (Eds.): INTERACT 2007, LNCS 4663, Part II, pp. 156–168, 2007.

attitudes regarding privacy correspond better to actual privacy related behaviors, one possibility is to contextualize inquiry with the use of scenarios, i.e. to inquire regarding particular actions in the context of a specific situation described in a scenario.

Human-computer interaction research and interaction design practice have endorsed scenarios as a means to contextualize inquiry and design activities (e.g., see [7]). Scenarios for human-computer interaction are typically delivered as narrative texts, but are often also shown as storyboards or short videos. Indeed several recent empirical investigations concerning privacy and ubiquitous computing systems are based on participant surveys about their reactions to scenarios delivered to them in textual or video form [1, 13, 24]. Textual scenarios were used in [1] as a means to investigate how people would respond to situations where personal information is collected. Participants were asked about their concerns through specific scenarios involving online data collection. One scenario, for example, asked respondents whether they would be more or less likely to provide data to a Web site with a privacy policy that explained that their information would be removed from the site's database if they did not return to the site for three months. Video scenarios were used in [24] to illustrate RFID technology, its benefits and drawbacks in a neutral way. Two groups of participants were shown the same video, except for the PET available to consumers for controlling their privacy. Afterwards, participants were questioned about perceived control in the scenario presented to them.

In this study, it is examined whether the interpretation of scenarios relating to privacy are affected by the medium in which the scenario is delivered. In the following section, the context of this study and the reasons behind the hypothesis that a medium effect exists with respect to the ability of informants to discuss privacy-related issues are presented.

The study presented is useful to HCI in two ways. The results of this study provide insight into the reliability of text or video scenarios for surveying attitudinal responses to different system designs. Secondly, the results provide quantitative evidence regarding the difficulty of conveying privacy related functions and policies to users; earlier research has shown that users often do not read such policies [17, 19] or are not able to comprehend them [15, 19].

1.1 Privacy Guidelines for Embedded User Modeling

A growing body of work in the domain of ubiquitous networked applications concerns privacy, including analyses of fundamental concepts [21, 6] and discussions of different cases. Researchers have proposed collections of design principles and guidelines for ensuring privacy through interaction design. Jiang and Landay [16] proposed principles for regulating the flow of information in ubiquitous systems. Chung et al. [8] proposed a set of design patterns to solve privacy problems. Others have adopted principles originating from legislation for technical systems and privacy, such as the five principles of Fair Information Practices [9, 18].

For the purpose of this study the focus is on one such set of guidelines, namely those by the OECD [20]. These guidelines were originally intended for assisting governments, business and consumer representatives in shaping policies and practices that protect privacy and personal data while preventing unnecessary restrictions to data flows across borders, both on- and off-line. OECD guidelines are the basis of the discussion by M. Langheinrich on designing for privacy in ubiquitous computing [18]. This study is often cited and has significant influence over work on privacy and ubiquitous computing/ambient intelligence. However, it did not attempt to provide empirical evidence to demonstrate that these principles do indeed lead to higher acceptance of such systems by end-users. The same holds for the other sets of principles cited above; currently they represent hypotheses that need to be validated empirically or through repeated application in practice.

The broader research aims to complement that work by providing empirical evidence regarding the importance of compliance to the OECD guidelines for users. In a recent study reported elsewhere [10], subjects were required to indicate their preferences regarding the relative importance of individual OECD guidelines by means of a scenario relating to tele-monitoring for healthcare. As a methodological precaution, a pre-study experiment was conducted, discussed in [11], where the ability of participants to answer correctly whether a particular system complied to a particular guideline or not was tested. Surprisingly, this pilot study revealed a very limited comprehension of the system's privacy policy. While this was improved substantially by rephrasing the text scenarios in the eventual experiment, many participants still could not recognize the system's privacy policy, even though the scenario contained the guideline text almost verbatim.

Based on this study it was suspected that the subtleties of the wording of OECD guidelines are not understood with common sense; people tend to make assumptions regarding the use of their personal information when they are told the purpose of its collection, or to assume policies regarding purpose by a description of the nature of information collected, etc. Further, it was suspected that a minimalist scenario lacking a narrative structure and a believable context is hard to understand. Hopefully, a video scenario, (which is typically used in informal evaluations with during interviews or focus groups to assess how a particular technology might be used), could provide a more compelling and easily comprehensible version of the scenario and would allow users to better express their preferences. (See for example, the study by Spiekermann [24] where privacy preferences were solicited after informants viewed two video scenarios for an RFID-based automated supermarket check-out). It was set to test experimentally whether providing a video-scenario would improve matters. A formal experiment was conducted to test these hypotheses. The main aim was to compare the degree of variance in interpretation across video- and text-based scenarios.

2 Method

The experiment involved comparing the medium (video or text) in which a scenario was presented to participants. A within-subject design was chosen, so participants were exposed to both the text-based and video-based scenario. Some participants were interviewed face-to-face and others over the internet. Participants were given judgment tasks, i.e. to indicate whether a given scenario complied or not with the guidelines presented to them in a shorthand manner. For each guideline, there was a correct answer. The dependent variable was the correctness of the response for each guideline and the overall correctness of the interpretation for each scenario.

2.1 Apparatus and Materials

The original text descriptions of the eight OECD guidelines [20] were adapted in such a way that they cover the essence of each guideline, without being too elaborate and especially omitting those parts of the guideline that are meaningful only as legal text rather than as design guidance. In this spirit, also the guideline of accountability was omitted, as it serves a legal purpose stipulating compliance with all other guidelines.

In this study Collection Limitation (CL) refers to the fact that data is collected with the knowledge of the user, or in other words, that the user is informed about the type of data that is collected. The part of the original guideline that requires collection by lawful and fair means is omitted.

Data Quality (DQ) pertains to the relevance of the collected data to the purposes for which they are to be used. The original OECD guideline requires also that this data be accurate, complete and kept up-to-date.

Purpose Specification (PS) requires that the purposes for which the data are collected be specified. The OECD guideline also prescribes that the timing of Purpose Specification, limitation of data use to the fulfillment of those purposes, and each occasion of change of purpose should be specified as well.

Use Limitation (UL) in this study refers to the fact that data is not used for purposes other than those specified. The OECD guideline also states that the data is not be disclosed, or made available for purposes other than those specified, and that there are exceptions in case of consent of the data subject and by authority of law.

The guideline for Security Safeguards (SS) refers to the protection of data by reasonable security safeguards. In the OECD guidelines it is specified that it offers protection against such risks as loss or unauthorized access, destruction, use, modification or disclosure of data, but this addition was again considered more relevant in the legal context and is omitted for this study.

Openness (OP) requires that the user is informed about the other parties that have access to the collected data. This is somewhat different from the original OECD guideline that implies a general policy of openness about developments, practices and policies with respect to personal data, and the availability of means to establish the existence and nature of personal data, and the main purposes of their use, as well as the identity and usual residence of the data controller.

The OECD principle of Individual Participation requires being able to get a confirmation about collected data, or getting data communicated; if either of these is denied then the reasons should be given, and the person should be able to challenge data. To allow compliance questions to be asked unambiguously, this principle was split in this study to two parts, Insight (IN) and Modification (MO). Insight refers to the possibility of inspecting stored data (rather than getting a confirmation or having data communicated). Modification pertains to the possibility to modify or erase collected data.

The scenario describing the healthcare system was a slightly improved version of a scenario used in the pre-study reported in [11]. It was adapted to eliminate some of the comprehension problems that were identified there and to provide a more coherent and natural narrative structure. The scenario describes how a diabetic patient called

John is checking his diabetes condition using his newly installed health-support system. The system informs him that data is being collected to monitor this, and only this. In the menu of his health-support system, John can see that his data can be used for other purposes as well and shows him a list of people and organizations that may access his data. John is not one of these people. He may not inspect, modify or erase data collected about him. In the same menu, he can also see that the system does not protect his data with any security safeguards.

Fig. 1. The text used for both versions of the scenario

John uses a health-support system for monitoring diabetes. The same text (see figure 1) was given in printed form and was read out as a voice-over to a related video. The text describes a system that clearly meets only three of the eight OECD guidelines for privacy and security (namely PS, DQ, OP).

The video shows a character, presumably John, interacting with a machine, presumably the health-support system (see Figure 2). The exact nature of this interaction could not be discerned from the video image since John remained unexpressive and the machine was not shown in detail (to avoid drawing attention to interaction details unimportant for this experiment).

Fig 2. A screenshot of the video-based scenario, showing 'John' taking a physiological measurement; the video does not make more explicit than the text what John is measuring

2.2 Participants

Participants for the face-to-face survey were recruited amongst University employees who were not familiar with the purpose of the experiment. Participants for the online survey were gathered through invitation on email lists and message boards and through asking department secretaries in other departments of the University to forward an email invitation to their colleagues. Because of high level of education and knowledge of the English language, it could be expected that their comprehension should be no worse than participants recruited for the purposes of evaluation studies. (User studies to which these methodological results need to apply, typically do not assume a higher level of education or knowledge of privacy issues; often they concern the general public or large consumer groups, including people of lesser education, or even elderly, with less familiarity with technology than the young adults participating in the present study).

In total 104 participants took part in the study: 25 people participated in the face-to-face survey; 79 participated in the online survey. The used procedure for recruiting ascertained that all participants were familiar with websites/computers and the English language. Participants had various backgrounds.

2.3 Procedure

Participants were first introduced to John and the function of the health-support system in his daily life through a short text before being shown one of the two scenarios. Participants were asked to read or watch each scenario before answering if they agreed with eight statements about the system described to them. These statements described compliance with an individual guideline, so in effect participants were asked whether the system met the guidelines or not and which guidelines it met (see Table 1). Participants were allowed to refer back to the scenario while answering these questions. When finished with answering the questions for one scenario, participants were then presented with the same scenario via the other medium and the experiment was repeated. The experiment was conducted under two conditions: face-to-face and online.

Table 1. Overview of possible system features. Participants were asked to indicate for each feature whether the system provided them or not.

Provided System Features (Yes/No)
The user is informed about the type of data that will be collected.
The user is informed about the main purpose for which the data will be used.
The system only collects data that is relevant to the main purpose of the system.
The data will be used solely to serve the main purpose of the system.
The user is informed about which other parties have access to the collected data.
The data is securely stored.
The user can inspect the stored personal data.
The user has the possibility to make changes in the stored data

This experimental set-up allowed for a number of experimental controls. First, conducting simultaneous face-to-face and online surveys allowed a double-check for bias. If the results for each of the experimental conditions were the same then it could be concluded that there was no interviewer bias during face-to-face surveys or spoiled results due to the absence of social control during online surveys. Systematic variation was employed during the presentation of the two scenarios. Face-to-face surveys varied presentation of text- or video-based scenarios on a strict every-second-participant basis. Online surveys varied presentation of media randomly per participant.

Importantly, the survey was conducted as a single-blind test. Participants were introduced to the experiment under the belief that they were going to be shown two scenarios and that they were then to be asked questions about these scenarios. They were not informed that they were going to be shown either a text- or video-based scenario or that both scenarios would be 'identical'. This set-up prevented participants from guessing the purpose of the experiment and so, intentionally or not, influencing its outcome. The face-to-face and online surveys used exactly the same text and formatting and were divided across three identical pages.

Given this set-up the experimental rationale was as follows: If the text- and video-based scenarios are identical, control has been made for the presentation of the media and participants do not suspect that the medium is being tested then it can be concluded that any variance in participants' answers across the media will be due to the effect of that medium.

3 Experimental Results

Since both online and face-to-face research was conducted, it is necessary to examine the differences between these two methods. The face-to-face condition did not involve an interview but it did involve spoken explanation and a continuous presence of the interviewer. However, the tasks, their layout, and the procedure were kept the same in both conditions. This led to the hypothesis that there would be no significant influence upon the test results caused by the method of data gathering. Thus, it was expected that there is no effect caused by potential interview bias or lack of social control.

The first task performed to check this assumption was to conduct t-tests on aggregated results. On the total number of correct responses within each method a t-test showed no significant difference between the two methods (p=0.878). After establishing this result for the aggregated data, a t-test was performed on the difference between the two data gathering methods for both the text-based scenarios and the video-based scenarios separately. Within the text based scenario there was no significant difference between the Internet and the face-to-face condition (p=0.831). The same was true for the video-based scenario (p=0.969).

Finally, before the results were aggregated between these two methods of data collection for further analysis, one extra check of the reliability of the assumption was performed. To check for differences on individual items between the internet and face-to-face surveys, a Chi-square tests for every individual guideline was conducted. The Chi-square test can be used to check for a relation between two variables of nominal measurement level. Table 2 presents the results of these individual Chi-square tests per item by presenting the Chi-squared value, the degrees of freedom and the significance level. Since there is no significant relationship between the data collection method and the number of correct responses the assumption that there is no effect for the method of data collection is supported.

Table 2. Comparison of face-to-face and Internet results per question

Item	Chi^2	Df	Sig.
Collection Limitation (**CL**)	0.42	1	0.516
Purpose Specification (**PS**)	1.08	1	0.299
Data Quality (**DQ**)	0.45	1	0.501
Use Limitation (**UL**)	2.32	1	0.128
Openness (**OP**)	2.31	1	0.128
Security Safeguards (**SS**)	0.40	1	0.525
Insight (**IN**)	1.88	1	0.171
Modification (**MO**)	0.15	1	0.702

Results were obtained by calculating the percentage of correct answers given for each question relating to one of the guidelines in each of the following conditions:

1. The text-based scenario shown first to participants;
2. The video-based scenario shown second (i.e. immediately after the text-based scenario had been shown);
3. The video-based scenario shown first;
4. The text-based scenario shown second (i.e. immediately after the video-based scenario had been shown).

The overall result for the whole scenario in each condition was also calculated.

Initial interpretations showed interesting results. On average, overall scores for each condition were approximately the same, with text performing slightly better. However, large variations in scores were obvious between the guidelines for each condition. Table 3 shows the percentage of good answer per guideline for each condition. Rows in this table show the condition and columns show the percentage of correct results for each guideline. The final column shows the overall percentage of correct answers per condition.

Table 3. The percentage of correct answers and per question by condition

Condition	CL	PS	DQ	UL	OP	SS	IN	MO	$\overline{X}$
Text read first	83.0	66.0	34.0	84.9	73.6	94.3	86.8	98.1	77.6
Video after the text	68.0	66.0	43.4	75.5	71.7	94.3	83.0	100.0	75.2
Video seen first	47.1	78.4	58.8	72.5	70.6	82.4	82.4	96.1	73.5
Text after the video	66.7	72.6	51.0	86.3	86.3	92.2	98.0	96.1	81.1

Of the participants who read the text-based scenario first, 83.0% correctly interpreted the Collection Limitation guideline based on text while only 68.0% correctly interpreted the guideline in the case of video, which the participants were shown second. The other group was exposed to the video-based scenario first. Of these 47.1% of the participants correctly interpreted the guideline in the case of video while 66.7% interpreted it correctly for the text-based version. For the Data Quality guideline, there were large differences in interpretation between the four conditions. This guideline is more often correctly interpreted for the video-based scenarios (51.1%) than for the text-based scenarios (42.5%). It is also clear that for the group who saw text version first, for the Purpose Specification and Secure Storage of data guidelines that there were no differences between text and video version of the scenario. Compared to other systems features, the last three features (Secure Storage, Insight and Modification) were answered most correctly. The least correctly answered question in the test was regarding Data Quality (34.0%). When text was shown first, it slightly improved if video was shown after the text (43.4%). The aggregated percentage of good answers on the text-based questions and aggregated percentages of good answers on the video-based questions was 79.4% and 74.4%. Multiple analysis of variance, using both the order and the medium as independent variables, showed a significant effect for medium (p=0.001).

No significant effect was found for order (p=0.715), showing that results were not affected by learning effects (either because of the purpose of the experiment or the content of the scenarios). This result confirmed that medium was the main effect. However, an indicative effect was found for interaction between medium and order (p=0.077). Taken individually, both text and video performed a little better when shown second – a different measure to checking for an order effect which tested the average score of both media when-shown-first against the average score of both media when-shown-second. This 'interaction effect' means, for example, that text performed better when shown second not for the fact of being shown second – it is already known that there was no effect for order – but because it was preceded by the video-based scenario. Scores for video improved also when preceded by text but by a lesser degree. Thus, the best results were obtained when the text scenario was preceded by the video scenario.

The above points are more clearly illustrated in Figure 3, showing the estimated marginal means of the percentage of correct answers for the four different conditions: Text shown first, text shown second, video shown first, and video shown second. Figure 3 shows clearly that there is a higher overall score for the text-based questions, which is the main effect mentioned above. In addition, it shows that the difference between the score of each medium when shown either first or second does not differ that much, explaining why the order effect was not significant.

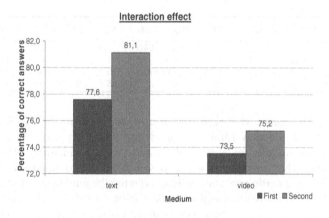

Fig. 3. Graph of the interaction effect

The interaction effect, which was significant at a ten-percent level, is reflected in the difference in increase between the first and second showing of the different media. It clearly shows that the increase in text shown first to being shown second is larger than the increase in video.

4 Discussion

As has been explained, the experiment aimed to investigate the variance in interpretation between video- and text-based scenarios. First of all, both type of scenarios showed poor understanding of the compliance with privacy guidelines. On average the text-based scenario resulted in 79.4% correct interpretation, while for the video-based scenario this was 74.3%. This means that about one fifth to one quarter of the privacy guidelines in this experiment were interpreted incorrectly. Jensen and Potts [15] explain that text with long words and/or long sentences are more difficult to read. The text used in the scenarios consisted of fairly short sentences and yet proved difficult to read.

Furthermore, the results showed that the interpretation of the both scenarios varied greatly. While on the whole, the text-based scenario performed better than the video-based scenario, it only did so to the order of 6.7%. However, more importantly, underlying these averages were great variations in answers given to individual questions. This variance between individual answers, and thus the interpretation of privacy and security guidelines between text- and video-based scenarios is the most significant finding of this study. It shows that caution must be exercised when surveying users regarding scenarios, whether this is for research purposes or as part of an iterative interaction design process.

The obtained results call into question the reliability of scenarios – both text- and video-based – for surveying users' attitudes regarding privacy-related issues. As mentioned, it is common practice to use scenarios of this kind as a means to explain a system to users and facilitate discussion regarding privacy. Clearly, results from such studies are contingent upon sufficient user comprehension, so future studies should include appropriate checks of the users' comprehension of the (sometimes) futuristic scenarios presented to them.

Another striking result is the interaction between media. Video, when shown first, "lifted" the results of the text-based scenario shown afterwards more than the text scenario did for video. This has led to the hypothesis that what may be happening is that video-based scenarios are more suited to act as contextualizing overviews to the more detail-affording qualities of text. Such a hypothesis does not take account for, much less explain, the differences in answers given for the individual guidelines between video and text.

To further analyze the outcomes of the study a hypothetical 'best-answer' medium was also looked at. The results of this medium consist of a combination of both text and video. To compute the percentage of correct answers for this hypothetical medium the best scores of text and video (when shown first) for each OECD guideline were combined. When adding all these 'best-answers' the following results emerge:

- 73.5% correct overall for video when shown first;
- 75.2% correct overall for video when preceded by text;
- 77.6% correct overall for text when shown first;
- 81.1% correct overall for text when preceded by video;
- 82.2% 'correct' overall for a hypothetical 'best-answer' medium shown first.

What is striking here is that the combined 'best-answer' medium does not score significantly higher than text scenarios when preceded by video. This result suggests that the problems posed by the phenomenon of variation in understanding between media by offering a 'best of both worlds' option can be avoided. Rather than make the pitfall of exposing users to one medium or the other, the best qualities of both may be able to be exploited if a text-based scenario is used, and preceded by a video-based version. Use of these scenarios should be framed in such a way that discussion is limited to the text-based version only, to avoid the shortcomings of video when shown first. In interaction design practice, the implication of this finding is that where a video scenario is made to solicit reactions of uses to a particular design concept it can be wise to offer a corresponding text, which they will consult after viewing the video in order to answer detailed questions that require in depth understanding of the concept described.

To help explain the results further, seven of the face-to-face participants were contacted again approximately three months after the experiment to discuss the study's findings with them. These return interviews were undertaken first to double-check for flaws in the experiment design and second to elicit explanations, which might have been overlooked. All seven interviewees could remember the experimental set-up with accuracy and the general function of the device in the scenario. Participants were then presented with the two prototypes once again in the order in which they had been shown in the original experiment. They were then informed that both were the same and provided with the answers, which they had given in the original experiment. These interviews took the form of a discussion of these answers with participants.

A number of participants argued that the video imagery did not provide extra detail regarding interaction with the device. While this point is true, it was necessary in order to maintain equivalence between both media and thus necessary for the experiment as a whole.

On the matter of the experiment results, half of the re-interviewed participants had performed better on the video prototype. However, regardless of their actual results, participants insisted on normative explanations of differences between text and video, contradicting the results data, mainly suggesting that text is vastly easier or that there was a learning effect. One participant did refer to the interaction effect, pointing out that for her, the benefit of video is that it helps frame a subject while text solidifies it. This opinion was reflected in the responses of other participants. They argued that overall they would prefer a mixed-medium, criticizing both video and text on their own. While the benefits of video were that it acted as a guide to a topic and can be digested passively, "once it's gone, it's gone." Another participant linked it to TV news, where text and video appear on screen at once, and others talked of the benefits of being able to "cross-reference" between video and text. These points, raised by participants, support the suggestion for the use of both video and text scenarios in succession.

Further to the methodological implications noted, the flawed understanding of privacy-related consequences of system use is noteworthy. Similar (and usually even more complex) texts to the scenarios are presented as privacy policies in commercial websites; this may lead to wrong assumptions about systems. When users realize the inaccurateness of their assumptions, they experience an invasion of their privacy [3]. It has to be noted that the concepts that were presented to the participants were based on legal documents and perspectives unfamiliar to most people. However, it is precisely such concepts that are translated into privacy policies used on websites. These policies are known to present comprehension problems to users [15, 19] and often are used to inform the interaction design for such systems, e.g., [18, 14].

5 Conclusions

The experiment examined differences in understanding of privacy guidelines between text and video scenarios. This paper has shown that a variation exists, both overall and more importantly in users' understanding of individual issues. It is also shown that the order in which text and video are shown has a significant effect on the level of understanding. Text scenarios resulted in slightly better understanding. However, if a video-based scenario is shown first then the interpretation of a text-based scenario improves. As a result of this study many questions are raised. Why does video appear to support text more than the other way around? What is the underlying process of this phenomenon? And why is there such a great variance in the answers for individual questions between media? This study cannot yet explain the reasons underlying these results.

For the time being, it is recommended that text-based scenarios preceded by a video-based version should be used for the purposes of privacy- and security-related user surveys. Future research into methodologies for investigating privacy should compare how video and text scenarios relate to actual or staged (e.g. Wizard of Oz) experiences of pervasive systems.

A similar advice can be given for the use of text and video scenarios during the interaction design process. Future work should examine whether similar results are obtained outside the specific context of privacy. Extending this inquiry can provide methodological guidance as to when different media are appropriate for presenting scenarios.

References

1. Ackerman, M.S., Cranor, L.F., Reagle, J.: Privacy in e-commerce. Examining user scenarios and privacy preferences. In: ACM Conf. on Electronic Commerce, ACM Press, New York (1999)
2. Acquisti, A., Grossklags, J.: Losses, Gains and Hyperbolic Discounting: An Experimental Approach to Information Security Attitudes and Behaviors. In: 2nd Annual Workshop of on Economics and Information Security (2003)
3. Adams, A., Sasse, M.A.: Privacy in multimedia communications. Protecting users, not just data. In: Blandford, A., Vanderdonckt, J., Gray, P. (eds.) People and Computers XV. Interaction without frontiers. Joint Proceedings of HCI2001 and IHM2001, pp. 49–64. Springer, London (2001)
4. Ajzen, I., Fishbein, M.: The Influence of Attitudes on Behavior. In: Albarracín, D., Johnson, B.T., Zanna, M.P. (eds.) The Handbook of Attitudes, pp. 173–221. Erlbaum, Mahwah (2005)
5. Berendt, B., Günther, O., Spiekermann, S.: Privacy in E-commerce: Stated Preferences vs. Actual Behavior. Communications of the ACM 48, 101–106 (2005)
6. Boyle, M., Greenberg, S.: The Language of Privacy: Learning from Video Media Space Analysis and Design. ACM Transactions 12, 2 (2005)
7. Carroll, J.M.: Scenario-Based Design. Wiley, New York (1995)
8. Chung, E., Hong, J., Lin, J., Prabaker, M., Landay, J.A., Liu, A.: Development and Evaluation of Emerging Design Patterns for Ubiquitous Computing. In: Proceedings DIS 2004, pp. 233–242. ACM Press, New York (2004)

9. Culnan, M.J., Armstrong, P.K.: Information Privacy Concerns, Procedural Fairness, and Impersonal Trust: An Empirical Investigation. Organization Science 10, 104–115 (1999)
10. van de, G-P.E., Markopoulos, P., de Ruyter, B.: On the relative importance of privacy guidelines for ambient health care. In: The fourth Nordic Conference on Human-Computer Interaction NordiCHI 2006, pp. 377–380. ACM Press, New York (2006)
11. van de, G-P.E., Markopoulos, P., de Ruyter, B.: Privacy Policies and Text-Based Empirical Research: Methodological Issues. In: CHI 2006 Workshop on Privacy and HCI. Methodologies for Studying Privacy Issues (2006)
12. van de, G-P.E., Markopoulos, P., de Ruyter, B.E.R., Eggen, J.H., IJsselsteijn, W.: Investigating privacy attitudes and behavior in relation to personalization. Social Science Computer Review 26,1 (in press 2008)
13. Günther, O., Spiekermann, S.: RFID and the Perception of Control. The Consumer's View. Communications of the ACM 48, 73–76 (2005)
14. Iachello, G., Abowd, G.D.: Privacy and proportionality: adapting legal evaluation techniques to inform design in ubiquitous computing. In: Proc. CHI 2005, pp. 91–100. ACM Press, New York (2005)
15. Jensen, C., Potts, C.: Privacy Policies as Decision-Making Tools. An Evaluation of Online Privacy Notices. CHI Letters 6, 471–478 (2004)
16. Jiang, X., Hong, J.I., Landay, J., A.L.: Approximate Information flows. Socially-Based Modeling of Privacy in Ubiquitous Computing. In: Miesenberger, K., Klaus, J., Zagler, W. (eds.) ICCHP 2002. LNCS, vol. 2398, pp. 176–193. Springer, Heidelberg (2002)
17. Kobsa, A., Teltzrow, M.: Contextualized Communication of Privacy Practices and Personalization Benefits. In: Martin, D., Serjantov, A. (eds.) PET 2004. LNCS, vol. 3424, Springer, Heidelberg (2005)
18. Langheinrich, M.: Privacy by Design. In: Abowd, G.D., Brumitt, B., Shafer, S. (eds.) Ubicomp 2001. LNCS, vol. 2201, pp. 273–291. Springer, Heidelberg (2001)
19. Milne, G.R., Culnan, M.J.: Strategies for reducing online privacy risks: Why consumers read (or don't read) online privacy notices. Journal of Interactive Marketing 18, 15–29 (2004)
20. OECD: OECD Guidelines on the Protection of Privacy and Transborder Flows of Personal Data (1980)
21. Palen, L., Dourish, P.: Unpacking "Privacy" in a Networked World. In: Proceedings of CHI 2003, pp. 129–146. ACM Press, New York (2003)
22. Patil, S., Romero, N.A., Karat, J.: Privacy and CHI. Methodologies for studying privacy issues. In: CHI'06 Extended Abstracts on Human Factors in Computing Systems, pp. 1719–1722. ACM Press, New York (2006)
23. Romero, N.A., Perik, E.M., Patil, S.: Appropriate methodology for empirical studies of privacy. In: Costabile, M.F., Paternó, F. (eds.) INTERACT 2005. LNCS, vol. 3585, pp. 87–89. Springer, Heidelberg (2005)
24. Spiekermann, S., Grossklags, J., Berendt, B.: E-privacy in 2nd Generation E-commerce. Privacy Preferences Versus Actual Behavior. In: Proc. ACM conference on Electronic Commerce, pp. 38–47. ACM Press, New York (2001)
25. Wright, D. (ed.) Safeguards in a World of Ambient Intelligence. Final Report, SWAMI Deliverable D4. A report of the SWAMI consortium to the European Commission under contract 006507 August 2006 (2006), http://swami.jrc.es

Strategic Tabletop Negotiations

Tokuo Yamaguchi[1], Sriram Subramanian[2],
Yoshifumi Kitamura[1], and Fumio Kishino[1]

[1] Human Interface Engineering Laboratory, Osaka University,
Suita, Osaka 565-0871, Japan
[2] Department of Computer Science, University of Saskatchewan,
110 Science Place, Saskatoon, Saskatchewan, Canada S7N 5C9
{yamaguchi.tokuo, kitamura, kishino}@ist.osaka-u.ac.jp,
sriram@cs.usask.ca

Abstract. Strategic negotiations in digital tabletop displays have not been well understood. There is little reported in the literature on how users strategize when group priorities and individual priorities conflict and need to be balanced for a successful collaboration. We conducted an observational study on three digital tabletop systems and a real-world setup to investigate similarities and differences in real-world and digital tabletop strategic collaborations. Our results show that in the real world, strategic negotiation involves three phases: identifying the right timing, using epistemic actions to consider a task plan and evaluating the value of the negotiation. We repeated the real-world experiments with different digital tabletops and found several differences in the way users initiate and perform strategic negotiations.

Keywords: Face-to-Face Collaboration, Digital Tabletops, Strategic Negotiations, Collaborative Tables, Single Display Groupware.

1 Introduction

When working in groups, we often conduct face-to-face meetings to accelerate the exchange of ideas or opinions, or to complete a cooperative task. Many studies and systems have been proposed to facilitate face-to-face collaboration during group meetings or discussions [4, 6, 11, 16-18].

Collaboration may be sought personally or imposed managerially. A variety of collaborative situations arises in everyday situations and has been analyzed by many researchers (e.g. [1, 21]). Some types of collaborative tasks, especially in business situations, fundamentally include both competitive and collaborative aspects. For example, at a meeting where sports team managers gather to trade baseball players, each participant attempts to increase individual benefit while the final goal of the meeting is prosperity of the sporting world. Similar examples can be found in a meeting on reshuffling of personnel in a company or an organization where managers or directors of some sections participate. Other examples can be found in various trading floor-like and auction scenarios.

In a collaborative task that includes both competitive and cooperative aspects, one of the fundamental actions of participants is to achieve their desired results through

C. Baranauskas et al. (Eds.): INTERACT 2007, LNCS 4663, Part II, pp. 169–182, 2007.

negotiation with other participants. A participant has to observe the transition of the task and find the ripest timing and best partner with whom to negotiate. Through the negotiation with a particular partner, each participant attempts to increase his individual benefit and this leads to an increase in the group's benefit. This process can be called "strategic negotiation" and is complex because conflicts between the personal and group priorities frequently arise. While it has been discussed in business situations (e.g. [3]), there is no investigation of this aspect with respect to designing tabletop systems.

Strategic negotiations in face-to-face collaboration require users to support transitions between personal and group work, and when we negotiate with others while sharing information, we often have to be careful about which parts of the information can and cannot be shared [2]. It offers them the opportunity to consult hidden information to make an informed decision or to present information at the most appropriate time to maximize its impact and increase its value to the presenter. However, digital tabletops today are either clumsy or not capable of effectively handling strategic negotiations. A special framework is often required to allow multiple users to deal with private as well as public information.

To design better digital tabletops, we need to have an understanding of the low-level dynamics of user actions that accompany strategic negotiations. We conducted an observational study to investigate strategic negotiations in various digital tabletop settings. Our results show that in the real world, strategic negotiation involves three phases: identifying the right timing, using epistemic actions to draw attention and evaluating the value of the negotiation. We repeated the real-world experiments in different digital tabletops and found several differences in the way users initiate and perform strategic negotiations. We identify many implications for the design of digital tabletops that arise from our findings.

2 Related Work

Recently, there has been a proliferation of systems and techniques that support digital tabletop interactions. Here we review the literature in two related areas – we present previous efforts in prototyping novel tabletop systems and investigations into the dynamics of face-to-face collaboration and various tabletop designs for managing user privacy in public information spaces.

2.1 Tabletop Systems

From time immemorial, tables have been used to discuss and make important decisions by a group of co-located people. The example of King Arthur's fabled Round Table still persists in the popular imagination. Today, we often have discussions while standing or sitting around a table to accelerate the exchange of ideas with multiple persons. Focusing on this type of interaction, there is much literature devoted to interactive tabletop displays to support face-to-face cooperative works. For example, InteracTable allows a group to annotate digital content on a computationally-enhanced table [17], and DiamondTouch is a touch-sensitive tabletop display for multiple users [4]. ConnecTables allows users of combined mobile desks to create a larger horizontal workspace and share and exchange documents, and a rapid sub-grouping in an office environment can be elegantly achieved [18]. An approach to tangible interface that uses phicons and phandles on the tabletop can be found in metaDESK [22] and Sensetable [9]. Augmented Surfaces [11] is an example of a shared continuous workspace that combines walls, tabletops and laptops. Other tabletop displays are surveyed in [15].

Many researchers have investigated tabletop collaboration and proposed some characteristics as foundations for the design of interaction techniques. Pinelle et al. [10] propose the *mechanics of collaboration* as a set of low-level actions and interactions that must be supported if team members are to accomplish a task in a collaborative fashion. Basic actions include communication, coordination, planning, monitoring and protection. Kruger et al. [7] studied the *role of spatial orientation* on communication and collaboration, through observational studies of collaborative activity at a traditional table. They found that orientation is important in establishing personal and group spaces and in signaling ownership of objects. Ryall et al. [12] explored the effect of table size and number of collaborators on collaboration. They found that even larger groups were successfully able to manage work at a small table. In order to avoid interference, collaborators usually separated the workspaces based on their seating positions and the task semantics [20]. Scott et al. [13, 14] took a closer look at how *territoriality affects* collaboration in tabletop workspaces. They found that three types of territories were common – personal, group, and storage territories – and that these spatial divisions helped coordinate people's activities in shared tasks. Recently, Tang et al. [19] investigated various forms of collaborative coupling, the manner in which collaborators are involved and occupied with each other. They identified six distinct styles of coupling based on whether users work in the same area of the shared workspace or if they perform similar tasks.

Most of the above research focused on designing systems for face-to-face cooperation and understanding users' pragmatic actions in cooperative settings. Most of the collaboration characteristics describe physical actions that allow users to cooperate better. It is not clear if these findings transfer directly to strategic collaborations. There is no reported investigation on the dynamics or characteristics of managing the various spaces during a strategic negotiation.

2.2 Privacy in Public Information Spaces

The space between users can be broadly divided into private, personal, shared and public spaces. Private space can be defined by the area where the owner can see and manipulate data but others cannot see the data or observe the owner's detailed manipulations of the data; personal space is the area where the owner can see and manipulate data while at the same time other users can observe the owner's actions in that area (without being able to observe the details of the data); a public space is defined by the area that allows all users to see and manipulate all data in it; a shared space is a form of public space that is created for a specific subgroup of users.

Because all the pieces of information displayed on the aforementioned tabletops can be easily observed by all participants equally, these systems do not provide appropriate support for strategic negotiations. For the purpose of strategic negotiations, a participant should be allowed to maintain parts of the information in a private space that is not readily observable by other participants until the opportunity is ripe for sharing all or part of that private information. The next paragraph describes digital tabletop examples that protect private information in public spaces.

In Augmented Surfaces [11], the authors support a private space that is integrated with the public space through an interaction technique called hyperdragging. Users can control which space to put the information in by using an amplified dragging gesture to move data between the private and public spaces. In RoomPlanner, users can create a private space on the table in front of them using a hand gesture that physically occludes the information from the other user's view [23]. The Lumisight Table provides different images to different users around the tabletop and has private spaces for individual users but lacks a public space in which information can be shared by multiple users [8]. UbiTable allows two users to transfer digital media from their laptops (private space) to a tabletop display (public space) where it can be shared and annotated [16]. It also includes a personal space along the boundary between the private and public space where users can observe each other's actions. Storage Bins is a mobile storage mechanism that enables access to stored items anywhere on the tabletop [14]. The electronic pile of stored items may be useful for hiding information from the other users and relies on social protocols to prevent others from manipulating them. A tabletop display system that allows multiple users to interact with both private and public information on a shared display in a face-to-face setting was proposed in [6]. The system relies on head tracking and users' viewpoints to dynamically create private spaces that can overlap with other users' private spaces to create shared and public spaces.

While system designers have built several tables that support private and public spaces, investigations into tabletop collaboration suggest the need for dynamic personal and public spaces. It's not clear from the literature what the interplay is between private, public and personal spaces with regards to strategic negotiations.

3 Study of Strategic Negotiations in Real World

In order to better understand the characteristics and factors that influence strategic negotiations during face-to-face collaboration, we conducted an observational study in various collaborative settings at a real-world table. The results of this study were used to help focus our study of a digital table.

3.1 Task and Method

We designed three strategic tasks for groups of four to six people at a single table. The tasks were designed to leverage various types of digital tabletop settings. We were interested in three types of negotiations: public-space negotiations like on an auction floor, shared-space negotiations like on a trading floor, and shared-public negotiations like in a boardroom meeting.

Task 1: Here participants build a story based on a given theme on a large sheet by linking 10 images into a storyboard. Each participant was given 10 different images from which they had to select five to help build the story. After selecting their images, each participant had to convince the others to use as many of their five selected images as possible to create the story line. Since there were only 10 spots available for the storyboard, not all images from all participants made their way into the storyboard. Participants were instructed to build the storyboard with the intention of using as many of their images as possible. This task requires users to negotiate strategically in the public space where everyone could observe and interact with everyone else.

Task 2: The primary objective of this task was to examine strategic negotiations when users have to perform shared-public negotiations with several different partners at a table. The task is similar to the first one, but participants build two small stories and combine them into a big story by adding an image at the end. As with Task 1, after selecting their five images, participants are divided into two groups and asked to build two small stories. In this task, the story built by each group must have eight images, so each participant has to convince the others to use as many of their own five selected images as possible for the storyboard. Then, one image out of the remaining images has to be selected to serve as a link between the two stories. Participants try to convince each other that one of their own images best represents the two stories. This task requires the users to negotiate with partners in a dynamically created shared space followed by negotiations in the public space.

Task 3: The third task was a card game called "Pit" that uses 52 playing cards. Each participant starts with five cards and one card is placed face-up in the center of the table. Participants take turns exchanging cards to acquire a hand consisting of five cards of a similar suit (a flush in Poker). There are two ways to exchange cards - participants can either swap one of their own cards for the card in the center of the table or can choose another participant with whom to negotiate and trade. In the second case, either of the participants can reject the negotiation before the transaction is completed. This game examines strategic negotiations when partners use private spaces in conjunction with shared spaces to engage with negotiating partners.

Participants and Method: Six groups participated in this study in a between participants design. For Tasks 1 and 2, each group consisted of four participants. Task 3 consisted of one group of four and one group of six participants. All 26 participants were university students aged 24-30 and included both females and males of varying ethnic origins. Prior to the task, each group received instructions on how to perform the task. Tasks 1 and 2 lasted 15 minutes each, whereas Task 3 lasted approximately 30 minutes. During each task, participants were comfortably seated around the table.

All sessions were videotaped and analyzed to compare and contrast the sharing of both the tabletop workspace and the objects on the table.

3.2 Results and Discussion

Figure 1 shows a snapshot of each task. Based on the analysis of the video, we observed that participants went through three successive stages when accomplishing strategic negotiation: Timing, Epistemic Action and Proposition Evaluation.

Fig. 1. Building a story in Task 1 (left), building stories in groups in Task 2 (middle), and playing a card game called "Pit" in Task 3 (right)

Timing: Capturing and retaining attention is important for strategic negotiations. In real-world setups, this is left to the charisma of the user. So users need to interrupt and gain others' attention to be able to efficiently negotiate. In Tasks 1 and 2, participants had to convince others to use as many of their own five selected images as possible. The center of the table (public space) and the spaces surrounding and between participants (shared space) were used to perform the main activities. During negotiation (when a participant suggested the use of his/her own image for the story), it was observed that the participant switched from his personal space to public space many times. For example, when the participants discussed transportation in their story, one participant suggested using an image of ships instead of an image of airplanes. He tried to gain the others' attention and negotiated strategically by moving the images back-and-forth between the personal and public spaces.

In Task 3, it was difficult for participants to be time efficient, because of the turn-taking nature of the game. Participants could speculate on which suits were being collected by observing the card in the public space or the cards requested for exchange. Despite the limited value of timing in this task, we found that participants were conscious of the value of timing. Most often participants indicated their sense of urgency or preparedness by moving their next card (face-down) into a make-shift personal space.

Epistemic Actions: Kirsh and Maglio [5] introduced the idea of epistemic actions to understand how users perform certain actions to improve their cognition of the world. They argue that epistemic actions are physical actions that users perform to reduce the memory, number of steps or probability of error involved in a mental computation. In our task, we found that participants performed three types of epistemic actions: i) checking the details of images or the card's suit repeatedly, ii) shuffling the image with no apparent reason or rearranging card positions in order of suit in preparation for the next negotiation, and iii) hesitating and shuffling the image and card repeatedly just before starting a negotiation. All participants performed these actions, which enabled them to create a strategy or a plan-of-attack in several places.

We found that participants frequently performed epistemic actions before initiating or terminating a negotiation. For example, in Tasks 1 and 2, participants often arranged the images with the storyline in their mind and tried to advocate use of their own image through repeated shuffling motions during discussion of the story. In Task 3, we observed that participants checked a card's suit endlessly while awaiting their turn and also rearranged the card's position when comparing their own cards and the card indicated for exchange. They also rearranged the card's position after exchange in preparation for the next negotiation. They were often observed to hesitate or reconsider their move when starting the negotiation.

Proposition Evaluation: We found that there were two steps in evaluating the value of a proposition to the current negotiation. The initial step is a coarse grain evaluation of the value of the negotiation. It means that a decision is reached without much consideration, and the object of negotiation is either deemed to be potentially valuable or not interesting at the current moment. The second step is accepting that the object could have potential value and performing a detailed examination of its value to the current negotiation.

For example, in building a story, when a participant suggested a different plot for the story by using his own images, he tried to indicate his image to the others via hand and body gestures that pointed to the images in his own personal space. Other participants recognized his actions and evaluated his proposal in a two-step process. If the initial examination suggests that the proposal is attractive, he is allowed the opportunity to place the images in the public space (Task 1) or the shared space (Task 2), and then present his case to further the discussion and evaluation. These actions were often observed and considered to be a more useful method for efficient collaboration. In Task 3, the cards introduced for transaction were carefully placed in front of the other participant by the giving participant. The exchanged card was usually quickly evaluated in the receiving participant's personal space (fast initial evaluation). If this card was rejected, it was moved back to the personal space of the giving participant. However, if the card was not immediately rejected, it was moved to the private space where it was evaluated again, this time more carefully in comparison with the other cards in the hand. Then if this card was not accepted for exchange, it was moved back to the personal space of the giving participant.

Summary: In all tasks, we observed the above sequence of actions for strategic negotiations. In general, users rely a lot on their personal space to effectively time the negotiation and use various forms of hand and body gestures to draw attention to their proposition or evaluate another user's proposition.

4 Study of Strategic Negotiations at Digital Table

In order to further explore the sequence of actions for strategic negotiations and examine similarities and differences between digital and real-world tabletop negotiations, we conducted a similar study using digital setups.

4.1 Tasks and Method

Our study in digital setups involved observing six groups (four participants each) performing in the same setting. We carried out our observations using three digital tabletops inspired by existing systems. All experimental setups used a table of size 1261×1530 sq mm and a horizontal display of size 635×1030 sq mm. Users could stand comfortably in front of the table. To keep the total experiment time to a reasonable amount, we restricted the task to Task 1 of the real-world setup. Similar to

Task 1, 40 images were used for each task. Participants were only allowed to change image locations; no other image manipulations were allowed.

At the beginning of each session, the groups were given instructions indicating how to perform the task. Following the instructions, the participants had a three-minute practice session before beginning the experimental task on each setup. For each setup, the task duration was 15 minutes.

(a) UbiTable-Inspired   (b) DiamondTouch-Inspired   (c) SharedWell

Fig. 2. Three digital setups

4.2 Tabletop Setups

Figure 2 shows the different experimental setups on the table. The three digital tabletop systems were inspired by UbiTable [16], DiamondTouch [4] and the strategic negotiation table described in [6], which we call "SharedWell." These systems were chosen for their different use of private, personal and shared spaces.

UbiTable-Inspired: Figure 2(a) shows the digital setup inspired by the UbiTable system. This system uses four small computers (two notebooks and two tablet computers) as the users' private space, and each user's screen top is connected to a large display. Users can handle their contents on their own screen as private space and transfer them to the large display as public space by moving them to the top of their own screen. Essentially, users can use the large display and their own small computers seamlessly, but cannot access each other's small computers. This system did not support personal or shared spaces.

DiamondTouch-Inspired: This digital setup is inspired by the DiamondTouch system in the sense that it's a large public space without any private, personal or shared spaces. Figure 2(b) shows the setup using a large single display. Participants can see all of the contents and can control their own cursors via an input device.

SharedWell: Figure 2(c) shows the users, whose head positions are tracked, looking through an aperture in the table to view their digital contents. This aperture allows users to maintain a private view of their contents even when they move around the table. To show or share their own contents, users have to come close enough to each other so that their views through the aperture overlap. The overlapping region creates a shared space for users to show or share contents. If a user wants to show or share contents with a particular partner, he puts the contents in the overlapping area by approaching the partner.

In all systems, participants were divided according to four colors (red, green, blue and yellow) and could recognize their own images and cursor by the color. A game controller was used as an input device for each participant to control the digital contents. All sessions were videotaped and analyzed to compare and contrast the sharing of both the tabletop workspace and the objects on the table.

4.3 Results

Based on the analysis of the video and the image movements, we describe our observations on strategic negotiation in the different digital tables.

UbiTable-Inspired: Participants had 10 different images to view on their private screens (private spaces) at the beginning, where they often rearranged the images. These epistemic actions helped them create a storyline. Soon after determining the images to be used, some participants moved them to the public space as the selected images. However, we also observed that others kept relocating the images (including images to be used in their own storyline) in their own private spaces. As their recommendations, these participants gradually moved the images into the public space as the session progressed. We believe that they preserved these images in their own private spaces so as to strategize and wait for the right timing to present them. In addition, we also observed that when participants initiated a discussion or negotiation with the others, they pointed at their image in the public space by using their own cursor or hand. If the image was not accepted after the group evaluation (this is considered the second step of the evaluation), the owner typically moved it back to his/her private space.

DiamondTouch-Inspired: This setup allowed all participants to see and handle all images during the entire session. At the beginning, these 40 images were distributed to each participant and placed in front of her at the edge of the table. In order to create their own storylines, participants rearranged their images within the area where the images were delivered. After determining images to be used for their own storylines in their minds, they moved the unnecessary images to the corner of the table, whereas they left the necessary images stationary in front of them as the selected images. We noticed that all participants handled their images only in the public space. They did not wait for the appropriate timing to present a particular image to the others efficiently because they could see all the images all the time during the session. Here a participant had to move the images by a cursor, and this seemed to present cognitive uncertainty to the other participants about the operator's intentions and so on. The epistemic actions occurred in the form of redundant movements of images, however they were not effectively used among the participants because of the cognitive uncertainty of the cursor operation. From the observation, they seemed to be used only for the careful consideration of the participant. When a participant tried to propose a particular image to be used in the storyline shared by all participants, she moved the image from the area in front of her to the public space. If there were images forming a storyline in the public space, we often observed that a participant put his image on top of these images, occluding them. By using these actions he could initiate negotiation and force a group evaluation of the proposal. Evaluations were often done in a single step.

SharedWell: The SharedWell system was designed to improve strategic negotiation by supporting shared spaces. Because of the nature of this system, participants performed many more physical movements for initiating or starting negotiations than with any of the other systems investigated. At the beginning, we observed that participants positioned themselves away from the table, therefore, distances among participants were long enough to preserve their own private spaces, avoiding the overlapping of their spaces to create the shared spaces. When a participant tried to initiate negotiation or discussion, he moved himself closer to the other participant(s) to create a shared space. This space was used as the public space for the discussion and negotiation between the two (or sometimes more) participants. Actually, they initiated negotiation or discussion by moving images from their private spaces to the shared space when the timing was right. All of the actions mentioned here could be observed in all of the participants, and they demonstrated the epistemic actions as well. Soon after the images were moved to the shared space, others evaluated them quickly. This was the first step of evaluation and was repeated several times by changing partners. Through a sequence of negotiations, images were gradually collected in the public space to form a storyline. These images were finally re-evaluated carefully. This was the second step of the evaluation process.

5 Discussions

From the results of the experiment, it is clear that there are differences in how participants engage in strategic negotiations in real-world and digital setups.

5.1 Real-World Setups vs. Digital Tabletop Setups

Based on the observations of the real-world setups and digital setups, we found many problems with the current digital tabletops. These problems relate to differences in user actions at different stages of strategic negotiation.

Timing: For strategic negotiation, users typically use their private spaces to examine information that needs to be shown to the other participants at the most appropriate time to maximize its impact. In the UbiTable-inspired system, we found that the participants could not use their private spaces effectively. We observed that some participants moved their selected images from the private space to the public space directly soon after the session started. Here, they did not create their own personal space explicitly, and thus they missed a chance to strategize and present information at the most appropriate time. In the DiamondTouch-inspired system, participants could not determine the best timing to propose their images since all information was visible to all participants from the beginning of the session. On the other hand, in the SharedWell system, participants could determine the most appropriate timing by observing the other participants' explicit movements; however, the physical movements forced participants to miss some opportune moments and at the same time quickly fatigued them.

Epistemic Actions: In the real-world settings, all participants easily noticed all negotiations and actions, including epistemic actions performed by a participant. Through these actions, a participant could understand the status of the collaboration taking place on the table, e.g. who was negotiating with whom, and results of the negotiation. At first we thought that the DiamondTouch-inspired system was the most similar to the real-world settings except that it required indirect manipulation using a cursor. However, we noticed that participants had difficulties in recognizing epistemic actions made by others because of the cognitive uncertainty of the cursor operation. On the other hand, in the other two systems, participants could perform the epistemic actions. In the UbiTable-inspired system, participants had their own private spaces and showed epistemic actions by rearranging their images while they considered their own storylines. Similarly, in the SharedWell system, they also had their own private spaces, and through physical motions such as enlarging the private space to be shared with adjacent participants or moving images from their private spaces to the shared spaces, they showed epistemic actions.

Proposition Evaluation: We found that users often evaluated a proposition by transitioning attention between spaces, especially from the private space to the personal space and from the personal space to the shared/public space. Explicit transitions between spaces attract other persons' attention and help provide cues of the evaluation process to all participants. From observations in the real-world settings, we understand that the two-step evaluation is important for the strategic negotiations. Moreover, through the investigation of digital tables, we found that the facility of providing personal spaces is especially important for proposition evaluation. The SharedWell system was designed to transfer the information between spaces because of the nature of this system. Therefore, participants could often perform the two-step evaluation efficiently. In the DiamondTouch-inspired system, participants could see and manipulate all the images on the display; therefore, they had to transfer the images by using explicit actions such as hand gestures or utterances. On the other hand, the participants on the UbiTable-inspired system moved their images from the private space to the public space without paying special attention to the timing; therefore, they often missed the chance to do a first-evaluation at the most appropriate time.

5.2 Supporting Strategic Negotiations on Digital Table

Digital tables can be made more efficient for strategic negotiation by improving various aspects of timing, epistemic actions and proposition evaluation.

Value of Personal Space: One of the crucial elements of strategic negotiation in real-world collaboration was a users' ability to maintain a personal space. Users often moved valuable negotiation data to the personal space, which served two purposes; first it informed others that this user had something that could be perceived as useful to the negotiation without giving them insights to evaluate the value of the data. This gave the user the opportunity to initiate negotiation when the moment was ripe. The second benefit of having information in the personal space was that at the right moment the user could easily introduce data to the public space for negotiation, and because others were anticipating this, they were more willing to listen to the user's proposition and were not taken by surprise. We believe that digital tables should support both personal and private spaces for enhanced strategic negotiations. Scott et al. [13, 14] suggest that digital tables do not have to support personal spaces because users generate these spaces by themselves. However, as described in the case of the UbiTable-inspired and DiamondTouch-inspired systems, very few participants created personal spaces because they either failed to appreciate their value or had insufficient workspace area. Systems could provide a default personal space that can be fluidly and intuitively moved around. We agree with Scott et al. [15] that it is important that users are able to flexibly and dynamically increase, decrease or relocate personal space within the workspace.

Sensitivity to User's Hand and Body Gestures: In the real-world task, users often created opportunities for negotiation by using various hand and body gestures. This rich communication language provided all users with awareness of each other's intentions allowing them to anticipate forthcoming actions. Hand and body gestures like rearranging cards within in the hand and drifting an image in-and-out of the public spaces provide rich awareness cues that users often pay attention to subconsciously. When a person tries to negotiate with others profitably, it is reasonable to expect this person to be aware of the other users' actions without compromising their privacy. It is this awareness of details that enables users to efficiently strategize negotiations in a group. Therefore, in order to support these negotiations, digital tables should be sensitive to users' actions related to body or hand gestures, and at the same time have the ability to keep private information private.

Interruptability and Epistemic Actions: We often observed that users interrupt each other with finesse to grab attention and propose an item for negotiation. While we did not explicitly examine interruption in our study we feel that digital systems should be proactive in providing support for interruptability. Systems could leverage a variety of multimodal information channels to further enhance strategic negotiation. As outlined in the results section, users rely on various epistemic actions to propose and evaluate negotiations. These could range from explicit transitions between spaces to attract other persons' attention to pondering and fiddling with the hands to indicate serious contemplation of the value of a proposition.

5.3 Implications for Design

The results of our investigation into strategic negotiations in digital tables have several implications for the design of future digital tabletop systems.

Support Creation of Personal Spaces: In our study of real-world strategic negotiations, we found that users often create personal spaces to negotiate efficiently. Tabletops that support strategic negotiations should not rely solely on private or public spaces and transfer information from private to public space directly. When designing strategic negotiations efficiently, an important implication is that the system must support creation of personal spaces.

Support Flexible and Fluid transition between Spaces: In all our digital systems, users repeatedly transferred information between private, personal and shared/public spaces. Fluid transition of information between these spaces is important for conducting strategic negotiations efficiently. Many researchers are exploring novel interaction techniques to support flexible and fluid transitions between different spaces. Our results reaffirm the need to do so.

Tabletop Systems should be Sensitive to Body and Hand Gestures: We observed that users relied on their hand and body gestures to negotiate in real-world setups. For strategic negotiation, these gestures also helped users to know the intentions of another other person's actions exactly. Therefore, we believe digital tables should be sensitive to these gestures while at the same time not demanding from users explicit gestures as with the SharedWell system. We believe that future systems must harness the body and hand gestures of users with greater finesse for strategic negotiations.

Provide Greater Support for Epistemic Actions: We repeatedly observed that users performed many epistemic actions during collaborations. While the digital tabletop systems did not explicitly factor in epistemic actions in their designs, the users were able to perform some of the epistemic actions observed in real-world settings. However, for digital tabletops to attain the flexibility and fluidity of real-world collaboration, we need to explicitly take into consideration typical epistemic actions when designing future tabletop systems.

6 Conclusions and Future Work

We investigated strategic negotiations in real-world face-to-face collaborations and compared the findings with three digital tabletop systems. We found that users strategize at multiple levels, preferring to use a personal space of dynamically re-changing size. We also identified several characteristics of group dynamics that can be valuable for designing next generation tabletop systems. Our results show that in the real-world, strategic negotiation involves three phases: identifying the right timing, using epistemic actions to draw attention and evaluating the value of the negotiation. We repeated the real-world experiments with different digital tabletops and found several differences in the way users initiate and perform strategic negotiations. In the future we plan to look into studying strategic negotiations with a variety of personalities and leadership qualities to see if there are any differences. We are also exploring novel ways to extend tabletop systems like the SharedWell to capture the nuances of negotiation that are evident in the real world.

References

1. Bui, T.X., Shakun, M.F.: Introduction of the negotiation support system minitrack. In: Proceedings of HISS, Hawaii, 23 (2000)
2. Elwart-Keys, M., Halonen, D., Horton, M., Kass, R., Scott, P.: User interface requirement for face to face groupware. In: Proceedings of the ACM CHI, pp. 295–301. ACM Press, New York (1990)
3. Dietmeyer, B., Kaplan, R.: Strategic negotiation: A breakthrough four-step process for effective business negotiation. Kaplan Business (2004)
4. Dietz, P., Leigh, D.: DiamondTouch: A multi-user touch technology. In: Proceedings of the 14th Annual ACM UIST, pp. 219–226. ACM Press, New York (2001)
5. Kirsh, D., Maglio, P.: On distinguishing epistemic from pragmatic action. Cognitive Science 18(4), 513–549 (1994)
6. Kitamura, Y., Osawa, W., Yamaguchi, T., Takemura, H., Kishino, F.: A display table for strategic collaboration preserving private and public information. In: Proceedings of IFIP ICEC 2005, pp. 167–179 (2005)
7. Kruger, R., Carpendale, S., Scott, S.D., Greenberg, S.: Roles of orientation in tabletop collaboration: comprehension, coordination and communication. Journal of Computer Supported Cooperative Work 13(5-6), 501–537 (2004)

8. Matsushita, M., Iida, M., Ohguro, T., Shirai, Y., Kakehi, Y., Naemura, T.: Lumisight table: A face-to-face collaboration support system that optimizes direction of projected information to each stakeholder. In: Proceedings of ACM CSCW, pp. 274–283. ACM Press, New York (2004)

9. Patten, J., Ishii, H., Hines, J., Pangaro, G.: Sensetable: A wireless object tracking platform for tangible user interfaces. In: Proceedings of ACM CHI, pp. 253–260. ACM Press, New York (2001)

10. Pinelle, D., Gutwin, C., Greenberg, S.: Task analysis for groupware usability evaluation: modeling shared-workspace tasks with the mechanics of collaboration. ACM Transactions on Computer-Human Interaction 10(4), 281–311 (2003)

11. Rekimoto, J., Saitoh, M.: Augmented Surfaces: A spatially continuous work space for hybrid computing environments. In: Proceedings of ACM CHI, pp. 378–385. ACM Press, New York (2000)

12. Ryall, K., Forlines, C., Shen, C., Morris, M.R.: Exploring the effects of group size and table size on interactions with tabletop shared-display groupware. In: Proceedings of ACM CSCW, pp. 284–293. ACM Press, New York (2004)

13. Scott, S.D., Carpendale, S.T., Inkpen, K.M.: Territoriality in collaborative tabletop workspaces. In: Proceedings of ACM CSCW, pp. 294–303. ACM Press, New York (2004)

14. Scott, S.D., Carpendale, S.T., Habelski, S.: Storage Bins: Mobile storage for collaborative tabletop displays. IEEE Computer Graphics and Applications 25(4), 58–65 (2005)

15. Scott, S.D., Grant, K.D., Mandryk, R.L.: System guidelines for co-located, collaborative work on a tabletop display. In: Proceedings of ECSCW, pp. 159–178 (2003)

16. Shen, C., Everitt, K., Ryall, K.: UbiTable: Impromptu face-to-face collaboration on horizontal interactive surfaces. In: Dey, A.K., Schmidt, A., McCarthy, J.F. (eds.) UbiComp 2003. LNCS, vol. 2864, pp. 281–288. Springer, Heidelberg (2003)

17. Streitz, N., Geibler, J., Holmer, T., Konomi, S., Muller-Tomfelde, C., Reischl, W., Rexroth, P., Seitz, P., Steinmetz, R.: i-LAND: An interactive landscape for creativity and innovation. In: Proceedings of the ACM CHI, pp. 120–127. ACM Press, New York (1999)

18. Tandler, P., Prante, T., Müller-Tomfelde, C., Streitz, N., Steinmetz, R.: Connectables: Dynamic coupling of displays for the flexible creation of shared workspaces. In: Proceedings of the 14th Annual ACM UIST, pp. 11–20. ACM Press, New York (2001)

19. Tang, A., Tory, M., Po, B., Neumann, P., Carpendale, S.T.: Collaborative coupling over tabletop displays. In: Proceedings of ACM CHI, pp. 1181–1190. ACM Press, New York (2006)

20. Tse, E., Histon, J., Scott, S.D., Greenberg, S.: Avoiding interference: How people use spatial separation and partitioning in SDG workspaces. In: Proceedings of ACM CSCW, pp. 252–261. ACM Press, New York (2004)

21. Tyler, T.R., Blader, S.L.: Cooperation in groups: Procedural justice, social identity and behavioral engagement. Psychology Press (2000)

22. Ullmer, B., Ishii, H.: The metaDESK: Models and prototypes for tangible user interfaces. In: Proceedings of the 10th Annual ACM UIST, pp. 223–232. ACM Press, New York (1997)

23. Wu, M., Balakrishnan, R.: Multi-finger and whole hand gestural interaction techniques for multi-user tabletop displays. In: Proceedings of the 16th Annual ACM UIST, pp. 193–202. ACM Press, New York (2003)

A Fundamental Study for Participating in Multiple Teleconferences

Hironori Egi[1,2], Hisashi Anzai[1], Itaru Takata[1], and Ken-ichi Okada[1]

[1] Faculty of Science and Technology, Keio University
3-14, Hiyoshi, Kohoku Ward, Yokohama City, 223-8522, Japan
{egichan,anzai,takata,okada}@mos.ics.keio.ac.jp
[2] Information Media Center, Tokyo University of Agriculture and Technology
2-24-16, Naka-Cho, Koganei City, Tokyo, 184-8588, Japan
egichan@cc.tuat.ac.jp

Abstract. The purpose of this research is to support office workers to participate in multiple teleconferences simultaneously. In order to achieve this goal, we have investigated how people understand multiple voices that differ in conditions of overlapping rates. We have evaluated comprehension of the context and the keywords in multiple voices, which is necessary for the users to participate in multiple teleconferences. In addition, we have described the psychological load of the users by using NASA-TLX as the workload index and the physiological load by examining the brain waves of the users. From the experiment, we can show three factors. First, we found more than half of the examinees understand the context when the voices are overlapped completely. Second, little of no difference is observed in the level of comprehension of keywords, between when the voices are half overlapped and overlapped completely. Third, it can also be suggested that examinees are more uncertain of their answers when the voices are overlapped completely compared to when they are only half overlapped. As for the load of the users, our results suggested that imperfect overlap amplifies the psychological load. Based on these results, we will discuss the necessity of selecting appropriate overlap rates and design the environment of multiple teleconferences.

Keywords: multitask, multiple voices, multiple teleconferences, overlap rate.

1 Introduction

The developments of the office work techniques help employees perform tasks such as making documents and managing business. On the other hand, the speed-up of individual work and reduction in the number of workers by systematization of working has increased their workloads. To solve such a workload problem the research about workload in offices started[1]. The research shows us that many of the present IT systems are designed for neither task interference nor switching. They are only designed to support individual tasks like e-mail or preparing documents [2]. Keeping this in mind we focused on the multitasking researches.

C. Baranauskas et al. (Eds.): INTERACT 2007, LNCS 4663, Part II, pp. 183–196, 2007.

The multitasking researches engage two or more tasks at the same time and especially look at the combination of two tasks. We classified the office work as shown in Table 1.

Table 1. Categorizing office works

		Sub Work	
		Conversational Work	non-Conversational Work
Main Work	Conversational Work	e.g. Participating in two conferences simultaneously	e.g. E-mailing while participating in a conference
	non-Conversational Work	e.g. Listening to people's conversation while making documents	e.g. Reading documents and e-mailing simultaneously

In Table 1, we define "conversational work" as work involving live, real-time communication such as a business meeting. In conversational work, it is difficult to control the timing of interruptions. We define "non-conversational work" as work involving live, non-real-time communication such as e-mail and forming document. In non-conversational work, it is easy to control interruptions. When we consider the difficulty in the level of multitasking from the aspect of control, we hypothesize that the combination of conversational work is the most difficult combination to be engaged. We believe that thorough consideration of conversational work is the key to designing an effective multitasking system.

One of the multitasking studies discusses the necessary of the multitasking researches. They have a negative perception of it from the field of brain science because it is difficult for our brain to handle multiple tasks from the perspective of memory capacity. They also suggest that if we can handle multiple tasks simultaneously, it doesn't produce the desired effect compared to doing each task in part. That study implies the damage of memory function in our brain. However they say these results only when we handle multiple tasks by just using human pure function. And they also take a positive view of multitasking. They say it may be inevitable circumstance in the future from an institutional standpoint. So that means there's a possibility multitasking will become one of the office-work styles. To achieve the multitasking style, we try to design the multitasking system supporting human information-handling ability.

As an effort to adapt to such an environment, office workers are forced to work on two or more tasks simultaneously. One of the multitasking studies discusses the necessary of multitasking. In recent days, there is a growing need for ability to manage two or more tasks effectively while participating in other works. For example, if a person is required to attend to a meeting in which he/she only has to listen and does not have to speak, he/she might feel that it would be more productive if he/she could finish other works during the time of the meeting. In a similar way, many people may feel that it would be more productive if they could attend to two meetings at the same time. Although many serious objections to the efficiency of multitasking are claimed, we believe in the positive possibilities of multitasking. We have been examining such multitasking studies and believe in the possibility of multitasking, even though the multitasking system is not yet widespread in the world. The future aim of our research is to create a system where the users are able to participate in two or more tele-conferences. When we assume participation in two or more teleconferences, we need not only to listen to other participants, but also to understand statements of others and respond to them. The existing research of multitasking involves the study of dual-task interfaces, visualization systems, and so on. For instance, one of the previous researches describe that how secondary displays should be shown while users work on their main task on another computer. The experiment shows us that users are required to maintain awareness of the changing color or size of character and background on the secondary display. However in such a field of multitasking, little or no research quantitatively focuses on human ability to hear multiple voices. Therefore we aim to reveal the influence of human hearing ability of multiple voices. Our study investigates the comprehension level of the users and confidence of their answers under two various voice-conditions. The results produce a possible design of a multitasking system for participating in multiple teleconferences.

This paper is organized as follows. In Section 2, previous studies related to the multitasking are presented. The details of the proposed design for the experiment are described in Section 3. The procedure of the experiment and the results of the experiment are discussed in Section 4 and Section 5 respectively. In Section 6, the evaluation of the experiment is discussed. The concluding remarks and future works are noted in Section 7.

2   Related Work

Many of the studies, which stimulated our research, stemmed from previous studies on efficiency and attention in the aspects of multitasking. Because this paper describes how users are affected their attention under two various voice-conditions and our goal is designing the effective system of multiple teleconferences, these studies are of critical interest to us.

D.Smith et al.[3] describe the efficiency of multitasking by giving tasks to participants. The tasks, such as solving math problems and classifying geometric objects, indicate that multitasking may be less efficient especially for complicated or unfamiliar tasks. This is caused by the difficulty involved in switching mental gears every time the participant changes from task to task. However, the study also says that there is the possibility of success under certain environmental conditions and that it is worth challenging. H. Schumacher et al.[4] also describe the efficiency of multitasking. The research investigated the difference of reactive time and error rate between dual-task and single-task by making participants solve both visual and oral problems. As a result, the study says that there is no significant difference between dual-task and single-task after they perform them two or more times. Although the experiment gives oral tasks to the participants, it does not refer to anything about comprehension and imposition load in cases where participants hear multiple voices. This research stimulated our study of multitasking.

One of the important researches in the field of multitasking is the study about the dual-task system. Many of such dual-task researchers focus on visual aspects of multitasking. Since the dual-task system requires participants to switch quickly between the tasks using two visual displays, some of the previous evaluations focused on the combination of two tasks and the display of the secondary task. C.M. Chewer et al[5] analyze the rate of correct answers of various types of problems involving visual information in a dual-task system. In this experiment, participants work on a game task as the main task and a quiz as the secondary task. The visual appearance is varied in information, colors, positions, and sizes. According to their analysis, they stress the importance of designing a multitasking system from a cognitive viewpoint of human ability. Although our research focuses on the oral information in multitasking system, we share a common belief in the importance of the cognitive viewpoint. Jacob Somervell et al[6] attempt to know how to design information visualizations intended for the periphery and to investigate how quickly and effectively users can understand information visualizations while they are working other tasks hard. They focus on how several factors of a visualization (visual density, presence time, and secondary task type) impact user's abilities to keep working a primary task and to complete secondary tasks related to the visualization. They describe these significant results as follows: (1) We can introduce the peripheral display without reduced performance of main task. (2) Although it is difficult to understand complex visualization, it is effective if they work it with relaxed time pressure and reduced visual information density. Blair MacIntyre et al[7] also think that peripheral display is effective to achieve the multitasking system and try to investigate the design of the peripheral display for that system. They use not only the main display but also the white board as peripheral display which is displayed peripheral information to help their awareness.

Rooms[8] is a multitasking system designed to support task switching and focuses on six characteristics proposed by Banon[9]: reducing the mental load due to switching processes, suspending and resuming of activities, maintaining records of activities, functional grouping of activities, multiple perspective on the work environment, and interdependencies among items in different workspaces. Based on such characteristics, Rooms supports switching tasks more quickly. However, Rooms focuses on switching text information on computer displays, which differs from our approach, we focuses on the information of multiple voices in multiple teleconferences.

We were also stimulated by other researches including the task of teleconferences. Kawahara et al[10] experimented with three overlapped tasks simultaneously. After the experiment, participants answered a questionnaire about overlapping. These tasks include performing personal tasks such as participating in a teleconference and watching a video of a lecture. Although as a result, this study indicated the difficulty of comprehension contents in two overlapping voices and three simultaneous tasks. Therefore multiple voices in teleconferences should be investigated from a more quantitative approach.

Our research is different from the other researches in that it investigates the comprehension level of two overlapped voices quantitatively and discusses multiple teleconference system based on the results of our experiment.

3 Design Concept

The multitasking researches for office work environment described in the previous section focus on the visual element of switching of tasks. In order to discuss the design of multiple teleconferences, we quantitatively investigate three factors throughout the following experiments: user comprehension levels, psychological loads, and physiological loads of multiple voices.

This experiment is designed to quantitatively evaluate the voice overlapped tasks, assuming two teleconferences. In our experiment, we define the condition of a "Serial" as the most primitive model. This is a condition where two voices are presented one by one, and the voice that gives information is composed of two parts; one in the first half and one in the second half. The result is used as a comparison to the result of overlapped voices. It is also important to discuss the assumed condition of multitasking. For instance, when thinking about attending to two conferences at the same time, we can easily imagine that the difficulty level of oral comprehension depends on the amount of conversation. Therefore, we focus on the rates of overlapping voices in this experiment and use 0%, 20%, 60% and 100% as the overlapping rate of voices. When the overlapping rate is 0% it means that the two voices do not overlap, and when the overlapping rate is 100% it means that the two voices completely overlap. Detailed information about the overlapping rates is explained the nest section.

3.1 Overlapping Rate

When the overlapping rate is 0%, two voices are presented alternately. We show the switching process of these voices in Figure 1.

Story 1 consists of voice part A and B. Story 2 consists of voice part C and D. In this Figure, although the switch from "A → C," "C → B," and "B → D" involves cognitive processing, there is semantic and integrated processing involved especially in "C → B" and "B → D". Meanwhile, the condition of the series above also includes the switch from "B → C". It is different in the sense that integrated processing is not required. When the overlapping rate is 20%, the cognitive load in the human aspect of successive processing is the same as 0%. In addition, however, participants are required to process the overlapped voices and switch their cognition. Switching is done when they change their mind from processing one voice to the other overlapped voice and vice versa. The cognitive load of processing the voice at the overlapping rate of 60% is the same as the overlapping rate of 20%, although the time of the overlapping voices increases. When the overlapping rate is 100%, the voices completely overlap from

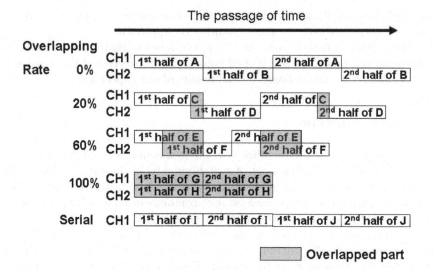

Fig. 1. Overlapping rate of two voices. Story 1 (channel 1 from left speaker) consists of voice part A and B. Story 2 (channel 2 from right speaker) consists of voice part C and D.

the beginning to the end. We hypothesize that the cognitive load of successive processing is the same as the cognitive load when the overlapping rate is 60%, even though participants may be experiencing voice processing on a micro level.

At the end of this paper, we will examine the result of Serial and each overlapping rate.

3.2 Experimental Design

We assume the experimental environment to be multiple teleconferences. We define the rate to which two voices come in succession as the "overlapping rate" and define the time the two voices overlap as "overlapping time".

The application used in our experimental environment is written in JAVA. As part of the experimental environment, we present two overlapped voices to the participants by using two speakers; one on the left and the other on the right hand side. We evaluate the level of comprehension of the voices by making participants solve problems related to the contents of the voices heard from the two speakers after the participants finish hearing the two voices. For instance, when voices of 40 seconds is played with the overlapping rate of 20%, the two voices overlap for eight seconds. We show the overall flow of the experiment in Figure 2.

The experimental environment in our research is composed of two components: two displays to present the problem, a stereo speaker on the right and left side of the participant to output the voices. As the experimental voices, we use the voice of a robotic machine in this experiment. The purpose of this is to remove nonverbal information included in the human voice, which facilitates the

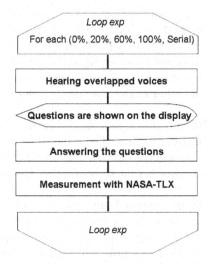

Fig. 2. Overall flow of the experiment

transmission of information. It is thought that the possibility of the multitasking system under difficult conditions can be verified. Our participants are required to answer questions about the content of voices heard from the stereo speaker to their left and right hand side, using desktop computers placed in front of them. They must check what they consider to be the correct answers, from the provided answer groups. The problems include both context problems and keyword problems. Context problems are presented before the keyword problems. The reason behind not presenting both problems simultaneously is to keep participants from anticipating the answer to the keyword problems using information from the answer group of the context questions.

4   Experiment

4.1   The Outline of the Experiment

In order to empirically investigate the comprehension level of the two voices, we test on twenty-eight participants and record their performance throughout our environment. Participants of our experiment are students of Keio University. As previously explained in section 3.1, Story 1 and Story 2 in Figure 1 consists of voice part A and B and part C and D respectively. Each voice part A~D is 40 seconds long. Story 1 is output from the left speaker and Story 2 is output from the right speaker. Two voices overlap according to the overlapping rate, 20%, 60% and 100%. We investigate the comprehension level, the psychological load and also measure the physiological load by examining the brain waves of randomly chosen 11 participants. We describe the method of each evaluation later on.

First of all, in order to accustom participants to the multitask situation, participants listen to the voice of the overlapping rate 80% for practice. Next, participants are required to hear the voices of stories. We adopt 0%, 20%, 60%, and 100% as the experimental overlapping rate and Serial as a comparison. The overlapping rate 0% is different from Serial in the point of task switching though the overlapped time is 0 second same as Serial. For the experimental order, we divide our participants into two groups, one in the ascending order (0% → 20% → 60% → 100%) and the other in the descending order (100% → 60% → 20% → 0%).

After that, they solve the problems concerning the contents of the voices displayed on the left and right display. These questions include two types; two context questions that show whether the participants are able to grip the context roughly or not and five keywords that show whether the participants heard the words or not.

The participants check the answer forms that they think is correct from the displays. In addition, they check the convincing level to the answer by five stages on the same displays. After hearing all patterns of overlapped voice and answering questions, we evaluate their psychological load by using NASA-TLX.

Finally, we also give them Serial task that two voices are presented one by one and evaluate their comprehension level and the psychological load.

4.2 Evaluation Method

We use the NASA-TLX as the evaluation method of the psychological load. NASA-TLX is the technique for requesting the load index of the task based on a multi-dimensional average of subjective information. In our research, we use the Japanese Version of NASA-TLX proposed by S.Haga et al[11]. The evaluation of this experiment include measures of the physiological load by examining their brain waves as well as the psychological load by using NASA-TLX. We measure the two loads of eleven randomly chosen participants in the experiment. We measure the α wave peak frequency which indicates the maximum value of the α wave in the brain waves which reflects the influence of mental operations. The α wave peak frequency moves to the high frequency as the work load rises.

5   Results

The result of this experiment include measures of the comprehension level of the overlapped tasks and Serial task as well as the psychological load and the physiological load. Analyzing these measured values separately allows us to examine the following; the comprehension level to the overlapped voices when it is assumed to participate in multiple teleconference, the mental load when participating in multitask system. The following sections summarize the results of the experiment.

5.1   The Result of Comprehension Level

The recorded correctness of the context questions and keyword questions for both overlapped voices and Serial in the experiment are shown in Figure 3 and Figure 4.

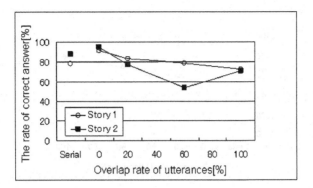

Fig. 3. Correctness of the context questions. In overlapped tasks, story 1 is spoken from the left speaker and story 2 is spoken from the right speaker.

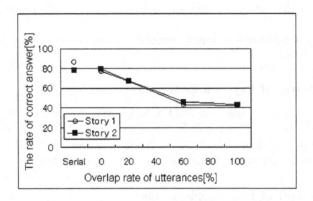

Fig. 4. Correctness of the keyword questions: In overlapped tasks, story 1 is spoken from the left speaker and story 2 is spoken from the right speaker

Figure 3 gives the correctness of the context problems. This result shows the following three factors:

- The correctness of overlapping rate of 0% is 10% higher than the correctness of Serial assumed as the present work style.
- There is a response variance to the correctness of right and left voices in overlapping rate 60%. The correctness of the right voice is lower than the correctness of the left voice.
- The correctness of overlapping rate 100% is higher than 70%.

Figure 4 gives data comparing correctness to keyword questions. As well as the context problem, this result shows the following two factors:

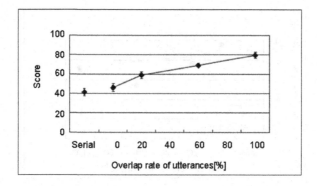

Fig. 5. The result of NASA-TLX

- The correctness of overlapping rate 0% is almost the same as Serial. This means that the correctness of overlapping rate 0% is higher than correctness 80%.
- Little or no difference is found between the correctness of overlapping rate 60% and 100%.

5.2   The Result of Psychological Load

We analyze the result using NASA-TLX to investigate their psychological load to the multiple voices. This result is shown in Figure 5. It indicates that there is highly significant difference (t(27) = 3.688 ∼ 9.280), p ≥ .01). This result excludes the combination of Serial and the overlapping rate 0%.)

5.3   The Result of Physiological Load

The result of the α wave peak frequency is shown in Figure 6. This result gives us that there is significant difference ((t(10) = 2.472), p ≥ .05)) for only the combination of the overlapping rate 20% and 60%.

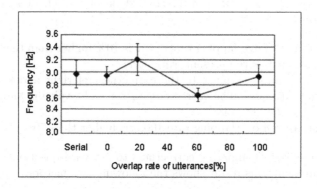

Fig. 6. The result of the α wave peak frequency

6   Evaluation

The results of the experiment are summarized in the following sections.

6.1   The Evaluation of Comprehension Level

Following factors are considered from the result of the correct answer rates.

- There is a possibility that the context can be understood even if two voices overlap completely. In Figure 3, the correctness of overlapping rate 100% is higher than 70%. This result describes participants are able to understand the context roughly when two voices are completely overlapped. This indicates that users who participate in two teleconferences are able to understand both contents.
- In correctness of keywords, little or no difference appears between the correctness of the overlapping rate 60% and 100%. Table 2 shows the detailed correctness values of keywords. From Table 2, we can understand there are actually only several differences between the correctness of the overlapping rate 60% and 100%. This result gives us that little or no difference of comprehension level appears when we compare the case that two voices are overlapped completely with the case that two voices are overlapped halfway. We think overlapping two voices completely is more effective than overlapping halfway because the former case produces reduction of working hours compared to the latter case.

Table 2. The values of correctness for keyword questions. In overlapped tasks, story 1 is spoken from the left speaker and story 2 is spoken from the right speaker.

	Serial	0%	20%	60%	100%
Story 1 (%)	86.4%	77.1%	67.1%	43.2%	42.1%
Story 2 (%)	78.2%	79.3%	67.5%	46.1%	43.2%

6.2   Individual Difference

Although there is no polarization in the comprehension level, we can divide 14 participants into six participants who acquire high correctness and eight participants who acquire low correctness. High correctness means that participants acquire correctness higher than 20% of the average correctness of all participants and low correctness means that participants acquire correctness lower than 20% of the average. We describe this separation in Figure 7.

This result shows us that there is a large difference between the correctness of the left voice and the right voice in the high score group (the difference of correctness is from 8.0% to 21.7%) compared to the low score group (the difference of correctness is from 2.5% to 13.8%). In addition, this figure shows that the participants of the high score group are able to acquire stable correctness

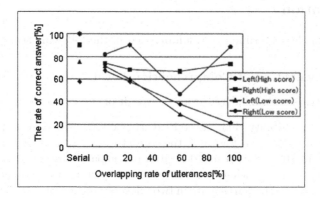

Fig. 7. The result of individual difference

to the right voice in overlapping voices. This result indicates that the participants of the high score group can divide their attention to both left and right.

6.3   The Evaluation of Psychological Load

The result of psychological load indicates that there is a possibility to make their psychological load lower by decreasing of overlapping rate.

6.4   The Evaluation of Physiological Load

The characteristics of the change in the α peak frequency are shown as follows:

- For overlapping rate 0%: equivalent to Serial.
- For overlapping rate 20%: becomes bigger than Serial.
- For overlapping rate 60%: becomes lower than Serial.
- For overlapping rate 100%: equivalent to Serial.

We analyze these results from the aspect of human processing. When the experimental environment has been changed from Serial to the overlapping rate 0%, participants are required to process the switching and the integration of their sense. When it has been changed from the overlapping rate 0% to the overlapping rate 20%, participants are required to process part of the overlapped voices and to shift their mind from the part of overlapped voices to the part of the single voice. We consider these processes are added to the participants as loads. On the other hand, the overlapping rate 20% is changed to 60%, we consider that the shift from the overlapped part to the non-overlapped part directly effects the differences of the correctness between the overlapping rate 20% and 60%. We see that the overlapping rate 60% requires the highest process of cognition. The reason for this is that the participants give up hearing overlapped voices. When it has been changed from the overlapping rate 60% is changed to the overlapping rate 100%, the cognitive process consists of only processing the part of the overlapped voices. It means they are not required to process the switching, the integration and the shift. This is why the α peak frequency is same as Serial. In addition, considering the result that the peak frequency of the overlapping rate 20% is higher than the overlapping rate 100%, it is supposed that the shift from the overlapped part to the single part is a significant factor from the aspect of physiological loads.

7   Conclusion

In this research, we focused on the fundamental study of participating in multiple teleconferences. Although many researchers focused on the field of multitasking researches, most of the studies aim to visualize dual tasks or to present secondary tasks to the main task. But there is a need to empirically investigate the comprehension level of users and loads of cognition. We prepared an environment which enables the change of the overlapping rate of two story voices and present it to participants.

From our experiment, the following three factors can be described:

– Participants are able to understand the context roughly even if two voices overlap completely. However, it is difficult to understand the keywords, the average of the context correctness of the overlapping rate 100% is 71.4% and the keyword correctness is 42.7%.
– In physiological loads of the overlapping rate 0% and 100%, these loads are almost the same for Serial. And the shift from the overlapped part to the single part is a significant factor as well as the process of overlapped part.
– Individual difference appears. There is a large difference between the correctness of left voice and right voice in the high score group compared to low score group.

This work is placed as a fundamental study that aims at designing multitasking systems.

References

1. O'Conaill, B., Frohlich, D.: Timespace in the workplace: dealing with interruptions. In: ACM Proc. CHI'95, pp. 262–263 (1995)
2. Gonzales, V.M., Mark, G.: Constant, Constant, Multi-tasking Crazines. In: Proceedings of CHI'04, pp. 113–120 (2004)
3. Smith, D.: Multitasking undermines our efficiency,study suggests. In: Proc. ACM SIGCOMM'95, pp. 342–356 (1995)
4. Schumacher, E.H., Seymour, T.L., Glass, J.M., Fencsik, D.E., Lauber, E.J., Kieras, D.E., Meyer, D.E.: Virtually perfect time sharing in dual-task performance: Uncorking the central congnitive bottleneck. Psychological Science, 101–108 (2001)

5. Jacob, S., McGrickard, D.S., Ndiwalana, A., Narth, C., Pryor, J., Tessendorf, D.: Secondary Task Display attributes-Optimizing Visualizations for Cognitive task suitability and interference avoidance. In: ACM Proc. VisSym'02, pp. 165–171 (2002)
6. Jacob, S., McCrickard, D.S., North, C., Shukla, M.: An evaluation of information visualization in attention-limited environments. In: Proceedings of the symposium on Data Visualisation '02, pp. 211–216 (2002)
7. MacIntyre, B., Mynatt, E., Voida, S., Hansen, K.M., Tullio, J., Corso, G.M.: Support for multitasking and background awareness using interactive peripheral displays. In: Proceedings of the 14th annual ACM symposium on User interface software and technology, pp. 41–50 (2001)
8. Card, S.K., Henderson Jr., A.: Tivoli: A Multiple, Virtual-Workspace Interface to Support User Task Swetching. In: Proc. SIGCHI Bulletin'87, pp. 53–59 (1987)
9. Banon, L., Cypher, A.: Evaluation and analysis of users' activity organization. In: Proc.ACM CHI'83, pp. 54–57 (1983)
10. Kawahara, T., Kobayashi, T., Takeda, K., Minematsu, N., Ito, K., Yamamoto, M., Utsuro, T., Shikano, K.: Sharable software responsitory for Japanese large vocabulary continuous speech recognition. In: Proc. ICSLP'98, pp. 3257–3260 (1995)
11. Haga, S., Mizukami, N.: Japanese version of NASA Task Load Index: sensitivity of its workload score to difficulty of three different laboratory tasks. Japanese Journal of Ergonomics 32, 71–79 (1993)

ICEbox: Toward Easy-to-Use Home Networking

Jeonghwa Yang and W. Keith Edwards

Graphics, Visualization and Usability Center
College of Computing
Georgia Institute of Technology
{jeonghwa, keith}@cc.gatech.edu

Abstract. Home networking is becoming an essential part of everyday life. However, empirical studies and consumer reports indicate that the complexities of configuring and maintaining the home network impose a high barrier for most householders. In this paper, we explore the sources of the complexity of the home network, and describe a solution we have built to address this complexity. We have developed a prototype network appliance that acts as a centralized point of control for the home network, providing device provisioning and reprovisioning, security, discovery, and monitoring. Our solution provides a simple physical UI for network control, using pointing to introduce new devices onto the network, and a physical lock to secure network access. Results of our user studies indicate that users found this appliance both useful and usable as a network configuration and management tool.

Keywords: Home networking, usability, user interface, and ICEbox.

1 Introduction

Increasingly, networking technology is finding its way into the home. Recent studies, for example, indicate that 43 million households in the US have broadband access, and many of these have a home network [5]; similar trends exist in much of the industrialized world. However, despite this rapid uptake of networking technologies, there are severe user interface hurdles. Data from consumer research firms and the mainstream press, for example, cite home networking technology as *the most returned item* at "big box" electronics stores [20]; consumers typically cite complexity of installation and configuration as the key impediment to adopting a home network [15]. As recently as this year (2006), roughly a quarter of the people who purchased wireless networks returned them because they were unable to properly configure and install them [16].

The user interface hurdles posed by home networking include not just the initial problems of configuring and installing the network and the devices on it, but also the ongoing monitoring and management of the network, troubleshooting when things break, and — occasionally — reconfiguring the overall network itself (such as when the network topology or service provider changes).

The networking concepts that are exposed to home network users today are fundamentally unchanged from those that were exposed to trained system- and network-administrators during the mid 1970's when the current Internet protocol suite

C. Baranauskas et al. (Eds.): INTERACT 2007, LNCS 4663, Part II, pp. 197–210, 2007.
© IFIP International Federation for Information Processing 2007

Fig. 1. The ICEbox hardware prototype and its location in the home network topology

was developed [3]. In order to effectively install and securely manage a network, users must understand basic network architecture (that a router separates the internal network from the external), terminology (Domain Name Service, IP addresses, ports), security (firewalls, Network Address Translation, port forwarding), and more. And while technologies such as the Dynamic Host Configuration Protocol (DHCP) [6], Zeroconf [4], and others address certain aspects of network usability, they have clearly not solved the problem, as shown by the return rates and user frustration noted above. Thus, we believe there is a need for HCI researchers to focus on new mechanisms and tools that can provide a better user experience for home networking.

Based on earlier empirical work designed to uncover problem areas in home networking, we have created a network appliance designed to reduce the complexity and increase the usability of the home network (Figure 1). This appliance, called the *ICEbox* (for *installation, configuration,* and *evolution* box), acts as a logical front door to the home network, serving as a central point of control for the home network, and providing a unified interface for home network management that shields the user from the technical details of the network.

The ICEbox addresses common problems with device configuration, network security, and monitoring and troubleshooting. A simple physical pointing interface is used for initial client device configuration; a graphical interface combined with physical controls on the ICEbox provides access to management functions, including network security. The architecture and interface effectively minimize user interaction with client devices in the management of the network.

In the following sections we present an overview of previous work in addressing the usability issues of home networking, and use this work to motivate a discussion of the specific problems that arise in home networking, which the ICEbox addresses. Next, we describe the ICEbox system and its features. We then describe a user study, in which we examined the usability of the key features of the ICEbox. Finally we close with future research directions.

2 Related Work

Much of the literature from the HCI community that has explored networking has focused on improving the tools of trained administrators (e.g. [8, 24]). The emphasis on tools for use in managed networks in unsurprising given the prevalence of such networks; however, these tools are typically very technical in nature and are often designed for "heads down" use—meaning, for use as a management console by a professional whose job it is to monitor the network. These characteristics make such tools a poor fit for home users who have neither the expertise nor the desire to manually manage the minutia of their networks.

While some empirical work has focused on the home, this work has largely focused on home *computing* rather than home *networking*. With a notable early exception [22], most of this work has been conducted in the last few years as home computing adoption has grown (see, e.g. [11, 14]). When the home network appears in these studies it is usually indirectly, through the use of networked applications (such as web browsing and home shopping) rather than the setup, management, and troubleshooting of the network itself. One exception to this categorization [13] does confirm the problematic aspects of home networking, noting that 89% of families in their study needed support from an external help desk during the first year of their Internet use.

Two empirical research studies have focused on the user experience of networking per se. These include an investigation of "early adopter" home network users [9] and an investigation into the user-visible consequences of applications that make use of discovery technology [23]. Both of these have informed the specific approaches taken by the ICEbox, as described in the next section.

In addition to this HCI-driven work, research from the networking community has also focused on new technologies, tools, and protocols to improve the user experience of home networking. PARC's Network-in-a-box (NiaB) system [2] is the work most closely related to ours. NiaB allows users to add laptops to a secure wireless network by walking up to an access point and physically pointing a laptop at it. The functionality of NiaB, however, is restricted only to secure wireless configuration. NiaB uses a short-range communication mechanism to facilitate the exchange of certificates needed for 802.1x wireless security. The goal of the ICEbox, on the other hand, is to deal with other aspects of secure device provisioning, as well as higher-level service and application configuration, and monitoring of the network.

Although NiaB uses a pointing interface based on a short-range communication mechanism similar to ours, the use of such interfaces for device identification was introduced in the GesturePen system [21]. GesturePen allows users to select devices through a pointing gesture using custom tags and a custom stylus, instead of navigating through traditional user interface widgets such as lists.

Sony's FEEL and SyncTab [18, 19] also demonstrate the effectiveness of leveraging short-range communication and direct manipulation for ease of configuration, especially for establishing connections between two devices such as a camera and a printer or a PC and a TV. FEEL uses short-range wireless data transmission to exchange information necessary for setting up a connection; users point one device at another or put two devices in close proximity to create a network connection between them. SyncTab uses synchronous actions for establishing network connections. When users want to establish a connection between two devices, they synchronously press a button on both devices.

Techniques similar to both of these have been adopted in commercial products, such as recent Linksys Access Points that use a technique similar to SyncTab. Other commercial systems have focused on techniques that, while more cumbersome than the physical pointing or button interfaces, can provide a degree of automatic configuration. For example, Windows Connect Now (WCN) [17] provides an alternative mechanism for home wireless configuration in which users run a Wireless Network Setup Wizard that configures their computer for a new wireless network, and saves the configuration details on a USB key. Users then use the USB key to update the settings of the wireless access point and to set up other computers. While WCN clearly simplifies the process of setting up a wireless network, it only deals with basic SSID and WEP key provisioning for wireless networks. Further, it requires significant interaction (running the Wireless Network Setup Wizard) at each device.

In addition to these systems, there are a number of technologies that try to remove all user interaction from certain aspects of network configuration, including the Dynamic Host Configuration Protocol (DHCP), the Simple Service Discovery Protocol (SSDP) used by UPnP [7], and Zeroconf [4]. While all of these technologies share a similar focus on removing the complexity of configuration, they only deal with a small subset of the overall networking problem. They do not, for example, deal with lower-layer configuration details (such as link layer or physical layer configuration, including WiFi provisioning), trust associations (such as WEP keys, 802.1x certificates), nor higher-layer application defaults (such as printers or file shares). They also do not provide monitoring functionality that may be necessary for users.

We build upon the approach taken by NiaB, FEEL, and GesturePen by also using a short-range pointing technique to bootstrap device associations. In our case, this pointing interface is layered on an extensible introduction protocol amenable to other interaction techniques (such as the USB key mechanism used by WCN). Further, however, we *extend* all of these systems by going beyond initial network-layer configuration to provide a host of functions for link-, service- and application-layer configuration, and ongoing network monitoring.

3   Home Networking: What's the Problem?

This section discusses the key usability problems inherent in home networking today. Our description of these problems is based in analysis of earlier empirical studies undertaken by our group [9, 24]; here we report only on the high-level findings from these studies.

One of the primary sources of complexity concerns correctly **provisioning devices** for the home network. This task involves configuring or adapting devices to the particular circumstances and context of a specific home network, and includes not just network-layer configuration, but also higher-layer details of the home network, such as which printer to use and where file shares reside. Provisioning is especially arduous, as it requires not just knowledge of how to operate the new client device, but also the *particulars* of the home network it is joining (what form of security—if any—is used on this network? What form of addressing? What is the network's topology?). Many of these details are hidden from users, leading to problems with setting up new devices correctly. The difficulty of provisioning suggests that removing as much of this manual work as possible from the user is essential to improving network usability.

In addition to initial setup, another particularly troubling aspect of provisioning is that it is also *fragile*. Any **change to the topological structure** of the network, for instance, adding a new access point for example or change of Internet Service Provider, may necessitate *all existing clients* being reprovisioned to work on the reconfigured network. Likewise, tasks such as swapping out a printer require that the existing machines on the network be reconfigured to know about the new device.

The creation and management of **security and trust associations** are likewise problematic. Few networks in our studies had strong security (no 802.1x or MAC access controls, for example). Several participants had no wireless security enabled at all. Of course, with most commercial access points, householders can connect to the Internet without configuring any security at all. This suggests that any secure networking solution must be as easy to use *or easier* than using no security at all. The heavyweight and static nature of most network security technologies also conflicted with users' desires to support visitors or neighbors. Many in our studies expressed a desire to allow network access (perhaps transiently) to visitors or to neighbors. This need suggests that more lightweight security mechanisms are required, especially ones that can grant selective access to network resources, potentially with the ability to revoke access. These mechanisms must again be as easy to use as not, or householders will be unlikely to take advantage of them.

Ongoing network and device monitoring is another problematic area for home users. While few users outside of hobbyists *want* to do this work, it is occasionally necessary. Especially since users may have enlisted help from a friend or neighbor to set up their networks, they may not have any clue about how to repair the network if it stops working. The logical and sometimes even physical infrastructure of the home network is often invisible to its users. This invisibility makes it hard to check home network status and is also problematic at the time of troubleshooting. This suggests that we need tools that can support visual monitoring and management of the home network, designed not for constant use, but for occasional use during troubleshooting.

Lastly, even technologies designed to simplify network management may break down in complex networks. For example, current multicast-based **discovery protocols** do not cross link boundaries. This was apparent in a number of our subjects' homes, notably when trying to set up music streaming between wired and wireless machines. Of course, one common alternative to discovery protocols—using a managed directory service—requires human administration in order to populate the directory service. This experience suggests that new approaches are needed for service discovery that can operate at the small scale of the home network, but yet can cope with the potentially complex topology of the home.

4 ICEbox Overview

Based on the problems noted above, we have created an architecture designed to eliminate—or at least mitigate—user interface problems with provisioning, evolution, trust management, monitoring, and discovery. Our contribution is on new interfaces for existing network technologies, rather than on new networking or security technology.

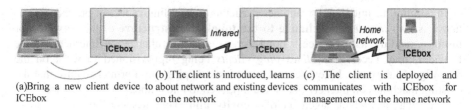

(a)Bring a new client device to ICEbox

(b) The client is introduced, learns about network and existing devices on the network

(c) The client is deployed and communicates with ICEbox for management over the home network

Fig. 2. The ICEBox device configuration steps

Our approach is based on simple physical actions by the user (such as pointing and turning a key in a lock), which then drive an architecture in which clients securely delegate configuration tasks to a centralized management node, the ICEbox.

By entrusting the ICEbox—rather than individual clients—with configuration responsibility, we separate those aspects of configuration that *must* be done by a user (because they cannot be intuited by systems, and therefore require human agency) from those that are incidental technical details (and thus can be automated).

In our model, users bring new devices onto the home network through a simple "introduction" step at the ICEbox (Figure 2). This step is through a physical pointing gesture, leveraging the proximity afforded by short-range communication to bootstrap communication and a trust relationship between the device and the ICEbox (Figure 2-a). This step effectively tells the ICEbox, *"This new device should be considered a part of my home network."* The client at that point delegates all future configuration responsibility to the ICEbox.

During this introduction phase, software on the client provides the ICEbox with details about itself, such as its type, network MAC addresses, what services it may offer, and so forth (Figure 2-b). This information is used by ICEbox to build up a model of client devices that exist on the home network.

Next, the ICEbox provides the new client device with a set of configurations that allow it to operate on the home network (also Figure 2-b). These configurations contain not only information necessary for link- and network-layer operation (SSID, WEP keys, address and router assignments, netmask, and so forth), but also application- and service-layer settings. These latter include, for example, information about printers deployed on the home network and fileshares on the network; for clients such as laptops, this information is used to install necessary printer configuration information as well as shortcuts to fileshares on the desktop. Such application- and service-layer information comes from the ICEbox's model of devices on the network, built up through repeated earlier introductions; this model can be used alongside network monitoring tools to drive a range of interactive monitoring and troubleshooting tools.

After introduction, the ICEbox adds the device to its model of the home network, and then notifies existing devices of the addition of the new one if necessary. For example, introducing a new printer onto the network will cause the ICEbox to communicate information about this new printer to all computers already installed on the home network. This mechanism moves from a model of linear complexity (adding a new device requires manual update of all existing clients on the network) to constant complexity (adding a new device is a single operation, no matter how many clients are already on the network).

Once deployed, the client device and ICEbox communicate using normal TCP/IP-based protocols. The client provides the ICEbox with details about its location in the network (based on which provisioned address it is using), and communicates status information back to the ICEbox. The ICEbox can use this protocol deliver new configuration information to the client remotely, to reprovision it when new devices appear (Figure 2-c).

This model yields a number of benefits. First, it can better support novice users by reducing the complexity of bringing new devices onto the network correctly. Users need only perform a simple introduction step to associate a device with the ICEbox and thus bring it onto the network, rather than hassling with tedious network configuration parameters; likewise, the addition of new clients can cause *existing* devices on the network to be updated to know about these new clients. Second, this model can support "UI-free" client devices, such as small, single-purpose information appliances that may not have mice, keyboards, or screens. Client devices need no UI in order to communicate with the ICEbox. Third, this model allows us to avoid some of the problems with multicast-based discovery protocols in complex multi-link home networks, by using the ICEbox as a self-populating directory service. Finally, the network model maintained by the ICEbox, coupled with the management protocols it uses for ongoing communication with clients, can drive a range of interactive tools that can support end-users' understanding, monitoring, and troubleshooting of the network. In the following section, we describe these features of the ICEbox in detail.

4   ICEbox Features

4.1 Physical Form

We investigated a number of physical form factors for the ICEbox, including integrating it into an existing home gateway router and building a software-only version that could execute on arbitrary PCs. While these approaches have the advantage of not requiring an extra "box" in the home, they restrict the UI approaches we could take. Namely, existing home gateway routers have no screen that could be used for the monitoring functions of the ICEbox; and, while we could create an arbitrarily complex UI on a PC platform, we felt it was important to move away from "PC-style" interfaces that require mice and keyboards.

Thus, our initial ICEbox prototype is implemented as a stand-alone mini networked appliance, which has several unique features, one of which is a color LCD touch screen that is used as an input and display device. The ICEbox is equipped with an infrared transceiver and a standard Ethernet port; the infrared transceiver is used for communication between the ICEbox and devices yet not attached to the home network, while the Ethernet port is used for communication between the ICEbox and devices attached to the home network. Another salient feature of the ICEbox is a physical key lock. This is used to restrict the ICEbox's ability to add devices to the network or configure devices on the network, as described below.

This form factor closely resembles a standard home security pad. It is roughly the same size as such a pad, has a small screen and lock, but otherwise no physical controls. Our previous studies indicated that network infrastructure equipment, such as access points and routers, is often hidden from view in users' houses. Such "invisibility" means that these devices are not positioned to easily notify users of problems—users are unlikely to notice a red light flashing, for example. By making the ICEbox resemble a home security pad, and by making it a vertical device, our goal is to explore placement opportunities that might be more amenable to visibility (such as placing the device on a wall near the security controls or a light switch).

The ICEbox is logically located at the boundary between the home network and the Internet, sitting just behind the home gateway router in our current implementation. In a future implementation the ICEbox will likely subsume the functionality of the router.

4.2 Interfaces for Device Introduction

As noted in the related work section, a number of earlier projects have demonstrated the benefits of short-range communication techniques for device association. Such mechanisms allow two devices to communicate in an ad-hoc, secure manner with no pre-configuration required. Thus, they serve as an ideal "bootstrapping" mechanism, since they can operate without explicit human involvement in configuration. Second, by limiting the range of such techniques, they provide an implicit interaction boundary, making them amenable to physical gestures such as pointing or touching two devices together.

However, pointing can also be problematic. One would not wish, for example, to have to point an Internet-enabled refrigerator at the ICEbox in order to provision it for the home network. Also, such mechanisms require the client device to be powered on in order to communicate; while this may not be an issue with laptops, it complicates the use of pointing techniques for devices such as desktops and printers (we will return to this issue in the Concluding Remarks section).

To support a range of introduction techniques—including pointing, as well as others—we have defined an abstract introduction protocol that can be carried over a number of different transports. In our current implementation, however, we carry this protocol over infrared (and thus use a short-range pointing interface) as our sole introduction mechanism. Our goal at this stage of our research is to refine the introduction protocol sufficiently that it can work for a range of devices, and then later to explore how this protocol can be manifested in a variety of specific interaction techniques. Thus,other short-range mechanisms could also be used, as long as they support the ability to transfer data bi-directionally and to detect packet loss. For example, this might include digital over-the-air audio, short-range RF, and inductive communication. Further, the introduction protocol could be layered over an existing TCP/IP protocol, or even "sneakernet" mechanisms (such as shuttling a USB key back and forth between devices).

4.3 A Physical Lock for Securing the Home Network

Protecting the network from unwanted access is another source of complexity for home users. It requires that users understand the security syntax and semantics of their specific home network. By automating the provisioning step—including passing WEP keys and SSIDs—the ICEbox hides basic security configuration, requiring no knowledge on the part of users about security. Since security configuration happens automatically at the time of introduction, we obviate the possibility that users might neglect to set up security.

But this model introduces new factors into the security equation. By requiring physical access to the ICEbox in order to add to or change the network, this approach transforms the problem of network security to one of physical security—as long as physical access to the ICEbox itself is restricted, then interlopers cannot easily add an unauthorized device to the home network. For some users, in some circumstances, this level of security may be sufficient. However, for more security-conscious users, there are times when even physical security might be insufficient. For example, home visitors (neighborhood teenagers for example) might have access to the ICEbox while they are in the home. Therefore, we provide an additional layer of security to optionally restrict access to the ICEbox functions.

There are many potential ways to add this extra security layer. One is to require users to enter a password (on either the device or the ICEbox) in order to complete the introduction step. While such a solution is simple to implement, it has all the problems of traditional password solutions [1]: it requires that users remember the password, requires that they perform an extra step at each introduction, and requires that we provide extra UI mechanisms to enter, change, and manage the password.

Instead, the ICEbox provides a hardware-based solution that maps to existing practices and metaphors. As mentioned before, our metaphor is that the ICEbox is a logical door to the home network. Thus, like a physical door, the ICEbox appliance is equipped with a physical lock that enables access to its introduction and management features. A homeowner uses a key to unlock the ICEbox when he or she wants to attach a new device to the home network, and can also unlock the ICEbox when a visitor appears with a device the owner wishes to provision onto the network. In much the same way that users may leave a copy of a physical key with trusted friends, users may also leave the key to the network with associates. Likewise, users who are not concerned with additional security can simply leave the device unlocked.

This door lock metaphor can provide a greater degree of security to prevent unauthorized devices or users from joining the home network. The physical lock allows users to restrict access in a natural way while not requiring any network- or system-level security knowledge from users, nor requiring the use of mechanisms such as passwords or access control lists.

4.4 Visual Interface for Device Monitoring

The model of the home network created by the ICEbox is used to drive a graphical display of the network. The touchscreen display on the ICEbox displays the devices on the home network and lets users monitor them. Each device that has been introduced to the network is represented by an icon on the display. Touching a device icon brings up details of that device, including device and service descriptions and real-time connectivity status (whether the device is reachable or not) for all devices on the home network. To determine device connectivity, the ICEbox uses a simple monitoring protocol, sending out periodic connectivity status check messages to all devices and updates their connectivity in its model and on the display (Figure 3).

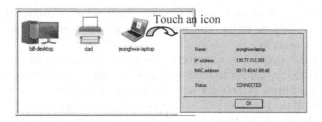

Fig. 3. Touch screen visual interface for device monitoring

4.5 Directory and Discovery Features

As noted earlier, typical multicast based discovery protocols such as mDNS used by Zeroconf [4], and SSDP used by UPnP [12], suffer from problems when used in complex network topologies. Because these protocols generally work only on a single network segment (given their multicast time-to-live radius), users find that devices that should automatically discover each other sometimes do not. Correcting such problems requires an understanding of physical layer network topology.

The typical solution to multi-segment discovery involves the deployment of a directory service (such as is used by the Service Location Protocol, SLP [10]). In the home setting, however, such approaches are untenable because they require explicit administration to deploy, configure, populate and maintain the contents of the service as devices come and go.

In contrast, a key advantage of the centralized network model of the ICEbox is that it can provide a robust mechanism for device and service discovery without the administrative hassles of a managed directory service. Since the ICEbox maintains a list of all devices currently on the network, it acts as a *self-populating* directory service; clients use a simple lookup protocol to query it for devices that match specified types. This approach mitigates many of the scoping problems seen with multicast-based discovery protocols without adding additional administrative burden.

5 User Experience

We performed an evaluation to investigate the usability and utility of the three key features of the ICEbox user interface: introducing devices to the home network, securing the home network, and monitoring the home network. Our goal with this study was to get a sense of the overall usability and utility of our approach, rather than to perform an in-depth usability analysis and task metrics. The first task compared ICEbox device introduction with a common method for manual setup of devices on the home network. The second task examined securing the home network. The third explored the usability and utility of the visual interface and monitoring features the ICEbox.

We built a networked home environment in our laboratory, instrumented with a Netgear 54WRG614 wireless access point, an ICEbox appliance, a networked printer, and several wireless laptops. Participants were invited to our laboratory to participate in the study. While there are limits to studying home networking in a lab, controlled conditions give us repeatability that would be unobtainable on a real network, which is essential in studying usability rather than the network technology itself.

Ten users, 3 males and 7 females, aged 20-35 years old, participated in our study, all of whom have a network at home. Half of the participants described themselves as novices who had never set up networked devices before (their roommate, friend, or spouse had configured their networks for them). The other half had previous experience setting up networked devices in their homes. Their knowledge varied, with some users describing themselves as "familiar" with network setup, while other "beginners" still had experience installing and configuring network devices at home.

5.1 Device Configuration

The configuration task consisted of two sub-tasks: adding a new laptop to an existing secure home network, and then configuring the laptop to use a new networked printer. We used a WEP-enabled secure network for our tests since we believe users do desire security on their networks at home if it can be provided easily. We chose a wireless laptop and a printer to test both network-level and application-level configuration, respectively, since these are common in many networked households.

We used a within-subjects design in which each participant performed trials using the ICEbox and the existing manual methods. For each trial, each participant was first asked to add an unconfigured wireless laptop to the home network; then, the laptop correctly configured, he or she was then asked to configure access to the printer from the laptop. For the manual trials these tasks involved using the existing tools provided by the OS and access point, and the "Add Printer" Wizard, respectively. We gave a brief verbal overview of both systems and provided participants the instructions that come with the Netgear access point and with an ICEbox instruction sheet; participants were told that they could refer to either as necessary.

Participants were asked to think out loud during the study, and we recorded audio from these trials. Trials ended when the participant claimed to have finished or gave up.

Experienced users succeeded in configuring the laptop and the printer for both the manual setup and the ICEbox setup, with the ICEbox allowing faster configuration. Novice users, however, showed a more noticeable difference between the two methods. Four of five novice participants gave up configuration in the manual task. Some of them referred to the instruction manual for assistance; however, despite this, they eventually gave up since they could not understand the manual. Meanwhile, all novice participants succeeded in configuration with the ICEbox. After the study, we administered a post-study questionnaire to gain insight into participants' subjective impressions of each method and overall method preference. Participants were very positive about using the ICEbox as a configuration tool. Nine of the ten participants preferred using the ICEbox to the manual set up method, and eight of these strongly preferred using the ICEbox. One experienced user still preferred the manual setup because it was more familiar to her. All participants agreed that the ICEbox was an easier way to configure devices.

5.2 Securing the Home Network

We ran a pre-study session in which participants were asked to secure the home network using the existing Netgear wireless security setup method. Only two out of ten participants succeeded in securing the wireless home network. They used the wireless network wizard or the Netgear access point web interface for this task. The other eight participants were unable to complete the task, despite having the product manuals available. On the other hand, all participants understood and were able to use the ICEbox key lock interface. Based on our interviews with them, most users understood the lock as a way to "keep outsiders out" of the network. Qualitatively, all of our participants preferred the key lock interface to the manual security set up method; users noted the physicality of the interface as being important in making is the functionality both apparent and intuitive.

5.3 Monitoring the Home Network

We were interested in gaining a qualitative sense of the utility as well as the usability of the monitoring features of the ICEbox. Overall, most network-experienced users and some novice users expressed their interest in this functionality, with several providing suggestions for refining the feature set. Meanwhile, three novice users reported that they did not need this feature since they had no need for network monitoring.

Other users, more familiar with network configuration and troubleshooting tasks, expressed interest in having an easily available depiction of network status, and an interest in having an icon for the entire network in addition to the individual devices on it (for controlling network and firewall parameters, for instance). A number of suggestions revolved around desires to add functionality behind network configuration and monitoring, such as remote control of devices in the home.

5.4 Study Summary

Although we view our study as a high-level exploration of the usability and utility of centralized network management in the home, we do believe that it points to the promise of this model. For the majority of our users, the ICEbox significantly reduced the complexity of certain home networking tasks. We found that even novice users were able to configure wireless devices easily, secure the network, and monitor devices' connection status without deep knowledge of networking. We believe that these experiences highlight the utility of *removing* as much interaction as possible from the network setup process.

We also noted during our study that, although few participants referred to manuals (as might be expected), none of the ICEbox users referred to the instruction sheet in order to accomplish tasks. We believe that this demonstrates the utility of a simple set of physical interactions for network configuration, and especially the value of having tangible, physical affordances to functionality that is often hidden (such as security configuration).

There were, however, several features that our participants did not like. Many of these concerned the difficulty of infrared communications: finding and facing infrared ports on two devices was not familiar to most users, which suggests that further work on introduction protocols is necessary. Likewise, some users advocated for a "mini ICEbox" in the form of a cellphone or other device, which would allow them to bring the ICEbox to the device, rather than the device to the ICEbox. Finally, although users were generally positive about the key mechanism for network security, a number of participants worried about the possibility of loss of the key. At the same time, these users expressed a desire to incorporate other functions into the lock, such as parental access controls for the network.

6 Concluding Remarks

In this paper, we analyzed why home networking is difficult for users and then introduced a novel type of network appliance, called the ICEbox, designed to reduce the complexity and increase the usability of home networking. The ICEbox simplifies device configuration through a pointing interface based on a short-range communication; it provides easy-to-use security through a door lock metaphor. Visual monitoring capabilities provide a graphical display of the devices on the network and their current status for easy monitoring of the network.

There are a number of open questions regarding the physical form of the ICEbox, as well as the mechanism used for the introduction protocol; these two issues interrelate with one another. For example, one approach may be to detach part of the ICEbox (a "provisioning wand") that you touch to client devices. Another approach—reminiscent of WCN—is to use a USB memory key. Some of these mechanisms are restrictive from a systems perspective, because they make multi-round communication between the ICEbox and client difficult (you'd have to walk back and forth with your USB key to perform the multi-round introduction protocol, for example). Balancing the systems benefits of two-way communication against users' effort is necessary to find the "sweet spot" of low-overhead, automated introduction.

In parallel with this, we are planning a series of studies to inform other future goals of the project. For example, one issue that the current ICEbox implementation does not deal with is easy revocation of access to the home network, especially for "transient" devices such as those of visitors. Many users now provide access to their home networks to visitors or neighbors. While the current ICEbox implementation allows easy access to the network for these users, we have no easy way to close the network to them after they leave. What are the most flexible (and socially appropriate) ways to allow such transient access? The interface challenge here is in providing easy access without overburdening the introduction step with a checklist of possible rights and time periods for which access is granted, nor with requiring that users remember to revoke visitor access once they leave.

Finally, our current protocols work best when the ICEbox is the first entity deployed onto the network. This allows it to build up its network model as new devices are introduced to it. We plan to explore techniques to allow post hoc introduction of the ICEbox onto the network.

References

1. Adams, A., Sasse, M., Lunt, P.: Making Passwords Secure and Usable. In: Proc. HCI'97 (1997)
2. Balfanz, D., Durfee, G., Grinter, R., Smetters, D., Stewart, P.: Network-in-a-Box: How to Set Up a Secure Wireless Network in Under a Minute. In: USENIX Security Symposium (2004)

3. Blumenthal, M.S., Clark, D.D.: Rethinking the design of the Internet: the end-to-end arguments vs. the brave new world. ACM Transactions on Internet Technology 1(1) (2001)
4. Cheshire, S., Steinberg, D.: Zero Configuration Networking: The Definitive Guide. O'Reilly Associates (December 2005) ISBN 0596101007.
5. Consumer Electronics Association, Broadband and the Home of Tomorrow (March 30, 2006)
6. Droms, R.: Dynamic Host Configuration Protocol, Internet Engineering Task Force Request for Comment (RFC) 2131 (1997)
7. Goland, Y., Cai, T., Leach, P., Gu, Y., Albright, S.: Simple Service Discovery Protocol/1.0: Operating Without an Arbiter. Internet Engineering Task Force Draft, (October 28, 1999)
8. Goodall, J.R., Lutters, W.G., Komlodi, A.: I Know My Network: Collaboration and Expertise in Intrusion Detection. In: Proc. ACM CSCW, pp. 342–345 (2004)
9. Grinter, R.E., Edwards, W.K.: The Work to Make a Home Network Work. In: Proc. European Conference on Computer-Supported Cooperative Work (ECSCW'05) (September 2005)
10. Guttman, E., Perkins, C., Veizades, J., Day, M.: Service Location Protocol, Version 2. Internet Engineering Task Force Request for Comments (RFC) 2608 (1999)
11. Jackson, L.A., Von Eye, A., Barbatsis, G., Biocca, F., Fitzgerald, H.E., Zhao, Y.: The Impact of Internet Use on the Other Size of the Digital Divide. Communications of the ACM 47(7), 43–47 (2004)
12. Jeronimo, M., Weast, J.: UPnP Design by Example: A Software Developer's Guide to Universal Plug and Play. Intel Press, Hillsboro (2003)
13. Kiesler, S., Zdaniuk, B., Lundmark, V., Kraut, R.: Troubles With the Internet: The Dynamics of Help at Home. Human Computer Interaction, 323–351 (2000)
14. Kraut, R., Scherlis, W., Mukhopadhyay, T., Manning, J., Kiesler, S.: HomeNet: A Field Trial of Residential Internet Services. In: Proc. CHI'96, pp. 284–291 (1996)
15. Laszlo, J.: Home Networking: Seizing Near-Term Opportunities to Extend Connectivity to Every Room. Jupiter Research (BRB02-V01) (2002)
16. MacMillan, R.: Plugged In: Wireless Networking Baffles Some Customers. Reuters news report (March 10, 2006)
17. Microsoft Corp. Windows Connect Now Architecture whitepaper (April 11, 2005), http://www.microsoft.com/whdc/device/netattach/WCN.mspx
18. Rekimoti, J., Ayatsuka, Y., Kohno, M.: SyncTab: An Interaction Technique for Mobile Networking. In: Proc. Mobile CHI, pp. 104–115 (2003)
19. Rekimoto, J., Ayatsuka, Y., Kohno, M., Oba, H.: Proximal Interactions: A Direct Manipulation Technique for Wireless Networking. In: Proc. INTERACT2003, pp. 511–518.
20. Scherf, K.: Parks Associate Panel on Home Networking. In: Proceedings of Consumer Electronics Association Conference (2002)
21. Swindells, C., Inkpen, K.M., Dill, J.C., Tory, M.: That one there! Pointing to establish device identity. In: Proc. ACM UIST, pp. 151–160 (2002)
22. Vitalari, N.P., Venkatesh, A., Gronhaug, K.: Computing in the Home: Shifts in the Time Allocation Patterns of Households. Communications of the ACM 28(5) (1985)
23. Voida, A., Grinter, R.E., Ducheneaut, N., Edwards, W.K., Newman, M.W.: Listening Practices Surrounding iTunes Music Sharing. In: Proc. CHI2005 (2005)
24. Whittaker, S., Amento, B.: Seeing: what you are hearing: Co-ordinating responses to trouble reports in network troubleshooting. In: Proc. ECSCW'01, pp. 219–283. Kluwer Academic Publishers, Dordrecht (2003)

Selective Analysis of Linguistic Features Used in Video Mediated Collaboration: An Indicator of Users Sense of Co-presence

Paulo Melo[1] and Leila Alem[2]

[1] LAIV [Interactional Analysis and Videography Lab],
Federal University of Pernambuco, Recife, Pernambuco, Brazil
[2] CSIRO ICT Centre, Cnr Pembroke & Vimiera Roads,
Marsfield NSW 2122 Australia
paulomelo@gmail.com, leila.alem@csiro.au

Abstract. Studies in video mediated collaboration are going beyond traditional measures of time on task and task accuracy by attempting to qualify specific aspect of users' experience. This paper explores users' sense of co-presence as the extent to which they feel co-present with their partner when building collaboratively a toy over a video conferencing system. A linguistic analysis of the way users are referring to remote objects and places has been conducted in order to investigate the correlation between co-presence score and the frequency of local and remote deixis. Our results indicate that co-presence score is positively correlated to the frequency of local deixis as reported previously [1] and negatively correlated to remote deixis. We conclude that the words used by users when referring to remote objects and places may indicate aspects of user's experience while engaged in remote collaboration.

Keywords: Co-presence, CMC, linguistic analysis, Video mediated collaboration.

1 Introduction

Traditional video mediated collaboration studies have focused mostly on measures of task performance and user satisfaction. Recent studies in video mediated collaboration research report on measures of user's sense of presence when collaborating with others over a distance. One study [2] reports on the sense of physical presence a specialist doctor experiences when engaged in a remote consultation of a patient. The measure focuses on the extent to which users of video conferencing systems feel physically present in the remote location. Others studies [3, 4] report on the sense of social presence users experience when negotiating with remote partners using a video conference link. In these studies the presence measure focuses on the extent to which users feel connected with their remote partners. One important observation from those studies is the effort to go beyond traditional measures of time on task and task accuracy by attempting to qualify user's sense of presence.

This paper follows this trend and reports on a video mediated collaboration study in which a worker and a helper are assembling jointly a Lego toy. In this study the

C. Baranauskas et al. (Eds.): INTERACT 2007, LNCS 4663, Part II, pp. 211–214, 2007.
© IFIP International Federation for Information Processing 2007

helper's sense of co-presence (i.e. the extent to which they feel in the same room as their remote partner) was assessed. Another work [1] reports an experiment with a similar design where researchers have found that local deixis[1] and remote deixis[2] were positively correlated to presence. In that study the sense of presence was measured by a set of questions developed by the authors. We were interested in replicating some aspects of these previous promising findings by this time using a tool based on an existing and established measure of co-presence [5]. In this paper we have used an average measure of co-presence of the whole trial. This average co-presence score and a general measure of the linguistic features were used for investigating potential correlation between co-presence score and linguistic features such as local and remote deixis.

2 Our Experiment

Our study was conducted in the context of a more comprehensive experiment which investigated the effects of two different representations of gesture (hand/ pointer) in a remote collaboration on physical task[3]. Thirty-four participants were grouped into randomly assigned 17 pairs of one worker and one helper. Much of the technical setup was based on another work [6]. Each participant faced a standard desktop monitor and had a mat on their desk as the shared workspace. A camera was positioned directly above the mat with a field of view encompassing the entire mat (Figure 1). The Virtual Tea Room technology developed by CSIRO functioned as the technical platform for this experimentation.

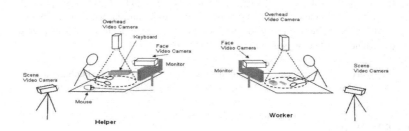

Fig. 1. The technical setup used in the experiment

In this study we have used two methods: a set of subjective measures of co-presence and a linguistic analysis based on full transcription of the trials. The sense of co-presence was measured using a set of questions inspired in Schroeder's work [5]. The transcriptions were fed to a text analysis software [7]. The software determined the rate at which the speakers used 70 dimensions of language. Based on [8], we hypothesized that we would find a positive correlation between the frequency of local deixis and co-presence score as established in [1]; and a negative correlation between local deixis and remote deixis as opposed to findings reported [1].

---

[1] Local deixis include words such as: here, this and these.

[2] Remote deixis include words such as: there, that and those.

[3] Initial findings of the more comprehensive study are reported in another paper.

2.1 Participants and Procedures

Helpers were asked to guide remotely their partner in assembling the object. While the worker had access to the pieces of Lego toy, the helper had access to the instructions for building the toy. The pair had to built collaboratively the Lego toy under three media conditions administrated in a randomized order. In a final step the pair was asked to assemble the body parts assembled in previous conditions. A post questionnaire was administered after each condition as well as after completion of the final step. A final questionnaire was also administered consisting of demographic information, and preference questions. Then the participants were debriefed and compensated with AU$ 40,00. Each session took approximately 80 minutes.

3 Results

An initial analysis indicated a high positive correlation between the co-presence score and the frequency of local deixis, and a negative correlation between presence score and the frequency of remote deixis, and finally, a high negative correlation between local and remote deixis (Table 1). A regression analysis was performed in order to check the linguistic features ability to predict co-presence score. The regression used the frequency of local deixis and the frequency of *We category* (words as we, our and us). Results indicate that those linguistic variables can predict about 38% of the whole the co-presence score (R Square = .381; F [12,680] = 4.31).

Table 1. Correlations between local and remote deixis and presence score (N=17). ** p < 0.01; * p < 0.05 level (2-tailed).

	Remote deixis	Local deixis	Co-presence
Remote deixis	1	-.667(**)	-.379
Local deixis	-.667(**)	1	.581(*)
Co-presence	-.379	.581(*)	1

4 Discussion

In this paper, the use of a co-presence measure developed and used by the presence research community increased our confidence in the interpretation of our findings. Aligned with previous results [1] we have found a high positive correlation between the co-presence score and the frequency of local deixis. In opposition with the same study [1] we also have found a negative correlation between the co-presence score and remote deixis and a negative correlation between the frequency of local deixis and remote deixis. Our results validate what we have hypothesized. It seems reasonable to assume that users during their remote interaction with their partner will either mostly use local deixis (i.e. their linguistic behavior is as if they were co-present with their partner), or mostly use remote deixis (i.e. their linguistic behavior is indicative that they do not feel in the same place as their partner). Users' verbal behavior is hence one indicative of some aspects of their experience while engaged in remote collaboration, more specifically their sense of co-presence. From a methodological point of view, our contribution was showing the analysis of specific linguistic features while requiring a lot of effort (full transcription of the trials) is a good candidate method for developing an objective measure of co-presence.

It is proposed to target future work in developing a more cost/effective way of deploying linguistic analysis methods and in exploring relevance of the linguistic approach for measuring/evaluating other aspects of user's experience such as their sense of social presence. Future works will also explore the predictability power of co-presence score through linguistic analysis.

Acknowledgements

We would like to thank Anja Wessels and Susan Hansen for their help during the data analysis. As well Aiden Wickey, Cara Stitzlein, Alex Krumm-Heller, and Jane Li for their contribution in running the overall experiment. Finally we thank Networking Research Lab at CSIRO for funding this study.

References

1. Kramer, A., Oh, L., Fussell, S.: Using Linguistic Features to Measure Presence in Computer Mediated Communication. In: CHI 2006 Notes, pp. 913–916. ACM Press, New York (2006)
2. Alem, L., Hansen, S., Li, J.: Evaluating Clinician Experience in a Telemedicine Application: a Presence Perspective. In: Proceedings of OZCHI'06, Sydney, Australia (2006)
3. Stitzlein, C., Alem, L.: When Mixing Physical Presence and Telepresence. In: Proceedings of Presence 06, Cleveland, Ohio, USA (2006)
4. Hauber, J., Regenbrecht, H., Hills, A., Cockburn, A., Billinghurst, M.: Social Presence in Two and Three Dimensional Videoconferencing. In: Proceedings of ISPR (2005)
5. Schroeder, R., Steed, A., Axelsson, A.-S., Heldal, I., Abelin, A., Widestrom, J., Nilsson, A., Slater, M.: Collaborating in Networked Immersive Spaces: as Good as Being There Together? Computer & Graphics 25, 781–788 (2001)
6. Kirk, D.S., Fraser, D.S., Rodden, T.: The effects of Remote Gesturing on Distance Instruction. In: Proceeding of the International Conference on Computer Supported Collaborative Learning, Taipei, Taiwan, pp. 301–310 (2005)
7. Pennebaker, J.W., Francis, M.E., Booth, R.J.: Linguistic Inquiry and Word Count (LIWC): a Computerized Text Analysis Program. Erlbaum, Mahwah (2001)
8. Gergle, D., Rosé, C., Kraut, R.: Modeling the Impact of Shared Visual Information on Collaborative Reference. In: Proceedings of CHI 2007, pp. 1543–1552. ACM Press, New York (2007)

Gender Talk: Differences in Interaction Style in CMC

Xiaoning Sun, Susan Wiedenbeck, Thippaya Chintakovid, and Qiping Zhang

Drexel University, College of IST, 3141 Chestnut Street Philadelphia PA 19104, USA
{xs27, sw53, tc79, qiping}@drexel.edu

Abstract. Qualitative analysis was used to investigate the nature of the interactions of different gender pairings doing a negotiation task via computer-mediated communication (CMC). Preliminary results indicate that female pairs used more language of fairness, saving face, and acknowledgement in their conversation than did male pairs. Male pairs made more procedural statements about meeting management and actions than female pairs. The study provides a preliminary understanding of how gender interactions may affect performance in CMC tasks.

1 Introduction

A well-known phenomenon to linguists and socio-psychologists is that linguistic styles are relatively different for men and women, and these differences are rooted in different ways of learning speech from childhood [5]. Men tend to be sensitive to the power dynamics of interaction, speaking in direct ways that position themselves as one-up; women tend to react more strongly to the rapport dynamics, speaking in indirect ways that save face for others and avoid putting others in a one-down position [5]. These patterns are also reflected in the ways males and females interact with computers [6]. For example, meta-analysis revealed gender-related stereotypical patterns in CMC environments, in which female communication, compared to male, is more socio-emotionally oriented [2].

Our work on CMC and gender (summarized in Section 3) has shown that gender differences affect trust and performance in computer-mediated tasks [4]. However, there has been little qualitative research on the nature of the interactions of different gender groups that helps explain these results. In this study, we used qualitative methods to take a closer look at the social mechanisms employed by different gender pairings. This work-in-progress provides a preliminary understanding of how gender pair collaboration may affect trust and group performance in two CMC modes, video conferencing (VC) and Instant Messaging (IM).

2 Methodology

This study is a 3x2 between subjects design. The gender pairing factor included male/male (MM), male/female (MF), and female/female (FF) pairs; the media condition factor included VC and IM. In the VC condition gender information was known by passively seeing the partner in the video. In the IM condition, the gender of the partners was revealed by the experimenter immediately before doing their task.

C. Baranauskas et al. (Eds.): INTERACT 2007, LNCS 4663, Part II, pp. 215–218, 2007.
© IFIP International Federation for Information Processing 2007

A total of 120 undergraduate students (60 pairs) took part in the study. Participants were frequent users of IM technology, but less frequent users of VC technology. Pairs of participants did not know each other before the experiment.

Using a negotiation task [7], participants played the roles of marketing managers of two competitive companies in which they had to agree on prices for their three common drugs. The profits were constructed so that for one participant a particular price would bring about great payoff, but the same price created a loss for the other participant. In this situation, the best way to make money overall is to choose a set of three prices that are reciprocally beneficial—one player will receive a high payoff while the other takes a loss, and then the reverse for another product.

Pairs were run one at a time. Members of a pair were put in different rooms so that they did not see each other face-to-face. They were randomly assigned to perform the task using the VC or IM channel. Pairs had 30 minutes to do the task. Subsequently, they completed a trust questionnaire; the Alpha reliability was .82.

3 Analysis and Results

The analysis of the communication process was based on a coding scheme. Initial codes were developed based on the literature of pair negotiation and communication [1, 3]. Two researchers iteratively refined the codes and rules for their application. Then, they independently coded 18 randomly chosen transcripts. The inter-rater reliability was 91%. Considering the high reliability, one rater coded the rest of the transcripts. Table 1 shows the final coding scheme.

In a previous paper [4], we reported the results of the quantitative analyses of trust and performance. First, we found that female pairs perceived higher levels of trust

Table 1. The coding scheme

Code Name	Description
Fairness	Evaluative statements considering both parties' benefit. E.g., "[Drug] Alpha 2 is not in my best interest but if other prices work out I am willing to take a loss."
Clarification	Statements repeating information already mentioned. E.g., "You said [Drug] alpha1 is not good for you, right?"
Meeting Management	Statements that move negotiation ahead. E.g., "Where do you want to start, [Drug] Alpha?"
Action	Statements proposing negotiation strategies. E.g., "We should each come up with a list of [Drug] Alpha strategies that we would not accept just to narrow things down."
Saving face	Statements saying no in an indirect way. E.g., "The price is not very good to me."
Acknowledge-ment	Statements appreciating partner's work. E.g., "It's nice working with you."
Tentative Speech	Statements asking partner's opinions. E.g., "Do you agree with me on [Drug] Alpha 6?"

than male pairs when gender information was passively seen via the VC channel. Second, female pairs perceived higher levels of trust than male pairs when gender information was mutually revealed via the IM channel. Third, male/female pairs had better performance outcomes than female pairs.

To date, communications from a total of 27 out of 60 pairs have been analyzed. For the analysis of the communication process data, we conducted an ANOVA on each code. Table 2 shows the mean of each code frequency and p-value for the MM, FF, and MF pairs. Interaction effects were tested if gender and media were significant. For each gender-media condition, there were 4 or 5 pairs. In the presentation of the results we focus mostly on the MM and FF pairs.

Table 2. Mean and p value (from ANOVA) of codes among three gender pairings

	FF		MF		MM		p-value		
	IM	Video	IM	Video	IM	Video	Gender	Media	Interaction
Fairness	5.8	7.8	4.8	7.0	3.2	3.5	**.00**	**.04**	.48
Clarification	5.0	15.5	4.2	19.3	3.4	12.3	**.01**	**.00**	**.02**
Meeting Management	3.6	5.8	2.8	8.5	3.4	2.8	**.00**	**.00**	**.00**
Action	1.0	0.5	1.6	1.5	3.2	1.5	**.02**	.09	----
Saving face	5.0	0.5	2.0	1.0	1.6	1.0	**.01**	**.00**	**.00**
Acknowl-edgement	2.6	0.8	0.2	0.0	2.0	0.0	**.00**	**.01**	.07
Tentative Speech	2.0	3.3	2.8	1.8	2.2	0.8	.78	.53	----

There were several gender effects: (1) FF pairs had more collaborative communication language, including fairness ($F (2, 21) = 8.94$, $p < .00$), saving face ($F (2, 21) = 5.76$, $p < .01$) and acknowledgement ($F (2, 21) = 7.93$, $p < .00$); (2) MM pairs used more direct language and more calls for planning and action, including meeting management ($F (2, 21) = 14.54$, $p < .00$) and action ($F (2, 21) = 4.78$, $p < .02$); (3) FF pairs used more clarification statements ($F (2, 21) = 5.50$, $p < .01$). Also, there were media effects of VC on meeting management ($F (1, 21) = 37.16$, $p < .00$) and clarification ($F (1, 21) = 28.73$, $p < .00$). All pairs did more meeting management and clarification in the video condition. Furthermore, there were also media effects of IM on saving face ($F (1, 21) = 25.32$, $p < .00$) and acknowledgement ($F (1, 21) = 7.73$, $p < .01$). Overall, pairs used more cooperative language, such as acknowledgement words, in the IM condition. Generally, the MF pairs' conversational behavior in IM fell in between the FF and MM pairs, while in VC the MF pairs' conversational behavior was more variable. There were interaction effects of gender x media on meeting management ($F (2, 21) = 21.78$, $p < .00$), clarification ($F (2, 21) = 4.48$, $p < .02$) and saving face ($F (2, 21) = 18.95$, $p < .00$).

4 Discussion and Conclusion

As discussed above, females tend to use a collaborative conversational style focusing on harmonious relationships, whereas males tend to be sensitive to power in conversational interactions, speaking in direct ways and focusing on status [5]. Our communication process analysis is largely consistent with these ideas, in that FF pairs used more languages of fairness, saving face, and acknowledgement in their conversation; MM pairs used more direct statements about meeting management and action when communicating with each other and were less prone to use a collaborative style.

The qualitative analysis provides more detailed data to explain the results from our previous quantitative analyses, especially with respect to trust [4]. The higher levels of trust perceived by FF pairs in the VC and IM channels may be partly due to the conversational styles they used. It appears that FF pairs tried to create a smooth relationship by considering both parties' benefit and reinforcing that with language expressing mutual respect and appreciation of others' efforts. On the other hand, MM pairs showed lower sensitivity to group harmony in the competitive negotiation context. This may have influenced MM pairs' lower levels of trust. MF pairs' conversational behaviors have been less often studied, and we plan to focus on these mixed pairs in further analysis of these data. Our results are tentative because we have only analyzed about half of the pairs. If the full analysis of 60 pairs shows consistent results, we will have a much clearer understanding of linguistic mechanisms that support collaborators in competitive CMC settings.

In conclusion, it appears clear that gender is a factor that should be considered in CMC. As the workplace becomes more diverse in terms of gender and culture, leaders of virtual teams will need to become even better at interacting with diverse team members and more flexible in adjusting their own styles to different group compositions.

References

1. Fisher, R., Ertel, D.: Getting ready to negotiate: The getting to YES workbook. Penguin, New York (1995)
2. Li, Q.: Computer-mediated communication and gender difference: a meta-analysis. In: Presented at the Annual Meeting of the American Educational Research Association, Montreal (2005)
3. Rafaeli, S., Sudweeks, F.: ProjectH Codebook. [On-line] (1993), available: arch-sci.arch.su.edu.au/pub/projectH/coding.docs/ codebook
4. Sun, X., Zhang, Q., Wiedenbeck, S., Chintakovid, T.: The effect of gender on trust perception and performance in computer-mediated virtual environments. In: Proc. ASIS&T'07 (to appear)
5. Tannen, D.: The power of talk: who gets heard and why. Harvard Business Review 73(5), 138–148 (1995)
6. Turkle, S.: Computational reticence: Why women fear the intimate machine. In Technology and women's voices: Keeping in touch. In: Kramarae, C. (ed.) New York, pp. 41–61 (1988)
7. Zhang, Q.P., Olson, G.M., Olson, J.S.: Does video matter more for long distance collaborators? In: Proc. XXVIII International Congress of Psychology (CD-ROM) (2004)

Focus+Context Visualization Techniques for Displaying Large Lists with Multiple Points of Interest on Small Tactile Screens

Stéphane Huot[1,2] and Eric Lecolinet[1]

[1] GET/ENST – CNRS UMR 5141, 46 rue Barrault, 75013 Paris, France
[2] LRI (CNRS) & INRIA Futurs, Bât. 490, Univ. Paris-Sud, 91405 Orsay, France
Stephane.Huot@lri.fr, Eric.Lecolinet@enst.fr

Abstract. This paper presents a focus+context visualization and interaction technique for displaying large lists on handheld devices. This technique has been specifically designed to fit the constraints of small tactile screens. Thanks to its spiral layout, it provides a global view of large lists on a limited amount of screen real-estate. It has also been designed to allow direct interaction with fingers. This technique proposes an alternative to multi-focus visualization, called "augmented context", where several objects of interest can be pointed up simultaneously. We propose two implementations of this approach that either use spatial or temporal composition. We conducted a controlled experiment that compares our approach to standard scrollable lists for a search task on a PDA phone. Results show that our technique significantly reduces the error rate (about 3.7 times lower) without loss of performance.

Keywords: Mobile interfaces, focus+context visualization, spiral layout, finger interaction, one-handed interaction.

1 Introduction

During the last years, mobile devices have evolved from cell phones to handheld computers, introducing new usages, but also challenging new problems. Whereas hardware buttons were efficient to manage most of basic phones functionalities, modern handheld devices (PDA, PDA-Phones, etc.) can manage more and more data and include new functions that require more efficient interaction. However, most applications for handheld devices still rely on traditional GUI paradigms that have been developed for desktop computers. This model does not fit well on small devices because of their limited screen size and input capabilities. In fact, interacting with large quantities of data with small devices is still a challenging problem that is aggravated when several objects of interest must be highlighted simultaneously. This case is related to multi-focus visualization, but with the additional constraint that a very limited amount of screen real-estate can be used to represent multiple points of interest. Finally, the fact that handheld devices should be usable in mobility conditions is another key factor. Most applications for tactile screen devices require using a stylus, a way of interacting that is not very well suited for mobile interaction.

C. Baranauskas et al. (Eds.): INTERACT 2007, LNCS 4663, Part II, pp. 219–233, 2007.
© IFIP International Federation for Information Processing 2007

The next section describes some limitations of graphical representations and interaction techniques that have been proposed so far. Section 3 introduces some general principles we propose to solve these limitations. They have been implemented in two ways that are presented in the same section. The following sections include an experimental evaluation, related work and the conclusion and perspectives.

2   Challenges of Mobile Devices

2.1   Stylus Interaction

Stylus interaction is not very well suited for handheld devices for several reasons. It requires users to pull out the stylus, an operation that may be uneasy in mobility conditions (besides, users must be careful not to lose the stylus). Using a stylus also makes it impossible to interact with only one hand and it requires interaction to be performed very precisely by clicking on tiny widgets (thus reducing performance according to Fitts' Law [8]). This causes pointing errors, especially when the user is moving, and users may find this interaction style unpleasant because it requires too much attention [19]. Despite these limitations, most existing GUIs on mobile devices make use of tiny WIMP widgets and require using a stylus.

Ideally, the user should be able to interact directly with fingers by using only one hand while performing another activity [15]. But "thumb interaction" arouses several problems:

- The small size of touch screens limits tapping efficiency, especially when there are many UI objects on the screen. Conversely, the large contact area between the finger and the tactile screen makes tapping imprecise.
- Finger interaction causes screen occlusion.
- Some screen regions may be hard to reach, especially when the thumb is used.

To solve these problems, we propose an interaction technique based on a "Touch-Drag-Lift" strategy. Instead of directly tapping targets on the screen, the user manipulates a shifted cursor in a continuous manner. This technique, which is presented in section 4, limits screen occlusion while enhancing pointing precision.

2.2   Compact and Multi-focus Representations on Small Screens

The most common strategy for displaying a large amount of data on small screens consists in using scrollable viewports that reveal a subpart of the data. But viewports have several annoying drawbacks, especially on small screens. First, they are not well adapted for multi-focus representation as they rely on clipping. Clipping prevents highlighting a point of interest that is not currently located in the viewport (although some approaches, such as [3], show marks on scrollbars to indicate where interesting data could be found). As viewports hide most of the data, they provide very limited contextual information to users. This is especially true on small screens, where few items can be displayed (as shown in **Fig. 5d**). Focus+context (F+C) visualization techniques partially fit these constraints with a visual layout that combines:

- A *focus area*, where the data of most interest is displayed at full size or with full details,
- A *context area*, which is a peripheral zone where elements are displayed at reduced size or in a simplified way.

Depending on the techniques, the difference in representing elements in the focus and the context areas can be purely geometrical or make use of the semantics of the data [11], as semantic zooming [20].

F+C techniques enable to represent much more elements simultaneously than representations based on viewports. Elements that have a high degree of interest at a given time are displayed with a size that is large enough to make them more readable. Such techniques provide effective solutions to compensate the lack of screen real-estate on small displays. However, they generally do not suffice to solve the multi-focus problem when it is necessary to highlight elements that are located anywhere in the representation. This ability is crucial for applications that need to notify alerts or useful dynamical information about the elements they display. Some F+C techniques provide several focal points [23,24] but do not solve our problem efficiently because elements that must be highlighted may stay in the context zone. They are also likely to use too much space as the number of highlighted points increases.

3   New Techniques for Displaying Lists on Small Screens

3.1   Spiral Representation and Augmented Context

The list visualization techniques we propose use a spiral layout divided into sectors to display items (**Fig. 1**). In contrast with linear clipped lists, this compact layout makes it possible to show a large number of items. However, all items can not be shown if their number exceeds a certain limit (which is the number of sectors in the spiral). Moreover, items located in the innermost revolutions cannot be displayed with full details because their text labels would be too large. We thus combined this spiral representation with a focus+context strategy to increase the length of displayable lists in a limited amount of screen real-estate. It is interesting to notice that a tabular layout

Fig. 1. Spiral sectors and DOI zones

could be even more space efficient than a spiral representation. However, its 2D nature would not make it very well suited for representing lists, especially when F+C visualization techniques are used. Besides, a spiral layout is well adapted to thumb interaction because it is contained in a circular area that is easy to reach when holding the device in one hand.

F+C visualization techniques generally use geometrical distortions to display objects with a high degree of interest (DOI) at a larger scale in the focus area (like FishEye techniques [9]). In our case, such distortions would make textual data illegible, especially on low resolution handheld screens. We favored a semantic approach [20] where the graphical representation depends on data characteristics. The DOI of an item depends on its location in the spiral, on the spelling of its name and its neighbors' names, and on its intrinsic characteristics (as for instance, the requirement that it must remain visible). The visibility function does not involve geometrical distortions but controls if the label of this item is shown and how many letters are displayed (their number depends on the position of the item relatively to the focus and context zones). The label of an item located in the outermost revolution (the focus zone) is fully visible. Conversely, only the first letters of item labels are shown in the innermost revolutions (the context zone) where 3 letters are shown, then 2 and then only 1 (**Fig. 1**).

Item visibility in the context zone also depends on the spelling of labels. Items which labels start with the same letters are collapsed together in order to use less space. They can be expanded by moving them interactively in the focus zone. However, certain items conveying important information can remain always visible, whatever their location in the spiral. We call this principle "augmented context" as it allows to highlight objects of interest in the contextual view. Thanks to this property, there is no need to use intrusive or space consuming interaction techniques such as pop-ups or a dedicated label zone. Visual artifacts such as colors, blinking effects, special marks can also be used to provide various information about these items.

The next subsections describe two variants of the principles proposed so far. The first variant is founded on a purely spatial approach while the second makes use of a temporal approach. A preliminary version of the first variant was presented in [12].

3.2 A Spatial Focus+Context Strategy: SpiraList

This technique is based on a spatial strategy that follows a focus+context paradigm. Items are displayed in alphabetical order on the spiral layout in such a way that the first visible item and the last one are contiguous in the list (**Fig. 2a**). The *focus area* is located on the bottom of the outermost revolution so that the labels are fully visible on a handheld screen in portrait mode (in landscape mode, the focus appears at the right of the spiral). The selected item ("Piotr" on **Fig. 2a**) appears in the middle of the focus zone. The rest of the spiral contains the *context area*. According to the techniques presented in the previous subsection, item labels are progressively clipped and grouped while advancing inside the spiral. To avoid text overlapping, the labels are rotated according to their position in the spiral. Some visual cues are used to improve the representation: labels that start with a different letter than the previous label in the list are displayed in bold font. Similarly, colored sectors indicate items that are never collapsed because they convey some useful information (for instance a group call or an email if items represent persons).

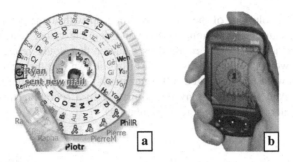

Fig. 2. SpiraList: a screenshot (a) and a picture of SpiraList in action (b)

Moving the cursor over items triggers a tooltip that shows their complete labels (**Fig. 2a**). Once the cursor reaches the item the user is looking for (or the group of items that contains it) he can move this item to the focus area just by releasing the finger. A fast animation is then performed to help the user to understand how the list is reorganized. If the desired item is grouped with other ones, the same action expands the group and moves corresponding items to the focus (or close to it if the group contains too many items). Another selection is then necessary to select the appropriate item. Alternatively, the list can be "scrolled" inside of the spiral by dragging the blue arrows located on its right hand side (**Fig. 2a**). This technique is useful to select items that are already located in the focus area, or to get information on their neighbors.

A noticeable characteristic with our technique lies in the way of changing the focus. Instead of most other focus+context techniques, the focus area always remains at the same place but the data moves to appear in the focus zone. This design tries to better take into account the form factor of handheld devices (**Fig. 2b**). Because of the limited available space and the rectangular shape of the screen, it is advantageous to display details in a fixed area below the spiral: this makes it possible to use the full screen width to display the spiral.

3.3 A Temporal Focus+Context Strategy: SnailList

A preliminary pilot study has shown that the SpiraList technique was well appreciated by users and considered to be time efficient in their subjective evaluations. However, actual measurements gave slightly disappointing results for lists containing more than 100 items. While this technique provides an efficient solution for displaying data at arbitrary locations in a global view, it is most suited for lists that do not exceed this size. These results lead us to analyze how to improve this initial design to obtain better performance for larger lists (we considered lists containing up to 500 items in the experiments).

The most obvious problem was that the automatic grouping algorithm used in the context zone was not efficient enough for large lists. This is because most items are likely to be collapsed in this case, thus reducing the chances of selecting the appropriate item with a single click. Moreover, the number of items that are collapsed together can be quite large if they start with a frequently used letter. The desired item may then appear quite far from the focus zone, thus requiring a second visual search to find it. It can even remain collapsed with other items, thus requiring further user interaction.

Besides, all the revolutions of the spiral are filled up with items when large lists are used. This may cause information overload and degrade visual search performance. Finally, we also identified text rotation as a factor that could reduce performance. Some previous work on tabletop displays [26] has shown that the effect of text orientation was somewhat overestimated in former work performed in the field of perception [16]. However, this effect may be significant in a searching task that requires scanning many elements with different orientations.

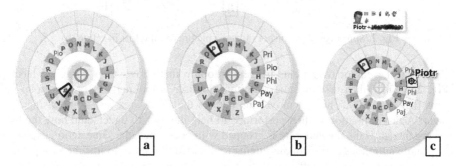

Fig. 3. SnailList: (a) context, (b) intermediate view and (c) focus

The new proposed technique, called *SnailList*, is based on a so-called "temporal" strategy. In contrasts with the previous technique it does not provide a focus and a context zone with a variable level of detail according to the location in the spiral. Instead, the context zone appears first in the innermost part of the spiral and is always shown at the same location (**Fig. 3a**). This zone contains all alphabetical letters and the objects of attention that must remain visible, like the "Pio" item in **Fig. 3a** (according to our augmented context principle). The level of detail is the same for all items (only one letter appears) and none of them are collapsed. The user must select one of them to make the focus to appear. If the chosen item is an alphabetical shortcut the list of all items starting with this letter appears on the spiral (**Fig. 3b**). This new list is displayed at the end of the context zone and it can be seen as an intermediate level of detail between context and focus. The three first letters of the items labels are displayed without text rotation. The user must then find the desired item and click on it to select this element. This makes it to appear with full details in the focus area, at the top of the spiral as shown in **Fig. 3c**.

The main difference with the former technique is that it deals with three representations, corresponding to three different levels of detail (context, intermediate and focus) that appear successively in time. Hence, the level of detail depends on time (*i.e.* the number of successive selections) rather than spatial location and it does not vary progressively with the revolution depth. This reduces the number of items that are displayed simultaneously, and thus, the number and the difficulty of visual searches. Therefore, searching an item follows an incremental alphabetical search scheme. The first search consists in finding the first letter of the desired item in the context zone. As it is always displayed in the same way, users may learn the approximate positions of letters after some practice time. The second visual search takes more time because the user must find the appropriate element in a list that has variable length and content, and that may contain items with the same three first letters (the full label must then be read in the tooltip). However, as the content of this list is filtered by the selected first letter, the number of items that the user must scan is noticeably smaller than with the first technique.

This intermediate view is not large enough if the list contains too many elements that start with the same letter (45 items by default). The number of visible items could be increased by augmenting the number of revolutions but this would decrease font size and make labels harder to read. Fortunately, this case seldom occurs except for very large lists or badly balanced ones. Alternate solutions could consist in using the same grouping strategy as in SpiraList or in improving filtering by adding supplementary alphabetical items in the context zone (e.g. "Aa" for accessing items that starts with "A" to "Al" and "Am" for remaining items).

4   Interacting with Fingers

The visualization techniques proposed so far have also been designed to fit the need of one-handed finger interaction, a very useful feature in mobile usage [15,19]. As explained in section 2, finger interaction (and more especially thumb interaction) brings two annoying problems: imprecise tapping and occlusion.

Imprecision. Imprecise tapping is due to the large contact area between the finger and the screen. It is thus difficult for the user to figure out which object is going to be selected. A solution can consist in using the touch screen as a relative input device. The position of a cursor in the screen space is then controlled by the movements of the finger in the motor space. Imprecision mostly affects the absolute location of press gestures. Drag gestures allow controlling the relative shifting of the cursor much more precisely. They are also less likely to be triggered accidentally than tapping [21].

Our interaction technique is based on this idea but still preserves some kind of absolute positioning. It follows a "touch-drag-lift" paradigm, which is related to the "take-off" technique [22]. *Touching* the screen anywhere with the thumb makes the cursor to appear above this location. The user can then *drag* this cursor all over the screen. Finally, *lifting* the thumb performs an interaction that depends of the last position of the cursor (over a list item, in an action triggering zone, etc.). Cursor moves are stabilized to withdraw the lack of precision of touch-screens: as continuous interaction with a finger involves multiple moving contact points and can lead to erratic and vibrating cursor jumps, the cursor trajectory is smoothed by means of a real-time adaptive low-pass filter that is optimized to avoid lag and does not slow down the cursor.

This technique makes it possible to achieve very good accuracy, even in the case of displaying dense information. It is also quite fast as it combines absolute (but imprecise) positioning with a relative (but precise) correction of this position.

Finger Occlusion. A fixed (but user adjustable) vertical offset is applied to the cursor as a simple but efficient way to avoid fingertip occlusion. An adaptive horizontal offset is also calculated to improve access to the left and right borders of the screen. It is computed according to the equation in **Fig. 4**:

$$\delta x = \frac{\left(x - W/2\right)^3}{W * \lambda}$$

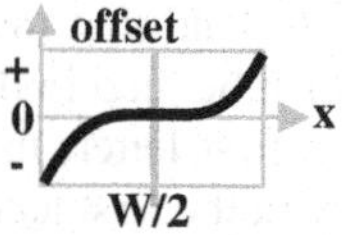

Fig. 4. Adaptive horizontal offset function

In this equation, x is the non-corrected position along the horizontal axis, W the width of the screen and λ the strength of the offset. This offset grows as the cursor goes away from the center of the screen as shown on **Fig. 4** (right). The λ parameter controls the offset around the central position. An experimental value of 80 gave good results: the offset is then unnoticeable around the center of the screen and augments slightly when the cursor reaches the edges.

5 Experiment

We conducted an experiment to compare the efficiency of SnailList (SN) and standard Scrollable Lists (SC) for finding items in one-handed interaction conditions.

5.1 Experimental Setup

Subjects. 10 unpaid subjects, aged from 24 to 40 (7 males and 3 females) served in the experiment. 4 of them are daily users of handheld devices (PDA or PDA-Phones), 3 are occasional users and 3 had never used one. One of them is left-handed. At the beginning of each session, the two techniques were explained to the participant during 10 minutes and s/he performed 10 training tasks with each technique.

Apparatus. We used a QTEK S200 PDA (TI 200MHz CPU and 320x240 tactile screen). The program, written in C#, implements the SnailList widget and an instrumented version of the standard WM 5.0 Contacts application. It automatically logs actions performed by the subject (taps, lifts, items fly over or selection, etc.), errors and the time needed to complete a trial.

Task. The task performed by the participants consisted in retrieving contacts from an address book in a mobility situation. They had to operate with the thumb of the hand that carries the device. However, to limit subjects' weariness, they were seated and could lean their arm (but not their hand) on a table or on their legs.

At the beginning of each trial, the name of the item to find was presented to the subject in the same way as it appears in the contact list (Name then First name). When s/he was ready, the subject started the trial by tapping the "Start" button (**Fig. 5a**). The name remained displayed during the whole trial at the top of the list (**Fig. 5c&d**).

When using SC (**Fig. 5d**), the user can use the scrollbar and the shortcut buttons above the list. These buttons make it possible to scroll the list automatically at certain alphabetical positions. When s/he finds the correct contact, s/he just has to tap on it to validate the trial. With SN (**Fig. 5c**), the user can display different parts of the list by lifting the cursor over the appropriate alphabetical item in the context zone. When s/he finds the desired contact, s/he must lift the cursor over it to validate the trial.

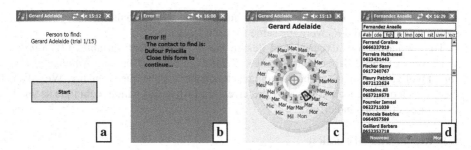

Fig. 5. Experiment: start of a trial (a), error form (b), SnailList (c) and Scrollable List (d)

When an erroneous contact is selected, an error notification appears (**Fig. 5b**) and the user is invited to close it to pursue the trial. When the right item is found, a new trial starts and the subject continues the experiment until all trials are performed.

5.2 Hypothesis and Experiment Model

Our hypotheses are:

Hypothesis 1: SnailList (SN) has equivalent or better performance than standard Scrollable Lists (SL) for retrieving items.

Hypothesis 2: SnailList (SN) generates fewer errors than Scrollable Lists (SC).

We chose three different sizes (100, 250 and 500 items) to compare the performances of the techniques. This choice was based on observations informally gathered by colleagues working on mobile phone usage. 100 items was observed to be an appropriate number for ordinary users, 250 for professionals that use mobile phones frequently and 500 as an upper limit for such usage. Those conditions involve 2 independent variables: *Techniques* (SC and SN) and *List Size* (100-250-500):

2 techniques (*SN* and *SC*) x 3 list sizes (*100, 250* and *500 items*) = 6 tasks

After a training of 10 trials with each technique (with 250 item lists), each subject performed 15 trials for every task. We grouped the tasks in 3 blocks of 30 trials, one block for each list size with the two technique conditions, in balanced order. Inside each block, subjects performed successively the 15 trials with the 2 techniques.

1 block of 30 trials x 3 list sizes = 90 trials per subject

We built several dummy contact lists using randomly chosen French names. As both techniques display lists in alphabetical order, we tried to minimize the effect of the alphabetical balance of the lists on experimental results. For each technique, the index of difficulty (ID) for searching a given item depends on N_l (the number of items that start with letter l) and on R_{it} (the rank of the item in the sub-list). When using SC to find an item that starts with letter l, a high value of N_l is likely to increase scanning and scrolling times (scrolling time depends on R_{it}). For SN, a high value of N_l augments the visual density and a high value of R_{it} augments the scanning time. To ensure that experiment results would not be biased by this balance effect, the same lists were used for each condition for a given subject and the 15 trials were organized in such a way that N_l and R_{it} were the same for each technique.

To summarize, our experimental design has 2 independent variables (*Technique* and *List Size*) and 2 dependent variables: *Trial Completion Time* and *Number of Errors*. Finally, we also asked the participants to answer a short questionnaire. We asked them which of the 2 techniques they preferred (and why) and which technique seemed to be more efficient and errorless.

5.3 Results and Discussion

We performed a repeated measures ANOVA on the *Completion Time* and found no significant main effects for *Technique* ($F_{(1,9)}$ = 0.69, p=0.4164). As shown in **Fig. 6a**, mean performance time are close for the 2 techniques when considering global conditions (list sizes). This result validates our first hypothesis when considering the 3 sizes of lists together (SN performs equally well as SC).

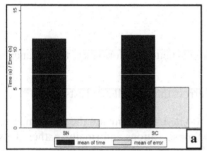 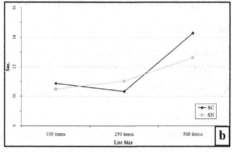

Fig. 6. Mean Time and Errors by Technique (a) and Mean Time by Technique and List Size (b)

We found a significant main effect on *Completion Time* for *list size* ($F_{(2,18)}$ = 12.43, p < 0.001). Paired t-tests indicated that the *100 items* and *250 items* size conditions are faster than the *500 items* condition when considering both techniques ($t_{(9)}$ = 2.3892, p < 0.1 and $t_{(9)}$ = 2.4886, p < 0.05). When restricting to the *SC* technique, paired t-tests indicated that *100* and *250 items* conditions are faster than *500 items* condition ($t_{(9)}$ = 1.7485, p < 0.05 and $t_{(9)}$ = 2.3169, p < 0.1), whereas for the *SN* technique the difference is not significant ($t_{(9)}$ = 1.6292, p < 0.1 and $t_{(9)}$ = 1.0828, p < 0.2). This tendency is visible in the line graph of **Fig. 6b**.

Even if there is no significant interaction effect of *Technique*Size*, those results suggest that the completion time for retrieving an item with SnailList augments slightly when the list size increase whereas the completion time augments more abruptly with the standard Scrollable List. These results are not significant enough to formally validate the fact that our technique outperforms standard Scrollable Lists for very large lists, but they seem to indicate that SnailList is especially robust to scaling (increasing list size) for what concerns performance.

We performed a repeated measures ANOVA on the *Number of Errors* and found a significant main effect for *Technique* ($F_{(1,9)}$ = 18.74, p < 0.001), without significant interaction effects for *Technique*Size*. T-test confirmed that the *SC* technique produced significantly more errors than the *SN* technique ($t_{(9)}$ = 4.1778, p = 0.0001). This result validates our second hypothesis that SnailList produces fewer errors than standard Scrollable List in mobility situations. In fact, the mean of errors with SN (when considering all list sizes) is 4 times less than with SC. The graph in **Fig. 7a** shows that this ratio is close to 7 in the case of 500 item lists.

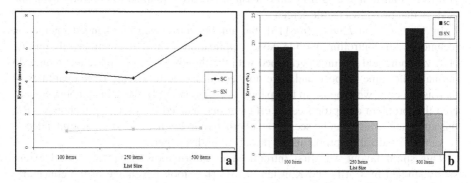

Fig. 7. Mean of errors (a) and Percentage of faulty trials (b) by Technique and by List Size

If we consider a trial to be erroneous if at least one error occurred during it, we obtain a percentage of 20.1% faulty trials for Scrollable List against 5.4% with Snail-List. This makes SnailList 3.7 times more accurate than Scrollable List. **Fig. 7b** shows that this percentage is almost constant for Scrollable Lists when the size of the list increases, while it is almost proportional to the list size when SnailList is used. This result suggests that the design of SnailList make its index of difficulty mainly dependent on the list size. In fact, errors with SnailList are mainly due to confusion between adjacent items with close labels and this case is likely to occur more frequently for large lists than for small ones. Conversely, the index of difficulty of Scrollable Lists is almost constant and at a high value in mobility situation for all list sizes. We attribute this result to the imprecision of tapping when performed with fingers (we noticed that users accidentally validated items whereas they wanted to scroll or to click on a button).

In subjective evaluations, most of the participants were convinced that they completed tasks faster with SnailList and with fewer mistakes than with Scrollable List (9 of 10). These estimations correspond to reality for errors, but not for completion time (performances was mostly similar for both techniques). 9 of 10 subjects said that they preferred using SnailList over the scrollable list. The novelty of the technique aside, they argued that its design made it well-adapted to finger interaction on a small screen. They also highlighted the fact that SnailList was less frustrating to use because they made less errors than with the scrollable list.

6   Related Work

Designing interactions techniques for mobility requires taking into account devices form-factor constraints and users' tasks together. Recent studies that focused on this topic [15,19] showed that one-handed mobile interaction is preferable because it is less distracting for the user (a principle called "Minimal Attention User Interfaces" in [19]). These studies have also emphasized the use of the thumb as a good way for interacting in such conditions. Other approaches consist of augmenting handheld devices with alternative input modes, like in physical embodied techniques [10]. However, thumb interaction is more feasible and well-adapted to currently available devices that provide a tactile screen.

In *AppLens* and *LaunchTile* [13], the authors introduced one-handed interaction techniques for controlling mobile device applications. These interactions rely on discrete zooming and gestures performed with the thumb. However, these techniques do not have the same purpose and have not been designed to display large quantities of data as the ones we propose in this paper. In *FaThumb* [14], the same authors considered this problem and proposed an efficient one-handed data seeking technique. But this approach, which can be seen as an alternative to textual queries, is not intended to solve the visualization problems we presented in this paper.

This spiral layout was first introduced in information visualization and extensively studied by Carlis and Konstan in [6]. They took advantage of the concentric layout of the Archimedean spiral for the visualization and interpretation of serial and periodic data. The same idea is used in *SpiraClock* [7], with a spiral that is augmented by an analog clock to provide a non intrusive display for upcoming temporal events. *RankSpiral* [25] also uses spiral layout to display large results of multiple search engines. This last approach is the most similar to our but it was designed for desktop PCs and does not take into account the display and input constraints of small devices.

In [6], Carlis and Konstan suggested the idea of extending the spiral layout with a focus+context scroll mechanism. We considered this idea as a good way for displaying more items in the spiral. Focus+context methods can be used to improve the overall visibility of large lists [4,17], but only a few items are readable because of their focus-dependant geometrical zoom, especially when a small screen is used. The compact display of our approach achieves the same level of visibility. But its non-geometrical strategy, which is somewhat related to semantic zooming, overcomes the legibility problem that arises with F+C techniques based on geometrical zooming. In [18], one of the problems addressed by the authors is close to ours but on standard displays: displaying large binary trees with several points of interest. They had shown that *Pan & Zoom* techniques outperform F+C techniques for navigating in this case. However their techniques rely on geometrical deformations that can have a strong impact on interaction performance and deals with 2D localization problems (as in [1]). Those conditions are quite different than ours that deal with 1D linear data on small screen, without geometrical deformations.

Various advanced new interaction techniques have been proposed for touch screens in recent studies (such as [2]) but they are not specifically designed for handhelds. Our work extends the "Take-off" technique [22] in the case of mobile devices. In particular, our adaptive horizontal cursor offset, that could be annoying on large touch screens [2], gives promising results on small screens.

7 Conclusion and Future Work

We have presented *SpiraList* and *SnailList*, two new visualization and interaction techniques for manipulating large lists on handheld devices. These techniques provide (a) one-handed operation using the thumb, a feature that is especially well suited for mobile interaction; (b) focus+context visualization and an augmented representation of context that allows to display objects of interest permanently. An experimental comparison of standard scrollable lists and *SnailList* on a PDA phone has shown that this new technique significantly reduces the error rate (to about 3.7 times lower) without loss of performance when interacting with the thumb.

The proposed technique for finger and thumb interaction improves the "Take-off" method [22] and allows precise interaction even when many small objects are displayed on the screen. It is based on a differentiation between the visual space and the motor space of the touch screen device. An interesting extension would consist in studying how methods that perform advanced control/display ratio adaptation, such as semantic pointing [5], could be integrated in our technique to improve selection.

We are now aiming at improving the performance time of the proposed technique. Items could for instance be filtered according to their second and third letters by selecting the alphabetical items located in the center of the spiral multiple times. This successive dichotomy approach would reduce the number of items displayed in the peripheral zone and could improve search time. Finally, we also plan to perform further experiments with more participants to obtain a more detailed comparison of the considered techniques for large lists.

Acknowledgments. This work has been done in collaboration with Guillaume Dorbes and Bruno Legat from Alcatel-Lucent R&D. We want to thank them for their useful advices and their help in evaluating SpiraList and SnailList. Many thanks to the people that accepted to participate in our experiment and also to Gilles Bailly and Anne Roudaut for their useful help while conducting it.

References

1. Baudisch, P., Rosenholtz, R.: Halo: A Technique for Visualizing Off-Screen Locations. In: Proc. Of CHI'2003 (Fort Lauderdale, FL, USA), pp. 481–488. ACM, New York (2003)
2. Benko, H., Wilson, D.A., Baudisch, P.: Precise Selection Techniques for Multi-Touch Screens. In: Proc. of CHI'2006 (Montréal, CA), pp. 1263–1272. ACM, New York (2006)
3. Bederson, B.B., Clamage, A., Czerwinski, M.P., Robertson, G.G.: DateLens: A fisheye calendar interface for PDAs. ACM Transactions on Computer-Human Interaction (TO-CHI) 11(1), 90–119 (2004)
4. Bederson, B.B.: Fisheye Menus. In: Proc. of UIST 2000 (San Diego, USA), pp. 217–226. ACM, New York (2000)
5. Blanch, R., Guiard, Y., Beaudouin-Lafon, M.: Semantic pointing: improving target acquisition with control-display ratio adaptation. In: Proc. of CHI'2004 (Vienna, Austria), pp. 519–526. ACM, New York (2004)

6. Carlis, J.V., Konstan, J.A.: Interactive Visualization of Serial Periodic Data. In: Proc. of UIST 98 (San Francisco, USA), pp. 29–38. ACM, New York (1998)
7. Dragicevic, P., Huot, S.: SpiraClock: A Continuous and Non-Intrusive Display for Upcoming Events. In: Extended Abstracts of CHI'02 (Minneapolis, USA), pp. 604–605. ACM, New York (2002)
8. Fitts, P.M.: The information capacity of the human motor system in controlling the amplitude of movement. Journal of Experimental Psychology 47(6), 381–391 (1954)
9. Furnas, G.: Generalized Fisheye Views. In: Proc. of CHI'86 (Boston, USA), pp. 16–23. ACM, New York (1986)
10. Harrison, B.L., Fishkin, K.P., Gujar, A., Mochon, C., Want, R.: Squeeze me, hold me, tilt me! An exploration of manipulative user interfaces. In: Proc. of CHI'98 (Los Angeles, USA), pp. 17–24. ACM, New York (1986)
11. Herman, I., Melançon, G., Marshall, M.S.: Graph Visualization and Navigation in Information Visualisation: a Survey. In: IEEE Transactions on Visualization and Computer Graphics, vol. 6(1), pp. 24–43. IEEE, Los Alamitos (2000)
12. Huot, S., Lecolinet, E.: SpiraList: A Compact Visualization Technique for One-Handed Interaction with Large Lists on Mobile Devices. In: Proc. of NordiCHI'06 (Oslo, Norway), pp. 445–448. ACM, New York (2006)
13. Karlson, A.K., Bederson, B.B., SanGiovanni, J.: AppLens and LaunchTile: Two Designs for One-Handed Thumb Use on Small Devices. In: Proc. of CHI'2005 (Portland, USA), pp. 201–210. ACM, New York (2005)
14. Karlson, A.K., Robertson, G.G., Robbins, D.C., Czerwinski, M.P., Smith, G.R.: FaThumb: a facet-based interface for mobile search. In: Proc. of CHI'2006 (Montréal, Canada), pp. 711–720. ACM, New York (2006)
15. Karlson, A., Bederson B.B., Contreras-Vidal, J.: Studies in One-Handed Mobile Design: Habit, Desire and Agility, Tech. Report 2006-02, HCIL, Washington (2006)
16. Koriat, A., Norman, J.: Reading Rotated Words. Journal of Experimental Psychology: Human Perception and Performance 11(4), 490–508 (1985)
17. Lecolinet, E., Nguyen, D.: Focus+context visualization of zoomable hierarchical lists. In: Proc. of French-Speaking Conference on Human-Computer Interaction (IHM 2006) (Montréal, CA), pp. 195–198. ACM, New York (2006)
18. Nekrasovski, D., Bodnar, A., McGrenere, J., Guimbretière, F., Munzner, T.: An evaluation of pan & zoom and rubber sheet navigation with and without an overview. In: Proc. of CHI'06 (Montréal Canada), pp. 11–20. ACM, New York (2006)
19. Pascoe, J., Ryan, N., Morse, D.: Using while moving: HCI issues in fieldwork environments. ACM Transactions on Computer-Human Interaction (TOCHI) 7(3), 417–437 (2000)
20. Perlin, K., Fox, D.: Pad: an alternative approach to the computer interface. In: Proc. Of SIGGRAPH '93, pp. 57–64. ACM, New York (1993)
21. Pirhonen, A., Brewster, S., Holguin, C.: Gestural and audio metaphors as a means of control for mobile devices. In: Proc. of CHI'02 (Minneapolis, USA), pp. 291–298. ACM, New York (2002)
22. Potter, R.L., Weldon, L.J., Shneiderman, B.: Improving the Accuracy of Touchscreens: An Experimental Evaluation of Three Strategies. In: Proc. of CHI'88 (Washington, USA), pp. 27–32. ACM, New York (1988)
23. Sarkar, M., Snibbe, S.S., Tversky, O.J., Reiss, S.P.: Stretching the rubber sheet: a metaphor for viewing large layouts on small screens. In: Proc. of UIST 93 (Atlanta, USA), pp. 81–91. ACM, New York (1993)

24. Shipman, F.M., Marshall, C.C., LeMere, M.: Beyond Location: Hypertext Workspaces and Non-Linear Views. In: Proc. of Hypertext'99 (Darmstadt, Germany), pp. 121–130. ACM, New York (1999)
25. Spoerri, A.: RankSpiral: Toward Enhancing Search Results Visualizations. In: Proc. Of InfoVis 2004 (Austin, USA), pp. 18–19. IEEE, Los Alamitos (2004)
26. Wigdor, D., Balakrishnan, R.: Empirical investigation into the effect of orientation on text readability in tabletop displays. In: Proc. of ECSCW 2005 (Paris, France), pp. 205–224. Springer, Heidelberg (2005)

Techniques for Interacting with Off-Screen Content

Pourang Irani[1], Carl Gutwin[2], Grant Partridge[1], and Mahtab Nezhadasl[1]

[1] University of Manitoba
Computer Science
Winnipeg, MB
irani@cs.umanitoba.ca, umpartr3@cc.umanitoba.ca,
umnezhad@cs.umanitoba.ca
[2] University of Saskatchewan
Computer Science
Saskatoon, SK
gutwin@cs.usask.ca

Abstract. Many systems – such as map viewers or visual editors – provide a limited viewport onto a larger graphical workspace. The limited viewport means that users often have to navigate to objects and locations that are off screen. Although techniques such as zooming, panning, or overview+detail views allow users to navigate off-screen, little is known about how different techniques perform for different types of off-screen tasks, and whether one technique works well for all tasks. We carried out two studies to explore these issues. The first study compared the performance of three classes of techniques (zoom, overview+detail, and proxy) in six types of off-screen tasks. We found that the techniques show substantial differences across different tasks and that no one technique is suitable for all types of off-screen navigation. This study led to the design of two novel hybrid navigation techniques – WinHop and Multiscale Zoom – that combine properties of multiple simpler approaches in an attempt to broaden support for off-screen navigation. We carried out a second study to assess the hybrid techniques, and found that they do provide reliable performance on a wide range of tasks. Our results suggest that integrating complimentary properties from different approaches can significantly improve performance in off-screen navigation tasks.

Keywords: Navigation techniques, offscreen navigation, small displays.

1 Introduction

In many applications such as map browsers or visualization systems, the workspace can be larger than the user's viewport. In order to retrieve and inspect content in these systems, users spend a substantial amount of time and effort navigating to off-screen locations. Researchers have developed a variety of different navigation techniques to alleviate some of the problems with navigating large workspace on small displays. However, most studies have investigated the performance of these navigation techniques with only a limited range of tasks. For example, several studies have investigated scrolling, but primarily on tasks related to navigating to known off-screen content [7,10]; panning and zooming have been investigated primarily in the context

C. Baranauskas et al. (Eds.): INTERACT 2007, LNCS 4663, Part II, pp. 234–249, 2007.

of off-screen targeting and navigation [9,13], and focus+context techniques have been studied primarily with reading, targeting, and steering [3,8].

This approach has successfully demonstrated the performance benefits of different systems in particular situations, but it does not provide much information about what would be the best technique in a real-world setting. Although we have evidence about individual techniques with individual tasks, little is known about how off-screen navigation techniques perform across a wide range of tasks. This knowledge is crucially important for designers, who must choose techniques that can adequately support a range of user activities, rather than just a few tasks.

In this paper, we explore several off-screen navigation techniques and tasks within one main type of activity – that is, finding and making decisions about off-screen objects in a 2D workspace with a clear spatial reference frame. The canonical application for these activities is a map browser with specific objects of interest that appear as annotations. Within this domain, we explore several questions:

- Which techniques are best suited to which task types, and is there one technique that performs well on all tasks?
- What are the characteristic properties of the techniques that lead to success with particular tasks?
- Can we combine these properties in new techniques, to increase the range of off-screen tasks that are supported?

To investigate these questions, we first built a framework that describes three different classes of off-screen navigation techniques (time-multiplexing, space-multiplexing, and proxy-based), and two different classes of off-screen tasks: spatially relative and spatially absolute tasks. Relative tasks involve identifying relationships between objects in a workspace, and absolute tasks involve interpreting the relationship of an object to the workspace.

We then conducted two studies. In the first, we compared the performance of representative techniques from each class, on six different off-screen tasks (three spatially relative, and three spatially absolute). We found that none of these basic techniques perform well on all tasks: time-multiplexing techniques such as zooming perform better on spatially-relative tasks, and proxy-based techniques such as hop perform better on spatially-absolute tasks.

The results of the first study led to the development of two hybrid techniques that combine different principles in order to better support a range of tasks. Our second study compared these new techniques–WinHop and Multiscale Zoom–to the 'pure' techniques used in the first study. The results show that both hybrid techniques improved on the originals, and that one hybrid, Multiscale Zoom, performed as well as the best 'pure' techniques for all task types. Overall, this work demonstrates the importance of breadth in evaluating navigation techniques, and suggests that narrow techniques can be broadened by incorporating elements from other approaches.

2 Related Literature

A number of existing navigation techniques can be used to interact with off-screen content. These techniques can be organized into three groups: time-multiplexing, space-multiplexing, and proxy-based techniques.

Time-Multiplexing Navigation

Time-multiplexing techniques allow users to interact with different regions of the workspace at different times – as a result, different views of the workspace are available in a serial fashion. Scrolling, panning, and zooming are the three most common techniques in this group.

Scrolling and Panning allow users to adjust the viewport without changing the scale of the view. Scrolling and panning have been studied extensively (e.g., [7,10]). However both require considerable effort and several variations have been developed to facilitate navigation [12,17]. *Zooming* allows people to navigate by changing the scale of the viewport. With a zoom technique, 'off-screen' is relative to the current zoom level – and if required, any amount of the workspace can be brought into view, albeit at the cost of detail [5]. The overviews that result from zooming out provide awareness of off-screen content to users, and these can perform better than regular scrolling systems [14]. However, to find a particular off-screen object from a set of candidates, the user may have to perform multiple zoom operations.

Space-Multiplexing Navigation

Space-multiplexing techniques allow users to concurrently view different regions of the workspace. The main method of showing multiple regions is to divide the viewport into two or more windows; as a result, these techniques use more display space than time-multiplexing techniques. Common space-multiplexing techniques include overview+detail systems, focus+context views, and portals.

Overview+detail techniques present a miniature view of the entire workspace in a small inset window [4,16]; the main display shows a zoomed-in view. Users move the detail view either by panning or by dragging a viewfinder in the overview. DragMag [20] is an overview+detail technique, but in which the main window shows the overview, and a smaller inset window shows a detail region. The detail window follows the viewfinder in the overview. Overview+detail views have been shown to be effective [3]; but they require additional cognitive overhead to switch between the different scales of the two views and occlude some of the context in the main window.

Focus+context techniques such as fisheye views [21] eliminate the need for multiple windows by presenting a distorted view of the entire workspace. They provide a smooth transition between an enlarged focus region and the surrounding context. The drawback with many focus+context views is that they can make tasks that require targeting more difficult [11], and the distortion caused by fisheye views can degrade performance in tasks that have a clear spatial component.

Portals allow the user to view remote content of large displays through a window that is overlaid on top of the user's viewport. With Frisbees [15], for example, users pan and zoom into the off-screen space using a porthole metaphor. WinCuts [19] allows users to interact with off-screen regions by providing a local replica of the off-screen content. Unlike most other space-multiplexing techniques, portals do not provide users access to the entire workspace. As a result, additional operations such as zooming in and out of portals are necessary to view the overall context.

Proxy-Based Techniques

The emergence of large screens and multi-display systems has led to proxy-based navigation techniques that bring distant objects closer to the user's interaction space. For example, drag-and-pop [2] and the vacuum filter [6] create local copies of distant objects, in response to a gesture from the user. These forms of interaction have shown significant savings in the time required to select distant objects in comparison to conventional dragging. However, neither drag-and-pop nor the vacuum filter was designed as off-screen navigation techniques. Hop [13] is a proxy-based technique that was developed to adapt the proxy approach to the needs of off-screen navigation. Hop uses halos [1] to provide awareness of off-screen objects, and allows users to create proxies by interacting with the visible halos.

3 Off-Screen Navigation Tasks

Within the general scenario defined earlier (objects of interest located on a spatially-organized workspace), there are a wide variety of tasks that users carry out with off-screen objects. There are many ways to categorize tasks, but in 2D workspaces a main distinguishing factor is the spatial relationship between objects and the space. From this perspective, tasks can either be spatially relative, involving relationships between two or more objects; or spatially absolute, involving relationships between an object and the underlying workspace. The list of tasks in each group is not exhaustive and many other spatial tasks are performed on graphical workspaces. However, the following list captures the types of tasks that are routinely performed in canonical object-workspace settings (such as those seen in a map browser application).

Spatially Relative Tasks

These tasks require people to determine and understand spatial relationships between objects in the workspace. Main types of spatially relative tasks include determining the proximity of an object to a reference point, the proximity of objects to one another, or identification of clusters of objects that match certain criteria.

Proximity to Point of Reference. Users often need to locate an object that is closest to a point of reference such as finding the bus stop that is closest to the user's current position. These tasks are carried out by first locating the point of reference, and then by searching outwards to locate candidate objects. For each candidate that is located, the user needs to remember the current best candidate; when all likely candidates are checked, the user can determine which was closest to the reference.

Proximity between Pairs of Objects. A number of tasks involve finding a pair of items that are close together – but location in the workspace is not important – such as locating a 3-star hotel that is close to a railway station. To complete this task, the user must locate all pairs of items in the workspace, perform distance comparisons to determine which candidate pair are closest together (or below some 'close enough' threshold), and remember the best pair.

Clusters. Cluster tasks are a more complex variation of the proximity between objects. These tasks involve locating an object in the vicinity of other objects. For example, a user may wish to locate a 4-star hotel that is near a supermarket, a bus route and a seafood restaurant. In this task, the user has to perform a visual query over the entire workspace to locate the required cluster of objects.

Spatially Absolute Tasks
Spatially absolute tasks involve determining the relationship of an object to the workspace that contains the item. Some examples of spatially absolute tasks include determining whether an item is in the workspace at all, the number of occurrences of a certain type of item, or the location of an object in the workspace.

Existence. A common question when browsing a graphical workspace is to ask whether a specific type of object exists. For instance, a user may want to determine whether a zoo, an art gallery, or a library exists on a map. In such tasks, the user scans the workspace until the desired object is found. In the worst, case the user needs to scan the entire workspace to locate the object.

Object Count. Another common task is to determine the number of objects of a specific type. For example, counting the number of 5-star hotels or cinemas may be necessary, if the user wishes to compare hotels or decide where to see a movie. In counting tasks, the user scans the entire workspace and mentally maintains a tally (and possibly the locations) of the objects found.

Location. Location tasks involve determining the position of an object in the workspace. This task is carried out at a particular level of granularity – that is, sometimes a user will need to know only the quadrant of the city in which an object appears, and sometimes a more detailed location is needed. In this task, the user scans the workspace until the object has been found, and then establishes the location of the target with respect to the entire workspace.

4 STUDY 1: A Comparison of Representative Navigation Techniques

The goal of the first experiment was to compare different classes of off-screen navigation techniques on a variety of different tasks. The results from experiment 1 also serve as a baseline for understanding the features of various techniques that make them suitable to different tasks.

Study 1 Methods

Participants
Eighteen volunteers (12 men, 6 women) were recruited from a local university. Ages ranged from 22 to 32 years (mean of 24.5 years). All participants were familiar with mouse-and-windows software (more than 8 hrs/wk); 10 were also familiar with mapping applications.

Navigation Techniques
We selected one navigation technique from each of the categories described above (time-multiplexing, space-multiplexing, and proxy-based).

Zooming was chosen to represent the time-multiplexing class, since prior results show that zooming is superior to panning and scrolling for off-screen navigation [13]. We implemented a two-level zoom, where users move from overview to full detail by clicking the barrel button on the tablet pen.

DragMag was selected from the space-multiplexing class; a pilot study with three participants suggested that this technique performs better than either an over-view+detail display or a fisheye view. In our implementation, an inset detail window magnified the area below a viewfinder that users could drag in the overview. Users could select items in either the overview or the detail view.

Hopping was picked from the proxy class, since it is the only proxy-based tech-nique that is designed for off-screen navigation [13]. Hop shows halos of off-screen objects; the user can invoke proxies by sweeping a 'laser beam' across the halos. Users can then 'teleport' to the actual location of any object by clicking on its proxy.

Apparatus

An experimental system was built in C#.NET, and deployed on a Windows Tablet PC with 1024×768 screen resolution. The system presented a simulated map-browsing application with a visual workspace that was larger than the viewport. The workspace contained a 2600×2400-pixel map and the viewport was 800×600 pixels; therefore, the map extended 900 pixels past the viewport in all directions.

The system also displayed several icons on top of the city map. Icons were 24×24-pixel orange squares that represented items of interest such as hotels, restaurants, and bus stops. On each icon, a capital letter indicated the object category, and smaller symbols represented further information such as the number of stars for the hotel or the bus routes servicing a particular stop. Twenty-four icons were randomly placed in the workspace, including the particular target icons used in different tasks.

Tasks

Participants completed all of the six tasks described earlier. Off-screen navigation was required for all tasks. Trials were completed, depending on the task, either by clicking a target in the workspace, or pressing a button on the tablet.

- *Existence.* Participants were asked to determine if there was a four-star hotel icon on the map. There was a 50% chance of the target being present.
- *Location.* Lines were added to the map to divide it into a 3×3 grid. Participants were asked to determine which section of the map contained the four-star hotel.
- *Object Count.* Participants were asked to count the number of four-star hotels on the map. The system randomly placed 2-6 targets for each trial.
- *Proximity between Objects.* Participants were asked to find the four-star hotel that was closest to a metro station. The system randomly placed three metro-hotel pairs on the map. One pair was always clearly closer together than the others, so that no precise measuring was required.
- *Proximity from Reference.* Participants were asked to find the closest four-star hotel to the centre of the map. The system randomly placed three targets; one of these was clearly closer upon inspection.
- *Cluster.* Participants were presented with a set of targets (e.g., a four star hotel, a four star restaurant, and a metro station), and were asked to find a cluster of exactly

these targets. The system randomly placed three clusters, of which only one contained the correct targets.

Study 1 Procedure and Design

The study used a 3×6 within-participants factorial design. The factors were:

- *Navigation technique*: Zoom, DragMag, Hop
- *Task*: Existence, Location, Object-Count, Proximity between Objects, Proximity from Reference, Cluster.

Navigation technique and task were fully counterbalanced using a Latin square. Within each condition, participants carried out one demonstration trial, one practice trial, and five test trials. The workspace was reset to its initial state (viewport centred) after each trial. Participants completed all six tasks in a condition before moving to a new technique (rests were provided between conditions).

With 18 participants, 3 navigation techniques, 6 tasks, and 5 test trials, the system recorded a total of 1620 trials. The study system collected completion times and error information for each target.

Study 1 Results

Completion Time

A repeated-measures ANOVA showed significant main effects of both *navigation technique* ($F_{2,34}$=15.17, p<0.001) and *task* ($F_{5,85}$=29.67, p<0.001). However, there was a significant interaction between navigation technique and task ($F_{10,170}$=37.88, p<0.001), and so our analysis is organized below by task.

For each task, we carried out a one-way ANOVA to look for effects of navigation technique. Figure 1 shows the average completion times by task and technique. There are obvious differences between the two main classes of tasks (absolute and relative), and so we organize the results by class (note, however, that we cannot collapse the data into these classes since there are different tasks in each group).

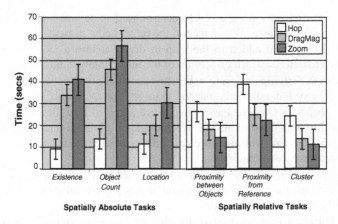

Fig. 1. Average completion time for each technique with each task. Error bars show standard error.

Spatially Absolute Tasks. For all three absolute tasks, one-way ANOVA found significant main effects of *navigation technique*: for Existence, ($F_{2,53}$=54.06, p<0.001); for Object Count, ($F_{2,53}$=50.635, p<0.001); for Location, ($F_{2,53}$=23.875, p<0.001). Tukey's post-hoc tests for all three tasks showed significant differences between all three techniques (Hop was significantly faster than DragMag, which was significantly faster than Zoom; all p<0.05).

Spatially Relative Tasks. For all three relative tasks, we also found significant main effects of navigation technique using a one-way ANOVA: for Proximity between Objects, ($F_{2,53}$=7.724, p<0.001); for Proximity from Reference, ($F_{2,53}$=9.544, p<0.001); for Cluster, ($F_{2,53}$=3.975, p=0.025). Post-hoc Tukey's tests show consistent significant differences between the fastest two techniques (Zoom and DragMag) and the slowest (Hop) (all p<0.05), but no differences between Zoom and DragMag.

The completion time results show that for the spatially absolute tasks, Hop was consistently fastest, followed by DragMag and Zoom (all differences significant). In spatially relative tasks, however, there was an exact reversal: Zoom was fastest, followed by DragMag and Hop.

Errors

A repeated measures ANOVA on error rates did not show a significant main effect of *navigation technique* ($F_{2,34}$=3.102, p=0.058) but did show a main effect of *task* ($F_{5,85}$=19.105, p<0.001). There was an interaction between navigation technique and task ($F_{10,170}$=4.114, p<0.001). Overall the error rates reaffirm the performance measure collected from the completion time data.

Study 1 Discussion

The main result of the first study is that there are strong differences in the effectiveness of the different techniques. For absolute tasks, Hop was best and Zoom was worst, and for relative tasks, the opposite ordering occurred. The limitations and strengths of the techniques in absolute and relative tasks provide guidelines for designing new off-screen navigation techniques. Our goal is to add elements together from different techniques to produce a hybrid that can potentially be effective for a wider range of tasks. In the next sections, we describe two hybrids: WinHop, which combines the proxy-based interaction of Hop with a space-multiplexing inset window; and Multiscale Zoom, which combines the time-multiplexing character of Zoom with the full-detail view of objects from proxy techniques.

5 Winhop

WinHop is an off-screen navigation technique that adds space-multiplexing and time-multiplexing elements to a proxy-based approach. Like Hop, it uses halos and proxies as the mechanism for finding off-screen objects. WinHop is space-multiplexing as it provides a view of off-screen regions through an inset window and is time-multiplexing as it allows zooming and panning in the portal.

Proxy-Based Characteristics

WinHop is an extension of Hop, and so shares that technique's basic characteristics (see Figure 2): (i) WinHop uses modified halos to inform users of the distance and direction to off-screen objects; (ii) users invoke proxies with a 'laser beam': the user places the pen on the workspace background and drags toward the edge of the screen, which draws a line to the screen edge. The user then sweeps the beam around with a circular motion, and as the laser beam touches a halo, the corresponding proxy is created near the pen; (iii) proxies are identical to the objects they represent, with the addition of a thin black and white border to distinguish them from true objects. A layout algorithm positions the proxies near the cursor, without occluding existing objects in the workspace; (iv) when the user moves the cursor over a proxy, WinHop provides additional information. To show direction, the system draws a thick arrowed line from the proxy to the actual off-screen object.

Space- and Time-Multiplexing Properties

In Hop, tapping on a proxy would teleport the user to the off-screen region. However, this approach is relatively slow (teleportation involves an animated scene transition), and participants sometimes felt that they got lost or disoriented through repeated teleportation. WinHop introduces a space-multiplexing inset window to let users explore

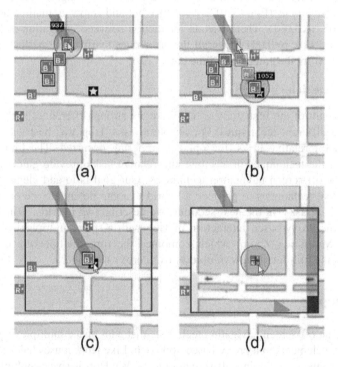

Fig. 2. The appearance of the WinHop window and translation from proxy to off-screen object. Clicking on a proxy (a), shifts the proxy to the center (b) and then opens a portal into the off-screen region around the object represented by the proxy (c & d).

the distant region without actually leaving their current location. When the user taps a proxy (Figures 2.a and 2b), a secondary viewport 'grows' out of the proxy (Figure 2.c. and 2.d); this new window teleports to the off-screen location, but nothing changes in the main view. The user may pan and zoom in the portal: panning by dragging the cursor; and zooming by moving a slider at the side of the portal window. The user can close the WinHop window by clicking on any region outside the window. Proxies that were previously displayed remain visible, so that the user can inspect other off-screen regions without re-sweeping the laser.

6 Multiscale Zoom

The main problem with the Zoom technique in the first study was that object details could not be seen in the overview (i.e., the zoomed-out view). Our second hybrid addresses this problem by incorporating full-detail object representations that are fundamental to proxy techniques.

The technique works by using different zoom functions for different elements in the workspace. In particular, object data has a greater endpoint, so that when the user zooms out to the overview, objects are not reduced in scale as much as the rest of the map (Figure 3). The end result is that objects remain above the threshold of visibility and readability in the overview. This idea is an extension of semantic zooming, which presents different representations at different scales (e.g., more detailed representations at larger scales). In our technique, it is the scaling rate of the zoom function that is 'semantic' – different data zooms at different rates. In the two-level zoom of the experimental system, we change the scale rates so that icon details remain visible in the overview, but are normally sized (with respect to the surrounding map) when zoomed in. We note that a simpler version of this idea has been seen in previous commercial applications: for example, mapping and GIS systems often lock the minimum size of the text tags and place names so that they remain readable at any zoom level.

Multiscale Zoom still preserves spatial relationships between targets (almost as well as regular Zoom), but also ensures that object details will be visible. This approach,

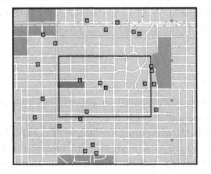

Fig. 3. Overview (zoomed-out view) with conventional Zoom (left), and with Multiscale Zoom (right). In multi-scale zoom the objects maintain their original size.

however, leads to certain challenges. Since objects take up more space in the overview than they should, some maps will appear cluttered, and objects will occlude each other. To overcome the occlusion problem, our multiscale zoom brings objects to the top of the stack when the user hovers the cursor over them.

7 STUDY 2: Hybrid Versus 'Pure' Navigation

We carried out a second experiment to determine whether the combination of elements allowed the two hybrid techniques to support a wider range of tasks. To compare the new techniques to those used in the first study, we asked participants from the first study to come back for the second, and then analyzed data from both studies together. (We recognize that there is a possible learning effect between the two studies that could improve relative performance on the new techniques; nevertheless, this method does at least allow the identification of large differences).

Study 2 Methods
Participants. Twelve subjects (8 male and 4 female) who participated in the first study volunteered to return.

Navigation Techniques and Tasks. WinHop and Multiscale Zoom were used as described above; the analysis also incorporated data from the earlier techniques (Hop, Zoom, and DragMag). Study two used the same six tasks described earlier, and participants also carried out the same number of trials.

Apparatus. The same tablet computer was used as that of Experiment 1; the custom study system was extended with implementations of the two new techniques.

Procedure and Design. Including data from the earlier study results in a 5×6 within-participants factorial design. The factors were Navigation technique (WinHop, Multiscale Zoom, Hop, Zoom, and DragMag), and Task (Existence, Location, Object Count, Proximity Between Objects, Proximity From Reference, and Cluster).

The second study, as mentioned above, gathered data from only the two new techniques (WinHop and Multiscale Zoom). For these two conditions, navigation technique and task were counterbalanced using a Latin square. With 12 participants, 2 navigation techniques, 6 tasks and 5 test trials, the system recorded a total of 720 trials.

Study 2 Results

Completion Time
The 12 participants from experiment one also participated in experiment two and therefore the analysis was performed across all techniques. A repeated-measures 5×6 ANOVA showed significant main effects of both *navigation technique* ($F_{5,55}=14.738$, $p<0.001$) and *task* ($F_{4,44}=31.326$, $p<0.001$). There was a significant interaction between navigation technique and task ($F_{20,220}=23.315$, $p<0.001$), and so our analysis is organized below by task.

For each task, we carried out a one-way ANOVA to look for effects of navigation technique. Figure 4 shows average completion times for task and technique by task category.

Spatially Absolute Tasks. For all three absolute tasks, one-way ANOVA found significant main effects of *navigation technique*: for Existence, ($F_{4,55}$=62.922, p<0.001); for Object Count, ($F_{4,55}$=44.265, p<0.001); for Location, ($F_{4,55}$=34.679, p<0.001). Post-hoc Tukeys's test for all three tasks showed significant differences between the fastest technique (Multiscale Zoom) and the slowest techniques (Zoom and DragMag; all p<0.001). Performance with Multiscale Zoom was also significantly faster than the two proxy-based techniques (WinHop and Hop; all p<0.05) in the Location task but there is no significant difference between Multiscale Zoom, WinHop and Hop for the Existence and Object Count tasks. sWinHop was significantly faster than both Zoom and DragMag in all tasks (all p<.001). There was no significant difference between WinHop and Hop.

Spatially Relative Tasks. For all the relative tasks, we found significant main effects of navigation technique: for Proximity Between Objects, ($F_{4,55}$=8.187, p<0.001); for Proximity from Reference, ($F_{4,55}$=12.196, p<0.001); for Cluster, ($F_{4,55}$=3.084, p=0.023). Post-hoc Tukey's tests show that Multiscale Zoom is significantly faster than all the other techniques in the Proximity between Objects and Proximity from Reference tasks (all p<0.05), but in the Cluster task Multiscale Zoom is only significantly faster than Hop (p<0.01). Interestingly, WinHop was significantly faster than Hop in the Proximity from Reference (p<.001) but not in the other two tasks. However, there were no significant differences between WinHop, DragMag and Zoom across all spatially relative tasks.

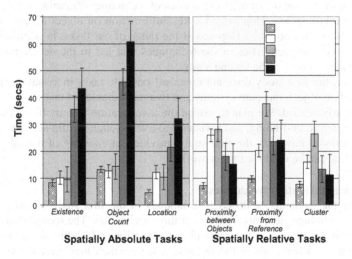

Fig. 4. Average completion time for each technique.

8 Discussion

The two studies described above provide answers to the questions posed at the beginning of the paper, and serve as an example of how a broader understanding of the characteristics of navigation techniques can be achieved by examining them over a wider range of tasks. The main findings are:

- No single basic technique performed well on all of the tasks, and performance was strongly affected by the characteristics of the task;
- WinHop offers improved performance on tasks where Hop performed poorly (relative tasks), and Multiscale Zoom dramatically improved performance on tasks where Zoom performed poorly (absolute tasks);
- Overall, Multiscale Zoom was the fastest technique, and its performance was consistent across all tasks;

In the following sections we reflect on the underlying goals of the two studies (testing breadth, and hybridization), and summarize the main lessons for practitioners.

Broader testing of navigation techniques
The exploration of the first study – to determine the performance of representative navigation techniques on six different tasks – provides an initial perspective of the uncharted territory between the known performance peaks for the three different navigation styles.

Whereas 'point studies' with carefully-chosen tasks allow researchers to establish that a novel technique is advantageous at a single location, survey studies of the kind carried out here help to show the regions of task space where a particular technique will be valuable. Comparing techniques on a range of tasks provided insight into some of the key strengths of different classes of techniques: Zooming is good for seeing spatial relationships, Hop provides key information on object details, and Drag-Mag falls between Zoom and Hop across the range of our tasks. In addition, the first study identified characteristics of the techniques that led to the development of the new techniques tested in the second study.

However, the first study does not cover all possible tasks in visual workspaces – we focused on object-and-map systems and two main classes of tasks – and so further work is clearly needed. We plan to extend the investigation to activities such as measuring, steering, route-finding, and revisitation. Even though we did not test an exhaustive list of tasks, however, the first study provides an example of a methodological approach that can be used for further work.

Hybridizing navigation techniques
Identifying the strengths of different techniques in the first study led to two hybrid designs that combine elements from two or more techniques. The second study provides evidence that this process was successful: both WinHop and Multiscale Zoom appeared to make up for deficiencies in the techniques from which they were derived. In spatially-relative tasks, WinHop improved the performance of the proxy-based approach to a level that is comparable to Zooming and DragMag. Similarly, Multiscale Zoom provided an enormous improvement over regular Zoom in spatially-absolute tasks.

In particular, Multiscale Zoom worked well across the entire range of tasks in our study. However, this result must be tested across even more tasks – just as we cautioned that individual techniques can be over-fitted to particular tasks, it is also possible that Multiscale Zoom is over-fitted to the two classes of tasks that we studied. The potential limitation of Multiscale Zoom is that in environments where many objects have been identified, the oversized overview icons can occlude the map, and can reduce object visibility when they overlap one another. Although there are solutions to these problems (as described above), we need to test this technique in other classes of tasks.

Nevertheless, augmenting navigation techniques by combining features is a promising design approach. We note that other researchers have also had similar success by integrating features of multiple techniques to improve performance [19]. However, the idea of hybridization also has limitations. Embedding a large number of features into a system creates overhead, increases training time, and can make simple tasks harder to accomplish. Clearly, there is a threshold beyond which adding new features to a technique will result in reduced performance. This threshold may have been crossed, in fact, in the design of WinHop: performance on the Location and Existence tasks actually decreased in comparison to Hop, and one explanation is that the new features required more effort (e.g., users had to open a portal before initiating a move toward the object). At the same time, however, we note that for this same task users made fewer errors with WinHop. This example suggests that integrating multiple features may enhance some performance aspects but at the expense of others.

Lessons for practitioners

This work provides three main lessons for designers of visual-workspace systems:

- Designers of object-and-workspace systems should consider using a hybrid technique – particularly Multiscale Zoom – to support offscreen navigation;
- Off-screen navigation techniques should show both spatial relationships and object detail with minimal navigation effort;
- Designers can develop new techniques by investigating the limitations of prior techniques with a range of tasks, but should add features cautiously to avoid reducing performance in other areas.

9   Conclusion and Future Work

Many techniques exist for navigating to off-screen content in a visual spatial workspace. However, any particular technique may not be suitable for a wide variety of tasks. We present the results of two studies that explored the effectiveness of different techniques for a wide range of off-screen navigation tasks. In the first experiment, we compared three techniques that represent three different approaches to off-screen navigation. In the second study, we tested two new techniques that are constructed by combining elements from the representative techniques. Both of these new techniques (Multiscale Zoom and WinHop) significantly improved user performance, particularly on tasks that are not easily supported by the earlier techniques.

In practical terms, designers cannot expect to produce a technique that fits all different possible off-screen navigation tasks. Similarly, we cannot expect users to switch between techniques to execute different types of tasks. At best, we can produce new techniques that are effective on many common tasks. With this outlook, our future work will proceed in three directions: studying navigation performance in other classes of tasks such as steering, measuring, and revisitation; studying the performance of hybrid techniques with datasets that can test their limits; and applying the idea of testing task breadth in an entirely different application domain, such as image editing or text browsing.

References

1. Baudisch, P., Rosenholtz, R.: Halo: a technique for visualizing off-screen objects. In: Proc. CHI 2003, pp. 481–488 (2003)
2. Baudisch, P., Cutrell, E., Robbins, D., Czerwinski, M., Tandler, P., Bederson, B., Zierlinger, A.: Drag-and-pop and drag-and-pick: techniques for accessing remote screen content on touch- and pen-operated systems. In: Proc. Interact 2003, pp. 57–64 (2003)
3. Baudisch, P., Good, N., Bellotti, V., Schraedley, P.: Keeping things in context: a comparative evaluation of focus plus context screens, overviews, and zooming. In: Proc. CHI 2002, pp. 259–266 (2002)
4. Baudisch, P., Xie, X., Wang, C., Ma, W.: Collapse-to-zoom: viewing web pages on small screen devices by interactively removing irrelevant content. In: Proc. UIST 2004, pp. 91–94 (2004)
5. Bederson, B., Hollan, J.: Pad++: a zooming graphical interface for exploring alternate interface physics. In: Proc. UIST 1994, pp. 17–26 (1994)
6. Bezerianos, A., Balakrishnan, R.: The vacuum: facilitating the manipulation of distant objects. In: Proc. CHI 2005, pp. 361–370 (2005)
7. Cockburn, A., Savage, J.: Comparing Speed-Dependent Automatic Zooming with Traditional Scroll, Pan and Zoom Methods. In: Proc. CHI 2003, pp. 87–102 (2003)
8. Gutwin, C.: Improving Focus Targeting in Interactive Fisheye Views. In: Proc. CHI 2002, pp. 267–274 (2002)
9. Gutwin, C., Fedak, C.: Interacting with big interfaces on small screens: a comparison of fisheye, zoom, and panning. In: Proc. Graphics Interface 2004, pp. 145–152 (2004)
10. Hinckley, K., Cutrell, E., Bathiche, S., Muss, T.: Quantitative analysis of scrolling techniques. In: Proc. CHI 2002, pp. 65–72 (2002)
11. Hornbæk, K., Frøkjær, E.: Reading of electronic documents: the usability of linear, fisheye, and overview+detail interfaces. In: Proc. CHI 2001, pp. 293–300 (2001)
12. Igarashi, T., Hinckley, K.: Speed-dependent automatic zooming for browsing large documents. In: Proc. UIST 2000, pp. 139–148 (2000)
13. Irani, P., Gutwin, C., Yang, X.: Improving selection of off-screen targets with hopping. In: Proc. CHI'06, pp. 299–308 (2006)
14. Kaptelinin, V.: A comparison of navigation techniques in a 2D browsing task. In: Proc. CHI 1995, pp. 282–283 (1995)
15. Khan, A., Fitzmaurice, G., Almeida, D., Burtnyk, N., Kurtenbach, G.: A remote control interface for large displays. In: Proc. UIST 2004, pp. 127–136 (2004)
16. Lam, H., Baudisch, P.: Summary thumbnails: readable overviews for small screen web browsers. In: Proc. CHI 2005, pp. 681–690 (2005)

17. Moscovich, T., Hughes, J.: Navigating documents with the virtual scroll ring. In: Proc. UIST 2004, pp. 57–60 (2004)
18. Sarkar, M., Brown, M.: Graphical Fisheye Views of Graphs. In: CHI 1992, pp. 83–91 (1992)
19. Tan, D., Meyers, B., Czerwinski, M.: WinCuts: manipulating arbitrary window regions for more effective use of screen space. In: Proc. CHI'04, pp. 1525–1528 (2004)
20. Ware, C., Lewis, M.: The DragMag image magnifier. In: Proc. CHI 1995, pp. 407–408 (1995)

CandidTree: Visualizing Structural Uncertainty in Similar Hierarchies

Bongshin Lee[1], George G. Robertson[1], Mary Czerwinski[1], and Cynthia Sims Parr[2]

[1] Microsoft Research
One Microsoft Way
Redmond, WA 98052, USA
{bongshin, ggr, marycz}@microsoft.com
[2] Human-Computer Interaction Lab
Institute for Advanced Computer Studies
University of Maryland
College Park, MD 20742, USA
csparr@umd.edu

Abstract. Most visualization systems fail to convey uncertainty within data. To provide a way to show uncertainty in similar hierarchies, we interpreted the differences between two tree structures as uncertainty. We developed a new interactive visualization system called CandidTree that merges two trees into one and visualizes two types of structural uncertainty: location and sub-tree structure uncertainty. We conducted a usability study to identify major usability issues and evaluate how our system works. Another qualitative user study was conducted to see if biologists, who regularly work with hierarchically organized names, are able to use CandidTree to complete tree-comparison tasks. We also assessed the "uncertainty" metric we used.

Keywords: Uncertainty visualization, Structural uncertainty, Tree comparison, Graphical user interfaces.

1 Introduction

Most current visualization systems generally suggest certainty. This means that when we show visualizations to users, they believe that what is currently displayed is ground truth. However, there are many cases where this is not true. For example, there exist several biological taxonomies and phylogenetic trees because not all biologists agree on one taxonomy or one phylogenetic tree and some analysis methods produce multiple possible trees. Current tree visualizations such as TaxonTree [10] and Hyperbolic Tree [9] typically show one taxonomy at a time without any certainty information, which often may not be easily computed. Hence, there is no way to see which parts of the tree are certain or uncertain. To address this problem, we interpreted the differences between two tree structures as uncertainty and developed a new interactive visualization system, called CandidTree (see Fig. 1), to visualize the differences.

C. Baranauskas et al. (Eds.): INTERACT 2007, LNCS 4663, Part II, pp. 250–263, 2007.

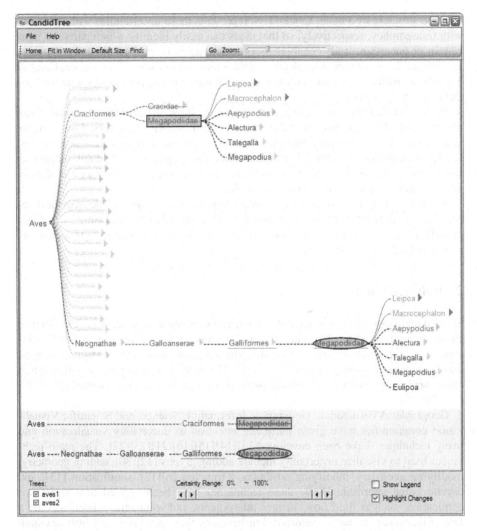

Fig. 1. CandidTree shows two types of structural uncertainty: location and sub-tree structure uncertainty, respectively, with color and transparency so that users can easily identify which parts are most certain or uncertain. CandidTree merges two trees into one and shows the merged tree in the tree browser at the top. The view of the paths at the bottom shows paths to the root in each tree from the currently selected node.

One of the most common approaches to comparing two tree structures is to use paired views side-by-side, using coupled interaction to allow users to compare and navigate two trees. This approach helps users identify where the differences are in two trees (usually by highlighting), but does not explicitly show the degree to which two parts are different.

CandidTree merges two tree structures into one and computes two types of structural uncertainty for each node: 1) location of a node relative to its parent and 2) sub-tree structure of a node. CandidTree represents these uncertainties with color and with transparency, respectively, so that users can easily identify which parts are most certain or uncertain. It also enables users to interactively explore the merged tree to investigate those parts in more depth. Furthermore, when users select a node, Candid-Tree shows paths to the root in each tree so that they can see how its absolute location differs in the two trees.

While CandidTree was originally developed to show structural uncertainty, it can also be applied to visualize the differences between two tree structures. For example, when we have two (backup) directory structures (for two different time points) containing backups for the same folder, CandidTree can help users find added, deleted, or moved files, in addition to modified folders. Furthermore, it enables users to identify which folder has been changed the most or least.

After reviewing related work, we explain how these two types of the structural uncertainty are defined. We describe how CandidTree visualizes them using a set of two classifications of scientific names. We also report two user studies we conducted and then conclude with future work.

2 Related Work

To provide a complete and accurate visual representation of data, it is important to show uncertainty within the data. Uncertainty has been very broadly defined to include concepts such as error, inaccuracy/imprecision, minimum-maximum ranges, data quality, and missing data [21][23][26]. For more than a decade, much research has described approaches to handling these various aspects of uncertainties [2][3][20] [25][26][28].

Geographic Visualization, Geographic Information Science, and Scientific Visualization communities have given particular attention to uncertainty visualization and many techniques have been developed [4][14][15][16][21][23][27]. The main techniques used to visualize uncertainty include adding glyphs [12][30], adding geometry, modifying geometry, modifying attributes, animation [6][12], sonification [13], and psycho-visual approach. While these techniques have been applied to a variety of applications such as fluid flow, surface interpolants, and volumetric rendering, only a few of them were actually evaluated. Furthermore, there has been very little research on visualizing uncertainty in tree structures. To our knowledge, only Griethe and Schumann proposed visual representations to represent uncertainty in parent-child relationship in structures [7]. For example, for node-link diagrams they used blurred or dotted links to indicate less certain relationships. However, they did not describe how to represent the degree of uncertainty. Moreover, while these authors brought up example applications for uncertainty visualization on structure information, their solutions were neither thoroughly investigated nor properly tested. In fact, it was beyond the scope of their paper to find effective metaphors in more challenging situations [7]. Since there is no formal definition of structural uncertainty, we propose two types of uncertainty for tree structures: location and sub-tree structure uncertainty, which will be explained in Section 3.

An error can be defined as a difference between a computed, estimated, or measured value and the true or correct value. There are many cases where we do not know correct values but can estimate those using different techniques or algorithms. It is common to use the differences between two results as an error (or uncertainty). For example, Pang and Freeman visualized differences between 3D surfaces generated by various rendering algorithms [22]. In fact, side-by-side comparison is one of the most commonly applied existing uncertainty visualization methods [23]. Therefore, theoretically we can use these kinds of visualization tools to show uncertainty in tree structures.

In the biology domain, there exist several biological taxonomies and phylogenetic trees because not all biologists agree on one taxonomy and one phylogenetic tree. In order to assess the quality of taxonomies and phylogenetic trees, it is important to understand which parts of two trees agree or disagree [19]. One of the commonly used approaches to comparing two trees is to use paired views side-by-side, using coupled interaction. In fact, many submissions to the InfoVis 2003 contest, Visualization and Pair Wise Comparison of Trees (http://www.cs.umd.edu/hcil/iv04contest), used side-by-side views. For example, TreeJuxtaposer automatically matches nodes in two trees based on the shared ancestors, and highlights where the differences are [18]. Info-Zoom transforms a tree into a tabular representation, in which each leaf is represented as a column and the path from the root is stored in the attributes (rows) [24]. It displays both trees (in a tabular form) side-by-side and marks the cells of differences. Some visualizations provide a merged tree by combining two trees into one. For example, TaxoNote shows the merged tree on left, first tree at center, and second tree on right [17]. It uses multiple tables to provide taxonomic names that are common or different. Zoomology also provides a single overview of the merged tree with the indication of difference, and uses matched twin detail windows to show similarities and differences via a zoomable interface [8]. While these tools show where the differences are, they do not show the magnitude of the differences.

3 Structural Uncertainty

As for the cases where we do not know the correct tree structures, we interpret the differences between two tree structures as uncertainty. For each node, we measure two types of uncertainty; location and sub-tree structure.

3.1 Location Uncertainty

Within a tree structure, the location of a node can be represented in two different ways: 1) absolute path from the root and 2) relative path from its parent. The main drawback of the first representation is that a small difference close to the root would affect its whole sub-tree. Therefore, we decided to use the relative path to compute the uncertainty in node location. The location uncertainty is not scalar but categorical in value and three possible categories are as follows.

1) A node is in both trees at the same location (i.e., under same parent) – most certain
2) A node is in both trees but at different locations (i.e., under different parents)
3) A node is included in only one of the trees – most uncertain

3.2 Sub-Tree Structure Uncertainty

Whether or not a node is in the same location in two trees, its sub-tree structures can be different. We compute the sub-tree structure uncertainty by measuring how many links overlap in two sub-trees. So, the sub-tree structure uncertainty function for a node v can be defined as follows.

$$\text{sub - tree structure uncertainty}(v) = 1 - \frac{n(L_1(v) \cap L_2(v))}{n(L_1(v) \cup L_2(v))},$$

where $L_i(v)$ is the set of links in the sub - tree of v in the ith tree.

4 CandidTree

We developed a visualization system, named CandidTree, to show the structural uncertainty described in the previous section. CandidTree automatically merges two tree structures into one and computes uncertainty based on the differences between them. As shown in Fig. 1, it consists of two views: 1) a tree browser to show the merged tree and 2) a paths view to show paths to the root in each tree from the currently selected node.

To describe how CandidTree works in this chapter, we use a set of two classifications of scientific names of birds; one from the National Center for Biotechnology Information (NCBI, http://www.ncbi.nlm.nih.gov) and the other from the Animal Diversity Web (ADW, http://animaldiversity.ummz.umich.edu). The fact that these two authoritative sources disagree on these classifications illustrates the degree of uncertainty in biological classifications, which CandidTree helps expose.

4.1 Visualizing Structural Uncertainty

CandidTree shows the location uncertainty of a node relative to its parent by color (of the node label). The color black means that the node is included in both trees under the same node. Red and blue show that the node is included in the first and second tree, respectively. If the node is included in both trees but under different nodes, this means that the node moved from the first tree to the second one. To represent this move case, CandidTree shows the red node in the first tree with a strikethrough and the blue node in the second tree with an underline. For example, "Megapodiidae" was under "Craciformes" in the first tree and then moved under "Galliformes" in the second tree (Fig. 1).

CandidTree shows the sub-tree structure uncertainty of a node by transparency (of the node label). To make the node readable, even if uncertainty is very high, CandidTree uses 128 as a minimum alpha value (50% transparent). From the usability study, we learned that it is difficult to distinguish small differences (e.g., the difference between 1 and .9). To help users distinguish the 100% certain information from less certain data, CandidTree uses a solid link only when the sub-tree structure uncertainty is 0. For example, in Fig. 1, among the children of "Megapodiidae," the sub-tree structure uncertainty of "Leipoa" and "Macrocephalon" is 0 and that of the others is non-0.

We also decided to use four discrete alpha values; 1) 255 (0% transparent) when u (uncertainty) = 0, 2) 214 (≈ 16%) when .5 <= u < 1, 3) 171 (≈33%) when 0 < u < .5, and 4) 128 (50%) when u = 1. To enable users to compare uncertainties in the same range, CandidTree provides exact values in a tooltip. The default set of alpha values means that the more certain the data, the more opaque (and readable) it is. However, users may want to focus on uncertain (different) information depending on data and tasks. CandidTree reverses the order of alpha values when users check the "Highlight Changes" check box (bottom right of Fig. 1) to make more uncertain information more readable.

Children of each node are grouped by location uncertainty; 1) nodes only in the first tree, 2) nodes moved from first tree, 3) nodes in both trees, 4) nodes moved to the second tree, and 5) nodes only in the second tree. This helps users capture only one tree from the merged tree. For example, if users want to focus on the first tree, they can ignore group 4) and 5). Within each group, children are sorted by sub-tree structure uncertainty.

4.2 Changes in Paths to the Root

When users click on a moved node (either red with strikethrough or blue with underline) in the tree browser, CandidTree finds the matching node in the other tree and opens them together. The selected node is indicated by a light blue background with a rectangular border and the matching node with an oval border. In the example of Fig. 1, once users click on "Megapodiidae" (in the first tree) under "Craciformes," "Megapodiidae" (in the second tree) under "Galliformes" is automatically opened.

CandidTree's tree browser and paths view are tightly coupled. So, when users select a node in the tree browser, paths to the root in both trees from the selected node are shown in the paths view. If the selected node is included in only one tree or its absolute location is the same in both trees, only one path is shown. When two paths are different, CandidTree vertically aligns the nodes with similar labels from two paths; the similarity of the labels is computed by Levenshtein distance [11]. This helps users see what changes are made between two trees. For example, two levels – "Neognathae" and "Neoaves" – are added to the second tree between "Aves" and "Strigiformes" (Fig. 2). This could also help users identify possible errors in node labels. For example, the parent of the "Musophagidae" is supposed to be "Musophagiformes" as in the first tree and "Musphagiformes" in the second tree is a typographical error (Fig. 3).

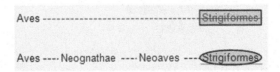

Fig. 2. CandidTree shows paths to the root in each tree from the selected node and its matching node (if exists) in the paths view

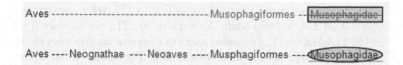

Fig. 3. CandidTree aligns nodes with similar labels from two paths. "Musophagiformes" is aligned with "Musphagiformes" because it is the most similar one among three nodes ("Neognathae," "Neoaves," and "Musphagiformes") from the second tree.

When users click on a node in the paths view, CandidTree temporarily highlights the corresponding node in the tree browser with a thick purple rectangle surrounding the node so that users can recognize where the node is. In addition, if the corresponding node is off-screen, CandidTree pans the tree to view the node.

4.3 Emphasizing Nodes of Interest and Search

As users browse through the tree, especially for the trees with large fan outs, the selected node and its matching node could be very far away from each other and the matching node could be off-screen. Even when there is no matching node, the screen could be still cluttered. We assume that users are mainly interested in the selected node and its children, siblings, and ancestors. So, when users select a node, Candid-Tree uses a fisheye technique [5] and deemphasizes all other nodes by making them smaller and less opaque (Fig. 1). If it exists, the same rule is applied to the matching node of the selected node.

For the cases where users are only interested in the nodes with a specific certainty range, we provide a double-headed range bar (bottom center of Fig. 1) in the control panel to allow users to un-highlight nodes that do not meet the certainty requirement. Users can focus on one tree by manipulating the check boxes in the Trees list (bottom left of Fig. 1); the unchecked tree is un-highlighted. Since 128 (50% transparent) was used as an alpha value for the most uncertain nodes for readability, CandidTree uses 64 as an alpha value (75% transparent) for un-highlighted nodes.

CandidTree provides support for search, providing simple substring match with node labels. Typing a word and pressing the "Go" button displays the search results colored in orange and restricts the view to the nodes relevant to the search results (Fig. 4).

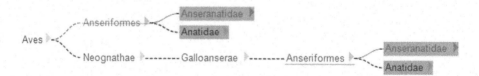

Fig. 4. A search for "Anatidae" shows four search results (containing the keyword) and nodes relevant to them.

4.4 Implementation Details

CandidTree is implemented in C# with Piccolo.NET, a shared source toolkit that supports scalable structured 2D graphics [1] (http://www.cs.umd.edu/hcil/piccolo). It uses a classical tree layout by Walker [29].

CandidTree reads data from files in an xml format. Each node is represented with a "node" element having two attributes; "id" and "name." The id attribute, which should be unique, serves as an identifier to be used to match nodes in two trees. The name attribute is used as a label of the node. The current implementation can be extended to show other node attributes or handle other data formats.

CandidTree builds the merged tree in memory and computes uncertainty at startup. It loads the first tree and then merges the second tree with the first one. The location uncertainty is computed during this merge process. Once the merged tree is built, CandidTree computes the sub-tree structure uncertainty using the equation in Section 3.2 after recursively counting the number of links in the sub-trees of each node.

5 Evaluation

5.1 Study 1: Usability Study with Computer Scientists

To identify major usability issues, we conducted a preliminary usability study with six participants: two researchers, three developers, one research intern (all male computer scientists). We used two sets of backup directory structures, each with two trees representing the data at two different time points. Trees in these sets contained about 150 nodes and 500 nodes.

Participants were given a brief tutorial of the system for up to 15 minutes including the time to play with the system and ask questions. Next, they were asked to perform 10 tasks (1-5 for the small tree and 6-10 for the large tree) with the system, which were timed and scored for correctness. The tasks were meant to cover major tree-comparison tasks and to evaluate the usability of main features to represent structural uncertainty. All participants were asked to perform the tasks as quickly and accurately as possible. Once they completed all of the tasks, participants were asked to fill out a satisfaction questionnaire. Each session lasted about 30 minutes and participants were given a $5 snack coupon for their participation. The list of tasks follows.

1) How many files were deleted from the "DynaVis" folder?
2) Among the sub-folders of "DynaVis," which folder has been changed the most? (We asked users to ignore added or deleted folders.)
3) Describe the changes made to the "DynaVis\DynaTestWin\obj" folder.
4) Which file was moved from the "DynaVis\DynaVis\obj\Debug" folder?
5) Where did the file move to?

Tasks 6-10 were equivalent to tasks 1-5 but applied to a large tree.

There were only 6 incorrect answers provided out of 60 questions across participants. Three participants answered all questions right and the other three each incorrectly answered one, two, and three questions, respectively. Task 2 (and 7 for the large tree) got the most wrong answers because participants had difficulty distinguishing between the colors black and green (green was the color of the second tree at the time of experiment). Two participants each gave wrong answers to Task 4 and 9, respectively. Overall, average task times were fast. While Task 8 took longer than the others (46.5 seconds on average), it was because it takes time to describe all the changes not because participants had a hard time finding the changes.

Table 1 below shows the average satisfaction ratings on a 7-point Likert scale, with 1=Disagree and 7=Agree. There was clear user frustration around the use of transparency to represent the sub-tree structure change. This is related to the readability issue participants raised. The ratings are fairly consistent with the usability issues we identified. We here summarize the major iterations made to CandidTree based on the first user study.

1) Do not use the fourth color for the moved nodes; instead use strikethrough and underline.
2) Use solid links only when the uncertainty is 0; otherwise dotted links.
3) Use four discrete alpha values.
4) Provide an option to highlight changed (uncertain) information.
5) Provide a legend to show the color scheme.

Table 1. Average Likert scale ratings for CandidTree, using the scale of 1=Disagree, 7=Agree. Study 1 refers to the Usability Study with Computer Scientists and Study 2 refers to the Qualitative User Study with Biologists described in the next section.

	Study 1	Study 2
Overall, the system was easy to use	5.0	5.7
I felt comfortable using this system	5.3	5.7
It was easy to learn to use this system	5.2	5.7
It was easy to navigate through this system	6.0	5.7
It was easy to read the labels of the nodes	4.7	4.6
Colors representing the node location change was clear	4.2	4.5
Transparency representing the sub-tree structure change was clear	3.5	3.0

5.2   Study 2: Qualitative User Study with Biologists

We conducted a qualitative study with biologists who regularly work with hierarchically organized names, with two main goals. First, are these users able to use Candid-Tree to correctly and quickly complete tree-comparison tasks, and which tasks pose more difficulty for users? Second, does CandidTree support advanced information understanding and insight? Gaining insight from data does not lend itself easily to the metrics typically used in quantitative studies. Finally, we were interested in an assessment of the "uncertainty" metric we used.

Participants. We recruited 8 volunteers (3 females and 5 males, 28 to 59 years old) from the Smithsonian Institution and University of Maryland. They included two graduate students, two post-doctoral fellows, and four curators or research faculty. All were unfamiliar with the testing datasets, though all had previously used data from the same source before. Two were familiar with the tutorial data. Three mentioned regularly working with datasets of more than 150 terminal taxa (leaves); typical datasets include between 40 to 150 leaves (median 143). However, several of the biologists were associated with NSF projects dealing with trees of names of thousands of organisms and two participants mentioned that CandidTree might be useful for those projects. Each participant was given a $20 Amazon.com gift certificate for his/her participation.

Datasets. For both demonstration and testing we used classifications of scientific names from the National Center for Biotechnology Information (http://www. ncbi.nlm.nih.gov) that were downloaded on different dates: December 14, 2005 and September 19, 2006. Tutorial data were from the Lepidoptera branch (moths and butterflies; tree 1=4103 nodes, tree 2=6262 nodes) while the test data were from the Aves branch (birds; tree 1=6912 nodes, tree 2=8140 nodes).

Procedure. Each participant filled out a background survey. They received a demonstration of CandidTree features and were told to freely explore and ask questions, for a total tutorial time of up to 20 minutes. The search feature was not described or tested, nor were default settings for transparency or filtering changed or described. Nodes that were darker were those with higher uncertainty scores. Participants who asked were told how uncertainty was calculated. Participants were then asked to perform eleven tasks, described below. Participants then completed the same preference survey as in the usability study (Table 1). We videotaped the computer screen throughout the tutorial and testing. Each session lasted 45 to 60 minutes.

Tasks. Biologically meaningful tasks (Table 2) were chosen based on 30-minute interviews with three biologists (one of whom was subsequently a participant). They were presented in order of increasing complexity. The first nine had single, correct answers. Task 10 was judged by the number of insights given by the participant, and Task 11 was an opinion.

Results. Overall ease of use improved slightly over the usability study (Table 1). Still, transparency as an indicator of the sub-tree structure change scored particularly low. "Color representing the node location change was clear" and "It was easy to read the labels of the nodes" also received relatively low scores.

Of 72 possible answers (8 participants x 9 tasks), only 8 were incorrect (Table 2). The oldest participant had the most difficulty, answering incorrectly for 3 out of the 5 most complex tasks. Task 4, which required understanding the coding of location uncertainty, was missed most often. Task 7, which required understanding whether the location change was up or down a level, was missed by two participants but they both admitted a lack of concern about the utility of biological ranks.

Coding of location uncertainty continued to be problematic despite the iteration and the addition of a legend. Several participants answered question 4 incorrectly at first and then corrected themselves after glancing at the legend (they were counted as correct answers). Those who missed it gave all red names as answers instead of just the names in red with strikethrough. One participant remarked that she expected the

Table 2. Biologist user study tasks, with results from eight participants

Task	# Missed	Mean duration (s)
1. Which branch (child) of the Neognathae is the most uncertain, from tree 1 to tree 2?	0	73
2. In the children of Bucerotidae, are the changes additions, deletions, or changes in the placement of taxa?	1	28
3. How much growth (in number of new taxa) has Lampornis experienced from tree 1 to tree 2?	0	19
4. Of the children of Passeriformes, name all the taxa that are placed differently in the different trees.	3	31
5. For Estrildidae, describe the difference in the placement.	0	29
6. The genus Agelaius moved from one group to another. Did all of the other genera in its group move too?	1	51
7. Was the parent of Icterus promoted or demoted in rank?	2	104
8. What happened to the family Cracticidae?	1	57
9. Overall, how would you characterize the uncertainty or change in the tree: changes in deep relationships, mid-tree relationships, or among terminal taxa?	0	137
10. Summarize the changes to Furnariidae and to Sylviidae.	--	275
11. In your opinion, which of the two groups Furnariidae and Sylviidae is the most uncertain?	--	73

two red codes to be additive: "It implies a hierarchy but in fact they signify different rather than nested ideas."

Average times to complete biologically relevant tasks were somewhat longer than in the usability study (Table 2). Some participants took 1 to 2 minutes for Task 1, either to orient to the testing protocol (giving answers verbally) or to the sort order of uncertainty. Otherwise, the simplest tasks each typically took less than 30 seconds. For task 10, most participants explored for 3 to 6 minutes before being satisfied they had given a good summary.

For task 10, participants reported 3 insights (the participant with the least domain expertise who spent only 110 seconds exploring) to 9 insights (participant 4, who systematically explored for 6 minutes). Overall, approximately 18 unique insights were given. Five of the 8 participants found a typographical error correction that required a correct interpretation of transparency, and 3 found a subtle location change that required understanding of location coding and the paths view. The example in Box 1 shows how Participant 4 built his insights in steps while exploring CandidTree. Participants also reported some insights that were unprompted during both the tutorial and test. For example, participants mentioned that the datasets were obviously large, had few changes, were different from a dataset they were familiar with, and had a sub-tree with lots of "problem children."

For task 11, six of 8 participants that sub-tree Sylviidae was more uncertain than the other. However, though the certainty scores were very close, half of the participants thought Sylviidae was much more uncertain because the changes involved numerous

---

Box 1. Participant 4 used CandidTree to make the following insights. Insight 9 builds on 6 and 7 which build on 5 which builds on 4.

Furnariidae sub-tree

1. Immediately identifies that there has been a spelling change between tree 1 and [requires opening the least certain sub-tree]
2. Counts 17 new genus-level nodes added
3. Finds in a sub-tree that there has been a new species added

Sylviidae sub-tree

4. Three nodes in tree 2 are not in tree 1
5. Two of these are entirely new subfamilies [judged by interpreting the label]
6. They contain both taxa that have been moved here from the first tree
7. and also include some taxa entirely new to the second tree
8. Elsewhere, some new subspecies have been added that were not in the first tree
9. Says, "Basically, taxa which had not previously been in subfamilies [a particular rank in the hierarchy] were moved into Acrocephalinae"

---

rearrangements and addition of internal nodes rather than simple addition of nodes at the leaves. Two participants thought it was not reasonable to compare them because the kinds of uncertainty were so different.

Consistent with the preference survey, the most common complaint was that transparency differences were too subtle to be usable. Also, two participants thought the more transparent names should be those with less sub-tree structure certainty. However, generally high task performance shows that these issues did not pose significant problems. Two participants thought that the colors should be reversed (red should represent the second, more recent or important tree). Several had trouble managing opening and then closing sub-trees and two suggested it would be useful to have a way to open or close one level of children all at once across the whole tree.

Participants offered many ideas for additional features or applications. Three participants wanted to use CandidTree to compare more than two trees, particularly with particular scientific datasets and websites such as NCBI or Tree of Life (http://www.tolweb.org). Some expressed interest in linking nodes to further information such as the GenBank sequence or host plants.

6   Conclusion and Future Work

We proposed two types of uncertainty for tree structures – location and sub-tree structure uncertainty – based on the differences between them. To visualize those structural uncertainties, a new interactive visualization system called CandidTree was developed. Since CandidTree computes uncertainty by comparing two trees, we were able to apply it to visualize the differences between them. For example, CandidTree helps users find added, deleted, or moved files as well as modified folders within two (backup) directory structures containing backups for the same folder.

We conducted two user studies to identify major usability issues and evaluate how our system works. Our qualitative study with biologists showed that while we have improved the uncertainty representation so that task performance and insight-building is high even with large trees, ways to improve satisfaction are needed. Also, while most users concur with relative uncertainty scores, there is not universal agreement on how to weigh the kinds of uncertainty. We are planning to conduct a controlled experiment to compare CandidTree with a traditional files and folders comparison tool to see whether users could perform better with CandidTree.

While the current implementation works only for two trees, we can handle more than two trees by providing the list of possible combinations of multiple trees and showing only one combination at a time. By ranking each combination based on the sub-tree structure uncertainty of the root node, we could enable users to easily identify most certain/uncertain (similar/dissimilar) tree combinations. As mentioned before, CandidTree loads each entire tree and builds the merged tree in memory, which is impractical for large trees. We can preprocess building of the merged tree and the computing structural uncertainty, and store them in a database. By accessing the data from a database when needed, CandidTree can be scaled up to support very large trees and with multiple attributes.

Acknowledgments. We would like to thank the participants of our two user studies for their participation and comments. Charlie Mitter and Ashleigh Smythe helped define biologist tasks as did Nathan Edwards who also provided NCBI data. Danyel Fisher reviewed our paper and gave thoughtful comments.

References

1. Bederson, B.B., Grosjean, J., Meyer, J.: Toolkit Design for Interactive Structured Graphics. IEEE Trans. on Software Engineering 30(8), 535–546 (2004)
2. Cleveland, W.S.: The Elements of Graphing Data (1985)
3. Eaton, C., Plaisant, C., Drizd, T.: Visualizing Missing Data: Graph Interpretation User Study. In: Costabile, M.F., Paternó, F. (eds.) INTERACT 2005. LNCS, vol. 3585, pp. 851–872. Springer, Heidelberg (2005)
4. Fegeas, R.G., Cascio, J.L., Lazar, R.A.: An Overview of FIPS 173, The Spatial Data Transfer Standard. Cartography and Geographic Information Systems 19(5), 278–293 (1992)
5. Furnas, G.W.: Generalized Fisheye Views. In: Proc. of CHI 1986, pp. 16–23 (1986)
6. Gershon, N.D.: Visualization of Fuzzy Data using Generalized Animation. In: Proc. of VIS 1992, pp. 268–273 (1992)
7. Griethe, H., Schumann, H.: The Visualization of Uncertain Data: Methods and Problems. In: Proc. of SimVis 2006, pp. 143–156 (2006)
8. Hong, J.Y., D'Andries, J., Richman, M., Westfall, M.: Zoomology: Comparing Two Large Hierarchical Trees. In: Posters Compendium of InfoVis 2003, pp. 120–121 (2003)
9. Hyperbolic Tree for the Green Tree of Life, http://ucjeps.berkeley.edu/TreeofLife/hyperbolic.php
10. Lee, B., Parr, C.S., Campbell, D., Bederson, B.B.: How Users Interact with Biodiversity Information using TaxonTree. In: Proc. of AVI 2004, pp. 320–327 (2004)
11. Levenshtein, V.I.: Binary codes capable of correcting deletions, insertions, and reversals, Doklady Akademii Nauk SSSR 163(4), 845–848 (1965) (Russian). English translation in Soviet Physics Doklady 10(8), 707–710 (1966)
12. Lodha, S.K., Pang, A., Sheehan, R.E., Wittenbrink, C.M.: UFLOW: Visualizing Uncertainty in Fluid Flow. In: Proc. of VIS 1996, pp. 249–255 (1996)

13. Lodha, S.K., Wilson, C.M., Sheehan, R.E.: LISTEN: Sounding Uncertainty Visualization. In: Proc. of VIS 1996, pp. 189–196 (1996)
14. MacEachren, A.M., Robinson, A., Hopper, S., Gardner, S., Murray, R., Gahegan, M., Hetzler, E.: Visualizing Geospatial Information Uncertainty: What We Know and What We Need to Know. Cartography and Geographic Information Science 32, 139–160 (2005)
15. Moellering, H.: Continuing Research Needs Resulting from the SDTS Development Effort. Cartography and Geographic Information Systems 21(3), 180–189 (1994)
16. Morrison, J.: The Proposed Standard for Digital Cartographic Data. American Cartographer 15(1), 9–140 (1988)
17. Morse, D.R., Ytow, N., Roberts, D.M., Sato, A.: Comparison of Multiple Taxonomic Hierarchies Using TaxoNote. In: Posters Compendium of InfoVis 2003, pp. 126–127 (2003)
18. Munzner, T., Guimbretiere, F., Tasiran, S., Zhang, L., Zhou, Y.: TreeJuxtaposer: Scalable Tree Comparison using Focus+Context with Guaranteed Visibility. Proc. of SIGGRAPH 2003, published as ACM Transactions on Graphics 22(3), 453–462 (2003)
19. Nye, T.M.W., Lio, P., Gilks, W.R.: A Novel Algorithm and Web-based Tool for Comparing Two Alternative Phylogenetic Trees. Bioinformatics 22(1), 117–119 (2006)
20. Olston, C., Mackinlay, J.D.: Visualizing Data with Bounded Uncertainty. In: Proc. of InfoVis 2002, pp. 37–40 (2002)
21. Pang, A.: Visualizing Uncertainty in Geo-Spatial Data. In: Proc. of the Workshop on the Intersections between Geospatial Information and Information Technology
22. Pang, A., Freeman, A.: Methods for Comparing 3D surface Attributes. In: Proc. of SPIE-VDA 1996, pp. 58–64 (1996)
23. Pang, A.T., Wittenbrink, C.M., Lodha, S.K.: Approaches to Uncertainty Visualization. The Visual Computer 13(8), 370–390 (1997)
24. Spenke, M., Beilken, C.: Visualization of Trees as Highly Compressed Tables with Info-Zoom. In: Posters Compendium of InfoVis 2003, pp. 122–123 (2003)
25. Sulo, R., Eick, S., Grossman, R.: DaVis: A Tool for Visualizing Data Quality. In: Posters Compendium of InfoVis 2005, pp. 45–46 (2005)
26. Taylor, B.N., Kuyatt C.E.: Guidelines for Evaluating and Expressing the Uncertainty of NIST Measurement Results, NIST Technical Note 1297 (1994)
27. Thomson, J., Hetzler, B., MacEachren, A., Gahegan, M., Pavel, M.: A Typology for Visualizing Uncertainty. In: Proc. VDA 2005, pp. 146–157 (2005)
28. Tukey, J.W.: Exploratory Data Analysis (1977)
29. Walker II, Q.: A Node-Positioning Algorithm for General Trees. Software-Practice and Experience 20(7), 685–705 (1990)
30. Wittenbrink, C.M., Pang, A.T., Lodha, S.K.: Glyphs for Visualizing Uncertainty in Vector Fields. IEEE Trans. on Visualization and Computer Graphics 2(3), 266–279 (1996)

Tagscape: Navigating the Tag Landscape

Lauren Haynes, Aylin Selcukoglu, Sunah Suh, and Karrie Karahalios

University of Illinois at Urbana-Champaign
Urbana, IL 61801, USA
{lnhaynes, selcukgl, sunahsuh, kkarahal}@uiuc.edu

Abstract. Recent years have seen an explosion in online collaborative tagging, the most prevalent visualization of which are tag clouds. Despite their popularity, tag clouds suffer from limitations of separation from tagged items, lack of relational information between tags and a less-than-fully interactive experience. In this paper we introduce Tagscape, a tag system interface that attempts to address these issues. Tagscape uses a magnet analogy to represent relationships between tags and tagged items as attractions and repulsions. Preliminary informal evaluations of the interface were positive and revealed avenues for future work.

1 Introduction

Tagging systems have played an important role in the popularly termed Web 2.0 movement, garnering much academic interest. Most of the recent work in this area, however, has concentrated on the semantic aspects of tagging, termed *folksonomy*. This research provides a strong basis for the usage trends in and semantic problems with tagging [3] as well as current tagging system designs [6], but does not examine the applied aspects of user interaction with these systems.

The limited work involving tag browsing has focused on the tag cloud due to growing popularity among social tagging-based systems such as Flickr, Del.icio.us, Technorati and Last.fm. The tag cloud is an alphabetic list of words where font size indicates frequency of tag use. Once a user clicks on a tag, a new page is displayed presenting items associated with that label. Research of tag clouds has concentrated on the effect of layout and font size on information retrieval and recall [4,8].

Researchers have proposed modifications to the traditional tag cloud including abandoning alphabetical listings for an algorithm that clusters tags within a cloud based on semantic relationships [5] and re-shaping the boxed form into a circular structure with distance to the center and font size indicating importance [1]. Another attempt visualizes the relationship between tags by proposing a graph with tags as nodes and edges (distance between nodes) as similarity between tags [9]. Additionally, third-party tag visualization tools are available (e.g. Extisp.icio.us, Fac.etio.us, and Tag.alicio.us). While these modified versions present improvements upon traditional tag clouds, they do not address both issues of separation between tags and tagged items and lack of information about the relationship between tags.

Though the tag cloud is widely used, it may not be the best method for tag visualization [4]. Issues with tag clouds include separation between tags and tagged items, lack

C. Baranauskas et al. (Eds.): INTERACT 2007, LNCS 4663, Part II, pp. 264–267, 2007.

of information about relationships between tags and a less interactive user experience, especially when compared to their context of use.

Tagscape contributes to this research by presenting a rich interface that allows simultaneous browsing of both tags and tagged items. By interacting with both aspects of tagging systems at once, users can see more meaningful metadata about not only the number of items tagged with a certain phrase but also the relationships between tags.

2   Tagscape

The current Tagscape prototype uses flyers as the tagged content, based on data from 100 unique flyers on corkboards in a university's computer science building. It was implemented using Processing and Jeffrey Traer Bernstein's physics library [7,10]. The interface relies on the metaphor of magnets – each tag acts as a magnet, attracting or repelling flyers which are represented as dots.

The layout consists of a left-hand tray containing the first-level tags, and a right-hand tray containing the most popular tags under the selected first-level tag. The magnets in the left-hand tray are static features of the system, determined from the physical flyers studied. The last magnet in the left-hand tray is blank, facilitating user-defined tag search if the 35 pre-selected options are not adequate. The right-hand tray is populated

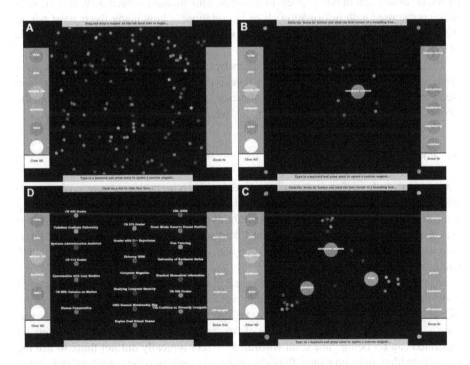

Fig. 1. (**A**) Tagscape in idle state. (**B**) Flyer-tag interaction. (**C**) Multiple magnet interaction. (**D**) Zoomed in view of flyers.

upon reload, and has five different configurations based on the currently selected first-level tag. The items themselves move around the centerfield in the idle state (see Fig. 1. A), where they also interact with user-placed magnets.

Although this specific adaptation uses a two-level tag hierarchy, the system could easily be applied to a flat tagging scheme with limited modification. The main benefit of the two-level scheme in this implementation is color association of the top-level tags with related flyers – more information is integrated in the visualization. The color saturation levels of the flyer dots integrate additional information about time – higher color saturations imply events approaching the present, while flyers far from the present are less saturated.

In order to browse tags, the user drags a magnet onto the field. This attracts all flyers having that tag to the area around the magnet and repels irrelevant flyers to the corners of the field (see Fig. 1. B). A spring-based algorithm creates these attractive and repulsive forces in a method similar to Visual Who [2]. The user removes magnets by dragging them back into the tray or by using the "Clear All" button at the bottom of the left-hand tray.

The system is best suited for exploring relationships between multiple tags. If two tags are placed some distance apart on the field, flyers that are pertinent to both settle between the two magnets, while flyers that are relevant to only one tag come to rest outside the two tags (see Fig. 1. C). Similarly, if the user wishes to filter irrelevant flyers, he or she can move magnets to a corner. This method immediately and visually presents the user with information about tag relations – how many flyers exist within the system pertaining to the placed tags as well as how many flyers relate to multiple placed tags.

The user can zoom in on interesting flyers by clicking and dragging in negative field space around the flyer. The zoomed view reveals the titles of the flyers within that region (see Fig. 1. D). From the zoomed view, the user can either return to searching using the "Zoom Out" button or double click on a dot, which opens the flyer in a new window.

3   Evaluation

An informal study of Tagscape was conducted with 16 users. Users were given time to play with the interface and were then asked to complete a set of tasks such as finding a specific flyer. Following interaction with the system, users were given an anonymous survey composed primarily of five-point Likert scales. Users generally rated the interface well, giving it an average score of 4.06 with 1 being "extremely unsatisfied" and 5 being "extremely satisfied."

Many users found the system engaging and most indicated they would use it again if given the opportunity. While users initially required some instruction, given in the form of a help bar at the top of the interface, they quickly grew comfortable with Tagscape. This is reflected in the average ranking of frustration of 3.81 with 1 being "extremely frustrated" and 5 being "not at all frustrated." Users typically did not think to use the magnets to filter away unwanted flyers by dragging magnets to the corner, an anticipated behavior. However, some users developed their own ways to use the system – arranging the magnets in patterns or chasing dots with magnets. Users commented that "the UI was relatively intuitive" and that it "makes searching easy."

4   Future Work

The next step in Tagscape's development will involve improving the user interface to emphasize current aspects of tag cloud representations that were less salient in Tagscape. One such aspect includes the information conveyed about the popularity of a tag; with tag clouds this is quantified using the font size of the tag word – the larger the word the more popular the tag. In Tagscape the popularity of a tag is not revealed until the user interacts with it. This could be improved upon by varying the size of the magnets based on popularity – the larger the magnet the more popular the tag.

Another possible improvement is to implement the interface using AJAX, which not only affords the user a more integrated experience in its normal context of use but also allows the interface to be as large as the user's browser window instead of the fixed resolution of a Processing applet. Following such changes, detailed user studies will be conducted comparing Tagscape to current tag cloud implementations.

References

1. Bielenberg, K., Zacher, M.: Groups in Social Software: Utilizing Tagging to Integrate Individual Contexts for Social Navigation. Masters Thesis The Program of Digital Media, Unisersitat Bremen (2006) (Submitted)
2. Donath, S.J.: Visual Who: Animating the affinities and activities of an electronic community. In: Proceedings of ACM Multimedia Electronic (1995)
3. Golder, S., Huberman, B.A.: The Structure of Collaborative Tagging Systems. HP Labs technical report (2005), Available from: `http://www.hpl.hp.com/research/idl/papers/tags`
4. Halvey, M., Keane, M.T.: An Assessment of Tag Presentation Techniques. In: WWW2007 Conference Proceedings (2007), Available from: `http://www2007.org/posters/poster988.pdf`
5. Hasan-Montero, Y., Herrero-Solana, V.: Improving Tag-Clouds as Visual Information Retrieval Interfaces. In: Proceedings of International Conference on Multidisciplinary Information Sciences and Technologies (2006)
6. Marlow, C., Naaman, M., Davis, M., Boyd, D.: Tagging Paper, Taxonomy, Flickr, Academic Article, ToRead. In: Proceedings of Hypertext 2006 (2006)
7. Processing, `http://www.processing.org`
8. Rivadeneira, A.W., Gruen, D.M., Muller, M.J., Millen, D.R.: Getting Our Head in the Clouds: Toward Evauation Studies of Tagclouds. In: Proceedings of CHI 2007 (2007)
9. Shaw, B.: Utilizing Folksonomy: Similarity Metadata from the Del.icio.us System. Project Proposal (2005), Available from: `http://www.metablake.com/webfok/web-project.pdf`
10. TRAER.PHYSICS, `http://www.cs.princeton.edu/~traer/physics/`

Visual Tagging Through Social Collaboration: A Concept Paper

Andrea Bellucci[1], Stefano Levialdi[1], and Alessio Malizia[2]

[1] [1]Department of Computer Science
University Sapienza of Rome
Via Salaria 113, 00100, Rome, Italy
{bellucci,levialdi}@di.uniroma1.it
[2] DEI Laboratory, Computer Science Department
Universidad Carlos III de Madrid
Avda. de la Universidad, 30. 28911-Leganés, Madrid (Spain)
alessio.malizia@uc3m.es

Abstract. Collaborative tagging has grown on the Internet as a new paradigm for web information discovering, filtering and retrieval. In the physical world, we use visual tags: labels readable by smartphones with cameras. While visual tags are usually related to a web site address, collaborative tagging, instead, provides updated, recommended information contributed and shared by users. In this paper we investigate the combination of collaborative tagging systems with visual tags. We present a prototype of a semiautomatic system generating visual tags which gather information from collaborative tagging. The user can interact with a list of relevant tags (built by clustering closely related tags) that can be further encoded in a visual tag, according to user's preferences. The user experience is enriched by retrieving multimedia content linked to the selected tags, present on the web. We finally show a case study illustrating our approach.

1 Introduction

Collaborative tagging[1,2] is the process by which users add metadata, by means of descriptive terms (tags), to community-shared content in order to classify or organize documents for further navigation, filtering or search. These tags are usually appended informally and personally by the author/creator of a document. Based on social structures, tagging is an adaptable process; it takes the form best supported by the content, letting users decide the categorization, rather than imposing a rigid structure on it. Nowadays there are a number of eminent web sites that rely on collaborative tagging: these systems allow users both to add tags and share content, so they can browse content categorized by other users as well as categorize information for their own purposes. An example of such sites is Flickr (http://www.flickr.com), a service giving to users the possibility to tag photographs they own. In the real world we assist to another tag proliferation: the one of visual tags[3]. Barcodes are the first example of visual tags; in this

C. Baranauskas et al. (Eds.): INTERACT 2007, LNCS 4663, Part II, pp. 268–271, 2007.

sense tagging simply places a machine-readable label on a physical object. The main advantage of visual tagging is that the actual modification on the object is minimal, as its cost. Visual codes can be easily incorporated when designing the package or printed on labels, but they must be scanned using a camera, or a code reader, and they need to display the retrieved information. Smartphones seem to embody the natural solution: small mobile devices that incorporate a tag reader (the mobile camera), a display and an online connection into a single device. The prevalent use of visual tags is to associate physical objects to digital information. Systems like the Japanese QR Code[4] provide visual tags, easy to generate and print, that are readable with a mobile camera. QR Codes appear in the most unpredicted places in Japan: for example one common use is placing codes, related to a web site address, on magazines or advertisements. You can also find QR Codes on the timetable at a bus stop, linked to real-time data on traffic and bus schedules. It follows that the real power of mobile visual tagging is in providing complementary information when and where a user actually need it. In this paper we investigate the possibilities offered by collaborative tagging activities on the web combined with visual tags.

2   Motivation

In practice web sites have a static meaning since the content is only organized by the web master. Collaborative tagging systems, instead, usually contain information shared by users, frequently updated and providing hints (e.g. tags suggesting whether or not something was appreciated by the "tagger", for example recent photos of a vacation trip, and so on). Such systems also contain individuals' structural knowledge about documents. Structural knowledge has been defined as the knowledge of how concepts in a domain are interrelated (Diekhoff and Diekhoff 1982)[5]. Therefore, in a collaborative tagging system, tags encode the knowledge of relationships among documents and concepts represented by the tags. Moreover, as users with similar interests tend to have a shared vocabulary, tags created by one user turn useful to others, particularly those with similar interests as the tagger's.

However while tagging systems claim to have many advantages over controlled vocabularies or taxonomies, they still suffer from some limitations, such as the lack of lexical relations[6] or information overload[7]. Searching and retrieving may turn very limited if we ignore lexical relations, especially in a system where many users with different backgrounds have added different tags. A solution to these handicaps can be found by clustering techniques within the tag space: starting from a seed word, we identify 'families' of tags having a strongly related meaning.

We suggest that if we use individuals' knowledge of a given concept (i.e. about *Rome*), revealed through the set of personal tags, in conjunction with clustering sets of tags related to *Rome*, we may then identify a core group of *key tags*: such *key tags* make up a family of potentially interesting tags for the user. Such tags best describe an associated concept that the system user required: for instance Rome can be followed by *Tiber* and *bridge*, representing different Roman bridges whilst followed by *Vatican* and *church* will depict Roman churches. Once identified, these *key tags*, can be encoded into a visual tag. The visual tag can be placed in a variety of physical objects (books, ads, historical ruins) and the contained information allows retrieval of online multimedia content in order to enrich the user experience. In this way, we have firstly established a bridge between the information contents (digital and online) provided by a group of people and the final user but also the possibility of sharing such information between a wide range of users so increasing the expressive power of such visual tag. The user may always retrieve the updated contents produced by other users in the world.

3   The System

We distinguish two classes of users: the editor of visual tags and the final user interested in retrieving multimedia content (images in our case) corresponding to her interests through the visual tag. The editor will submit a seed word and the underlying collaborative system (Flickr in our case) will firstly provide a list of strongly related tags established by clustering performed directly from the Flickr web site. The editor will choose those tags representative of her intended aim. For example if the seed word is *Rome* and the editor wants to provide pictures representing bridges on the Tiber river, she will select the tag *bridge* and the tag *Tiber* from the list (see Fig.1).

The editor will test her new tags by looking at corresponding images and either leave the chosen ones or add/delete other tags after checking their correspondence to her target concept. We next encode such tags into a Quick Response Code (QR Code) such as that shown on Fig. 2 (step 4). On the final user side, she will read the visual tag (on the site, totem or physical object) by means of a camera phone enabling her to retrieve updated information from Flickr.

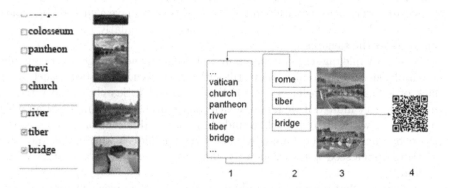

Fig. 1. List of tags for the seed word *Rome*

Fig. 2. The encoding process: input list (1), selected tags (2), corresponding images (3) and final, visual tag (4)

4   Case Study

Our test example is in the area of sightseeing and vacation guides. Such booklets provide printed indications about places to see and their related history. This information is traditionally static (printed) and contains few (expensive) images of the site: such drawbacks may be overcome by using our visual tags that may be printed on a page of such travel book. The tourist with her camera phone may read the visual tag so obtaining recent (daily updated) images, related to the site she will be visiting, taken by other visitors of the same site.

5   Conclusion and Future Work

In this paper we suggest to combine online collaborative tagging with visual tags. We have presented a semiautomatic system for generating visual tags starting from a list of semantically related tags of a given seed word. We have briefly described a case example to illustrate our approach, using Flickr. Our system may overcome the digital divide by providing information obtained from other countries in the world (travelers in our case) so expanding the knowledge of the final user to a limit similar to the one of the rest of the world. We are currently investigating the use of other collaborative tagging systems, such as Youtube (http://www.youtube.com) in order to extend the retrieval process to a wide range of multimedia contents; at the same time we will explore different clustering techniques so as to maximize the semantic closeness of our tags.

References

1. Mates A.: Folksonomies - Cooperative Classification and Communication Through Shared Metadata, Computer Mediated Communication, LIS590CMC (2004)
2. Hammond, T., Hannay, T., Lund, B., Scott, J.: Social Bookmarking Tools (I): A General Review. D-Lib Magazine 11(4) (2005)
3. Holmquist, L.E.: Tagging the World. ACM Interactions 13(4), 51 (2006)
4. DENSO WAVE (2004), http://www.denso-wave.com/qrcode/index-e.html
5. Diekhoff, G.M., Diekhoff, K.B.: Cognitive maps as a tool in communicating structural knowledge. Educational Technology 22(4), 28–30 (1982)
6. Begelman, G., Keller, P., Smadja, F.: Automated Tag Cluestering: Improving search and exploration in the tag space. In: WWW2006, May 22-26, 2006, Edinburgh (2006)
7. Wu, H., Zubair, M., Maly, K.: Harvesting Social Knowledge from Folksonomies. In: HYPERTEXT '06. Proceedings of the seventeenth conference on Hypertext and hypermedia, pp. 111–114. ACM Press, New York (2006)

Visualizing Activity on Wikipedia with Chromograms

Martin Wattenberg[1], Fernanda B. Viégas[1], and Katherine Hollenbach[2]

[1] IBM Research
[2] Massachusetts Institute of Technology
{mwatten, viegasf}@us.ibm.com, kjhollen@mit.edu

Abstract. To investigate how participants in peer production systems allocate their time, we examine editing activity on Wikipedia, the well-known online encyclopedia. To analyze the huge edit histories of the site's administrators we introduce a visualization technique, the chromogram, that can display very long textual sequences through a simple color coding scheme. Using chromograms we describe a set of characteristic editing patterns. In addition to confirming known patterns, such reacting to vandalism events, we identify a distinct class of organized systematic activities. We discuss how both reactive and systematic strategies shed light on self-allocation of effort in Wikipedia, and how they may pertain to other peer-production systems.

Keywords: Wikipedia, Visualization, Peer Production, Visualization.

1 Introduction

The past decade has seen a surge of activity in peer-production projects, where work is conducted by volunteers who make their own decisions about what to work on and when to work on it. Benkler [2] has argued that the success of these projects is partly due to the efficiency with which individuals allocate their own efforts. While several studies have examined what motivates contributors to these projects and the processes behind them [9,11], the mechanisms by which individuals allocate their effort are not fully understood.

One of the archetypes of peer production is Wikipedia, an online encyclopedia which anyone on the internet may edit. Not only is Wikipedia an influential example of peer production, but it is one for which a great deal of information is available. The Wikipedia community makes public nearly complete data on article edits and the discussions surrounding them.

Our investigation is based on this data, in particular the edit histories of Wikipedia "administrators," a key subset of active contributors. Since these histories are large and unstructured the analysis is a challenging problem. Our solution is to use a new visualization method, which we call a chromogram, that converts textual data to colors, producing a data-dense display that can fit a vast edit history onto a single screen. Because the method is simple and general we believe it is of interest in its own right, with potential applications in other areas.

We apply the chromogram technique to the activities of Wikipedia administrators. One clear result is heterogeneity of individuals' work habits at every time scale.

C. Baranauskas et al. (Eds.): INTERACT 2007, LNCS 4663, Part II, pp. 272–287, 2007.
© IFIP International Federation for Information Processing 2007

Almost every editor we studied engaged in task switching, rarely working on one article or type of task continuously. At the same time, most editors we studied also had at least one area of concentration: this focus could relate to content categories (for example ships, television shows, or alcoholic beverages) or to process (e.g., fighting vandalism, welcoming new users).

We identify two broad classes of focal activities: reactive edits (such as repairing vandalism), and "systematic" projects characterized by a sequence of repetitive activity. A common systematic strategy, for instance, is to make the same type of edit to a long sequence of related pages in alphabetical order by title.

We conclude by discussing potential explanations for these phenomena. In particular, we suggest that both the reactive and systematic strategies arise in response to the fact that work in Wikipedia often consists of a large number of very small tasks. It has been hypothesized [2] that a division of labor into many small modular tasks is a general characteristic of successful peer production projects, and so we discuss how our findings may relate to other peer production systems. We also show how these usage patterns suggest design principles for systems aimed at collaborative creation of content.

2   Background and Related Work

It is worth reviewing some of the mechanics of Wikipedia and how they may affect decisions about work. We start by narrowing our view to the English language version. This site is made up of several different types of pages lying within distinct "namespaces". The "Main" namespace holds the actual encyclopedia articles. Other key areas include "Main:Talk" where discussions about particular articles take place, "Image" where pictures are kept, and "Wikipedia," where guidelines are held. See [Viegas07] for more details.

Wikipedia's prominence, influence and transparency make it a natural target for research. A recent set of studies have addressed social and technical aspects of the system. Viégas et al. [16, 17] have investigated the collaboration and self-organization surrounding articles. Forte & Bruckman [6] have examined the incentives for individuals to contribute to Wikipedia, and Bryant et al. [4] suggested that people can make the transition from newcomer to Wikipedia expert via legitimate peripheral participation [10].

Many of the questions asked about Wikipedia—how does a system convince people to contribute their time for free? Why do people do it?—have also been investigated in the realm of open-source development. Several studies [9, 11], have examined what motivates people to perform for free what is normally highly paid work. A common thread in the findings is that contributors view open-source projects as an opportunity for intellectual stimulation and a chance to make tools for their own use.

Yochai Benkler [2] posits that Wikipedia and open-source development both fall into a general category of "peer production" systems. His argument is grounded in a broad review of existing practices and suggests that peer production systems thrive when they break work into fine-grained, modular tasks. Benkler argues that these systems can work well partly because the volunteer participants can allocate their own labor very efficiently.

The mechanics of this efficient allocation, however, remain mysterious. Indeed, none of the treatments described above examines the details of the day-to-day choices of individual participants. The closest may be the work by Bryant et al. [4]; our analysis of detailed edit histories is complementary to theirs, which is based on in-depth interviews with Wikipedia members. Just as with recent investigations of open-source projects and work on online communities such as listservs [5] the methods to date have largely relied on interviews and surveys of community members.

Before describing our own methods and results, it is worth discussing some of the ways that Wikipedia editors might choose what to work on. First, users often look for articles on specific topics of interest [4]. They may also respond to requests for help on a Talk page [17]. Technical mechanisms exist as well. Several investigations have noted the importance of watchlists, which allow users to monitor all changes to a customized set of pages, along with the "recent changes" and "random article" pages [6, 16, 17].

A final explicit way that Wikipedians organize work is through "Wikiprojects". A wikiproject is a set of pages that defines a focused area of activity, describing the scope of work, listing participants and work items, and offering identifying markers that can be placed on talk pages to advertise the project. Wikiprojects have distinctive social atmospheres. On "Wikiproject: Mathematics" a typical participant introduces himself with, "Ph.D. in mathematics from Caltech, with a specialization in mathematical logic" while on "Wikiproject: Beer" a representative self-description reads only "mmm, beer." Each project thus represents a community of interest.

3 Methods

The raw material for our investigation is the edit histories of Wikipedia administrators. An administrator (or "admin") is a user who has access to special functions such as page deletion and protection. A full description of the role of admins in the community and how they are selected is beyond the scope of this paper, but as a trusted, active, and influential set of users they play a core role in Wikipedia. In some respects they are analogous to "committers" on an open-source software project. Furthermore, such users are one of the big mysteries of Wikipedia: some average more than 100 edits per day over the course of a year, which seems surprising for volunteer labor. As of 2006, roughly 14% of edits on the English Wikipedia site have come from administrators.[1]

3.1 Data Collection

To ensure a sample of users with a substantial history as admins, we selected all "active" administrators as of October 2005. For these users we downloaded edit histories that ran until August 2006. The list contained histories for 514 users, but irregularities in the data format meant five of these had to be discarded, leaving a total of 509 histories.

An edit history for an individual user is a sequence of timestamped edit events, where an event consists of the title of the article edited and an optional user comment.

---

[1] Based on a 2006 Fig. of 81,132,479 edits from [23] and a total of 10,972,403 edits from more than 900 admins reported on [22].

We observe that Wikipedia comments tend to follow certain conventions. They are usually brief, to the point, and employ standard terms for user actions. For example, "rv commercial promotion" describes the action of reverting an edit that had been made to promote a company.

3.2 Privacy

The data discussed in this paper is publicly available on the Wikipedia website, both as an easy-to-download database dump and in aggregated form via prominently linked HTML pages. In addition editors have agreed that their work will be released under the GFDL license [7], which grants a wide range of permissions to third parties to copy the data. Nonetheless, individuals may not expect their data to be analyzed as we have done in this paper, so we anonymized user names in all visualization diagrams and discussions. We have also made efforts to omit ancillary information that might easily identify the real usernames.

3.3 Basic Descriptive Statistics

Some basic statistics provide a sense of the data. Of the 509 selected administrators, the number of edits per person ranged from 789 to 122,387. The average number of edits was 16,704 and the median was 12,337. At the high end, this works out to an edit roughly every 10 minutes since May 2004! Admins spread their work over many pages, touching an average of 7,872 different titles, ranging from a minimum of 322 to a maximum of 87,976.

3.4 Exploratory Analysis

How might one analyze these histories, going beyond simple descriptive statistics? To begin with, consider an abstracted version of the problem: how to study a sequence of timestamped text "tokens" (representing either comments or article titles). The distinguishing features of the data we face are:

1. Large scale: on the order of 100,000 events.
2. Diversity: up to 80,000 distinct text tokens.
3. Irregular structure: most edit histories we looked at had few precisely repeated subsequences or even long runs of a single token.

These three qualities make analyzing the data a challenge. The large scale means simply reading lists of edits is overwhelming. The fact that the data is textual rather than numeric rules out a range of statistical methods aimed at time series.

4 The Chromogram Visualization Technique

For these reasons we decided to use a visual exploratory method. While there is significant work in visualizing sequences of non-numerical data, the large space of tokens and irregularity again cause difficulty in applying existing techniques. Methods such as arc diagrams [20] that rely on finding precisely repeated subsequences do not work.

Techniques that do handle large, noisy sequences of discrete events, such as those used in visualizing traces from software profilers (e.g. [3]) or development activity [13]), frequently rely on color-coding. The idea is to avoid the use of lengthy labels by representing tokens by colors; this tactic allows extremely efficient use of space.

Typically color coding either relates to a small set of discrete values for which distinctive colors can be chosen by hand, or take continuous values which can be naturally mapped to a portion of color space. In our case, however, mapping text tokens to colors is a subtler problem. For any mapping of thousands of different strings to colors, many strings will inevitably receive nearly indistinguishable colors. To minimize this problem it is obviously desirable to make use of a large color space. In addition, it is desirable that the color mapping be consistent from one data set to the next, so users might recognize the colors of common words. Finally, one might hope that "similar" words would receive similar colors.

To balance these criteria, we decided on a scheme in which the first three letters of a string determine the color of its representation. The first letter determines the hue; the second letter the saturation, and the third the brightness. Saturation and brightness were both kept in a restricted range so that the hue was easily perceived. (Many variations of this method were tried, but this seemed to bring out patterns in the data better than other hue/saturation/brightness permutations, possibly due to the categorical nature of hue perception. We also tried mapping the first three letter values to the three RGB components but the resulting diagrams were hard to read.) As a special case, titles or comments that begin with a number were converted to a shade of gray based on the initial digits.

Fig. 1 shows how sample text tokens—in this case, typical words from user comments in Wikipedia—translate into colors. Note, for example, how "added" and "arbitration" differ largely in saturation, while "articles" and "arbitration" differ only in brightness.

At first this may look like an arbitrary way to encode text. Strings with opposite meanings can have identical colors (*terrible* and *terrific*) and strings with similar meanings can map to contrasting colors (*dog* vs. *the dog*). Similar colors may be hard to discriminate, and the perception of a given color will be influenced by its neighbors. The encoding does meet our criteria, however, of spreading colors over a large section of color space and of remaining consistent from one sequence to the next. In practice, moreover, we found the method effective at revealing structural features. The Findings section illustrates the broad variety of patterns that this encoding exposes, and in the Discussion section we suggest reasons for this unexpected efficacy.

Fig. 1. Sample Translations from Words to Colors

4.1 Drawing the Sequence

The color mapping described above allows us to display long edit histories on a single screen, using what we call a "chromogram". The idea of a chromogram, as illustrated in Fig. 2, is straightforward. Fig. 2a shows a hypothetical list of edits. To visualize this sequence, focusing on the comments, we can create a histogram (2b) where each row corresponds to a day, and contains one rectangle for each edit, ordered by time and colored with the alphabetical scheme above. Fig. 2c shows a "block view," in which edits are simply placed in a block, time-ordered left to right and then top to bottom (just as we read). This saves space at the expense of obscuring temporal rhythms; to keep some idea of time we label the beginning of each row with the date of the first edit in the row. Finally, Fig. 2d shows a compressed block view: here the rectangles for each edit are made small and labels are omitted.

The distinguishing feature of a chromogram is the method of mapping text to color. The layout is simple; similar methods have been used in systems such as the pixel-oriented visualizations of Keim [8]. The geometry is also similar to actograms, e.g., as used by Begole et al. [1] to visualize work rhythms. Unlike an actogram, however, the *x*-axis encodes not time but sequence, which allows more efficient use of space for bursty sets of activities.

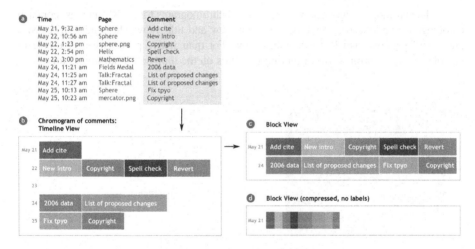

Fig. 2. Creating a Chromogram

4.2 The Chromogram Application

We implemented this visualization technique in a Java desktop application. The software reads edit history files in a tabular format and creates a chromogram of the results. Fig. 3 shows a screenshot, with blurring where text might identify the editor. Here the chromogram shows a block view (as in Fig. 2c).

The labels on the *y*-axis show the date of the first edit in each of the rows and the labels on the *x*-axis count the numbers of edits in each row's sequence. As the user moves the mouse over edit rectangles in the chromogram, a popup window shows details about article title, comment, and date. In addition to the central chromogram, some other user interface elements proved helpful. The top gray bar holds elements that let an analyst switch between visualizations of edit comments and titles of edited articles, and search for edits that contain particular words or phrases.

At right is a list of the most common words in the chromogram, arranged alphabetically. This list provides a quick color key for the most frequent titles or comments. Next to each word on the list is a bar indicating its frequency, which makes it easy for a user to get a sense of where and how the editor is spending their time. The items on the list are clickable so that a user can highlight only the edits that begin with a particular word of interest.

Fig. 4 shows a timeline chromogram view (corresponding to Fig. 2b). The data is the same as in Fig. 3. Because the timeline view is usually far less space-efficient than the block view, a scrollbar is often needed. The vertical gray stripe in Fig. 4 shows the scrollbar, which contains a histogram showing a wider view of the distribution of edits. The orange area highlights the region currently on screen. Note that Fig. 3, the block view, displays the entire sequence of edits on screen.

5 Findings: Patterns of Activity

Using the chromogram application we examined chromograms for all 509 admins. For each chromogram we looked at both the comment view and title view. This study suggested a number of patterns, which we describe below. For quantitative patterns we were able to corroborate our findings by computing statistics on the total set of administrators.

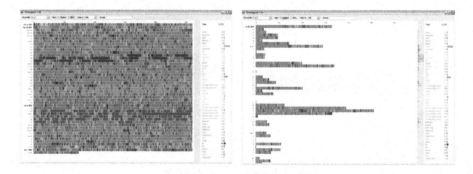

Fig. 3. The Chromogram Application: Block View

Fig. 4. The Chromogram Application: Timeline View, same data as Fig. 3

5.1 The Shape of Activity: Focal Tasks + Sporadic Edits

Although each editor we examined had a distinctive activity chromogram, some commonalities emerged. First, activity often occurred in bursts. The temporal view made this clear, as in Fig. 5. (To save space, in this and several subsequent Figures we show only a subset of the full chromogram.) This comment chromogram shows activity over the course of nine days. The first burst is largely typo fixing and the second burst—peaking at more than 300 edits in a day—involves adding disambiguation messages to pages. These bursts of activity correlate with type of edit, but we also saw patterns related to article content and calendar features such as weekends, weekdays, and holidays.

Fig. 5. Timeline comment chromogram with activity bursts. Blue: typo removal. Red: adding disambiguation messages.

Fig. 6. Title chromogram: purple edits relate to U.S. ships, green to lists of ships

A second feature seen in the chromograms was switching between articles and between tasks. Editors seemed to move between several activities, sometimes at a small time scale and sometimes at a large one. For 99% of admins studied, the majority of edits were followed by an edit to a different article. Sequences of consecutive edits to a single article were generally short in comparison to the lengths of edit histories overall. Across all admins, the average ratio of a user's longest sequence of single-article edits to the total number of edits was below 0.01.

Despite the heterogeneous nature of the activity, a degree of organization was evident in many user histories. In particular, many editors had a small set of tasks, defined by a set of similar edit comments (e.g., "revert vandalism") or related article titles (e.g., wine-related topics), that comprised a significant fraction of their edits. We term such an activity a *focal task*. Users displayed a great diversity of focal tasks, but they seemed to fall into two main categories: systematic activites and reactive actions. We describe both below.

5.2 Systematic Activities

Many users engaged in what we called systematic activities: that is, a sustained related sequence of edits. Some editors seemed to concentrate on particular topic areas. Fig. 6, a title chromogram, is typical: this user focused on naval history. The dominant color is a purple shade that corresponds to the prefix "USS" (United States Ship) used in the names of American naval vessels. Occasional edits with a different color are evident, but exploration of the data shows that they remain on the naval theme. Many of the green edits are to lists of ships, e.g., "List of all ships in the United States Navy, M" and "List of U.S. Military Vessels Named After Women."

Despite the intense topic focus the actual types of edits are diverse, as the comment chromogram for the same user and time period shows (Fig. 7). Although certain shades are frequently seen (the light brown corresponds to adding category information), the many different colors reflect many different actions: adding images, changing content, and so on.

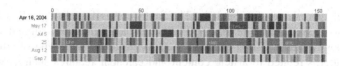

Fig. 7. Comment chromogram for same edits as Fig. 6: Highly irregular

Fig. 8 shows a title-based chromogram of a different type of systematic activity, covering roughly 900 edits over the course of four days in 2005. This user is "stub sorting," or putting category information in the small incomplete articles known as "stubs." The most visually interesting feature of this chromogram is the rough rainbow pattern: there is a clearly visible progression through the hues of the spectrum. Since the hue of an item represents the position of the first letter in the alphabet, this user seems to be methodically moving through an alphabetically ordered list of tasks.

Fig. 8. Rainbows: Alphabetical order effects in a title chromogram for 900 edits

The actual subjects of the articles are diverse, ranging from zoology ("Humphead wrasse") to pop culture: "Push (Professional Wrestling)". How did this editor find this sequence? The comments for the edits tell the answer: each edit refers to the stub-sorting wikiproject, where the admin is a listed participant and where lists are kept of stubs to be sorted.

We also observed list-guided activities that did not seem to be driven by Wikiprojects, but rather by lists in the main content area of the encyclopedia. One example can be seen in Fig. 9. Recall that gray items in our chromogram represent numbers. This sequence shows an editor making a systematic, ordered series of changes to a set of pages representing yearly compilations (e.g., "1922 in Literature"). The ordering is made visible through the light-dark gradient of some of the sequences in the middle row, indicating an ordered set of editing of pages starting with 1 to pages starting with 9. There is no Wikiproject on years in literature, but there is a "List of Years In Literature" article that links to pages edited by this user.

It is also worth noting that in this history a diverse set of edits interrupted the systematic edits. Interspersed with the gray areas are bars of many different colors. These represent changes to other content areas, for instance reverting an edit on the "Torah" article; correcting spelling on a television show page; editing articles on famous mathematical conjectures.

The pattern of alphanumerically ordered edits turned out be common. We found extended, strictly increasing alphabetical sequences of titles in many revision histories.

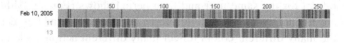

Fig. 9. Title chromogram: edits on pages with numerical titles (in gray)

(We say "strict" to exclude sequences that contain the same title twice in a row, so that a long sequence of edits to the same article does not count.) Although one would expect to see some short ordered sequences by chance, what we observed went well beyond random effects. A simple test illustrates this point. If $p(n, k)$ represents the probability of a strictly increasing alphabetical subsequence of length k occurring in a sequence of n revisions, a straightforward calculation shows

$$p(n, k) < (n - k + 1) / k!.$$

By this measure, 307 out of 509 (60%) of admin revision histories contained an alphabetically ordered subsequence of titles whose length was statistically significant. More precisely, 307 histories had a length n and an alphabetical subsequence of length k with $p(n, k) < 10^{-5} < .01/509$. In 13 histories we observed alphabetical runs of more than 100 consecutive titles.

A natural question is whether ordering effects can be seen in Wikipedia itself. One may conjecture that if alphabetical lists guide a portion of work then titles that appear early in the alphabet may see the most edits. In fact analysis of a 2005 snapshot of Wikipedia data does suggest a weak negative relationship between alphabetical order and editing activity. The Spearman rank correlation between alphabetical order of first letter of article title and average number of edits is -0.47 ($p<.05$). A full investigation of this phenomenon is beyond the scope of this paper, but it would be interesting to test this trend by performing the same analysis on foreign-language versions of Wikipedia.

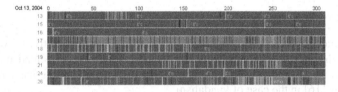

Fig. 10. Comment chromogram of about 2,900 copy edits. Green items are changes from "it's" to "its".

Stub-sorting is just one example of a whole range of organizational activities. Other organizational tasks include the creation of disambiguation pages and redirection pages. Yet another type of project involves "cleaning" a set of pages with known problems. Cleaning can cover grammar, spelling, or wiki syntax. It may also involve adding or modifying templates, changing formatting, or searching for copyright violations. An example is shown in the comment chromogram of Fig. 10.

A second common type of systematic activity was editing associated with maps and images. Fig. 11 shows a pattern we observed in several admins: switching between uploading images and then editing articles to include them. In the case of Fig. 11, which encompasses about 1,500 edits made over the course of a single week, the interspersed rainbow-like segments represent article edits, and the patches of near-uniform color represent images. The uniformity of color stems from naming conventions for these images: at top are maps of regions in Maryland, and their names all begin with "MDMap".

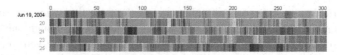

Fig. 11. Title chromogram: Switching between images (purple and light blue) and articles (rainbows)

A final type of systematic activity involves the use of "bots," or programs for making automated edits. Certain admins have written these programs as labor-saving devices. Because bots are technically users in Wikipedia, we could examine their edits histories in the same way we examined the activities of humans. Not surprisingly, the chromograms of robot users generally exhibited far more regularity than human users. Fig. 12 shows an example of a subset of a comment chromogram for one such program, "AFD_Bot". (AFD stands for "Articles for Deletion".) While the AFD_Bot is not human, we include this image because the bot was written by a human admin and thus may be considered part of the overall human editing strategy on Wikipedia, marking the extreme end of the systematic type of activity.

Fig. 12. Title chromogram for "AFD bot". Note the small range of colors and regular rhythm of edits.

5.3 Reactive Activities

A second category of activities seemed to be reactive. For these activites, which were essentially driven by external events and time-sensitive, users seemed to set themselves up to watch over certain aspects of the site. Reactive editing has already been described by [16] in the case of vandalism.

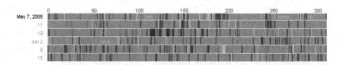

Fig. 13. Comment chromogram: Reverting vandalism and other bad edits

Fig. 14. Title chromogram for same edits in Fig. 13.

Fig. 13 shows a comment chromogram for a user whose focus is reversion. The diagram contains about 2,000 edits. The light blue corresponds to comments beginning with "revert." For a contrast, consider the corresponding title chromogram for the same series of edits, in Fig. 14. There is no clear pattern, since the reversions occur on a diverse set of pages. (It is interesting to compare these two diagrams with Figures 7 and 8, where the reverse is true: the titles were uniform and the comments diverse.) An analysis of all 509 admins showed that the behavior in Fig. 13 is extreme but not unique. For seven admins in our sample, the majority of edit comments referred to either reversion or vandalism[2]. For 152 (30%) of admins, at least 10% of edit comments were revert- or vandalism-related.

As with systematic edits, we see task switching and a diverse set of edits apart from the core focus task. Although the majority of edits are marked as reverts, there is other activity interspersed as well. Articles are "wikified" with correct syntax and links, and some general content is added.

Vandalism is by no means the only type of event that drives edits. The arrival of a new user has obvious importance for the Wikipedia community, and we observed several editors who took on the task of welcoming new users. (This corroborates the engagement between experienced users and newcomers described in [4].) There are also many events that are related to steps in various Wikipedia. Requests for peer reviews, featured article status, admin privileges, the removal of admin privileges, and arbitration are all events that drive subsequent actions.

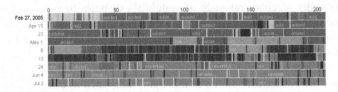

Fig. 15. Comment chromogram with about 2,000 edits between February and July 2005. Long-term task focus switches are evident. Brown: categorization; blue: reverts.

5.4 Mixtures of Strategies

For clarity, the preceding section focused on portions of edit histories that illustrated a single task focus. Many admins, however, seemed to switch between task foci at a large time scale. Fig. 15 shows a typical example. The brown, red, and cyan areas correspond to categorization activities. The blue area at bottom, on the other hand, represents vandalism repair.

6 Discussion

What do these editing patterns tell us about how admins allocate their effort? At a broad scale, we have seen that many of them make a vast number of edits. At the same time, we observe a high degree of diversity within a single editor's history, with sustained uninterrupted attention to a single article or task type being uncommon.

---

[2] We counted all comments that contained the text "revert" or "vandal," or began with "rv," a common abbreviation for reversions.

On the other hand, given that the individuals in our sample sometimes made upwards of 10,000 edits, the diversity of edit types raises a question. How is it that the self-allocation of effort by individuals can be efficient, as described by Benkler [2]? Making a good decision a few times might be easy, but making 10,000 smart decisions seems hard by any standard. In other words, there seems to be an inherent tension between Benkler's hypothesis that large-scale peer-production systems should break work into fine-grained units, and the desire for workers to make as few decisions as possible about what to work on next.

A resolution to the mystery may lie in our second main observation: that editors tend to have focal tasks that, despite interruptions, take up a significant percentage of their time. In some cases they may make a single decision to react to a certain type of event, such as the arrival of a new user or an act of vandalism. In other cases, the editor may join a Wikiproject or find a list of pages that need work, make a single decision to work on every item in a list, and then systematically move through a set of tasks that others have aggregated.

In each case, the editor has greatly reduced their own cognitive burden. Instead of making a separate decision about the value of each individual potential edit, they make a decision to focus on a particular type of work and then perform a large set of related tasks. For reactive activity this set of related tasks may come through semi-automatic filtering mechanisms such as watchlists or posts to special pages such as "votes for deletion". In other cases, such as Wikiprojects, a purely human phenomenon is occurring: one set of people is collating, listing, and sorting tasks, which are then performed by others.

These cases form an interesting example of non-hierarchical flow of information about where work is needed. Viewed in this light, tasks such as categorization of pages are as much about organizing work as they are about organizing content. That is, the beneficiaries of Wikipedia's many lists and categories are not just readers looking to make connections between topics but also editors looking for new work items.

An important direction for future work would be to deepen our analysis via qualitative research methods. Although part of the impetus for our research was to look at quantitative issues, we believe our findings have raised questions that may be best answered through qualitative investigations. A second future direction would be to make comparative studies, for example between new and experienced users or active non-admins versus admins. Such comparisons might lend quantitative support (or could falsify) hypotheses about the trajectory from new user to admin.

6.1 Chromograms

Considering the simplicity of the color mapping, the chromogram technique seems to be surprisingly effective. One explanation is that even a random encoding technique will reveal some patterns, e.g., with high likelihood distinguishing between a run of 10 identical tokens and a sequence of 10 distinct tokens. Furthermore, coloring based only on the beginning of the word means that stemming occurs automatically, abbreviations are often handled correctly, and effects of alphabetical ordering are clear.

Some of the benefits of chromograms come from the consistency of the coloring across users. In our experience with the tool, we quickly grew to recognize colors associated with common words such as "list" and "revert." Moreover, we were able to recognize similarities across users: having seen one user who made many comments starting with "birth" and "death," it was easy for one of the authors to spot that pattern in other users' chromograms.

Another explanation may lie in the nature of Wikipedia titles and comments. Comments from administrators often employ conventional terminology ("revert", "fix", "wikify", etc.) and rarely start with content-free words such as "the" or "of". Many article titles start with a helpful keyword: for instance "list" for lists, or "HMS" for British ships. These conventions add structure to the data that helps make the visualization legible. The technique might therefore be less successful with less well-structured text.

Given the initial promise of the chromogram technique, it is natural to look for other applications and possible extensions. One direction for future research is simply to test the tool by applying it to other domains that feature timestamped snippets of text such as commits to software projects or email headers.

There are also several possible improvements to the basic technique. It would be interesting to explore the space of color mappings. What are the optimal constants for the letter-to-color translation (i.e., for the code in Appendix One)? What schemes are best for users with color deficiencies? More broadly, are there useful non-alphabetical schemes, for instance based on custom ontologies? (Our initial experiments in this direction using the Wikipedia category scheme gave mixed results.) There is also room for improvement in the simple layout. Would it be possible to show additional dimensions such as the size of an edit?

6.1.1 Directions for Design

One set of implications for design comes from the ways in which Wikipedia editors have reinvented wiki technology. Wikis are remarkably flexible, and so the community can use the same interface that supports articles to create, without reprogramming, de facto discussion boards (as in Talk pages) and bug databases (as in lists of needed work). Examining the conventions the community has created may provide design ideas for other systems where such features would need to be programmed.

In fact it is illuminating to compare the Wikiproject pages with standard bug databases in open source projects. Wikiprojects can easily describe a set of overlapping concerns, while providing a central page and discussion of that topic. While bug databases such as Bugzilla support overlapping concerns to some degree through tagging, they do not offer users the same sense of purpose and "place" that Wikiprojects do. Perhaps it would help to let users create special project areas with their own discussion sections and membership lists.

A second set of design implications stems from the systematic list-driven activites we observed. It might be useful, for example, to allow users to declare their intentions to work through a list. Given that the pervasive use of alphabetically ordered lists may actually be biasing which pages get edited, it might also be worthwhile to include different sorting mechanisms. For example, putting the oldest items at the top of a list might distribute effort more evenly.

At the same time, we may draw lessons from the flexiblility of wiki technology. The Wikipedia community has been able to coopt and reinvent [15] the basic wiki framework for many coordination tasks. When the underlying technology does change, it is often to formalize methods that have been "prototyped" by Wikipedia users. In this sense Wikipedia can be viewed as a grand experiment in participatory design [12]. Finding ways to add rapid user prototyping capabilities to other communities is an interesting general area for exploration.

7 Conclusion

This paper described a broad study of Wikipedia administrator activity. To explore edit histories of administrators, we introduced a new visualization technique, the chromogram. The new technique is a space-efficient way of displaying sequences of words and phrases by mapping text to color using an alphabetical code.

Despite the simplicity of the coding scheme, the chromogram technique turned out to be effective in distinguishing between various patterns of activity, and helpful in viewing small- and large-scale structures. Because of its simplicity and generality, the technique may be useful in contexts aside from Wikipedia.

Through examination of chromograms of editing patterns, we found that admins usually switched between multiple tasks, rarely concentrating on the same type of work continuously. At the same time, certain focal tasks seem to occupy a significant proportion of their time. These focal tasks fell into two types. Some were systematic; one tell-tale signature of such activities is a long alphabetically ordered sequence of article titles in the edit history. Other tasks were reactive, as admins reacted to vandalism or requests from other Wikipedia users.

While other studies have examined reactive activities such as vandalism, the existence of systematic, sustained sequences of edits has received less attention. The existence of such organized behavior suggests that devices such as lists, categorization schemes, and Wikiprojects play a strong role in what individual admins choose to work on. The fact that these organizational devices exist helps resolve a tension in peer-production work: having many fine-grained tasks has benefits, but to reduce the cognitive burden on workers, it is important to provide organizing devices that help them allocate their time at a higher level of granularity than an individual task.

References

1. Begole, J., Tang, J., Smith, R., Yankelovich, N.: Work Rhythms: Analyzing Visualizations of Awareness Histories of Distributed Groups. In: CSCW 2002 (2002)
2. Benkler, Y.: Coase's Penguin, or, Linux and The Nature of the Firm. 112 Yale Law Journal 369 (2002)
3. Bosch, R., Stolte, C., Rosenblum, M., Hanrahan, P.: Performance Analysis and Visualization of Parallel Systems using SimOS and Rivet: A Case Study. In: Int'l Symposium on High Performance Computer Architecture (2000)
4. Bryant, S., Forte, A., Bruckman, A.: Becoming Wikipedian: Transformation of Participation in a Collaborative Online Encyclopedia. In: GROUP 2005 (2005)
5. Butler, B., Sproull, L., Kiesler, S., Kraut R.: Community Effort in Online Groups: Who Does the Work and Why? In: Weisband, S., Atwater, L. (eds.) Leadership at a Distance (2002)
6. Forte, A., Bruckman, A.: Why do people write for Wikipedia? Incentives to contribute to open-content collaboration. In: Proceedings of GROUP 2005 workshop (2005)

7. GNU Free Documentation License v. 1.2 (2002), Downloaded from www.gnu.org/copyleft/fdl.html
8. Keim, D.: Pixel-Oriented Database Visualizations. SIGMOD Record 25(4) (1996)
9. Lakhani, K., Wolf, R.: Why Hackers Do What They Do: Understanding Motivation and Effort in Free/Open Source Software Projects. In: Perspectives on Free and Open Source Software, MIT Press, Cambridge (2005)
10. Lave, J., Wenger, E.: Situated Learning: Legitimate Peripheral Participation. Cambridge University Press, Cambridge (1991)
11. Mockus, A., Fielding, R., Herbsleb, J.: Two Case Studies of Open Source Software Development: Apache and Mozilla. ACM Trans. Software Engineering and Methodology 11(3), 309–346 (2002)
12. Schuler, D., Aki, N. (eds.): Participatory Design: Principles and Practices. LEA (1993)
13. Seeberger, M., Kuhn, A., Girba, T., Ducasse, S.: Chronia: Visualizing how developers change software systems. In: CSMR 2006 (2006)
14. Sherif, M., Harvey, O.J., White, J., Hood, W., Sherif, C.W.: Intergroup conflict and cooperation: the robbers cave experiment. University Book Exchange, Norman, OK (1961)
15. Sproull, L., Kiesler, S.: Connections: new ways of working in the networked organization. MIT Press, Cambridge (1991)
16. Viégas, F., Wattenberg, M., Dave, K.: Studying Cooperation and Conflict between Authors with history flow Visualizations. In: CHI 2004 (2004)
17. Viégas, F., Wattenberg, M., Kriss, J., van Ham, F.: Talk Before You Type: Coordination in Wikipedia. In: HICSS 40 (2007)
18. Wagner, C.: Breaking the Knowledge Acquisition Bottleneck Through Conversational Knowledge Management. Information Resources Management Journal 19(1), 70–93 (2006)
19. Ware, C.: Information Visualization: Perception for Design. Academic Press, London (2000)
20. Wattenberg, M.: Arc Diagrams: Visualizing Structure in Strings. In: IEEE InfoVis 2002 (2002)
21. Wikipedia: Active Administrators, English (September 2006), http://en.wikipedia.org/wiki/Wikipedia:List_of_administrators
22. http://en.wikipedia.org/wiki/Wikipedia:List_of_administrators_by_edit_count
23. http://en.wikipedia.org/wiki/Special:Statistics

MatLink: Enhanced Matrix Visualization for Analyzing Social Networks

Nathalie Henry[1,2] and Jean-Daniel Fekete[1]

[1] INRIA/LRI, Bat. 490, Univ. Paris-Sud, F91405, Orsay, France
[2] Univ. of Sydney, Australia

Abstract. Visualizing social networks presents challeges for both node-link and adjacency matrix representations. Social networks are locally dense, which makes node-link displays unreadable. Yet, main analysis tasks require following paths, which is difficult on matrices. This article presents MatLink, a hybrid representation with links overlaid on the borders of a matrix and dynamic topological feedback as the pointer moves. We evaluated MatLink by an experiment comparing its readability, in term of errors and time, for social network-related tasks to the other conventional representations on graphs varying in size (small and medium) and density. It showed significant advantages for most tasks, especially path-related ones where standard matrices are weak.

Keywords: Node-Link Diagram, Matrix Visualization, Social Network.

1 Introduction

Social network analysis has been a growing area of the social sciences recently for many reasons: Internet social activities that can be automatically instrumented and analyzed: Peer-to-Peer file exchanges, chat, blogs, and collective development such as Wikipedia and Open-Source Software projects; intelligence agencies seeking to discover terrorist networks; monitoring to detect and contain outbreaks of diseases such as avian influenza and SARS.

Many of these new social networks are large, complex and continuously changing, which creates challenges for analysis tools. Information visualization can be an effective approach to help social science researchers both explore relationships between actors and present their findings to others. For both purposes, it is critical to make the visual representations of social networks *readable*.

Examination of the "International Network for Social Network Analysis" software repository (http://www.insna.org) reveals that most of the 55 software referenced for visualizing and exploring social networks use Node-Link diagrams (NL). Unfortunately, social networks are locally dense, and NL have been shown by Ghoniem et al. [1] to behave poorly on dense networks even for the simplest tasks such as checking if one node is connected to another. NL remain useful to show the overall structure of a network (Figure 1a), but details about dense sub-graphs within them are frequently impossible to read. [1] also showed that matrix graph representations (MAT) (Figure 1b), the primary alternative to NL, are poor for path-finding tasks. These are crucial to social network analysis [2].

C. Baranauskas et al. (Eds.): INTERACT 2007, LNCS 4663, Part II, pp. 288–302, 2007.
© IFIP International Federation for Information Processing 2007

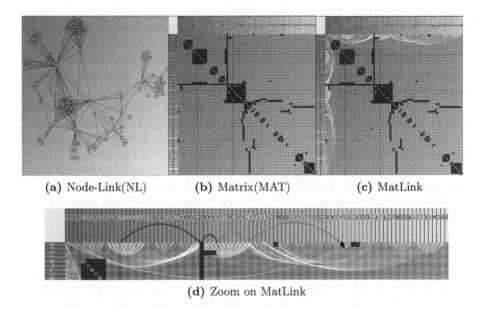

(a) Node-Link(NL)   **(b)** Matrix(MAT)   **(c)** MatLink

(d) Zoom on MatLink

Fig. 1. Three representations of a social network

To address these limitations, we developed MatLink, an enhanced matrix-based graph visualization that overlays a linear node-link diagram on the edges and adds dynamic feedback of relationship between nodes (Figure 1c). To assess its effectiveness, we performed an experiment comparing user performance with NL, MAT and MatLink on a set of representative social network analysis tasks.

The rest of the paper is organized as follows: the next section describes previous work on social network characterization, evaluating graph visualizations and analysis tasks, visual exploration systems and layout algorithms. We then describe our novel visualization and present an experimental evaluation comparing it to existing network visualizations. A discussion on the results and their implications follows.

2   Related Work

2.1   Social Network Characterization

Social networks involve persons or groups called actors and relationships between them, with a lot of variety in the kind of actors and relationships. As described in Wasserman and Faust [2], actors can be people, subgroups, organizations or collectivities; relations may be friendship (relationships), interactions, communications, transactions, movement or kinship. However, the nature of actors and relations does not really matter: we focus on their structure.

Very often in the literature, social networks are confused with small-world networks. After studying real social networks, we identified three categories.

Almost trees are trees with additional links forming cycles with a low probability. They include genealogy data and Sexually-Transmitted Disease transmission patterns.

Almost complete graphs are complete graphs with missing relations, such as data about trade between countries, cities or companies. They usually carry values on their edges.

Small-world networks have been studied extensively since they were first described in Watts and Strogatz [3], who defined them as graphs with three properties: power-law degree distribution, high clustering coefficient and small average shortest path. They are locally dense (sparse with dense sub-graphs.)

Ghoniem at al. [1] showed that NL are very poor at visualizing almost complete graphs and more generally dense networks. Conversely, NL are very well suited to visualizing "almost trees" networks. Since Small-World networks are locally dense, NL readability is questionable.

2.2 Evaluating Graph Visualizations and Task Taxonomies

Selecting representative and comparable tasks to compare visualization performance is difficult. Most early visualization system evaluators chose tasks they considered representative and that they knew their system could perform. However, evaluating multiple systems calls for a more systematic approach.

Task taxonomies have been proposed for many kinds of visualizations. Amar et al. presented a list of 10 basic tasks on multivariate data visualizations [4] Plaisant et al. adapted it to graphs [5]. Unlike multivariate data tables where the objects of interest are records with uniform attribute sets, networks have attributes associated with edges as well as vertices, and a more complex topology including compound objects such as paths or sub-graphs. Thus the task set is different. However, their tasks are generic and need extension for social networks.

Reference books on social network analysis such as [2] list the following important high-level concepts: *centrality, cohesive subgroups, positions* and *roles*. Each of these concepts are formalized with several measures, all of them requiring computations on the network. However, visually, they all rely on path-related properties. For example, centrality measures include *betweenness centrality*: the most central being the person who is on most shortest-paths. Cohesive subgroups, positions and roles also rely on path-related measures. Therefore, we consider that a good representation of a social network should visually support path-related tasks.

Ghoniem et al. published an experimental evaluation comparing performance in NL and MAT, but only for low-level readability tasks [1]. We are not aware of comparisons targeted at social networks.

2.3 Systems for Social Network Exploration

We distinguish two categories of social network visualization systems: systems for end users to visualize their personal networks, and those designed for professionals analyzing entire networks.

Systems such as Vizster [6] or flickrGraphc (http://www.marumushi.com/apps/flickrgraph) are in the first category. They are an easy and entertaining means for users to explore their personal networks by interactive navigation. They do not provide an overview of the full network and only use NL.

Systems in the second category focus on professional analysts willing to spend significant time and effort to learn the system and analyze their data. Pajek [7], the most popular system among social science researchers, offers a sometimes-intimidating set of menus and functions to analyze large social networks. JUNG (http://jung.sf.net) also provide a rich set of drawing functions. Guess [8] takes a different approach, letting users write simple script-language programs. All these systems use only NL, except that Pajek can perform block modeling [9] and print (but not display) their adjacency matrices.

MatrixExplorer [10] uses NL and MAT representations in parallel to visualize and explore social networks. Users can perform each task on the most appropriate representation, maintaining a visual relation between them by interactive brushing and linking. However, alternating between two representations imposes a significant cognitive load. Also, MatrixExplorer requires at least two screens to be used effectively.

2.4   Layout for Node-Link and Matrix Representations

Besides choosing an appropriate representation, its layout must be correct if it is to be readable, revealing the network's overall structure and important features. Layout algorithms compute positions for each vertex from the graph topology, sometimes augmented with a (dis)similarity function between vertices. For NL, a position is a 2D or 3D point; for MAT, a 1D ordering. Some layout methods are specific for one representation, while others can be applied to both. We review those considered most effective for social network visualizations.

Good introductions to NL layout algorithms can be found in [11]. For social networks, the biggest problem is that the distribution of edge numbers is not linear but power-law. Most vertices have few edges but few — often the most interesting ones — have many, with a very skewed distribution. Simple force-based graph layout algorithms behave poorly on such networks. Recently, Noack presented important improvements [12]. His layout behaves as well as possible on social networks. However, the dense sub-graphs around high-degree vertices remain difficult or impossible to read.

Several strategies have been investigated to overcome the link density problem: clustered graphs [13] in which dense graph parts are collapsed and Pivot-Graphs [14] where the graph is only visible according to the values of selected vertex attributes. Network details these solutions hide remain accessible by navigation or interactions.

Matrix representations have also been used to visualize social networks. There is a long tradition of matrix block modeling in the social sciences [9]. As Bertin stated, when adequately reordered, a matrix can reveal both global and local structures in a network [15]. While block modeling tries to gather equivalent roles into blocks, other reordering algorithms collect vertices with similar connection patterns. Several methods attempt to gather clusters that exhibit structural features such as cliques or quasi-cliques, bridges or articulation points, communities and outliers. Henry and Fekete [10] compared several categories of methods. They showed that Traveling Salesman Problem (TSP) approximation and Clustering methods produce better results when applied to the distance matrix of the graph instead of its boolean adjacency matrix. A survey remains to be done to clearly understand the advantages and drawbacks of each method.

Matrices display dense networks without edge overlap, but have display area quadratic in the number of vertices. Techniques have been designed to navigate effectively on very large matrices. Abello and Van Ham [16] introduced matrices augmented with clustering trees. Van Ham [17] described smooth navigation techniques for matrices whose vertices possess several hierarchical levels.

3   MatLink

To address matrix-based graph representations' weaknesses on the path-related tasks social network analysis requires, we designed MatLink, a matrix representation with links overlaid on its borders and interactive drawing of additional links and highlighting of the cells included in a path from the cell under the mouse pointer.

MatLink displays the full graph using a linearized node-link representation we call the full linear graph (Figure 1d). Its links are curved lines drawn interior to the vertex displays at the top and left edges of the matrix. Links are drawn over the matrix cells, using transparency to avoid hiding them. Longer links are drawn above shorter ones. The linear graph conveys detailed and long-range structure together without hiding any detail of the matrix: a feeling for link densities and sub-graphs, but also paths and cut points.

When the user has selected a vertex in the rows or columns, it is highlighted in red, and the shortest path between this vertex and the one currently under the mouse pointer is drawn in green on the vertex area, mirror-imaged to the links drawn in the matrix border[1]. This dynamic visualization of the shortest path is designed to make paths preattentively visible on the matrix. Early versions of MatLink drew these dynamic paths over the full linear graph, but users complained about visual complexity and difficulty seeing cells under the path links. This was not the case with paths drawn in the vertex area.

When several vertices are selected, their related rows or columns are highlighted in red, and the shortest path is visualized using red curved links in the vertex area. When the user moves the mouse pointer, the shortest path between the last selection and the vertex under the pointer is drawn in green.

We display only one shortest path even if several equivalent ones exist. To avoid confusion, we ensure that the same path is always displayed between two vertices. If the path from A to E contains C, then the same links will be displayed when only the path between A and C is visible. We considered also showing a shortest cycle within a subset of vertices but decided it would be

---

[1] A video is available at http://insitu.lri.fr/~nhenry/matlink/matlink.mov

confusing, because adding one vertex to the selection could completely change the links drawn. Moreover, when the selection grows, computing a shortest cycle requires noticeable time. Other analytical attributes could be displayed on the linear graph, statically or dynamically. In this article, we focus on the shortest path.

Displaying the linear graph of a randomly permuted matrix is useless and even confusing. However, after the matrix is reordered using the modified TSP algorithm described in [10], the matrix representation shows clusters clearly. Also, the linear graph appears well organized with mostly short links connecting nearby vertices and some long edges connecting the clusters. Although our layout algorithm does not guarantee that the total number of crossings is minimized, it is very small compared with a random layout. This layout also reveals that some vertices primarily belonging to one cluster also have a few links to vertices in other clusters, sometimes not visible on the screen when the network is large and requires scrolling. Finally, the linear graph seems to facilitate the understanding of the matrix representation when users are familiar with NL.

MatLink is implemented with the InfoVis Toolkit [18], so all the attributes of the network can be assigned as visual attributes such as color, or label for the vertices and the edges.

4   Experimental Evaluation

We performed a controlled experiment to compare MatLink with MAT and NL. We designed a 3x6x5 within-subject experiment, comparing the 3 visualizations of 6 social networks asking subjects to complete 5 different tasks for each.

4.1   Selected Tasks

This experiment evaluated primarily mid-level readability tasks. Low-level tasks have been evaluated by Ghoniem et al. [1] for MAT and NL (whose paradigms MatLink combines) while performance on high-level interpretation tasks depends more on the domain and the subject's background, requiring an subjective and time-consuming evaluation.

We selected the three most important high-level tasks in social network analysis: evaluating connectivity, finding central actors and identifying communities. We evaluated performance on one or two medium-level tasks within each of these high-level tasks. We also chose tasks we could easily explain to novice users, and for which answers could be objectively validated.

1. *commonNeighbor*: given two actors, find an actor directly linked to both;
2. *shortestPath*: given two actors, find a shortest path linking them;
3. *mostConnected*: find the actors with the highest number of relations;
4. *articulationPoint*: find a cut point, i.e. an actor linking two sub-graphs;
5. *largestClique*: find the largest set of actors who are all linked to each other.

4.2   Dataset Selection

To avoid scrolling and navigation issues, we limited dataset sizes to what all three representations could display on one screen, slightly less than a hundred nodes. We also only considered undirected networks and used the largest connected component.

Because existing social network generators did not provide realistic data (for details, see http://www.infovis-wiki.net/index.php/Social_Network_Generation),we collected examples of real social networks from Pajek, UCINET, Complex Networks, Graph Drawing contests and the InfoVis 2004 contest. To select a representative subset of networks, we drew a portrait of each dataset's characteristics: vertex number (S), edge number (E), density (D) and clustering coefficient (CC). Controlling the average path length is difficult, and we also did not attempt to control degree distribution, considering that our small networks might not have enough vertices to exhibit a power-law degree distribution. Therefore, we attempted to counterbalance S, CC, and D while including networks representative of all three structures we identified (almost-trees, small-world, and almost-complete). We excluded three kinds of graphs for which we considered the results obvious or already proven in Ghoniem et al. experiment: very small graphs containing less than two dozen vertices, small and very sparse graphs for which NL performs very well, and very dense graphs obviously better visualized with MAT. We selected the following datasets: *Infovis* (S=47, E=114, D=0.23, CC=0.83), *Dolphins* (S=47, E=202, D=0.30, CC=0.42), *Fraternity* (S=47, E=294, D=0.36, CC=0.72), *Genealogy* (S=94, E=192, D=0.15, CC=0.59), *Collaboration* (S=94, E=313, D=0.19, CC=0.90) and *USairports* (S=94, E=990, D=0.33, CC=0.84).

To minimize extraneous interpretation issues, we anonymized all actors. To reduce memorization effects, we assigned different labels when presenting the same graph twice. To match the selected graphs in size, we produced a set of randomly filtered graphs for each instance and selected the filtered graphs with D and CC properties similar to the originals. We relaxed the constraint on D when shrinking large graphs, as it is difficult to keep a low D with a high CC when filtering it.

4.3   Experimental Setup

Adding interactive highlighting can affect the performance of visualizations. For example, finding the shortest paths between two actors can become preattentive with highlighting. For these reasons, we decided to augment both MAT and NL with interactive highlights to run a fair comparison with MatLink. Subjects were limited to three interactions: mousing over an element, clicking on an element, and dragging on several elements using the left mouse button. Clicking on a row or column header selected one element, indicated by displaying it in red. Similarly, dragging the mouse over a group of elements selected them all. Only vertices were clickable, not edges. In addition, the space bar was used to start and terminate each trial.

We drew NL diagrams using the LinLog algorithm [12]. To reorder matrices, we chose the augmented TSP algorithm described in [10]. We were careful to maintain readability of vertex labels in all conditions. We used the same node sizes for small and large graphs. Since NL visualizations are usually more compact than MAT, we considered it fair to enlarge their nodes to increase their readability.

4.4 Subjects and Apparatus

We used a total of thirty-six subjects, divided into two distinct groups of eighteen. The first group was composed of students and researchers from Univ. of Sydney, mostly from a graph drawing research group. The second group consisted of students and researchers from Univ. of Paris-Sud, primarily specialists in HCI. Only one subject in each group was familiar with matrix-based representations. Both groups used a 3GHz Pentium IV computer with 1GB of RAM and one 19" screen oriented vertically. The screen was divided in two parts: the upper part displayed the question and the lower the visualization.

4.5 Procedure

Before starting the experiment, subjects were given a brief interview to gather information about their previous experience with graphs and visual representations. A tutorial sheet introduced the visualizations, and an experimenter demonstrated the experimental environment, how each representation worked and how to complete the tasks. Subjects could then practice with the program for a few minutes. The training ended when the subject answered all questions correctly for all representations. Subjects spent an average of forty minutes on the training, usually longer than they did on the experiment itself.

The rule for the experiment was to answer correctly as rapidly as possible. If the subjects felt unable to answer a question, they were allowed to skip it. Each subject had a total of 90 questions to answer: 5 tasks performed on 3 visualizations of 6 graphs. To limit the experiment duration, the system limited the completion time (*Time*) to 60 seconds. To limit the subject fatigue, we split the experiment in two sessions with a ten-minute break in between. Moreover, subjects could rest after any question by delaying the start of the next trial.

Sessions were not balanced: the first session presented small datasets, while the second presented large datasets. Sessions were split into three blocks, one for each representation. The order of the representations was complete and counterbalanced across subjects. Each representation block was split into three blocks of three datasets (small for the first session, large for the second) counterbalanced across subjects using a Latin square. We alternated the order of representations to reduce memorization effects: subjects remembering the answer from the previous representation and dataset. However, we kept the order of datasets constant for each session and counterbalanced across subjects.

At the end of the experiment, subjects had to answer a questionnaire about their use of each representation, rating them by task and preference. Finally, a debriefing was conducted to answer any remaining questions and collect their final comments.

4.6 Data Collected

Our primary measure was answer correctness. We scored answer correctness on a scale of 0-3, with 0 meaning error and 3 the best answer. For example, analysts exploring a large network are interested in finding primary actors, but while finding the most important rated a 3, other main actors got partial credit. We consider *Time* as a secondary measure. In our analysis, it is reported for all trials, even those with errors. Therefore, caution should be used in evaluating this indicator where the error rate is high, because a fast wrong answer is not useful for data analysis.

5 Results

We performed an analysis of variance (ANOVA) whose results are reported in Table 1. We report Tukey's HSD Post Hoc test (TT) on all significant effects. Table 2 shows mean *Score*, *Time* and Errors.

5.1 All Tasks

Score and Time: A four-way ANOVA *Vis*Task*S*D* reveals a significant effect for *Vis* on *Score* ($F_{40,1400} = 29.7944, p < .0001$) and on *Time* ($F_{40,1400} = 235.5474, p < .0001$). Figure 2a shows the average *Score* per visualization, and TT reveals that MatLink performs significantly better than MAT and NL. Figure 2b shows the average *Time* per visualization. Clearly the speed of NL is much higher than both MatLink and MAT, although TT also indicates significance for the advantage of MatLink over MAT. Figure 2c shows the average number of errors per Task and *Vis*. This information is important to avoid misleading interpretations of the *Time* for Tasks and Visualizations with a high number of Errors. As predicted, MatLink reduces the number of errors produced with MAT for the connectivity tasks (T1 and T2). MatLink produces less errors on all Tasks except T4 (articulationPoint).

User Feedback: Overall, for both group and all tasks, 18/36 users preferred MatLink, 13/36 preferred NL and 4/36 could not decide between MatLink and NL. All users spontaneously reported that they liked MatLink at first sight. After the experiment, they commented that they preferred NL for sparse networks and MatLink for dense networks. Most commented that MatLink was a good compromise for all tasks and graphs except for the articulation point (Task 4). We noticed a difference between groups. Subjects with a graph drawing background showed equal interest in NL and MatLink (8/18 MatLink, 8/18 NL) whereas those from the HCI field preferred MatLink (11/18 MatLink, 5/18 NL).

5.2 Task 1 and 2: Connectivity Tasks

Predictions: We predicted that for both connectivity tasks (commonNeighbor and shortestPath) MatLink *Score* would be better than MAT, and that it would

Table 1. ANOVA for each Task for *Vis*, *S*(Size), *D*(Density) and their interactions

		Task 1 commonNeighbor	Task 2 shortestPath	Task 3 mostConnected	Task 4 articulationPoint	Task5 largestClique
Score						
Vis	$F(2,70)$	11.7262 ***	48.2368 ***	70.2711 ***	068.2356 ***	36.9626 ***
S	$F(1,35)$	1.4318	18.2947 ***	9.5485 **	0.9167	1.1485
D	$F(1,35)$	0.5154	2.8872	71.2042 ***	147.0766 ***	74.4772 ***
S*D	$F(1,35)$	8.2470 *	0.7724	0.5085	18.5628 ***	1.4031
Vis*S	$F(2,70)$	0.6157	11.8654 ***	8.6931 ***	1.2031	1.275
Vis*D	$F(2,70)$	0.902	8.7654 ***	19.032 ***	30.9444 ***	9.2798 ***
Vis*S*D	$F(2,70)$	7.7745 ***	0.0335	5.5856 **	2.2344	17.9178 ***
Time						
Vis	$F(2,70)$	83.4673 ***	56.4941 ***	17.0372 ***	206.8297 ***	5.9018 **
S	$F(1,35)$	11.2244 ***	218.5899 ***	14.8107 ***	14.7163 ***	30.9148 ***
D	$F(1,35)$	31.0351 ***	93.5538 ***	36.2844 ***	248.3838 ***	152.5933 ***
S*D	$F(1,35)$	6.2936 *	74.9258 ***	0.0009	40.4718 ***	1.3117
Vis*S	$F(2,70)$	1.0601	8.0762 ***	0.8878	4.4137 *	3.3366 *
Vis*D	$F(2,70)$	0.207	0.963	5.2016 **	49.5183 ***	0.3993
Vis*S*D	$F(2,70)$	8.7874 **	11.0777 ***	1.9474	0.3012	8.4249 ***

$$***p < .0001 \quad **p < .01 \quad *p < .05$$

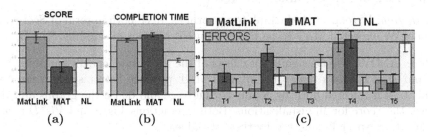

(a) (b) (c)

Fig. 2. Overall average *Score* and *Time* by visualization. Average number of error by task and visualization.

Table 2. *Score* and *Time* for all visualizations and tasks. Average (Standard Deviation)

	Task 1 commonNeighbor	Task 2 shortestPath	Task 3 mostConnected	Task 4 articulationPoint	Task5 largestClique	All
Score						
MatLink	**2.95** (0.05)	**2.94 (0.08)**	**2.72 (0.07)**	1.84 (0.09)	**1.89 (0.08)**	**2.47 (0.04)**
Mat	2.64 (0.05)	1.99 (0.08)	**2.68 (0.07)**	1.81 (0.09)	**2.00 (0.08)**	2.19 (0.04)
NL	**2.92 (0.05)**	2.52 (0.08)	1.72 (0.07)	**2.91 (0.09)**	1.20 (0.08)	2.24 (0.04)
Time						
MatLink	10.08 (0.66)	**15.97 (0.78)**	15.15 (0.80)	32.66 (1.32)	22.18 (1.25)	19.12 (0.58)
Mat	17.04 (0.66)	22.70 (0.78)	**11.42 (0.80)**	33.74 (1.32)	20.80 (1.25)	21.44 (0.58)
NL	**7.91 (0.66)**	15.22 (0.78)	11.06 (0.80)	**8.55 (1.32)**	18.43 (1.25)	**12.24 (0.58)**

not be affected by S and D. We also expected that MatLink would be faster than NL.

Score: ANOVA reveals a significant difference by *Vis*. As expected, TT shows that MatLink is significantly better than MAT for both connectivity tasks. MatLink and NL are not significantly different for commonNeighbor, but surprisingly MatLink performs significantly better than NL for shortestPath. D has no significant impact for either task and visualizations. S has a significant effect on shortestPath: subjects have higher scores on small graphs for all visualizations. ANOVA reveals that interactions $Vis*S$ and $Vis*D$ are significant for shortest-Path; MAT is particularly affected by both of them. $Vis*D$ reveals a surprising effect for NL, where users had higher scores for higher D.

Time: ANOVA reveals a significant effect on *Vis*, S and D. As expected, TT shows that MatLink is significantly faster than MAT for both tasks. However, MatLink is only significantly faster than NL for the shortestPath. We predicted that the *Time* would increase for large and dense graphs on both tasks. However, the interaction $Vis*S$ for shortestPath shows that all visualizations including MatLink are affected by S.

User Feedback: Most of the users preferred MatLink.

5.3   Task 3: Most Connected Actor

Prediction: We expected MatLink to perform as MAT both in term of *Score* and *Time*. We expected MAT to be faster than NL and not affected by S or D.

Score: ANOVA reveals significant effects of the three independent variables *Vis*, S and D. TT shows that MatLink and MAT produce better scores than NL. This task is affected both by S and D: the large and dense the graphs are, the lower the *Score* for all visualizations. Both interactions $Vis*S$ and $Vis*D$ reveal that NL is especially affected by these variables.

Time: This indicator is to be interpreted carefully for NL as the error rate is 28% for this task. ANOVA reveals significant effects for *Vis*, S and D. For all visualizations, *Time* increases with S and with D. TT shows that MatLink is slower than the other representations. The interaction analysis of the interaction $Vis*D$ reveals that MatLink is particularly affected by D whereas the interaction $Vis*S$ is not significant.

User Feedback: Most of the users preferred MAT. Several subjects report that MatLink lacked a highlight or mouse-over effect to ease the comparison of actors, especially to help them counting the number of edges in the matrix row/column.

5.4   Task 4: Articulation Point

Prediction: We predicted that NL would outperform MatLink and MAT both in term of *Score* and *Time*. We expected MatLink to show higher Scores than MAT especially for sparse graphs.

Score: As predicted, ANOVA reveals significant effect of *Vis*. TT shows that NL produces significantly higher scores. The *Score* for this task is affected by *S* and by *D*. The interaction *Vis*D* reveals that MatLink and MAT are affected by *D* for this task: dense graph produce significantly lower scores for both representations. Unexpectedly, ANOVA reveals no significant difference between MAT and MatLink for sparse or dense graphs.

Time: ANOVA reveals that *Vis*, *S* and *D* have a significant impact on the *Time*. TT confirms that NL outperforms significantly MAT and MatLink for this task. *User Feedback:* All subjects except two preferred NL for this task. Their level of confidence was very high and their performance good with this representation. Almost all subjects report that this task was the most difficult one when dealing with MAT and dense graphs. Several subjects commented that MatLink was slightly better for sparse graphs.

5.5 Task 5: Clique

Prediction: We expected MatLink to perform slightly better than MAT in terms of *Score*. We also predicted NL would present low scores for dense graphs. We did not expect any significant difference in *Time*.

Score: ANOVA reveals significant difference by *Vis* and *D*. As expected, TT shows that MatLink and MAT produce higher scores than NL. However, ANOVA does not reveal any significant difference between MatLink and MAT. TT shows significantly smaller scores for all visualizations with dense graphs. The interaction *Vis*D* shows that NL scores are significantly reduced on dense graphs.

Time: ANOVA reveals a significant difference by *Vis*: NL is faster than MatLink and MAT. However, this indicator should be interpreted carefully, because NL's error rate is 48% for this task: users who gave up immediately were counted as having a fast (if erroneous) completion. ANOVA shows also that *S* and *D* affect the *Time*. The interaction *Vis*D* is not significant, whereas the interaction *Vis*S* is significant: MatLink and MAT are slower when *S* increases.

User Feedback: Almost all subjects preferred MAT or MatLink for this task. They comment that they had a much higher level of confidence identifying if a visual cluster was a clique or not. However, several added that finding the largest clique was difficult without reordering the MAT to place sub-parts next to each other. Most reported that links were not useful, but several argued that links helped them find a member of the clique distant from the others in the representation.

6 Discussion

For the social networks and tasks we studied, users were significantly more accurate with MatLink than with MAT for most tasks. Although NL is usually more accurate than MAT for path-based tasks, MatLink was more accurate than NL for one task in our study (shortestPath). MAT was known to be more accurate than NL on dense and large graphs for mostConnected, but on this dataset it was also better for largestClique. Using the best layout for each representation, MAT and MatLink were both better than NL for the clique-finding task. Moreover, we confirmed Ghoniem et al. [1] results that MAT outperforms NL for low-level tasks on our selected social networks.

As we predicted, for the path-related tasks (1 and 2), MatLink performance is much better than MAT and is competitive with NL, outperforming it for the shortest path task even when the path is highlighted. A surprising detail is that users had fewer errors with NL on dense graphs than sparse ones. This appears to be an artifact of the highlighting of the shortest paths. From our observations, it seems that users ignored the highlighting information in our NL implementation when the network was sparse and thus missed the shortest path, whereas they systematically used highlighting on dense graphs.

For task 3 (mostConnected), as predicted, users were more accurate using MAT and MatLink than with NL. However, surprisingly, the time was longer for MatLink than MAT. Our interpretation is that the added overhead of drawing the auxiliary visualizations created a small time lag that impacted this task. We did not provide continuous feedback about the vertex under the mouse, and several users complained about the lack of this feature when they clicked near but not on the most-connected vertex.

Interestingly, although we expected a difference between the two groups of subjects, one of which had a strong background in graph drawing using NL, our results do not show a significant difference between groups. Users usually performed tasks faster with NL than with MAT and MatLink, but this finding should be interpreted carefully, because users had many errors with NL than with MatLink and MAT (except for task 4 articulationPoint).

7 Conclusions

This article describes and evaluates MatLink: an enhanced matrix visualization of graphs that overlays a linear node-link representation on the matrix and adds dynamic feedback of path-relationship between nodes.

We assessed the effectiveness of this visualization by a controlled experiment comparing user performance for representative social network analysis tasks, performed on realistic social networks fitting in full screen. The three tools assessed were MatLink, conventional matrix representations (MAT), and node-link diagrams(NL). The experiment showed that MatLink significantly outperforms ordinary matrix visualizations for path-related tasks — known to be difficult on MAT — that are required for social network analysis. It also performs as well or better than MAT on other analysis tasks that cannot be effectively performed on NL because of the inherent tendency of social networks to be locally dense. Therefore, MatLink is a good compromise for visualizing and analyzing social networks with a single representation. However, on some tasks related to overall graph structure, NL is still superior.

Other improvements are possible for all three visualizations. For example, we assigned shortest-path for the dynamic feedback, but other kind of paths could be computed and highlighted based on user preferences. We also need to assess the effectiveness of MatLink for larger networks when scrolling or other navigation techniques are required. Now that users can visualize and analyze denser social networks, we need to understand better the kind of supports they will need. Longitudinal user studies would help us understand user needs and preferences. Which representation will they choose when all are available? For which tasks? Will they alternate between representations? How often?

Acknowledgments

We would like to thank Howard Goodell for improvements to the article and to Yann Riche for helping with the accompanying video.

References

[1] Ghoniem, M., Fekete, J.D., Castagliola, P.: On the readability of graphs using node-link and matrix-based representations: a controlled experiment and statistical analysis. Information Visualization 4(2), 114–135 (2005)

[2] Wasserman, S., Faust, K.: Social Network Analysis. Cambridge University Press, Cambridge (1994)

[3] Watts, D.J., Strogatz, S.H.: Collective dynamics of 'small-world' networks. Nature 393, 440–442 (1998)

[4] Amar, R., Eagan, J., Stasko, J.: Low-level components of analytic activity in information visualization. In: Proceedings of the IEEE Symposium on Information Visualization, pp. 111–117 (2005)

[5] Plaisant, C., Lee, B., Parr, C.S., Fekete, J.D., Henry, N.: Task taxonomy for graph visualization. In: BEyond time and errors: novel evaLuation methods for Information Visualization (BELIV'06), Venice, Italy, pp. 82–86. ACM Press, New York (2006)

[6] Heer, J., Boyd, D.: Vizster: Visualizing Online Social Networks. In: Proceedings of the IEEE Symposium on Information Visualization 5 (2005)

[7] de Nooy, W., Mrvar, A., Batagelj, V.: Exploratory Social Network Analysis with Pajek. In: Structural Analysis in the Social Sciences, Cambridge University Press, Cambridge (2005)

[8] Adar, E.: Guess: a language and interface for graph exploration. In: CHI '06. Proceedings of the SIGCHI conference on Human Factors in computing systems, New York, NY, USA, pp. 791–800. ACM Press, New York (2006)

[9] Doreian, P., Batagelj, V., Ferligoj, A.: Generalized Blockmodeling. In: Structural Analysis in the Social Sciences, Cambridge University Press, Cambridge (2005)

[10] Henry, N., Fekete, J.D.: MatrixExplorer: a Dual-Representation System to Explore Social Networks. IEEE Transactions on Visualization and Computer Graphics 12(5), 677–684 (2006)

[11] Di Battista, G., Eades, P., Tamassia, R., Tollis, I.G: Graph Drawing: Algorithms for the Visualization of Graphs. Prentice Hall, Englewood Cliffs (1998)

[12] Noack, A.: Energy-based clustering of graphs with nonuniform degrees. In: Healy, P., Nikolov, N.S. (eds.) GD 2005. LNCS, vol. 3843, pp. 309–320. Springer, Heidelberg (2006)

[13] Auber, D., Chiricota, Y., Jourdan, F., Melancon, G.: Multiscale visualization of small world networks. In: Proceedings of the IEEE Symposium on Information Visualization, pp. 75–81 (2003)

[14] Wattenberg, M.: Visual exploration of multivariate graphs. In: Proceedings of the SIGCHI conference on Human Factors in computing systems, Montréal, Québec, Canada, pp. 811–819. ACM Press, New York (2006)

[15] Bertin, J.: Semiology of graphics. University of Wisconsin Press (1983)

[16] Abello, J., van Ham, F.: Matrix zoom: A visual interface to semi-external graphs. In: Proceedings of the IEEE Symposium on Information Visualization (INFO-VIS'04), Austin, Texas, pp. 183–190 (2004)

[17] van Ham, F.: Using multilevel call matrices in large software projects. In: Proceedings of the IEEE Symposium on Information Visualization, Seattle, WA, USA, pp. 227–232 (2003)

[18] Fekete, J.D.: The InfoVis Toolkit. In: Proceedings of the IEEE Symposium on Information Visualization, pp. 167–174 (2004)

CodeSaw: A Social Visualization of Distributed Software Development

Eric Gilbert and Karrie Karahalios

University of Illinois
Urbana-Champaign, Illinois, USA
{egilber2, kkarahal}@cs.uiuc.edu

Abstract. We present CodeSaw, a social visualization of distributed software development. CodeSaw visualizes a distributed software community from two important and independent perspectives: code repositories and project communication. By bringing together both shared artifacts (code) and the talk surrounding those artifacts (project mail), CodeSaw reveals group dynamics that lie buried in existing technologies. This paper describes the visualization and its design process. We apply CodeSaw to a popular open source project, showing how the visualization reveals group dynamics and individual roles. The paper ends with a discussion of the results of an online field study with prominent open source developers. The field study suggests that CodeSaw positively affects communities and provides incentives to distributed developers. Furthermore, an important design lesson from the field study leads us to introduce a novel interaction technique for social visualization called spatial messaging.

1 Introduction

A recent study suggests that nearly 1.1 million software developers in North America participate in open source development [1]. Major companies and governments have adopted open source software for critical infrastructure. Projects like Linux, Apache and Mozilla have propelled the open source "movement" into the popular consciousness through their media attention.

Open source software development operates quite differently than traditional software development. Developers do not meet face to face. There are few schedules. In all but the most prominent projects, there is no plan. Developers choose what they work on and how much time they spend working on it. In almost all cases, developers do not get paid for their work. Traditional mechanisms for coordinating work (e.g., schedules, plans, face to face meetings) are absent [2], yet studies show that distributed development needs coordination more than collocated development [3]. We are just starting to learn what drives these communities.

At the same time, many open source communities also represent vibrant online social spaces [4]. Developers have heated emailed exchanges on the project mailing list about feature additions. Legal issues concerning software licensing get vigorously discussed. Code is checked out, checked in and reviewed by community leaders in cycles of iterative development. The code and email archives left behind tell the story.

C. Baranauskas et al. (Eds.): INTERACT 2007, LNCS 4663, Part II, pp. 303–316, 2007.

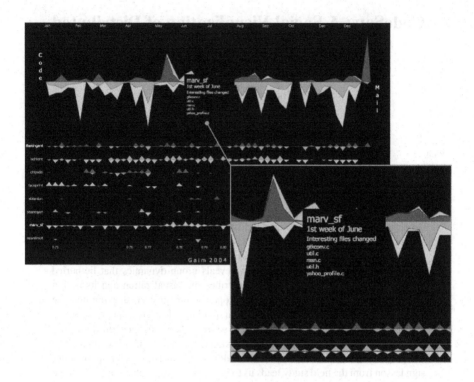

Fig. 1. CodeSaw showing Gaim in 2004. Small timelines denote developers, with time progressing from left to right. The top of each axis represents code contributions; the bottom represents project communication. The user has compared two developers by dragging their timelines into the investigation area at the top. By hovering, the user sees the top 5 files changed by a developer.

Yet, for the most part, projects leave these archives untapped. The sheer size of the archives may play a significant role. A typical open source project can generate over 20,000 CVS code checkins. A project mailing list may hold years of conversations, comprising thousands of individual email messages. While a long history of group dynamics lives in these archives, the current state of technology leaves it buried.

In this paper, we present CodeSaw, a social visualization of distributed software development. CodeSaw combines code repository information with project communication to visualize a software community from two independent perspectives. By bringing together both shared artifacts (code) and the talk surrounding those artifacts (project mail), CodeSaw reveals group dynamics that lie buried in existing technologies. Code-Saw's interface allows users to compare developers, dig deeper into archives and leave messages on the visualization itself (Figures 1 and 4). CodeSaw underwent an iterative design process, and we evaluated CodeSaw in an online field study with lead open source developers.

CodeSaw can benefit both community insiders and outsiders. For outsiders, Code-Saw provides an opportunity to compare open source projects and dig deeper into particularly relevant ones. For project developers, the foundation of the community, CodeSaw offers a chance to reflect on their community and their contributions. Especially because most open source developers do not get paid for their work, seeing their contributions in the community context can be powerful. One user study participant said that CodeSaw recalled an important time when she worked closely with another developer who had left the project. Another told us that CodeSaw made him feel "vindicated." Our contributions include: the CodeSaw visualization, an example of how CodeSaw can reveal roles in open source projects, the evaluation of CodeSaw and a novel interaction technique for social visualization called spatial messaging.

2   Related Work

We begin by reviewing related work in distributed software development, our target audience. Afterward, we review related work in visualization.

Distributed Software Development. Gutwin, et al. interviewed open source developers to learn more about the mechanisms that underlie their collaboration [5]. In their study, they found that developers do maintain awareness of one another, and that text-based communication (e.g., mailing lists and chat systems) is the primary vehicle for maintaining it. Along the same lines, LaToza's study claims that 40% of a developer's time is devoted to communicating about code [6].

Researchers have also looked at open source communities from an organizational perspective. Mockus, et al. studied two well-known and successful open source projects, Apache and Mozilla [2]. In their study, they looked into the assignment of roles in each community. They found that a core group of about 10 - 15 developers used mailing lists to coordinate and assign work. Kraut and Streeter stressed the uncertainty, interdependence and informal communication of software development [7]. Noting the distinct problems of scale inherent in large software systems, they point out that "many software systems ... are very large and far beyond the ability of any individual or small group to create or even understand in detail." In the context of maintaining large software systems, Singer found that code repositories (e.g., CVS) are important sources of information for programmers [8].

Our work leverages the lessons of these studies. For example, incorporating Gutwin's analysis, CodeSaw uses mailing list email communication in its visualization. CodeSaw aims to address the need for a visualization that promotes awareness, both social and work-related, among distributed developers.

Visualization. A number of projects have visualized software projects [9, 10, 11, 12, 13, 14]. SeeSys [9] takes an overall project approach, using a treemap visualization of the source code file system. SeeSys works particularly well for very large projects that are also relatively stable. Augur [11] adopts a line-oriented style, presenting one user with an integrated visual-diff display of CVS records. Augur, as in [12, 13], also gives users a social network view of the code and a temporal view. While Augur shows a line-oriented temporal history, CodeSaw abstracts that information. CodeSaw shows one year in the life of a project, and is not tied to any one file. CodeSaw also differs from Augur by adding spatial messaging and email communication, social features, to its visualization. We designed CodeSaw as a community mirror, a visualization for an entire group.

Collaborative contribution has been studied outside of the source code context. History Flow [15] and Authorlines [16] visualize Wikipedia and Usenet postings, respectively. History Flow focuses on the interaction of collaborators on one Wikipedia entry. Authorlines deals with one user's posts to Usenet.

CodeSaw builds on the research presented here. CodeSaw seeks to visualize one year in the life of a project in an informative and intuitive way. Secondly, CodeSaw aims to present an aesthetically intriguing visualization. An aesthetically intriguing visualization can invite play, an important part of interacting deeply with data [17]. CodeSaw primarily differs from existing work by visualizing two important and contrasting information sources: code repositories and project communication. CodeSaw also presents a new, social approach to visualizing software development, exemplified by its spatial messaging and its focus as a community mirror.

3   CodeSaw's Iterative Design Process

Exploring the Design Space. To establish baseline requirements for CodeSaw, we conducted informal interviews about the collaborative software process with eight colleagues at our university. Five of our colleagues had worked on open source projects before; the other three had worked on many academic or commercial software projects.

Results. From our interviews we observed the following:

- *Developers felt disconnected from the rest of the community.* While working hard on one area of the code base, a developer may have a difficult time appreciating the work happening in other areas. This observation motivates tools that promote awareness and sociality inside the community. Such a tool could help confer value onto developers' contributions. However, developers noted that one metric alone would not capture the multiple dimensions of their work.
- *Developers used the project mailing list to maintain awareness.* This observation echoes the findings of Kraut and Streeter [7]. Developers used informal communication on the project mailing list to coordinate work and to get to know one another.

Iterations. CodeSaw evolved from a prototype to its current form over the course of four major iterations. After the development of each iteration, we conducted formative evaluations with between three and four software developers. In these sessions, developers used CodeSaw to explore a typical open source community, thinking aloud during the process. While it might be useful to present each of the iterations, for the sake of brevity we condensed this discussion into the following section. Next, we present CodeSaw's design rationale as a series of design implications learned from our formative evaluations.

4 CodeSaw

CodeSaw shows up to eight developers over the course of one year (Figure 1) [18]. Prior work pointed out that most projects have around 10 core developers. Our own experiments support this. In trials with 20 randomly selected open source projects, not one had more than 8 core developers.

4.1 Design Rationale

Design Implication: Focus on people. Users of the prototype started by asking simple social questions. "When was I most active?" "Who writes more code than me?" "What was going on on the mailing list then?" From the start it was evident that the prototype had difficulty answering these simple questions. We noticed that users of the visualization asked questions that revolved around people: themselves and the others working in the periphery. Therefore, CodeSaw focuses first and foremost on the people in the community.

Social Data Analysis. During formative evaluations, users would often call over other people to look at their discoveries. In one instance, a user noted that a particular developer only contributed code during the summer, wondering "if this developer might be a student." In another instance, a user commented that with the exception of one developer, no one had contributed to a particular project during the last week of December. Talking about the one developer that contributed, the user said, "the holidays must not have been good, since this guy worked so much." The developer contributed only code during this period; the mailing list was silent, implying that the developer worked alone. We feel that our focus on people directly lead to the social data analysis we observed.

Design Implication: Allow users to explore context. While early CodeSaw iterations achieved a simplicity that users liked, some felt that it hid too much information. They asked for a way to uncover some of the information that CodeSaw aggregated or discarded. For example, a number of designers wanted to know on what files the developers were working, or what phrases the developers were most commonly writing in emails at the time of a release.

To uncover the email discussion, CodeSaw shows excerpts from the email dialog on the project mailing list. In the same way that the source files are listed by their activity levels, email words are sorted by their frequency of appearance in the email exchange (Figure 2). The choice to include salient words from an email dialog mirrors the design choices made in the recent Themail [19]. In Themail, Viégas, et al. used prominent words from email exchanges to paint a portrait of relationships. In addition, users wondered aloud many times if release dates coincided with spikes in activity. To provide this contextual information, CodeSaw plots release names along the bottom of the visualization. This simple addition provides some interesting insights about releases and milestones.

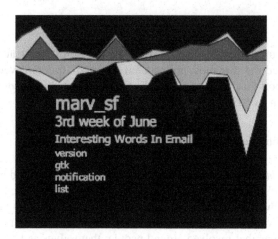

Fig. 2. CodeSaw exposes project email dialog to reveal informal communication. This design choice helps users explore the online social space. In this example, a user has hovered over the timeline of particular developer to find out what he was saying on the mailing list.

Design Implication: Only visualize essential information. The CodeSaw prototype used a large portion of the available information in the visualization: number of lines added, number of lines subtracted, recency of changes, etc. Initially, we hypothesized that code developers would want such a high level of detail. However, users told us that it exposed too much information. If they wanted such high levels of detail, users could more easily go back to the CVS archives and the code itself. Only the information items indicated as very useful by users made their way into CodeSaw.

Design Implication: Keep it quick and simple. In early iterations, a technical constraint made users wait for all of the data to load from the database before showing the visualization. CodeSaw requires a number of complex database queries that can take a considerable amount of time. Users often felt frustrated with the long time they had to wait to see anything. Following the lead of Wattenberg in NameVoyager [20], the data for all eight developers loads in parallel. The small timelines animate from left to right as data fills into them. Many have commented on the aesthetic beauty of this technique.

CodeSaw presents an easily graspable concept for code contributions: raw number of code lines added. Although this choice throws away some important information about a developer's actions, most designers and developers considered it a fairly accurate representation of work. We made a similar decision with email. CodeSaw goes with a simple metric, the number of words written in email on the project mailing list.

This simplified representation is very powerful. Most existing tools focus on only one archive. CodeSaw, on the other hand, incorporates two archives, visualizing the community from two important and separate perspectives. CodeSaw intuitively made sense to users, since it did not incorporate complex measurements that were hard to understand quickly. Unlike our experience with early iterations, many people said that they would not need to go back to CVS to see the things that CodeSaw told them.

4.2 The Visualization Details

The area under each triangle is calculated as follows. The raw number of code lines added to a source file by a developer determines the area under the top triangles. The raw number of words written on the project mailing list determines the area under the bottom triangles.

The timelines in CodeSaw employ Tufte's small multiples concept [21]. Small multiples are representations of information that repeat a common design and scale, inviting comparison. In Envisioning Information, Tufte writes, "for a wide range of problems in data presentation, small multiples are the best design solution." The small timelines in CodeSaw allow a user to compare developers. By adding any combination of developers to the detail graph, a user can learn much more about the people involved. While resembling a Zooming User Interface [22], our technique differs by reserving screen space for drag-and-drop comparison which affords any combination of timelines in the investigation.

5 Using CodeSaw to Find Trends and Roles

Having described CodeSaw's design, we turn now to using CodeSaw to find trends and roles in an open source community. In the example that follows we applied CodeSaw to the popular open source project Gaim [23]. Figure 1 shows Gaim broadly, looking at all core developers over the year 2004. Figure 3, on the other hand, shows a detailed view of two developers. Both views give us insight into the community.

A glance at Figure 1 tells us that Gaim was very active in 2004. A closer look at Figure 1, however, also shows us that one or two people do the majority of the work. We have seen this trend in all 20 open source projects we have analyzed with CodeSaw. A handful of leaders emerge who keep the project moving.

A closer look at the developers in Figure 3 offers insights into their behavior patterns. Until May, marv_sf wrote only mail (a). In the last few weeks of April, marv_sf and thekingant write a large amount of mail corresponding to a project release (b). Code-Saw denotes a project release by a thin gray line. Almost directly after April's mail surge, marv_sf starts coding for the first time, backed up by thekingant (c). marv_sf makes significant contributions to Gaim during these couple of months. Did thekingant convince marv_sf to code for Gaim?

By July, marv_sf has stopped coding for the most part. He contributes almost no code for the rest of the year, in fact (d). We can also see that thekingant and marv_sf tend to peak in project mail at the same times, usually connected to a release (e). In the first week of October, right before a release, both developers go silent–no code or mail (f). Did the project go down, or did both developers happen to take a break at the same time? Do they know each other personally?

Viewing CodeSaw from the outside, we can try to project a story onto the visualization. Did the surge in production by the thekingant inspire marv_sf? Did marv_sf finish a hard semester at school and suddenly find a lot of time on his hands? However, CodeSaw is primarily designed as a community mirror. From the outside we can learn important things about a project, but we do not get the critical context that only the community itself can provide. In this respect, we feel that CodeSaw achieves a good

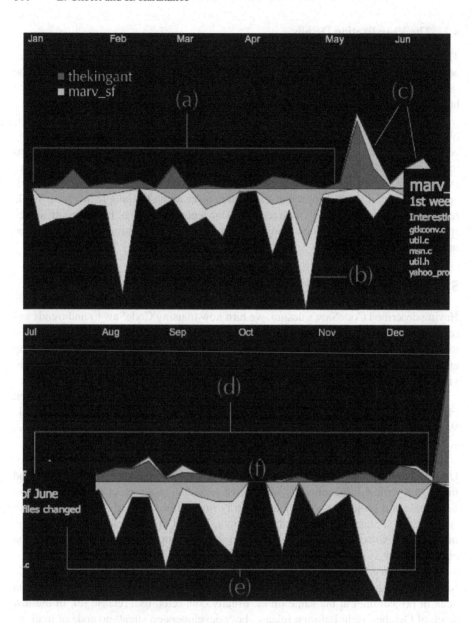

Fig. 3. A closer look at two core developers in Gaim. Until May, marv_sf writes almost no code (a). Then, following a surge in mail by both developers (b), marv_sf makes a big code contribution (c). However, his coding is short-lived (d). thekingant and marv_sf write mail at about the same time (e), and they take a break during the same week (f). What is their relationship?

balance between revealing private information to the world and leaving enough of it ambiguous so as to not invade privacy.

6   Online Field Study

Since we wanted to test CodeSaw "in the wild," we distributed CodeSaw via the web to developers around the world. We wanted developers to integrate CodeSaw into their regular routines and projects, which we could not accomplish in the lab. We recruited by targeting project mailing lists and lead developers of open source projects. The projects were all hosted on SourceForge.net. In total, nearly 500 recruitment messages were sent over the course of one month. Subjects received a $20 gift certificate to an online retailer for their participation in the study.

Our approach allowed developers to see their own project history visualized. After interacting with CodeSaw from somewhere between 30 minutes to one hour, participants completed an online survey. We asked users to complete the survey no more than one hour after they finished using CodeSaw. Participants were free to continue using CodeSaw after completing the survey. Because we wanted to do an in situ study, and the participants were scattered across the world, we could not do interviews. So we replaced interviews with the best thing we could: an in-depth online survey. The survey asked participants about their satisfaction and enjoyment with CodeSaw. In addition, the survey asked participants about the effectiveness of CodeSaw in visualizing their community.

6.1   Participants and Their Projects

Nine participants took part in the evaluation of CodeSaw. Two were female and seven were male. The subjects ranged in age from 19 to 61. Five came from open source projects; four belonged to the same project at a research laboratory. The four from the research laboratory spent about half of their time in the same office and about half at a distance. They used email on the project mailing list to coordinate work. The research project had been ongoing for three years at the time of the study. In terms of code, the project consisted of 801 source code files.

Each of the five open source participants worked on a distinct project. Each project was among the top 200 most active projects hosted on SourceForge.net [24]. The duration of the projects ranged from one to four years. In terms of code, the projects ranged from 376 source files to 1785 source files, with a mean of 980. We chose these projects because they are representative of open source projects generally.

Each participant had developed software for more than three years. Six of the nine participants had used CVS for more than three years; the other three participants had used it for between one and three years.

7   Results

Overall, participants enjoyed using CodeSaw to investigate their project's history. When asked, using a 5-point Likert scale, how easy CodeSaw was to use, participants responded, on average 1.6 (1 being the most and 5 being the least). Not including watching a one minute introductory video, 8 of 9 participants said that it took them 10 minutes or less to get comfortable with CodeSaw, validating our design goal of a visualization that novices can access quickly. When asked how often they would use CodeSaw if it were deployed into their community, 7 of 9 said they would use it on a monthly basis or at release time. Since many projects go through 5 to 20 releases a year, we feel that this result is positive. Although participants were, for the most part, positive about their experience with CodeSaw, some pointed out flaws. We address these design lessons in the section entitled Incorporating Field Study Results.

7.1 Community

Many of the participants reported seeing confirming and surprising aspects of their community in CodeSaw:

> *It was interesting to see the contributions over time in an easy graphical interface. I am not sure it was surprising, rather confirming.*

> *It gave me a better idea about what the overall community is doing.*

Other participants noted that CodeSaw exposed roles in the community:

> *It confirmed my long-held suspicions about the community. It was easy to see who was doing the development and who was doing the commentary. Often they were not the same people.*

> *It was interesting. At first I felt as though I had not contributed much, but then I realized that I had a 'surrogate'. I was working closely with another developer who committed the changes to the code base.*

While most participants felt that CodeSaw seemed most relevant to core developers, one participant felt that CodeSaw would be of better use to outsiders looking in:

> *As a developer I pretty much knew what was happening, but this would be more useful to an outsider who wanted to understand the activity of each contributor.*

In this case, CodeSaw could be of use to newcomers to a project. They could discover at a glance who contributes when and to what parts of the code base.

Two participants that worked on projects with less than 5 developers commented on the loneliness that CodeSaw engendered:

> *I feel a bit lonely. It doesn't reflect the community in a whole. There's a lot of people passing by in the forums. People sending bug reports and patches are not taken into account.*

> *Viewing/visualizing the [anonymous] traffic on the forums and the lists would be great.*

We did not explicitly design for projects with just a few developers. However, in retrospect it seems clear that CodeSaw does not serve these projects well. The participant behind the first comment above said, "I don't feel like using it again. As I'm almost the only contributor, it doesn't make much sense." The Incorporating Field Study Results section specifically addresses these feelings of loneliness.

7.2 Incentives for Developers

Participants also remarked on the incentives CodeSaw provides to developers:

> *I'd love to have it in the "activity page" of the project to show the "pulse". It might be interesting as an immediate reward for developers. CodeSaw might show the "most active people" in the community very easily, and it could show the history of the project (some project leaders might want to erase some parts of it though). :-)*

> *It made me appreciative of who was doing the work.*

When asked how CodeSaw made him feel about his contributions to his project, one participant simply responded, "Vindicated. :-)"

Two of the participants commented on the potential for CodeSaw as a project management tool, an application we did not explicitly design for:

> *For example, if one looks at <username> in 2005, he did no development work that year. If the project were waiting for him to do something and a milestone was not met, we could get after him.*

> *I found some surprises - some developers were not attributed as working on the code I *thought* they were working on in a given period. Others were not contributing much code during periods when I thought they should have been.*

No one worried about privacy or about a boss having this tool. Since only one participant described himself as a project manager, we found this result somewhat surprising.

8 Incorporating Field Study Results: Spatial Messaging

In the field study, we learned that CodeSaw helped users better understand their communities and provided incentives for developers. However, we also learned that CodeSaw created feelings of loneliness in communities with only a few developers. We view this as the major design lesson from the field study and hope that designers of other social visualizations can learn from our experience.

As a response to this lesson, we added spatial messaging to CodeSaw (Figure 4). Spatial messaging allows users to leave comments on the visualization *itself*. These comments are linked to visualization state (i.e., the configuration of timelines in the detail graph). When a user brings the visualization back into the state where the comment was made, the comment appears. We do not intend to replace traditional communication channels (e.g., the project mailing list) with spatial messaging. Developers do not need yet another communication medium to monitor. In fact, we explicitly designed spatial messaging to supplement existing communication channels. A spatial message automatically generates mail to the mailing list. The message includes a link that brings the visualization into the right state.

We designed CodeSaw as a community mirror for developers and users that rarely meet face to face, yet construct a vibrant online social space. Using spatial messaging,

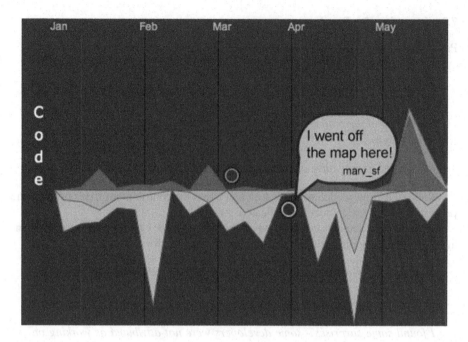

Fig. 4. CodeSaw incorporates spatial messaging to create a socially activated visualization. A user hovers over a spatial message, represented as a disk filled with the developer's color, to reveal its contents. Spatial messaging allows users to mark up a social visualization in a novel way.

developers and users can reflect on their shared history in the same place where they see it. We feel that spatial messaging represents a novel interaction technique for social visualizations.

9   Discussion

Overall, users found CodeSaw informative and intuitive. Users enjoyed interacting with CodeSaw and reported finding both confirming and surprising results. The field study suggests that CodeSaw positively affects users' conceptions of their own communities. In addition, the field study reveals that the visualization serves as a motivation to developers. This is key in open source communities, since developers volunteer their time. Based on user comments, we believe that introducing CodeSaw into an open source project may lead to increased production. We also believe that developers would feel more valued in the community. However, without a longitudinal study we cannot make concrete claims. We intend to follow up on this work with quantitative measures in a longitudinal study.

Since CodeSaw reveals deeply buried, although public, information, we expected privacy to be a serious concern. The field study showed otherwise. Not a single participant reported any concerns about privacy. It could turn out that under constant use and constant observation, CodeSaw would cause users to express privacy concerns.

Because we engaged in four iterations of a user-centered design process, we feel that CodeSaw reflects the needs of distributed software communities. As suggested by one of the participants in our field study, we plan to explore options for incorporating CodeSaw into real open source communities. Sourceforge.net is one option. A longitudinal, ecologically-valid user study would provide valuable information to the HCI community and definitively answer the privacy questions expressed above.

Our field study provides a compelling analysis of the introduction of a social visualization into real-life open source communities. The field study also motivated the creation of a novel interaction technique for social visualization, called spatial messaging. Many visualizations revolve around scientific data or highly personal data, like email or health data. Since the data visualized in CodeSaw lies in a space between the familiar and the foreign, we believe our field study contributes in an often-overlooked area of visualization research.

10 Conclusion

We have presented CodeSaw, a social visualization of distributed software development. CodeSaw visualizes a software community from two unique perspectives: code repositories and project communication. Using two distinct project archives reveals patterns not available in current technology.

Following an iterative design process, we have explained the rationale behind Code-Saw as a series of design implications that can be used by other designers. Our online field study suggests that CodeSaw positively impacts distributed developers' notions of community, and that CodeSaw provides incentives for distributed developers. Following a design lesson from our field study, we have also presented a novel interaction technique for social visualization called spatial messaging. Spatial messaging allows users to leave comments on the visualization itself.

Acknowledgments

We thank the very busy developers in our study for contributing their time to our project. We also thank the UIUC Social Spaces group for their helpful feedback.

References

1. Orgell, E.: More than 1.1 million developers in north america now working on open source projects (2006), http://evansdata.com/n2/pr/releases/dps2004.shtml
2. Mockus, A., F.R., Herbsleb, J.: Two case studies of open source software development: Apache and mozilla. ACM Trans. Softw. Eng. Methodol. 11(3), 309–346 (2002)
3. Herbsleb, J.D., Grinter, R.E.: Splitting the organization and integrating the code: Conway's law revisited. In: ICSE '99: Proceedings of the 21st international conference on Software engineering, pp. 85–95. IEEE Computer Society Press, Los Alamitos (1999)
4. SourceForge.net: (2006), http://sourceforge.net
5. Gutwin, C., Penner, R., Schneider, K.: Group awareness in distributed software development. In: CSCW '04: Proceedings of the 2004 ACM conference on Computer supported cooperative work, pp. 72–81. ACM Press, New York (2004)

6. LaToza, T.D., Venolia, G., DeLine, R.: Maintaining mental models: a study of developer work habits. In: ICSE '06: Proceeding of the 28th international conference on Software engineering, pp. 492–501. ACM Press, New York (2006)
7. Kraut, R.E., Streeter, L.A.: Coordination in software development. Commun. ACM 38(3), 69–81 (1995)
8. Singer, J.: Practices of software maintenance. In: ICSM, pp. 139–145 (1998)
9. Baker, M.J., Eick, S.G.: Space-filling software visualization. Journal of Visual Languages and Computing, 119–133 (1995)
10. Eick, S.G., Steffen, J.L., Sumner, E.E.J.: Seesoft-a tool for visualizing line oriented software statistics. IEEE Trans. Softw. Eng. 18(11), 957–968 (1992)
11. Froehlich, J., Dourish, P.: Unifying artifacts and activities in a visual tool for distributed software development teams. In: ICSE '04: Proceedings of the 26th International Conference on Software Engineering, Washington, DC, USA, pp. 387–396. IEEE Computer Society Press, Los Alamitos (2004)
12. Ducheneaut, N.: Socialization in an open source software community: A socio-technical analysis. Comput. Supported Coop. Work 14(4), 323–368 (2005)
13. Medynskiy, Y.E., Ducheneaut, N., Farahat, A.: Using hybrid networks for the analysis of online software development communities. In: CHI '06: Proceedings of the SIGCHI conference on Human Factors in computing systems, pp. 513–516. ACM Press, New York (2006)
14. Bernard Kerr, L.T.C., Sweeney, T.: Growing bloom: design of a visualization of project evolution. In: CHI '06 extended abstracts on Human factors in computing systems, pp. 93–98. ACM Press, New York (2006)
15. Viégas, F.B., Wattenberg, M., Dave, K.: Studying cooperation and conflict between authors with *history flow* visualizations. In: CHI '04: Proceedings of the SIGCHI conference on Human factors in computing systems, pp. 575–582. ACM Press, New York (2004)
16. Viégas, F.B., Smith, M.: Newsgroup crowds and authorlines: Visualizing the activity of individuals in conversational cyberspaces. In: HICSS '04: Proceedings of the Proceedings of the 37th Annual Hawaii International Conference on System Sciences (HICSS'04) - Track 4, Washington, DC, USA, p. 40109.2, IEEE Computer Society Press, Los Alamitos (2004)
17. Vande-Moere, A.: Form follows data: the symbiosis between design and information visualization. In: CAADfutures, pp. 167–176 (2005)
18. Gilbert, E., Karahalios, K.: Lifesource: two cvs visualizations. In: CHI '06 extended abstracts on Human factors in computing systems, pp. 791–796. ACM Press, New York (2006)
19. Viégas, F.B., Golder, S., Donath, J.: Visualizing email content: portraying relationships from conversational histories. In: CHI '06: Proceedings of the SIGCHI conference on Human Factors in computing systems, pp. 979–988. ACM Press, New York (2006)
20. Wattenberg, M.: Baby names, visualization, and social data analysis. In: INFOVIS '05: Proceedings of the Proceedings of the 2005 IEEE Symposium on Information Visualization, Washington, DC, USA, p. 1. IEEE Computer Society Press, Los Alamitos (2005)
21. Tufte, E.R.: The Visual Display of Quantitative Information. Graphics Press (1983)
22. Bederson, B.B., Hollan, J.D.: Pad++: a zoomable graphical interface system. In: CHI '95: Conference companion on Human factors in computing systems, pp. 23–24. ACM Press, New York (1995)
23. Gaim: (2006), http://gaim.sourceforge.net
24. SourceForge.net: (2006), http://sourceforge.net/top/mostactive.php?type=week

The Use of Information Visualization to Support Software Configuration Management*

Roberto Therón[1], Antonio González[1], Francisco J. García[1], and Pablo Santos[2]

[1] Departamento de Informática y Automática, Universidad de Salamanca,
Plaza de la Merced s/n. 37008, Salamanca, Spain
{theron, agtorres, fgarcia}@usal.es
[2] Códice Software, Edificio Centro, Parque Tecnológico de Boecillo
47151, Valladolid, Spain
psantos1@codicesoftware.com

Abstract. This paper addresses the visualization of the collaboration history in the development of software items using a simple interactive representation called Revision Tree. The visualization presents detailed information on a single software item with the intention of supporting the awareness of the project managers and developers about the item evolution and the collaboration taking place on its development. We considered that repositories of Software Configuration Management tools are the best information source to extract relevant information dealing with the relationships between the programmers and software items, as well as information regarding the creation of baselines, branches and revisions, and useful date and time details for the arrangement of the development timeline and collaboration representation.

Keywords: Software Configuration Management (SCM), Information visualization, Focus + context, Time line, Polyfocal display, Interaction, Revision Tree.

1 Introduction

The software development process and the collaboration that it involves are difficult to understand and represent, due to the large number of software items that constitute a software product. Moreover, the collaboration taking place in the development of each item is concurrent and may be distributed across several geographical locations. Software Configuration Management (SCM) controls the evolution of complex systems [1] taking into consideration the communication at every level of the organization as well as the changes of code and documentation. To accomplish this purpose, the tools supporting such a process must provide services for the management of the component database, enhancing the environment of the developers, managing concurrency and collaboration, and recording changes including time, date, which modules were affected, how long the modification took and information about who did the change.

---

* This work was supported by the Education and Science Ministry of Spain under projects TSI2005-00960 and TIN2006-06313.

C. Baranauskas et al. (Eds.): INTERACT 2007, LNCS 4663, Part II, pp. 317–331, 2007.

The IEEE Standard 828-1990 [2] states that "SCM activities include the identification and establishment of baselines; the review, approval, and control of changes; the tracking and reporting of such changes; the audits and reviews of the evolving software product; and the control of interface documentation and project supplier SCM". Hence, the importance of SCM repositories as the information source to extract the collaboration activities taking place during project developments, as well as key information as the identification and establishment of baselines and revisions and the tracking of changes including dates and times. However, in spite of the richness of this data source and decades after the first SCM systems were released, there is an important lack of mechanisms with which to convey, by means of proper representations, how the contribution and collaboration of team members occurs in a particular project.

In recent years, the field of information visualization has played an important role in providing insight through visual representations combined with interaction techniques that take advantage of the human eye's broad bandwidth pathway to the mind, allowing experts to see, explore, and understand large amounts of information at once [3]. Traditionally, the software development process has been a subject of interest for information visualization practitioners. Thus, the software visualization community is providing excellent results which are being featured in main stream IDEs. Nevertheless SCM tools can still be enhanced by using highly interactive visualizations rather than mere "static" representations.

The interactive visual solution we propose in this paper considers both space and time strategies: the space strategy uses layout and graphic design to pack appropriate information in one view, while the time strategy uses view transitions to spread information over multiple views [4]. Additionally, we take into consideration several techniques to support navigation, interpretation of visual elements and understanding relationships among items in their full context [5].

There are also many information visualization techniques, each one with its advantages and disadvantages; the use of a sort of combination to provide a real solution to end users is very frequently required. Spence [6] and Card et al. [7] provide excellent surveys of information visualization mechanisms and techniques. We support our visualization through the use of a grid-based structure, selection, navigation, filtering and zoom interaction mechanisms, in addition to polyfocal display, a tree hierarchy (a directed graph) and a time line as visualization techniques.

We considered what is going on in the project in our design, who else is working on the project, what they are doing, how long they have been working on a revision, how their work may impact the work of others and the overall framework designed by Storey in [8] for describing the visualizations of human activities in software engineering.

This paper is devoted to present the first contribution to the SCM tool (PlasticSCM) developed by Códice Software (http://www.codicesoftware.com); an interactive 2D visualization, named Revision Tree, which allows visualizing the contributions of the team members, through several revisions, baselines and long periods of time, on the same item or document within the software project. This way, the rest of the paper is organized as follows: Section 2 reviews some related works applied to the visualization of software evolution and software visualization techniques; Section 3 discusses the design of the Revision Tree visualization; Section 4 analyzes a case study in which the results of the Revision Tree are compared with the ones offered by a 3D version tree present in the current version of PlasticSCM tool; and, finally, Section 5 discusses the conclusions and future work.

2 Related Work

Considerable work has been dedicated to study the software visualization and information visualization areas. Gracanin [9] states that Software Visualization is "a discipline that makes use of various forms of imagery to provide insight and understanding and to reduce complexity of the existing software system under consideration". As a consequence, it is important to identify the tasks that will be performed by the visualization as well as its scope and content, who the audience will be, what data source is going to be represented, how it will be represented, which medium will be used for the representation, the forms and techniques that will be used by the presentation and how the user is going to interact with the visualization.

Although we concentrate on the evolution of individual items and the collaboration of software teams on its development, in this section we will review some useful ideas that have been applied in the visual representation of Software Configuration Management tools repositories.

Xie et al. [10] list a set of questions that can be used to guide the design of visualizations of SCM tools repositories; for the purposes of this paper, it is relevant to determine which authors worked on the same file, when a modification was made and how many authors worked on the release of the system.

Moreover, Eick et al. [11] accurately state that a fundamental problem in visualizing software changes is to choose effective visual representations or metaphors and review some of them, as well as some combinations showing different data perspectives filtered by developer, basic statistics about changes, size of the changes, activity carry out by developer, etc.

Voinea and Telea [12] support the idea that software configuration management repositories are valuable for project accounting, development audits and understanding the evolution of software projects. We strongly agree with these authors about the richness of software repositories; thus, the effective design of the repository of SCM tools can provide information about the development process that is not possible to acquire from any other source and through a well-designed visualization, it is possible to navigate the repository data and get an insight of what is going on in the project. The same authors also propose two visualizations for software management configuration repositories in [13] and [14]. Those proposals demonstrated that the adequate use of 2D visualizations in conjunction with colors and textures contribute to the development of powerful multidimensional visualization solutions.

Gall et. al. [15] developed an interesting approach using 3D representations and color coding applied to software evolution through the time, thinking over structure and attribute changes. The attributes are the revision number, item size and complexity. This approach visualizes the version and each item attributes every time, using one color for each attribute.

There are several proposals addressing the representation of temporal spaces using many different structures. Morris et al. [16] worked with the visualization of temporal hierarchies plotting research documents along a horizontal track in the time line and placing related documents according to the hierarchical structure produced by the clustering phase. Card et al. [17] developed a visualization that allows exploring hierarchies that change with time by using searches, navigating through a hierarchical presentation and filtering results with the assistance of a time slider control. Therón [3] proposed a tree-ring metaphor to represent hierarchical time-based structures and applied it to browse and discover relationships in the history of computer languages. Kumar and Garland [18] proposed a solution for the visualization of time-varying graphs, where the users can slide to different time periods to explore the graph or discover trends interacting with the presentation.

The visualization presented by Lanza in [19] deals with the visualization of software attributes throughout the time using an evolution matrix with variable rectangular-sized boxes inside each cell; the width of the boxes represents the number of methods and the height the number of attributes in the class. This visualization method is powerful and could be improved borrowing some ideas about colors and textures from [15].

At this point, it is relevant to reference the work developed by Koike [20][21], which describes a representation, called VRCS, that shows the evolution of items from the repository of the software management configuration tool. On this visualization, each software item is represented by using two dimensions and the overall visualization with three dimensions, as illustrated in figure 1. This visualization will be analyzed further, in the presentation of the case study.

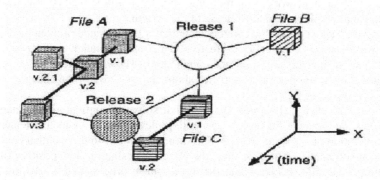

Fig. 1. Software history visualization using 3D presentation for several items

Finally, Perforce (http://www.perforce.com/) is a software configuration management system that includes a visualization module; a sample of which is displayed in figure 2. The visualization offered by this tool is two dimensional and uses a graph to show the relationships between baselines, branches and revisions. It features an overview + detail approach rather than a more convenient focus + context approach [22] and will also be discussed in section 4.

3 Revision Trees: Visualization of the Collaboration History of Software Items

In this section we propose a 2D representation for the collaboration history of software items. The Revision Tree was designed to visualize the contributions of the team members through several revisions, baselines and long periods of time, on the same item or document within the software project. In this context it is important to consider that the evolution of every software item implicitly holds a temporal attribute, which is the most important and critical element needed to understand the software development process of any system. The problem at hand presented several challenges that were addressed in the proposed visualization: the representation of large revision trees, where the baselines have several branches and each branch many

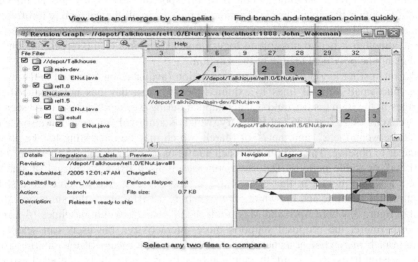

Fig. 2. Visualization of the evolution of a software item with Perforce

item revisions; the navigation through the version tree offering a focus + context view; support to interactivity to enable the inspection of more than one baseline at a time, exhibit the collaboration of developers for every baseline and correlate all the information with the time line. The full evolution is displayed for a complete analysis in figure 3 (it was turn around due to page constrains), and a piece of this representation is examined further in figure 4.

At this point, it is important to highlight that we decided to use a grid-based structure because it provides an intuitive mechanism to visualize the working relationship between authors and baselines by using the rows to represent the authors and the columns for the baselines (when changes expand during a number of baselines, the column is named after that interval of baselines). Moreover, grid and matrix structures are widely known by developers and the cells can be used as containers for the drawing of nodes of the directed graph representing the flow of revisions for the item.

Figure 3 depicts three sketches of the same revision tree and figure 4 shows a zoom through a piece of this design in order to better review the details. The first sketch (the one on the top) exposes the normal vista of the design; it uses variable width columns to accommodate the revisions in each baseline, the distribution of the rows is uniform, the first row is used for the baseline numbering, the second row represents the timeline and includes information about the date and hour of creation of a revision, the horizontal blue lines with arrows on both ends emphasize an individual day and the vertical blue lines indicate the end of one day; the dark blue small lines in between the parallel vertical blue lines point out the absence of work, the rounded rectangular nodes are used to emphasize the creation of branches and the orange line connecting the blue ovals outline the main code version. This sketch allows us to appreciate all the baselines and revisions of the item at a glance, as well as the relationships among baselines and the hierarchical association between baselines and revisions.

The second and third sketches show the use of the bifocal display expanding the column of the twelfth baseline and the row corresponding to Borja, while the information of the other baselines shrinks, keeping in the screen all the versioning information of the item and allowing us to concentrate on the area in which the item has more activity; although it is also possible to focus on several points of the representation at a time using the polyfocal feature of the solution.

An interesting key point of this representation (available on figure 4) is the use of dark blue small vertical lines to exhibit times when a day has not produced any changes in the item (as it would usually happen during weekends); this can be seen for the weekend of 25th and 26th of February, which is a normal situation, but also for the period between the 2nd and the 7th of March, which may be interesting for the project manager to observe. This simple approach allows us to discover intuitively these "nonworking" or stable periods. The same approach is used when the period of stability covers a whole month; in that case, a small, blue circle is used to represent a stable month in the timeline and the white-gray switching is maintained (this situation can be seen in figure 3, where April and May produced no changes within baselines 14-22).

Furthermore, the proposal supports more interactivity;, the users can select the main branch or regular branches of the application as a means of uncluttering complex revision trees; as a result, the application will bring out all its first level associations along the presentation, they can also select any node to highlight its connections. By means of the interaction, the representation can be modified in order to show the user the exact information he/she wants to see.

One of these interaction techniques in the proposed visualization is a focus + context technique: the use of variable width columns depending on the number of revisions in the baselines and the use of bifocal and polyfocal displays. The bifocal display consists of the capacity of the visualization to expand the rows and columns intersected in the area of interest; the polyfocal display has the same distortion behavior but allows focusing on more than one area.

On the other hand, filtering is another useful possibility: it may be interesting to have the same representation but for a particular period of time, or including only the information of selected developers.

We recommend reviewing all these design details carefully on figure 4 and use table 1 for a listing and description of the variables and visual elements in the representation.

When assessing the proposed Revision Tree, it becomes evident that it is possible to obtain a great amount of information at a glance and that a detailed explanation to discover data of relevance is not required; it is easy to follow up on contributions to the development of a software item and understand how it has evolved throughout. This visualization also provides useful information for project managers; they can become aware of who has been working most in the development of the item, if someone has quit or been fired from the company, as well as discover if the last revisions made by that programmer to the item were merged or if there is a merge that has never been done for any other reason. They can also get information about the periods

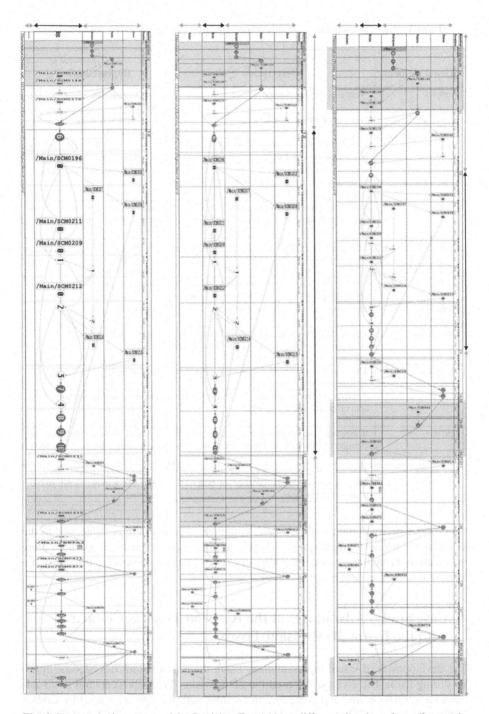

Fig. 3. Representation proposed for Revision Trees (three different situations depending on the interaction are shown).

Table 1. Visual elements and variables represented on the Revision Tree visualization

Visual element	Description	Representation
Authors	Names of the developers.	Label with the name of the developer.
Baseline	Number of the baselines.	It is displayed at the top of the visualization.
Date	It indicates the creation date of branches, baselines or revisions.	Label with the date. It is exhibited on the timeline.
Day column	It is the graphical space for the representation of a day having activity in the creation of branches, baselines or revisions.	A dark blue line with arrows on both ends.
Time	Shows the time when a new branch or revision has been created in the main branch or any other.	Label with the time. It is shown on the timeline.
New main branch	Indicates the creation of the main branch.	Purple large oval
New branch	It shows the creation of a new branch.	Yellow large oval
Main branch line	It highlights the main branch.	orange arrows
Arches	Connect the branches and revisions created by the developer working on the main branch.	Green arches.
Main branch revisions	Revisions created in the main branch.	Blue nodes
Branch line	The branch line connects the main branch with other branches and the revisions within that branch or between two branches.	Green arrows.
Revision	This symbol represents the creation of a new revision of the software item.	Yellow nodes
Merge	A merge occurs when one or more branches are combined with the branch.	Incoming arrows coming from other branches into the main branch.
Idle day	It denotes a day without any activity in the creation of baselines, branches or revisions.	A small vertical blue line in the timeline, for each day with no activity.
Idle month	This symbol represents an entire month without any activity in the creation of baselines, branches or revisions.	A small blue circle is used to represent a stable month in the timeline

with more activity in the component and recognize when the item is stable, due to the fact that it is not suffering frequent changes. At present, it is possible to get a lot more information through the careful checking of every visualization detail, particularly if a large real-life set of data is used.

4   Case Study: Advantages of the Revision Trees as Compared with the Use of 3D Revision Trees

The development of visual representations using three dimensions has become popular during the last few years. We used the 2D Revision Tree representation to visualize a large revision tree and compared the results with the ones produced by Códice Software's PlasticSCM and its visualization 3D version tree tool, VRCS and Perforce.

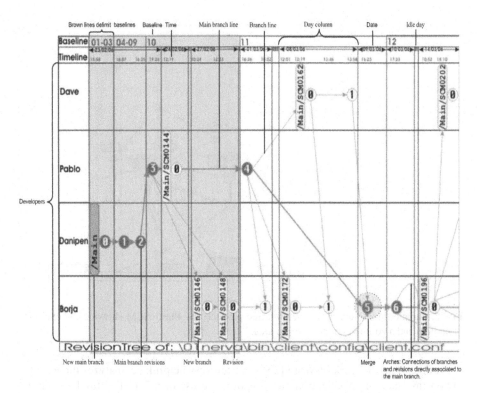

Fig. 4. Revision Tree layout showing all design features and the use of the bifocal display

Figure 5 shows the 3D version tree for the same example as the one shown in figure 3 and a zoom in for the first 11 baselines.

The 3D version tree is eye-catching; it has a line representing the main line of the development and green arrows showing the merge of revisions. Along with the nodes, there are labels indicating some information about the baselines and revisions. Although the representation is visually appealing, it shows a number of drawbacks, the first one being that it is a static representation: the user can only change the point of view or choose how far he/she is looking at it (i.e, it is only possible to turn around the tree and zoom into a region to get closer to a node or area). When zooming in, the size of the node increases and it is harder to manipulate the tree and the context is lost because the visualization lacks a context + focus view, so the user becomes disoriented; when we zoom out, the tree becomes a 3D shape with no special SCM meaning. Moreover, even after zooming in, you cannot see all the information represented due to occlusion; the front nodes hide the other nodes representing revisions.

Although the 2D revision tree performs better in a large screen, even a small space such as the one used in figure 3 (1 third of a page in a colored print out) can help the user to obtain a general idea of what was the evolution of a particular item.

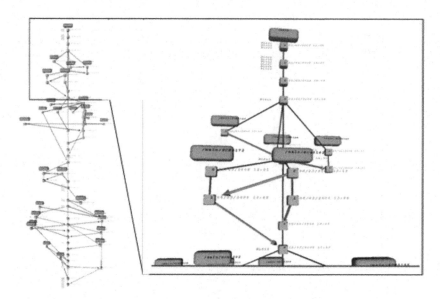

Fig. 5. Sample three dimensional version tree produced by PlasticSCM showing the evolution of an item and a zoom in on the selected area.

At this point, the work of Ware [23] has been very helpful: he analyzes the use of 3D on information visualization and proposes the use of a 2 1/2D attitude when designing representations. It basically addresses many of the drawbacks of 3D visualizations and suggests the use of 3D consciously in combination with 2D for producing better visualization solutions.

Before going on with our analysis, we will discuss some details VRCS and the Perforce visualization tool. Our main concerns with the visualizations presented in [19][20] and illustrated in figure 1 are the lack of a focus + context view, the navigation through the structure, and how it can behave with the presentation of complex systems due to the high processor and memory demands of three dimensional visualizations and occlusions. As we discussed above, the visualization of large revision histories for one item using the three dimensional version trees has some limitations. Therefore, the visualization of large repositories with many items containing lots of baselines and revisions would result in a very large hard to navigate visualization and probably would not provide, within a short time, the information required by the user.

Besides, the representation produced by Perforce (figure 2) offers an overview + detail approach, loosing this way a great amount of screen real state. It shows information about branching and merges and it is possible to obtain the date and time of revisions by clicking over the nodes and reviewing the information on the Details tab on the left panel. However, it does not provide information about the programmers contributing to the development of the item, how long the developers have been working on the item, nor in regards to periods without activity; furthermore, it is not possible to compare two baselines or see the time line at a first sight. In conclusion, this visualization is static and does not offer interaction options.

Table 2. Comparison of visualization tools for the representation of revision trees

Questions	PlasticSCM	VRCS	Perforce	Revision Tree
Does the visualization provide a focus + context view?			X	X
How many developers are participating in the development of the software item?				X
Who are the developers contributing to the evolution?				X
Who is the programmer with more contributions to the evolution of the item?				X
How many baselines constitute the whole evolution process?	X	X		X
Does the tool offer information about dates and times of the creation of baselines and revisions?			X	X
Is there a revision without been merged after a long time?			X	X
How long has been the development of the item?	X	X	X	X
Which baseline has more branches and revisions?				X
Which branch has more modification activity?			X	X
Which is the period of time that does not show any activity?				X
Is there a period when the item was stable and then suddenly started having a lot of activity?				X
Is it possible to compare baseline activity?				X

The table 2 presents a list of questions to compare the visualization tools discussed above with our design, showing an X mark when the tool demonstrate evidence of answering a question within a short time and little effort while visualizing a large version tree.

Currently, in order to show the validity of our proposal, we have implemented a prototype that features the main ideas exposed above. An incomplete evolution corresponding to the first twelve baselines of the software item, used as an example, is shown in figure 6. It is easy to realize that Borja has done many contributions on versions 10, 11 and 12 (it was rotated due to page constrains). Revision 1 pointed out by the node 4 in the main development line has not been merged, the development of the item started on February, 23rd and revision no. 11 was reached 15 days later; the baseline with more branches and revisions is number 12; branches 0162 and 0172 are tied into the number of revisions. There are two periods of time in which there is no activity in the item and whose dates are between February 24th - February 27th and March 1st – March 8th, also, the comparison between the baselines is immediate in this case, due to the short period of time under consideration.

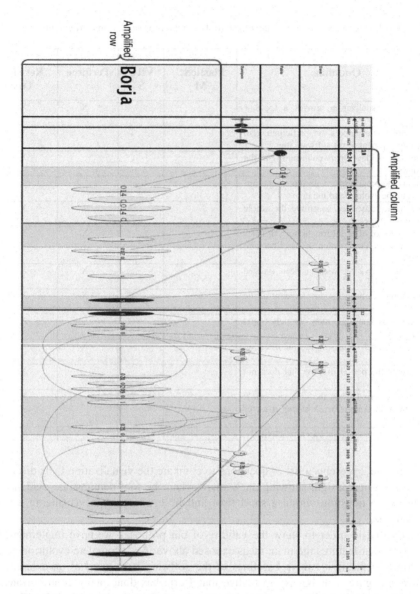

Fig. 6. Revision tree of the first twelve baselines of the overall evolution example

The brackets on the figure 6 highlight the use of bifocal display, the row corresponding to Borja has been amplified as well as the column associated to baseline 10, to show specific details. This figure also shows the use of a focus + context view; it allows getting information about specific areas while showing the general picture.

We consider that, after doing this comparison, our proposal is a valid representation for the visualization of revision trees and its complete development incorporating the features described in this paper as well as others that will result from its evaluation by users, and which will end in a powerful visualization easy to use and learn while providing the information needed by the users.

5 Conclusions

Revision Tree provides a focus + context view, a grid structure to which all programmers are familiar with, a timeline to guide and position users in time and space and several interaction possibilities to make the information the user needs available. With this presentation, the user can get many answers about how the evolution of the item is progressing and the team is always aware about who is working on the different baselines and revisions.

Whereas the visualization is always visible for all revisions, the users can review all the baselines and revisions in a very short period of time, therefore, there is no hidden information or an occlusion.

The timeline representation is clear, showing the complete time interval since the item was created, it also supports temporal comparisons and it made the concurrency of the programmers evident. Besides, the interactivity adds functionality to filter or focus on specific areas: in synthesis, the two-dimensional visualization offers a clear and functional presentation.

On the other hand, the three dimensional visualization does not support a focus + context view and only provides useful information at the detail level; to get the required information the user has to interact with the system for a long period of time. It allows the inspection of only one revision at a time, while nodes and labels could occlude the presentation at a general level.

The visualization presented in this paper shows enough evidence to state that for the representation of the evolution and collaboration in the development of software items a two dimensional representation offering several interaction possibilities can result in a powerful solution for the visualization of multidimensional data.

Future improvements will consider the improvement of interaction techniques, the use of linked views for the visualization of the directory structure of baselines and the comparison of several baseline structures. Furthermore, a usability test to compare the three dimensional representation and Revision Tree will be conducted.

There are other challenges also related with this problem; the representation of the collaboration between programmers and all the items stored in the repository of SCM tools.

References

1. Estublier, J.: Software Configuration Management: A Roadmap. ACM Press, New York (2000)
2. Berlack, H., Updike-Rumley, M.: IEEE standard for software configuration Manager plans (1990)

3. Theron, R.: Hierarchical-temporal Data Visualization using a Tree-ring Metaphor. In: Butz, A., Fisher, B., Krüger, A., Olivier, P. (eds.) SG 2006. LNCS, vol. 4073, pp. 70–81. Springer, Heidelberg (2006)
4. Mackinlay, J.D., Robertson, G.G., Card, S.K.: The perspective wall: detail and context smoothly integrated. In: CHI '91. Proceedings of the SIGCHI conference on Human factors in computing systems, pp. 173–176 (1991)
5. Leung, Y., Apperlley, M.: A review and taxonomy of distortion-oriented presentation techniques. ACM Transactions on Computer-Human Interaction 1(2), 126–160 (1994)
6. Spence, R.: Information Visualization. ACM Press, New York (2000)
7. Card, S.K., Mackinlay, J., Shneiderman, B.: Readings in Information Visualization: Using Vision to Think. Morgan Kaufman, Seattle, Washington (1999)
8. Storey, M.D., Cubranic, D., German, D.M.: On the use of visualization to support awareness of human activities in software development: a survey and a framework. In: Proceedings of the 2005 ACM symposium on Software visualization 2005, St. Louis, Missouri, May 14-15, pp. 193–202 (2005)
9. Gracanin, D., Matkovic, K., Eltoweissy, M.: Software visualization, Innovations in Systems and Software Engineering. A NASA Journal 1, 221–230 (2005)
10. Xie, X., Poshyvanyk, D., Marcus, A.: Visualization of cvs repository information. In: WCRE '06. Proceedings of the 13th Working Conference on Reverse Engineering (WCRE 2006), Washington, DC, USA, pp. 231–242. IEEE Computer Society, Los Alamitos (2006)
11. Eick, S.G., Graves, T.L., Karr, A.F., Mockus, A., Schuster, P.: Visualizing software changes. IEEE Trans. Softw. Eng. 28(4), 396–412 (2002)
12. Voinea, L., Telea, A.: An open framework for cvs repository querying, analysis and visualization. In: MSR '06. Proceedings of the 2006 international workshop on Mining software repositories, pp. 33–39. ACM Press, New York (2006)
13. Voinea, L., Telea, A.: Mining software repositories with cvsgrab. In: MSR '06. Proceedings of the 2006 international workshop on Mining software repositories, pp. 167–168. ACM Press, New York (2006)
14. Voinea, L., Telea, A.: Multiscale and multivariate visualizations of software evolution. In: SOFTVIS 2006. Association for Computing Machinery Inc. (2006b)
15. Gall, H., Jazayeri, M., Riva, C.: Visualizing software release histories: The use of color and third dimension. In: ICSM '99. Proceedings of the IEEE International Conference on Software Maintenance, Washington, DC, USA, p. 99. IEEE Computer Society, Los Alamitos (1999)
16. Morris, S.A., Yen, G., Wu, Z., Asnake, B.: Time line visualization of research fronts. Journal of the American Society for Information Science and Technology 54, 413–422 (2003)
17. Card, S., Suh, B., Pendleton, B., Heer, J., Bodnar. J. TimeTree: Exploring Time Changing Hierarchies. IEEE Symposium on Visual Analytics Science and Technology (2006).
18. Kumar, G., Garland, M.: Visual Exploration of Complex Time-Varying Graphs. IEEE Transactions on Visualization and Computer Graphics 12(5) (2006)
19. Lanza, M.: The evolution matrix: recovering software evolution using software visualization techniques. In: IWPSE '01. Proceedings of the 4th International Workshop on Principles of Software Evolution, pp. 37–42. ACM Press, New York (2001)
20. Koike, H.: The role of another spatial dimension in software visualization. ACM Trans. on Information Systems 11(3), 266–286 (1993)

21. Koike, H., Chu, H.-C.: VRCS: Integrating version control and module management using interactive 3d graphics. In: VL '97. Proceedings of the 1997 IEEE Symposium on Visual Languages (VL '97), Washington, DC, USA, IEEE Computer Society, Los Alamitos (1997)

22. Rao, R., Card, S.K.: The table lens: merging graphical and symbolic representations interactive focus + context visualization for tabular information. In: CHI '94. Proceedings of SIGCHI conference on Human factors in computing systems, pp. 318–322. ACM Press, New York (1994)

23. Ware, C.: Designing with a 2 1/2D Attitude. Information Design Journal 10(3), 255–262 (2001)

Enhancing Interactivity in an Online Learning Environment

Luciane Maria Fadel and Mary C. Dyson

The University of Reading. Department of Typography & Graphic Communication
2 Earley Gate, Whiteknights, Reading, RG6 6AU, UK
+ 44 118 9312107
luciane_fadel@hotmail.com, m.c.dyson@rdg.ac.uk

Abstract. This study focuses on of the use of animation to alert students to incoming messages and system updates in an online environment. It describes an experiment which compares an animation- and a text-based interface in terms of how the students perceived the alerting system. Relationships between the number of interactions, performance, and perceived social presence are examined. The results indicate that the animation-based interface group interact more than the text-based interface group and perceptions of social presence might be stronger for those students who post more messages. In addition, the results suggest that those students who perceived a stronger social presence also performed better. These findings have implications for designing online course environments where the design of the interface should be considered as a variable that enhances social presence.

Keywords: interactivity, social presence, animation, online environment.

1 Introduction

The wide use of computer networks to deliver education on the one hand and the emergence of people-centred online education on the other hand has dramatically increased the demand for systems that support social interaction [1,2]. Much of the effort to enhance the participation and interaction of people has taken tools focus (e.g., chat tools, bulletin boards, instant messaging) rather than interface design focus that is crucial for the success of any computer application [3]. In particular, the user interfaces of many online learning systems suffer from their web page origins. The design of interfaces for online learning applications offers many more challenges than the design of web pages, because information that is not relevant for web pages has to be integrated [4]. The interface must provide information about others to efficiently support social interactions – it must enhance social presence [5]. Social presence in this study is defined as the extent to which virtual entities, which represent others, are perceived as real in an online learning environment.

This paper explores the design of interfaces to present system feedback which might enhance social presence in online learning applications. More specifically, this paper discusses the design, implementation and evaluation of an alerting system based on animation and another based on text in order to promote interactivity.

C. Baranauskas et al. (Eds.): INTERACT 2007, LNCS 4663, Part II, pp. 332–344, 2007.

Interactivity is a dimension associated with social presence and includes the communication style and learning activities in which the users engage [6]. One of the most important components that affects interactivity is response time. When an expected response is not received a feeling of low interactivity is generated, thus diminishing the perceived social presence. Therefore, animations alerting students to incoming messages and system updates might contribute to the perception of responses, thereby increasing interactivity and perceived social presence.

This experiment investigates the use of animation to alert participants to incoming messages and system updates. Incoming messages encompass new instant mailing, web mail or forum messages while system updates are related to modifications to the agenda, tasks page or lecture content.

A number of studies have shown that the human visual system is extremely sensitive to the motion of objects [7-11]. It is hypothesised that animation might attract participants' attention without disturbing them. If too much information is presented, it might become difficult for the students to concentrate on the essential aspects of their study [12]. However, animation might be introduced to support interactivity without generating information overload or having a disruptive effect.

2 Animation

2.1 Perception of Animation

Animation might be used to attract the attention of the students because the perception of motion is crucial from an evolutionary point of view. The eye has evolved to function essentially as a motion-detecting system [13]. For example, a camouflaged animal might not be noticed until it moves [14].

Animation uses the principle that the mind fills in the gaps between frames when a rapid series of still images are presented. The illusion of continuous motion is called apparent motion [10]. Ramachandran and Anstis [10] suggest that the visual system applies strategies that limit the number of matches the brain needs to consider to detect which parts of a successive image reflect a single object in motion. Among the features that the visual system might attempt to extract from images Ramachandran and Anstis [10] found that brightness and texture serve as cues for detecting correspondence. Correspondence means that the visual system must determine which parts of successive images reflect a single object in motion. In this case, introducing animation of an object by altering its brightness might not generate information overload because the visual systems tends to match areas of similar brightness before it detects more detailed outlines. Thus, animation based on changing brightness could be used to direct students' attention to a specific point of the interface without generating information overload.

2.2 The Effects of Animation

The literature on audio-visual communication contains many references to the effects on learning that occur when animation is used to represent information. Animation may enhance descriptive and procedural text [13-16]. Large, Beheshti, Breuleux, & Renaud [14-16] indicated that the presence of animation can help students to understand a text which outlines a series of steps that must be undertaken to achieve a goal. In addition, they suggest that animation is likely to be most effective when combined with text whose content is related to motion. Animation may concentrate attention on those aspects of a text which deal with motion. A similar recommendation is made by Rieber [17, 18]. The experimental evidence brought together by Rieber led him to recommend that animation should be used when visualisation, motion or trajectory are needed for successful completion of an instructional task. Although the use of animation as an alerting system differs in nature to animation as illustration of text, the idea of motion is implicit. In this case the actual state of the system is altered by an incoming message or update.

Although the findings of Large, Beheshti, Breuleux, & Renaud and Rieber support the use of animated graphics to present information better than static display, Morrison, Tversky and Betrancourt [19] argue that the findings are due to greater information in the animations than in the static display. This means that if the animation and static display had the same amount of information, the results could be less encouraging. Morrison, Tversky and Betrancourt [19] suggest two principles specifying conditions for successful animated graphics. The Principle of Apprehension which establishes that animation must be readily perceived, and the Principle of Expression which establishes that conceptual knowledge to be conveyed must be apparent from animation.

These two principles specify conditions that the animation must fulfil in order to be successful. One condition is that the animation must be readily perceived. In order to achieve this, the animation was produced in a simple manner by altering button sizes and/or brightness. The other condition states that conceptual knowledge should be apparent from the animation. The conceptual knowledge associated with the animation in this experiment was that a new message had arrived or the system had been updated. To make this idea apparent, the animation was conceived to represent the change in the system. To test if the animation was simple and communicated the change in the system a pilot study was carried out [20]. The results of the pilot study suggested that:

1. The animation did not cause disruption;
2. The contrast of the circular sections should be enhanced, and;
3. The tutor's messages should have the highest priorities.

3 The Aim of This Experiment

A series of experiments were designed to study the relationship between the interface design and social interaction among students in an online learning environment [21-24]. This experiment reports the findings of the fifth in the series.

The aim of this experiment is to compare two different interfaces to an online course, one based on text, referred to as the text-based interface and the other based on animation, referred to as the animation-based interface. Measurements are made of perceived social presence, and the number of interactions.

The following hypotheses were tested:

1. Alerting the participants to incoming messages and system updates using an animation-based interface results in a greater number of interactions among students compared to the number of interactions with a text-based interface.
2. Alerting the participants to incoming messages and system updates using an animation-based interface results in a stronger social presence compared to the social presence perceived by the students with a text-based interface.
3. The degree of social presence perceived by participants is positively related to the quantity of their interactions. This means that a greater number of interactions correlates with a stronger degree of social presence.
4. The performance of participants is positively related to the degree of social presence. This means that a stronger degree of social presence correlates with a better performance.

4 Experimental Plan

4.1 Interface Design

The interfaces used in this experiment were developed in a previous experiment [21] and were modified in this experiment to present an alerting system. In the text-based interface the alerting system is represented using text (see Fig 1). The text is located below the grey bar in the same column as the bulletin board.

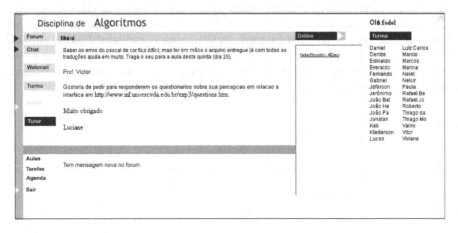

Fig 1. Home page for the text-based interface showing the text '*Tem mensagem nova no Forum*' (There is a new forum message) alerting the students to new forum message

The animation-based interface uses animated buttons to alert students to incoming messages and system updates. A priority is associated with each button. This means that only one animated button will be shown each time the user reaches the home page (see Fig 2).

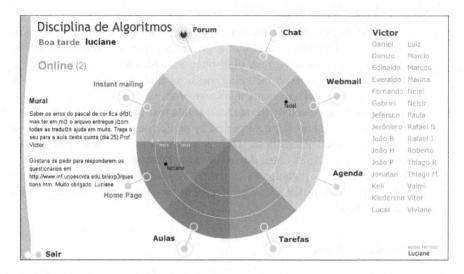

Fig. 2. Home page for the animation-based interface showing an animated forum button alerting the students to new forum posting

The Animated Button

Fig. 3 shows a storyboard for the animated buttons. Modifying the size of a copy of the button's external circle and the colour of the button's internal circle creates the animation. The copy of the circle was used so the original form of the button was not modified. The copy of the grey external circle's radius is increased from its original size until it touches the circular sector. There is also an increase in the size of the contour and brightness of this circle. The increasing size of the external circle might look like the concentric waves caused by a stone thrown into the water.

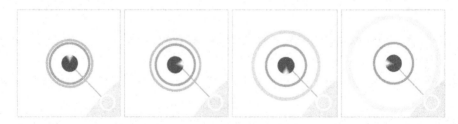

Fig. 3. Storyboard of animated button 4 frames showing the increasing size of the grey circle and the increasing brightness

The colour of the internal circle is dark red and a bright triangular shape rotates 360°. The internal circle is red for incoming instant mailing, web mail and forum messages and blue for system updates buttons, i.e., changes in the agenda, tasks and lecture contents. The red colour used in the internal circle might be associated with something important, while the rotation of the triangular shape might remind the participants of a radar form which searches for something new.

4.2 Participants

The course 'Algorithm' is a mandatory course offered to 1st year Computer Science students at the Universidade do Oeste de Santa Catarina (UNOESC) in Videira, Brazil. Thirty students were recruited for the experiment. The sample consisted of six women and twenty-four men. Participants were assigned to use one of the two interfaces such that equal numbers of participants used the text-based interface (15 students) and the animation-based interface (15 students). The criteria used to assign the students to groups were age, gender and the report from the tutor about each student's previous performance in another course. The aim in assigning students to groups was to ensure that, as far as possible, both groups were equivalent in terms of these factors (age, gender and level of performance).

4.3 Data Collection Procedures

Data was collected using a questionnaire, participants' grades and system logs. The questionnaire collected perceptions of social presence from the students. The system logs included data from the Web server access log (name of the user, date and time), pages visited and messages exchanged (content, sender, receiver). Using these logs it is possible to record the number of interactions (messages sent and received), the content of messages, and number of page hits for each individual page. Students' performance in this experiment was measured by their final grades which are the total points the student received during the course. The tutor was responsible for marking and assessments.

4.4 Questionnaire Content

The items of the questionnaire used to assess the perception of social presence in this experiment was developed iteratively, based on previously published research, piloting the questionnaire and analysing data from previous experiments [21,22] . The aim was to design a questionnaire concise which assessed the students' perception of the presence of the others supported by the interface in an online learning environment.

The questionnaire consisted of 7 items and aimed to find out the degree of social presence sensed by the students, investigating their perceptions about feelings of being part of a group and group belonging. Indicators of their feeling of being part of a group were obtained from the first four items. Indicators of group belonging were obtained from the last three items. The seven items used to assess each participant's perceptions of social presence were a set of statements with which students were asked to agree or disagree. The responses used a five-point Likert-scale where 1=strongly disagree, 2=disagree, 3=neither disagree nor agree, 4=agree, 5=strongly agree. A scale of five points was chosen because it encompasses a clear set of options. The wording of statements varied so that agreement might indicate either a strong or a weak sense of social presence. This was done to try to ensure that each question was read, rather than the same response ticked for each item. This questionnaire was answered at the end of the course.

4.5 Procedure

The course was structured around reading and weekly discussions. In addition, practical tasks were required which were designed to get students to use their acquired knowledge. The tasks were related to the week's topic. The tasks could be an essay or developing an algorithm based on the theory. The students were supposed to work alone but they could ask for help from the other students or from the tutor using email, forum or chat.

The course was organised into fifteen weeks. During the first four weeks the course was delivered using face-to-face meetings at the University. The next five weeks the course was delivered in the form of distance learning using the site. After that, the students had one face-to-face meeting at the University followed by four weeks of online meetings. The last lecture was a face-to-face meeting.

One week before the first online meeting the students were trained to use the interfaces. The tutor explained to each group separately what they were supposed to do, how they should study, how they would be assessed and how to use the environment. In addition, the groups were aware of the same functionalities of the different interfaces. Finally, the experiment was explained and they were asked to sign a consent form as part of the University of Reading's Research Ethics Committee procedure.

When the course was delivered online, the lecture's topic was presented to the students using the online learning environment. The students had a week to read the material and to prepare the tasks. On Thursdays they met in a chat session to discuss the topic. The completed tasks were sent to the tutor using web mail. The chat sessions were scheduled for Thursday evenings and lasted for two to three hours depending on how many questions the students had.

The chat sessions used a chat room on a different server from the environment because the system chat did not support the whole group at the same time. Both groups used this chat room outside the online learning environment. The chat room used is located at http://batepapo.bol.com.br/Outrostemas/Computacao1. This chat room had no restricted access and therefore unfortunately allowed people other than the students to participate in the chat session. The messages exchanged among these non-students and the students were discarded.

5 Results

The results are organised in four sections. The first two sections describe the results from the groups separately. These results are considered in relation to hypotheses 1 and 2. These hypotheses concern the relationship between the use of text and the use of animation to alert participants to incoming messages and system updates, and the number of interactions and social presence. The last two sections describe the results from both groups combined and these results are used to evaluate hypotheses 3 and 4.

These hypotheses deal with the relationship between social presence, number of interactions and performance.

5.1 Number of Postings

The text-based interface group sent a total of 158 messages during the course. These postings were produced via chat (106), forum (17), web mail (21) and instant mailing (14). The total number of postings of individual students in this group ranged from 0 to 43 with a mean of 12.1.

The animation-based interface group sent a total of 502 messages during the course. These postings were produced via chat (208), forum (10), web mail (44) and instant mailing (240). The total number of postings by individual students for the course ranged from 0 to 75 with a mean of 38.6.

The number of postings in chat, web mail and instant mailing is higher for the animation-based interface group. A t test to examine the differences between the total means found t = 3.63 (26df, $p<0.05$) and it is therefore concluded that the mean number of postings from the animation-based interface is significantly more than from the text-based interface group.

The animation-based interface group sent many more messages using the instant mailing feature than the text-based interface group. There were a total of 240 messages posted using the instant mailing feature for the animation-based interface group against 14 for the text-based interface group (t= 4.36, 26df, $p<0.001$).

The number of messages posted via web mail was 44 for the animation-based interface group and only 21 for the text-based interface group. Almost all the messages (total of 18) posted by the text-based interface group were replies to original messages originated by the animation-based interface group using the instant mailing.

5.2 Text- and Animation-Based Interfaces and Social Presence

The groups did not differ significantly in relation to the perceived social presence and it is therefore concluded that there is no difference in the perceived social presence between groups.

5.3 Number of Postings and Degree of Social Presence

Table 2 shows the number of postings and the degree of social presence. There were a total of 660 postings during the course. This total includes all the messages exchanged between students and between student and tutor but does not include the postings from the tutor. These postings were produced via chat (314), forum (27), web mail (65) and instant mailing (254). There is a low correlation between the number of postings and the degree of social presence across the two groups, with a correlation coefficient (r) of 0.2, which is not statistically significant (t=1.09, 24df, $p>0.05$). However, Fig 3 illustrates a positive significant relationship between the number of instant mail postings and the perceived social presence for the animation-based interface group (t=2.24, 11df, $p<0.05$).

Table 1. Number of postings and degree of social presence

Text-based interface group			Animation-based interface group		
Student	Number of postings	Social presence	Student	Number of postings	Social presence
1.	0	2.7	1.	64	4.0
2.	1	3.4	2.	23	2.6
3.	2	3.3	3.	51	3.3
4.	1	3.7	4.	15	4.0
5.	20	3.3	5.	30	3.7
6.	9	3.1	6.	39	3.3
7.	6	3.7	7.	26	2.9
8.	29	3.7	8.	24	2.9
9.	43	4.3	9.	49	2.5
10.	0	2.4	10.	69	3.9
11.	5	2.9	11.	17	2.9
12.	2	3.0	12.	20	3.3
13.	40	3.3	13.	75	4.3
Total	**158**	-	**Total**	**502**	-
Mean	**12.1**	**3.3**	**Mean**	**38.3**	**3.4**
SD	**15.6**	**0.5**	**SD**	**20.8**	**0.6**

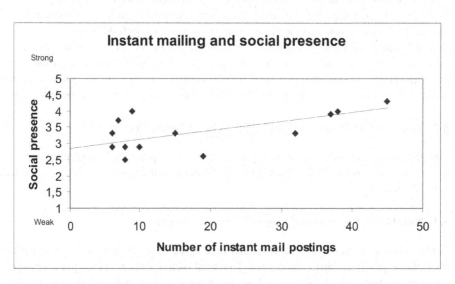

Fig. 3. Scatter diagram illustrating correlation between the number of instant mail postings and the perceived social presence for the animation-based interface group

5.4 Degree of Social Presence and Performance

Students' performance in this study was measured by their final grades which are the total points the student received during the course. Point scores for each graded item (participation, tasks and exam) were converted to a grade point (GP) scale. The participation score (PS) was the sum of grade points from the number of messages related to the subject posted at forum, instant mailing, web mail and the number of chat sessions the students participated in.

The overall grade for the course is calculated based on a weighted average, as follows: Final grade=0.3*(participation GP)+0.2*(tasksGP)+0.5*(Final Exam GP).

Those participants who did not answer the questionnaire on perceived social presence were not considered in the correlation between performance and social presence. Fig 4 shows a significant relationship between the degree of social presence and the student's performance with a correlation coefficient (r) of 0.48 (t=2.7, 24df, p<0.05). This means that those students who perceived a stronger social presence also performed better.

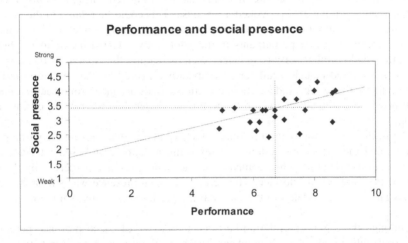

Fig. 4. Scatter diagram illustrating correlation between the degree of social presence and student's performance represented by their final grades

A more detailed analysis of the relationship between performance and social presence shows that there is a correlation between the task grade points and perceived social presence with a correlation coefficient (r) of 0.53 (t=3.04, 24df, p<0.05) and between the exam grade points and perceived social presence with a correlation coefficient (r) of 0.48 (t=2.7, 24df, p<0.05).

It was expected that those students who perceived a stronger social presence also performed better because the students were supposed to work together to solve tasks. To solve the tasks the students might have used the instant mailing feature to discuss a topic or to organise 'who does what'. In this case, interacting more might have contributed to a higher grade and a better performance. This assumption is based on the number of messages and further analysis on content of the messages should be carried out to establish causation.

6 Discussion

The purpose of this experiment was to compare a text-based interface with an animation-based interface to alert participants to incoming messages in an online course.

The results do suggest that alerting the participants to incoming messages and system updates using an animation-based interface results in a greater number of interactions among students compared to the number of interactions with a text-based interface. This suggestion is based on the fact that the animation-based interface group send more messages than the text-based interface group which might be related to animation directing students' attention to a specific point in the interface. The students responded to the animation by selecting the animated button and consequently posting messages. This sequence of actions might have been facilitated because the animated buttons appeared only in the home page from where other pages should be selected. In this case there were no other elements competing with their attention, such as, the content of the lecture. It seems that the animated button not only directed students' attention but also provoked a response. This could be related to the fact that the only way of stopping the animation is responding to it by selecting the animated button. Considering that participants in the pilot study selected the animated button when they had no other activity planned, such as reading the content of the next lecture, it is assumed that this call for participation triggered by the animation did not cause a disruptive effect. Indeed, the animation-based interface group seemed not be disturbed by the animation since they performed better than the text-based interface group.

The results of this study do not support the hypothesis that alerting the participants to incoming messages and system updates using an animation-based interface promotes a strong social presence compared to the social presence perceived by the students with a text-based interface. The perceived social presence was similar for both groups and might be related to the fact that the participants shared some face-to-face courses.

Although there is no correlation between the degree of social presence perceived by participants and the overall number of postings there is a correlation between the degree of social presence perceived by animation-based interface group and the quantity of their instant mail messages. This result might be related to the fact that the instant mailing feature is a service for exchanging messages between two online students. Thus, an instant mail message usually asks for an immediate reply. The message exchanging increases the interactivity and consequently the perception of the receiver/sender as a real participant.

The results showed that the performance of participants is positively related to the degree of social presence. This means that a stronger degree of social presence correlates with a better performance. Social presence appears to have a positive effect on performance because the students who perceived a stronger social presence might have the opportunity to cooperate with their peers to complete their tasks. If they perceived the presence of the others they might have felt more inclined to share experiences which would increase their task points and consequently exam grade points. These findings support prior research that established a correlation between perceived social presence and written assignments [25]. However, autonomous students who perform better in online learning environments also prefer immediate communication like for example instant mailing. Immediate communication is associated with a stronger social presence [26]. This means that good students might choose ways of communicating that enhance the perceived social presence.

7   Conclusion and Future Work

This study had shown that animation alerting the students to incoming messages results in a greater number of web mail and instant mail messages. The results also indicated that a greater number of instant mail messages had a positive effect on the perceived social presence. In addition, the students who perceived a stronger social presence performed better in tasks and written exams.

Future work should investigate social presence when the students do not have other courses with a face-to-face approach. In this case, the sense of presence would be informed only by the online experience and not influenced by their 'real life' relationships. In addition, the findings reported in this paper indicate that the students behave differently using different interfaces. Previous research has indicated that social presence is perceived differently by each user. Potentially research could include the creation of design solutions that are responsive to dynamic changes in information and the user's intention, i.e. adaptive interfaces.

The results of this experiment indicate that the design of interfaces should be carefully considered in the development of online learning environments. Students' behaviour may be driven by the interface design. These findings have implications for designing online course environment where the design of the interface plays a crucial role in enhancing social presence.

Acknowledgments. This study was sponsored by CNPq Brazil.

References

1. Anderson, T.: Getting the mix right again: An updated and theoretical rationale for Interaction. International Review of Research in Open. and Distance Learning 4(2) (2003)
2. McInnerney, J.M.: Online learning: Social interaction and the creation of a sense of community. Educational Technology & Society 7(3), 73–81 (2004)
3. Jung, Y., Lee, A.: Design of social interaction environment for electronic marketplaces. In: DIS'00 - Designing Interactive Systems: Processes, Practices, Methods, Techniques, ACM Press, New York (2000)
4. Kreijns, K., Kirschner, P.A., Jochems, W.: The sociability of computer-supported collaborative learning environments. Educational Technology & Society 5(1), 1–19 (2002)
5. Lee, A., et al.: Fostering social interaction in online spaces. In: INTERACT 2001, IOS Press, Amsterdam (2001)
6. Tu, C.-H., McIsaac, M.: The relationship of social presence and interaction in online classes. The. American Journal of Distance Education 16(3), 131–150 (2002)
7. Cutting, J.E.: Perception with an eye for motion. The MIT Press, Cambridge, Massachusetts (1986)
8. Imura, T., et al.: Perception of motion trajectory from the moving cast shadow in human infants. Vision Research 46, 652–657 (2006)
9. Limoges, S., Ware, C., Knight, W.: Displaying correlations using position, motion, point size or point colour. In: Graphics Interface (1989)
10. Ramachandran, V.S., Anstis, S.M.: The perception of apparent motion. Scientific American 254(6), 80–87 (1986)
11. Johansson, G.: Visual motion perception. Scientific American 232, 76–89 (1975)

12. Sohlenkamp, M.: Supporting group awareness in multi-user environments through perceptualization, in Dept. of Computer Science. Paderborn: Sankt Augustin, Germany. p. 151 (1998)

13. Large, M.-E., Aldcroft, A., Vilis, T.: Perceptual continuity and the emergence of perceptual persistence in the ventral visual pathway. Journal of Neurophysiology 93, 3453–3462 (2005)

14. Large, A., et al.: Multimedia and comprehension: a cognitive study. Journal of the American Society for Information Science 45(7), 515–528 (1994)

15. Large, A., et al.: Multimedia and comprehension: the relationship among text, animation, and captions. Journal of the American Society for Information Science 46(5), 340–347 (1995)

16. Large, A., et al.: Effect of animation in enhancing descriptive and procedural texts in a multimedia learning environment. Journal of the American Society for Information Science 47(6), 437–448 (1996)

17. Rieber, L.: Animation in Computer-Based Instruction. Educational Technology Research and Development 38(1), 77–86 (1990)

18. Rieber, L.: Using computer animated graphics in science instruction with children. Journal of Educational Psychology 82, 135–140 (1990)

19. Morrison, J.B., Tversky, B., Betrancourt, M.: Animation: Does It Facilitate Learning? International Journal of Human Computer Studies 57(4), 247–262 (2002)

20. Fadel, L.M., V.F. Jr.: Enhancing interactivity using animation to alert students to incoming messages. In: ICBL2007, Florianopolis, SC (2007)

21. Fadel, L., Dyson, M.C.: Comparing a text- and visual-based interface presenting social information in an online environment. In: IEEE Symposium on Visual Languages and Human-Centric Computing, Brighton, UK (2006)

22. Fadel, L., Licheski, L., Paz, L.: A comparison of the complexity in the perception of social information in text and visual-based interfaces. In: ICOS 2006. interfacing society, technology and organisations: The International Conference on Organisational Semiotics, Campinas, Brazil (2006)

23. Fadel, L.M., Dyson, M.: The effect of interface design on the enhancement of social presence in online courses. In: ICL2006., Kassef University Press, Villach, Austria (2006)

24. Fadel, L.M., Dyson, M.C.: A Comparison of the perception of social information in text and visual-based interfaces. In: 12th International Conference on Technology Supported Learning & Training - Online Educa Berlin, Germany (2006)

25. Picciano, A.G.: Beyond student perceptions: issues of interaction, presence, and performance in an online course. JALN 6(1), 21–40 (2002)

26. Tu, C.-H.: The impacts of text-based CMC on online social presence. Journal of Interactive Online Learning 1(2), 1–24 (2002)

Reading Companion: A Interactive Web-Based Tutor for Increasing Literacy Skills

Keith Grueneberg[1], Amy Katriel[1], Jennifer Lai[1], and Jing Feng[2]

[1] IBM T.J. Watson Research, 19 Skyline Drive Hawthorne, NY 10532
[2] Fordham University, New York, NY 10023
{kgruen, amygk, jlai}@us.ibm.com, jfeng@fordham.edu

Abstract. This paper discusses learnings from the development of Reading Companion, a web-based system that uses speech recognition technology to help children and adults increase their literacy skills. An animated tutor character both 'speaks' and 'listens' to the reader, guiding them as they read e-books selected by their teacher from a virtual library. The system creates detailed performance reports for each student and because it is available on the internet, the learners can continue reading where they left off once they get home to share their progress with their family. We discuss implementation challenges that were overcome, as well as feedback from users and teachers. To our knowledge this is the first successful implementation of real-time interactive speech recognition using Flash on the internet. We believe this presents a valuable model of how speech can be used on the web as part of interactive applications.

Keywords: Literacy, web, speech recognition, animated tutor character.

1 Introduction

Approximately 90 million adults in the United States have limited literacy skills [4]. The key to increasing literacy skills is practice, and successful practice requires immediate feedback. The concept of using speech recognition technology as an aide to improving reading skills has been around for a decade; however none of the earlier solutions were available through secure access on the worldwide web. Previous applications [e.g. 1, 2, 5] required CD-ROM installation of the software. Watch Me! Read, [3] was the precursor to Reading Companion, using speech recognition with an interactive tutor to lead the student through the process. Like other solutions of its ilk, it required a CD-ROM installation. A lack of centralized results required teachers to go to each computer in the classroom to view student results, and for each student to use the same machine every time. Further, students could not continue their work at home and have those results appended to the results acquired at school. Reading Companion (RC) is a web-based literacy solution that addresses these problems. It has recently been made freely available through grants to not-for-profit organizations such as elementary schools and adult learning centers, operating in over 200 sites with almost 10,000 registered users.

C. Baranauskas et al. (Eds.): INTERACT 2007, LNCS 4663, Part II, pp. 345 – 348, 2007.

2 Reading Companion

Reading Companion engages students with an animated character who provides help-ful instruction on how to interact with the e-book (e.g. "ok, now you read the words in red") and 'listens' to the reader using speech recognition technology, providing real-time feedback to emerging readers (e.g. "you sound great"). A screen shot of the ap-plication is shown in Figure 1. Automatic changes in scaffolding levels, where the tutor reads more for novice readers and less for more advanced readers, make the same books accessible for different levels of readers.

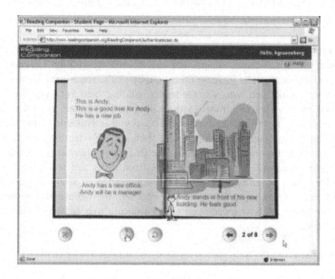

Fig. 1. An online e-book for adults

Speech recognition over the web can be accomplished either by deploying a speech recognizer on a server and sending the compressed speech over the network, or by embedding the speech capabilities in the browser and doing the decoding locally. Server-based speech recognition systems are optimized for telephony applications (i.e. automated phone answering systems), but do not work as well for web browser-based applications. Calls from a web client to a server-based recognizer are subject to latency problems due to the cost of transmitting audio over a network. An initial ver-sion of Reading Companion (RC) that used a server-based recognizer revealed laten-cies in schools that varied from 1 to 32 seconds. As a result, we had to re-architect the system to use an embedded speech recognizer rather than a server-based recognizer. RC uses a lightweight VoiceXML browser that is launched from Internet Explorer (or Firefox), which allows communication directly from Flash to the speech recognizer. This browser, runs on top of the IBM Embedded ViaVoice engine. To our knowledge this is the first time speech recognition has been embedded into a browser and used interactively on the web as part of a Flash application.

When a user accesses Reading Companion for the first time, they are prompted to download the speech software using a browser plug-in. The speech recognizer runs in the background as a student is reading. Because the application knows what words are displayed on the page that is being presented, it can load a dynamic vocabulary, which creates very accurate speech recognition even for people with heavily accented English. Sample data collected in the field, showed a word error rate of 6.7% for the adult speech engine, and 4.6% for the child engine. Currently, when the companion 'speaks' the audio consists of pre-recorded human speech. This speech is recorded at the time the book is created. All speech recognition takes place on the client and the data for RC is stored on a centralized server. The DB2 database stores information on each student's performance, registration data, classroom settings, user session data (e.g. where the student left off in the book), as well as the book library.

The teacher, or a computer admin person, usually sets up RC on all the machines since first and second grade students are not sufficiently literate, in either computer or reading skills, to follow even the simple directions (e.g. click here to download). Each student had his/her own headset with microphone, and they log in by picking their name from a list of students. The reader (either adult or child) is presented with a library of books that the teacher has pre-selected for the class. Usually the teacher will also direct the student which book to pick since often these correspond to concepts or vocabulary that is currently being taught in class. Adult learners are presented with books geared toward things like finding employment, getting a driving license or gaining American citizenship. They receive feedback reading in English, obtain the necessary vocabulary to find a job, and increase their computer skills (e.g. mouse usage). Since RC is available on the internet, students can continue to access it from home. Reading Companion saves the user's session on the web server, so they can continue reading wherever they left off in school.

3   Feedback from Users

Similar to reading with a parent or teacher, the companion character provides support by modeling words (i.e. reading to the student), highlighting the text to be read, and giving both encouragement and immediate feedback. We use a panda character while the adults now interact with a stick-like figure (see Figure 2). Initial software trials used a character for adults shaped like a microphone who 'spoke' even though it did not have a mouth and it said things like "Click on my picture to start reading". It also 'listened' even thought it had no ears, and thus suffered from a credibility problem. We observed that the majority of our adult immigrant users would click on all pictures in the book in response to the instruction "click on my picture", without realizing that the microphone was talking about itself! The switch to a character which was more suggestive of human characteristics (such as ears and a mouth) alleviated all traces of this confusion.

Fig. 2. Adult, child and microphone characters

Tutoring applications need an effective way of modeling the student's progress, so that the system can adapt to the student's current skill level. The RC student model incorporates an extensive dictionary of words that are mapped to sound spellings (e.g. the silent "e" rule) and word features (e.g. consonant blends). The system stores results for each student in a database, and as the reader improves, less scaffolding is provided. The scaffolding levels are automatically adjusted based on the progress of the reader and we had to modify the highest level based on feedback from teachers who wanted additional room for growth for the most proficient readers.

Reading Companion provides detailed reporting for teachers, giving them visibility into the reader's areas of strength and weakness. The top of the report contains a summary of the overall accuracy of the student's reading, along with a visual sequential representation of all the words read by the student. The correct words are shown in green and the incorrect words are shown in red, thus allowing large patterns to be easily detected. As the teacher mouses over a red or green line, a popup shows the details of the word. Teachers really liked the visual display and the summary information since they often did not have the time to read the detailed findings for each student, but wanted to get an overview of the student's progress.

4 Conclusion

This paper describes the architecture, rationale and findings for a web-based literacy application called Reading Companion that is used by both adults and children. Feedback from users suggests that using speech recognition over the web to help learners increase reading skills is not only a viable solution, but one that is well accepted by the user populations. With RC we introduce a method that can be used by other interactive applications that wish to use speech technologies on the web.

There are many advantages to having a literacy tutor available over the web. The centralized web server makes it easy to administer and update the software, which is a huge advantage in terms of maintenance and adding new books to read. From the user's standpoint, the web provides anytime/anywhere access and a familiar browser interface. The ability to access Reading Companion from home allows the family members to stay involved with the reader's progress, and the learner can access the same content at home as in the classroom. Lastly, with RC we are able to impact emerging readers around the globe – all joining and building our web-based community of learners, teachers, and book-authors.

References

1. Mostow, J., Beck, J.E.: Project LISTEN's Reading Tutor: Interactive Event Description. In: Supplemental Proc. AIED 03, pp. 30–32 (2003)
2. Price, P., Luc, J.: Using speech and language technology to coach reading. In: Proc. HLT '01, Association for Computational Linguistics, pp. 1–2 (2001)
3. Williams, S.M., Nix, D., Fairweather, P.: Using Speech Recognition Technology to Enhance Literacy Instruction for Emerging Readers. In: Proc. ICLS 2000, pp. 115–120. Erlbaum, Mahwah (2000)
4. http://www.nifl.gov/nifl/facts/facts_overview.html
5. http://soliloquylearning.com/

PASTEL: Pattern-Driven Adaptive Simulations

Mark K. Singley, Peter Fairweather, Tracee Wolf, and Dick Lam

IBM T.J. Watson Research Center, 19 Skyline Drive,
Hawthorne, New York, USA
{ksingley, pfairwea, tlwolf, rblam}@us.ibm.com

Abstract. We propose a new kind of learning environment called an adaptive simulation that more deeply explores and exploits the potential of simulations as pedagogical and explanatory tools. In an adaptive simulation, the simulation configuration is not fixed but rather can be modified by an instructional agent for optimal pedagogical effect. Types of adaptations include manipulations of simulation time and state, changes in representation to facilitate explanations and/or task performance, and adjustments in simulation complexity by the addition and/or removal of components. We briefly describe a system we are developing called PASTEL that is designed to enable these kinds of adaptations. Open research issues include precisely how to perform these adaptations and when to employ them for optimal effect.

Keywords: adaptive user interface, simulation, HCI patterns, systems thinking.

1 Simulations as Learning Environments: Unrealized Potential?

There is a long history of interest in simulations as learning environments, primarily because of their ability to support conceptual exploration and learning-by-doing in authentic, risk-free, immersive settings. In the face of mounting global challenges requiring deep insight into the complexities of economic, biological, and social systems, interest in simulations as exploratory conceptual tools only appears to be growing [1]. Although widely regarded as having great promise, simulations can have a number of associated learning problems, primarily having to do with learner understanding, management of system complexity, and the lack of built-in instructional support [2]. In our work, we are striving for a tight linkage between the design of simulations and the design of associated instructional components. Specifically, we are considering what value may result if the simulation itself is put under much more direct and masterful control of an instructional agent.

2 Radical Adaptation

In developing our vision of adaptive simulations that can reconfigure themselves radically in service of instructional goals, we are investigating three broad categories of adaptation:

C. Baranauskas et al. (Eds.): INTERACT 2007, LNCS 4663, Part II, pp. 349 – 352, 2007.
© IFIP International Federation for Information Processing 2007

2.1 Control of Simulation Time and State

The instructional agent should be able to arbitrarily set the simulation's time and state for its own pedagogical purposes. (This goes beyond the standard simulation tactic of time compression in order to achieve future states faster than real time). We are envisioning a system that can "rewind" the simulation to an earlier critical juncture and either step through what happened with the learner as a form of review or to give the learner another opportunity to practice with either the same simulation state first encountered or a similar one. Another potential use of this capability would be to provide episodic summaries of learner behavior to an interested third party such as a teacher, mentor, or fellow learner cast in the role of critic.

2.2 Adjustment of Simulation View and/or Representation

In order to promote perceptions of authenticity as well as maximize the overlap between learning and performance environments, simulations often strive for a high-fidelity representation of the system and/or setting being modeled. However, such realistic representations might not always be best for instructional purposes. In some circumstances, it may be beneficial to expose the hidden workings of a device or the internal state of a process. Additionally, it may be beneficial to strip away what might be considered the extraneous detail of a complex situation and focus on the truly important and meaningful elements. Such representations that expose hidden elements and remove extraneous details might be termed *schematic*. The tutor should be able to change the outward view or representation of the simulation, moving along the realistic/schematic continuum to suit the current pedagogical goal.

Aside from swapping in more schematic representations of the simulation model, we are also exploring the use of scaffolded representations of the interface to provide transitional support during all phases of learner behavior. Here are some brief examples: (a) **Perceiving:** In complex situations where there are multiple information streams whose monitoring and integration is critical to understanding, a useful simplification might be to reconfigure the interface so that these sources are placed together in a prominent position. (b) **Acting:** Learner action can be scaffolded by activating only task-appropriate controls, and conveying this action space through highlighting, shading, or some other graphical technique.

2.3 Selection of Simulation Components

Finally, aside from just changing the outward representation, the instructional agent should be able to change the underlying deep structure of the simulation as well. By adding and/or removing components, the instructional agent should be able to adjust simulation complexity and focus attention on current instructional goals. The challenge here is to author the simulation in such a way as to enable this kind of decomposition and modular assembly on the fly. This is the focus of much current work on simulation in the learning objects community.

All of these factors combine into what might be called a *scaffolding gradient*, a multi-dimensional space of possibilities that can be navigated by the instructional agent for optimal pedagogical effect. Just how, when, and where to navigate in this space is a subject of active research interest.

3 Overview of PASTEL System Components

Simulation Model. A key feature of our approach is that we make use of semantically-rich, domain-general patterns to build our simulation models. These patterns, which are better characterized as schemas or frames [3], are declarative abstractions that specify common, recurring inter-related roles and/or behaviors. An example of a schema is the SUPPLY schema, which is quite general and can be used to describe processes in many domains. A listing of the SUPPLY schema's roles and their instantiations for a simple flashlight example is shown in Table 1.

Table 1. SUPPLY schema roles and example instantiations

Role	Definition	Flashlight Example
Producer	produces the provision for the consumer	battery
Consumer	consumes the provision	bulb
Provision	that which is supplied	electricity
Control	enables or controls the process	switch
Indicator	reveals the state of the process	bulb
Path	path by which the provision gets to the consumer	CIRCUIT schema

To build a simulation model, the user selects schemas from the PASTEL schema library (which has been stocked by mining such sources as FrameNet [4]) and instantiates their roles with elements drawn from the system being modeled. To describe a complex system, schemas have to be composed both "horizontally" and "vertically." A horizontal composition involves having a single system element fill multiple roles across multiple schemas (a system element may also fill multiple roles within the same schema, as shown by the bulb element in Table 1). A vertical composition involves having a role within a schema instantiated by another schema (again shown in Table 1, where the *Path* role is instantiated by a CIRCUIT schema). Providing these multiple, hierarchical, schematic descriptions of the system provides the leverage necessary for many of the adaptations described earlier. The schematic approach is also valuable pedagogically because it encourages the modeler to describe the system using general semantic frames. These frames activate general knowledge learners already have and use to understand the world.

User Interface. Every instantiated schema role element defined in the simulation model potentially has a representation in the user interface. Some elements (those that are typically visible in a realistic depiction of the system) will be displayed in an authentic view, whereas others (those that are either ordinarily hidden in a realistic depiction or represent abstract, latent variables that typically have no physical manifestation) may be revealed in more schematic views. It is often these hidden elements that, once exposed or reified, provide true insight into the operation of a complex system.

The creation of the user interface is coordinated semi-automatically with the creation of the simulation model. Those elements cast as *Controls* in the simulation model are initialized as actual user controls in the interface; those elements cast as

Indicators become dynamic elements of the interface that are updated in response to changes in the internal states of the simulation. Those elements that are neither controls nor indicators become static elements in the interface.

Instructional Agent. The purpose of the instructional agent is to project different views of the simulation model onto the interface, in accordance with pedagogical goals either stated by the user (e.g. "tell me more about this element" or "explain how I got into this state") or generated by some other agent, such as an intelligent tutor. Thus, the simulation model, interface, and instructional agent can be regarded as an instance of the traditional model-view-controller pattern.

The instructional agent uses the schematic descriptions of the simulation model in combination with its own pedagogical heuristics to decide what view to project. Its operations are organized into three levels (cf. [5]) :

Operators. Each element of the interface can respond to the following basic commands, which when applied individually and in combination form the basis for realizing many of the adaptations: create/destroy, attach graphic(s), move/stop, enlarge/shrink, hide/show, dissolve/emerge, blur/glow, raise/lower, compose.

Tactics. The above operators are combined into pedagogical tactics such as *highlight* (e.g. move nearby elements aside, move and enlarge element of interest), *reveal* (dissolve occluding element and apply glow to element of interest), or *categorize* (e.g. move similar elements to the same location). There may be many methods defined within each tactic that accomplish the same goal but involve different combinations of operators.

Strategies. Finally, tactics are combined to form pedagogical strategies, such as *give overview* (traverse upper level of a functional schematic description of the system and highlight elements in turn), *disassemble* (recursively unpack elements of a spatial schematic description), and *reify hidden state* (traverse functional schematic description and reveal hidden elements).

References

1. Thompson, C.: Saving the World, One Video Game at a Time. New York Times (July 23, 2006)
2. Hayes, R., Singer, M.: Simulation Fidelity in Training System Design. Springer, Heidelberg (1989)
3. Barsalou, L.: Frames, Concepts, and Conceptual Fields. In: Lehrer, A., Kittay, E. (eds.) Frames, Fields, and Contrasts: New Essays in Semantic and Lexical Organization, Erlbaum, Hillsdale (1992)
4. FrameNet website: http://framenet.icsi.berkeley.edu
5. Seligmann, D., Feiner, S.: Automated Generation of Intent-Based 3D Illustrations. SIGGRAPH Computer Graphics 25(4), 123–132 (1991)

Online Communities Administration:
Defining Tools for Different Profiles

Elton José da Silva[1,2] and Silas Sallaume[1]

[1] Departamento de Computação, Universidade Federal de Ouro Preto,
Campus Morro do Cruzeiro, Ouro Preto – MG, 35400-000, Brasil
elton@iceb.ufop.br, ssallaume@ic.uff.br
[2] Semiotic Engineering Research Group
Departamento de Informática, PUC-Rio, Brasil

Abstract. There occur a great number of breakdowns in online communities caused by the natural gap between face-to-face and virtual relationships. In addition to this shortcoming, creating, managing and promoting participative online communities is frequently arduous work, and there usually are few tools to help the administrators through this endeavor. So, in this paper we present some results of a research carried out for the implementation of a tool for managing online communities called *OriOnGroups,* which aims to help in the administrator's decision-making when creating and managing communities. We introduce a categorization for communities profiles and make use of *personas,* which helped us to select different tools for each one of these profiles.

Keywords: Online Community Administration, User/Group Profiles, *Personas.*

1 Introduction

OriOnGroups is a virtual environment for supporting online communities, developed at PUC-Rio's Department of Informatics and UFOP's Department of Computer Science. The first release of that environment basically made available a discussion forum tool for supporting discussions brought about by online academic orientation to graduate students. Subsequent releases were based on a study of expectations towards this kind of environment as evidenced by a group of potential users who were involved in academic research [2]. Over the course of this time, some of the tools included in *OriOnGroups* were, for instance, bulletin board, members' profiles, forum participation assessment, polls, file repository, search engines, among others. These new functionalities, which were added in a poorly planned and unstructured manner by the users themselves – Computer Science students, in Human-Computer Interaction courses –, have caused the system to become more complex and the code to become unstable. In order to resolve these setbacks, we proposed a total redesign of *OriOnGroups* by using an object-oriented structure and design patterns [3]. These modifications improved the *OriOnGroups* structure and were beneficial to its development since we had in mind a generic tool for the creation of online communities, in which the activities of defining, configuring and managing different types of communities were to be included. These features also facilitated code maintenance (by the development team) and interface configuration (by the end-users).

C. Baranauskas et al. (Eds.): INTERACT 2007, LNCS 4663, Part II, pp. 353–356, 2007.

2   Online Communities Administration

It is true that there exist many problems in present online communities, and one that can be cited is connected with the disparity between the social-virtual and social-real relationships [1], such as, for example, the way in which the hierarchical relationships among the members of a group are built. With the traditional computer architecture and programming techniques, it is difficult to build a virtual community that works in the same manner as that of a real community [2]. We believe that a way of reducing the gap between real and virtual is through a proper intervention by one or various persons in charge of an effective management of the community. By 'management' we understand a series of activities which include, for example, administration, moderation, mediation and facilitation. The goal of such intervention is to provide an environment which is more flexible and agreeable to the end-user, in such a way that the participants feel compelled to engage actively in the forums, thus making the group and the discussions more productive.

Each community has unique characteristics, requiring therefore different tools and leadership styles. However, virtual communities are designed either specifically for a certain type of group – which makes its use by another type of group inadequate – or in a very generic way – which makes it likely for a group not to realize its full potential when employing a nonspecific kind of virtual community. Unfortunately, in most existing group environments it is rather troublesome to make a change in the environment structure or in its leadership style. With the aim of defining the different types of groups which can be configured under *OriOnGroups*, we are utilizing a division of communities into classes as proposed by [5], as shown in Figure 1.

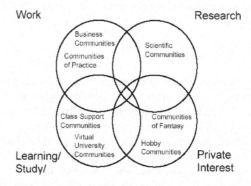

Fig. 1. Different Online Communities Profiles (extracted from [5])

The *Work* profile comprises communities for corporate environments and design teams. Communities of scientific research – such as those used in the early versions of *OriOnGroups* – could be named as typical representatives of the *Research* profile. E-learning communities are typical representatives of groups in the *Learning/Study* profile. The *Private Interest* profile includes entertainment communities (such as many Orkut communities) or discussion groups on private matters, such as *health communities*. Figure 1 also indicates that some communities can be placed in intersections of different profiles, which conveys different customization combinations at the level of the groups' administration.

3 Setting Up Different Types of Communities

From the categorization of communities in [5], we began to identify and build *personas* – archetypical representations of real or potential users – in each presented profile. For instance, Figure 2 shows the description of a *persona* in a medical community domain belonging to the *Research* profile.

Persona: Fabio Figueiredo

Fábio is 23 years old and a medicine graduate-to-be at UFOP. During his second semester in college he decided to specialize in Cardiology. Nowadays, he tries to keep up with the news in his field of study, especially Chagas disease, about which he has frequent discussions with his colleagues. He plans to take a Master's Degree at USP, where he already participates in a research group. This is one of the reasons for his intense use of the Internet, as he needs to maintain long-distance contact with other doctors and researchers of his group.

Fabio's goals are:
-To get ahead in academic life, acquiring knowledge in Cardiology and producing scientific articles.
-To achieve financial stability in order to marry soon.

Psychology kind: (Extroverted – Sensorial – Thinker – Judger – Planner)

Fig. 2. Excerpt of a *persona*'s description in a typical *Research* community

The identification and creation of *personas* in the different types of community profiles has helped us to define the tools and possibilities for customization under *OriOnGroups*. In the *Work* profile, the environment shall be configured so as to make available tools like: project follow-up and management, bulletin board, individual and group appointment book, etc. Participants shall be provided with indicators of updates in group events and community usage rules. Options of moderation and inclusion of moderators shall also be allowed. The issue of information security and confidentiality shall be highly relevant in this kind of community, in which the information exchanged among participants is typically strategic to the organization. In the *Research* profile, the environment shall be configured so as to make available tools for helping with scientific research, such as files repository, links repository, online collaboration in article production, among others. Users shall be provided with indicators of content updates as well as quantitative and qualitative indicators related to the group as a whole and to each user, so that the production of knowledge by the group can be assessed. With regard to the community's rules, these are more flexible in this kind of environment, which has a nearly horizontal hierarchy, dispensing with the use of moderators in most cases. Here, the issue of information security and confidentiality is also important, although not as crucial as in the *Work* profile. Access to group knowledge is normally granted to previously invited participants only. In the *Learning/Study* profile, the community's administrator is provided with tools that enable him to assess each participant individually, as well as tools for publishing grades obtained by the participants in the proposed activities. In the *Private Interest* profile, basic tools shall be made available, such as: files and links repository, polls, photo album, blog, chat rooms, among others. Regarding the community's rules, options of moderation and inclusion of moderators shall be allowed, aiming at censoring certain themes and uploads, since, by default, any person can take part in the group.

In *OriOnGroups*, the group administrator can create communities under this profile classification. He/she can then configure the group, easily including and excluding some tools, customizing the environment to different types of groups [4]. Important is to point out that, when configuring each tool, the administrator is provided with its description and the most likely consequences of its enabling/disabling to that specific type of group (e.g.: possible effects of a chat room in a research community in which one wants to motivate more deeper discussions among participants).

4 Conclusion

In this paper we presented *OriOnGroups*, a tool for creating and configuring online communities. We believe that good tools for administering these communities can help in the job of dealing with – and possibly reducing – the gap between virtual and face-to-face group relationships. For example, it is fundamental to provide the administrators with descriptions of how the selected configurations can affect a specific type of group. Using a categorization of different online communities profiles, we created *personas* to help us to understand for whom we were creating a community and the types of tools to put available to its participants.

We expect these results to foster discussion on how to design more participative online community environments, and also how the use of *personas* can help teams in the design of interactive software. The next steps in this work will be to improve the present implementation of *OriOnGroups* and evaluate the management and use of virtual communities with different profiles.

Acknowledgments. *"For from Him and through Him and to Him are all things. To Him be the glory forever!"* (Romans 11:36)

References

1. Ackerman, M.: The Intellectual Challenge of CSCW: The gap between social requirements and technical feasibility. Human-Computer Interaction 15, 179–203 (2000)
2. da Silva, E.J, Sieckenius, C.S., Prates, R.O., Nicolaci-da-costa, A.M.: What they want and what they get: A study of light-weight technologies for online communities. In: CLIHC'2003. Proceedings of Latin-American Conference on Human-Computer Interaction, Rio de Janeiro, RJ. Conference, pp. 135–146 (2003)
3. da Silva, R.F.: Projetando uma nova estrutura para uma Comunidade Online. Trabalho de Conclusão de Curso, Departamento de Computação, UFOP, junho de (2006) (in Portuguese)
4. Sallaume, S., da Silva, R.F.: Gerenciamento em Comunidades Online: Um módulo de administração para o OriOn, XII Seminário de Iniciação Científica da UFOP (2005) (in Portuguese)
5. Seufert, S.: Design and Management of Online Learning Communities. In: Proceedings of the European Academy of Management (EURAM), Stockholm (2002)

Building Communities with People-Tags

Stephen Farrell, Tessa Lau, and Stefan Nusser

IBM Almaden Research Center
San Jose CA 95120, USA
sfarrell@almaden.ibm.com

Abstract. Social tagging has been applied to many applications including image sharing, bookmarking and music recommendations. We have developed a application for the social tagging of *people* to support contact management and browsing profiles in an enterprise directory. As we expected, we found that users tag people for personal organization and for "social" motivations just as in other systems. However, an unexpected result is that users tag other users in order to create communities. By tagging, encouraging others to tag, and sharing links to tags, an active minority of users is using people-tagging to bring people together.

1 Introduction

Social tagging has been applied widely to enrich applications for sharing bookmarks, photos, videos, music, podcasts and other resources. We have built a social tagging application for enterprise contact management called "Fringe Contacts" which enables employees to place themselves and their fellow employees in a folksonomy of skills, interests and projects [4].

More recently, we have integrated social tagging into our enhanced directory prototype "Fringe". Through usage statistics, surveys and interviews, we learned that tagging is useful for personal organization, enables an active minority to contribute useful and accurate information to other's profiles, and that tag frequency provides a basis for ranking people. Moreover, early evidence suggested that users policed themselves and that inappropriate and undesired tags were rare in this environment [5].

An unexpected result that emerged from our interviews, which was not reported in previous work, is that users frequently tag people for the benefit of others. They wanted users to find out about each other and to encourage them to start using the tagging feature. They included snapshots of tag groups in presentations, they shared links to tag-based groups of people, and they used tags to construct *ad hoc* mailing lists. In short, they used people-tagging to define and socially manage communities. In this paper, we report on this result and speculate on what it means for the design of future tagging communities.

2 Related Work

Social bookmarking systems enable users to tag web pages and contribute to an emergent folksonomy of web pages [1] [2]. Social tagging has also been successfully

C. Baranauskas et al. (Eds.): INTERACT 2007, LNCS 4663, Part II, pp. 357–360, 2007.

applied to other media including images (flickr.com), videos (youtube.com) and music (last.fm). Marlow et al surveyed tagging systems and have developed a taxonomy of system design parameters and user incentives. They have found tags used for *future retrieval, contribution and sharing, attracting attention, play and competition, self presentation*, and *opinion expression* [3].

3   Interviews

We have found a substantial number of users—3,726, more than 1% of all employees—contributing tags to our system. We asked a number of the top users to participate in a 30 minute interview. We selected these users based on the number of people who had tagged them, the number of people they had tagged, and the duration of time they have been using the system. In the end, we conducted 19 semi-structured interviews.

4   Results

We found that many of the same incentives that applied to other social tagging systems also applied to person-tagging. Most respondents reported using tags to organize their contacts to help with *future retrieval*. Most reported clicking on a tag to recall people, and about half mentioned that they found it useful to see their own tags while browsing others' profiles, reminding them what they knew of the other person.

We were surprised to learn how many respondents reported using tags for *contribution and sharing*. 15 of the 19 respondents described sharing (or interest in sharing) tags to inform others about a group or to inform members of the group about each other. This was not necessarily altruistic behavior: many respondents had an interest in the success of the community and found people-tagging a means to that end.

Community builders were resourceful in finding ways to leverage person-tags. One respondent tagged participants in a program he was running `tap-innovator` so he could demonstrate to his management the range of people involved. Another lead a cross-organizational study on patterns in software development and tagged its members by subtopic and embedded links to these groups in the project wiki. Others shared tags by directing people to their profile, emailing links, or even including screen-shots in presentations. Two respondents had not thought of sharing tags, but, upon the suggestion, wanted to try it. Some of these respondents reported using the list of email addresses that appears on the tag page as an *ad hoc* mailing list.

Some community builders have taken person-tagging to the next level. Realizing that users could tag themselves or anyone else, they enlisted the community to manage itself. One respondent described her practice of sharing links and encouraging *reuse* of tags as "helping the community to self-organize".

We learned about the first example of self-organizing communities prior to our interviews with the `chi2006` tag. One user had tagged everyone he knew that was attending the CHI conference that year. He then sent them an email that included a link to the group and instructions to tag anyone who was missing. In the end, a comprehensive list of everyone attending the conference had been produced by a few people in an unstructured way. This behavior has recurred with web20forbiz, p-vista and, recently, chi2007.

One of our respondents described how he used person-tagging to help build a community around the virtual reality program Second Life. He described an early practice of asking people in email, web pages and presentations to tag themselves "secondlife" so they could find each other. However, he backed off of this practice when the community reached into the thousands.

In other cases, this application of tagging failed to reach critical mass. One respondent commented on a tag that had only been used twice: "Bob is trying to get that going". Since taggees are not notified upon being tagged, the ability for tags to spread virally is limited. All of the successful examples we know of have had champions using other channels to encourage the spread the use of the tag.

We also uncovered some interactions with an existing system for managing groups called "Bluegroups". One respondent started creating a community with a tag but then switched to Bluegroups so he could use the membership list for access control. Conversely, another respondent translates the names of Bluegroups that appear on users' profiles into tags. Yet another respondent manually synchronizes the two. A final respondent felt that a Bluegroup was too large to be useful to him, so he tagged just the "key people" in the group.

We found users took advantage of the flexibility of the semantics of person tagging in community building. One respondent explained the tag webdevlounge: "we use this tag to organize everything". Indeed, they also use it for social bookmarks, blogs, wikis, and other tools. For this community, tagging a person webdevlounge in Fringe means that the person is *of interest* to the team, not a member. A Bluegroup serves the purpose of managing team membership.

An interesting variant of community tagging, perhaps related to *play and competition*, was shaming. One respondent wanted to encourage his colleagues to upload photos to their profile. He tagged them no-picture-in-bluepages and removed the tag once this had been rectified. There is no one with this tag now.

We also found examples of other incentives enumerated by Marlow including *attracting attention* and *self presentation*. Users tag *themselves* with their skills and projects, in effect enabling others to find them by browsing and influencing the tags that appear on their profiles. We also found tags used for *play and competition*. For example, we found the use of sassy and needs-a-shave. We found that respondents did not use these tags to describe themselves suggesting that they serve a social rather than informative role. We also found this result with affirmative tags like organized and rockstar.

Finally, we found evidence of *disincentives* to tagging people. Respondents *withheld* tags due to presumed consequences. One respondent reported that he did not tag a colleague with the name of a former project because he knew the colleague did not want to be contacted about it. While some respondents suggested it could be useful, all were reluctant to use people-tags for *opinion expression*. One respondent put it: "I try to be very conservative, and not make judgments and aspersions about them.... I try to use this as a very positive thing."

5   Conclusion

We have found that people-tagging as implemented in Fringe fits well into the family of other tagging systems as outlined by Marlow et al. The same basic motivations of self-interest and "social" contribution play major roles.

We think *creating community*, while related to *contribution and sharing*, is itself a distinct incentive. Users already motivated to create communities have found people-tagging a useful tool to demonstrate the community to others and introduce the members to each other. Moreover, they have leveraged the openness of tagging to enable the community to maintain itself.

We expect to find the incentive of *creating community* in other tagging applications. For example, someone might use the tag "sanfrancisco" on flickr not only to associate the photo with a topic area, but also to help photographers in San Francisco find each other.

In the future, we would like to study how these tag-defined communities compare with opt-in or administered communities on Facebook and other social network sites. We are also looking at extending email and instant messaging tools to enable users to contact people by tag. We may also introduce features to help "viral" spreading of tags by enabling users to notify others of the tags as they assign them. As person-tags are more widely used and the tools to leverage them become more powerful, we will continue to watch user's reactions to being tagged and report on our findings.

References

1. Golder, S., Huberman, B.A.: Usage patterns of collaborative tagging systems. Journal of Information Science 32(2), 198–208 (2006)
2. Millen, D.R., Feinberg, J., Kerr, B.: Dogear: Social bookmarking in the enterprise. In: CHI '06. Proceedings of the SIGCHI conference on Human Factors in computing systems, pp. 111–120. ACM Press, New York (2006)
3. Marlow, C., Naaman, M., Boyd, D., Davis, M.: HT06, Tagging Paper, Taxonomy, Flickr, Academic Article, ToRead. In: HT '06. Proceedings of Hypertext, ACM Press, New York (2006)
4. Farrell, S., Lau, T.: Fringe contacts: People-tagging for the enterprise. In: Workshop on Collaborative Web Tagging, WWW 2006 (2006)
5. Farrell, S., Lau, T., Wilcox, E., Nusser, S., Muller, M.: Socially augmenting employee profiles with people-tagging. Submitted to UIST (2007)

Interactive Floor Support for Kinesthetic Interaction in Children Learning Environments

Kaj Grønbæk[1], Ole Sejer Iversen[2], Karen Johanne Kortbek[3],
Kaspar Rosengreen Nielsen[3], and Louise Aagaard[4]

[1] Department of Computer Science, University of Aarhus,
Åbogade 34, 8200 Århus N, Denmark
kgronbak@daimi.au.dk
[2] Department of Information Science,
Helsingforsgade 14, 8200 Aarhus N, Denmark
imvoi@hum.au.dk
[3] Alexandra Institute Ltd., Åbogade 34, 8200 Århus N, Denmark
{kortbek,kaspar}@alexandra.dk
[4] Aarhus School of Architecture, Nørreport 20, 8000 Aarhus C, Denmark
louise.aagaard@aarch.dk

Abstract. This paper introduces a novel kinesthetic interaction technique for in-teractive floors. The interaction techniques utilize vision-based limb tracking on an interactive floor – a 12 m² glass surface with bottom projection. The kines-thetic interaction technique has been developed for an interactive floor imple-mented in a school square. The paper discusses the kinesthetic interaction technique and its potentials in the domain of learning applications: Kinesthetic in-teraction supports body-kinesthetic learning as argued in the learning literature. Kinesthetic interaction is fun and motivating thus encourages children to explore and learn. Kinesthetic interaction on large display surfaces supports collaborative, co-located play and learning through communication and negotiation among the participants. Finally, the paper discusses prospects and challenges in development of kinesthetic interaction for interactive floors.

1 Introduction

The work reported was conducted in a project on interactive school environments. The objective was to create new types of IT-based learning experiences for school children. The work has been inspired from several sources namely empirical research in school environments [2,10], literature studies within multiple learning styles [5], and movement based interaction techniques [13,18]. Others have pointed to the fact that computer supported learning artifacts can stimulate learning through kinesthetic interaction. Underkoffler & Ishii's [26] Illuminating Light workbench lets students learn about optical systems by designing them. In a use survey of the commercial Dance Dance Revolution[1], Höysniemi [6] points to the fact that playing the kines-thetic interaction game has a positive effect on the social life and physical health of players, and improves endurance, muscle strength, and sense of rhythm by the users.

---

[1] www.konami.com

C. Baranauskas et al. (Eds.): INTERACT 2007, LNCS 4663, Part II, pp. 361–375, 2007.
© IFIP International Federation for Information Processing 2007

A more thorough study of how bodies matter in interaction design is described in Klemmer et al. [12]. The empirical research in schools revealed challenges in moving it-support for multiple learning styles beyond the pure audio/visual styles and take advantage of kinesthetic learning styles. This challenge made us look into the field of interactive floors [3,15,13,14,16].

Traditional computer games and learning-systems, running on PCs and laptops only challenge limited parts of the human body - usually only eyes, ears, and the pointing finger. But Gardner's [5] theory of multiple intelligences implies a need for multiple learning styles to provide optimal learning for a broader range of children.

Thus we developed an interactive floor platform for games and learning applications – it is called iGameFloor [6]. The platform has been implemented in Møllevang-skolen school in Aarhus, Denmark, where is has got the nickname "Wisdom Well". However we denote the platform iGameFloor [6]. The iGameFloor is placed in a school department square where pupils spend both learning time and break time. It consists of a 12 m^2 bottom projected interactive floor with vision based tracking of user movement. The work behind this paper has been carried out using this large scale installation for experimentation. A number of learning applications have been developed for iGameFloor.

iGameFloor supports three types of applications. *Collaborative learning games.* The kids work together through direct communication and kinesthetic interaction on the shared surface. The collaborative presence provides the social qualities of e.g. traditional board and card games. *Knowledge sharing applications.* A central placement of the iGameFloor in a department square makes it ideal for creating awareness of activities among classes. The floor is a remarkable [23] interface that draws attention to displayed information and encourage exploration. *Simulations.* The iGameFloor surface is ideal for simulating scenarios in a scale that immerses the kids beyond traditional computer displays. Learning about geometrics, physics, geography, and biology involves many examples of scenarios where there are learning potentials in simulations that may scale the content, simulating the users to be, e.g. nano particle size or stellar size.

Fig. 1. iGameFloor in use at school

The applications have been developed in a participatory design process [1,9] with children and teachers as participants. We particularly used the 'Fictional Inquiry' technique, [2,9,10], which establishes a shared narrative design space between stakeholders in the design process; in this case among teachers, children and designers. This paper focus on the novel kinesthetic interaction techniques supported by iGameFloor.

2   Interactive Floors

Interactive floors with movement based interaction have emerged in recent years. They fall in two main categories: sensor-based and vision-based interactive floors.

Sensor-based interactive floors are typically utilized in dance and performances like set-ups, e.g. Magic Carpet [22] and Litefoot [3]. The prototypes are sensor intensive environments for tracking movements of feet. In Magic Carpet the sensor floor has been supplemented with sensor technologies for tracking the movements of the upper body and arms. To serve different shaping and sizes of an interactive floor the Z-tiles concept [16,24] was developed. As the above-mentioned systems the Z-tiles interactive floor is based on sensor technologies. Input from the sensors is used to control and manipulate sound providing the idea of playing an instrument with body movements. Another system exploring multi-user spatial interaction by means of a sensor based floor is the Virtual Space project [14]. The sensors are here used to enable spatial interaction and control of a computer game projected on a vertical positioned display. BodyGames [15] is a system consisting of tiles with touch sensors and light diodes supporting games where players invoke certain light patterns with their feet to gain points in the game. These sensor-based floors are typically limited to a discrete interaction with relatively large floor tiles. Finally, LightSpace™ (www.interactivefloor.com) is a commercial product based on tiles and sensors providing entertainment environments like dance floors

In contrast to the sensor-based floors, the vision based floors supports a more fluid and natural interaction on a floor surface. iFloor [13] introduces an interactive floor facilitating debate based on SMS and email contributions. A projector mounted on the ceiling is connected to a local computer to provide a display on the floor. The floor interaction works on the basis of a vision-based tracking package [27] analyzing the rim of the interface based on a video feed from a web-cam also mounted on the ceiling. The tracking of people's position and movement are interpreted as "magnetic" forces attracting a cursor with its home position at the center of the floor display. The force is proportional to the size of the shadow blob generated by a person moving under the projector. iFloor maintains precise tracking of up to 10 people at one time in a 4 * 5 m rectangle. People are tracked in a one meter band surrounding the display which is 3 *4 m in size. A visual feedback is given in form of a projected string connecting the cursor and the user while being in the tracked area, thus people were made aware that they were taking part in the interaction. Finally, Natural Interaction[2] has developed several prototypes of interactive floors based on tracking with vision technology.

---

[2] www.naturalinteraction.net

The iGameFloor is built on the vision principles, but utilizing tracking of limb contact points from the bottom of the display. In the following, we will present the kinesthetic interaction technique in relation to children learning.

3 Kinesthetic Interaction for Learning

In recent years there has come focus on children and the need for more body movement. The tendency towards sedentary game playing in front of a TV or computer screen has generated a focus on lack of body movement and exercise. These gaming activities have been related to an increasing number of overweight children[3]. One way to address this problem is to combine body movement and the attractive digital game elements, as seen e.g. in EyeToy™ from Playstation2™, Dance Dance Revolution and Nintendo Wii™.

Body movement is a central learning area for children [5], but the body is not limited to being a basis for movement activities or an instrument to impact on the surrounding environment. Body and movement stimulate the sensory system, which gives the individual experience and knowledge of her/his own identity as well as the physical and social outside world. This sense perception makes a basis for reflection and abstraction - this way body movement also relates to cognition. The role and significance of the body movement in children's learning processes is crucial, especially in the pre-school age, not only concerning health and exercise questions, but also sensuality, aesthetic, social and personal learning. Children sense and learn through the body. Merleau-Ponty's phenomenology [17] of the body gives the body an essential significance in relation to the individual's recognition of her/himself and others.

Within the HCI community the discussion of human-computer interaction has primarily been discussed from a cognitive concern. With the rapid penetration of technology into everyday life and the following "aesthetic turn" in HCI [25] a concern for the human body as a locus of sensory-aesthetic appreciation is gaining acceptance. Moen [18] provides an account of design aspects of human movement when used as interaction modality between people and technology. She calls this modality for kinesthetic interaction. An examples is, the BodyBug, being a way to experience and interact with technology by use of the full faculty of the human body [19].

A popular kinesthetic interaction based game is the commercially available Nintendo Wii that utilizes accelerometers and gyroscopes in measuring user movements and transforming them to tennis or golf swings. Another example is the EyeToyPlay game (http://www.eyetoyplay.com/) for Playstation 2™. It is a TV game platform utilizing web camera input. The time-out based selection technique introduced by EyeToyPlay is also well-suited for vision based interactive floors, see section 4.

The kinesthetic interaction approach is especially interesting when it comes to IT support in learning environments. Gardner [5] provides a theory of multiple intelligences emphasizing that each individual child possesses a unique combination of relatively autonomous intelligences including a body-kinesthetic intelligence. Traditional class-room teaching emphasizes the development of logical intelligence and linguistic intelligence excluding body-kinesthetic learning to the gyms.

---

[3] E.g. http://www.msnbc.msn.com/id/7722888/

According to Moser [20], educational research confirms that movement based playing can be relevant in developing social skills, and in this way social skills attached to body and movement may lead to improvement of speech. The iGameFloor sets a stage for this kind of activities, whether it is concrete sound/speech training according to a bottom-up method or a dialogue in "free" games according to a top-down method. The iGameFloor is a motivating place to train vocabulary through games – the Stepstone application being described in Section 6 is an example of this kind of training.

4   iGameFloor Infrastructure

In this section we briefly describe the infrastructure, a more extensive description can be found in [6]. The iGameFloor is built into the physical floor of a school department square. The iGameFloor is a 3 m deep hole covered with a projection surface. The projection surface is 3*4 m glass of approximately 9 cm thickness divided into four tiles. The glass surface consists of carrying glass, diffusion layer, and a hard protection surface glass. The four tiles are supported at the outer edges and with an internal conic frame resting on a supporting pillar in the center (see Fig. 2). The projection is created by 4 projectors with a resolution of 1024*768 pixels. They are placed vertically covering each their tile of glass. The projectors are driven by a PC with a graphics board with 4 DVI outputs. Each projector is associated with a Web cam tracking limb contact points on the tile covered by the given projector.

The four Web cams associated with the projectors are managed by a separate PC running the vision software supporting fine-grained tracking of limb positions. The limb positions are communicated to the application PC feeding the four projectors. The tracking PC can be switched to a mode, where it uses a ceiling mounted wide-angel Creative webcam for coarse-grained tracking of body contours from above.

The iGameFloor supports sound through ceiling mounted loudspeakers and a subwoofer placed nearby the iGameFloor. The start up/shut down of computers and

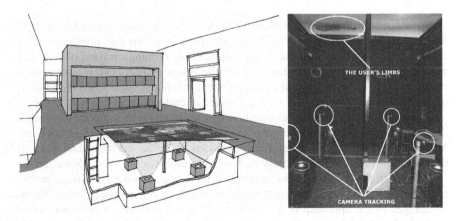

Fig. 2. Sketch and picture of the iGameFloor beneath the surface

projectors is handled by a Creston control panel on a nearby wall. The panel also controls lighting and curtains. Having powered up the iGameFloor from the Creston panel, it can be fully controlled by body movement on the surface. A traditional key-board and mouse is located on a nearby shelf to be used for editing purposes.

The basic software architecture is described in detail in [6], it consists of three layers: Server layer, client layer and sensor layer. The *server layer* consists of a web-server with a database. The database holds data and settings for the learning game applications and more general objects that can be referenced across applications. E.g. when a game is created in an application the user can specify type and the level of difficulty for the children. The *client layer* consists of a common Flash plus .NET framework for a num-ber of learning game applications. This way Flash can tap into the power of .Net for storage connectivity, user interface widgets and operating system integration while maintaining the power of Flash for 2D game development. The general selection princi-ple used is time-out based, i.e. sticking to a selection for a few seconds starts the invoca-tion of an action. A Dashboard for switching applications and handling settings has been developed, in addition to the range of awareness, gaming and simulation applications. The *sensor layer* consists of four basement mounted cameras. The cameras track the location of the users and send the location to the application running on the floor. The basement mounted cameras also track the location of the users but does so by tracking the silhouette of the user's limbs through the glass plates on the floor. This will be de-scribed in greater detail in the following section.

Data from the cameras is sent to a tracking machine in the client layer that processes the data and applies an algorithm for assigning and maintaining identifiers for limb contact points between frames for use in the applications running on the floor. The algo-rithm compares the previous frame with the current frame of the camera input and if the two tracked limbs are within a specified number of pixels from each other they are most likely the same limb and will thus be assigned the same identifier between frames. Oth-erwise the limb will be assigned a new unique identifier.

5 Kinesthetic Interaction Based on Limb Tracking

One of the major innovations in the setup is the use of the basement mounted cameras for tracking the user's limbs like hands and feet. Positions and identifiers of limb contact points are used as input to the applications running on the floor. A ceiling mounted camera approach, as known from the iFloor project [13], is well suited for moving along a ribbon around the projection but it is not suitable when trying to track the position of the user in order to, e.g. activate a "button" on the floor. Another prob-lem with the ceiling tracking approach is that users are seen in perspective and not directly from above making it hard to separate user's contours from each other. Moreover, it is hard to calculate precise positions to use for the individual users since the contour "blob" is quite big compared to the users contact points with the surface.

In contrast, the limb-based interaction technique offers a solution to these problems even though it is not as light-weight as the ceiling mounted approach. One of the main advantages in the approach is the elimination of the perspective problem since the user's limbs are in direct contact with the glass plates and only limbs in contact with the glass surface are tracked. The limbs can be tracked with a webcam since the contact points with the surface create a sufficient contrast from both the projection and the rest of the body under suitable light conditions, see Fig. 3. Limb positions are piped via TCP/IP to the applications. It is thus possible to hit a button in an application even though other users are standing close. Since only the center and not the contour of the limbs are being tracked the users are much less likely to disturb other users while interacting with the system. Fig. 3 shows a user's feet being tracked on the floor. The black circles indicate the center position of the user in the system and are very accurate compared to the physical location of the user.

Conditions for Reliable Real-Time Limb Tracking

There are some demands that need to be fulfilled for the system to track the user's limbs in a reliable way. One demand is a calibration in the tracking software based on various factors in the environment like ambient light and shadows. Another demand is that the light from above the iGameFloor must be strong enough to reduce the light emitted from the projectors in order to give the required contrast on the user's limbs when standing on the glass surface. Tests show that at least 300 lumen ambient light are required to obtain the desired contrast for tracking. Otherwise the dark areas in the projected interface will be tracked as input to the applications. This means the iGameFloor must be put in a controlled environment where the light on the iGame-Floor is adjusted according to changes in the environment. To achieve this we use indirect light on the floor since the reflection from direct light can be disturbing for the users.

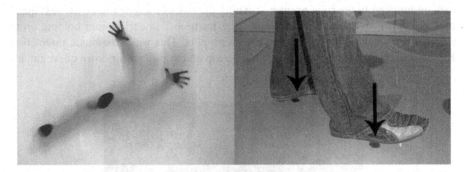

Fig. 3. Limb contact with the surface is tracked. The black dots to the right show the estimated positions of the users' limbs that are used in the applications.

When the system has been calibrated and adjusted to the light settings in the environment it is very robust and is able to track multiple users accurately. Tests have shown that up to fifteen users, i.e. at least 30 limb contact points can be tracked simultaneously on the floor though space is limited.

There is, however one limitation, to be aware of when designing the game play for applications on the iGameFloor. The problem may occur when the user places limbs directly on the reflection from the projector lens in the glass. This way the silhouette of the user's limb will be lighted up and can hardly be tracked by the system. Thus there are four dead spots in the current setup – one for each projector.

6   Applications Utilizing the Kinesthetic Interaction Technique

In this section a brief introduction to some of the applications developed or redes-igned for the iGameFloor is provided. The applications were developed as part of our research in limb-based tracking and kinesthetic interaction.

Pong
One of the first games implemented on iGameFloor was Pong - the classic video-game. Pong is a tennis-like game, and it calls for kinesthetic interaction in that the players may use their body movement to move the bat from side to side similar to real tennis or ping pong. On iGameFloor, it can be played by two players – one on each side of the iGameFloor and the side wards movements of their feet are tracked. The system keeps track of the players' scores and the player who first scores ten points has won the game. This game can be started by the children in the school breaks.

iFloorQuest
iFloorQuest is a floor game for four players inspired by Trivial Pursuit™. During the game a series of questions are "thrown at" the individual players from the center of the floor. Players then have a few seconds to jump to the one of the two spot with the possible answers. If a correct answer is selected both the player and the team will score a point since there is both an individual and collaborative score. In this way players can both play with or against each other. In most cases the children get very engaged and try to help each others in answering either through communication or by explicit jumping to the right answer - running the risk of missing ones own next ques-tion. As shown in Fig. 4, children sometimes team up 2 in each corner holding on to each other to make joint jumps to the answer spots. This way kinesthetic interaction has introduced engaging physical activity on top of a traditional sit down quest game.

Fig. 4. iFloorQuest in use with 8 players

Stepstone

Stepstone is a learning game application for up to four players. During the game a series of exercises are issued in speech and text, and the children must quickly use their hands and feet to combine a selection of several game elements to provide the correct solution. Stepstone functions as a framework in which different learning content can be implemented as required (e.g. the multiplication table, mapping language concepts to broader language concepts etc.), as well as the graphical environment can be varied (e.g. sea, rainforest, the city, the universe etc.). In this specific scenario, the setting is a beach with four shores in the corners and in the middle a sea filled with piranhas and stones for players to step on. Exercises require each player to select a combination of stones to provide a solution. The only way to avoid getting bitten is not to step in the water - or to solve the exercises correctly.

The objective in the game is to score as many points as possible by mapping pictures of concepts to categories over a specified amount of rounds. The players must select the correct answers by placing their hands or feet on the stones within the given time limit (visualized by movements in the water). Since the amount of correct answers exceeds the number of players, the players will have to use both hands and feet in order to score as many points as possible. When the time is up the selected answers will be evaluated and the player's collaborative score will be updated.

The interaction in the Stepstone application depends solely on kinesthetic interaction. Inspired by Twister released in 1966 by Milton Bradley Company, Stepstone uses body movement in a collaborative game frame. Whereas Twister is an edutainment game, Stepstone combines collaborative solving of learning exercises with the entertaining and engaging aspects of kinesthetic interaction. A variant of Stepstone was developed for hearing impaired children [11].

Fig. 5. Various stages in a Stepstone application

Dashboard

To avoid use of mouse and keyboard for controlling iGameFloor applications, a so-called dashboard has been developed. It is capable of performing standard task like switching between applications and basic control settings of the applications.

Since the dashboard has to function as a layer on top of the other iGameFloor applications, it is activated by a rare sequence of movements. The user walks from one

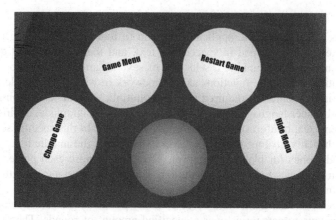

Fig. 6. Screen dump of the dashboard for application management

side of the floor to the other side and ends the sequence at the floor center. Here the Dashboard pops up in front of the user standing in the middle of the floor. It is a half pie variant of pie menus [8] that folds out in front of the user who can now select the action to take. Available options are e.g.: "Restart Game", "Hide Menu", "Game Menu" and "Change Game". If the "Change Game" option is triggered another half pie menu will fold out with available learning applications.

7   Kinesthetic Interaction Lessons

In the following, we describe qualitative lessons learned from the research and development phase. During the design project, participant observations of children's interacting on the iGameFloor were undertaken. Preliminary analysis of the observations brought about some general lessons regarding kinesthetic interaction and it's relation to learning environments.

Achievements and Successes

Full control possible through Kinesthetic Interaction. The iGameFloor can be fully operated using body movement. Children are able to interact with the iGameFloor using body movement as the only mean of interaction. When playing the iFloorQuest Application, children answered the questions by moving their body to the position of the right answer. The kinesthetic interaction was initiated without further instructions. When playing the Stepstone application, children immediately grasped Stepstone's metaphor and started stepping on the stones. Selections (corresponding to click and double click) are implemented by timeout triggers, i.e. standing still for 3 seconds may invoke a selection. Standing still for another 3 seconds may invoke an operation on the selection. Finally, generic functionality in the Dashboard can be invoked by a little rare movement sequence as described in Section 6; this kinesthetic sequence corresponds to pushing the Windows button on a PC or invoking the Dock on a Mac. One operation which we found hard to make kinesthetic is entry of data similar to keyboard entry. Thus a wireless keyboard is available close to the floor.

Kinesthetic interaction stimulates collaborative learning. Children perceive the iGameFloor as a collaborative learning environment. During the games, children communicate with other participants and with the spectators in order to find the right solutions to the given game challenges. In the iFloorQuest as well as in Stepstone, the children treated each other as teammates on a team assignment; Exercises and challenges were discussed during the games with other team members and with spectators and strategic agreements were quickly negotiated in the teams with respect to prior experiences on the floor. Engaging shouting of proposals across the floor is often observed, and individual scores were less important than collective scores.

Kinesthetic interaction is fun and motivating. Children were generally engaged by the use of kinesthetic interaction and described the learning games as 'fun', 'motivating', for instance they were eager to make their own content for the games. When doing an assignment in geography a group of six graders themselves made 50 questions to the iFloorQuest application on geography. Then their classmates were invited to a 'battle' on the iGameFloor; A battle of capitals and famous sights worldwide. This particular iFloorQuest game was played with 8 participants and the rest of the class cheering or advising the participants in the geographical questions. Afterwards both children and the teacher found the activity rewarding.

Limb-tracking is more precise than contour tracking. Both iFloor [13] and Eye-ToyPlay interpret the contour of the users' shadows and use that as the "cursor" representing the user. In iFloor this makes it quite hard to conduct precise selections since the cursor position is set to the center of the shadow blob. In EyeToyPlay, it is the edge of the shadow blob that constitute the cursor, this makes it possible to cheat, e.g. in games expecting the player to jump, you may just wave your hand over your head, since a jump is detected as a generating a higher shadow. In contrast limb contact points are pretty small and assigning a cursor to the center or the edge of a limb contact point will both be precise and easy to interpret in relation to ones body.

Limitations and Challenges

Hard to identify individual players. A central issue for the game play is identification of individual players. Identifiers are relevant if the system was to keep track of the individual user's score. But it is hard to identify individuals solely based on shadows generated on a glass surface. For the first version of iGameFloor, we have made collaborative gaming applications that get around the identification issue either by associating a location to a specific player or to make the game a complete collaborative endeavor for a group of players to solve a common mission. In iFloorQuest, identification is handled by giving all users a base to stand on to not move freely around on all of the iGameFloor. In the Pong game, each end of the court is associated with a player. In the Stepstone learning game users can select stones all over the floor making it hard to track the score of a given user. Thus the game play was made collaborative for the group by calculating a common score. A possible future solution may be to identify users with different LED-light colors similar to MultiLightTracker [21]. If users interact with both hands and feet this will involve marking up both hands and feet with the same unique color. Another approach could be shape or visual tag tracking.

Children expecting a touch-sensitive surface. Some children assumed that they could interact with the iGameFloor using their feet as point and click/drag and drop. iGameFloor has some similarities with well-known interfaces from the familiar PC, thus it was quite common that children started stamping on icons and the like, expecting the computer to respond to kinesthetic clicks. In other incidences children double stamped on the iGameFloor during game as an attempt to generate a response by the computer as if they were double clicking a mouse. These observations all points to the need for a conceptual framework and standard audio/visual cues for kinesthetic interaction such that the interface doesn't lead to wrong expectations.

Missing the third dimension. Since the limb-based tracking is only 2D, we lack the possibility of taking advantage of users' movement in the third (vertical) dimension. Children expected iGameFloor to "be aware" of their hand gestures in the air. During a game session two 10 years old were moving their body as if the computer could track their body movement away from the floor. They wanted to be able to control a virtual ball on the floor by moving their upper body. To address this issue, we consider combining the limb-tracking with other sensors, e.g. taking advantage of the capabilities of children cell phones, e.g. Nokia 5500 and some Samsung models includes accelerometers and Bluetooth communication, thus it might be able to let the cell phone send signals about movements above the surface to iGameFloor. Another possibility might be to utilize a camera from the side tracking in the third dimension.

8 Comparison to Related Work

BodyGames [15] and LightSpace™ (www.interactivefloor.com) are two sensor and tile based floors with abstract light diode feedback. Compared to BodyGames and LightSpace™ the iGameFloor provides a much richer visual multimedia feedback with extensive guidance on the activities undertaken.

Compared to the vision based iFloor system [13], the iGameFloor supports tracking of multiple users directly on the projection surface. iFloor only facilitated tracking on the edge of the floor. The iGameFloor also reduces the problems of shadowing the projection since the projection comes from beneath the users' bodies and do not disturb the projection except from what they hide with their feet on the surface. The iGameFloor also provides a much more fine-grained and precise tracking of users. The tracking is targeted to the contact points of limbs and not just the contour of the entire body as was the case in iFloor.

9 Conclusion and Future Work

This paper has introduced a novel kinesthetic interaction technique for a large scale interactive floor installation. The kinesthetic interaction technique utilizes vision-based limb tracking from the bottom of the interactive floor. Four cameras provide fine-grained tracking of limb (e.g. foot, hand, knee, and elbow) contact points. The setup allow real-time tracking of 30+ limb contact point, thus providing large scale multi-user interaction in an interactive space. The kinesthetic interaction technique has been utilized to develop learning applications including games for school environments. It has been illustrated how the kinesthetic interaction technique can support real-time co-located collaborative learning games with many participants. Several new applications of the kinesthetic interaction technique is under development, and applications are not limited to school environments – experience environments like museums, attractions, and playgrounds or shopping malls are among the new application domains.

We thus see many possible extensions to the concept. We could e.g. start detecting difference between hands and feet and we may be able to track different foot gestures or patterns that could be used to invoke different actions in the applications.

We also wish to investigate how limb-tracking may be supported without the expensive bottom tracking of floors, since many of the applications may be executed on a much cheaper platform with projection from above or in some future with new "electronic paper" based display put on top of floors.

A structured evaluation of the kinesthetic interaction and learning potentials on specific educational tasks will take place when the system is finally released at the school.

Acknowledgements

This work was supported by ISIS Katrinebjerg, Center for Interactive Spaces. We wish to thank all our center colleagues as well as the staff at Department of Education, Aarhus Municipality and Møllevangskolen for contributions to the work. We would also like to thank the sponsors of the physical installation: the Oticon Foundation, Boligfonden Kuben, NNC, Arkitema, Søren Jensen Engineering, and Dansk Data Display.

References

1. Bødker, S., Grønbæk, K., Kyng, M.: Cooperative Design: Techniques and Experiences from the Scandinavian Scene. In: Baecker, et al. (eds.) Readings in Human- Computer Interaction: Toward the Year 2000, Morgan Kaufman Publishers, San Francisco, USA (1995)
2. Dindler, C., Eriksson, E., Iversen, O.S., Lykke-Olesen, A., Ludvigsen, M.: Mission from Mars: a method for exploring user requirements for children in a narrative space. In: Proceeding of the 2005 Conference on interaction Design and Children. IDC '05, Boulder, Colorado, June 08 - 10, 2005, pp. 40–47. ACM Press, New York (2005)
3. Fernström, M., Griffith, N.: Litefoot – Auditory Display of Footwork. In: Proceeding of ICAD'98, Glasgow, Scotland (1998)
4. Fogarty, J., Forlizzi, J., Hudson, S.E.: Aesthetic Information Collages: Generating Decorative Displays that Contain Information. In: Proceedings of UIST'01, pp. 141–150. ACM Press, New York (2001)
5. Gardner, H.: Frames of Mind: The theory of multiple intelligences. In: Britain by Fontana Press, 2nd edn., p. 466. Basic Books, New York (1993)
6. Grønbæk, K., Iversen, O.S., Kortbek, K.J., Nielsen, K.R., Aagaard, L.: iGameFloor - a Platform for Co-Located Collaborative Games. In: Proceedings of the International Conference on Advances in Computer Entertainment 2007, Salzburg, Austria (June 13-15, 2007)
7. Höysniemi, J.: International survey on the Dance Dance Revolution game. ACM Computers in Entertainment 4(2) (2006)

8. Hopkins, D.: The Design and Implementation of Pie Menus. in Dr. Dobb's Journal (1991)
9. Iversen, O.S., Brodersen, C.: Bridging the Gap between users and children - A socio-cultural approach to designing with children in Springer's journal Cognition. Technology and Work for the special issue on Child-Computer Interaction: Methodological Research 9(2) (2007)
10. Iversen, O.S.: Participatory Design beyond Work Practices - Designing with Children, Ph.D. Thesis, Dept. of Computer Science, University of Aarhus (2006)
11. Iversen, O.S., Kortbek, K.J., Nielsen, K.R., Aagaard, L.: Stepstone- An Interactive Floor Application for Hearing Impaired Children with a Cochlear Implant. In: Proc. of IDC07 6th International Conference on Interaction Design and Children, Aalborg, Denmark (June 6-8, 2007)
12. Klemmer, S.R., Hartmann, B., Takayama, L.: How bodies matter: five themes for interaction design. In: Proc. of the 6th ACM Conference on Designing interactive Systems. DIS '06, University Park, PA, USA, June 26-28, 2006, pp. 140–149. ACM Press, New York (2006)
13. Krogh, P.G., Ludvigsen, M., Lykke-Olesen, A.: Help me pull that cursor - A Collaborative Interactive Floor Enhancing Community Interaction. In: Proc. of OZCHI, University of Wollongong, Australia. CD-ROM, 22-24 November, 2004 (2004) ISBN:1 74128 079
14. Leikas, J., Väätänen, A., Räty, V.: Virtual space computer games with a floor sensor control: human centred approach in the design process. In: Brewster, S., Murray-Smith, R. (eds.) HH-CI. LNCS, vol. 2058, pp. 199–204. Springer, Heidelberg (2001)
15. Lund, H.H., Klitbo, T., Jessen, C.: Playware Technology for Physically Activating Play. Artificial life and Robotics Journal 9 (2005)
16. McElliot, L., Dillon, M., Leydon, K., Richardson, B., Fernstrom, M., Paradiso, J.: ForSe FIElds – Force Fields for Interactive Environments. In: Proc. of Ubiquitous Computing. 4th Int. Conference, Göteborg Sweden, pp. 168–175 (2002)
17. Merleau-Ponty, M.: Phenomenology of Perception translated by Colin Smith. Humanities Press, New York (1945)
18. Moen, J.: KinAesthetic Movement Interaction: Designing for the Pleasure of Motion, dissertation from KTH, Numerical Analysis and Computer Science, Stokholm, Sweden (2006)
19. Moen, J., Sandsjö, J.: BodyBug - Design of KinAesthetic Interaction. In: Digital Proceedings of NORDES In the Making, Copenhagen, Denmark (2005)
20. Moser, T.: Bevægelse i sproget – sproget i bevægelse (in Danish) http://kidlld.dk/temaer/krop/beveagelse/ PloneArticle_view
21. Nielsen, J., Grønbæk, K.: MultiLightTracker: Vision based simultaneous multi object tracking on semi-transparent surfaces. In: Proc. of the International Conference on Computer Vision Theory and Applications (VISAPP 2006), Setúbal, Portugal, 25-28 February, 2006 (2006)
22. Paradiso, J., Abler, C., Hsiao, K., Reynolds, M.: The Magic Carpet - Physical Sensing for Immersive Environments. In: Proc. of CHI' 97, Atlanta, GA, USA (1997)
23. Petersen, M.G.: Remarkable computing: the challenge of designing for the home. In: Proceedings of CHI'2004, pp. 1445–1449. ACM Press, New York (2004)
24. Richardson, B., Leydon, K., Fernstrom, M., Paradiso, J.A.: Z-Tiles: building blocks for modular, pressure-sensing floorspaces April 2004 Extended abstracts of the 2004 conference on Human factors and computing systems (2004)
25. Udsen, L.E., Jørgensen, A.H.: The aesthetic turn: unraveling recent aesthetic approaches to human-computer interaction. In Digital Creativity 16(4), 205–216 (2005)

26. Underkoffler, J., Ishii, H.: Illuminating light: An optical design tool with a luminous-tangible interface. In: Proc. of the SIGCHI conference on Human factors in computing systems, ACM Press, Los Angeles (1998)
27. Valli, A.: RETINA - video tracking software available at (2004-06-18),
    http://alessandrovalli.com/retina/

Was Vygotsky Right? Evaluating Learning Effects of Social Interaction in Children Internet Games

Franca Garzotto

HOC – Hypermedia Open Center
Department of Electronics and Information, Politecnico di Milano
Via Ponzio 34/5, 20133 Milano (Italy)
franca.garzotto@polimi.it

Abstract. The social basis for learning, particularly in childhood, has been acknowledged since the seminal research of the Russian psychologist Lev Vygotsky. Although his theory is very often cited in HCI literature as a theoretical basis for the design of multi-user interactive artefacts, little empirical data is available that assess Vygotsky's thesis in this domain. This paper presents an empirical study that investigated the learning impact of social interaction in the context of *children online edutainment.* We developed "multiplayer" and "individual" configurations of an educational internet game and measured the learning benefits of *"playing together"* and *"playing alone"* in 54 children from a local elementary school. Not surprisingly, our findings confirm that Vygotsky was right. They provide some empirical evidence that in contexts of online gaming, the presence of interpersonal communication, collective goals, and social activities has measurable beneficial effects on children learning.

Keywords: edutainment, social interaction, multiuser online game, children, learning, evaluation.

1 Introduction

The Russian pedagogist Lev Vygotsky (1896-1934) is one of the most cited researchers in HCI literature on social interaction and learning. The major theme of his theoretical framework is that the social dimension plays a fundamental role in the development of human cognition and learning, especially in childhood [24]. Although his work is very often invoked as a theoretical basis for the *design* of multi-user interactive artefacts, little data are available that empirically assess Vygotsky's thesis in situations of ICT mediated social interaction, particularly in the domain of *children edutainment[1]*.

In this paper we discuss an empirical study that investigate the learning benefits of social interaction on children engaged in *internet educational games,* in order to

---

[1] The term "edutainment" - standing for "educational entertainment" - denotes a form of entertainment designed to educate as well as to amuse.

C. Baranauskas et al. (Eds.): INTERACT 2007, LNCS 4663, Part II, pp. 376 – 389, 2007.

empirically establish whether, in this context, "playing *with peers*" is more conductive to learning than *"playing alone"*, and whether *different conditions of social interaction* induce different measurable learning effects.

For the purpose of our study, we developed multiple configurations - multiplayer and individual - of an internet game and compared the learning effects in three groups of elementary school children using the system "alone" and "together". We also investigated the role of *competition* in multiuser gaming, obtaining some empirical data on how "playing *against others*" may affect learning.

Not surprisingly, our findings confirms Vygotsky's general thesis, highlighting that, at least in young children, *internet game experiences involving social interaction are more conductive to learning than playing alone*. The results of our study also show that children using the multiplayer *competitive* version achieved slightly better results that those using the multiplayer non-competitive version, suggesting that, in some situations, competition may foster learning.

The rest of the paper is organized as follows. We first present the game used in our research, describing its various configurations. Then we introduce the procedure adopted in our empirical study and discuss its main findings. We conclude with a brief overview of related works and some final considerations.

2 The Online Game

The online game used in our study is called *Pirates Treasure Hunt* ("Pirates" for short). It was built by our laboratory[2] in the context of a larger project [9] [5] that collaborates with elementary and high schools to design, develop, and evaluate internet based edutainment experiences for children. The general educational goal of Pirates is to stimulate children interest in and attention for "other" cultures and ways of life - a subject of primary school curricula in our country. The game exposes children to contents and knowledge tasks related to the culture of two non-European countries – Morocco and Japan. To complete the game, players must apply what they have previously studied and learnt about these subjects. At a deeper level, Pirates fosters concept understanding and meaning-making, as well as recognition and recall skills.

For the purpose of our study, we developed three different versions of the game: a *Multiplayer Collaborative* and *Competitive* version (MCC Pirates), a *Multiplayer Collaborative* version (MC Pirates) and an *Individual* version (I Pirates). In the rest of this section, we introduce the general gaming rules holding in all configurations, and then describe the peculiar characteristics of each version.

2.1 Pirates: General Rules

Pirates is a *discovery* game where players act like pirates, exploring a virtual archipelago and discovering hidden "treasures". In the virtual space, a user is represented as a small ship (see figure 1 - #3) and can navigate the archipelago either

---

[2] Using Flash Communication Server and XML technology.

in a continuous way (using cursors) or "by jumps" (selecting an area on a map). The Pirates' world is populated with interactive objects - animals or environmental elements. Some of them, e.g., rocks and sharks, are "dangerous" (see figure 1 - #2): when casually encountered or explicitly activated, they cause a penalty and a brief (10 seconds) suspension of the player's activity, during which any interaction is inhibited. Others are "treasure objects": they hide "treasures" that appear when these objects are "clicked". A treasure is a quiz card that shows an image and a quiz (see figure 2). The image represents a typical aspect of the culture of Morocco or Japan, i.e., a traditional Japanese food or a typical piece of furniture of Morocco. The quiz is a yes/no question about the image meaning, such as: "Is this Moroccan dressing?"

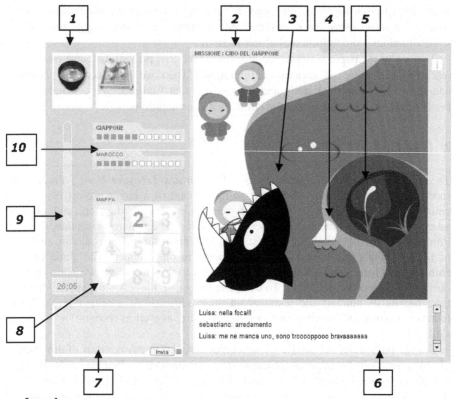

Legend:
1: Collected Treasures (Miso Soup and Sushi, in this case); 2: Player's Mission (Japanese Food in this case) 3: Dangerous Object; 4: Player's "Avatar"; 5: Treasure Object; 6: Chat Messages;
7: Chat Authoring Box; 8: Interactive Map; 9: Timer; 10: Teams' Progress Status (partially or totally removed in other configurations)

Fig. 1. Pirates interface – MCC configuration

A Pirates player has a *mission*: to discover and collect all treasures (i.e., cards) that concern a specific "cultural aspect" (food, dressing, tradition, or furniture) of a country. If a player's answer to a treasure question is wrong, he gets a penalty and a

10 seconds suspension. If his answer is correct *and* the image corresponds to the player mission, he gains points and the card can be "picked up" (appearing on the treasure bag on the top left side of the screen - see figure 1 - #1), contributing to the progress towards game completion.

The treasure objects hidden in the archipelago are the same in all game sessions (as discussed in section 3.2); also the images on the treasure cards are the same, but the quizzes are dynamically customized to the current mission of the player who clicks on the object and discovers the treasure. For example, a shark may hide a card showing the image of cous-cous plate but the quiz is "Is this Japanese food?" only for the player whose current mission is to collect Japanese food; another question will appear on the same card for a player who has a different mission.

2.2 Pirates Configurations

For the purpose of our study, we need to ensure that in all Pirates configurations players have an *equivalent exposure to learning contents*[3] and the only aspect that is modified in the user experience concerns the *social conditions* in which children are exposed to such contents. To meet this requirement, in all game versions the player's tasks are the same ("explore and collect"); also the set of treasure cards hidden in the archipelago are the same, thus providing equivalent knowledge spaces to explore. We only change the rules to end the game: in all its configurations, Pirates is over when *all* missions for a country are completed, but in the two multiplayer modes there are both "individual" missions and a "collective mission" that must be fulfilled in order to terminate the game.

2.2.1 Multiplayer Collaborative and Competitive Version (MCC)

This version (see figures 1, 2 and 3) involves *eight* simultaneous remote players, who are organized in *two competing teams,* each one representing a country - Morocco or Japan. A different mission is assigned to each player, but the victory is assigned to a team only if *all* members complete their mission and they achieve this result before the other team. In other word, the challenge is to discover and pick up *all* treasures (cards) for the own team country *before* the other team (see figure 4). This *collective goal* is the key motivator for collaboration and communication. A player should feel that the completion of the others' missions in his team is as important as his own mission's achievement; he is motivated to continue searching for team treasures and to offer mutual assistance even after his individual mission is completed.

The communication and collaboration tool is the *chat* (see figure 1 - #7). A player can send messages to invoke or provide help, to alert the other members about pitfalls or dangerous objects in a given area, or to inform his team mates when he discovers a treasure that is relevant for the rest of the team.

---

[3] Here we use the term "content" in a broad sense, to denote two aspects: i) the information pieces that are available in the game (i.e., the treasure cards) and players get exposed to; ii) the knowledge tasks in which children get involved.

Treasure Card

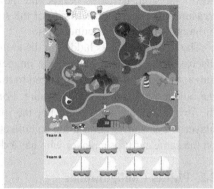

Fig. 2. MCC Configuration: treasure card

Fig. 3. MCC configuration: Players are logging-in (One player in team A – Morocco - hasn't logged in yet)

Fig. 4. End-game screen shot - MCC configuration. It shows collected treasures, gained points, penalties, and play time of each team

2.2.2 Multiplayer Collaborative Configuration (MC)

In this version, *four* remote children play *together* for the *same* country. The interface is essentially the same as in the MCC version, but the progress bar now presents the progresses of one country only (see figure 5), and the end-game screen displays the final results for that country only. In absence of competition, what are the motivations for social interaction? One motivation could be enjoyment for "getting in touch" with remote peers (via chat) and feeling part of a community. Or a child may be in trouble and may need to ask the others for help. Or he may contribute to other's missions for the purpose of speeding up the game conclusion: minimizing the session duration is a form of challenge – a kind of self-competition at group level, and a self-rewarding feature per se.

2.2.3 Individual Player Configuration (I)

In the individual version, the player is initially assigned to a country and a mission (as in the multiplayer versions), and a new mission for the same country is *automatically* assigned after the current mission is completed. As in the MC version, the game terminates when all treasures for the current country have been discovered.

In the individual configuration, the chat has the role of personal "notebook", where the user can take notes and record information that can be useful later, e.g., annotating where he find the dangerous objects or the locations where treasures for future missions can be found.

Fig. 5. Pirate's interface - MC configuration

2.3 Educational Support Material

In order to properly answer treasure quizzes, children must have previously acquired some "domain knowledge" about the game subjects. For this purpose, we provided some printed educational material and integrated the game with an online, individual, 3D learning space. Both are intended to be used before gaming. The printed material, which can be studied in the classroom or at home before gaming (see next section),

Fig. 6. The 3D learning space

comprises information sheets about the various cultural topics of the game, including images and texts describing the subjects of the treasures hidden in the game.

The online learning space (see figure 6) provides two cartoon-like 3D worlds that reproduce "typical" environments of Morocco or Japan (e.g., a Japanese house or a Moroccan "suk"); these virtual spaces include a number of interactive objects that show "in context" the game cultural elements of each country (examples of food, dressing, traditions, furniture that represent the game treasures) . When an interactive element is selected, the corresponding information sheet appears (see figure 6- right). The printed material and the information sheets in the learning environment both use the same images as the treasure cards in the game.

4   Evaluation Procedure

The general goal of the study was to assess empirically two hypotheses:

i) social interaction in online edutainment promotes children's learning; in particular, playing an online educational game *together* is *more effective for learning* than playing *alone*;

ii) *different conditions of social interaction* induce different learning effects.

For the purpose of our study, we measured and compared some learning results achieved by three groups of elementary school children who used Pirates in the different configurations discussed in the previous section. We considered learning benefits at two levels of Bloom's taxonomy of the learning domain [1]: the *cognitive* level (which involves knowledge and intellectual skills) and the *affective* level (which involves the manner in which learners deal with things emotionally – e.g., feelings, values, appreciation, enthusiasms, motivations, and attitudes). At the cognitive level, we focused on the cognitive skills of recall, recognition, and understanding of specific facts or concepts. At the attitude level, we considered motivation to learning new subjects and interest to "other cultures and ways of life", which are the subject of the educational content of Pirates.

The study involved *54* children aged 8-9 (28 girls and 26 boys), from three third grade classes of a public elementary school in our city. All children had a sufficient level of skills in the use of mouse and keyboard, and a homogenous exposure to interactive experiences. We randomly organized participants in *three* groups, one per game configuration, composed of 16 children. Children played with the game in the two computer laboratories of the school, which is the conventional context where children in our country use computers in their normal school activity. When using the multiplayer configurations of Pirates, we simulated the effect of playing with "remote" peers by allocating children of the same team in different computer labs. Rooms were quite wide, and children in the same lab were placed far enough so that they could not peep nor could be distracted by what the others in the same space were doing. Six teachers (two per class) were also involved in the study; they offered assistance during the play sessions and were interviewed afterwards.

Each group playing a *multiplayer* configuration (MMC or MC) was split in *four subgroups*, each one composed of *four* randomly selected children. Subgroups

Table 1. Children' allocation to game configuration in the laboratory sessions (MCC=Multiplayer Collaborative Competitive; MC=Multiplayer Collaborative; I = Individual)

Lab Session #	Configuration	Kids	Sub-groups
1	MCC	8	2
2	MCC	8	2
3	MC	4	1
4	MC	4	1
5	MC	4	1
6	MC	4	1
7	I	16	n.a.

playing the competitive configuration were *paired* to play one against the other. We conducted *seven laboratory sessions with children,* of the average *duration of 2 hours,* involving children and sub-groups as described in the following table.

For all groups, the work was organized in three phases:

Phase 1 – Study and learning pre-test. Some days before a laboratory session, children studied and discussed the printed material in the classroom for one hour, and spent approximately 45 minutes using the 3D learning space of Pirates with their teachers. This activity aimed at supporting a homogeneous level of domain knowledge in all children in our study. At the end of this work, we submitted a learning test to assess children learning level on game subjects. Knowledge and intellectual skills (recognition, recall, concept understanding) were operationalized in terms of children' capability to assign meaning to images. The test included *ten* "quizzes". A quiz was a checklist question. It showed an image of the culture of Morocco or Japan (e.g., a Moroccan dress) randomly selected from the set of the game treasure cards, asking "what is this..?"; the four alternative answers were defined in terms of country and cultural type aspect, e.g., "Japanese Food".

Phase 2 – Play. Before playing the game, children were trained about game rules and spent approximately 10 minutes to practice with interaction commands, on a demo-version of Pirates. Finally, they played the real game *twice,* each time changing country and initial mission (see figure 7 - left side).

Phase3 – Learning post test and questionnaire. After gaming, we submitted a second learning test, similar to the first one but with a different set of quizzes. In addition, children filled a simple questionnaire (see figure 7 – right side) aimed at giving us some quantitative and qualitative information about *learning benefits at the affective level,* and about *satisfaction* and *enjoyment.* The questionnaire included few open and close ended questions, asking children how much they liked the gaming experience, what they liked and disliked more, and similar. A suggested in [19], we adopted a "Smilemyometer" ☺☺, ☺, ☺, ☺ as rating metric for children, instead of numerical scores.

Beside learning tests and questionnaires, we collected qualitative data by *observing* children behavior and by *interviewing* the teachers. During play, an observer sat side-by-side each child and took notes about his behavior (voice comments, movements, strategies, interaction mistakes, focus of attention,...) on a structured evaluation form. Interviews with teachers were held some days after the test sessions, and mainly attempted to get insights about learning benefits at attitude level.

Fig. 7. Playing Pirates (left) and filling the questionnaire (right)

5 Findings

The main measure for learning at the *knowledge* level was the difference in the scores (number of correct answers) of pre and post test learning tests. The average difference of correct questions in the three groups (MMC, MC, I) is shown in fig. 8, that highlights that in all configurations the gaming experience induced some learning benefits at knowledge level.

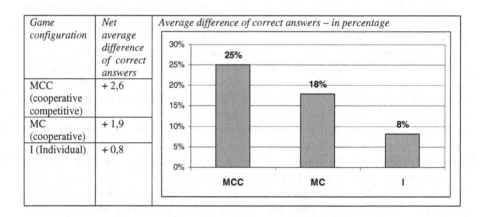

Fig. 8. Measuring Learning Benefits at Knowledge level: means of score differences in pre-post learning tests

To measure the learning benefits at the *affective* level (motivation to learning new subjects and interest to "other" cultures and ways of life) we analyzed various sources: quantitative and qualitative results of children' questionnaire, teachers' answers during interviews, and observers' notes. In the questionnaire, for example, we asked children to rate ☺☺ , ☺ , ☺ , or ☹ their appreciation of each of the

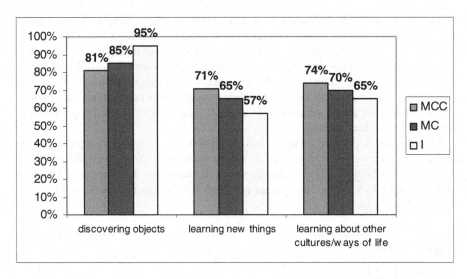

Fig. 9. Children' ☺☺ ratings for question "How much did you like...?"

other countries and ways of life".   Figure 9 visualizes the percentages of children in the three groups who rated ☺☺ a specific aspect. It shows that the discovery features of the game is the aspect that children appreciated more – this is, indeed, the truly "gaming" aspect of Pirates' experience, common to all configurations.

The fact that in all three groups more that 50% of children gave the highest possible rate also to "Discovering new things" and "Learning about other cultures and ways of life", highlights that the overall experience fostered positive feelings towards the educational content of the game. Still, the number of children who rated learning aspects as ☺☺ was larger in those playing together (the MCC and MC groups) than in those playing alone (I group). These data may be interpreted as a positive result achieved at affective level by the MMC and MC groups. At least, they reveal that children playing in the two contexts of *social* gaming became *more* self-conscious of the fact that *they learned something new,* or were *more willing* to acknowledge this aspect as positive, than their peers playing alone. This affective aspect seems slightly stronger in presence of competition (MCC group).

Qualitative data analysis partially confirms these results. We coded the "free notes" reported in children questionnaires and their voice comments transcribed by the observers. Then we clustered the contributions denoting positive feeling towards "learning new things" or "learning about other countries and ways of life. (Examples of children' comments in this cluster are: *"I didn't' know that my favorite cartoons are from Japan! It's great! Now I understand why characters always eat that funny rice!"*(written comment)*; "Look at origami! Do children in Japan build origami at school as we do?"*(voice comment) [4]. The number of contributions that externalized

---

[4] In the above comments, children refer to "manga" comics, sushi, and origami, appearing in Pirates as treasures for missions related to Japan. Origami is an activity that some of our children practiced at school.

positive feelings about learning was higher in the groups playing in a social mode than in the individual mode (50% and 35% more in the MCC and MC groups respectively, than in the I group). Still, at the affective level no significant difference among the three groups was reported by teachers. Teachers involved children in classroom and home "conventional" activities on the game subjects (discussion, storytelling, drawing). In all participants they noticed interest and enthusiasm for such topics, which were totally new for most students, and do not observed any significant difference in the three groups.

As a further input for analysis and reflection, we considered *enjoyment*. We analyzed the scores given to the questionnaire question: *"How much did you enjoy playing Pirates?"* ☺☺ ☺ ☺ ☹ . As shown in the following diagram, more people in the MCC group (75%) rated enjoyment very high ☺☺, against the 64% of MC group and the 41% of I group.

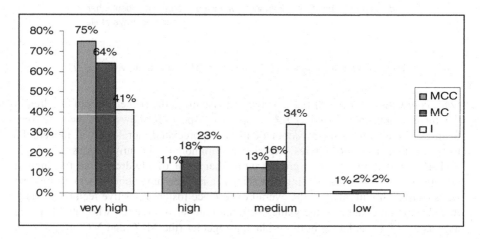

Fig. 10. Percentages of children' high rating ☺☺ for enjoyment

The analysis of qualitative data confirmed this trend. We considered the number of comments in the questionnaire, transcripts of voice comments, and observers' notes about children' behaviour during the game that denoted high degree of enthusiasm, appreciation, or engagement (e.g., *"I would like to do Pirates thousands times!!!"*, *"I wish I had Pirates at home thus I could play it every day!"*). The number of contributions coded as "enjoyment" resulted higher in the MCC group than in the MC group, who in turn showed more enjoyment than the I group. For example, in the MCC group the progress bar was wept franticly under control (more constantly than the other groups), and any progress of the own team was outlined by enthusiastic comments. The happiness of victorious children was enormous (they shouted and jumped for 5 minutes).

6 Discussion

As we expected, the findings of our study provide an empirical validation of Vygotsky's general thesis in the context of internet edutainment: in young children, *online game experiences involving social interaction are more conductive to learning than playing alone.* We measured stronger educational benefits in social gaming w.r.t. individual play at both the knowledge and the attitude levels of Bloom's taxonomy. In this section, we attempt an interpretative analysis of our findings. In our case study, social interaction took three forms: communication, remote cooperation, and competition.

Communication, enabled by the chat, created the feeling of "being there with many" ("co-presence" [14]) and of being "a member of a group" ("community" [26]). The "experience of connection" enhanced the sense of social *identity* and enforced the feeling of *self-recognition* without which learning attitudes, in children, may be weakened [21]. Discussing strategies and solutions with others was a way "to make thinking visible" and created a more tangible context for what had been learned, building the conditions for *situated learning* [12].

Remote cooperation with distant peers (implicit in the concept of "multiplayer online" game) was founded on *shared* goals, which pinpointed in children the need for more than one person to be involved and for complementary abilities, and increased their *motivation* for applying individual skills and knowledge.

Competition was a powerful motivator for being engaged in educational content. Children gained satisfaction from competing against and beating other people; competition added emotions that made the gaming experience more exciting and fun [4][13][15][23][25] – all aspects that fostered learning.

The results of our study also support our second hypothesis, i.e., *different conditions of social interaction* induce different learning effects. Our data show some correlation among *learning* and *intensity of social interaction*. As observed in the previous subsection, communication and collaboration among remote peers was more intense in the MCC group, which apparently achieved stronger learning benefits than in the MC, and became stronger towards the end of the game. Higher intensity of social interaction may be induced, in our case, by the only two aspects in which the MCC and MC configurations differ: the number of players involved (8 against 4) and the competitive nature of the MCC game experience. Although competition is in antithesis of cooperation, the need or desire to compete with others is a very common impetus that motivates individuals to cooperate with each other in order to form a stronger competitive force. After completing their individual mission, MCC children showed a more intense desire to continue playing if compared to the MC group, and cooperation and communication became more intense – they wanted to win!

Our study also provides some empirical evidence of some other emotional factors that are induced by social interaction and foster learning. A correlation that our data pinpoints (see figure 10) is between *learning* and *enjoyment*, showing that children who learnt more (the MCC group) also had more fun. The relationship among these two factors has been largely investigated [18]. In our case, the main variable that seemed to affect enjoyment (and, through enjoyment, increased learning) is *competition*. In this respect, our results differ from other studies (e.g., [17]) that found that the competitive nature of a social experience may hamper reflection and well-though decision making, and induce less learning benefits that a non competitive version of the same experience.

7 Related Works and Conclusions

The combination of social interaction and gaming was investigated by Vygotsky himself: although he is less known for his research on play, he studied children gaming as a psychological phenomenon and acknowledged its role in the child's development, both in individual and social contexts [24].

Since the advent of multimedia technology, the educational potential of *multiplayer interactive games* has been acknowledged by many empirical studies in HCI [3][7][10][11][20][22] and has its theoretical foundation in a number of classical and modern theories in cognitive science and pedagogy [21][26]. Still, relatively few *empirical* studies exist that investigate the educational benefits of social *online* gaming *for young children*. Most of HCI empirical research on *online* multiplayer games scarcely addresses this target [22], mainly focusing on adults [6][11] or adolescents [5] (and marginally considering educational aspects). The HCI literature reports a number of empirical results on social playing and learning for pre-school or primary school children, but most of the published studies exploit "complex" technological settings for the social gaming experience (tabletops, tangibles, robots, mobile devices, augmented reality systems, etc.) [3][7][16]; apparently, the main goal of these studies is more to test the design of *novel forms of interactions* than to evaluate how the social dimension of these innovative solutions may affect learning.

The main contribution of our work is to empirically investigate game-based learning [18] and social interaction in *young children* and in a conventional technological domain – the Internet - that is becoming more and more popular in education, both in conventional settings and in home-schooling situations.

Acknowledgments. The author is grateful to the technical staff of HOC Lab. Special thanks go to the children and the teachers of elementary school "Nolli Arquati" in Milan who participated so enthusiastically in the evaluation study.

References

1. Bloom, B.S., Mesia B.B., Krathwohl D.R.: Taxonomy of Educational Objectives New York. David McKay., (1964)
2. Csikszentmihalyi, M.: Flow: The Psychology of Optimal Experience. Harper Perennial, New York (1991)
3. Deguchi, A., et al.: A system for supporting childrens face-to-face collaborative learning by integrating personal and shared spaces. In: Proc. IDC'2006, Tampere, Finland, ACM Press, New York (2006)
4. Desurvire, H., Maplan, M., Toth, J.A.: Using heuristics to evaluate the playability of games. In: Extended Abstracts of CHI 2004, Vienna, pp. 1509–1512. ACM Press, New York (2006)
5. Di Blas, N., Paolini, P., Poggi, C.: Educational benefits: testing and evaluation of a collaborative 3d world. In: Proc. ED-MEDIA 2005, AACE, pp. 1002–1011 (2005)
6. Ducheneaut, N., Yee, N., Nickel, E., Moore, R.: Alone Together Exploring the social dynamics of massively multiplayer online games. In: Proc. CHI2006, pp. 407–416. ACM Press, New York (2006)
7. Druin, A. (ed.) The Design of Children Technology. San Francisco (CA) (1999)

8. Fisch, M.S.: Making Educational Computer Games "Educational". In: Proc. IDC'05, Boulder (Colorado), ACM Press, New York (2005)
9. Garzotto, F., Forfori, M.: FaTe2: Storytelling Edutainment Experiences in 2D and 3D Collaborative Spaces. In: Proc. IDC '06, Tampere (Finland), ACM Press, New York (2006)
10. Hanna, L., Neapolitan, D., Risden, K.: Evaluating Computer Game Concepts with Children. In: Proc. IDC 2004, College Park (Maryland), pp. 49–56. ACM Press, New York (2004)
11. Nardi, B., Harris, J.: Strangers and Friends: Collaborative Play in World of WarCraft. In: Proc. CSCW'06, Banff (Canada), pp. 1–10. ACM Press, New York (2006)
12. Lave, J., Wenger, E.: Situated Learning: Legitimate Peripheral Participation. Cambridge University Press, Cambridge (1990)
13. Lazzaro, N., Keeker, K.: What's my method? A game show on games. In: Extended Abstracts of CHI 2004, Vienna, pp. 1093–1094. ACM Press, New York (2006)
14. MacIntyre, B., Bolter, J.D., Gandy, M.: Presence and the aura of meaningful places. In: Proc. Presence 2004, Valencia (October 2004)
15. Pagulayan, R., Keeker, K., Wixon, D., Romero, R., Fuller, T.: User-centered design in games. In: Jacko, J.A., Sears, A. (eds.) The HCI Handbook, pp. 883–905. Lawrence Erlbaum Associates, Mahwah (2003)
16. Piper, A.M., O'Brien, E., Morris, M.R., Winograd, T.: SIDES: A Cooperative Tabletop Computer Game for Social Skill Development. In: Proc. CSCW'06, Banff (Canada), pp. 1–10. ACM Press, New York (2006)
17. Pal, J., Pawar, U., Brewer, E., Toayama, K.: The case for multiuser design for computer aided learning in developing regions. In: Proc. WWW 2006, pp. 781–789. ACM Press, New York (2006)
18. Prensky, M.: Digital Game-Based Learning. McGraw-Hill, New York (2001)
19. Read, J.C., MacFarlane, S.J.: Using the Fun Toolkit and Other Survey Methods to Gather Opinions in Child Computer Interaction. In: Proc. IDC'2006, Tampere, Finland, ACM Press, New York (2006)
20. Revelle, G.: Educating via Entertainment Media: the Sesame Workshop approach. ACM Computer and Entertainment 1(1), 1–9 (2003)
21. Rogoff, T.: Apprenticeship in Thinking: Cognitive development in social context. Oxford University Press, Oxford (1990)
22. Steiner, B., Kaplan, N., Moulthrop, S.: When play works: Turning game-playing into learning. In: Proc. IDC'2006, Tampere, Finland, ACM Press, New York (2006)
23. Sweetser, P., Wyeth, P.: Game Flow: A Model for Evaluating Player Enjoyment in Games. ACM Computer and Entertainment 3(3), 1–23 (2005)
24. Vygotsky, L.S.: Mind and Society: The development of higher psychological Process. In: Cole, M., John Steiner, V., Scribner, S., Souberman, E. (eds.), Harvard University Press, Cambridge (1978)
25. Vorderer, P., Hartmann, T., Klimmt, C.: Explaining the enjoyment of playing video games: The role of competition. In: Proc. of the 2nd International Conference on Computer Games (Pittsburgh, PA) (2003)
26. Werger, E.: Communities of Practice, Learning, Meaning, and Identity. University Cambridge Press, Cambridge (1999)

Daily Activities Diarist: Supporting Aging in Place with Semantically Enriched Narratives

Georgios Metaxas[1], Barbaros Metin[1], Jutta Schneider[1], Panos Markopoulos[1], and Boris de Ruyter[2]

[1] USI Programme, Eindhoven University of Technology,
The Netherlands
{g.metaxas,b.metin,j.m.schneider,p.markopoulos}@tue.nl
[2] Philips Research
{boris.de.ruyter@philips.com}

Abstract. The Daily Activities Diarist is an awareness system that supports social connectedness between seniors living alone and their social intimates. The Daily Activities Diarist extracts automatically an Activity-of-Daily-Life (ADL)-journal from data collected through a wireless sensor network installed at the home of the seniors. We describe the design of the system, its implementation and the lessons from two trials lasting 2 weeks each. The paper makes the case for narrative presentation of awareness information and for seamful design of awareness systems of this ilk.

Keywords: Computer-mediated communication, awareness systems, assisted living, ubiquitous computing.

1 Introduction

The well known aging of Western societies has prompted a growing interest into technologies that supports "Aging in place" and "Assisted living". Systems designed to support awareness through continual and partly automated flow of information between seniors living alone and their social intimates can help bridge geographical distance, discrepant lifestyles and daily routines, potentially providing peace of mind to both parties and feelings of being connected.

By now, there is a substantial body of work on Awareness systems supporting informal social communication at the home. An early influential project was Casablanca [7] which constituted a first exploration of the relevant design space. It proposed concepts that are still current today such as notice boards shared between households, or using decorative objects (e.g. a lampshade) to provide friends or family with an indication of a user's presence.

The Aroma project [17] let users stay in touch by adding to everyday means of communication (such as telephone and email) with a shared media space. The media space was organized as a pair of windows on different workstations, each displaying abstract visual and auditory effects, all together reflecting the state of affairs at the remote site. The visual effects were represented as an abstract, dynamic painting in

C. Baranauskas et al. (Eds.): INTERACT 2007, LNCS 4663, Part II, pp. 390–403, 2007.
© IFIP International Federation for Information Processing 2007

which the dynamics reflect the changes in the combined auditory and the visual state of the remote site.

Astra [12] was an exploration of intentional communication for the extended family that was shown to enhance feelings of connectedness and to prompt direct communications. Projects such as Intel's CareNet [3] and Honeywell's I.L.S.A [6] have examined the use of similar systems for supporting aging in place; they focus on providing professionals care-givers information about elder's medication, nutrition, falls etc. A related light-weight communication-oriented concept was the Digital-Family-Portrait (DFP) [19]; DFP was designed to provide peace of mind to adult children regarding a lone parent living at a distance. DFP presents graphically the activity level of the senior and other contextual information at their location (e.g. weather). This system constituted a significant advance over earlier such systems as it was deployed and tested in the field whereas earlier systems (e.g., [15]) were only tested briefly in the lab or activity sensing was simulated by Wizard of Oz techniques (for example, CareNet [3] relied on telephone interviews with participants to feed the display with awareness information). Recent projects such as SharedLife[22] explore the possibilities of extracting and encoding "personal memories" using contextual information and sensor input either for personal use or for sharing among individuals.

Looking at current research prototypes of awareness systems connecting households, it is noteworthy that they are still semantically impoverished with little progress made towards system interpretation of awareness information. The Interliving project [8] explored several communication appliances to connect family members; whereas interesting concepts were produced and the project has accomplished long term field deployment (6 months), the information communicated does not involve any system interpretation. The Digital Family portrait mentioned above [19] only goes so far as visualizing an aggregation of sensor firings over the day rather than attempting a more meaningful interpretation of this data. An important reason for this is that it is difficult to obtain reliable interpretations of user activity and to prevent false alarms.   This does not represent only a technical challenge; improvements in technology may improve the quality of the data obtained but the inherent design challenge remains of basing awareness on potentially flawed inferences regarding human activity.

In the present study, we examine the feasibility of providing semantically rich interpretations of sensor activity and applying the concept of 'seamful design' [2], in order to support users who are exposed to the imperfections of the sensing technology. We examine the use of narrative information to disambiguate graphical status presentations of awareness information, in line with Gershon et. al. who argue that images are susceptible to uncertainties and require some declarative statements for clarification [5].

The study reported in this paper explored the feasibility of automatically generating a detailed journal of daily activities, and through several iterations of design and evaluations explored how such information can by usefully presented. This iterative process lead to the lead to the conception and the design of the Daily Activities Diarist, a wireless Activity-of-Daily-Life (ADL)-journal from data collected through a wireless sensor network installed at the home of seniors. Two field trials were conducted with the Daily Acitivities Diarist lasting two weeks each. In each case, the household of an elderly person living alone was connected to that of their adult children. The field trials provide an initial assessment of whether awareness of such information is valued by the elderly and their children.

In the remainder of this paper we sketch out the user studies that lead to the design of our awareness system, we explain the motivation behind its design, and summarize its implementation briefly. Finally we describe two trials that we run, for two weeks each and outline future work.

2 User Studies

By its nature awareness can be seen as the flip side of privacy [1], requiring the capture and disclosure of information about an individual. Continuous presentation of awareness information about one's social intimates can lead to an information overflow [9] or at least to regular disruption of the receiver of this information. These trade-offs were investigated by a user study that involved interviews, focus group sessions, and questionnaires with both seniors and social intimates.

User Profiles
In this paper the term '*Senior adults*' refers to people over the age of 65, retired, that have children, and do not suffer from any serious illness. Our target group of senior adults mostly approximates *Healthy Hermits* [14], i.e. senior individuals remaining in relatively good health yet somewhat withdrawn socially. Healthy hermits have experienced at least one life-changing event such as the death of a spouse. They don't like their isolation or that they're expected to act like old people. Adults who are 85 years old constitute the upper age limit of this population, as they tend to become frailer and have more health problems after that age. The senior adults targeted live alone. However, they have a good and close relationship with their children. They communicate with each other on a regular basis.

The second target group consists of '*intimate socials*' (or social intimates) of the senior adults, such as sons and/or daughters (Neustaedter et al. [16]). This group consists of people in the age of 45 to 60 years old who have a close personal relationship with their parents, but live a certain distance away from them (e.g. at a different city), and mostly have a different life rhythm than their parents.

Interviews
Interviews were conducted with seniors (N=4, 69 to 85 years old) and intimate socials (N=3, 54-57) to realize their attitudes and patterns of communication. Staying up-to-date with events in the other's life, communicating their own experiences, exchanging practical information, showing interest, reinforcing the relationship and giving or receiving emotional support were reported as the main reasons of communication by both groups. Elderly are more interested in everyday happenings in the lives of their social intimates; the latter want to know more about general activities of the elderly in the day and if there have any needs and/or problems.

The interviews revealed that seniors fear to bother or to annoy their children when they contact them too often or too long. On the other hand they feel checked up on by daily phone calls from their children. They don't want to share bad moods and feelings with their social intimates.

The intimate socials reported wanting to know how their parents feel, i.e. what their moods are. It is also important for them to know where they are (in or out the house), and if they are asleep or not. All in all they would like to get a general impression of their daily activities.

In both groups it was apparent that women more often mediate social and emotional contacts. Elderly men are more likely to initiate contact only if they have a clear and practical purpose in mind, such as a question they want to ask. The above-mentioned findings are consistent with earlier studies, such as [11] and [13], the NESTOR-LSN survey [4] and the Digital Family Portraits project [15] .

Focus groups

To confront the target groups with the notion of Awareness Systems and to evaluate our initial concept designs two focus group sessions were held; one with senior adults (N=6, 75-86) at the 'Wilgenhof' elderly home and one with intimate socials (N=5, 45-54) at the Philips High Tech Campus.

More specifically a collection of 9 related design concepts were presented to both groups, and used as a discussion basis in the focus group sessions (figure 1 shows two of the mockups we used as a prompt to examine a scenario). The mockups were presented as paper prototypes through a mechanical frame, that allowed flipping between the various drawings. This helped simulate the dynamic behavior of the system, showing the transaction between different awareness information at different moments in the day. It is worth mentioning that all the examples used in focus group sessions, were based on an analogy with a real world window. For example, figure 1, displays a greeting scenario where a social intimate is seeing through the window her parent greeting when the day starts.

Both groups were quite positive about prospective system-attributes such as its unobtrusiveness. Interestingly the main concerns about privacy arose at the social-intimate side, who did not wish to compromise the privacy of their elderly relative, while a typical response given by elderly was *"Anyhow, we know everything about each other"*. Social-intimates expressed an interest in being aware of the physical-status on the other side (e.g., sleeping, eating etc.), critical events such as rapid decline of the parent's health. They were also interested in knowing the feelings and moods of their parents; however seniors were reluctant regarding the communication of negative feelings.

Fig. 1. Two of the prompts used in the focus group sessions

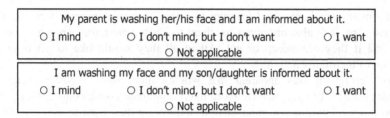

Fig. 2. Example question from the questionnaire for the elderly (top), and for the social intimates (bottom)

Questionnaires

Rather than taking a technology centric perspective of in surveying the acceptance of communicating different kinds of information that are possible to sense automatically, we aimed to understand privacy issues and user preferences regarding awareness information without reference to the way this information can be captured. A questionnaire was assembled based on various inventories of activities-of-daily-life (ADL) to examine what kind of activities the seniors (N=10, avg. age 81) want (or don't mind) to share on one hand, and what their social-intimates (N=15, avg. age 45) want to be informed about on the other.

The questionnaire was compiled from different published inventories such as the "Activities of daily life list" [11], the "Instrumental activities of daily life" [10] and the "Advanced activities of daily life" [18]. These inventories provide comprehensive lists of activities at minute-level detail initially intended for profiling the level of self-efficacy of an individual. By asking subjects to indicate the degree to which they would like their social intimates to be aware of the activities listed, we get a comprehensive understanding of their need to share awareness information. The activities that were more of interest for our design were:

- Day-to-day maintenance activities such as feeding, sleeping, personal hygiene, dressing, etc.
- Instrumental activities, such as shopping, calling, cooking, doing the laundry, using the phone, etc.
- Daily life concern activities, which arise out of individual abilities and interests, such as social activities.

The format of these questions is illustrated in figure 2. Each questionnaire included 49 such items. The outcome dictated that home presence/absence, bed-occupation, visiting friends/having visitors, followed by other activities like having a walk, cooking, shopping etc. could be shared from the senior side to the social-intimate side without jeopardizing their privacy. Another interesting finding was that the senior adults overall wanted to share good moods and feelings (N≥9) but not negative ones (N≤3).

Fig. 3. Graphical presentations of "away", "at home", "in bed", "at the kitchen", and "with Visitors"

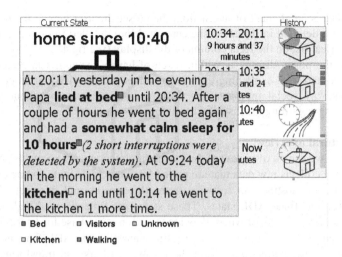

Current State		History

home since 10:40

10:34- 20:11
9 hours and 37 minutes

At 20:11 yesterday in the evening Papa **lied at bed** until 20:34. After a couple of hours he went to bed again and had a **somewhat calm sleep for 10 hours** *(2 short interruptions were detected by the system)*. At 09:24 today in the morning he went to the **kitchen** and until 10:14 he went to the kitchen 1 more time.

10:35 and 24 tes

10:40 utes

Now utes

▣ Bed   ▫ Visitors   ▫ Unknown
▫ Kitchen   ▪ Walking

Fig. 4. Screen shot of subject's A1 Daily-Activity-Diarist, showing all three levels of detail presented to users

3   Prototype Design and Implementation

Conceptual design

Based on the user studies described and more specifically on the senior adults' activities that could be shared with their intimate socials without putting privacy at risk, we chose activities such as walking, sleeping, having visitors, cooking and eating, to populate an auto-generated ADL-journal. Due to the stated preference of elderly to keep negative feelings private, we discarded from this journal moods and feelings. Apart from the synchronous exchange of real time activity data, the conceptual design was supplied with a history of logged activity data, to bridge the different life paces of the user groups.

Further to the graphical display of activities, we decided also to use a narrative presentation with more detailed feedback and reasoning about the displayed activities. The narrative feedback was chosen to address the problems that may rise from false-alarms and user-misinterpretations, when graphical information visualization is invoked. Our goal was to minimize these problems by providing semantic-cues and explanatory-statements using narration as a complement to graphical visualization of the extracted activities.

In order to maintain peripheral-awareness and light-weight interaction with the end-users (i.e. the social intimates), the features of the ADL-journal were presented through an 'interactive dynamic poster', assembling the following goals:

- Major changes in the poster can be identified from a long distance using icons (see fig. 3); therefore social intimates can maintain a peripheral awareness of the elderly activities at the other side.

- Distance is an element of interaction; the closer the user gets to the poster/display, the more detailed information she can get. More detailed information is offered as a historical list on the right column of the display (see fig 4)
- When the poster/display is within reach-of-hands, the user can directly invoke a detailed narrative explaining the system status and activity journal created (fig 4). In this way social intimates can acquire more information about the system's reasoning regarding the displayed activities.

Architectural overview

In figure 5 we see an overview of the system architecture. The Sensor-Network at the elderly side collects raw data that are pulled from the ADL-State Extractor. The ADL-State Extractor abstracts in software terms the sensors and interprets the collected signals to predefined ADL states. These states are time-stamped and pushed to the ADL-State Database Host where they are stored in a database for later process. When it is needed (e.g., on request, or on specific intervals), the ADL-Semantics Extractor pulls the corresponding states from the database, filters and transforms them to an ADL journal that is described in a XML-semantics file. Depending on the configuration, the XML data are pushed to, or pulled by the Presentation Server, which does the final transformation to HTML code. The location of Presentation Server is resolved from a Point to Point Server that redirects the Client requests to the resolved URL.

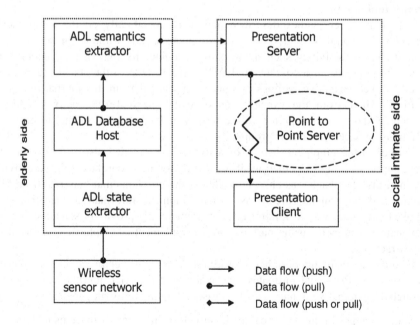

Fig. 5. Overview of the prototype architecture, its components, and their location in the current experimental configuration

Fig. 6. From left to right: mica2dot mote, key fold with mica2dot, and mica2 mote

Wireless Sensor Network and ADL-State-Extraction

A wireless sensor network was used to collect data from the elderly homes. Presence at home, mobility, sleep, and other activities are extracted using the raw data collected from this first layer. The wireless sensors are abstracted in software terms by ADL-State-Extractors, which transform the collected raw data to ADL-states.

The Sensor network is responsible for all the collected data that are fed in to the system. Presence at home, activity, sleep, and other activities should be extracted by using the data collected from this first layer. The implementation of this layer was based on Crossbow wireless sensors. These are small programmable wireless-communication motes that can be connected to a variety of sensors. The Crossbow motes are equipped with TinyOS, an open-source operating system designed for wireless embedded sensor networks.

With the aforementioned framework the Crossbow motes were programmed to support some basic functionality that initiates the activity extraction at the ADL-State extractor side.

Presence and Mobility detection

A subject's presence or absence detection is done using the Crossbow MICA2dot wireless coin-size mote (Figure 6). The mote is placed in the subject's key-fold. When the subject is present at home, any signal from the sensor can be detected from the sensor and interpreted as presence, and vice versa when a subject is absent.

In order to detect the mobility of a subject, an accelerometer sensor is added to the mote. When the subject is away the accelerometer records the subject's activity. The activity data can be interpreted later by the system, when the subject is back at home.

In order to make possible the above and to maintain low power consumption, the MICA2dot is programmed to transmit its state every 10 seconds. Additionally, every 30 seconds it gets 1 second of high sampling acceleration data. When the energy of the one-second acceleration samples is higher than a predefined 'walking' threshold, the 30 seconds interval is marked as high activity and vice versa.

On the ADL-state extraction side, the sensor is abstracted in software terms, and the collected data are transformed to presence/absence states. The high and low activity counters are compared with the latest known values in order to calculate the subject's mobility while the subject was away. Furthermore, some filters were introduced to overcome problems with lost messages. For example, although the system expects a signal from the sensor every 10 seconds, the subject is considered to be away only if no signal is received for more than a minute.

Kitchen activity detection

Activity in the kitchen and other rooms was identified by monitoring the light condition of cupboards. For example, by monitoring light emittance inside a refrigerator we can tell when the door was opened. The combination of these events from various sources, like cupboards and refrigerators, is used to extract information regarding activity in the kitchen (and possibly other rooms).

For the above purpose we equipped MICA2 motes (Figure 7 left) with photo-sensors and programmed the motes to measure light emittance every 2 seconds. If the measured light exceeds a 'cupboard open' threshold, the sensor sends a signal to the system. To avoid battery drain, the sensors are programmed not to transmit more than once per minute.

On the ADL-state-extraction side, a collection of these motes is abstracted in software, and the collected data are transformed to kitchen activity data. A sequence of 'open cupboards' is interpreted as high kitchen activity with the corresponding duration and intensity.

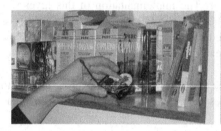 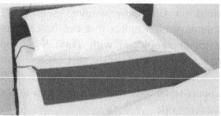

Fig. 7. Placing a wireless mote with a photo sensor in a cupboard(left), an illustration of a pressure pad used for bed-activity detection (right)

Bed/Chair/Visitors activity detection

A combination of a MICA2 mote and a pressure-pad (Figure 7 right) is used to detect whether a subject is lying on a bed or sitting on a chair. The MICA2 is programmed to make a measurement of the pressure-pad's analog output every 10 seconds, and the measured value is then transmitted to the system.

On start-up, the ADL-state-extraction component makes the assumption that initially the subject is not lying. Therefore the first readings are used to calculate a 'lying' threshold. The same assumption is done when the subject is away, making possible to adapt the 'lying' threshold to the changing physical condition of the pressure-pad. A sensor-reading higher than the 'lying' threshold is translated as a 'bed-active' state and vice versa. Time delay filters are used to overcome lost signals from the MICA2 mote similar to the presence detection.

Furthermore, on the ADL-state-extraction side, a collection of these motes can be used to detect the presence of visitors (e.g. when more than one chair's state is active, the system turns on the 'visitors' state).

ADL-Semantics Extractor and State Database Host

The states that are extracted from the ADL-state-extraction components are stored in a database at the ADL-State Database Host as a sequence of states. This sequence however may contain logical errors, or reliability errors that cannot be addressed from the previous layer (ADL-state-extraction). For example, a pressure-pad could turn on before presence is detected due to network traffic, or the presence sensor may not be detected at some intervals due to poor network signal resulting in a series of falsely alternating present/absent states.

The ADL-semantics extractor is a software component that is aimed at resolving these issues, by further processing the extracted state-data, and transforms the later to a nested XML ADL-journal. The XML formatted journal allows flexibility on the final rendering, and enables a higher level of semantic analysis.

Presentation Server
The presentation server makes the final analysis and rendering of the XML semantics to HTML. The tree structure of the XML ADL-journal is transformed using XSL to an HTML document that presents the argumentation regarding the presented activities in order to avoid misunderstandings and to give access to more detailed information. For example, when the duration of a "bed" state is less than three hours the interpretation is "nap", or when a "bed" state is interrupted more than 3 times the interpretation is "disrupted sleep" and so on.

The HTML document contains explanations like: "At 23:30 yesterday in the evening John went to bed and had a somewhat disrupted sleep until 07:45 today in the morning. Then (at 08:20) he went to the kitchen for half an hour". Further more, the system explains its argumentation on user request (e.g. "somewhat disrupted sleep" expands to "2 interruptions were detected by the system at 1:45 and at 4:30....". In figures 4 and 8 one can notice an actual instance from a subject's ADL-journal with a narrative explanation of some extracted activities.

4 Evaluation

Two field trials were conducted each involving two households, that of a senior participant and that of their social intimates. Each trial lasted two weeks. Our aim was to explore the overall experience of living with such a system, patterns of usage to the extent allowed by the duration of the study and affective benefits and costs incurred.

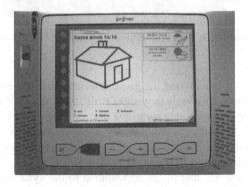

Fig. 8. Daily Activities Diarist displayed on a Philips iPronto device, showing the current state (left) and the history (right)

Participants
Family A included a male senior (80) (subject A1), his son (44) (subject A2), daughter in law (43) (subject A3) and their two children. The senior A1 is in good health but uses a so-called 'walker' when going out. Therefore, trips on his-own are restricted to, e.g., getting the newspaper or visits to neighbors. However, he is still an active person.

Family B included a female senior (85) (subject B1), her daughter (57) (B2) and her son in law (57) (B3). The senior B1 is in good health and although she also uses a 'walker' to go out, she is still very mobile.

Apparatus and Maintenance
The system was installed in the home of the senior participants. Both apartments were similar in size and layout (small bedroom, living room, kitchen, hallway, and bathroom). In their children's homes two Philips iPronto devices (originally intended as 'smart remote controls) were used to display the ADL journals.

In the end of the first week batteries were changed as scheduled, and then the system was left to run for seven more days. Interviews with each participant were conducted at the end of the second week. We also used standardized questionnaires to measure social connectedness using the ABC questionnaire [21] and well being through the subjective complaints questionnaire [20]. Given the small sample size these were not intended for quantitative analysis, but to prepare larger scale trial and to see if any interesting variations in connectedness/well being could be indicated by our participants.

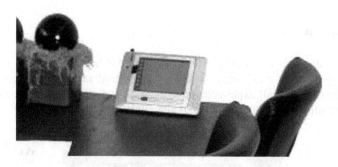

Fig. 9. Presentation Client (iPronto) at participant's B2/B3 living room

Results
Social intimates at both trials found the given information in the story telling function sufficiently explanatory, although they didn't all use it equally often - *"The story telling function was very explanatory, the information which I needed was all provided"* - subject A2. Subjects A2, and A3 consulted the narrative regularly (e.g., after waking up and after work). The other subjects were not that interested in acquiring in depth information so frequently.

Participants, A2 and A3, had to get accustomed to the system the first day, but as early as the second day they started relying upon it. Participant A2 used the system to check whether his father was at home or not before calling him, sometimes he checked what he had been doing during the day, if he was sleeping, etc. Some of the information they were interested in was not supported by the system's configuration - *"I would like to know if my father is within 'de Akkers', or outside 'de Akkers' or if he is at another place, such as the supermarket"* – subject A2. However, the information provided was experienced overall by participant A2 and A3 as sufficient and appreciated as meaningful.

In contrast, during the second trial technical problems lead to different reactions by participants B2, B3 who found no value in the information provided: "I did not really trust the system, it malfunctioned a lot, and I had to reset it quite a few times." - subject B2. Also, they did not feel comfortable with the unidirectional nature of the system fearing that it compromised their parents' privacy - *"My mother (in law) should be able to make contact through the system when she wants."*- Subject B3, *"The system makes me feel as a spy, and it makes her feel as being spied"* – subject B2. An erroneous system operation caused subject B2 to be unnecessarily alarmed regarding her mother; also the constant flow of information on her mother's activities made her nervous. She did not however react by immediately calling or visiting her - *"Yesterday the system showed that my mother was out at night, and this kept us awake all night. However, we were hesitant to disturb her."* – subject B2. Both participants thought the system should be made more obtrusive for alerting to critical or life-threatening events.

The participants noted that they prefer to be informed if sensors or other system parts not obvious to them malfunction, e.g., when batteries drain, or when the network is down. This could prevent them from misinterpretations caused by system failures.

From their side, seniors expressed no complaints about the sensors installed in their homes, claiming that they were oblivious to them. Perhaps surprisingly, none of the seniors felt their privacy was invaded. *"No privacy issues... it is my son"*- subject A1. This however should not be assumed as sufficient evidence that no privacy issues arise; a longer term trial would be more likely to uncover situations where privacy could be compromised or for both parties to better appreciate the privacy risks involved.

An unexpected positive finding (provisional given our small sample) was the reduction of agoraphobia of both participating seniors as measured by post-trial questionnaires. Both seniors reported going out more often than usual; this may be attributed to the safety they felt knowing that their children are aware of their activities.

5   Conclusion

Journaling ADLs and displaying them as peripheral social awareness cues can potentially help elderly and their social intimates to be connected. We have argued that a narrative presentation of awareness information that provides rich semantic feedback regarding the system reasoning offers practical advantages over impressionistic graphical presentations of the instantaneous status of the elderly. Clearly a larger empirical basis is needed, but it has to be noted that the difference between these displays is more reliably appreciated by test-participants during actual rather use of the system in the field, rather than lab-based evaluations.

Running longer term field trials of such systems poses significant challenges, as is evident from current state of the art. Longer term field trials of communication systems rely on capture and communication of raw audio-video data or text/graphical input by users. For example, the Interliving project involved field trials of up to x months of their communication appliances. On the other hand, the technical and social challenges of installing sensor based awareness systems at the homes of participants result in a long set-up phase to get the system reliable and a comparatively shorter term deployment and actual use of the system. For example, Mynatt et al report actual use of their DFP system by one subject for one week after a set up period of about a year.

Clearly, sensor based awareness systems need to become more robust and easily configurable, so that deployment is faster at many different households. In order to enable longer term user trials with larger sets of participants, we are currently re-engineering the Daily Activities Diarist to support end-user configurability of the information flow between the connected households. This is necessary to adapt to the different social and physical contexts of the participants' homes and to allow them to provide personalized descriptions of locations and activities that are meaningful to them and their social intimates.

Awareness systems even when aiming for peace of mind have a safety critical nature; the affective costs of an occasional malfunction can outweigh their benefits as they can unsettle relatives mistakenly. The need to portray the seams of the system, as argued recently by Chalmers et al [2], can be an appropriate design approach in order to avoid false alarms and to provide more meaningful explanations. For example, an other step towards seamful design would be to use network-health and battery-status metrics when reporting activities in order to insert into the narrative confidence qualifications, e.g. "your parent is probably outside", or "Papa might had a disturbed sleep" where "probably" and "might" can be expanded at the request of the user to an explanation about the sensor-network health and battery-status on demand.

References

1. Boyle, M., Greenberg, S.: The Language of Privacy: Learning from Video Media Space Analysis and Design. ACM ToCHI 12(2), 328–370 (2005)
2. Chalmers, M., Galani, A.: Seamful Interweaving: Heterogeneity in the Theory and Design of Interactive Systems. In: Proc. DIS 2004, pp. 243–252. ACM, New York (2004)
3. Consolvo, S., Roessler, P., Shelton, B.E.: The CareNet Display: Lessons learned from an in-home evaluation of an ambient display. In: Davies, N., Mynatt, E.D., Siio, I. (eds.) UbiComp 2004. LNCS, vol. 3205, pp. 22–29. Springer, Heidelberg (2004)
4. Dykstra, P.A., Knipscheer, P.M.: The availability and intergenerational structure of family relationships. In: Knipscheer, C.P.M., de Jong Gierveld, J., Tilburg, T.G., Dykstra, P.A. (eds.) Living arrangements and social networks of older adults, pp. 37–58 (1995)
5. Gershon, N., Page, W.: What storytelling can do for information visualization. Communications of the ACM 44(8), 31–37 (2001)
6. Haigh, H.Z., Kiff, L.M., Myers, J., Guralnik, V., Kirschbaum, K., Phelps, J., Plocher, T., Toms, D.: The Independent LifeStyle Assistant™ (I.L.S.A.): Lessons Learned. In: Proc. AAAI, pp. 852–857 (2004)

7. Hindus, D., Mainwaring, S.D., Leduc, N., Hagström, A.E., Bayley, O.: Casablanca: Designing social communication devices for the home. In: Proceedings CHI 2001, pp. 325–332. ACM, New York (2001)
8. Hutchinson, H., Mackay, W., Westerlund, B., Bederson, B.B., Druin, A., Plaisant, C., Beaudoin-Lafon, M., Conversy, S., Evans, H., Hansen, H., Roussel, N., Eiderbäck, B., Lindquist, S., Sundblad, Y.: Technology Probes: Inspiring Design for and with Families. Proceedings CHI 2003, CHI Letters, 5 (1), pp. 17–24 (2003)
9. Khan, J.V., Markopoulos, P., Mota, S.A., IJsselsteijn, W.A., de Ruyter, B.: Intra-family communication needs; how can Awareness Systems provide support? In: 2nd International Conference on Intelligent Environments (IE06), pp. 84–89 (2006)
10. Lawton, M.P., Brody, E.M.: Assessment of older people: self-maintaining and instrumental activities of daily living. Gerontologist 9, 179–186 (1969)
11. Mahoney, F.I., Barthel, D.W.: Functional evaluation: the Barthel Index. Maryland State Medical Journal 14, 61–66 (1965)
12. Markopoulos, P., Romero, N., Baren, J.v., IJsselsteijn, W., de Ruyter, B., Farshchian, B.: Keeping in Touch with the Family: Home and Away with the ASTRA Awareness System. In: Proc. CHI 2004, ACM, New York (2004)
13. Melenhorst, A.S., Rogers, W.A., Caylor, E.: The use of communication technologies by older adults: exploring the benefits from the users' perspective. In: Proceedings HFES (2001)
14. Moschis, G.P.: Life Stages of the Mature Market. American Demographics, 44–50 (1996)
15. Mynatt, E.D., Rowan, J., Jacobs, A., Craighill, S.: Digital Family Portraits: Supporting Peace of Mind for extended Family Members. In: Proceedings CHI 2001, pp. 333–340 (2001)
16. Neustaedter, C., Elliot, K., Greenberg, S.: Understanding Interpersonal Awareness in the Home. In: ACM CHI 2005 Workshop on Awareness systems (2005)
17. Pedersen, E.R., Sokoler, T.: AROMA: Abstract Representation of Presence Supporting Mutual Awareness. In: Proceedings of ACM SIGHI Conference on Human Factors in Computing systems, pp. 234–241 (1997)
18. Reuben, D.B, Laliberte, L., Hiris, J., Mor, V.: A hierarchical exercise scale to measure at the Advanced Activities of Daily Living (AADL) level. Journal of the American Geriatric Society 38, 855–861 (1990)
19. Rowan, J., Mynatt, E.D.: Digital family portrait field trial: Support for aging in place. In: Proc. CHI 2005, pp. 521–530. ACM, New York (2005)
20. SCL-90-R: Symptom Checklist-90-R: Administration, Scoring & Procedures Manual LR Derogatis - 1994 - National Computer Systems, Inc
21. van Baren, J., IJsselsteijn, W.A., Romero, N., Markopoulos, P., de Ruyter, B.: Affective Benefits in Communication: The development and field-testing of a new questionnaire measure. In: PRESENCE 2003, Aalborg, Denmark (October 2003)
22. Wahlster, W., Kroner, A., Heckmann, D.: SharedLife: Towards Selective Sharing of Augmented Personal Memories. In: Stock, O., Schaerf, M. (eds.) Reasoning, Action and Interaction in AI Theories and Systems. LNCS (LNAI), vol. 4155, pp. 327–342. Springer, Heidelberg (2006)

Head Up Games: The Games of the Future Will Look More Like the Games of the Past

Iris Soute and Panos Markopoulos

Faculty of Industrial Design, Eindhoven University of Technology,
P.O. Box 513, 5600 MB Eindhoven, The Netherlands
{i.a.c.soute,p.markopoulos}@tue.nl

Abstract. With the emergence of pervasive technology, pervasive games came into existence. Most are location-aware applications, played with a PDA or mobile phone. We argue that the interaction paradigm these games support, limits outdoor play that often involves spontaneous social interaction. This paper introduces a new genre of pervasive games we call Head Up Games. The paper describes these games and how they differ from current research prototypes of pervasive games. Also, it outlines their characteristics and illustrates our vision with Camelot, an outdoor game for children.

Keywords: Pervasive games, Children, Social gaming.

1 Introduction

Computer games are often criticized for reducing players to interact with their fingers, sitting still at a screen, having limited possibilities for social interactions. With the development of pervasive technology the genre of pervasive games has emerged: "[a] genre in which traditional, real-world games are augmented with computing functionality, or, depending on the perspective, purely virtual computer entertainment is brought back to the real world" [4]. We are interested in outdoor games for children, with the emphasis on social gaming: i.e. games that support and stimulate social interaction between players.

There has been a wealth of pervasive games reported in related literature. Examples of outdoor games for adults are Uncle Roy All Around You [1] and Catchbob! [6]. These games are location-based games, played with a GPS and/or Wifi device. Mobile players use a small display (PDA or mobile phone) to show location and game-related information. Fewer cases exist of pervasive outdoor games specifically designed for children: two pioneering examples are Savannah [2], and Ambient Wood [7]. In Savannah, children were equipped with PDA's with WiFi and GPS. A virtual savannah was overlaid on a school field, and children had to cooperate as "lions" to hunt the savannah. In Ambient Wood, children took a field trip in a wood that was augmented with mobile and fixed devices that provided contextually-relevant information. Each pair of children carried a PDA and a probe. The games mentioned above share three characteristics:

- **Location Bound Infrastructure.** The game narrative is supported by a location-specific investment of installation and maintenance of hardware, e.g.,

C. Baranauskas et al. (Eds.): INTERACT 2007, LNCS 4663, Part II, pp. 404–407, 2007.

placing the devices in the forest for Ambient Wood. One may expect that in the future both the hardware and the infrastructure will be more readily available but for the time being creating such a mixed reality game narrative remains an expensive undertaking requiring considerable expertise and effort. Moreover, assuming such infrastructure exists does not mean that spontaneous play at locations such as playgrounds, parks etc. becomes possible.

- **Location awareness.** All games assume a form of location awareness. However, GPS errors can adversely influence the game play, as has been noted in Savannah [2]. Nova et al. [6] report that players that used the automated location awareness tool did not perform better than other participants.
- **PDA as gaming platform.** Interactions with the virtual world are performed through a portable display, that acts as a window to the virtual world. This mode of interaction competes with the interaction between players and the physical world. Instead of looking at each other children have to walk head down attending to their devices.

2   Traditional and Head Up Games

Perhaps a good way to start discussing traditional outdoor children's games is by referring to a 16th century painting by Bruegel called 'Children's Games' [1]. Many of the games depicted are still played today, e.g.: tag, hide and seek or ball games. Traditional games have features in common: they require physical activity, and are played with little materials (like a ball, or a skipping cord). As these games are played with multiple players and are played in the same physical space, traditional games promote social interaction. Finally, the rules of traditional games are often few and simple. It is our assertion that it is feasible to transfer some, or all, of the features of traditional games to pervasive games and that this would lead to enjoyable and sociable gaming experiences.

Currently, the settings where children play games also mark a clear separation in the type of games that are played. Outdoor games require physical activity; indoor games are mostly played sitting down at a computer. We advocate a new class of games merging aspects of both worlds: games that can be played outdoors, requiring physical activity, and are enhanced by technology. We argue that these types of games should make minimal use of handheld displays, as this forces children to abandon physical activity; looking down on a screen, does not go together with wildly running around. Hence the name of the games: Head Up Games (HUGs). The defining characteristics of HUGs are:

- **Technology and game design.** Technology must be simple and work reliably so that its usage becomes transparent. We accept the argument that limitations (seams) [3] exist in most forms of technology and designers ought to address them, but we feel that current research prototypes in the field of pervasive gaming have focused too much on exploring the potential of new technologies rather than serving the purposes of game design. Simpler

---

[1] See http://www.khm.at/staticE/page2121.html

and more robust technologies can support pervasive gaming for children adequately, avoiding the pitfalls relating to technology imperfections.

- **Minimal installation.** If we look at current outdoor games, we see that the toys used are easy to bring along, and play with anywhere, anytime. We should keep this in mind when applying technology in HUGs.
- **Imagination vs. visualization of virtual worlds.** Traditional play relies heavily on a child's imagination: e.g., a broom stick can easily turn into a horse. Vygotsky (in [8]) stresses the importance of symbolic play, i.e. without explicit visualizations, as this presumably lays the foundation for development of abstract thinking. Furthermore, using location awareness and PDA's to connect virtual to real worlds neglects alternative possibilities such as the use of sensors to sense motion, proximity, or contact, opening up a richer foray of interactions. In HUGs we aim to investigate these alternative possibilities.
- **Rich, social interaction.** In many multi-player computer games social interaction is limited to online chat, i.e. using the keyboard to convey messages. With HUGs, like traditional games, we aim to have children use a broader range of social interactions, like spoken language and body language.

3   Camelot

Camelot [9] represents a first attempt to design a head up game. It was developed over a course of 4 months, and during development it was repeatedly evaluated with a group of 10 children between 7 to 10 year old (see Figure 1). In Camelot children compete in two teams to build a castle. To this end, the teams have to gather different types of resources that are spread around in zones on the play field. The first team to complete the castle wins the game. Randomly during the game, a ghost appears and tries to steal resources from the teams.

No display technologies were used in Camelot. Instead, small devices (collectors) were designed to acquire resources from the zones. For communication purposes, each collector and zone was equipped with infrared technology. Hence, there was no need for a centralized computer system. The collectors weighed very little and were easy to run around with for the children. Also, the zones

Fig. 1. Photos of the evaluation of Camelot with children in their school gym

were portable, so the game could be played anywhere. As Camelot was played in teams, players needed to discuss tactics to win the game. This automatically led to social interaction between the players. The evaluations showed that fun came from the social interaction, the competition between the teams but also the suspense added by the unpredictable appearance of the ghost.

4 Discussion and Conclusion

In his motivation for "La Casa Prossima Futura" [5], Marzano envisioned that with ambient intelligence technology: "The home of tomorrow will look more like the home of yesterday than the homes of today". This paper has sketched HUGs as an analogue to Marzano's vision in the world of pervasive games, where currently fun appears to be subordinate to concerns for the operation of technology. After the initial fascination with pervasive technology, the scene is set for designing games that provide entertainment in ways familiar, in settings where games have always been played and supporting the patterns of play that have traditionally been found when children meet outdoors to play together. We have argued in favor of this vision and outlined what we believe to be the defining characteristics for Head Up Games. We have discussed Camelot, an example of such a game. In our future research we plan to design more instances of HUGs in order to explore their possibilities and limitations.

References

1. Benford, S., Seager, W., Flintham, M., Anastasi, R., et al.: The Error of Our Ways: The Experience of Self-Reported Position in a Location-Based Game. In: Mynatt, E., Siio, I. (eds.) UbiComp 2004. LNCS, vol. 3205, pp. 70–87. Springer, Heidelberg (2004)
2. Benford, S., Rowland, D., Flintham, M., Drozd, et al.: Life on the edge: supporting collaboration in location-based experiences. In: CHI '05, pp. 721–730. ACM Press, New York (2005)
3. Chalmers, M., Bell, M., Brown, B., Hall, M., Sherwood, S., Tennent, P.: Gaming on the edge: using seams in ubicomp games. In: ACE '05, pp. 306–309. ACM Press, New York (2005)
4. Magerkurth, C., Cheok, A.D., Mandryk, R.L., Nilsen, T.: Pervasive games: bringing computer entertainment back to the real world Comput. Entertain. vol. 3, ACM Press, New York (2005)
5. Marzano, S.: True Visions: The Emergence of Ambient Intelligence. In: Aarts, E., Encarnacã, J. (eds.) Ambient Culture, Ch. 3, pp. 35–52. Springer, Heidelberg (2006)
6. Nova, N., Girardin, F., Molinari, G., Dillenbourg, P.: The Underwhelming Effects of Automatic Location-Awareness on Collaboration in a Pervasive Game. In: International Confernce on Cooperative Systems Design, pp. 224–238 (2006)
7. Rogers, Y., Price, S., Fitzpatrick, G., Fleck, R., et al.: Ambient wood: designing new forms of digital augmentation for learning outdoors. In: IDC '04, pp. 3–10. ACM Press, New York (2004)
8. Verenikina, I., Harris, P., Lysaght, P.: Child's play: computer games, theories of play and children's development. In: CRPIT '03, Australian Comp. Soc (2003)
9. Verhaegh, J., Soute, I., Kessels, A., Markopoulos, P.: On the design of Camelot, an outdoor game for children. In: IDC '06, pp. 9–16. ACM Press, New York (2006)

MarkerClock: A Communicating Augmented Clock for Elderly

Yann Riche[1,2] and Wendy Mackay[1]

[1] INRIA/LRI and Univ. Paris-Sud, France
[2] Univ. of Queensland, Australia
yann.riche@lri.fr, wendy.mackay@inria.fr

Abstract. This paper presents markerClock, a communication appliance embedded into a clock and designed for seniors as a simple and intuitive device. MarkerClock enhances seniors' connectedness to their social networks, particularly friends, neighbors and relatives, therefore increasing the potential of human communication for providing and receiving care. In doing so, markerClock supports reciprocal care behaviors observed during our initial user study, which could be used to leverage the need for institutionalized care. This paper describes markerClock and its implementation of both passive and active communications.

1 Introduction

In industrialized countries, the population is aging [1], forcing institutions to seek innovative ways to address this challenge. To date, many researchers are exploring how monitoring solutions fitted into our seniors' homes can leverage the stress on care facilities. Monitoring technologies are designed to support the caregivers' tasks - help the helper - by sensing the seniors' environment. However, monitoring systems are invasive solutions, often ignoring simpler ways in which technology can benefit a larger population, such as maintaining social connectedness and preventing isolation and loneliness. In this context, our project explores how *communication appliances* (CA) [2] can help seniors to better age in place while offering an alternative to monitoring care solutions.

2 Related Work

Our preliminary study [3] highlighted the role of peer support amongst seniors. Subsequently, we define PeerCare as the bilateral, reciprocal care relation amongst seniors. In this context, our approach extends current and past research on media spaces [4] and home computer mediated communication (CMC) to design a *communication appliance* [2] supporting the well-being of seniors aging in place. Communication appliances (CA) are defined as "[...]simple-to-use, single-function devices that let people communicate, passively or actively, via some medium, with one or more remotely-located friends or family" [2]. In particular, CA can establish shared awareness between relatives and friends through

C. Baranauskas et al. (Eds.): INTERACT 2007, LNCS 4663, Part II, pp. 408–411, 2007.
© IFIP International Federation for Information Processing 2007

the use of both passive and active communication. While home is becoming one of the major markets for interactive systems, it presents specific challenges by shifting the designer's focus from productivity to more intimate concerns such as closeness, intimacy, leisure, or entertainment. Recently, the interLiving project [5] studied the design of CA for intergenerational home communication and provided a context and a set of methods to study and design CMC in the home.

3 MarkerClock

MarkerClock (Fig. 2) is specifically designed to address the needs of the seniors by augmenting a simple clock into a communicating device. Communications are drawn around the clock as concentric colored spirals, each representing a different user. As a CA, markerClock supports active communication by using symbols, and passive communication by sharing activity values. Passive communication is a trace of motion captured by a camera fitted on the clock. Five levels of motion are visible (Fig. 1.b) from no motion (very light color) to extreme motion (very dense color). The motion trace does not require explicit user actions and provides peripheral communication among users. At the same time, the data exchanged is very limited and provides very little information, thus protecting the privacy of each participant. Moreover, the motion detection feature only captures motion occurring in the field of view of the camera. This also reinforces privacy protection since the data collection occurs only in a specific area decided by the user. Users can cheat and move the camera away, and decide whether to be in the field of view of the camera or not.

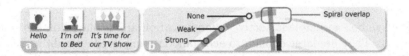

Fig. 1. Examples of a) users' codes, b) user's motion trace

Simple symbols, shaped to point at a particular spot on the motion trace, are used for active communication. By using the inherent time mapping of the clock, the time of the messages becomes explicit. For example, if Beatrice sends a droplet every morning to say she is all right, the same symbol sent at 8pm can convey a different meaning. Symbols are also explicitly chosen to carry no predefined meaning. Users are expected to build their own meaning and extend the available vocabulary using combinations of symbols (Fig. 1.a). The message is only explicit amongst people having the knowledge of the code and thus becomes part of the appropriation of the clock.

3.1 An Augmented Clock

While many existing products add extra functionalities to their designs, marker-Clock is a selection of features chosen for their simplicity and usefulness. Clocks are particularly suited to be augmented as they are ubiquitous in our homes. MarkerClock remains a simple clock and reuses existing interactions. Users can browse past communication by simply moving the hour hand clockwise or anti-clockwise. The time and date of the current focus is then displayed as text at the bottom left corner of the clock. Users can return to the present by either bringing the hands back to the present time or by waiting 3 seconds without touching the clock.

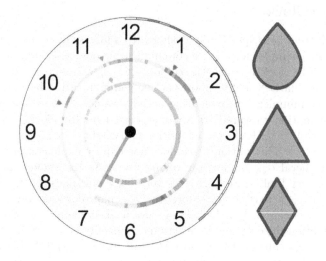

Fig. 2. Preview of a markerClock showing two connected users

The symbols available for active communication are displayed on the side of the clock. They are large enough to accommodate impaired eyesight and motor skills. Each user is also identified by his color, which is used for displaying his communication across connected clocks. The clock displays each message sent at the position of the hour hand for that time. For example messages sent at 3pm will be displayed in front of the number 3 on the clock. The thickness of the spiral depicting motion decreases over time so as to easily distinguish between present and past communication. The age of a symbol or portion of motion trace is also emphasized by decreasing their saturation as time advances. The half hour of activity also fades to disappear totally (See Fig. 1.b). MarkerClock provides similar representations of self and other users on each device. A clock can display between 1 and 4 users, which can be separated into groups so that the friends do not see what the neighbor sends. This is particularly important as the social networks of seniors are often made of many sub-networks, which do not necessarily communicate with each other.

3.2   Routines and Temporal Context

The history of the past 12 hours of activity and the exploration of past communications allow users to build a shared knowledge of each other's routines. Users can compare the existing traces and their intimate knowledge to interpret events and stay aware of each other's activities. For example, Marie's brother, Sam, is used to see her activity start before 9am every morning. If this does not happen one morning, he might call her to check that everything is right. Knowledge of particular events is already shared by usual means such as phone or emails, if that change was to be expected, we assume that the information was passed during other regular communications.

By using the familiar mapping between time and geometry, markerClock enhances the role of time in messages and makes the "historical" context important. This use of time to provide explicit context for communication extends existing asynchronous/synchronous paradigms found in the literature. For example, If the clock is situated in her friend's living room, Beatrice will know that if a motion occurred between 4 and 5am, this is not only a night snack. This may show a sleep disorder due to her friend's upcoming surgery. Beatrice can clearly see when her friend was up during the night because the information is not lost (the old information is replaced by a newer one) and is readily available.

4   Conclusion

MarkerClock is an augmented clock built upon seniors' stories of their daily life. It uses simple active communication and non intrusive passive communication to support shared awareness amongst seniors. The evaluation of markerClock has been initiated by its deployment in our lab between people located in different offices and its introduction to a few seniors. These initial stages of evaluation allowed the refinement of some details such as color contrasts, decrease of motion sampling frequency, and the suggestion of tactile interaction. A deployment in situ will allow the contextual evaluation of markerClock. Results will be used to design new communication appliances and to refine markerClock itself.

References

[1] UN: World population and world urbanization prospects (2005)
[2] Mackay, W., Riche, Y., Labrune, J.-B.: Communication appliances: Shared awareness for intimate social networks. In: ACM SIGCHI 2005 Workshop on Awareness Systems, Portland, OR, US, ACM Press, New York (2005)
[3] Riche, Y., Mackay, W.: Peercare: Challenging the monitoring approach. In: B-HCI WShop on Designing Technology for the Older Population, Edinburg, UK (2005)
[4] Bly, S., Harrison, S., Irwin, S.: Mediaspaces: Bringing people together in a video, audio and computing environment. Comm. of the ACM 36(1), 28–47 (1993)
[5] Hutchinson, H., Mackay, W., Westerlund, B., Bederson, B.B., Druin, A., Plaisant, C., Beaudouin-Lafon, M., Conversy, S., Evans, H., Hansen, H., Roussel, N., Eiderback, B.: Technology probes: inspiring design for and with families. In: ACM SIGCHI 2003 Conf., Ft. Lauderdale, USA, pp. 17–24. ACM Press, New York (2003)

Usability Study of Multi-modal Interfaces Using Eye-Tracking

Regina Bernhaupt[1], Philippe Palanque[2], Marco Winckler[2], and David Navarre[2]

[1] ICT&S Center, Universität Salzburg, Sigmund-Haffner-Gasse 18,
5020 Salzburg, Austria
Regina.Bernhaupt@sbg.ac.at
[2] IRIT, Université Toulouse III,
{palanque, winkler, navarre}@irit.fr

Abstract. The promises of multimodal interaction to make interaction more natural, less error-prone and more enjoyable have been controversially discussed in the HCI community. On the one hand multimodal interaction is being adopted in fields ranging from entertainment to safety-critical applications, on the other hand new forms of interaction techniques (including two-handed interaction and speech) are still not in widespread use. In this paper we present results from a usability evaluation study including eye-tracking on how two mice and speech interaction is adopted by the users. Our results show evidence that two mice and speech can be adopted naturally by the users. In addition, we discuss how eye-tracking data helps to understand advantages of two-handed interaction and speech.

Keywords: Multimodal interfaces, usability evaluation method, two mice, speech.

Introduction

Making interaction more natural is one of the promises of multimodal interfaces. Research on evaluating multimodal interfaces dates back to the mid 1980s [5] and since then it is seen as a promising approach to improve desktop interaction techniques. Multimodal interaction techniques are considered as a potential way to increase communication bandwidth between users and systems and to enhance users satisfaction and comfort by providing a more natural way of interacting with computer systems [5], [6].

Several studies have shown that using two pointing devices in a normal graphical user interface is a more efficient and understandable interaction than using basic mouse and keyboard [8], [19], [28]. On the one hand there exists a strong foundation on two-handed input (see [15] for an overview), on the other hand still two-handed interaction and speech is not in common use. This might have various reasons. In addition to subjective factors like comfort and satisfaction, increasing communication bandwidth between users and systems can have a significant impact on efficiency. For instance the number of commands triggered by the users within a given amount of time and the error rate (typically both the number of slips and mistakes made by the users [26]), are influenced by the user interface and its underlying interaction

C. Baranauskas et al. (Eds.): INTERACT 2007, LNCS 4663, Part II, pp. 412–424, 2007.
© IFIP International Federation for Information Processing 2007

techniques. While complementarity of modalities can be used to reinforce and clarify the communication between the users and the system [23], studies of Dillon et al. [9] and by Kjeldskov and Stage [21] "unsurprisingly" revealed that when multimodal interfaces are poorly designed they are neither better understood nor more efficient than any other user interface offering more standard interaction techniques. In order to determine the impact of modalities on interaction, many empirical studies have been carried out:

- *Showing how usability and user acceptance is influenced by new devices and novel interaction techniques*: [7], [16];
- *Showing that the perceived usability is impacted according to the kind of tasks performed* [10], [18] *and according to the context of use* (e.g. indoor x outdoor conditions, mobile applications) [2];
- *Trying to assess the accuracy of multimodal interaction for given tasks*: [3], [20].

Based on these findings, this paper reports research work aimed at exploring if two mice and a speech recognition system can be easily adopted by novice users. To investigate the usage of two mice and speech, in terms of usability we conducted a usability study including eye-tracking. We used eye-tracking to explore eye-gaze and hot spots when using various combinations of two mice and speech. We additionally explored possible interferences of multimodal interaction with cognitive load. This evaluation has been carried out on a multimodal interface of a safety critical interactive command and control system for satellite operations.

Evaluating Two Mice and Speech

We want to explore if two mice and speech (which a rarely used combination of input devices) can be naturally adopted by novice users. Our hypothesis is that two mice and speech are adopted quickly and new forms of interaction techniques are discovered by non-experienced users easily. We assume that speech becomes natural to interact with the system, even though combined with two mice as graphical input devices.

To prove our hypothesis that two-handed interaction and speech is adopted quite easily and quickly by users, we performed a usability study. Usability evaluation studies seem to be a preferred strategy for the evaluation of multimodal interfaces because it allows the investigation of how users adopt and interact with multimodal technology providing valuable information about the general usability and the user experience. Several types of user testing have been conducted for multimodal interfaces in both usability laboratories and in the field revealing user preferences for interaction modalities based on factors such as acceptance in different social contexts, noisy and mobile environments [18]. An overview on new forms of usability evaluation methods for multimodal interfaces is presented in [4].

We used eye-tracking to gain some insight in usage patterns for two mice, and how speech influences the usage of the two mice. Additionally we explored eye-tracking as a mean to measure users' cognitive load. Using eye-tracking in usability studies combined with some forms of think-aloud is still discussed controversially in the literature. One of the reasons is that think-aloud might increase people self-consciousness and thus prevents them from behaving naturally [11]. Additionally, we will evaluate to which extend eye-tracking data adequately represents cognitive load [25].

Usability Evaluation Study

The goal of this usability evaluation study was to show that two handed interaction and speech can be naturally adopted by users, and that two-handed interaction or speech helps to reduce the cognitive load and necessary attention compared to normal mouse input. Next section presents informally the system on which the usability evaluation has been carried out. Then, the experiment (participants, setup and procedure) will be detailed. The section is concluded with the presentation of the results of the experiment and their interpretation according to the hypothesis presented above.

Informal Description of the System Used

This system has been built within a research project funded by CNES (French National Study Center on Space). The project was meant at defining a formal description technique capable of describing multimodal interfaces and multimodal interaction techniques in a complete and unambiguous way.

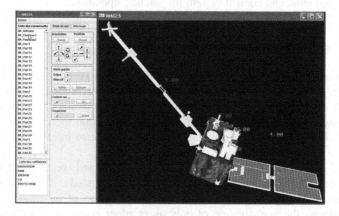

Fig. 1. Screen shot of the system showing a 3D representation of Demeter satellite for the study of ionospheric disturbances

This work defining extensions to an existing formal description technique called Interactive Cooperative Object (ICO) [1], which is based on object Petri nets and Objects. These extensions allowed us to describe unambiguous temporal behaviour of the speech-based interaction technique and how speech commands impact the temporal evolution of the graphical representation. The formal specification of the behavior of such multimodal interaction techniques is given in [22].Beyond these software engineering aspects, the usability of the system was one of the main concern of the part of the project reported in this contribution. Indeed, such safety critical systems require certification by independent authorities prior to deployment and human factor certification is a critical aspect of that certification phase.

The system lies in the domain of Space Ground Systems that can be found in satellite control rooms [24]. The main goal of the system is to monitor a satellite making it possible for the controller to access any component of the satellite. This goal is separated into three main tasks: monitoring temperature, monitoring electricity consumption and locating hardware components in the satellite by moving the 3D image representation (see Figure1). In this application multimodal interaction takes place both while using special buttons (Figure 2) for navigating and changing the point of view of the 3D model, and while interacting with a range slider widget for selecting the temperature and the consumption (see Figure 4). The speech recognition system recognizes two words: "fast" and "slow", which are used to increase or decrease the speed of visual display (movement of the 3D graphical representation of the satellite). The user can use speech interaction at any time she wants. Two-handed synergistic interaction is available on some interactors (see Figures 2 and 4) allowing users to manipulate both left and right input device at the same time.

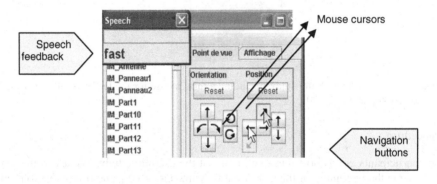

Fig. 2. Possible multimodal interactions using 2 mice for tow-handed interaction (rotating the satellite) and speech input

Participants

We asked 11 participants to take part in our usability evaluation study. Participants were recruited within the university including students and staff members. We selected four female and seven male participants, four of them with former experience on new forms of interaction techniques (pen input, special controllers and joy-sticks) and seven with low or no experience of new forms of interaction techniques. We excluded people wearing eye-glasses in the selection process. Thus we could unfortunately not reach an equivalent distribution of male and females. 8 participants use the right hand for mouse input, 3 participants the left hand for mouse input. Age ranged from 21 to 26 years, with a mean of 22.9 years. All participants used the PC for more than 4 years (mean 10 years of usage), around 4.5 hours per day for work and 2.95 hours per day for work with the Internet at every day of the week (except one participant using the PC only 5 days/week). 9 out of 11 participants stated that they play games, about one hour per day (mean).

Set-up

For the usability evaluation study the participant was seated in front of a table, the eye-tracking device in front, and a laptop on a box in front of the participant. Two mice (left and right from a normal keyboard) were positioned on the table (see Figure 3). The participant used a headset around the neck for speech input. Additional to the eye-tracking, we used two cameras and a microphone for recording the scene and the user interaction. Additionally we captured the screen of the application.

Fig. 3. Set-up for the usability study (including a third mouse for the leader of the experiment to start and stop applications)

Procedure

The participants got a short introduction about the usability study. We asked them to describe in the beginning of the task, what they intended to do, and if possible to think aloud during task completion. If participants naturally stopped the think-aloud because of the speech interaction, we did not force them to continue. We decided to use think-aloud as additional direct mean of providing useful insights in the usage of multimodal interaction, especially to offer insights in possible difficulties encountered while using the system. The data from eye-tracking thus has to be interpreted carefully, as think-aloud might interfere with cognitive load. However, the interaction technique was not influenced by the think-aloud, as speech was only used in two tasks of the study and simply consisted of two words. We will look into possible effects of thinking aloud in following studies.

Starting the usability study, participants answered some preliminary questions regarding the usage of other interaction techniques and games. Then the eye-tracking system was calibrated using 16 points on the screen to make calibration as good as possible. We used the Tobii x50 eye-tracker. None of the participants was wearing eye-glasses. One participant had lenses. The calibration was acceptable for all users.

After the calibration an introduction to the system and its basic functions was given (see Figure 1 for a screen-shot of the prototype in use). During the following training

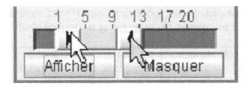

Fig. 4. Two-Handed synergistic interaction on a temperature-slider

phase the user was introduced to the possible usage of the system using two mice and speech. The usability study included 6 tasks. After the completion of the tasks we made a short interview and participants filled out a questionnaire. Task 1 was to make only one component of the system visible. This task was a slight variation of one of the tasks during training. All participants solved this task, showing that they were able to perform basic interaction on the system.

In task 2 all components of the satellite with a temperature higher than 4 degrees °C should be made visible. This task is only solvable if the participant goes through the long list of all the components and requesting display of the temperature of each component. Task 2 should involve two-handed interaction. Task 3 was to locate a special component and to show all the components surrounding it (using two-handed interaction and speech) Task 4 was a variation of task 2. All components between 4 and 9 degrees should be shown and the number of components should be given. The main goal was to show that after short training (in task 2) two-handed input becomes more frequent in use. In task 5 participants were requested to show the antenna of the satellite on the full screen as quickly as possible, and task 6 to show the anchor of the antenna as quickly as possible too. Task 5 and 6 should involve speech input. To enforce speech input usage, we made the system considerably slower displaying graphical output.

After the performance of the tasks, an interview was carried out. During that interview the participants were asked to fill in two questionnaires. One questionnaire addressed system's usability (SUS). The other questionnaire was used to indicate how active or passive the system was during usage. This active/passive questionnaire was adopted from the AttrakDiff [14].

Results

Table 1 gives an overview of number of tasks successful completed, the tasks completed with help (help was defined for each task, for example during task 3, after 3 minutes all participants needed a hint to look more closely on the available functions in the interface) and tasks not completed at all or not completed because of reaching the time limit. In addition, the mean duration for performing the tasks is given. During the task we tried to give hints for function and usage of the program, to avoid, that functions not found interfere with the usage of the interaction technique. This explains the high percentage of tasks completed with help. Participants started to perceive tasks as easier during the test. We interpret the better ratings as a natural adoption of the interaction technique. The fact of easier usage was also reported by nearly all participants during the interview.

Table 1. Overview of completed tasks and their ratings. (*) unfortunately one rating could not be reconstructed during transcription, the mean rating is based on N=10.

Task	Completed	Completed with help	Not Completed	Rating (Mean/SD)	Task duration (mn:sec)
T1	11	0	0	1.45 (0.52)	0:54
T2	0	5	6	3.91 (0.70)	5:55
T3	0	11	0	3.09 (0.83)	4:36
T4	5	3	3	2.73 (0.90)	3:37
T5	9	2	0	1.70 (1.06)(*)	1:39
T6	7	4	0	2.36 (1.03)	0:55

Two-Handed Interaction and Speech

The participants adopted the interaction with two mice quite naturally. Most of them started to use two mice interchangeably. They selected a specific component in the list using left mouse, and then performing an action using the right mouse. This behavior (influenced by the relative position on the GUI) was even shown by left-handed participants. Table 2 gives an overview of the interaction techniques used by the participants during the execution of the six tasks.

During task 1 the participants mainly used the mouse of their dominant hand to solve the task. Task 2 already shows an increase in two-handed interaction. The increased usage of the two-handed interaction-technique was supported by selecting a task including many repetitive elements (each component had to be selected on its own to solve the task). Depending on the strategy of the participant to solve task 3 they started to use two-handed interaction or speech to solve the task. Task 4 was closely related to task 2. The increase of using the two-handed interaction is quite

Table 2. Interaction Techniques used during the performance of the six tasks: First column presents dominant vs non-dominant mouse usage (adding up to 11 participants); last column reports the number of time speech has been used additionally.

Task	One mouse	Two mice	Speech used additionally
T1	8	3	0
T2	4	7	0
T3	6	5	3
T4	1	10	0
T5	11	0	7
T6	10	1	9

impressive. This might be explained by the fact, that the attention needed for problem solving during the task is shifted, increasing the number of people using the two-handed interaction technique. The problem description of task 5 included the formulation "as fast as possible". 7 out of 11 participants started to use speech to solve the task faster. The other participants used a specific function in the system to solve the task (just taking seconds to reach the solution). Task 6 again included the request to solve this task in minimal time. 9 out of 11 participants started to use voice to speed up the visualization process.

Noticeable during the whole usability study is that one participant started to move the hand away from the non-dominant mouse during several tasks (for example during task 4; this was the only user not using other interaction forms). On the other hand, two participants started to use the two-handed input not only interchangeably but really synergistically in trying to rotate the point-of-view of the satellite not only for one axis but two (task 6), or to use the slider for the temperature left and right at the same time (task 4). In one case the user started to use two mice in parallel (Figure 4), but completely forgot to use speech (while ALL other users used speech and only one mouse to complete task 6).

The standard usability scale (SUS) indicated that participants thought that the usability of the system could be considerably improved. SUS scored 59,6 on a scale from 0 to 100 indicating quite some potential to improve usability. Ratings on the adjective scales showed, that people thought that the system is best described using attributes like new, original and innovative. The highest ratings for negative attributes referred to boring, unpleasing and clumsy.

Eye-Tracking

User intent and cognitive load is very difficult to asses during a normal usability study using thinking aloud [17]. To quantify cognitive load and user intent eye-tracking data is used as a possible objective measure. The three measures most commonly used are the number of fixations and the mean fixation duration, gazing time and saccade rates [25]. The number of fixations in each area of interest (AOI) is said to be negatively correlated with search efficiency and task efficiency [25]. Psychologists investigated eye-tracking as to provide insights on problem-solving, reasoning or search strategies. [17] gives an overview of measures used in eye-tracking studies and related evidence for corresponding cognitive processes. According to [12] the overall number of fixations indicates less efficient search. More fixations on a particular area indicate that this area is more noticeable, or more important to the viewer. Longer fixation duration can indicate difficulty in extracting information. We computed overall numbers of fixations, target fixations (fixations on targets divided by total number of fixations [13]), average fixation time and transitions between areas.

We defined several areas of interest, especially the navigation area, temperature slider, component list and satellite depiction. The overall number of fixations in the respective areas of interest defined, showed no significant trend of less efficient search in any of the areas. Same holds true for differences on number of fixations and target fixations. The average fixation time showed a tendency that areas related to navigation, selection of objects or temperature selection showed longer average fixation times compared with menu options or the satellite depiction. For example in

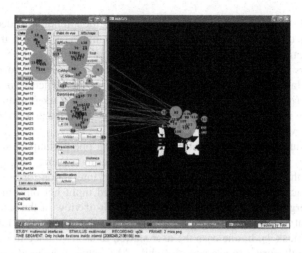

Fig. 5. Gaze plots when interacting with two mice, the left mouse was positioned on the selection of the item, the right mouse positioned on the menu entries and temperature slide

task two the average fixation time in the area of interest "temperature slider" was 386 ms compared to 259 ms for the satellite.

The extensive eye-tracking data analysis showed that average task duration was ways too high to allow meaningful and reliable interpretation of the data captured. Long task durations and variations within the interaction technique usage might deeply influence the eye-tracking data. We thus decided to look more closely on the specific usages of interaction techniques during task execution.

To interpret the eye-tracking data in more detail, we classified all scenes of two-handed mouse interaction and usage of mouse and speech. The interaction technique was used mainly alternating (selection of a component in a list with the mouse in the non-dominant hand, performing the action with the mouse in the dominant hand). We additionally looked closer at participants trying to interact synchronously (using two mice at the same time, using mouse and speech at the same time). For synchronous usage in technical terms we could only classify a small number of cases. To investigate the fact of synchronous usage in detail we will implement a logging tool.

From the tasks described above we want to explain the selection of the temperature as one typical example. We classified the selection of the temperature based on the interaction technique used. As the selection of temperature could be used in two tasks we could classify 17 cases for usage with only one mouse and 3 cases of multimodal usage. The mean number of fixations while solving the task with one mouse was 41.45 fixations, when using two mice only 9.73 fixations occurred. More overall fixations normally indicate a less efficient search [25]. We interpret this gap as support for multimodal interaction, making solution of the task more efficient when using two mice.

Comparing the multimodal selection of components in a list with the single-modality selection, the same trend can be shown, that multimodal interaction shows less fixations compared to normal interaction with one mouse.

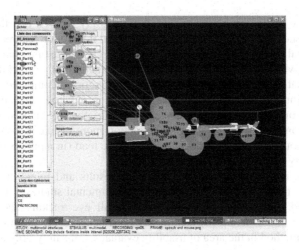

Fig. 6. Hot spots during speech interaction

We identified 14 instances of using *speech while rotating* the satellite. Unfortunately we could only identify one instance of synergistic usage of two mice to solve the same rotation task. Using speech the mean number of fixations in the areas of interest of the satellite (54.09 fixation in the AOI) , the orientation control area (4.36 fixations) and the position control area (5.18 fixations) show that number of fixations are lower when using speech compared to multimodal interaction. The interaction with two mice showed more fixations in these areas (62 fixations for the satellite but 8 for the orientation and 18 for the position). Speech reduces the number of fixations. Taking the overall fixation count, the number of fixations while using two mice is 643 fixations in the menu area compared to only 100 fixations in the same menu are while using speech. People tended to look at the satellite while using speech interaction (758 fixations compared to 332 fixations in the two mouse interaction condition).

Gaze-time shows the same trends as the number of fixation. The average fixation time was about the same for all interaction techniques (ranging from 300 to 500 ms). We currently explore these results in another usability evaluation study to measure time to first fixation more accurate. Observing the gaze during two-handed interaction shows that people are not looking at the mice while interacting. Participants tend to look at the interface elements. Figure 5 shows typical gaze plots when interacting with two mice.

Participants tended to look at the satellite while rotating with speech, ignoring additional input possibilities with the mouse. Figure 6 shows the hot spots during speech interaction.

Summary

The usage of three input devices (two mice and speech) is naturally adopted by users quite rapidly. Users reported in the final interview that they quickly adopted the interaction technique involving these devices, in terms of usage. They reported that continuous use made usage easier. The usability study showed that that eye-tracking data can be used to investigate usage of multimodal interaction technique. People tend to ignore visual input possibilities while using speech, on the other hand they forget to use speech, when performing two handed interactions Eye-tracking data shows tendencies that speech reduces the number of fixations compared to two handed interaction. Some cases indicated, that eye-gaze is reduced when using two mice, compared to one mouse. Multimodal interaction with two mice shows advantages compared to one mouse, making task completion more efficient. Usage of two mice or usage of mouse and speech shows less cognitive load (in numbers of eye fixations) than when only one mouse is used.

Due to the rather limited number of users, results and interpretations presented above have to be handled carefully. Further experimental studies have to show if the data presented above can be generalized. Overall eye-tracking should be used to further explore multi-modal interaction in experiments to lay the ground for further usage of this method in the area of usability evaluation of safety-critical systems.

Conclusion and Future Work

This paper has presented the evaluation of a multimodal user interface featuring synergistic multimodal interaction techniques exploiting two mice and a speech recognition system. We have shown that multi-modal interaction with two mice and speech can be quickly adopted by novice users. Eye-tracking data indicated that speech reduces the visual focus. Two-handed interaction does not result in additional eye-gaze compared with single mouse usage.

Some remaining issues are related to the low level interaction technique exploiting the input devices. Indeed, as stated in the introduction, the interaction technique has been fully modeled using the ICO formal description technique. While building the models we had to define aspects like acceleration of the mouse cursors (both for the dominant and non dominant hand) temporal interval for fusing the events produced by the various input devices, etc. Such temporal elements have been modeled using the notation and their actual value might have a significant impact on the usability results presented above. For instance, informal evaluation has shown that acceleration of mouse cursor should be smaller on the non dominant hand with respect to the dominant one.

To explore the eye-tracking data we want to connect the eye-tracking software with our modeling software PetShop (that allows editing, verifying and executing ICO models) to study first fixations and dynamic stimuli in more detail.

This work belongs to a more ambitious work aiming at providing methods, techniques and tools for the engineering of safety critical interactive systems. Beyond the low level interaction technique issues raised above we also consider higher level concerns like meaningful tasks carried out by users. This will be done by exploiting the formal models to support usabiliy evaluation. Such support can be achieved by generating test cases from the models and thus providing pertinent scenarios to be evaluated via usability techniques as the ones presented in this paper. Such scenarios will be designed in such a way that they will cover all the low-level interaction aspect that have to be evaluated and thus enable designer to assess whether the interaction technique requires additional improvement or if the new design has a positive or negative impact on users' performance (with respect to previous designs).

Acknowledgements

This work is partly funded CNES (National Center of Spatial Studies in France) and the European commission via the Network of Excellence ResIST IST-4-026764-NOE (www.resist-noe.org).

References

1. Bastide, R., Navarre, D., Palanque, P., Schyn, A., Dragicevic, P.: Model-Based Approach for Real-Time Embedded Multimodal Systems in Military Aircrafts. In: Proc. ICMI 2004, pp. 243–250. ACM Press, New York (2004)
2. Baille, L., Schatz, R.: Exploring Multimodality in the Laboratory and the Field. In: Lazzari, G., Pianesi, P. (eds.) ACM international conference on Multimodal Interfaces (ICMI'2005), pp. 100–107. ACM Press, New York (2005)
3. Balbo, S., Coutaz, J., Salber, D.: Towards Automatic Evaluation of Multimodal User Interfaces. Intelligent User Interfaces, Knowledge-Based Systems 6(4), 267–274 (2003)
4. Bernhaupt, R., Palanque, P., Winkler, M., Navarre, D.: Supporting Usability Evaluation of Multimodal Safety Critical Interactive Applications using Dialogue and Interaction Models. In: Law, E., et al. (eds.) Maturing Usability: Quality in Software, Interaction and Value, Springer, Heidelberg (2006)
5. Bolt, R.A.: Put-That-There: Voice and Gesture at the Graphics Interface. In: Proceedings of the 7th International Conference on Computer Graphics and Interactive Techniques, Seattle, pp. 262–270 (1980)
6. Bolt, R.E., Herranz, E.: Two-handed gesture in multi-modal natural dialog. In: Mackinlay, J., Green, M. (eds.) Symposium on User Interface Software and Technology (UIST'92), pp. 7–14. ACM Press, New York (1992)
7. Bowman, D., Gabbard, J., Hix, D.: A Survey of Usability Evaluation in Virtual Environments: Classification and Comparison of Methods. Presence: Teleoperators and Virtual Environments 11(4), 404–424 (2002)
8. Buxton, W., Myers, B.A.: A study in two-handed input. In: Mantei, M., Orbeton, P. (eds.) ACM Conference on Human Factors in Computing Systems (CHI'86), pp. 321–326. ACM Press, Boston, Massachusetts (1986)
9. Dillon, R.F., Edey, J.D., Tombaugh, J.W.: Measuring the true cost of command selection: techniques and results. In: Chew, J.C, Whiteside, J. (eds.) ACM Conference on Human Factors in Computing Systems (CHI'90), pp. 19–25. ACM Press, Seattle, Washington (1990)
10. Dybkjær, L., Bernsen, N.O., Minker, W.: New Challenges in Usability Evaluation - Beyond Task-Oriented Spoken Dialogue Systems. In: Proceedings of ICSLP, vol. III, pp. 2261–2264 (2004)
11. Godding, T. (2006) Eye tracking vs. Thinking aloud? (Retrieved December 15th, 2006), from http://staff.interesource.com/priority4/octover2006/eyetracking.htm
12. Goldberg, H.J., Kotval, X.P.: Computer interface evaluation using eye movements: Methods and constructs. International Journal of Industrial Ergonomics 24, 631–645 (1999)

13. Goldberg, H.J., Wichansky, A.M.: Eye tracking in usability evaluation: A practicioner's guide. In: HyÖna, J., Radach, R., Deubel, H. (eds.) The mind's eye: Cognitive and applied aspects of eye movements research, pp. 493–516. Elsevier, Amsterdam (2003)

14. Hassenzahl, M.: The Thing and I: understanding the Relationship Between User and Product. In: Blythe, M., Overbeeke, C., Monk, A., Wright, P. (eds.) Funology: From Usability to Enjoyment, pp. 31–42. Kluwer Academic Publishers, Dordrecht (2003)

15. Hinkley, K., Czerwinsky, M., Sinclair, M.: Interaction and Modeling Techniques for Desktop Two-Handed Input. In: Proc. IUI 1998, pp. 49–59. ACM Press, New York (1998)

16. Hinckley, K., Pausch, R., Proffitt, D., Kassel, N.F.: Two-handed virtual manipulation. ACM Transactions on Computer-Human Interaction 5(3), 260–302 (1998)

17. Jacob, R.J.K., Karn, K.S.: Eye tracking in human-computer interaction and usability research: Ready to deliver the promises (Section commentary). In: Hyona, J. (ed.) The Mind's Eyes: Cognitive and Applied Aspects of Eye Movements, Elsevier Science, Oxford (2003)

18. Jöst, M., Haubler, J., Merdes, M., Malaka, R.: Multimodal Interaction for pedestrians: an evaluation study. In: Riedl, J., Jameson, A., Billsus, D., Lau, T. (eds.) ACM International Conference on Intelligent User Interfaces (IUI'2005), San Diego, Unite State, pp. 59–66. ACM Press, New York (2005)

19. Kabbash, P., Buxton, W., Sellen, A.: Two-handed input in a compound task. In: Plaisant, C. (ed.) ACM Conference on Human Factors in Computing System (CHI'94), pp. 417–423. ACM Press, Boston, Massachusetts (1994)

20. Kaster, T., Pfeiffer, M., Bauckhage, C.: Combining Speech and Haptics for Intuitive and Efficient Navigation through Image Database. In: Oviatt, S. (ed.) ACM International Conference on Multimodal interfaces (ICMI'2003), pp. 180–187. ACM Press, New York (2003)

21. Kjeldskov, J., Stage, J.: New Techniques for Usability Evaluation of mobile systems. International Journal on Human-Computer Studies 60(5), 599–620 (2004)

22. Navarre, D., Palanque, P., Dragicevic, P., Bastide, R.: An Approach Integrating two Complementary Model-based Environments for the Construction of Multimodal Interactive Applications. Interacting with Computers 18(5), 910–941 (2006)

23. Oviatt, S.: Ten myths of multimodal interaction. Communications of the ACM 42(11), 74–81 (1999)

24. Palanque, P., Bernhaupt, R., Navarre, D., Ould, M., Rubio, R.: Model-based Measurement of the Usability of Multimodal Man-Machine Interfaces for Space Ground Segment Applications. In: Proceedings of SpaceOps 2006, AAAI Press, Stanford, California (2006)

25. Poole, A., Ball, L.J.: Eye Tracking in Human-Computer Interaction and Usability Research: Current Status and Future Prospects. In: Ghaoui, C. (ed.) Encyclopedia of Human Computer Interaction, Idea Group, USA (2004)

26. Reason, J.: Human Error. Cambridge University Press, Cambridge (1990)

27. Salber, D., Coutaz, J.: A Wizard of Oz Platform for the Study of Multimodal Systems. In: Interchi 93, pp. 95–96. ACM Press, New York (1993)

28. Zhai, S., Barton, A.S., Selker, T.: Improving browsing performance: a study of four input devices for scrolling and pointing tasks. In: Howard, S., Hammond, J., Lindgaard, G. (eds.) The IFIP Conference on Human-Computer Interaction (INTERACT'97), pp. 286–292. Chapman & Hall, Sydney, Australia (1997)

Investigating Effective ECAs: An Experiment on Modality and Initiative

Alistair Sutcliffe and Faisal Al-Qaed

Centre for HCI Design, School of Informatics, University of Manchester, UK
alistair.g.sutcliffe@manchester.ac.uk
faisal.al-qaed@postgrad.manchester.ac.uk

Abstract. This paper investigates the effectiveness of conversational agent-based delivery of task strategy and operational help for an interactive search tool. The study tested three modalities of advice (text-only, text-and-audio, and text-audio-and-agent) in addition to a control group with no advice. User- and system- initiated advice modes were also compared. Subjects in the text-only group outperformed other modality groups in usability errors, search performance, advice uptake and in their positive comments in the debriefing interview and post-test questionnaire. User-initiated advice was preferred and was more effective. Users criticized speech advice for being too long and difficult to control. The results suggested that the computer as social actor paradigm might not be effective for advisory applications.

Keywords: Multi Modal Interfaces, Advisor Agents, User initiative.

1 Introduction

Embodied Conversational Agents (ECAs) have attracted considerable attention as a means of enhancing user experience in e-commerce [1], and in social interaction on the Internet [10]. Following Fogg's [12] advocacy of computers as a persuasive technology, ECAs are being used in e-commerce as store guides to advise users [1, 31]. Although the computer as social actor theory [28] predicts that the use of human image and voice will invoke a powerful response by users, treating computers as if they were human agents, it is not clear how far these experimental findings generalize to interactive settings. Conversational agents or avatars can improve user engagement and motivation [3, 7]; however, evidence of task-related performance improvements is less clear.

ECAs using TTS (Text-To-Speech) voice have positively influenced users' preferences and purchasing behavior [8]; however, in another web-based study, the presence of animated agents that actively monitored users' behavior was found to decrease users' performance and increase their anxiety level [29]. Generally, there are few convincing demonstrations that ECAs or animated characters significantly influence users' behavior or improve task-related performance [11, 21]; indeed, Berry et al. [2] found that text-based advice was better than an ECA for persuading users to adopt healthy life styles, although the agent version with more natural dialogue and facial expressions was preferred. This paper extends previous studies by investigating the effectiveness of the CSA paradigm for task-based advice. Most previous evaluations have assumed system initiative and control of the conversation by the

C. Baranauskas et al. (Eds.): INTERACT 2007, LNCS 4663, Part II, pp. 425–438, 2007.

ECA.; however, given the well known user aversion to system initiated help, for instance the Microsoft Clippie agent; and politeness rules posited in [28] user initiated ECA advice might receive a more positive reaction. To complement previous studies we also investigated differences in user- and system- initiated interaction.

The context for the study is providing decision making advice based on strategies from the Adaptive Decision Making (ADM) theory [24] and online help for users using a visual browsing/search tool based on Shneiderman's Spotfire display [32]. Since users tend to access help and explanation systems when they perceive the task to be difficult, this scenario investigates the difference between task-based advice for decision making which may be useful but not essential, and online help which will be necessary if problems are encountered.

The paper is organized as follows: the next section provides a brief background of related research. This is followed by the discussion of the methods and results of the experiment. The discussion reviews the experimental findings and concludes with plans for future research.

2 Related Work

ECAs can emulate human behaviors and influence user behavior and judgment if they portray a believable human presence [7]. Substantial attempts [6, 7, 21] have been made to improve the design and responsiveness of ECAs with emotional reactions and appropriate facial expressions to provide an experience approaching the quality of natural human-to-human interaction. Preliminary evaluations of Cassel's RHEA showed that agent-based advisors for health topics can be effective. Pelachaud and Bilvi [25] presented a computational model for the creation of non-verbal behaviors associated with speech for natural ECAs that can emulate human behaviors, facial expressions, body gesture and speech. Informal evaluations of their GRETA agent also suggest the computer as social actor can be an effective advisor.

De Angeli et al. [9, 10] have shown that even limited capability ECAs or chatterbots designed with social anthropomorphic reactions can establish social relationships with users. In a Wizard of Oz study on help for online banking, they demonstrated that text-based dialogues with chatterbots closely resemble human-human conversations, and that people prefer ECA agents to text-based advice Similar limited capability ECAs based on Microsoft agents have been implemented as advisor agents in e-commerce applications [31] in which two or more agents converse with the user to advise on different aspects of a product. Once again informal evaluations seem to show that users respond well to agent-based advisors.

Commercial use of ECA-style shopping assistants is becoming widespread on the Internet. In a study of e-commerce websites, Keeling et al. [15] investigated the appropriateness of different ECAs (e.g. cartoon-like agents and human-like agents) for a variety of the websites and users. They concluded that great care should be taken in matching ECAs with websites, considering both the physical characteristics of the ECA and the goals and motivations of the users.

Riegelsberger et al. [30] illustrated how users respond more effectively and more naturally to rich media representations (video, audio, avatar, photos) compared to textual messages, and showed that video followed by audio gives the user the most detailed insight into expertise and promotes trust with agents. Oviatt et al. [22, 23] investigated natural modality integration patterns and proposed a predictive model for modality integration. This suggests that ECAs using speech with complementary non-verbal communication (facial expression and gesture) should be more effective than other single modalities. Overall it appears that, apart from Berry et al.'s study, most of the evidence points towards agent-based advisors as being more effective that standard text-based advice.

ECAs have tended to use speech to deliver advice; in contrast, chatterbots and avatars on the Internet tend to be text based. Guidelines for modality combination suggest that speech may be more effective than text when advice also involves inspecting a text-based resource, for example user interface menus, prompts and displays. The modality design guidelines and the Split-Attention principle developed by Moreno and Mayer [17] recommend avoiding using the same modality for two competing tasks, and that material delivered on different modalities should be complementary rather than dividing the user's attention. In contrast, multimedia design guidelines [14, 33] advocate presenting detailed material in text rather than speech. Interpretation may depend on how detailed the advice is and whether users can split their attention between two tasks (e.g. operating the interface and comprehending advice) and information presented on one modality.

3 Experimental Design

Forty subjects (25 males and 15 females, aged 20 to 39) from the University of Manchester participated in the experiment. Most subjects were postgraduate students with intermediate to expert Internet search experience. The subjects were paid £10 for their participation. The interview sessions were video-taped and lasted for 45 minutes, with experimental task durations ranging from 10 to 15 minutes.

The study tested three modalities of advice (text-only, text-and-audio, and text-audio-and-agent); in addition there was a control group with no advice, resulting in four between-subject groups with 10 subjects each. Following Moreno and Mayer's [17] multimedia design principle (Split-Attention Effect), the audio and text were not played concurrently, to prevent the audio from interfering with text advice.

In each modality group, two advice initiative conditions were used. In the user-initiative condition the subjects accessed the advice by clicking on appropriate buttons of the agent. In the system initiative condition the advisor delivered the advice automatically, although the speech/text delivery could be cancelled. The subjects were able to close the advisor window or get advice any number of times in both initiative conditions. The initiative conditions were counter-balanced for each modality group.

Prior to starting the experimental tasks, the subjects were given a brief tutorial on how to control the advisor. They were then given a scenario of finding an apartment to rent in Manchester using a student accommodation database with two tasks:
Use the Scatterplot filtering tool to:

- Find the best apartment that has 2 rooms and a weekly rental less than £200.
- Find the number of apartments that are 3-4 miles from the city centre and with popularity rating of at least 8. (Hint: You may need to re-configure the slider settings).

The hint directed subjects' attention to the need to change the sliders on the tool before the second search task could be completed. Thus the first task was relatively simple and could be achieved without help whereas the second task should be perceived as being more difficult; and motivate access to the agent's help. The Scatterplot filtering tool (see Figure 1), inspired by Shneiderman's [32] Filmfinder tool using the concept of dynamic query filters, was developed using Java applets that communicated with Java Servlet programs at the server-side to dynamically retrieve data from the database. Operation of the tool was reasonably intuitive although users had to guess that both ends of the slider could be manipulated to set a range. The advisor agent was implemented using Microsoft Agents toolkit, using a male agent with limited facial expressions and gestures. Text was presented in a separate window partition once the speech was completed. The two tasks required subjects to use different features of the tool. Two identical types of advice were given in each modality group, Strategy advice and Tool advice. Strategy advice provided decision strategies that could be employed with the selected tool, whereas Tool advice contained specific explanation about how to use different features of the tool. The control group subjects carried out the tasks without any advice. Finally, all subjects were presented with a post-test questionnaire eliciting their subjective assessment of the advisors, and a debriefing interview in which they were asked for their advisor modalities and initiative preferences; and to provide suggestions for improvements with explanations of any particular problems they had experienced.

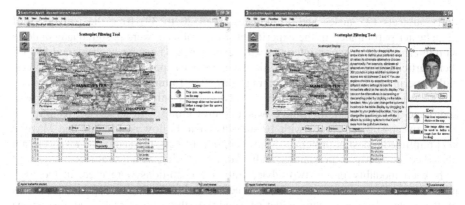

Fig. 1. Scatterplot Filtering Tool without the Advisor (left), and with the Advisor (right) showing the text appearing after the speech advice

4 Results

4.1 Task Times and Errors

The subjects' search performance times differed significantly between the groups (see Figure 2) in Task 1 (ANOVA, $F=13.876$, $df=3,39$, $p<0.001$) and for Task 2 ($F=12.431$, $df=3,39$, $p<0.001$). There were no differences in search times between tasks since users learned search tool operation in Task 1 (mean 507.6s) which compensated for the additional configuration actions required in Task 2 (mean 496.5s). All modality groups had better search performance times than the control group in both tasks (p<0.001, Tukey HSD post-hoc test). In Task 1, the control group was significantly worse that the text-only, text-and-audio, and text-audio-and-agent groups (henceforth agent group) (p<0.001, p<0.05 and p<0.01 respectively), while the text-only condition was better than text-and-audio and agent groups (p<0.05 andpP<0.05 respectively). In Task 2, similar significant differences were found between the control and all other groups (p<0.001, p<0.05 and p<0.05 respectively). In addition, the text-only condition was better than the text-and-audio and-agent modalities (p<0.05 and p<0.05 respectively). Similar inter-modality differences were found when times were adjusted to allow for the imposed latency in the agent and text conditions when subjects had to listen to the speech before the text advice appeared.

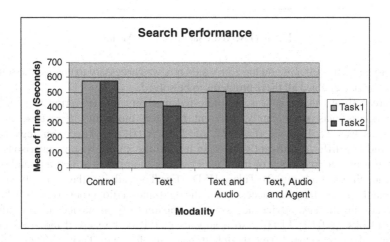

Fig. 2. Mean Search Times (not adjusted for imposed latency)

A one-way between-group ANOVA with observed usability errors as the dependent variable showed a significant difference between groups (F=6.063, df=3,39 p<0.01). The control group experienced significantly more errors than the advice text-only and agent groups (Tukey HSD post-hoc tests p<0.001 and p<0.05 respectively); however, the difference between the control group and text-and-audio group was not significant (see Figure 3). More errors occurred in Task 1 than in Task 2 (p<0.05 Binomial test on totals for all conditions) even though Task 2 was more difficult and involved configuration so the learning effect was minor. The agent group had fewer usability errors than the text-and-audio group even though the same advice was present in both conditions, although this difference was non-significant. Most of the usability errors were accounted for by four design problems: users couldn't find the sliders, they did not realize that both ends of the slider bar could be moved to create a range query, the sort results function was not clear as it required the user to click on the header bar to sort by the selected attribute (location, price), and the configuration cue was poor since users

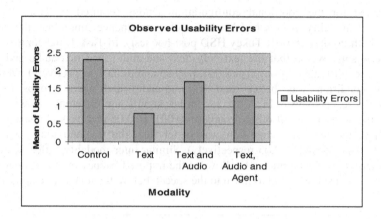

Fig. 3. Observed Usability Errors Means

had to guess that clicking on the x or y axis box was necessary to change the settings. The tool advice enabled all these problems to be solved.

Figure 4 shows that text was the preferred modality for delivering advice. Total advice access was significantly different between modalities (F=8.694, df=2,29 p<001), as was Tool advice (F=6.927, df=2,29 p<0.01); however, Strategy advice access did not differ significantly between modalities. In pairwise comparisons text-only had a higher frequency of total advice access compared to text-and-audio, and agent modalities (both p<0.01 Tukey HSD). For Tool advice, the text-only showed significantly more frequent access than the text-and-audio group (p <.01) but no differences in strategy advice access were apparent. Total advice access differed between tasks (p<0.01, T1>T2); so it appears that Task 1 received more advice but also caused more errors, even though it was simpler than Task 2. This apparent contradiction is analyzed further in section 4.4.

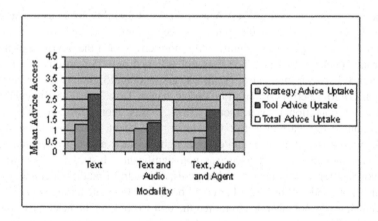

Fig. 4. Advice Access frequencies by Modality

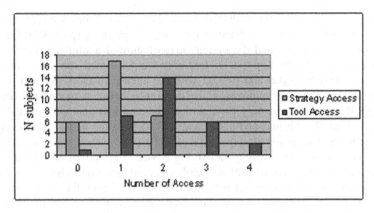

Fig. 5. Number of subjects accessing each type of advice

Tool advice was accessed more frequently than Strategy advice (see Figure 5) probably because it was perceived to be more useful, from debriefing interview comments. In the debriefing interview most subjects commented that the Strategy advice agreed with their normal approach to search tasks hence it had limited utility and they ignored it. Many subjects (56.7%) complained that the speech advice was too long, which may have caused them to access it less frequently than text presentations.

4.2 Questionnaire Ratings

Figure 6 shows users' ratings captured in the post-test questionnaire. In Q1 (The Advisor delivers the advice clearly) differences between modalities were significant

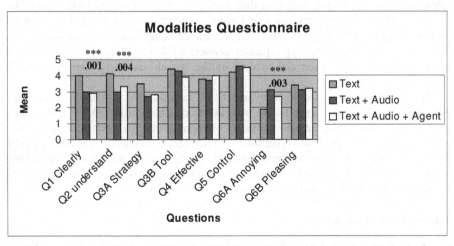

Note: Stars indicate significant differences between advisor modalities (Sig. level <0.05) and the numbers below them indicate the Sig. Value. Q represents question number explained within text.

Fig. 6. Post-test Questionnaires ratings

(F=9.165, df=2,39 p<0.001) with the text-only advisor outperforming the other modalities in delivering clear advice in pairwise comparisons (p<0.005). Q2 (I was able to follow and understand the system advice) showed a similar pattern between modalities (F=6.715, df=2, p<0.01); text-only outperformed the other modalities P<0.01 with text-and-audio and p<0.05 with the agent). In Q6A (System delivered advice in a way that was annoying), the difference between modalities (F=7.252, df=2, p<0.01), favored text-only presentation as being less annoying than the other modalities (p<0.01 with text-and-audio and p<0.05 with the agent). However, Q3A (The system was useful for Strategy advice), Q3B (The system was useful for Tool advice), Q4 (The advisor's way of delivering advice is effective), Q5 (User controls for getting advice are easy to use) and Q6B (System delivered advice in a pleasing way) showed no differences between the modalities. From the users' subjective opinion ratings the agent does not appear to have been treated as a social actor in this advisor context.

4.3 Debriefing Interviews

In debriefing interviews, 63.3% of the subjects stated that they preferred the agent advisor modality, followed by the text-only advice (16.7%); while 80% of the subjects preferred the text advice compared to audio and text. Their preference for the advisor modality was significant (Chi-Square = 37.3, df=4, p<0.001). Although they perceived the agent interface to be more attractive, most subjects (80%) suggested giving the advisor more personality to improve its social presence.

The audio was disliked by 80% of the subjects, who commented that it was annoying to have to listen to a long speech clip especially when they needed to access the advice more than once (the duration for the audio of Tool advice was 52 seconds and for Strategy advice was 24 seconds). In contrast, the subjects preferred the text advice because they could read it at their own pace. 55% of the subjects from audio groups disliked the artificial voice and recommended using more natural recorded speech. A third of the subjects (30%) recommended better matching of voice, accent and tone to the user group, e.g. speaker gender, while two thirds (70%) suggested better controls for the pace and content of the speech and use of smaller speech segments (65%).

The subjects were asked to state which advice initiative (system or user) they preferred. As expected, user initiative was preferred in both tasks (86.7%, Chi-Square = 16.1, df=1,pP<0.001). Several subjects commented that the system initiative was annoying, especially the audio conditions. Advice access frequency was controlled by the experimental condition, so only repeated access (second access after cancelling speech) could be compared; however, no significant differences were apparent between system and user initiative.

4.4 Behavior Analysis

In this section we explore the effects of advice initiative in more depth by analyzing the users' behavior patterns. Using the video recordings the subjects' search behavior was categorized into actions: using sliders to search, browsing and sorting the results table or getting advice. Usability errors were classified as attempting an action, e.g.

attempt use sliders. Sequences of behavior were analyzed by casting transition frequencies for all combinations of behavior categories in a matrix (i.e. frequencies where A was followed by B, B was followed by C, etc.) and then constructing behavior network graphs for all subjects. To test for significant sequence transitions, an expected value was calculated for each cell in the matrix by formula (1):

$$ExpA,B = \frac{FrequencyA \times FrequencyB}{NT} \tag{1}$$

where NT=total transition frequencies in the whole matrix divided by number of cells.

The expected value was then used in the Binomial test for sample sizes where N>25 in formula (2), where x = the observed transition frequency between behavior (A,B) and N was the expected value:

$$Z = \frac{(x \pm 0.5) - 0.5N}{0.5\sqrt{N}} \tag{2}$$

In the network diagrams, only frequencies above 1% of the overall total are reported, to make the diagrams more readable. This may cause inconsistencies between the total input and output transitions for some behaviors.

Figure 7 illustrates the behavior patterns for Task 1, user initiative condition. Most subjects either attempted to use the sliders or browsed, then accessed the Tool advice. Seven subjects cancelled the advice (all in the speech condition), while eight accessed the advice twice. After accessing the advice most users operated the tool successfully and completed the task, although few used the sort function. In the system initiative condition (see Figure 8) all users cancelled the strategy advice and most cancelled the tool advice before it ended. Four used the tool sliders successfully then browsed results, while four were unsuccessful even after accessing advice. Many users accessed the advice on their own initiative after experiencing difficulties. This explains the apparent anomaly of frequent advice access and more errors in Task 1; users were following a trial and error strategy and accessing advice after experiencing problems.

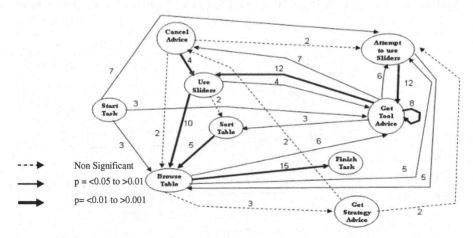

Fig. 7. Behavior Network for Subjects in Task 1 – User Initiative

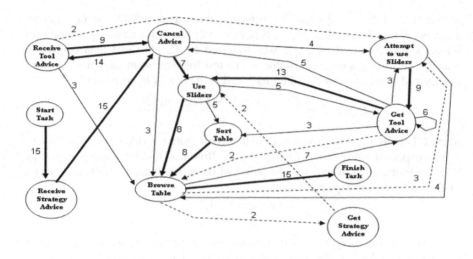

Fig. 8. Behavior Network for Subjects in Task 1 – System Initiative

In Task 2 the subjects were required to learn how to configure the slider settings to effectively finish the task. In the user initiative condition, depicted in Figure 9, most subjects accessed the advice before attempting to configure the tool. This may be due to a learning effect after Task 1, coupled with the greater perceived difficulty of configuring the sliders compared with simply operating the Scatterplot tool. Few errors or advice cancels were observed. In the system initiative condition (see Figure 10) all users cancelled the Strategy advice, but few cancelled the Tool advice, possibly reflecting a more positive perception of the utility of the advice for the more difficult configuration task. They then followed a variety of pathways before re-accessing the advice and proceeding with the configuration-search task.

Most subjects cancelled the speech advice before it ended in both tasks (75%). Advice accesses were more frequent in the text-only condition, while cancels were more

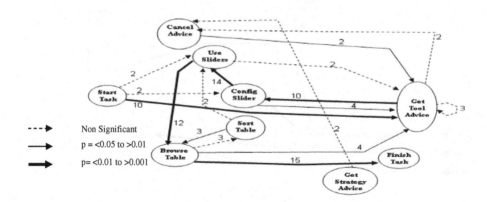

Fig. 9. Behavior Network for Subjects in Task 2 – User Initiative

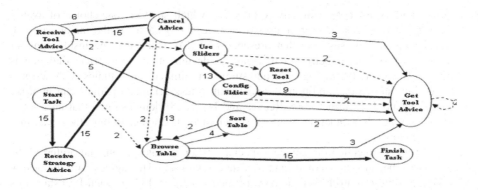

Fig. 10. Behavior Network for Subjects in Task 2 – System Initiative

frequent in the speech conditions (p<0.001 Binomial test on totals for all subjects). System initiative was bound to have more cancellations due to the experimental design; however, repeated access did not differ between initiative conditions.

Overall the behavior analysis shows that user initative was more effective, as might be expected; however, when the task is more difficult the difference between the patterns is less clear cut. Users appear to be more tolerant of system control if they perceive the advice may be important. Interestingly, when we examined the patterns by modality, it appeared that the agent condition had little impact on the pattern of user behaviour.

5   Discussion

Previous studies on using ECAs to improve the effectiveness of interaction have produced mixed results, with some showing positive effects [2, 4, 7, 11] while others showed no improvement over text-based advice [2, 27]. This study has added evidence to the contention that human-like agents are not always effective, suggesting that 'the computer as a social actor' paradigm [28] may not be manifest in certain conditions when usability errors may override the persuasive potential of human-like avatars. Whereas previous evaluations of ECAs have measured users' attitudes and perceptions such as social presence and flow [27], our study on task-related advice demonstrated that the agent was worse than text-only presentation in both performance and satisfaction measures. Berry et al. [2] also found no advantage for an ECA in a persuasion task, and that text-only was more effective for comprehensibility of advice. In our study, the subjects' comments and preference for the ECA condition indicated that the agent may have had some positive or 'social actor' effect; but when usability concerns became critical, as in the agent-speech condition, we conjecture that the positive social presence of the agent is over-ridden by the users' adverse reaction to the speech dialogue.

One reason for the ECA's poor performance may lie in design of the speech dialogue, since users can have an adverse reaction to inappropriate artificial voices [18]. However, experimental studies and speech dialogue principles [18, 19] suggest that users are tolerant of poor quality TTS speech [20]) and that male voices carry more authority for delivering advice [18, 19], which supports our choice of avatar. We suspect that lack of user control over speech proved to be the major cause of dissatisfaction. This suggests that presence of ECAs alone may be insufficient for delivering task-related help and that careful design of an appropriate dialogue is critical. However, the dialogue in our study was limited, and studies with scripted ECAs have shown that addition of social chat to task-oriented dialogue can improve trust in agents [3]; furthermore, Reeves and Nass [28] demonstrated that an agent's social presence is a function of its on-screen size. The agent in our study was in a small window.

Most users cancelled the advice, especially when it was spoken, and preferred the text advice because they could read it at their own pace. This agrees with the design principle of user control over the pace of media delivery [33, 34] and ISO standards [14, 33]; however, guidelines [16] are less forthcoming about the acceptable duration of speech segments. Our results indicate that simple stop controls, which we implemented, may not prevent user dissatisfaction, and the duration of speech segments should be short, possibly less than 10 seconds. The default assumption of using speaking ECAs to deliver task-related advice [7, 25] may have to be reconsidered. Speech may be used more profitably for giving background information and attracting the users' attention with the ECA, while detailed advice is delivered by text. This follows previous recommendations for partitioning topics in explanatory dialogues and matching the delivery modality to different types of information [26].

The decision strategy advice tended to be ignored by most subjects, probably because it was not relevant to the task in hand. However, the Tool advice was perceived as effective and it was accessed particularly after users had experienced difficulties. Furthermore, the Tool advice was accessed more frequently in Task 2, indicating that users' predisposition to help may be susceptible to experience and perceived difficulty of the task. This agrees with previous findings that users tend to access help and explanation only when they perceive the task to be difficult; otherwise, trial and error is the usual strategy [5, 13]. In our future work we will improve the advisor's presence and the quality of the advice itself and design experiments to evaluate configuration of the toolset and tool support for specific decision making tasks.

References

[1] Aberg, J., Shahmeri, N.: An Empirical Study of Human Web Assistants: Implications for User Support in Web Information Systems. In: Conference on Human Factors in Computing Systems, ACM Press, New York (2001)

[2] Berry, D.C., Butler, L.T., DeRossis, F.: Evaluating a Realistic Agent in an Advice Giving Task. International Journal of Human-Computer Studies 63, 304–327 (2005)

[3] Bickmore, T., Cassell, J.: Relational Agents:A Model and Implementation of Building User Trust. In: Conference on Human Factors in Computing Systems, pp. 396–403. ACM Press, New York (2001)

[4] Bickmore, T., Cassell, J.: Social Dialogue with Embodied Conversational Agents, in Natural. In: Intelligent and Effective Interaction with Multimodal Dialogue Systems, Kluwer Academic, New York (2004)

[5] Carroll, J.M., Rosson, M.B.: Paradox of the Active User, in Interfacing Thought: Cognitive Aspects of Human-Computer Interaction. MIT Press, Cambridge (1987)

[6] Cassell, J., Pelachaud, C., Badler, N.I., Steedman, M., Achorn, B., Becket, T., Douville, B., Prevost, S., Stone, M.: Animated Conversation: Rule-Based Generation of Facial Expression, Gesture and Spoken Intonation for Multiple Conversational Agents. In: Computer Graphics Annual Conference Series (SIGGRAPH-94), pp. 413–420. ACM Press, New York (1994)

[7] Cassell, J., Sullivan, J., Prevost, S., Churchill, E.: Embodied Conversational Agents. MIT Press, Cambridge (2000)

[8] Darves, C., Oviatt, S., Coulston, R.: The Impact of Auditory Embodiment on Animated Character Design. In: Falcone, R., Barber, S., Korba, L., Singh, M.P. (eds.) AAMAS 2002. LNCS (LNAI), vol. 2631, Springer, Heidelberg (2003)

[9] De Angeli, A., Johnson, G.I., Coventry, L.: The Unfriendly User: Exploring Social Reactions to Chatterbots. In: International Conference on Affective Human Factors Design, Asean Academic Press, London (2001)

[10] DeAngeli, A.: To the Rescue of a Lost Identity: Social Perception in Human Chatterbot Interaction. In: Virtual Agents Symposium, pp. 7–14 (2005)

[11] Dehn, D.M., VanMulken, S.: The Impact of Animated Interface Agents: A Review of Empirical Research. International Journal of Human-Computer Studies 52, 1–22 (2000)

[12] Fogg, B.J.: Persuasive Technology: Using Computers to Change What We Think and Do. Morgan Kaufmann, San Francisco (2003)

[13] Gregor, S.: Explanation From Knowledge-Based Systems and Cooperative Problem Solving: An Empirical Study. International Journal of Human-Computer Interaction 54, 81–106 (2003)

[14] ISO: ISO 14915 Multimedia User Interface Design Software Ergonomic Requirements, Part 1: Introduction and Framework; Part 3: Media Combination and Selection: International Standards Organisation (1998)

[15] Keeling, K., Beatty, S., McGoldrick, P., Macaulay, L.: Face Value? Customer Views of Appropriate Formats for Embedded Conversational Agents (ECAs) in Online Retailing. In: 37th Hawaii International Conference on System Sciences, IEEE Computer Society Press, Los Alamitos (2004)

[16] Luz, S., Bernsen, N.O.: A Tool for Interactive Advice on the Use of Speech in Multimodal Systems. Journal of VLSI Signal Processing 29, 129–137 (2001)

[17] Moreno, R., Mayer, R.E.: A Learner-Centered Approach to Multimedia Explanations: Deriving Instructional Design Principles From Cognitive Theory. Interactive Multimedia Electronic Journal oc Computer Enhanced Learning (2000)

[18] Nass, C., Brave, S.: Wired for Speech: How Voice Activates and Advances the Human-Computer Relationship. MIT Press, Cambridge (2005)

[19] Nass, C., Gong, L.: Speech Interfaces From an Evolutionary Perspective. Communications of the ACM 43, 37–43 (2000)

[20] Nass, C., Lee, K.M.: Does Computer-Generated Manifest Personality? An Experimental Test of Similarity-Attraction. In: Conference on Human Factors in Computing Systems, pp. 49–57. ACM Press, New York (2000)

[21] Oviatt, S.L., Adams, B.: Designing and Evaluating Conversational Interfaces with Animated Characters. In: Embodied Conversational Agents, MIT Press, Cambridge (2000)

[22] Oviatt, S.L., Coulston, R., Lunsford, R.: When Do We Act Multimodally? Cognitive Load and Multimodal Communication Patterns. In: Sixth International Conference on Multimodal Interfaces (ICMI 2004), ACM Press, New York (2004)

[23] Oviatt, S.L., Coulston, R., Tomko, S., Xiao, B., Lunsford, R.: Toward a Theory of Organized Multimodal Integration Patterns During Human-Computer Interaction. In: International Conference on Multimodal Interfaces, ACM Press, New York (2003)

[24] Payne, J.W., Bettman, J.R., Johnson, E.J.: The Adaptive Decision Maker. Cambridge University Press, Cambridge (1993)

[25] Pelachaud, C., Bilvi, M.: Computational Model of Believable Conversational Agents. In: Communication in MAS: Background, Current Trends and Future, Springer, Heidelberg (2003)

[26] Purchase, H.C., Worrill, J.: An Empirical Study of on-Line Help Design: Features and Principles. International Journal of Human-Computer Studies 56, 539–567 (2002)

[27] Qiu, L., Benbasat, I.: The Effects of Text-to-Speech Voice and 3D Avatars on Consumer Trust in the Design of 'Live Help' Interface of Electronic Commerce. International Journal of Human-Computer Interaction 19, 75–94 (2005)

[28] Reeves, B., Nass, C.: The Media Equation: How People Treat Computers, Television and New Media Like Real People and Places. CLSI/Cambridge University Press, Stanford CA/Cambridge (1996)

[29] Rickenberg, R., Reeves, B.: The Effects of Animated Characters on Anxiety, Task Performance, and Evaluations of User Interfaces. In: Conference on Human Factors in Computing Systems, pp. 49–56. ACM Press, New York (2000)

[30] Riegelsberger, J., Sasse, M.A., McCarthy, J.D.: Rich Media, Poor Judgement? A Study of Media Effects on Users Trust in Expertise. In: HCI 2005, Springer, Heidelberg (2005)

[31] Rist, T., André, E., Baldes, S.: A Flexible Platform for Building Applications with Life-Like Characters. In: International Conference on Intelligent User Interfaces, ACM Press, New York (2003)

[32] Shneiderman, B.: Dynamic Queries for Visual Information Seeking, in Readings in Information Visualization: Using Vision to Think. Morgan Kaufmann, San Francisco (1999)

[33] Silveira, M.S., de Souza, C.S., Barbosa, S.D.J.: Semiotic EngineeringContributions for Designing on line Help Systems. In: Smith, M., Salvenrdy, G., Koubek, R. (eds.) Proceedings of HCI International, San Franciso CA, pp. 31–38. Elsevier, Amsterdam (1997)

[34] Sutcliffe, A.G., Kurniawan, S., Shin, J.: A Method and Advisor Tool for Multimedia User Interface Design. International Journal of Human-Computer Studies 64, 375–392 (2006)

Towards a Physiological Model of User Interruptability

Daniel Chen, Jamie Hart, and Roel Vertegaal

Human Media Lab
Queen's University, Kingston, Ontario, Canada
{chend, jamie, roel}@cs.queensu.ca

Abstract. User interruptability has become an important topic of study in Human-Computer Interaction (HCI). However, automatically determining the availability of users is still problematic. In this paper, we present a preliminary study of the use of physiological measurements for predicting user interruptability status. We measured Heart Rate Variability (HRV) and Electromyogram (EMG) signals whilst users performed a variety of tasks; including reading, solving word puzzles, mental arithmetic, typing, and playing a racing game. Results show high correlations for both HRV ($r = 0.96$) and EMG ($r = 0.85$) with user self-reports of interruptability. We combined these two measures into a single linear model, which predicted user interruptability with a combined r^2 of 0.95, or 95% of the variance. Please note that our model, at this stage, describes interruptability across users rather than per individual. We describe an application of our findings in the Physiological Weblog, or 'Plog, a system that uses our model for automating online messaging status.

Keywords: Interruptions, Blogs, Attentive User Interfaces (AUIs).

1 Introduction

With the emergence of camera phones and other mobile imaging devices, many users are capturing their daily lives and posting them online [4]. One example of this recent trend is the mobile blog, or 'moblog [18], a wearable form of blogging. Another example is the movement towards continuous capture or archival of personal experience [2], for example, using video glasses like eyeTap [21] or eyeBlog [6] (see Figure 1).

With the availability of ubiquitous wireless devices, we have also seen an increase in communications between users. However, since these devices are not aware of the status or availability of their user, they often interrupt the user's tasks and thought processes at inopportune times [12]. Studies have shown that workplace interruptions via communication devices adversely affect productivity and lower worker performance [17, 23].

The Attentive User Interface (AUI) paradigm [29] attempts to address these challenges by allowing devices to allocate the attention that users have for their tasks and devices in a more optimal fashion. According to Shell et al. [29], AUIs achieve this through 1) sensing, 2) reasoning about, and 3) augmenting user attention. However, little research has been done on how AUIs might communicate attention to signal availability of others for online communications.

C. Baranauskas et al. (Eds.): INTERACT 2007, LNCS 4663, Part II, pp. 439–451, 2007.
© IFIP International Federation for Information Processing 2007

Fig. 1. Continuous archival of personal experiences using eyeBlog video glasses [6]

This paper extends work on the Physiologically Attentive User Interface (PAUI) [5], and presents a study on the use of physiological measures for automated detection of user interruptability. We discuss an application of our findings in the Physiological Weblog interface, or 'Plog for short. Like PAUI, this system allows online users to assess availability of mobile users through a web-based interface. We first discuss background literature on interruptability and the use of physiological measures in HCI. We then discuss our experiment, and conclude with a description of the 'Plog system.

2 Previous Work

There is very little work on the combination of blogging technologies and physiological interfaces. Since work on personal blogging tools is extensive, we restrict our discussion to studies involving interruptability. This section discusses previous work on interruptability, and the use of physiological measures in Human-Computer Interaction.

2.1 Interruptability

There has been a considerable interest in the modeling of user activity for the purpose of determining availability for notifications and communications [1, 3]. Horvitz et al. [13, 15] approached this problem using Bayesian reasoning models that allowed prediction of user interruptability on the basis of a variety of measures of interactive behaviors. They created attention-based models based upon analysis of keyboard and mouse events during interactions with applications such as, for example, Microsoft Outlook. Horvitz et al. also measured the effect of interruptions by calculating the cost of interruption, from user feedback on video recordings [14]. The cost of interruption varied according to the state of the user, with highly focused tasks obtaining a higher cost of interruption. In this way, attention-based states like driving and sleeping could be detected and correlated with a particular cost of interruption. Horvitz et al. [16] applied their Bayesian reasoning models in the Lumière project, which was used to provide automated assistance in popular software applications.

Hudson et al. [17] used a "Wizard of Oz" study in an office setting to gather attention-based data from video-recorded user interactions. They used a "beeper" approach to poll users for their current interruptability, rated on a linear scale. Like Horvitz, they were able to uncover correlations and build statistical models for the prediction of human interruptability based upon overt physical activities [10].

In [30], Siewiorek et al. presented SenSay, a context-aware mobile phone that sensed physical and environmental changes in order to determine current user interruptability. SenSay determined if a user was in a busy (uninterruptable) state based upon their electronic schedule, their movement, and any audible noise in the environment. However, the device was limited due to its reliance on external measures in the user's surroundings, which are not always related to interruptability.

2.2 Physiological Measures

Some of the earliest research that combined Human-Computer Interaction with physiology was by Picard et al. [25]. They used physiological sensors to analyse facial muscle tension, blood volume pulse, skin conductance, and respiration rate. After several weeks of data collection from one participant, they were able to create a feature-based algorithm using Sequential Floating Forward Search with Fisher Projection (SFFS-FP) [26] that was 81% accurate in the classification of eight emotional states (including anger, joy, and grief).

Our paper draws inspiration from this work, with the hopes of modeling interruptability by measuring physical and mental activity of the user without having to overtly identify specific user tasks. In taking this approach, we hope to correlate the user's physiological responses to their self-assessed interruptability, thereby creating a task-independent model of interruptability based purely on the user's current physiological state.

Determining Mental Load. To obtain a model, we first needed to determine which measures would most likely correlate with user interruptability. As a first candidate, we examined measures of user mental load during a task. In the past, the most common measure of mental load has been NASA's Task Load Index (TLX) [11], a subjective self-assessment of various mental and physical aspects of a task. Results take the form of a multi-dimensional rating, based on the weighted average of six subscales: mental demand, physical demand, temporal demand, performance, effort, and frustration.

Later, Rowe et al. [28] released a preliminary study indicating that mental effort may be reflected in Heart Rate Variability (HRV) [22]. In their experiment, participants' HRV was monitored whilst playing air traffic control games with varying levels of difficulty. After completing the task, participants were asked to fill out the NASA TLX Test for Mental Effort. Results from the TLX showed significant increases in mental load with task difficulty. HRV correlated well with measures from the TLX questionnaire, with the advantages that HRV can be determined in real time; and is an objective measure, not reliant on participants' self-assessment. We therefore decided to use HRV as our physiological indictor of mental load.

The Parasympathetic and Sympathetic Nervous Systems. Within the human nervous system there are two opposing systems at work: the sympathetic nervous system (SNS) and the parasympathetic nervous system (PNS). The SNS prepares the body for potentially dangerous or stressful situations by increasing both heart rate and blood pressure. Conversely, the PNS is the calming force that returns the body to normal after stimulation by decreasing heart rate and blood pressure. The balance between these two opposing forces is known as the sympathovagal balance, and it is these changes in the cardiac cycle that are reflected in Heart Rate Variability (HRV) measure [20].

Determining Physical Activity. To complement measures of mental activity, we also examined ways in which we could measure physical activity. In the past, electroencephalogram (EEG) was typically used to measure gross motor movement using *mu*-related desynchronisation [27]. This approach has been used in work by Chen and Vertegaal [5] on Physiologically Attentive User Interfaces. However, EEG can be quite invasive because it requires direct scalp contact and the use of electrolytic gels.

Instead, we chose to use electromyography (EMG), a direct measure of muscle activity. EMG is much less invasive than EEG, as it only requires the placement of one dry sensor on the muscle in question. This has the advantage that it can be used to measure signals throughout the user's body for detecting specific muscle contractions. In order to minimise the intrusiveness of data acquisition we decided to examine the use of EMG for our interruptability model.

3   Obtaining HRV and EMG Measurements

We will now discuss how measurements of both Heart Rate Variability and Electromyography were obtained and analysed for use in our model.

3.1   HRV: Analysing the ECG Signal

Measures of Heart Rate Variability (HRV) are obtained through the analysis of Electrocardiogram (ECG) signals [8]. A typical ECG signal is shown in Figure 2, with each peak consisting of a complex pattern of pulses labeled *PQRST*, as illustrated in Figure 3. The most recognisable feature is the *R* peak, which represents the point in time where the ventricles of the heart are completely depolarised. We used the time interval between subsequent *R* peaks in determining both the heart rate itself and Heart Rate Variability.

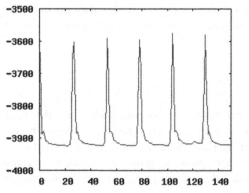

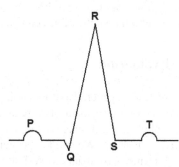

Fig. 2. Electrocardiogram (ECG) signal   **Fig. 3.** PQRST structure

A number of feature variables were used to explore how physiological signals correlated with interruptability (see [32] for a more detailed discussion):

1) ECG Heart Rate Variability (Time Series): This measure is found by taking the standard deviation of the time interval between R peaks.

2) ECG Heart Rate Variability (Frequency Domain): Here, measures of HRV are taken in the frequency domain. First, we take the Fourier transform of the R-R peak interval series, known as the tachogram. We then measure the resulting power in the 0.1Hz range, which has been shown to vary with mental load [28].

3) ECG RMSSD (Root Mean Square of Successive Differences): This measure is calculated by finding the square root of the mean squared differences between successive R-R peaks.

4) ECG Beats Per Minute: This is the heart rate itself, as defined by the time interval between successive R peaks; and is used as an indicator of physical activity.

3.2 Analysing the EMG Signal

The typical EMG signal is irregular in comparison to the ECG signal, extracting usable signals is therefore more difficult. The signal is a flat line prior to muscle contraction, then peaks with contraction, after which it becomes somewhat erratic.

The following feature variables were used to determine EMG activity:

1) EMG Count (Small and Large): Given a window of EMG data, this variable is incremented when a data point lies above a threshold. The use of small or large thresholds allows distinction of smaller versus larger muscle contractions.

2) EMG Standard Deviation (EMGSD): Given a window of EMG data, this variable takes the standard deviation of the EMG measurement. As the signal increases in contraction, the amount of variation and deviation from the mean will also increase.

3) EMG Power: Given a window of EMG data, this measures the overall power of the signal.

An advantage of the latter two EMG feature variables is that they do not require calibration, whereas the EMG Count variable requires visual inspection so that meaningful threshold values can be chosen.

4 Evaluation

To obtain a generalised physiological model of interruptability, we designed a preliminary experiment that related participants' self-perceived interruptability to their physiological state as measured by Heart Rate Variability (HRV) and muscle activity (EMG). We used a beeper-study approach similar to that used by Hudson [17], asking participants to verbally state their interruptability whilst performing five different tasks with varying levels of both mental difficulty and physical activity.

4.1 Participants and Design

A total of nine people participated in our experiment. Participants consisted of six males and three females with a mean age of 24.3 years; all were regular computer users. We employed a within-subjects design, meaning that all nine participants performed all five tasks. The order of presentation was counterbalanced between subjects to eliminate any bias due to ordering.

4.2 Apparatus

A wearable Procomp+ system by Thought Technology [35] was used to continuously acquire discrete real-time physiological data from four sensors placed on the participant's body. Each sensor consisted of three silver chloride electrodes in a triangular formation, with a spacing of 2cm between electrodes.

The ProComp+ system samples both ECG and EMG at 32 samples per second, which is sufficient for both HRV and EMG power analysis. Our software logged the physiological data with a time stamp for offline analysis. The computer system used a 2.0 GHz Pentium 4 processor, running a Debian Linux operating system.

4.3 Sensor Placement

We affixed four adhesive sensors to each participant (see Figure 4). One sensor was placed on the left side of the upper chest to measure HRV, while the other three sensors were used to measure EMG in the upper fibres of the trapezius in the right shoulder, the extensor carpi radialis in the right forearm, and the tibialis anterior in the lower right leg.

4.4 Task Description

Participants were first briefed about the experiment, and familiarised with each of the five tasks. The experimenter told participants that they would be interrupted every 30 seconds and asked to verbally state their interruptability. Participants were told to

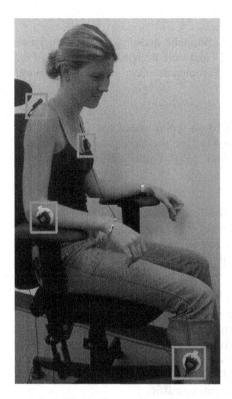

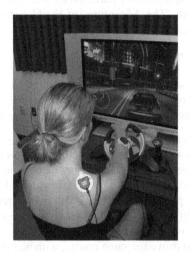

Fig. 4. Sensor placement   **Fig. 5.** Participant performing the racing game task

answer on a scale of one to five, with one meaning "I am completely available for interruptions", and five meaning "I do not wish to be interrupted". Each task took approximately three minutes to complete, and we therefore collected roughly 15 minutes of data for each participant. Participants remained seated during all five conditions.

4.5 Task Conditions

We selected the following five tasks, which varied in both mental difficulty and physical activity:

- *Reading*
  Participants were presented with a short reading passage of approximately 1100 words (taken from [9]). In order to encourage more thorough reading, participants were forewarned that they would be tested regarding the passage's contents through a multiple-choice comprehension test with 10 questions. Physiological data was logged for the duration of the reading period, but not whilst the subjects were answering the questions.

- *Mental Arithmetic*
  The experimenter read 30 simple mental arithmetic questions to the participant. The questions were in the form "9 – 4 + 2", and were designed such that all of the answers fell between one and nine. Participants were required to answer verbally, and as quickly as possible.

- *Typing*
  Participants were presented with a web-based typing speed test [33]. For fair comparison, all participants were required to type the same passage (an excerpt from "The Adventures of Huckleberry Finn" [36]). Participants were allowed to practice prior to the task.

- *Word Puzzle*
  We chose an online anagram puzzle called Text Twist® [34], where the user is presented with a number of scrambled letters. The task is to rearrange the letters in order to create as many words as possible. Participants were given three minutes to find as many permutations as possible.

- *Racing Game*
  Participants played a racing game on an XBOX console [24] connected to a 42" widescreen plasma display (see Figure 5). We chose the game "Need For Speed Underground 2" [7], as it provides a high-resolution simulation of a driving task. To provide participants with a more realistic experience we used a Madcatz MC2 [19] steering wheel and surround sound stereo equipment. All participants were allowed to practice prior to the task. All participants used the same car model, and drove the same course, with no opponents or traffic.

4.6 Hypothesis

We hypothesise that both HRV and EMG measures correlate with participants' self-perceived level of interruptability, as these measures predict both mental effort and physical exertion during a task.

5 Results

In order to achieve the most accurate results, we analysed all four HRV feature variables (see Section 3.1) and all three EMG feature variables (see Sections 3.2). We chose to use the standard deviation of Heart Rate Variability (Time Series) as our mental load metric and the standard deviation of EMG (EMGSD) as our muscle activity metric, as these measures proved to be the most consistent.

Figures 6 and 7 shows the relationship between the self-assessed interruptability and our mean measures for HRV and EMG respectively, averaged over all five tasks. Since both the HRV and EMG are measured in standard deviations, the y-axes of the graphs are unitless. As we expected, linear regressions showed a significant correlation of HRV with interruptability scores of $r = 0.96$ (p < 0.01). EMG measures also showed a significant correlation of $r = 0.85$ (p = 0.03).

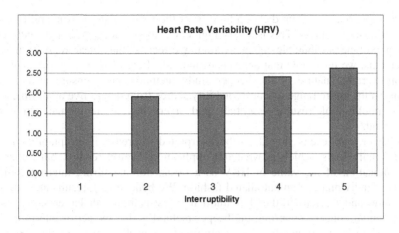

Fig. 6. Mean HRV levels with self-perceived interruptability

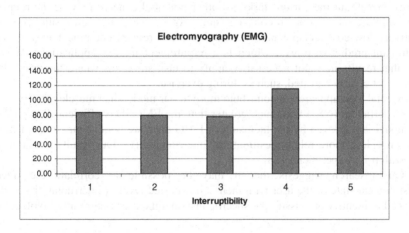

Fig. 7. Mean EMGSD levels with self-perceived interruptability

We combined the two measures into a single model, as follows:

$$Interruptability = a + b\ (HRV) + c\ (EMGSD) \qquad (1)$$

Multiple regression showed an excellent fit to the model, with $r = 0.98$ ($r^2 = 0.95$) and the following results for our constants a, b and c:

$$Interruptability = -8.12 + 6.89\ HRV - 0.04\ EMGSD \qquad (2)$$

6 Discussion

Results show that, as expected, both measures of HRV (Time Series) and EMGSD increased significantly with participants' self-perceived interruptability level.

Surprisingly, our model predicts up to 95% of the variance in interruptability scores, across a variety of tasks. This is a very high correlation indeed. Although such results may in part be attributable to an averaging effect of the linear regression across participants, we must note that analysis of individual correlations is problematic. The random variable nature of the beeper study method cannot ensure every subject reports on the entire range of interruptability scores from one to five at all times. This makes pooling of results essential, and averaging of individual correlations impractical.

However, our results should not be interpreted to predict interruptability for any *specific* individuals, which is what our applications would require, but rather as a clear indication of the value of HRV as a means for measuring interruptability of groups of individuals in an automated fashion. We believe such results are extremely promising, and warrant further longitudinal investigation with larger sample sizes. One potential concern regarding the beeper method is that the act of interrupting the user to ask their interruptability may itself affect the resulting measurement. However, our results make this unlikely, and indicate a significant variance in interruptability scores throughout the various tasks. Another potential concern may be the relatively low sampling rate of our Procomp+ system. Again, our regression results show that relatively low-cost and potentially wearable measurement equipment may generate significant predictive power, which is a requirement for our applications. We also note that results may not necessarily apply to task situations where the user's heart rate is particularly elevated, such as during exercise.

Mental load appeared to contribute more to our model than muscle activity, as the HRV coefficient (6.89) was much greater than the EMGSD coefficient (0.04). While the model is improved by the inclusion of EMG data, we believe measures of mental load provide a more reliable estimate of interruptability. Our results are largely in line with prior experiments [28].

Our research suggests that it may be possible to correlate the internal physiological state of the user with their self-reported level of interruptability without the need to identify or classify the specific task that the user is currently involved in.

7 'Plog: A Physiological Weblog

We applied our findings in 'Plog, an automated availability status system that blogs the user's physiological state, as well as their predicted interruptability (see Figure 8). The most important function of 'Plog is the *communication* of attention, thus allowing for an alternative approach to regulating interruptions. Note that because 'Plog relies on other users to interpret the recipients' states, a high degree of individual predictive power is not absolutely critical. In part, we believe 'Plog works by making others more aware of the need to be more considerate of recipients' interruptability.

'Plog continuously uploads physiological data information to a web server through a secure *ssh* protocol [31]. The system is tailored to each user's individual physiological signals, and uses both HRV and EMG to infer the user's current level of interruptability. This information is represented using a simple interface that displays the interruptability on a scale from one to five. This allows people to maintain

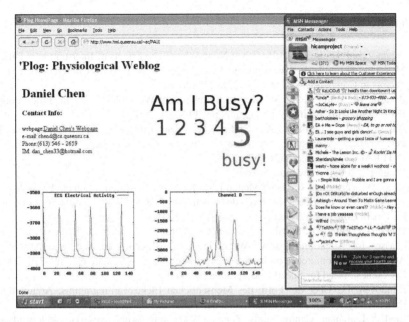

Fig. 8. Screenshot of the physiological weblog displaying the user's predicted level of interruptability

awareness of the interruptability of others, thus facilitating informed decisions on availability prior to actual communication. As such, we expect 'Plog to act as an attentive notice board that could reduce the number of inopportune interruptions by emails, instant messages or telephone calls. As a future direction of this work, we hope to evaluate the effectiveness of the 'Plog system as a means for determining and communicating user availability.

8   Conclusions

In this paper, we presented a preliminary study of the use of physiological measurements for predicting user interruptability status. We measured Heart Rate Variability (HRV) and Electromyography (EMG) signals whilst users performed a variety of tasks, including reading, solving word puzzles, mental arithmetic, typing, and playing a racing game. Results show high correlations for both HRV ($r = 0.96$) and EMG ($r = 0.85$) measures with user self reports of their interruptability. We combined these two measures into a single linear model, which predicted user interruptability with a combined r^2 of 0.95, explaining 95% of the variance. We note that our model describes interruptability across users, rather than per individual, and as such should be considered preliminary. We presented an application of our findings in the Physiological Weblog, or 'Plog, a system that uses our model of interruptability for automating online messaging status.

References

1. Adamczyk, P.D., Bailey, B.P.: If Not Now, When? The Effects of Interruption at Different Moments within Task Execution. In: Proceedings of the CHI'04 Conference on Human Factors in Computing Systems, pp. 271–278 (2004)
2. Aizawa, K., Ishijima, K., Shiina, M.: Summarizing Wearable Video. In: Proceedings of IEEE Conference on Image Processing, pp. 398–401 (2001)
3. Bailey, B.P., Konstan, J.A., Carlis, J.V.: The Effects of Interruptions on Task Performance, Annoyance, and Anxiety in the User Interface. In: Proceedings of INTERACT'01, pp. 593–601 (2001)
4. Blogger.: (2005), www.blogger.com
5. Chen, D., Vertegaal, R.: Using Mental Load for Managing Interruptions in Physiologically Attentive User Interfaces. In: Extended Abstracts of ACM CHI'04 Conference on Human Factors in Computing Systems, pp. 1513–1516 (2004)
6. Dickie, C., Vertegaal, R., Shell, J., Sohn, C., Cheng, D., Aoudeh, O.: Eye Contact Sensing Glasses for Attention-Sensitive Wearable Video Blogging. In: Extended Abstracts of ACM CHI'04 Conference on Human Factors in Computing System, pp. 769–770 (2004)
7. EA Games.: Need for Speed Underground 2 (2005)
8. Einthoven, E.: Über die Form des Menschlichen Elektrocardiogramms. Archiv für die gesamte Physiologie des Menschen und der Tiere 60, 101–123 (1895)
9. English Language Centre Study Zone.: (1997), http://web2.uvcs.uvic.ca/elc/studyzone/410/reading
10. Fogarty, J., Hudson, S., Lai, J.: Examining the Robustness of Sensor-Based Statistical Models of Human Interruptibility. In: Proceedings of the CHI'04 Conference on Human Factors in Computing Systems, pp. 207–214 (2004)
11. Hart, S., Staveland, L.: Development of NASA-TLX (Task Load Index): Results of Empirical and Theoretical Research. In: Human Mental Workload, pp. 139–183 (1988)
12. Ho, J., Intille, S.: Using Context-Aware Computing to Reduce the Perceived Burden of Interruptions from Mobile Devices. In: Proceedings of the CHI'05 Conference on Human Factors in Computing Systems, pp. 909–918 (2005)
13. Horvitz, E.: Principles of Mixed Initiative User Interfaces. In: Proceedings of the CHI'99 Conference on Human Factors in Computing Systems, pp. 159–166 (1999)
14. Horvitz, E., Apacible, J.: Learning and Reasoning about Interruption. In: Proceedings of ICMI 2003 International Conference on Multimodal Interfaces, pp. 20–27. ACM Press, New York (2003)
15. Horvitz, E., Koch, P., Apacible, J.: BusyBody: Creating and Fielding Personalized Models of the Cost of Interruption. In: Proceedings of CSCW '04, pp. 507–510. ACM Press, New York (2004)
16. Horvitz, E., Breese, J., Heckerman, D., Hovel, D., Rommelse, K.: The Lumiere Project: Bayesian User Modeling for Inferring the Goals and Needs of Software Users. In: Proceedings of the Fourteenth Conference on Uncertainty in Artificial Intelligence, pp. 256–265 (1998)
17. Hudson, S., Fogarty, J., Atkeson, C., Avrahami, D., Forlizzi, J., Kiesler, S., Lee, J., Yang, J.: Predicting Human Interruptability with Sensors: A Wizard of Oz Feasibility Study. In: Proceedings of the CHI'03 Conference on Human Factors in Computing Systems, pp. 257–264 (2003)
18. Ito, J.: Joi Ito's Moblog (2005), http://joi.ito.com/moblog
19. Madcatz.: (2005), www.madcatz.com
20. Malik, M., Camm, A.J.: Heart Rate Variability. Futura Publishing, Armonk, NY (1995)

21. Mann, S.: Wearable Computing: Towards Humanistic Intelligence. IEEE Intelligent Systems Special Issue on Wearable Computing and Humanistic Intelligence 16(3), 10–15 (2001)
22. McCraty, R., Atkinson, M., Tiller, W., Rein, G.: The Effects of Emotions on Short-Term Power Spectrum Analysis of Heart Rate Variability. The American Journal of Cardiology 76(14), 1089–1093 (1995)
23. McDaniel, M., Einstein, G.O., Graham, T., Rall, E.: Delaying Execution of Intentions: Overcoming the Costs of Interruptions. Applied Cognitive Psychology 18, 533–547 (2004)
24. Microsoft Game Studios. Xbox home (2007), http://www.xbox.com
25. Picard, R., Vyzas, E., Healy, J.: Toward Machine Emotional Intelligence: Analysis of Affective Physiological State. IEEE Transactions on Pattern Analysis and Machine Intelligence 23(10), 1175–1191 (2001)
26. Pudil, P., Novovicov, J., Kittier, J.: Floating Search Methods in Feature Selection. Pattern Recognition Letters 15, 1119–1125 (1994)
27. Ramoser, H., Muller-Gerling, J., Pfurischeller, P.: Optimal Spatial Filtering of Single Trial EEG During Imagined Hand Movement. IEEE Transactions on Rehabilitation Engineering 8, 441–446 (2000)
28. Rowe, D., Sibert, J., Irwin, D.: Heart Rate Variability: Indicator of User State as an Aid to Human-Computer Interaction. In: Proceedings of the CHI'98 Conference on Human Factors in Computing Systems, pp. 480–487 (1998)
29. Shell, J., Selker, T., Vertegaal, R.: Interacting with Groups of Computers. Special Issue on Attentive User Interfaces, Communications of ACM 46(3), 40–46 (2003)
30. Siewiorek, D., Smailagic, A., Furukawa, J., Moraveji, N., Reiger, K., Shaffer, J.: SenSay: A Context Aware Mobile Phone. In: Proceedings of the Seventh IEEE International Symposium on Wearable Computing, pp. 248–249 (2003)
31. SSH: Secure Shell Protocol (2005), www.ietf.org/html.charters/secsh-charter.html
32. Task Force of the European Society of Cardiology and the North American Society of Pacing and Electrophysiology: Heart Rate Variability - Standards of Measurement, Physiological Interpretation and Clinical Use. European Heart Journal 17, 354–381 (1996)
33. Testmytyping.com (2005), http://www.testmytyping.com/typing-speed-test.php
34. Text Twist Online Anagram Puzzle: (2005), http://games.yahoo.com/games/downloads/tx.html
35. Thought Technology: Procomp+ User Manual (2005), www.thoughttechnology.com
36. Twain, M.: The Adventures of Huckleberry Finn. Charles R. Webster & Company, New York (1885)

Evaluation of a Multi-user System of Voice Interaction Using Grammars

Elizabete Munzlinger, Fabricio da Silva Soares,
and Carlos Henrique Quartucci Forster

Instituto Tecnológico de Aeronáutica, Divisão de Ciência da Computação,
Praça Marechal Eduardo Gomes, 50 – 12.228-900 São José dos Campos, Brasil
{bety, p2p, forster}@ita.br

Abstract. This paper shows an experimental study about the design of grammars for a voice interface system. The influence of the grammar design on the behavior of the voice recognition system regarding accuracy and computational cost is assessed through tests. With the redesign of a grammar we show that those characteristics can be expressively improved.

Keywords: Grammar, multi-user interface, automatic speech recognition.

1 Introduction

Many speech recognition systems need every new user to train the system to recognize one's voice through the exhaustive reading of texts. This training is necessary because these systems often use extended vocabularies of words [1]. It is desirable to have a system independent of the training and able to recognize the same words when spoken by different voices, with different accents [5]. Applications that use recognized commands don't need such extended vocabulary, which can be restricted to the needs of the particular application. By the use of grammars associated to the application a limit of possible words to every context is determined. The right design of a grammar can make the application become a multi-user system.

The present document shows an experimental study about the design of grammars for a voice interface system for home application (Domotic). The design of grammars based on tests for accuracy and performance analysis made with an ASR (Automatic Speech Recognition) component used to recognize Brazilian Portuguese is described. The knowledge of improved design of grammars is a first step to the automatic generation of a grammar for multi-user interactive applications.

The grammar was used in a prototype of Domotic system that controls up to 32 devices through voice recognition. The system uses the parallel port of the computer and is connected to an electronic circuit that activates the devices. For the ASR system, IBM Via Voice was chosen because its acceptance of Brazilian Portuguese. The Domotic application was developed in Java and uses IBM Java Speech Technology API, which gives access and works together with the IBM VIA VOICE through the JSAPI API [4].

C. Baranauskas et al. (Eds.): INTERACT 2007, LNCS 4663, Part II, pp. 452–455, 2007.
© IFIP International Federation for Information Processing 2007

2 Grammar Design

A grammar is built from a set of sentences separate by production rules and structured as a tree composed by nodes. The nodes of the grammar are contained in a static structure describing a hierarchy of nodes from the main node and a set of nodes dependent on it. Every node of the grammar has a name who specifies its category [3]. In two-dimensional disposition (Figure 1) it is possible to see the possibilities of connections between the levels of the tree following its hierarchy until reaching the terminal symbols.

At first, we designed a grammar for general use (by systems with several contexts) based on the morphological analysis used in the sentences of the Portuguese language and made of many rules that determines, for example, verbs, subjects, treatments, pronouns and articles. Thus the rule that defines an article comprises other two sub-rules for definite articles and indefinite articles. In the end the grammar has a total of 64 sub-rules and 167 terminal symbols.

It was noticed that this complex grammar lowers the performance of the recognition system making it impossible to execute the application. It took at least 980 MB of memory and 100% of CPU occupancy during 1 minute for allocation and processing of the structure of the grammar. Therefore, there were no computational resources remaining to analyze any sentence.

To solve this problem, the grammar was restructured with changes to the rules composition resulting in the tree showed in Figure 1. The main node of the grammar is the rule *comando* that is composed by the sub-rules, *complemento*, *ação* and *objeto*.

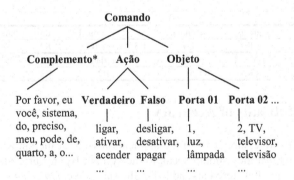

Fig. 1. Composition of rules of the grammar represented by the tree

The rule *ação* has two sub-rules, *verdadeiro* and *falso*, that controls the activation condition of the devices in the Domotic system. The rule *objeto* has one sub-rule for each one of the 32 devices to be controlled, all in the same level of the tree. Like the rule *ação*, this rule also must return the value of accepting of just one of its rules. The sub-rule *complemento* has no value of acceptation and contains 165 terminal symbols extracted from the 35 sub-rules morphologically separated beforehand. Using this grammar, the consumption of memory went down to an average of 423 MB and the duration of total use of the CPU was less than one second. In the new structure of the grammar the sub-rule *comando* employs the recursivity of the Kleene star operator, permitting 0 to n occurrences of its words in sequence and accepting command variations. Regular grammars have basically the same potentialities of the state machines [2]. Grammar rules can be represented by states of a machine as shown in Figure 2, where R1, R2 and R3 represent the rules *ação*, *objeto* and *complemento* respectively. The recursivity of R3 makes possible the acceptation of any sequences of terminal symbols.

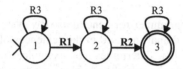

Fig. 2. Grammar represented through a state machine with a recursivity rule

With the recursivity in R3, replicated and interleaved with the other rules, the recognition of simple and complex commands described by the same grammar represented in the Table 1 becomes possible. In Brazilian Portuguese, many complements may appear either in the beginning, middle or in the end of the command (eg.: "*por favor*").

Table 1. Examples of simple and complex commands based in the rules of grammar

Ligar	Luz							
R1	**R2**							
Por favor	eu	preciso	acender	a	lâmpada	do	meu	quarto
R3	R3	R3	**R1**	R3	**R2**	R3	R3	R3
Sistema	você	pode	desligar	o	ventilador	para	mim	por favor
R3	R3	R3	**R1**	R3	**R2**	R3	R3	R3

3 Tests and Results of Accuracy

At first, 16 users were submitted to the application without the knowledge about the type of command that they should speak to the system. By this procedure, the natural spoken phrases were registered and added to the sub-rule *complemento*. As a high rate of acceptation was noticed, an important question was made: Is the system really recognizing what is spoken by the user? To answer this question, all the words (tokens) really recognized were logged. We could clearly detect incompatibilities between spoken and recognized words and as result of the log analysis we had:

1. The rate of acceptation of all the simple and complex commands was 98%. However just 24.1% really match what was spoken by the user, becoming 85.7% when disregarding the presence of definite articles.
2. The definite articles were recognized in 10.9% of the selected simple commands and from these commands 18.6% were not right. And curiously the rate was 35,3% for selected complex commands and just 6.5% of them were not right.

3. In tests with commands containing numbers from 1 to 32 written as words and in numeral form the recognition was alternated. The recognition in numeral form had the rate of 66.8%. For 34.3% of the numbers we just had the recognition in the numeral form that is what happened with the numbers 7, 14, 19, 23, 24, 25, 26, 28, 29 and 32.
4. The numbers with the highest rates of errors in the recognition was 21, 27 and 31. We noticed the system mistook words with similar sound for numbers like "20 eu" for the number 21. This happened in 70% of the cases in utterances of the number 31, being changed to characters like "trinta ele o", "trinta aí eu", "30 aí vou", "30 aí eu", "30 aí o", "30 aí os", "30 aqui os", "30 aqui eu", "30 eu", "30 em".

4   Conclusion

In this article we study the behavior of a voice interface system and the implications in the design of grammars to define the voice commands. This study was accomplished using experiments with users, redesigning of a grammar with recursive rules and creating a log to analyze and adjust the grammar. We noticed that the presence of many sub-rules, even with few terminal symbols, demands more computational resources than the opposite. So, the adoption of a small vocabulary in a grammar does not guarantee a low computational cost or accuracy in the recognition.

The use of the redesigned grammar made especially to the application and with good testing brings better recognition accuracy, because it will allow prediction of the next word. This is crucial to the critical systems and decision, where the recognition must be precise. Multi-user coverage without the need of training is a fundamental feature of the voice interfaces of the present days. From this study, we can create a methodology for automatic generation of grammars for interactive applications with proper care about the design of rules. This work intends to helping the coming of an era when interfaces will be more natural to people.

Acknowledgements. We acknowledge CAPES for the financial support and Hueber Candido de Lara and all the other colleagues that helped being part of the tests.

References

1. Burstein, A., Stolzle, A., Brodersen, R.W.: Using Speech Recognition in a Personal Communications System. In: Communications, 1992. ICC 92, Conference record, SUPERCOMM/ICC '92, IEEE, Los Alamitos (1992)
2. Pfaff, G.E.: User Interface Management Systems, p. 72. Springer, New York (1985)
3. Seneff, S.: TINA: A Natural Language System for Spoken Language Applications. Comput. Linguist. 18, 61–86 (1992)
4. Sun Microsystems Ltd, Java Speech API Programmer's Guide Version 1.0, [online at], http://java.sun.com/products/javamedia/speech/
5. Vieira, R., Lima, V.L.: Lingüística Computacional: Princípios e Aplicações. In: JAIA – ENIA, 2001, Fortaleza (2001)

An Eye Tracking Study of How Pictures Influence Online Reading

David Beymer[1], Peter Z. Orton[2], and Daniel M. Russell[3]

[1] IBM Almaden Research Center, 650 Harry Road, San Jose, California 95120 USA
[2] IBM Center for Advanced Learning, 20 Old Post Road, Armonk, New York 10504 USA
[3] Google, 1600 Amphitheatre Parkway, Mountain View, California 94043 USA
{beymer, porton}@us.ibm.com, drussell@google.com

Abstract. We present an eye tracking study to measure if and how including pictures – relevant or irrelevant to the text – affects online reading. In a between-subjects design, 82 subjects read a story on a computer screen. The text was accompanied by either: (a) pictures related to the text, (b) pictures unrelated to the text (advertisements), or (c) no pictures. Reading statistics such as reading speed and regressions were computed, as well as measures of picture gazes. When pictures related to the text were replaced with advertisements, we observed a number of significant differences, including speed, regressions, and re-reading.

Keywords: Eye tracking, viewing pictures, online reading.

1 Introduction

To understand the detailed structure of how people read text, psychologists and HCI researchers have turned to eye gaze tracking as a valuable analysis tool. In eye gaze tracking, a camera tracks and records where a subject's eye is looking; these gaze points are mapped to the text to follow the subjects' reading behavior. Eye tracking analysis has revealed how the eye moves during the reading process – see Rayner and Pollatsek [1] and Rayner [2] for excellent summaries. The eye reads a line of text in discrete chunks by making a series of fixations and saccades. A *fixation* is a brief moment, around 250 ms, where the eye is paused on a word or word group, and the brain processes the visual information. A *saccade* is a fast eye movement, usually forward in the text around 8-12 characters, to take in the next section of text. A *regression* is a backwards motion in the text, and it indicates confusion. The trace of these eye tracking parameters reveals much about the reader's cognitive state as well as the nature of the reading material. For instance, more difficult passages of text will yield longer fixations, shorter saccades, and a higher regression rate.

While eye tracking researchers have also studied how we process pictures (see Yarbus [3], Loftus and Mackworth [4]), surprisingly little work has been done on how we process the *combination* of text and pictures. Given our everyday exposure to rich combinations of text and pictures on the web, this gap is a little surprising. Carroll *et al* [5] studied how subjects view cartoons, looking at the processing of cartoon captions and graphics in *The Far Side* cartoons. They found that the text was read

C. Baranauskas et al. (Eds.): INTERACT 2007, LNCS 4663, Part II, pp. 456 – 460, 2007.

first and occupied most of the subjects' time. Similar results were reported by Rayner *et al* [6] for print advertisements and by Hegarty *et al* [7] for diagrams. The interplay between text and advertisements on web pages is being explored; Burke, *et al* [8] studied the negative effect of banner ads, showing that they slow down subjects in a web search task. In the Eyetrack III study [9], media researchers studied how subjects read online news sites. They found that (a) ads mixed in with the main text are viewed more than ads in the periphery, and (b) size matters for ads, with larger ones viewed more than smaller. The Norman Nielsen Group [10] recommends that pictures relate to content and don't look like ads.

An important unaddressed problem is how pictures influence the *reading for comprehension* task. That is, given an online article with accompanying pictures, how do the pictures affect the reader when asked to read the article for comprehension? This issue is important for online instructional material as seen in e-learning systems.

In this paper, we present an eye tracking study of how different types of pictures affect reading a fixed passage of text. For a fixed, single-page story, we present three conditions to subjects: (a) *on task* – pictures relate to the story, (b) *advert* – pictures are advertisements, and (c) *none* – pictures are replaced by blank space. Will the differences in pictures alone cause detectable eye tracking differences in reading? For example, will advertisements slow the reader down? Understanding the influence of pictures on reading could help extend cognitive modeling in psychology or put HCI/usability rules-of-thumb about the use of pictures on more solid footing.

2 Experiment

In our experiment, we collected eye tracking data from 82 subjects in a between-subjects design; Table 1 shows the breakdown between conditions (A) – (C). The subjects were employees of a major computer company. We recruited subjects at two company cafeterias, offering them a cafeteria voucher in return for their participation.

Table 1. Page layout for the story and pictures. N is the number of subjects in each condition.

	Picture Conditions		N
text	A) on task	pictures relate to text	27
	B) advert	pictures are ads, same size as A	27
	C) none	pictures replaced by blank space	28

The story presented to our subjects, taken from a science news web site written at an 8th-grade reading level, is on changes to the Earth caused by the 2004 Asian tsunami. The content was selected to go beyond common knowledge to allow for testing of retention. The story is 7 paragraphs long and contains 444 words total. In the *on task* condition, the two pictures include (1) an aerial shot of damaged coastline, and (2) a color-coded map showing depth changes in the ocean floor. In the *advert* condition, we selected ads for National Geographic and the New York Times as they were reasonably consistent with the science and news theme. Picture size is the same between conditions (A) and (B).

Our eye tracking setup includes the Tobii 1750 eye tracker, a camcorder taking a head-and-shoulders shot of the subjects, and three IBM T40 laptops. After sitting the subjects at a distance of around 60-70 cm from the Tobii and running a 5-point Tobii calibration, the experiment is presented in an instrumented browser. It includes: (1) instructions to read the story for comprehension, (2) a questionnaire asking for: name, first language, and a self-estimate of web usage, (3) the tsunami story itself, and (4) a 3-question, multiple-choice post-test of retention.

Data are recorded and analyzed by WebGazeAnalyzer (WGA) [11]. During reading analysis, WGA finds reading fixations by looking for a linear, horizontal grouping of fixations, calling the result a *gaze line*. Next, the analysis system uses a robust line- matching algorithm to match gaze lines against lines of text from the story itself. From these matches, we can measure where and what the subject read, the reading speed, regressions, and additional statistics that we now report.

3   Results

Table 2 summarizes a number of eye tracking statistics, grouping them into measures of speed, distraction, and retention. For all but two rows, there are significant differences between the *on task* and *advert* conditions. First, consider reading speed. Using a speed metric of the 1st-pass speed (equal to the 1st-pass gaze duration / characters read) [2], [12], *on task* readers are 19% slower than *advert* readers, a significant difference ($F(1,52) = 10.23$, $p < 0.005$). Furthermore, this speed difference is consistent with similar significant differences in fixation duration and saccade length. For *on task* subjects, fixation durations are 7.6% longer ($F(1,52) = 5.35$, $p < 0.03$) and saccade length is 15% shorter ($F(1,52) = 7.51$, $p < 0.01$) compared to *advert* subjects.

Table 2. Reading statistics reveal that on task pictures slow the reader's speed, and advertisements increase the regression rate (shown as reg. rate). All but two rows have significant differences between the *on task* and *advert* conditions; the p-value is given in the right column. Standard deviations are shown in parentheses.

Reading Statistic	Pictures			Significance level, p
	On task	Advert	None	
Speed: 1st pass speed (char/sec)	40.2 (7.8)	49.9 (13)	45.9 (13)	$p < 0.005$
Fixation duration (ms)	269 (35)	250 (26)	260 (42)	$p < 0.03$
Saccade length (char)	10.1 (1.8)	11.9 (2.9)	11.1 (2.7)	$p < 0.01$
Distractions: Reg. rate (reg/sec)	0.43 (.17)	0.54 (.19)	0.53 (.22)	$p < 0.03$
Picture gaze duration (sec)	1.26 (1.1)	0.86 (1.1)	n/a	*not significant*
Number of picture gazes	1.69 (1.3)	1.05 (.83)	n/a	$p < 0.05$
Re-read on picture return (char)	6.25 (14)	23.8 (26)	n/a	$p < 0.03$
Retention (% correct)	80.2 (19)	80.2 (24)	80.9 (21)	*not significant*

The second group of rows in Table 2 compares conditions based on measures of distraction. While the *on task* subjects spend more time viewing pictures than *advert* subjects, evidence from regressions and re-reading suggest that pictures are a distraction for *advert* subjects. Increased picture viewing for *on task* subjects comes as no surprise, because pictures do relate to story content. To measure picture viewing, we look at (a) picture gaze duration, and (b) the number of distinct picture gazes. First, for picture gaze duration, *on task* subjects spend 44% more time fixating on the pictures compared to *advert* subjects. Due to high variance in the time data, however, this difference is not significant (picture viewing is quite unstructured and variable among subjects). Second, subjects in the *on task* group have 60% more distinct picture gazes compared to the *advert* group, a significant difference ($F(1,52) = 4.471, p < 0.05$).

Despite *on task* subjects' increased attendance to the pictures, pictures seem to hurt *advert* subjects through increased regressions and re-reading. Subjects in the *advert* condition have a significantly higher rate of regressions than *on task* subjects ($F(1,52) = 5.014, p < 0.03$), which we attribute to the distracting nature of ads. Finally, to measure re-reading caused by a picture gaze, we note the text exit and re-entry points. If the re-entry point is located before the exit point, then the picture gaze is causing re-reading. As shown in the Table 2 row "re-read on picture return," the ads caused significantly more re-reading than the on task pictures ($F(1,29) = 5.34, p < 0.03$).

Finally, there are no significant differences between conditions for retention of the material as measured in the 3-question multiple-choice post-test. While the ads may have caused regressions and re-reading of the material, they did not impair comprehension.

4 Discussion

This paper is the first eye tracking study of the effect of different types of pictures (on task, advertisements, and no pictures) on the task of reading for comprehension. One finding is that on task pictures slow readers down, decreasing 1st-pass reading speed, lengthening fixation duration, and making saccades shorter. We attribute this to the extra effort the reader is making to relate the pictures to the text – the cognitive effort to relate pictures and text is slowing down the reader. On the other hand, advertisements appear to be distracting the reader by causing more regressions and re-reading of the material. No impact was found, however, from pictures on the retention of the material.

This study is important for design issues in e-learning. The negative impact of ads on the regressions and re-reading would argue against e-learning sites that are funded by ads placed on the same page as the instructional material. It would be better to charge users (or their organizations) up front and keep the site ad-free.

Returning to the issue of distraction from advertisements, it is interesting to note the rise of contextual advertising and its potential to increase the attraction of ads. In contextual ads, the web page content is scanned to determine those ads that may interest the reader, and only those ads are presented (Google AdSense, Chitika [13]). Thus, the ad will target the web page's intended audience, potentially creating a distraction that is hard to resist. The effect of contextual ads on a subject's performance and task completion would make an interesting future eye tracking study.

References

1. Rayner, K., Pollatsek, A.: The Psychology of Reading. Lawrence Erlbaum Associates, Mahwah (1989)
2. Rayner, K.: Eye Movements in Reading and Information Processing: 20 Years of Research. Psychological Bulletin 124(3), 372–422 (1998)
3. Yarbus, A.: Eye Movements and Vision. Plenum Press, New York (1967)
4. Loftus, G., Mackworth, N.: Cognitive determinants of fixation location during picture viewing. Journal of Experimental Psychology: Human Perception and Performance 4, 565–572 (1978)
5. Carroll, P., Young, J., Guertin, M.: Visual Analysis of Cartoons: A View from the Far Side. In: Rayner, K. (ed.) Eye Movements and Visual Cognition, pp. 444–461 (1992)
6. Rayner, K., Rotello, C., Stewart, A., Keir, J., Duffy, S.: Integrating Text and Pictorial Information: Eye Movements When Looking at Print Advertisements. Journal of Experimental Psychology: Applied 7(3), 219–226 (2001)
7. Hegarty, M.: The Mechanics of Comprehension and the Comprehension of Mechanics. In: Rayner, K. (ed.) Eye Movements and Visual Cognition, pp. 428–443 (1992)
8. Burke, M., Hornof, A., Nilsen, E., Gorman, N.: High-Cost Banner Blindness: Ads Increase Perceived Workload, Hinder Visual Search, and Are Forgotten. ACM Trans. On Computer-Human Interaction 12(4), 423–445 (2005)
9. Eyetrack III: Online News Consumer Behavior in the Age of Multimedia. The Poynter Institute, http://www.poynterextra.org/eyetrack2005/main.htm
10. Norman Nielsen Group, http://www.nngroup.com
11. Beymer, D., Russell, D.: WebGazeAnalyzer: A System for Capturing and Analyzing Web Reading Behavior Using Eye Gaze. In: CHI 2005 Extended Abstracts, pp. 1913–1916. ACM Press, New York (2005)
12. Liversedge, S., Paterson, K., Pickering, M.: Eye Movements and Measures of Reading Time. In: Underwood, G. (ed.) Eye Guidance in Reading and Scene Perception, pp. 55–75 (1998)
13. Tedeschi, B. Internet Banner Ads Look to Get More Interesting (and Thus Less Easy to Ignore). The New York Times (July 11, 2005)

Quantifying the Performance Effect of Window Snipping in Multiple-Monitor Environments

Dugald Ralph Hutchings[1] and John Stasko[2]

[1] Computer Science Department, Bowling Green State University
Bowling Green, OH 43403 USA
drhutch@cs.bgsu.edu
[2] GVU Center, College of Computing, Georgia Institute of Technology
Atlanta, GA 30332 USA
stasko@cc.gatech.edu

Abstract. Snip is a tool that allows a user to constrict the view onto any window. We report on a controlled study of the snip tool in the context of a multiple-monitor environment. The study was designed based on observed user behavior in a field study of multiple-monitor users' snipping habits. Analysis provided results that indicate that users can expect to reference information approximately 15% to 30% faster from snipped windows than from non-snipped windows. Further, users need to pay only a small overhead cost to perform the snip operation. The result extends to other recently presented region-based interface tools that aim to assist multiple-monitor users interact effectively and employ additional monitor space for information-referencing activities.

Keywords: multiple monitors, window management, evaluation, snip

1 Introduction

Over the last five to ten years there has been an increasing amount of interest in and attention paid to research about *multiple-monitor systems*, which are defined as a traditional, single computer with one or more graphics adaptors driving a total of two or more physical monitors. Multiple-monitor systems exhibit a physically separated display space (the physical area between monitor frame boundaries) but provide the user with a virtually contiguous space, often at a cost less than a single large display. With a single set of input devices such as keyboard and mouse, users can set the position of information to be on any of the monitors or across monitor boundaries. Initial results about multi-display systems are positive, showing that users can expect to experience rises in productivity [5, 6] despite frequent occurrences of inconsistent or counterproductive interface behaviors [6, 7]. Recent research has focused on ways to overcome or eliminate the behavior or further improve the interaction experience.

One of the noted uses of multiple monitors is in support of the display of reference materials in one or more inactive windows (*i.e.* windows not receiving input from the user) while interaction takes place in the active window [7, 9, 10]. Applications are typically designed with an active user in mind, with little or no attention paid to how people might use the information displayed by an application when the window is not

C. Baranauskas et al. (Eds.): INTERACT 2007, LNCS 4663, Part II, pp. 461–474, 2007.

active. Field research further indicates that users often try to set a group of windows to overlap in just the right way to show or hide information in each of the windows in the group when they are in "inactive use" because users have no direct way to force a window to show only a specific subregion [11]. The challenge of keeping just the right amount of information visible can become more difficult when multiple monitors are present since there is an increased chance that information that should stay hidden will become visible.

In response to the evident desire to control the information displayed by a window when in inactive use and the increasing percentage of display space showing inactive windows in the presence of multiple monitors, we proposed the notion of a window snipping operation that would allow a user to select a region of a window and show only that region [12]. Figure 1 illustrates the difference between snipping a window and resizing a window.

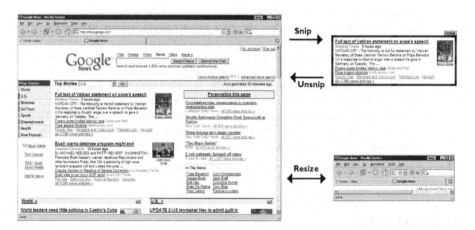

Fig. 1. Window snipping is portrayed in the upper-right corner. For comparison, window resizing is portrayed in the lower-right corner. Notice the difference in favoring the display of information (snip) or favoring the display of interaction components (resize).

Since proposing the idea of a region-based interface to control displayed information in windows [11, 12], we have developed a tool that implements the operation for everyday use in the Microsoft Windows XP system. We have also deployed the tool to a group of multiple-monitor participants in a field study of their window management practices with snip and without it [9]. The key finding from that study is that as compared to periods of time when the snip tool was not available, participants used snip to create space for more visible windows. In other words, multiple-monitor participants actually did use snip to simultaneously show more pieces of information, which can be described as a space-efficiency gain.

The question that remained was whether users could likewise expect to experience a complementary time-efficiency gain, *i.e.*, whether users could reference information more quickly from snipped windows than from non-snipped, normally-arranged windows. If so, we wanted to understand how much overhead was involved in using snip (the time needed to snip versus the time saved from each reference to the snipped window) to measure the expected true time-efficiency gain from employing window snipping. As a result, we developed a controlled laboratory study to measure the length of time needed to snip each member of a representative set of windows and the length of time needed to answer questions about information in those windows in both their normal, full-size states and their snipped states. Before we proceed to report the results of the study, we briefly provide some additional detail about the current methods users employ to snip a window.

2 How Snip Works

We built snip as a third party application for Microsoft Windows XP, which is both a window manager and operating system. When a user desires to snip a window, the user must set the window to be active. This results in a button labeled *Snip* appearing near the window's other operation interface buttons (close, maximize/restore, and minimize). The user then clicks the Snip button, which temporarily interrupts any interaction between the user and the interface components in the window's application.[1] In a fashion similar to drawing a rectangle in a graphical editing program, the user then indicates the region to be shown (to result in hiding the remainder of the window). The window becomes snipped and interaction resumes as normal. In particular, since the snip occurs directly on the window, interaction can still take place in the constrained region. For example, if a user snips a piece of a window containing a research document, then the user can copy the text from the snipped window's application and paste it into another window without having to unsnip the document window.

In addition to the window being "snipped," the tool provides a small border around the snipped region to allow the user to distinguish it from other windows. Since Windows XP generally allows users to move windows only through interaction with the title bar, the small border also facilitates the movement of the snipped window elsewhere on-screen. The border is larger when the snipped window is active to facilitate window movement and smaller when the window is inactive so as to reflect the normal border size of a window. Figure 1 (previous page) illustrates the result of window snipping.

3 Controlled Study of Snip

In this study we compared the time cost paid to make a reference to each of two sets of windows on a second monitor: (1) a set of snipped windows and (2) a corresponding set of non-snipped windows (in this section, we call these *regular* windows). We placed all snipped reference windows or regular reference windows on the second monitor because of a pattern that we observed in the aforementioned field study [9], namely that snipped windows tended to appear on a specific monitor. As a result, snipped windows did not overlap but regular windows did overlap. Thus a user potentially pays a higher cost in accessing a regular window because it might need to be brought forward before the reference can be made. Simultaneously, there is an up

---

[1] Refer to Hutchings' detailed description of snip for technical details [9].

front cost to reference a snipped window: it must be snipped. We arranged the regular windows in such a way that they could all be accessed with a single click by ensuring a fixed portion of each window was always visible. Further, this visible portion allowed the used to quickly identify the type of information in the window, making it as easy as possible for the participant to determine the correct window. In essence, we constructed the study to give as much advantage to the regular windows as was possible but also reflect the tradeoffs users make in choosing whether to snip a window.

This is a crucial point and deserves reiteration. We fully expect that users will be able to access information from snipped, non-overlapping windows more easily than from non-snipped, overlapping windows. This does not confound the study but rather completely describes the heart of the matter: is the initial, one-time overhead of snipping worth avoiding the repeated overhead of finding the overlapped window of interest and possibly bringing it to the top of the stack? In the study, we are addressing the tradeoff that users can consider but also making any possible additional adjustments to ensure that users can access the overlapped window as quickly as possible. We discuss other, future experimental strategies in Section 3.5.

The study examines the average time needed to make a snip to a window and the relative difference in time needed to make references to sets of snipped windows and regular windows. For the first part, participants snipped a variety of differently shaped windows in different on-screen locations. In the second part, participants answered a series of questions displayed on a left-hand monitor about content of a set of snipped windows and a corresponding, equivalent set of regular windows, both pre-arranged on a right-hand monitor.

3.1 Method

We recruited participants by word of mouth at Georgia Institute of Technology. We required that they were fluent in English and had never interacted with the snip operation. All interaction during the study occurred on a computer system with two monitors arranged side-by-side, a state-of-the-art video card designed to support 2D graphics for a dual-display configuration, and a standard optical desktop mouse. The system ran Microsoft Windows XP and was set to use the default mouse pointer speed. Each monitor was a 17" flat-panel LCD display running at native landscape resolution of 1280×1024 pixels for a total resolution of 2560×1024 pixels. Figure 2 (next page) is a photograph of the experimental setup. Note that the left-hand monitor was not used in the experiment.

In Phase 1 participants responded to 8 sets of 12 statements: 2 practice sets followed by 6 timed sets. Each set had the following structure. To begin a set, the participant clicks a "begin set" button on the left-hand monitor. A group of windows appears on the right-hand monitor in predefined locations. Participants have the opportunity to alter the z-order to see what is contained in each window but cannot otherwise move or resize the windows. After a fixed period of time (5 seconds per window; a group of four windows yields 20 total seconds of viewing time), the right-hand screen becomes blank so the user cannot see the windows. The left-hand monitor then displays a window containing a statement, the name of the window on the right-hand monitor to which the statement refers, and a "ready" button. The user reads the statement, understands the necessary reference window to respond to the statement, and clicks the ready button (again, note that the user knows *in advance* which window to use to respond to the statement). Simultaneously, (1) the right-hand screen re-appears and the user locates the reference window and (2) the left-hand screen displays a "true" button and a "false" button. Once the user ascertains whether the statement is true or false by viewing the appropriate window on the right-hand screen, the participant clicks the appropriate button on the left-hand screen. The right-hand screen then goes blank and the process repeats for each of the remaining 11 statements in the set.

Fig. 2. A photograph of the input and output devices used for the experiment

An example statement is "The top news story concerns a pharmaceutical drug company." The statement would be accompanied by the window description "news Web browser" so that the user would know where to look before clicking "ready." Note that complementary sets of windows contain equivalent questions. For example, if the answer to the example statement is true for a set of snipped windows, then there will be a statement about the news Web browser that will also be true. In this way, each statement should be able to be answered in the same amount of time.

Participants are timed only between clicking "ready" and clicking the response ("true" or "false"). During the practice trials we instruct participants that information in the window is likely to change in between statements and that they need to verify a response by actually looking at the window first. They are further instructed that upon introduction of the new group of windows they should become familiar with the configuration of the windows and the type of information contained in the windows, not the actual information, since the information will be different the next time that they look at it. Changing the information each time eliminates any potential advantage gained by memorizing information while answering. Figure 3 (next page) demonstrates a group of four snipped windows and a group of four regular windows.

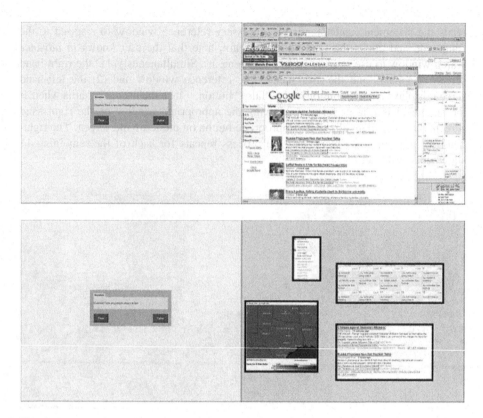

Fig. 3. A comparison of an overlapping group of four windows and a snipped group of four windows. Notice that each window in the overlapping group is visible.

There are three timed primary groups of windows: ($G2$) a group of two windows, which is a personal calendar and a news Web page; ($G4$) a group of four windows, which is group $G2$ plus an instant message buddy list and a weather map; and ($G6$) a group of six windows, which is group $G4$ plus an outline of a document and a road map. Each of the three primary groups Gi has two secondary groups Gi_r of regular windows and Gi_s of snipped windows, for a grand total of six timed window groupings and statement sets. Gi_r and Gi_s are equivalent in that for each question in Gi_r, there is a corresponding question in Gi_s that should take an equal time to answer. However, the *content* displayed in the sets does not overlap in any way. For example, if set Gi_r contained the statement "The top news story is about the Yellow Jackets" and the headline in the news window contained the word "Yellow Jackets" (thus the answer was true), then in the set Gi_s, for the corresponding news headline (say, "Falcons edge Rockets in overtime thriller"), there would be a statement containing a keyword from the headline (say, "The top news story is about the Falcons"). Both of these statements should thus be able to be answered in the same amount of time, so the entire set of statements is equivalent. Figure 3 illustrates $G4_r$ and $G4_s$.

An equal number of participants receive the primary window groups in each of the six possible orders. Within each ordering, half of the participants always receive the snipped windows first and the regular windows second and the other half receive the reverse ordering. Twelve participants are thus necessary to fill each variation in ordering and balance the study.

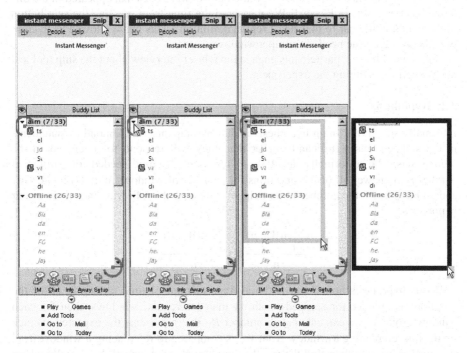

Fig. 4. A step-by-step breakdown of snipping: clicking the snip button, clicking the first region point, dragging toward the second region point, and releasing the button to complete the snip

Participants are not allowed to move the windows in the groups when responding to the statements in order to avoid confounding the timing data (further, participants are disallowed from accessing windows through other means, such as the TaskBar or keyboard shortcuts like pressing alt+tab). The group of snipped windows is always small enough to be placed such that they do not overlap. The group of regular windows is always too large to be arranged in a non-overlapping fashion. As a result, the regular groups are always pre-arranged such that (1) each window always has a piece visible regardless of the global z-ordering and (2), the "always visible piece" of each window reflects the type of information it contains. To further provide participants opportunities to most quickly respond to statements about regular window groups, when the group has n windows and since there are 12 questions per group, $n/12$ of the questions refer to a window that is at the top of the z-order and the participant does not need to bring any window forward to answer the question.

In Phase 2 participants are introduced to the actual window snipping operation (as opposed to simply the display of snipped windows) and given 5 practice trials to snip a series of different regions on a single window. Snip region points appear on the window to guide the user in snipping the desired region (Figure 4). This visual setup simulates an actual snip operation, where a user knows what region should be snipped before actually moving to snip it. After the practice trials, participants proceeded to make one snip in each of a series of seven windows and then repeated the sequence for a total of 14 timed snips. These seven windows were ones that appeared in the different reference sets in Phase 1. We measured the time from pressing the snip button in the window title bar to the end of region definition. This phase allowed us to compute the average time needed to snip a window.

Following Phase 2, participants engaged in a brief interview about the snip tool and their experiences during the experiment.

3.2 Hypothesis

Informally stated, our main hypothesis is that participants will respond to statements in the snipped sets significantly faster than they will respond to statements in the regular sets. More formally, let $A(W, p)$ represent the time needed for participant number p to answer all of the questions for each set of windows $W \in \{G2, G4, G6\}$ and let n represent the number of participants, yielding the following inequality as our hypothesis.

$$\frac{\sum_{p=1}^{n} A(W_r, p)}{n} >> \frac{\sum_{p=1}^{n} A(W_s, p)}{n}$$

If this hypothesis holds, *i.e.*, if the average amount of time to answer all of the questions is smaller for snipped windows than for regular windows, then for each window group W we can calculate a number R_W that represents the expected average savings in referencing a window from W_s as compared to referencing a window from W_r. Further, we can then find the smallest number N_W such that $R_W N_W > S(W_r)$ where $S(W_r)$ is the expected average time needed to snip the windows in W_r. N_W represents the number of references that a user needs to make to W before snipping becomes worthwhile. In other words, given that a user makes k references to windows in W, the user can expect to save $(k - N_W) \cdot R_W$ amount of time as compared to not snipping the windows.

3.3 Experimental Results

Thirteen participants enrolled in the study but one participant ultimately declined to participate, thus we collected data from twelve participants. For each participant p and for each set of windows W, we calculated the time needed to answer all of the questions in the regular set of windows W_r and the snipped set of windows W_s, which again are denoted $A(W_r, p)$ and $A(W_s, p)$ respectively. We then ran Student's paired-samples, one-tailed t-test on those total times. In Table 1, we report the means of the collected data, the associated standard deviations, and also the p-values returned by the t-tests. Participants answered questions in the snipped sets significantly faster than in the regular sets,

Table 1. *t*-test results for each of the three main window groups

t	$G2_r$	$G2_s$	$G4_r$	$G4_s$	$G6_r$	$G6_s$
$\bar{x}$ (sec)	92.1	65.4	92.9	62.9	79.2	66.3
σ	25.5	20.4	22.0	16.3	18.2	20.7
p	< 0.01		< 0.01		< 0.01	

with time improvements approximately ranging between 15% and 30%. Note that the average error rate over 12 questions was below 1 for all 6 sets of windows. There were no significant differences in error rate between the snipped sets of windows and the regular sets or windows.

Thus our main hypothesis holds; people answered questions more quickly for the snipped sets of windows than for the regular windows. Thus we can now calculate R_W, *i.e.*, the expected average savings in referencing a snipped window from W_s as compared to referencing a regular window from W_r for each $W \in \{G2, G4, G6\}$. For each participant p, we calculated $\Delta(W, p) = A(W_r, p) - A(W_s, p)$, which represents how much time participant p saved in the snipped set relative to the corresponding regular set. We then calculate the mean of these $\Delta(W, p)$ values, *i.e.* the average time savings across all participants for the whole set of windows, and divide by 12 (the number of questions in the set) to arrive at R_W:

$$R_{G2} = 2.22 \text{ sec}$$
$$R_{G4} = 2.51 \text{ sec}$$
$$R_{G6} = 1.07 \text{ sec}$$

Having calculated R_W, we would like to calculate N_W, which is the number of references that a user needs to make to the windows in W before snipping becomes worthwhile. In other words, we desire to find N_W such that $N_W \cdot R_W = S(W_r)$, where $S(W_r)$ is the total time required to snip all of the windows in W_r. This means that N_W is subject to the following equation.[2]

$$N_W = \left\lceil \frac{S(W_r)}{R_W} \right\rceil$$

As previously mentioned, each participant snipped each of the seven unique types of windows twice, for a total of 14 snips per participant. The mean time needed to perform a snip operation was 3.34 seconds with a standard deviation of 0.95. In order to create a more conservative estimate of snipping time, we constructed a confidence interval around the mean subject to the standard deviation and $\alpha = 0.01$, yielding a conservative mean of 3.53 seconds. Calculating $S(W_r)$ is thus accomplished by multiplying this conservative mean by the number of windows in W_r, providing the following values for N_W.

---

[2] We are not suggesting that users will consciously make a decision whether to snip based on this calculation. Rather, we are providing the analysis to demonstrate how low the overhead of snipping tends to be should users decide to snip.

$$N_{G2} = \quad 4 \text{ references}$$
$$N_{G4} = \quad 6 \text{ references}$$
$$N_{G6} = 20 \text{ references}$$

In other words, to overcome the overhead cost of snipping all of the windows in the groups of 2, 4, and 6 windows, the user must make 4, 6, and 20 references to windows in the set, respectively. This is a respective average of 2, 1.5, and 3 references per window. Once this overhead cost is paid, the users can expect a time savings of R_W per reference.

It is interesting to note that in our data analysis we do not consider the time needed to arrange the windows on the "reference monitor." In this study, we pre-arranged these windows for our users so that each window always had a piece visible, regardless of the z-order at any time. As the number of windows increases (especially above four windows, where a "four corners" strategy no longer works), the difference in arrangement time between the snipped windows and the regular windows becomes nontrivial. As a result, if we included arrangement time in the calculation of N_W, then we would expect the values to remain stable or decrease, particularly for N_{G6}.

We observed one additional interesting behavior. Seventy-five percent of the participants would move the mouse from the left monitor to the right monitor for every question in the regular sets of windows, even when the window containing the answer to the question was already on top. They would not move the mouse to the right monitor for the snipped windows. When mouse movement was unnecessary in the regular sets, there was nevertheless an expectation of locating the needed window and bringing it to the top of the z-order, causing unnecessary navigation time.

3.4 Interview Results

All participants concurred that regardless of the number of windows displayed on the right-hand screen, the snipped window sets were never overwhelming and they felt that they answered questions faster when windows were snipped. Participants varied however on how much faster they felt they could answer. Three participants felt twice as fast, with one even saying that he thought snipping allowed him to be exponentially faster as the number of windows linearly increased. Three participants indicated that they felt "just a little" faster with the snip operation and three others indicated that they had no idea how much faster they were. Other responses included 10% faster, 25% faster, and "a few seconds" faster.

All but one of the participants felt that the mechanics of the snip operation made sense, with one participant indicating that clicking a button to begin a snip was awkward; he would have preferred a keyboard shortcut. Half of the participants indicated that they would use snip for their everyday interactions, whereas the other half said that they "might use it" or "would use it depending on the circumstances of the day." Participants overwhelmingly indicated that they could use snipping for reference materials and notes or for email updates. Other responses included generally "Web browsing," calendars, sports scores, and traffic information. Interestingly, a number of participants indicated situations where they definitely would *not* use snipping: three said they would never use it for news and one said she would never use it for instant messages.

There were a few other comments of note. One participant requested that snipped windows also be able to be designated as always-on-top, especially when referencing information and using it elsewhere. This would be a technically simple capability to add to the currently implemented version of snip. There were two potentially conflicting opinions about virtual desktops. One participant indicated that she would like to have a virtual desktop of snipped windows to make it easy to bring reference information to the fore in a single action when multiple monitors are equally engaged in interaction (which is like Apple Macintosh OSX Dashboard though the participants did not explicitly mention this application). Another user indicated that he would avoid snipping because virtual desktops already allowed him to avoid overlapping windows. It is unclear how snip would interact with virtual desktop users, though currently snip operates correctly regardless of any virtual desktop system being run by a user.

3.5 Discussion

The results of this study show promise for snip: they complement the space efficiency gain showed in a previous field study [9] with an indication of a strong time-efficiency gain that a user can realize. The reader may rebut that sometimes a user might snip the wrong region of a window and will have to unsnip to get at information and possibly resnip back to the original size. Clearly this will have an impact on the time-efficiency increase to be expected by the user, but we do not currently know how often this situation arises. However, unsnip and resnip should cost about as much as an original snip. Devising studies to uncover the frequency of unsnipping, motivations for unsnipping and resnipping, and determining the cost of unsnipping and resnipping are obvious next steps in this line of research. Other variations to the presented study including allowing users the ability to move and resize the regular windows, which has the benefit of "personalized space" and might improve users' spatial memory of different windows, but also had the drawback of the validity in comparing times needed to answer questions about the windows (every user is looking at a different visual configuration). On the other hand, we could incorporate this window management time into the total time needed to answer a question. We could also provide more challenging sets of overlapping windows by, for example, having windows that occlude all others once selected.

Our laboratory-based evaluation results further show promise for several region-based tools that have recently appeared in various HCI venues. WinCuts is a window management tool very similar to snip but has the following two major differences: (1) WinCuts provides live *copies* of a region the source window instead of operating on the window itself, but (2) due to technical limitations of the Windows XP system, the copies are not interactive [18]. However, in the scenario of simply referencing information from a copy, the results of this snip study also apply to WinCuts. Metisse is a system that provides users with a variety of tools to manipulate windows as if the windows were images and Metisse runs on any X-based platform, including the Macintosh OS X system [4]. A demonstration of the capabilities of Metisse shows how WinCuts and snip can be implemented on the system, though Metisse improves on WinCuts by allowing interaction in either the source window or in the live copy [17].

Our results again help show the potential utility of Metisse and as a result extend past the Windows XP window manager to other systems.

4 Related Work

Controlled studies of window management tools appear infrequently in the literature. Two of the more recent systems to have been evaluated in laboratory studies are the TaskGallery [14] and Elastic Windows [13]. Both studies are similar to the snip study since the tools were compared to standard window manager systems and operations. However, both Task Gallery and Elastic Windows were tested on single-monitor systems and both concerned window grouping functionality rather than operating on individual windows. Another difference is that the snip study reflects observed multiple-monitor window management behavior whereas the other two studies did not collect field data prior to the design of the controlled study.

Other studies recorded data from use of an interface in the field but did not include complementary controlled studies. One prominent study is that of the Rooms system [8] (notably the design of the Rooms tool was motivated by field research [3] just as snip was motivated by field research [7, 9, 10, 11]). The Rooms study demonstrated the utility of what are today referred to as virtual desktops. More recently the GroupBar was evaluated over a 1-week period [15]. Both Rooms and GroupBar also relate to window grouping behavior rather than direct window operations like slight rotation and peeling [1], which, as mentioned, have not been evaluated in the field or in the lab.

Another line of research that is related to the snip tool is development of interfaces dedicated specifically to peripheral awareness (as opposed to snip, which operates on any window). This body of research is considerably large so we have selected a few representative examples. For example there is Sideshow, which provides small views onto many pieces of information in a single application. Sideshow is limited to certain types of information and further must be tethered to the edge of a monitor instead of anywhere in the display areas [2]. The InfoCanvas is an artistic rendering of important information such as news, stock prices, airline ticket prices, incoming email messages, or any piece of dynamic information from an Internet source [16]. This tool is specifically designed for use on a second monitor (or as a standalone, separate display) but occupies the entirety of that display space. Macintosh OS X includes the Dashboard and its widgets that provide small tools and views of peripheral information like weather and news. The Dashboard cannot bet set to be always visible and appears only when the user summons it as opposed to snipped windows, which can be persistently displayed (http://www.apple.com/macosx/features/dashboard/).

5 Conclusion and Future Work

We have demonstrated that the snip tool, designed to reduce the space needed to display information from a window, resulted in the ability to reference that information 15% to 30% more quickly than without the tool. Further, the overhead cost of performing a snip is rather low, especially for 2 or 4 windows of information. This suggests that the snip tool is valuable for multiple-monitor users. Other recently developed region-based tools should also exhibit similar time-efficiency gains for their users. The general result is intuitive (finding relevant information in a smaller space without the need for interaction should be faster) but the specific result demonstrating the magnitude of the difference is valuable in characterizing potential productivity benefits for users of multiple-monitor systems. Further the fact that the study was based on observed behavior of the tool among multiple-monitor users should provide a realistic estimate of real-world impact.

While our primary motivation for developing snip was to assist multiple-monitor users take better advantage of the extra space provided in a common context of use, *i.e.*, for displaying reference information, follow-up experiments could assess the effects of window snipping in physically large display environments, high-resolution displays, or in small display environments. In addition to broadening the display environments, we could also narrow the potential types of windows to specific classes of users or applications to see if any of the effects become magnified in the context of certain tasks.

Finally, we would like to explore an "anti-snip" tool that would allow a user to show everything in a window *except* for the selected region. This would allow users with the specific intent of hiding a piece of information (as opposed to showing it) a tool to potentially satisfy that need. A variation on both snip and anti-snip would be to automatically make the window full-sized and fully visible when active and then automatically re-snip (or re-anti-snip) the window when the user places input focus elsewhere. This variation could be useful for windows like instant messages so that the text of the conversation is only visible when that conversation retains input focus.

Acknowledgements. Thanks to the reviewers of this paper for providing additional points to add to the discussion sections. Thanks to the National Science Foundation for supporting this work under grant IIS-0414667.

References

1. Beaudouin-Lafon, M.: Novel interaction techniques for overlapping windows. In: Proc. UIST 2001, pp. 153–154. ACM Press, New York (2001)
2. Cadiz, J.J., Venolia, G., Jancke, G., Gupta, A.: Designing and deploying an information awareness interface. In: Proc. CSCW 2002, pp. 314–323. ACM Press, New York (2002)
3. Card, S.K., Pavel, M., Farrell, J.E.: Window-based computer dialogues. In: Proc. INTERACT 1984, pp. 239–243 (1984)
4. Chapuis, O., Roussel, N.: Metisse is not a 3D desktop! In: Proc. UIST 2005, pp. 13–22. ACM Press, New York (2005)
5. Colvin, J., Tobler, N., Anderson, J.A.: Productivity and multi-screen displays. Dept. Comm. Univ. Utah 2(1), 31–53 (2004)
6. Czerwinski, M., Smith, G., Regan, T., Meyers, B., Robertson, G., Starkweather, G.: Toward characterizing the productivity benefits of very large displays. In: Proc. INTERACT 2003, pp. 9–16. IOS Press, Amsterdam (2003)
7. Grudin, J.: Partitioning digital worlds: focal and peripheral awareness in multiple-monitor use. In: Proc. CHI 2001, pp. 458–465. ACM Press, New York (2001)

8. Henderson Jr., D.A., Card, S.K.R.: The use of multiple virtual workspaces to reduce space contention in a window-based graphical user interface. ACM Trans. on Graphics 5(3), 211–243 (1986)
9. Hutchings, D.R.: Making multiple monitors more manageable. Doctoral Dissertation, Georgia Institute of Technology, Atlanta, GA, USA (August 2006)
10. Hutchings, D.R., Smith, G., Meyers, B., Czerwinski, M., Robertson, G.: Display space usage and window management operation comparisons between single monitor and multiple-monitor users. In: Proc. Advanced Visual Interfaces, pp. 32–39. ACM Press, New York (2004)
11. Hutchings, D.R., Stasko, J.: Revisiting display space management: understanding current practice to inform next-generation design. In: Proc. Graphics Interface 2004, Canadian Human-Computer Communications Society, pp. 127–134 (2004)
12. Hutchings, D.R., Stasko, J.: Shrinking operations for expanding display space. In: Proc. AVI 2004, pp. 350–353. ACM Press, New York (2004)
13. Kandogan, E., Shneiderman, B.: Elastic windows: Evaluation of multi-window operations. In: Proc. CHI 1997, pp. 250–257. ACM Press, New York (1997)
14. Robertson, G., van Dantzich, M., Robbins, D., Czerwinski, M., Hinckley, K., Risden, K., Thiel, D., Gorokhovsky, V.: The Task Gallery: A 3D window manager. In: Proc. CHI 2000, pp. 494–501. ACM Press, New York (2000)
15. Smith, G., Baudisch, P., Robertson, G., Czerwinski, M., Meyers, B., Robbins, D., Andrews, D.: GroupBar: The Taskbar evolved. In: Proc. Australian Comp. Human Interaction Conf (OZCHI), pp. 34–43 (2003)
16. Stasko, J., Miller, T., Pousman, Z., Plaue, C., Ullah, O.: Personalized peripheral information awareness through information art. In: Davies, N., Mynatt, E.D., Siio, I. (eds.) UbiComp 2004. LNCS, vol. 3205, pp. 18–35. Springer, Heidelberg (2004)
17. Stuerzlinger, W., Chapuis, O., Phillips, D., Roussel, N.: User interface façades: towards fully adaptable user interfaces. In: Proc. UIST 2006, pp. 309–381. ACM Press, New York (2006)
18. Tan, D.S., Meyers, B., Czerwinski, M.: WinCuts: manipulating arbitrary window regions for more effective use of screen space. In: CHI 2004 Extended Abstracts, pp. 1525–1528. ACM Press, New York (2004)

Interacting with the Computer Using Gaze Gestures

Heiko Drewes[1] and Albrecht Schmidt[2]

[1] Media Informatics Group, LMU University of Munich,
Amalienstraße 17, 80333 München, Germany
heiko.drewes@ifi.lmu.de
[2] Fraunhofer IAIS and B-IT, University of Bonn,
Schloss Birlinghoven, 53754 Sankt Augustin, Germany
albrecht.schmidt@acm.org

Abstract. This paper investigates novel ways to direct computers by eye gaze. Instead of using fixations and dwell times, this work focuses on eye motion, in particular gaze gestures. Gaze gestures are insensitive to accuracy problems and immune against calibration shift. A user study indicates that users are able to perform complex gaze gestures intentionally and investigates which gestures occur unintentionally during normal interaction with the computer. Further experiments show how gaze gestures can be integrated into working with standard desktop applications and controlling media devices.

Keywords: eye-tracker, gaze gestures.

1 Introduction

Eye-trackers are video-based, and the cost of video cameras has dropped substantially in the past few years. Commercially available eye-trackers work with a resolution of 640 x 480 pixels and this is the resolution of a web cam, which can be bought as a consumer device for a few dollars. Most mobile devices sold today have a built-in camera and there are already the first laptops and desktop computers with built-in camera on the market. It is foreseeable that future monitors will have an integrated camera for no extra cost, as it is the case for integrated speakers today.

The processing power of a standard computer is sufficient to do real-time processing of a video stream. This means that within the near future eye-tracking technology will be available for no extra costs. There are already projects for low-cost or off-the-shelf eye-trackers [1], [2].

There are eye-tracker systems for disabled people to direct the computer and it is imaginable that eye-tracking could become an additional input modality for everybody. But the systems for the disabled are cumbersome to operate and less efficient compared to the classical way of interaction with keyboard and mouse. For this reason researchers from the field of human computer interaction think about new interfaces utilizing the eye-gaze.

1.1 Eye-Tracking

Quantitative research on eye-movements became possible with the invention of the motion camera and the first research dates back to this time. This kind of research was

C. Baranauskas et al. (Eds.): INTERACT 2007, LNCS 4663, Part II, pp. 475–488, 2007.
© IFIP International Federation for Information Processing 2007

mostly done by psychologists who wanted to understand perception. Most eye-tracker systems were built for analysis of the eye movement and its application in fields like advertisement. The first ideas to use the eye-gaze for interaction with the computer date back to the early 80s and 90s [3] [4] [5]. This was the time when it became possible to process a digital video stream in real-time. For an overview on eye-tracking see [6].

The technological basis of nowadays eye-tracking is easy to understand. An infrared LED causes a reflection spot on the eyeball. As the eye is perfectly round, the reflection spot stays at the same position no matter in which direction the eye is looking. A video camera detects the reflection spot and the center of the pupil. The direction of the eye-gaze can be calculated from the distance of both points by simple linear mapping.

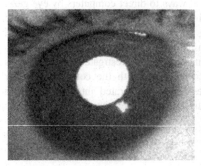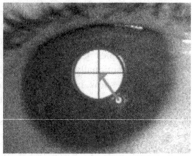

Fig. 1. Video-based eye-tracking uses the reflection of an infrared LED and the center of the pupil to calculate the direction of the eye-gaze. The reflection spot stays in the same position, while the pupil moves.

After a calibration procedure, for example gazing at the four corners of the display, the eye-tracker can deliver screen coordinates to the computer. The method requires that the head stays in the same position. Consequently, such systems need a head fixation or at least a chin rest, but this is no problem for the disabled person who can't move anything except the eyes. A typical commercial system of such an eye-tracker is the ERICA[1] system, which we used for our research.

To achieve freedom of movement in front of the display a head-tracker is necessary. Normally this is done by a second video camera. Such systems are more expensive, but also commercially available, for example the EyeGaze Eyefollower[2] or Tobii 1750 Eye Tracker[3].

1.2 The Problems of Eye-Gaze Based Interaction

Eye-gaze based interaction is now available for more than 20 years [7], but it is solely used in the domain of accessibility. Systems for eye-gaze based interaction typically

---

[1] http://www.eyeresponse.com
[2] http://www.eyegaze.com
[3] http://www.tobii.com

display a keyboard layout on the display and to enter a character the user has to gaze for a certain time, the dwell time, on the corresponding key. The time which could be saved by the proverbial quick movement of the eyes is eaten up by the dwell time. Reducing the dwell time leads to the Midas-Touch problem – inspecting the display causes unwanted actions [5].

The accuracy problem, which is not only a question of the resolution of the video camera but is intrinsic because of the jitter in the eye-movement, leads to big sizes for the keyboard layout. This causes a space problem on the display.

A general problem is the fact that the eye is mainly an input sensor and not an output actor. The eyes move to see something and not to trigger actions. Using the eyes for both, input and output, may result in conflicts [8]. On the other hand we can communicate with other persons by the direction where we look. As we know that other persons are aware of where we are looking, we keep our eyes under control as a part of our social protocol. The question how much output activity we can put on the movement of the eyes and how much unintentional eye movements interfere with intentional eye movements is not clear yet.

1.3 The Concept of Gestures

Gestures are a well-known concept for computer human interaction. Typical examples are Unistroke [9] and Cirrin [10]. A gesture consists of a sequence of elements, typically strokes, which are performed in a sequential time order. The advantage of gestures is that the number of commands can be increased by increasing the set of gestures. If commands are selected from a list, the increase of commands results in a bigger list und this can cause a space problem. For this reason gestures are used for interaction with small devices. As one problem of eye-gaze interfaces mentioned above is a space problem, gaze gestures are worth examining, especially for interaction with small displays.

1.4 Related Work

Most approaches to utilize the gaze position for computer control follow the concept of gaze as a pointing device and as an alternative for mouse input. There is only little research on different concepts like gestures.

Most work on gestures aims to identify the user's task or attention and use this as context information for smart interfaces. Qvarfordt and Zhai used eye-gaze patterns to build a dialog system [11]. They studied gaze patterns in human-human dialogs and used the results to mediate a human-computer dialog. In contrast to our approach the users did not learn gaze gestures to operate the system. The users were not even aware that they perform gestures.

Isokoski proposed the use of off-screen targets for text input [12]. To enter text the eye-gaze has to visit the off-screen targets in a certain order. The eye movements resulting from this are gaze gestures. The difference to the gaze gestures presented in this paper is that off-screen targets force the gesture to be performed in a fixed location and with a fixed size. The gaze gestures researched in our user study are scalable and can be performed in any location.

2   The Gaze Gesture Algorithm

As there was not much research done on gaze gestures the main research question is whether people are able to perform complex gestures with the eyes. The question which algorithm to use is secondary until the first question is answered.

2.1   Searching for a Gaze Gesture Algorithm

The popular and freely available mouse-gesture plug-in[4] for the Firefox web browser inspired us to implement a similar gaze-gesture algorithm. The mouse-gesture plug-in traces the mouse movements when a gesture key, normally the right mouse key, is pressed and translates the movements into a string of characters or tokens representing strokes in eight directions. Horizontal and vertical directions are given by the letters U, D, L, and R for up, down, left and right respectively. Diagonal directions are given by 1, 3, 7, and 9 corresponding to the familiar layout of the number pad on a standard keyboard. A gesture is defined by a particular string consisting of these eight characters.

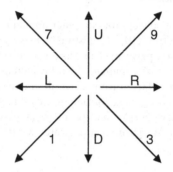

Fig. 2. The names of the eight directions of a stroke

The stroke detection uses a grid of size s. The algorithm maps every point reported by the mouse to a point on the grid by a simple integer division. The origin of the grid is the starting point of the stroke. If the integer division has a result different from zero for at least one of the coordinates, the algorithm calculates the direction. It outputs the corresponding character, but only if it is different from the character before.

The other gesture algorithm which inspired our work is EdgeWrite [13]. This algorithm starts with the four corners of a square and the six connecting lines. A stroke is a move from one corner to another corner and a gesture is a series of connected strokes. It is easy to see that all EdgeWrite gestures can be expressed with the tokens from the mouse gesture algorithm and consequently are a subset of the mouse gestures. This is interesting because the EdgeWrite gestures have the capability for a big complex alphabet.

---

[4] http://optimoz.mozdev.org/gestures

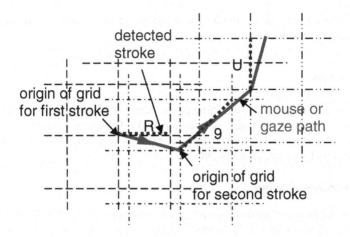

Fig. 3. The figure shows how a mouse or gaze path is translated into the string of characters R9U. The end point of a detected stroke is the origin for the grid to detect the next stroke.

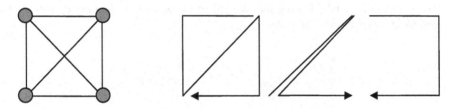

Fig. 4. The four corners and the six connecting lines used for the EdgeWrite gestures and three examples for EdgeWrite gestures (digits 0, 2 and 3)

2.2 Implementing a Gaze Gesture Algorithm

We liked the simplicity of the mouse gesture algorithm, but we disliked the need of a gesture key. So the first modification of the algorithm is the introduction of continuous recognition. Consequently the algorithm must divide between natural eye movements and gestures. The situation is similar for detecting commands with speech recognition.

To better separate the gestures from the natural movement we introduced a time aspect. During the performance of a gesture only short fixations and no long fixation should occur. A long fixation should reset the gesture recognition. We extended the algorithm with timeout detection and introduced a colon as the ninth token. The algorithm generates a colon as output if no other token was generated for time t.

The eye-gaze gesture recognition algorithm is a two-step process. In the first step the algorithm takes the x-y position of the current eye-gaze in pixels and maps this to strokes as described above. In the second step the algorithm recognizes the actual gestures by comparing the string to the given gesture pattern string. If the gesture pattern matches an action can be triggered.

The software is implemented for the Windows platform and the software is written in C++ with Visual Studio.

3   User Study

We conducted a user study with nine participants, six male and three female persons in the age from 23 to 47 years. All persons had a European cultural background and academic education. All of them used computers regularly, but none of them had experience with eye-tracking systems.

3.1 Experimental Setup

For the user study we used the commercial eye-tracker ERICA. The system consists of a camera and a tablet PC mounted together on a stand. The display has a size of 246 mm x 185 mm and a resolution of 1024 x 768 pixels. The distance of the eyes from the screen is 48 cm ± 2 cm. This values result in 0.028° visual angle per pixel or around 36 pixels for 1°. The accuracy of the system is ± 0.5°.

The ERICA system delivers a maximal update rate of 60 Hz or about one position every 17 milliseconds. During the movement of the eye no data are delivered. This results in a gap during a saccade.

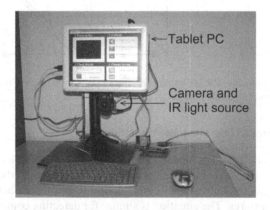

Fig. 5. The ERICA eye-tracker system used for the user study

The software written for the user study did the gesture recognition. The grid size was set to 80 pixels and the timeout parameter t was 1000 milliseconds. The program gave auditory feedback i.e. prompted the recognition of a gesture with a beep. It also had options to display helping lines or blank or structured background. The structured background was a screenshot of a spreadsheet application.

3.2 Design of the User Study

The user study consisted of three different tasks. Prior to the experiment the participant got a brief introduction to the system.

The first task was to close a dialog by using eye-gestures instead of the mouse. The participants were instructed to perform the action by visiting the corners clockwise for YES and counter-clockwise for NO. (Could also be OK and CANCEL). The gaze gesture recognition scanned for the patterns RDLU, DLUR, LURD and URDL for YES and for the patterns LDRU, DRUL, RULD and ULDR for NO. The time needed for the operation was recorded.

Fig. 6. The first task in the user study was to close a dialog with a gaze gesture

In the second task the users had to do three different gaze gestures of increasing difficulty on three different backgrounds. Again the software logged the gaze activity. To prove that the user is able to do the requested gesture, each gesture had to be repeated three times. This resulted in 27 gestures per candidate. The gestures used were RLRLRL, 3U1U and RD7DR7, see Figure 2 for an illustration. For each performed gesture the required time was recorded.

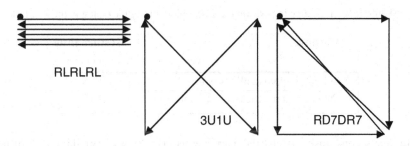

Fig. 7. The three gaze gestures shown had to be performed for the second task in the user study

The first background showed an outlined square with diagonal lines as shown in Figure 8. The helping lines were given to guide the gaze gestures. The second background was a screenshot of a desktop with an open spreadsheet document. This enabled the test users to choose positions for fixations. And the third background was just gray.

The third task was to surf the internet for three minutes. The gesture recognition software logged the resulting gesture string. The reason for this task was to find out which patterns occur during normal work, or at least during surfing.

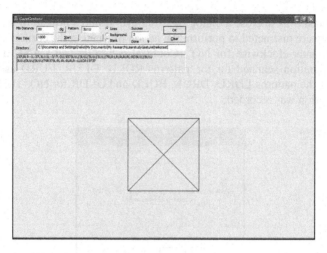

Fig. 8. Screenshot of the program written for the user study. The display modes are blank, structured background and display of helping lines.

3.3   Results of the User Study

All users were instantly able to close the dialogs by gaze with YES and NO using eye-gestures. The average time to perform the gesture was about 1900 milliseconds with a standard deviation of about 600 milliseconds. This time is in the same range than performing the action by mouse including a homing from keyboard to mouse and clicking a button. All participants reported this as an easy task.

Table 1. Average time to perform the gesture for closing the dialog in the first task

Gesture	Gesture time
	average over all subjects (ms)
YES (clockwise all corners)	1905
NO (counter-clockwise all corners)	1818

In the second task, where the participants had to perform the three different gestures, we were surprised that all users were able to perform all gestures on the helpline and text background, most of them with ease. The number of attempts to complete a gesture varied very much. In many cases users were able to perform the gestures instantly whereas for some others it took quite long to complete the task successfully. Table 2 shows the task performance times for the 3U1U gesture.

For the blank background all users could accomplish the gestures RLRLRL and 3U1U. Five of nine users were even able to perform the most difficult task (RD7DR7 on a blank background). In some of these cases it initially took quite long to get the gesture, but after the first success it took not much time to repeat the gesture again.

Table 2. Total time in milliseconds to perform three times the 3U1U gesture

Participant	Helping Lines	Text Background	Blank Background
P1	26808	30795	23915
P2	33528	28400	25407
P3	5899	35611	23513
P4	160370	38506	74567
P5	25106	33177	97240
P6	10355	9353	15022
P7	12789	60708	71633
P8	26849	32477	10926
P9	23724	114074	56722
Mean	**36159**	**42567**	**44327**
Std. Dev.	47452	29874	31216

Overall we learned that with a structured background such as text, tables or web pages, even difficult gaze-gestures can be performed reliably and that neither the background nor the complexity of the gesture has a significant impact on the completion time. The time for the gesture depends only on the number of segments. The average time required for a segment was 557 milliseconds.

Table 3. Average gestures time and standard deviation in milliseconds to perform the three different gestures on three different backgrounds in the second task. The data are from nine participants, except RD7DR7 on blank background, where only 5 participants were able to perform the gesture.

Gesture	Helping Lines	Text Background	Blank Background
RLRLRL	3113 (±627)	3089 (±728)	3288 (±810)
3U1U	2222 (±356)	2311 (±443)	2429 (±307)
RD7DR7	3163 (±490)	3563 (±651)	3569 (±520)

The third task recorded the characters produced by the gaze gesture recognition algorithm while surfing. The total time for the 9 users was 1700 seconds or 28 minutes, resulting in 2737 characters. This results in 1.6 characters per second or about 600 milliseconds for a stroke. This string was searched for the gestures of the first and second task.

Table 5 shows the occurrence of the gestures from the first and second task. Some of the eight gestures to enter YES or NO respectively in a dialog did not occur in the whole string and others at most 3 times. When restricting the recognition to the context of use (e.g. currently a dialog is open) the risk to answer a dialog unintentionally seems to be extremely low.

Table 4. Statistics for detected strokes within half an hour of web surfing

Stroke	Occurrences	Percentage	Stroke	Occurrences	Percentage
:	388	14,1%			
1	136	5,0%	D	178	6,5%
3	136	5,0%	U	229	8,3%
7	138	5,0%	L	685	25,0%
9	115	4,2%	R	732	26,7%

The RLRLRL gesture occurs very often (69 times in the sample of all participants), because this is the natural eye movement during reading and consequently should not be used for commands in general. The 3U1U and RD7DR7 gestures didn't occur during the half hour of surfing. In particular the 3U1U gesture seems to be a good candidate for a gesture that is generally applicable, relatively easy to perform, and very unlikely to appear during normal use.

Table 5. Occurrence of the gestures from task 1 and 2 within half an hour of web surfing

Gesture		Gesture		Gesture	
RDLU	0	DRUL	2	RLRLRL	69
DLUR	2	RULD	3	3U1U	0
LURD	1	ULDR	0	RD7DR7	0
URDL	1	LDRU	1		

4 Experiments with Standard Applications and Media Devices

After the positive results from the first user study, the next step was to look for fields of application for this novel type of interaction. The EdgeWrite gestures provide a full alphabet, but the gaze gestures are not adequate for text input. As seen in the user study a gesture needs 1 to 2 seconds to enter and even the standard dwell time method is faster and typing with the fingers is definitely the more efficient way of text input.

A useful application of gaze gestures is the field of accessibility. Because of the robustness against accuracy problems and immunity against calibration shift a gaze gesture is the perfect way to invoke a recalibration process for the disabled users of eye-tracker systems. It is also imaginable to use the gestures for general macro functions within accessibility systems. For example a gaze gesture could be used to save a document and close the application or to paste content from the clipboard.

One idea was to offer the macro functionality as an extra input modality for everybody. For this reason we implemented a software prototype which is able to recognize a list of gestures and trigger a corresponding command. We used the WM_APPCOMMAND of the Windows operating system to realize an open document, save document and close document function which works with standard

Windows software such as Word. When observing people working with documents and application we noticed that many users put the hands to the mouse to select the save option from the menu and return the hand to the keyboard for further text entry. With the use of gaze gestures it is imaginable to leave the hands on the keyboard - saving the lengthy time for homing and selection – and invoke the save operation with the eyes.

To test the idea we put some colleges, not involved in our research, in front of our system and asked them to type something and save the document with the gaze gesture. They were instantly able to perform the operation asked for. They told us that there is some fascination in the possibility to direct the computer without touching, but for not to grab the mouse they would press the short cut ctrl-s to save their document. The returned to their office and saved the next document by using the mouse. Of course every command invoked by a gaze gesture could also be invoked by a key press. Whether or how many people would use gaze gestures if offered as standard interaction is not clear.

This result motivated us to look for further applications. Gaze gestures could be useful in the case that keyboard and pointing device are out of reach. This situation is typical for controlling media devices, especially media center computers. Such devices normally come along with remote control.

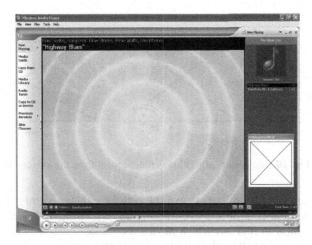

Fig. 9. Screenshot of the media player and a window with helping lines to perform the gestures. It turned out that it is more convenient to use the edges of the main display to enter the gesture and the helping lines are not necessary.

The accuracy of an eye-tracker is given in visual angle. In principle this means, that the spatial accuracy in millimeters or pixels on the screen gets worse with growing distance. But gaze gestures on a big grid are insensitive to accuracy problems and seem to be well suited to the situation.

Thus, we extended our software with additional commands for media control such as play, pause, stop, previous track, next track, media channel up and down and volume control. To test the system we placed candidates in a distance of one meter away from the display. The one meter distance is the maximum our eye-tracker optics is able to focus and it is longer than the arms of the candidates, so the couldn't reach the keyboard. The observations were encouraging.

The first observation was that people didn't need the helping lines offered. The corners of the display window or the screen provide a natural orientation to perform the gestures. The candidates had no difficulties to perform the gestures.

The next observation was that people experienced it easier to perform big scaled gestures than small scaled gestures. From our recorded data we know that the time needed for a saccade does not increase much if the saccade length gets bigger. A saccade above 5° visual angle lasts about 120 milliseconds (see also [14]). The influence of the scale used for the gesture does not have a big effect on the time to perform the gesture.

It also turned out that the grid size of the gesture algorithm is not critical. The big scaled gestures were reliably detected with the grid size settings for the small scaled gestures. People seem to perform horizontal and vertical eye movements with high precision.

Another observation from this category was the insensitivity of the gesture recognition to the aspect ratio. The gestures do not have to be in square shape. An aspect ratio of 4:3 and 16:9 for the corners also work well. See figure 10 for an illustration.

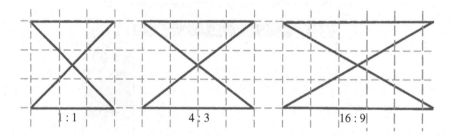

Fig. 10. The gesture algorithm is independent from the aspect ratio

There was already research to use eye-trackers for remote control [15]. Vertegaal et al. used one remote control and eye-trackers on several devices and used the eye-tracker information to find out which device the remote control is meant for. Using the gaze gestures would allow the remote control to be eliminated.

5   Conclusions and Future Work

It seems that the concept of gaze gestures has a potential to be used as an input modality. Gaze gestures solve some of the big problems of eye-gaze interaction. First of all the gaze gestures use only relative eye movements and consequently do not need a calibration of the eye-tracker. Accuracy is not an issue, because the gaze is not used for pointing. As the grid size of the gesture algorithm can be chosen as large as

10° visual angle and the time needed to perform a gesture segment is several hundred milliseconds, the gaze gesture detection does not demand high spatial and temporal resolution from the eye-tracker. This makes it possible to manufacture eye-trackers, which can detect gaze gestures only, with cheap standard devices. Finally the use of gaze gestures does not exhibit the Midas-Touch problem and the users do not feel stressed by not being allowed to look too long at something.

Research on this topic is still in the early beginning and the presented algorithm is not yet fully researched. Further user studies should be done on the question which gestures occur unintentional during normal looking, e.g. watching videos. The parameters of the algorithm, the grid size s and the timeout t, will be a subject for optimization. A bigger grid size up to the dimensions of the display will lead to fewer unintended gestures, because the eye movements normally stay within the display and typical saccade lengths are much smaller than the width or height of the display.

The question whether users will accept gaze gestures as an additional input modality is very interesting. In the field of accessibility the concept of gaze gestures will certainly bring benefit for the user, for example as a substitute of accelerator keys (ctrl-s) or to invoke a recalibration process. In addition to the application as a substitute for remote controls as mentioned above, the gaze gestures can be very useful in fields with high hygienic demands. A surgeon in the operating room could interact with electronic devices using gaze gestures.

It also seems worthwhile to think about alternative gesture algorithms. This will lead to a closer look on the low-level recognition algorithms. The eye-trackers of today are optimized for the detection of fixations and dwell times. Normally the eyes move in saccades, but some people are also able to roll the eyes smoothly.

Our future efforts will focus on gaze gestures on mobile devices, where eye-gaze input is difficult because of the small display size.

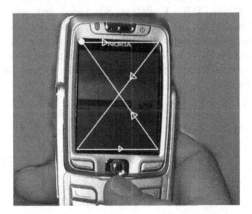

Fig. 11. Gaze gestures on small displays

Acknowledgments. The work has been conducted in the context of the research project Embedded Interaction ('Eingebettete Interaktion') and was partly funded by the DFG ('Deutsche Forschungsgemeinschaft').

References

1. Hansen, D.W., MacKay, D.J.C., Hansen, J.P., Nielsen, M.: Eye tracking off the shelf. In: ETRA 2004, pp. 58–58. ACM Press, New York (2004)
2. Li, D., Babcock, J., Parkhurst, D.: openEyes: a low-cost head-mounted eye-tracking solution. In: ETRA 2006, pp. 95–100. ACM Press, New York (2006)
3. Bolt, R.A: Gaze-orchestrated dynamic windows. In: SIGGRAPH '81, pp. 109–119. ACM Press, New York (1981)
4. Ware, C., Mikaelian, H.H.: An evaluation of an eye tracker as a device for computer input. In: Proceedings of the CHI + GI '87, pp. 183–188. ACM Press, New York (1987)
5. Jacob, R.J.: What you look at is what you get: eye movement-based interaction techniques. In: CHI '90, pp. 11–18. ACM Press, New York (1990)
6. Duchowski, A.T.: Eye Tracking Methodology: Theory and Practice. Springer, New York (2003)
7. Majaranta, P., Räihä, K.: Twenty years of eye typing: systems and design issues. In: ETRA 2002, pp. 15–22. ACM Press, New York (2002)
8. Zhai, S., Morimoto, C., Ihde, S.: Manual and gaze input cascaded (MAGIC) pointing. In: CHI '99, pp. 246–253. ACM Press, New York (1999)
9. Goldberg, D., Richardson, C.: Touch-Typing With a Stylus. In: CHI '93, pp. 80–87. ACM Press, New York (1993)
10. Mankof, J., Abowd, G.D.: Cirrin: a word-level unistroke keyboard for pen input. In: UIST '98, pp. 213–214. ACM Press, New York (1998)
11. Qvarfordt, P., Zhai, S.: Conversing with the User Based on Eye-Gaze Patterns. In: CHI '05, pp. 221–230. ACM Press, New York (2005)
12. Isokoski, P.: Text input methods for eye trackers using off-screen targets. In: ETRA '00, pp. 15–21. ACM Press, New York (2000)
13. Wobbrock, J.O., Myers, B.A., Kembel, J.A.: EdgeWrite: a stylus-based text entry method designed for high accuracy and stability of motion. In: UIST '03, pp. 61–70. ACM Press, New York (2003)
14. Abrams, R.A., Meyer, D.E., Kornblum, S.: Speed and accuracy of saccadic eye movements: Characteristics of impulse variability in the oculomotor system. Journal of Experimental Psychology: Human Perception and Performance 15(3), 529–543 (1989)
15. Vertegaal, R., Mamuji, A., Sohn, C., Cheng, D.: Media eyepliances: using eye tracking for remote control focus selection of appliances. In: CHI '05, pp. 1861–1864. ACM Press, New York (2005)

A Comparative Longitudinal Study of Non-verbal Mouse Pointer

Murni Mahmud[1], Adam J. Sporka[2,3], Sri H. Kurniawan[4], and Pavel Slavík[3]

[1] International Islamic University Malaysia
P.O. Box 10, 50728 Kuala Lumpur, Malaysia
murni@iiu.edu.my
[2] Hečkova 8, 14200 Praha 4, Czech Republic
adam@sporka.eu
[3] Czech Technical University in Prague
Karlovo náměstí 13, 12135 Praha 2, Czech Republic
a.j.sporka@fee.ctup.cz, slavik@fel.cvut.cz
[4] University of Manchester
PO Box 88, Manchester M60 1QD, United Kingdom
s.kurniawan@manchester.ac.uk

Abstract. A longitudinal study of two non-speech continuous cursor control systems is presented in this paper: Whistling User Interface (U^3I) and Vocal Joystick (VJ). This study combines the quantitative and qualitative methods to get a better understanding of novice users' experience over time. Three hypotheses were tested in this study. The quantitative data show that U^3I performed better in error rate and in simulating a mouse click; VJ was better on other measures. The qualitative data indicate that the participants' opinions regarding both tools improved day-by-day. U^3I was perceived as less fatiguing than VJ. U^3I approached the performance of VJ at the end of the study period, indicating that these two systems can achieve similar performances as users get more experienced in using them. This study supports two hypotheses but does not provide enough evidence to support one hypothesis.

Keywords: Voice-based interface, non-verbal vocal input, speech recognition, cursor control, continuous input, mouse cursor, acoustic gestures.

1 Introduction

Most recent days' interactive systems follow the WIMP (Windows, Icons, Menus, and Pointer) paradigm and can usually be controlled optimally using a mouse or equivalent pointing devices such as a trackball or touchpad. However, people with some impairments of upper limbs, especially those who have problems performing fine motor movement with their fingers, face difficulties when using these devices, and have to use alternative devices to accommodate their needs and capabilities. Many of these devices are based on dedicated hardware solutions, such as sip-and-puff controllers, feet-operated input devices, or eye trackers. Being typically produced in small quantities, they can be very costly and therefore are not affordable to some users.

C. Baranauskas et al. (Eds.): INTERACT 2007, LNCS 4663, Part II, pp. 489–502, 2007.
© IFIP International Federation for Information Processing 2007

Increasing reliability and deployability of the speech recognition on the lower-end computer systems make this technology a promising alternative. However, the speech recognition systems operate on a query—response basis, where the system usually waits for the user to complete the utterance before responding. This makes the speech recognition inconvenient to use in real-time continuous tasks, including mouse pointer movement, where the minimum delay of the system is a critical feature of the feedback loop of the system [22].

In the last decade, the non-speech (or non-verbal) input has started to emerge. It is based on production of sounds other than speech by the user's vocal tract. It can be considered a counterpart to the non-speech output modality, which is mostly used in presentation of data (such as [3, 7]). In non-speech input, the sound is analyzed and certain features are extracted, such as the pitch profile, or the sound timbre, in order to solicit information from the user. Depending on the application, these features may be assigned to different elementary controls of the user interface.

Recently, this form of input has been employed in several tools that implement a virtual mouse device. This paper aims at comparing two of these systems, Whistling User Interface (U^3I) [19] and Vocal Joystick (VJ) [10]. These two systems will be explained in more detail in Section 4.

2 Motivation

Many usability studies have pointed out that there is a considerable difference between involving so-called novice or expert users because these users may have different levels of experience with the system being evaluated. Therefore, it is important to study users over time as they develop expertise in using the systems to answer a key question of how the user's experience of a system's usability changes when they transform from being novices to being more expert, if usability problems really disappear over time when users get more familiar with a system [13]. This forms the motivation of the longitudinal nature of the reported study.

This study combines quantitative and qualitative methods to arrive at a better understanding of the usability and performance of the two tested systems by novice users, as it develops over time. This combination is expected to be able to complement the pictures provided by individual methods in regard to user performance and opinions on the tested systems.

Non-speech voice input as a user interface control modality holds the potential for offering effective input modality for individuals with physical or situation-induced motor impairment, but this space has been relatively unexplored. Through studying the adoptability of such techniques by novice users, we hope to gain a better understanding of whether such systems are indeed viable, and what their ease of use and learnability are. By combining results from prior studies that compare these systems to common input devices (e.g. VJ and the mouse in [4]), we can also place these novel input methods on the map of other existing input devices.

We decided to investigate user experience on VJ and U^3I for several reasons:

- Past studies had compared the performances and user opinions of one of the systems (VJ) with common input devices, and therefore, the comparison between VJ and U^3I can be placed on a 'bigger map' of input devices in general.

- Both systems share certain properties (based on non-speech vocal input and respond immediately to changing features of the sound), thereby minimizing the variability when investigating the causes of performance and opinion differences.

  There are three hypotheses that this study tests (the reasoning behind these hypotheses will be elaborated in the sections that explain how these two tools work):

  H1: U^3I is faster than VJ in emulating a click (reasoning: humming is easier to produce than the sound 'k' used by VJ to emulate a click).

  H2a: User performance is higher using VJ as opposed to using U^3I (reasoning: it is easier to associate the sounds and movements produced in VJ than it is in U^3I).

  H2b: User opinion of U^3I is better than that of VJ (reasoning: it is less tiresome to produce 'mmmm' than it is to produce 'aaah', 'iiih', 'uuuh', 'eeeh').

  H3: User performance and opinions regarding both tools would improve at the end of the study period.

3   Related Work

Non-speech input has been evaluated in many different contexts, such as computer games [10], interactive art [1], music training [17], or keyboard emulation [20]. In this section, an overview of the voice-based methods of mouse pointer control is given.

Non-speech Methods. Only non-verbal sounds are used to control the mouse pointer.
- Whistling User Interface (U^3I) [19] is based on the use of tones (in whistling or humming) where the difference between the initial pitch and current pitch determines the speed of motion.
- Vocal Joystick (VJ) [10] is based on the assignment of different vowel sounds ('aah', 'eeh', etc.) to four or eight basic directions. The movement continues for as long as the sound is being produced. The loudness governs the speed of motion.

Hybrid Methods. The hybrid methods make use of speech commands that are augmented by non-verbal vocalizations.
- Non-verbal quantification of speech-issued commands is proposed in [11]. The users would utter 'move down' and then produce sound such as 'aaah' for as long as they wished the movement to last.
- Migratory Cursor [16] combines the speech recognition for coarse approach of cursor towards the target and subsequent refinement of the position with a non-verbal sound.

Speech-based Methods. In speech-based methods, the mouse cursor is controlled by speech utterances only.
- Direction commands-based methods—such as SUITTEKeys [15] interface—make use of discrete speech commands such as 'move mouse left' (initiating motion in that direction), 'stop' (motion is stopped). The Dragon NaturallySpeaking® package, in addition to these basic commands, allows control the cursor speed by commands such as 'faster', 'much faster', etc.
- Grid-based systems, such as [12, 5] are based on recursive subdivision of screen by a grid, typically 3 by 3 cells, assigned numbers 1 through 9. Upon selecting a cell

by uttering a number, the cell becomes subdivided a similar manner. As soon as the focus is over the target, the user may utter a 'click' command.

- Voice Mouse [8] uses a similar assignment of vowels as VJ. However, the system requires the user to produce one sound to initiate the motion and another to end it.

4 Description of the Systems

The Vocal Joystick System. The Vocal Joystick (VJ) system [10] offers as one of its modes a cursor control mode that allows a user to move the mouse pointer by making vowel sounds that have been assigned to each direction. Figure 1 shows the mapping of the vowel sounds to the directions for the 4-way version of VJ, which was the version that was used in our experiment. An 8-way version is also available. A more detailed technical description of the VJ system can be found in [4].

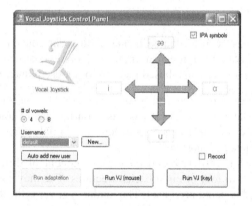

Fig. 1. Set-up Screen of the Vocal Joystick Application, showing the assignment of sounds to directions of mouse pointer movement

To move the mouse cursor, the user starts vocalizing one of the vowel sounds, and the cursor would immediately begin moving in the corresponding direction with a speed that is proportional to loudness. The user can continuously vary the vowel or the loudness, and the cursor stops moving as soon as the vocalization terminates. Clicking is achieved by making a short discrete sound (in this case the consonant 'k'), and toggling of the mouse button for dragging is performed by making the discrete sound 'ch'. The control panel of VJ is shown on Fig.1.

VJ can be used without any user specific training, but its performance can be improved by adapting the system to each user's vocal characteristics. This process involves the user vocalizing each of the vowel sounds for two seconds at their normal loudness, and the actual adaptation step takes less than a second.

The recognition of the vowels is very robust and accurate compared to recognizing words under conventional speech recognition systems.

Whistling User Interface. This system (U^3I) allows the users to operate the mouse by producing a series of acoustic gestures [19]. Depending on the length and pitch profile (melody) of the gesture the system moves the cursor in specific direction at certain speed or emulates a click.

The cursor may be moved along one of the x- and y-axis at a time. Depending on the initial pitch of the tone (either below or above a specified threshold), the gesture would drive the cursor either horizontally or vertically. A mouse click is emulated when a short tone is produced by the user. All gestures are shown in Fig. 2.

Originally, only whistling was received by the system, which gave the system its name. The analysis of humming (i.e. producing 'mmm' sound) was implemented as a user test [21] proved that humming was easier to produce and less tiresome for the users.

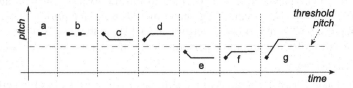

Fig. 2.   Example gestures of the U^3I system. a – click, b – double-click, c – downwards, d – upwards, e – to the left, f – to the right, g – a movement to the right.

The system runs as a standalone application on win32 platforms (see Fig. 3). Its user interface comprises of a single dialog window which also provides a visual feedback of the system for set-up purposes (checking proper function of the microphone, calibration of parameters, etc.) However, while used in normal operation, the system provides no additional feedback than the one provided by a common mouse.

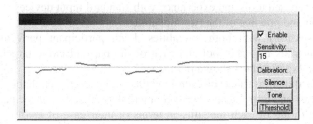

Fig. 3. Ser Interface of U^3I Application

5   Experiment

Participants. Ten participants were recruited from the university, high school and members of the public in the Manchester Area (mean age=18.8, SD=9.1). All participants (8 female, 2 male) have some computer and mouse experience (mean=3.2 years, SD=2.6). None of the participants was familiar with the target acquisition task. All participants signed informed consent forms before the experiment.

Apparatus. The experiment was conducted on a Dell Inspiron 630m laptop with 1.6 GHz Intel Centrino processor and 1 GB of RAM running the Windows XP Home operating system. The resolution of the 14.1" LCD was 1280 by 800 pixels. The experiment was conducted in full screen mode, with the user's head situated about two feet from the screen. A noise-canceling headset microphone (Altec Lansing AHS322) was used for audio input.

Design. A series of controlled experiments were executed longitudinally over five consecutive days. The experiment sessions were conducted at about the same time of day everyday. The study followed a 2×2×2×8 within-subjects design with repeated measures (3 trials per condition). The arrangement of the tools and the size of the target were counterbalanced. It was decided to run the experiment with an index of difficulty (ID in bits) of 3 (replicating one of the IDs used in a prior target acquisition work comparing VJ's and mouse's performances [4], as the results of this study will need to be extrapolated with mouse performance). The factors and levels were:

- Modality (M) {VJ, U^{3}I}
- Target shape (T) {bar – similar to the stimulus used in Fitts' 1954 experiment [6], circle}
- Target width-distance (to maintain ID=3, in pixels) {W=50, A=350; W=100, A=700}
- Approach angle (θ in degrees, counterclockwise) {0 = the direction to the right of the screen, 45, 90, 135, 180, 225, 270, 315}
- Day (D) {1..5}

Procedure. The experiment on day 1 consisted of the following (in the order it was conducted):

1. A demographics questionnaire to elicit age, experience with computer, experience with speech-based tools and experience with standard input devices.
2. Calibration and practice of the two modalities.
3. Training sessions with both modalities. Each participant performed 16 target acquisition trials for each tool and each of the bar and circle targets. A stimulus used in the experiment is shown in Fig. 4.
4. 48 target acquisition trials for each modality and each target shape. The sequence of modalities and target shapes were counterbalanced across participants.
5. Subjective rating of each modality in terms of their ease of learning, ease of use, level of fatigue, level of frustration, satisfaction and confidence.

On days 2-5 the participants performed activities 2, 4 and 5. In addition, on the last day the participants also performed a simple reaction time (SRT) task aimed at measuring how the two modalities process sounds intended to simulate a click.

The SRT test was performed using an online stimulus called The Online Reaction Time Test [2]. This was a simple operation where the participant clicked the right button to start, which caused the red light to turn on. The participant had to click this button as fast as they could as soon as the red light turned green. No cursor movement was measured in this experiment. Each participant was asked to click 20 times for each tested system. After 20 times, the data were analyzed to remove outliers. If there were outliers, the participants were asked to click some more times to make up 20 useful data points. The data were then averaged. To assist users, a printout of the mapping between the voices and movements was provided throughout the experiment to guide the participants (shown in Fig. 5).

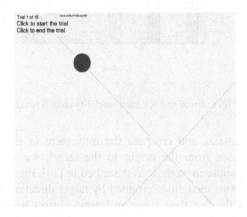

Fig. 4. A screenshot of a stimulus. The cursor position is at the crossing of the two diagonal lines.

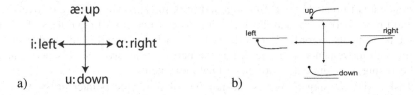

Fig. 5. Printout of mapping used in the experiment for (a) VJ and (b) U^3I

6   Results

In the rest of the paper, data we report as significant are at p ≤ .05 level.

6.1   Quantitative Results

The error rate (percentage of the trials in which the participant failed to acquire the target) over the five days for each of the modality is shown in Figure 6. Trials in which the participants failed to acquire the target were not included in subsequent analyses.

Figure 7 shows the movement times for each modality across the five days. The data had to be analysed separately for *cardinal* (horizontal or vertical) and *ordinal* (oblique) directions, as the index of difficulty of the ordinal targets were higher than those of the cardinal targets. Helmert contrasts showed that the day effect was not significant after day 4 for U^3I, but that it was not significant at all throughout the five day period for VJ, in support of H2b.

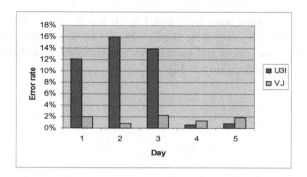

Fig. 6. Error rate for each modality over five days

In order to characterize and compare the movement of the pointer under each modality as it traverses from the origin to the target, we analyzed six different measures of mouse pointer movement as described in [14]. Figure 8 shows the plot of the measures for the two modalities grouped by target direction categories. The data was aggregated over the five days since no learning effect was observed for any of these six measures. The data on six measure support H2a (User performance using VJ is better than those using U^3I).

- Target Re-entry (TRE) is the number of times the pointer moved from within the target area to outside the target area and back in. This is a measure of overshoots, and Figure 7(a) shows that the TRE remains constant for VJ regardless of whether the movements are ordinal or cardinal, U^3I's TRE was significantly higher than VJ for both movements, with the difference between the two system's performances becoming more dramatic with the ordinal movement.
- Task Axis Crossing (TAC) is the number of times the pointer crossed the line connecting the starting point to the target centre (the task axis). It is expected that TAC is smaller for cardinal movements as the users only need to maintain the movement in one direction. However, in two directional movements, TAC shows that users have more problems in 'wobbliness' when using U^3I compared to when VJ was used.
- Movement Direction Change (MDC) is the number of points along the pointer path where the change in direction is parallel to the task axis.
- Orthogonal Direction Change (ODC) is the number of points along the pointer path where the change in direction is perpendicular to the task axis. MDC and ODC represent similar measures, the degree of overshoots along the task axis. It is interesting to note that users seem to have more problems with MDC than with ODC when using VJ at ordinal movement while the performance was pretty much constant when using U^3I. This might indicate that certain movement change using VJ is more difficult to make than other change (e.g., changing from 'aah' to 'uuh' might be more difficult than changing from 'uuh' to 'iih').
- Movement Variability (MV, in pixel) is the standard deviation of the distances of the points along the path to the task axis from their mean.

- Movement Error (ME, in pixel) is the average distance of the points along the path from the task axis. Both MV and ME are a detailed measure of wobbliness, and therefore these two diagrams depict similar trends to those of TAC. VJ was significantly lower than U^3I on all measures regardless of the target direction.

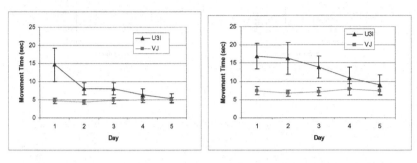

Fig. 7. Movement times over five days for VJ and U^3I for targets along (a) cardinal directions and (b) ordinal directions. The bars show the standard deviations.

6.2 Simple Reaction Time

This experiment aimed at testing H1 (U^3I is faster than VJ in emulating a click as humming is easier to produce than 'k' used by VJ to emulate a click). The results suggest that the U^3I was significantly faster in emulating a click (mean=578ms, SD=84) than VJ was (mean=857ms, SD=129) with ($F(1, 18)=32.744$, p <0.01). Therefore, the empirical data gathered in this study is in support of H1.

6.3 Subjective Ratings

Both tools were rated at the end of each day session on six aspects: Q1 through Q6 (Q1 = ease of learning, Q2 = ease of use, Q3 = level of fatigue, Q4 = level of frustration, Q5 = satisfaction and Q6 = confidence), with 1 = lowest and 5 = highest. For analysis, the ratings for fatigue and frustration were reversed so that lower numbers indicate better opinions regarding fatigue and frustration. Figure 9 and 10 shows the progress of ratings over five days. Both figures show that users' opinions regarding both systems improved by days, in support of H2b.

The changes in ratings by day suggest that overall the participants' perception of the two tools had improved. For each aspect, the results suggest that VJ received significantly better rating than U^3I as tested through t-tests. This suggests that there is not enough evidence to support H3.

However, the Table 1 shows that the improvement in user perception was not equal for both tools. The t-test analysis comparing day 1's and day 5's perceptions show that the mean ratings for both tools were not significantly different for ease of learning (Q1). The change in ease of use (Q2) was not significant for U^3I. The change in frustration (Q4) was not significant for VJ; with VJ receiving a higher rating than U^3I did for this aspect.

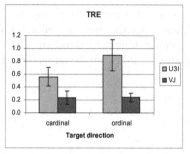

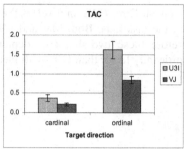

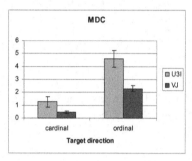

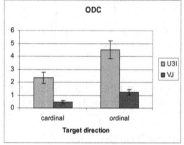

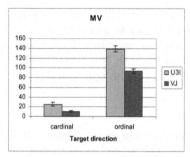

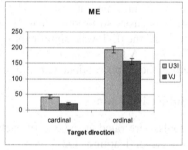

Fig. 8. Mouse pointer trail movements for VJ and U^3I grouped by directions

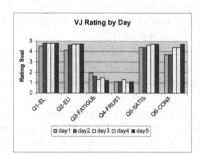

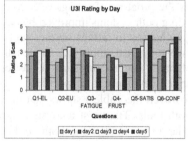

Fig. 9. Subjective rating across five days for (a) VJ and (b) U^3I

Table 1. t-test result of comparing day 1 and day 5 for each aspect (df=9)

Aspect	VJ T	sig	U^3I t	sig
Q1	-1.406	0.193	-1.103	0.299
Q2	-3.674	0.005	-2.181	0.057
Q3	2.689	0.025	4.583	0.001
Q4	same rating		2.941	0.016
Q5	-1.406	0.193	-2.372	0.042
Q6	-2.372	0.042	-5.075	0.001

6.4 Qualitative Data

The following qualitative data were derived from a combination of the participants' comments and the researchers' observation. Participants were generally optimistic about both systems.

Production of sounds. When using VJ, some of the participants had problems with articulating the appropriate vowel sounds. In situations where the participants were not able to replicate the sounds stored in the existing VJ profile (causing the cursor to move in undesired direction), a new profile was created.

The humming sounds in U^3I were much less challenging for the users in terms of articulation but people with pitch hearing would be in advantage when using U^3I. There key problem was for the users to memorize the threshold pitch. Users had to reselect their threshold pitch everyday, making U^3I sessions, in general, to last longer than VJ sessions.

Fatigue. The participants generally reported the VJ to be more fatiguing than the U^3I due to the need of keeping the proper articulation of the vowel sounds, especially when moving the cursor over large distances.

Cursor control. When using VJ, it was observed that when the cursor was close to the target, the users tended to decrease the volume to avoid overshooting. It was also observed that some participants could not reach the target in one continuous movement because of short of breath. One participant commented that there was a noticeable delay between the voice and the corresponding cursor movement.

In situations where the participants overshot the target and the cursor went off the screen, sometimes they could not rectify the problem even after producing various voices in an attempt to bring the cursor back. In these situations, the experimenter would use the mouse to reveal the position of the cursor.

One suggestion that the participants made was to implement a filter of unwanted noises. These include background noise (to which both systems were very sensitive) and vocalizations made by user other than the prescribed ones.

Ease of learning and use. Many participants mentioned that it was difficult to use the systems at the beginning but with practice, they were able to gain their skills. Participants were generally in agreement that VJ was easier to learn than U^3I. It was found more comfortable for voicing out vowels was a familiar activity for the users. Though humming sounds in U^3I were easier to produce, memorizing the threshold pitch was a hindrance. The voice—movement mapping printouts were helpful by most participants. The participants suggested improving both tools by providing a more user-friendly interface and cues that would help them recover from errors.

7 Discussion

The analysis of the SRT experiment supports H1, the users were faster when using U^3I. This suggests that producing a tonal gesture (i.e. 'mmm') is more practical and easier to pronounce than the consonant 'k'. Users were more frustrated when they were unable to produce the correct sound. As VJ is affected by the volume of the voice produced, when the users raised their voices, the sound 'k' was easily distorted and thus not recognized by VJ. The users reported that they felt that more extensive movement of lips was required to click using VJ than using U^3I.

Comparing the learning curves for the cardinal versus ordinal directions, it is interesting to note that the curve for U^3I is more gradual for the ordinal directions. This seems to reflect the observation that given the 4-way nature of the two input methods used, moving in a diagonal can take more getting used to than simply moving along one of the 4 directions, as the user will need to constantly change directions using the appropriate sounds.

Another point of intrigue is the fact that for the VJ, almost no learning effect was observed. This might suggest that the participants were able to get used to the VJ control very quickly and therefore plateaued, or that the learning curve is very gradual and that with longer usage time, their performance will improve further.

Comparing the two modalities, it appears that U^3I approached the performance of VJ at the end of the five day period, and suggests a need for a prolonged study to assess whether one would significantly outperform the other.

From the experiment, it can be concluded that:

- Overall, the participants' opinions improved by day for both systems (supporting H3 and highlighting the importance of longitudinal study).
- U^3I is significantly better than VJ in emulating mouse clicks (supporting H1).
- VJ was better than U^3I in various performance measures (supporting H2a).
- VJ received better user opinions than U^3I in various performance measures (indicating that there is not enough evidence to support H2b).

The results show that the participants' objective measures and subjective opinions improved longitudinally. One interesting thing to note is that there was contradiction between the ratings and comments for fatigue. Some participants stated that VJ was more tiring than U^3I as it required more lip movements. However, the quantitative ratings suggested that VJ was less tiring than U^3I.

One possible explanation was that, whilst VJ did require more extensive lip movement, there were more overshoots when controlling the cursor with U^3I, causing the users to perceive U^3I as more tiring in their ratings.

8 Conclusion

This paper presents a longitudinal study of two cursor control systems that share some characteristics: Both systems are non-speech and continuous. The observation of novice users over time through a mixed of qualitative and quantitative methods shows the change in user experience as they gain more expertise in using the systems.

The study reveals that the participants' opinions on both tools improved day-by-day. Both U^3I and VJ excelled in some aspects, but the performances of both systems became rather similar toward the end of the study period. Combining this finding with the finding from a previous study comparing VJ and speech-based cursor control system and a hand-operated joystick [10], where VJ can potentially approach the performance of a hand-operated joystick with expert users, we can argue that these two systems have the potential for being used as a standard input device (although as [10] shows, the performance is still three times slower than when a mouse is used).

There are some limitations of the study. In order to compare the user performance with standard input devices, this study should be interpolated with another study [10]. In future studies, it is important to ensure that mouse performance is captured. Secondly, only 10 users were involved in the study, over a period of 5 days (even though each user performed 96 trials per day).

A longer longitudinal study with more users would reveal more interesting findings, such as stronger evidence of performance plateauing, especially with U^3I. Finally, as this system would benefit user population with upper limb impairment the most, future studies should include this population to investigate their opinions and acceptance regarding these two systems.

Acknowledgements

We would like to thank Susumu Harada of University of Washington for providing the Vocal Joystick system, the platform for performing the target acquisition tasks, and his valuable advice on data analysis. We would also like to thank all the participants who volunteered to take part in the user evaluation.

This work has been partly supported by the Ministry of Education, Youth and Sports of the Czech Republic under the research program LC-06008 (Center for Computer Graphics).

References

1. Al-Hashimi, S.: Blowtter: A voice-controlled plotter. In: Proc HCI 2006 Engage, The 20th BCS HCI Group conference in co-operation with ACM, vol. 2, London, England (2006)
2. Allen, J.: The online reaction time test. On-line (retrieved August 2006) (2002), http://getyourwebsitehere.com/jswb/rttest01.html
3. Barra, M., Cillo, T., Santis, A.D., Petrillo, U.F., Negro, A., Scarano, V., Matlock, T., Maglio, P.P.: Personal webmelody: Customized sonification of web servers. In: Proc 2001 International Conference on Auditory Display (August 2001)
4. Bilmes, J.A., Li, X., Malkin, J., Kilanski, K., Wright, R., Kirchhoff, K., Subramanya, A., Harada, S., Landay, J.A., Dowden, P., Chizeck, H.: The Vocal Joystick: A voice-based human-computer interface for individuals with motor impairments. In: Proc Human Lang Tech Conf./Conf. on Empirical Methods in Natural Language Processing (October 2005)
5. Dai, L., Goldman, R., Sears, A., Lozier, J.: Speech-based cursor control: a study of grid-based solutions. SIGACCESS Access. Comput. 77(78), 94–101 (2004)

6. Fitts, P.M.: The information capacity of the human motor system in controlling the amplitude of movement. J. of Experimental Psychology 47(6), 381–391 (1954)
7. Franklin, K., Roberts, J.C.: Pie Chart Sonification. In: Proceedings Information Visualization, pp. 4–9. IEEE Computer Society, Los Alamitos (2003)
8. de Mauro, C., Gori, M., Maggini, M., Martinelli, E.: Easy access to graphical interfaces by voice mouse. Technical report, Universit? di Siena (2001)
9. Hämäläinen, P., Mäki-Patola, T., Pulkki, V., Airas, M.: Musical computer games played by singing. In: Proc of 7th Intl Conf on Digital Audio Effects, Naples, pp. 367–371 (2004)
10. Harada, S., Landay, J.A., Malkin, J., Li, X., Bilmes, J.A.: The vocal joystick: evaluation of voice-based cursor control techniques. In: Proc ASSETS 2006, Portland, Oregon (2006)
11. Igarashi, T., Hughes, J.F.: Voice as sound: using non-verbal voice input for interactive control. In: UIST '01. Proc 14th Annual ACM Symp on User Interface Software and Technology, New York, NY, USA, pp. 155–156. ACM Press, New York (2001)
12. Kamel, H.M., Landay, J.A.: Sketching images eyes-free: a grid-based dynamic drawing tool for the blind. In: Proc ASSETS 2002, New York, pp. 33–40 (2002)
13. Kjeldskov, J., Skov, M.B., Stage, J.: Does time heal?: a longitudinal study of usability. In: OZCHI '05: Proceedings of the 19th conference of the computer-human interaction special interest group (CHISIG), pp. 1–10, Australia (2005)
14. MacKenzie, I.S., Kauppinen, T., Silfverberg, M.: Accuracy measures for evaluating computer pointing devices. In: Proc CHI '01, pp. 9–16. ACM Press, New York (2001)
15. Manaris, B., McCauley, R., MacGyvers, V.: An intelligent interface for keyboard and mouse control - providing full access to PC functionality via speech. In: Proc 14th Intl. Florida Artificial Intelligence Research Society Conference, pp. 182–188. AAAI Press, Stanford, California (2001)
16. Mihara, Y., Shibayama, E., Takahashi, S.: The migratory cursor: accurate speech-based cursor movement by moving multiple ghost cursors using non-verbal vocalizations. In: Proc ASSETS 2005, pp. 76–83. ACM Press, New York (2005)
17. Nakano, T., Goto, M., Ogata, J., Hiraga, Y.: Voice drummer: A music notation interface of drum sounds using voice percussion input. In: Proc. of UIST 2005, pp. 49–50. ACM Press, New York (2005)
18. Sporka, A.J., Kurniawan, S.H., Slavík, P.: Accoustic control of mouse pointer. Universal Access in the Information Society 4(3), 237–245 (2006)
19. Sporka, A.J., Kurniawan, S.H., Slavík, P.: Non-speech operated emulation of keyboard. In: Clarkson, J., Langdon, P., Robinson, P. (eds.) Cambridge Workshop on Universal Access and Assistive Technology, CWUAAT 2006. Designing Accessible Technology, pp. 145–154. Springer, Heidelberg (2006)
20. Sporka, A.J., Kurniawan, S.H., Mahmud, M., Slavík, P.: Tonal control of mouse cursor (U^3I): A usability study with the elderly. In: Proc HCI International 2005, Lawrence Erlbaum Associates, Mahwah (2005)
21. Sporka, A.J., Kurniawan, S.H., Mahmud, M., Slavik, P.: Non-speech input and speech recognition for real-time control of computer games. In: The Proceedings of The Eighth International ACM SIGACCESS Conference on Computers & Accessibility, ASSETS 2006, Portland, Oregon, ACM, New York (2006)

ZWPS: A Hybrid Selection Technique for Small Target Acquisition in Pen-Based Interfaces

Jibin Yin and Xiangshi Ren

Kochi University of Technology, Kochi 782-8502, Japan
088402e@gs.kochi-tech.ac.jp, ren.xiangshi@kochi-tech.ac.jp

Abstract. In this paper a novel zoom-based technique with pressure (hereafter referred to as "ZWPS") is proposed to improve small target selection in pen-based interfaces. In this technique pressure is used as a switch mode to couple a standard pointing technique and a zoomable technique together. ZWPS allows both precise and normal selections. We conducted an experiment to examine the effectiveness of ZWPS. The experimental results indicate that ZWPS significantly enhance small target selections.

Keywords: pen-based interface, pressure, zoom-based, small target acquisition.

1 Introduction

Pen-based devices allow direct touch and data manipulation on screen with stylus pens, which has a very strong appeal to users. However, being direct between control and display, screens of pen-based devices have special limitations. First, users generally suffer from a small amount of parallax error due to the display being slightly below the touch sensitive surface; second, users' finger, hand and arm can obscure part of the screen. The limitations, to some degree, bring difficulties to target selection tasks, especially for small target selections. There are some researches that have proposed techniques to improve small target selection performance [1, 3, 4, 5, 6] in a pen-based environment. This issue was notably addressed by Sears, Shneiderman and colleagues [3, 5, 6]. Their basic technique, called Take-Off, provides a cursor above a pen-tip or the user's finger tip with a fixed offset when touching the screen to achieve precise selection.

Zoom pointing is also a typical technique for small target selection, which is currently used in many painting systems. For example, drawing a precise line from one dot (e.g., railway station) to another (e.g., a college) on a digital map requires the user to zoom in and click on one end, zoom out to find the other end, zoom in again to click on the other end, then zoom out again to look at both ends, all of which cause great inconvenience to users. Moreover, after zooming in, the user may lose information in the overview and the detailed windows. The switch between zooming in and zooming out often interrupts the user's attention. This awkward situation becomes our direct motivation to study alternatives to the current technique. We present ZWPS which integrates two techniques by using pressure as switch mode to allow both precise and normal selections.

C. Baranauskas et al. (Eds.): INTERACT 2007, LNCS 4663, Part II, pp. 503–506, 2007.

2   ZWPS Design and Implementation

We seek to find a selection technique that should satisfy the following conditions:

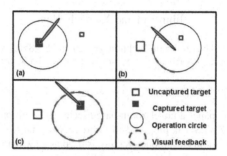

Fig. 1. A process for selecting a target using ZWPS: (a) shows the process of selecting a target of normal size in standard pointing mode. (b) and (c) illustrate the process of selecting a small target by zoom selection mode.

(1) have a zoom function to allow a small target selection; (2) Provide a flexible and seamless switch mode between zooming in and out; (3) zoom only a certain part of the display area to prevent the user from losing the information in overview.

Therefore, we present a novel technique called ZWPS to enhance small target selection. ZWPS, in essence, is a hybrid selection technique that includes two selection techniques: the standard pointing technique and the zoom technique. The standard pointing selection mode works in selecting common size targets while zoom selection mode works best when selecting small size targets.

To couple the two techniques in ZWPS a suitable switch mode is essential. The properties of pressure (easily producing discrete controlled states) make it competent to seamlessly switch modes in ZWPS. To determine a proper switch threshold, a pilot experiment with 10 subjects was performed. The task was to draw freehand strokes (arbitrary curves and straight lines), basic geometrical graphs (such as rectangles and circles) and a mixed set of Roman, Japanese, and Chinese (kanji) characters and signatures on a blank space in a natural manner. Pen-tip pressure was recorded in a 17ms sampling periods. Ninety-five percent of the force samples fell within the 210 to 810 units range. The results showed that pressure levels of more than 810 units were seldom used in a natural manner. Therefore, in ZWPS the threshold value is set at 970 units.

An operation circle (see Figure 1) is also defined to specify a zoomed area. Targets that are completely enclosed by the circle can be zoomed in by imposing heavy pressure, enough to surpass the switch threshold. By conducting a pilot experiment, the diameter of the operational circle was set at 24mm. When more than one target is enclosed by the operation circle, they are zoomed in or out together simultaneously. The parts that are beyond its border can be squeezed into its edge.

An arc with a dotted red line, which is attached on the border of the operational circle, is employed as visual feedback to indicate the current pressure state. When the arc, augmented by pressure from a pen, increases to a complete circle (surpassing the threshold) it means that the zoom technique is activated, Conversely, ZWPS still maintains the standard pointing technique, when effective pressure is not applied.

As illustrated in Figure 1 when selecting a target of normal or big size, the user, imposing light pressure on a pen-tip, taps the target directly to select it in the standard selection mode (Figure 1a). When selecting a very small target the target is first enclosed (Figure 1b) by the operational circle, and then the zoom selection mode is activated by heavy pressure to enlarge the target. The pen-tip slides into the zoomed target to highlight it (Figure 1c). When the pen is lifted from the screen, the target is selected and it recovers to its original size. Note that ZWPS only zooms in the operation circle area around the cursor, not the whole area in the view window, which enables the user to avoid losing the information in overview, even when it is in zoomed status.

3 Experiment

We compare the performance of ZWPS to other techniques for selecting small targets. We chose Take-off, a promising technique, as the baseline, because it is a very common baseline in many other evaluations of techniques for small-target selection reported to date [3, 5, 6].

Twelve subjects (11 male and 1 female) all with right-handed and previous experience using computers were tested for the experiment. The average age was 24.9 years.

3.1 Procedure

The experimental task was simple reciprocal target pointing. Two square targets of width W, separated by distance D were presented on the screen. The goal target was colored red and underlined, which alternated between the two. Participants were instructed to select the red target as quickly and, more importantly, as accurately as possible. When a desired target was selected correctly a beep sound played.

The design of the experiment was as follows: crossed Technique (T) x Width (W) x Distance (D). Since the focus of this study is precision pointing, target width W was set at 1, 4 and 8 pixels and distance D was set at 100, 250, 750. For each of the two techniques, 9 combinations (=3 target widths x 3 distances) appeared in random order. Each subject had a total of 63 attempts (7 blocks x 3 widths x 3 distances).

3.2 Results

A repeated measures analysis of variance showed that there was a significant difference between Take-off and ZWPS in selection time, $F(1,47)=39.9$, $p<.001$. Target size had a significant impact on mean selection time. There were also interaction effects between Techniques x Target size for selection time, $F(2,47)=12.5$, $p<.001$. ZWPS took less time than Take-off for 1, 4 and 8 pixels. The difference between them became more significant as targets became smaller. The results indicted that ZWPS delivered more benefits for small-target selections.

In particular, for 1 pixel or 2 pixel targets, Take-off was dramatically more error prone than ZWPS. For the large target (8 pixels), Take-off was still higher than ZWPS in error rate.

Subjects gave ZWPS a significantly higher rating than Take-off. ZWPS enables the user to easily select targets by zooming them, especially for very small (pixel level) targets.

4 Discussion

ZWPS utilizes pressure as a switch mode to couple two selection techniques (a standard pointing technique and a zoom technique) to enable it to be competent for both normal and precise selections. An experiment was conducted comparing it with Take-off, a current promising technique. Experimental results indicate that ZWPS can bring significant advantages to small target selection performances. In fitts' law [2] study ZWPS roughly fits Fitts' law with low $R^2 = 0.8$. Its reason is that when using ZWPS to select small targets the selection process is more complex than a typical single pointing task, which requires users to perform two steps, i.e., enlarge the target and select the goal target. In ZWPS pressure plays a successful state switch role, which suggests that pressure should be a good alternative to mode switch.

References

1. Albinsson, P.-A., Zhai, S.: High Precision Touch Screen Interaction. In: Proc. CHI 2003, pp. 105–112 (2003)
2. Fitts, P.M.: The information capacity of human motor system in controlling the amplitude of movement. Journal of Experimental Psychology 47, 381–391 (1954)
3. Potter, R.L., Weldon, L.J., Shneiderman, B.: Improving the accuracy of touch screens: an experimental evaluation of three strategies. In: Proc. CHI'88, pp. 27–32 (1988)
4. Ren, X., Moriya, S.: Improving selection performance on pen-based system: A study of pen-based interaction for selection tasks. ACM Trans. Computer-Human Interaction 7(3), 384–416 (2000)
5. Sears, A., Shneiderman, B.: High Precision Touchscreens: Design Strategies and Comparison with a Mouse. International Journal of Man-Machine Studies 43(4), 593–613 (1991)
6. Shneiderman, B.: Touch screens now offer compelling uses. IEEE Software 8(2), 93–94 (1991)

Investigation to Line-Based Techniques for Multi-target Selection

Jibin Yin and Xiangshi Ren

Kochi University of Technology, Kochi 782-8502, Japan
088402e@gs.kochi-tech.ac.jp, ren.xiangshi@kochi-tech.ac.jp

Abstract. This paper presents three selection techniques (called Rubber-ling-sweep, Line-string and Coupling-with-pressure) to enhance multi-target acquisition in GUIs and to overcome the drawback of the standard rubber-band box technique, i.e., the limitation of not being able to select an irregular layout of targets. Rubber-line-sweep utilizes a rubber-band line to select targets by "sweeping" them. Line-string employs a line stroke to "string" targets together and select them. Coupling-with-pressure couples these two techniques with pressure as a switch mode. Experiments were conducted to compare these techniques with the standard Rubber-band box, which used a two-dimensional grid which could include varied target sizes, distances and target layouts, and which is applied by using pens as input devices. Experimental results indicate that Rubber-line-sweep, Line-string and Coupling-with-pressure show significant advantages for targets with irregular layouts. Taking performance and subjective ratings together, Coupling-with-pressure outperforms the other three techniques.

Keywords: multi-target selection, pen-based interface, pressure.

1 Introduction

In user graphic interface (GUIs), fundamental computing operations commonly include single-selection tasks and multiple-selection tasks. Single target selection is usually accomplished by tapping; multiple target selection is usually accomplished using the rubber-band box. The rubber-band box works like this: the rectangular selection region is specified by extending the diagonal of the rubber band box by dragging; the targets interacted by the rectangular selection region are highlighted for selection. An obvious drawback of the rubber-band box is that it is difficult to select the multiple targets that are not included in the rectangular area (see Figure 1c). Conversely, it is impossible to exclude unwanted targets form the rectangular area without further clicks, taps or other maneuvers. So, when selecting multiple targets that are arranged irregularly, the user has to implement a variety of selection tasks such as using tapping the "Ctrl" key and the rubber-band box together. In some sense the rubber-band box limits the user's performance in multiple target selections. Thus we present three novel line-based techniques (Rubber-Line-Sweep, Line-String and Coupling-With-Pressure) to enhance multi-target acquisition. We conducted experiments to compare Rubber-Line-Sweep, Line-String, Coupling-With-Pressure

C. Baranauskas et al. (Eds.): INTERACT 2007, LNCS 4663, Part II, pp. 507–510, 2007.

and Rubber-band box by pen. In the experiments the selection task was the conjunctive selection of multiple targets (rectangles) in two-dimensional grids varied in terms of the sizes of the targets and layout complexity of targets.

2   Multi-target Selection Techniques Design

To overcome the shortcomings of the Rubber band box method we employ rubber-band lines or line strokes to select multi-targets instead of the rubber-band rectangle (see Figure 1). (1) Rubber-Line-Sweep: it utilizes rubber-band lines to select targets. Rubber-band lines are very common computer graphic elements, the length and direction of which can be easily adjusted. When the user wants to perform multi-target selection using the Rubber-Line-Sweep he/she first lands the pen-tip on the screen, then moves it to extend a rubber-band line. Targets swept by the rubber-band line are selected. Rubber-Line-Sweep uses "sweep" as the interaction manner of selection. In essence Rubber-Line-Sweep utilizes a rubber-band line to specify a selection area by "sweeping" so it can define irregularly shaped selection areas. To abort selection of a highlighted target the target is swept again by a rubber-band line (see Figure 1a). (2) Line-String: Line-String exploits a line stroke to select targets by stringing them together (see Figure 1b). To abort a highlighted target a line stroke is drawn through the target and the highlighted state is aborted. (3) Coupling-With-Pressure: Rubber-line-sweep and Line-string have their own special operational characteristics and advantages. It is even possible to combine the two techniques in special situations, e.g. when they are applied to a pen-based device they can be combined by using pressure as the switch mode between the two techniques, i.e. at light pressure one mode is active while at heavy pressure the other is active. This technique is called Coupling-with-pressure. The threshold value is crucial for achieving a free and stable switch between techniques. If the threshold is very low it is quite likely that the user will unintentionally pass the threshold and change from the currently desired method. Therefore, it should be set to a high value which would require a deliberate change in pressure to switch the operational state. To determine a

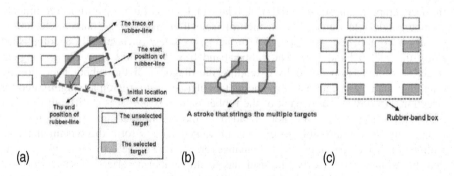

Fig. 1. Selection processes of Rubber-Line-Sweep, Line-String and Rubber-band box: (a) Rubber-Line-Sweep: dragging cursor extends a rubber-band line which is used to sweep targets to select them; (b) Line-String: drawing a stroke to string targets to select them.(c) an irregular layout of targets can not be completely included by a rectangle.

proper switch threshold a pilot experiment with 10 subjects was performed. The task was to draw freehand strokes (arbitrary curves and straight lines), basic geometrical graphs (such as rectangles and circles) and a mixed set of Roman, Japanese, and Chinese characters (kanji) and signatures on a blank space in a natural manner. Pen-tip pressure was recorded in a 17ms sampling periods. Ninety-five percent of the force samples fell within the 210 to 810 units range. The results showed that the pressure level of more than 810 units was seldom used in a natural manner. Therefore, in Coupling-with-pressure the threshold value is set at 970 units. Visual feedback which denotes the current pressure value is added to Coupling with pressure. Ramos et al.' study [6] shows that a good visual feedback is needed for pressure-based UI design. Inspired by the pressure cursor design by Ramos and Balakrishnan [5], in Coupling-with-pressure, pressure was displayed   in a wedge-shaped graphical widget. The transparent green area indicates the current pressure value. The top border represents the switch threshold. When pressure is beyond the top border the technique is changed from Rubber-line-sweep (default status) to Line-string.

3 Experiment

We explored the performance efficiency of the four multi-target selection techniques in different circumstances. The complexity of the layout of the targets and the number of targets were varied.

Twelve volunteers (10 male and 2 female) participated in Experiment. The average age was 24.3 years (ranging from 21 to 31). All were right-handed. The hardware used in Experiment was a Wacom DIT-520 interactive LCD graphics display tablet with a wireless stylus that has a pressure sensitive isometric tip, which reports 512 levels of pressure and has a binary button on its barrel.

3.1 Procedure

Conjunctive multi-target selection tasks are prescribed in Experiment. For each trial, thirty-six squares were shown on a 6 x 6 grid. Target squares were green in color, and the other (non-target) squares were white with a blue frame. With respect to the number of targets in a task, there are three types of tasks: four target tasks, nine-target tasks and sixteen target tasks. With reference to target layout, we provided three complexity degrees for the tasks: low complexity tasks, medium complexity tasks and high complexity tasks, which were determined by the subjects in pilot study. Thirty-six different target layouts were used in Experiment.

3.2 Results

For Low and Median complexity layout of targets repeated measures analysis of variance showed no significant difference in selection time between the four selection methods. For High complexity layout there was a significant difference in selection time between the four selection methods, $F(3,43)=6.3$, $p<.01$. The post hoc Tukey HSD test showed that Rubber-lines weep, line-string and Coupling-with-pressure were all faster than Rubber-band box ($p<.05$). There were no other significant differences across the selection methods. Coupling-with-pressure was the fastest method followed in older by Line-string, Rubber-line-sweep and Rubber-band box. No significant difference was found between the four selection methods in error rate. Subjects gave Coupling-with-pressure the highest rating followed in order by Line-string, Rubber-line-sweep and Rubber-band box. Some subjects mentioned that Coupling-with-pressure was more flexible and it enabled the user to choose a proper method (between Rubber-line-sweep and Line-string) depending on the conditions of the selection tasks at any particular time.

4 Discussion

In this study we present three techniques to enhance multi-target selection, especially for irregular layouts of targets. Experiment results suggest that Rubber-line-sweep, Line-string, and Coupling-with-pressure are all faster than Rubber-band box for complex layouts of targets. They are all comparable to Rubber-band box for simple and median layouts of targets. Overall, Coupling-with-pressure is the fastest technique and the most preferred by subjects. Pressure, as an additional input parameter, is seldom explored and applied into UI designs. Coupling-with pressure offers a promising instance of pressure-based applications. We believe that the results of our work uncovered several basic principles that are applicable directly toward the design of interaction techniques for multi-target acquisition, particularly in pen-based interfaces.

References

1. Accot, J., Zhai, S.: More than dotting the i's - foundations for crossing-based interfaces. In: Proc. of CHI'04, pp. 73–80 (2004)
2. Chipman, S.F.: Complexity and structure in visual patterns. Journal of Experimental Psychology: General 106(3), 269–301 (1977)
3. Miller, R., Myers, B.: Multiple Selections in Smart Text Editing. In: Proc. of IUI'02, pp. 103–110 (2002)
4. Mizobuchi, S., Yasumura, M.: Tapping vs. Circling Selections on Pen-based Devices: Evidence for Different Performance-Shaping Factors. In: Proc. of CHI'04, pp. 607–614 (2004)
5. Ramos, G., Balakrishnan, R.: Zliding: Fluid Zooming and Sliding for High Precision Parameter Manipulation. In: Proc. UIST'05, pp. 143–152 (2005)
6. Ramos, G., Boulos, M., Balakrishnan.: Pressure Widgets. In: Proc. CHI'04, pp. 487–494 (2004)

Usability Cost-Benefit Analysis:
How Usability Became a Curse Word?

Mikko Rajanen and Netta Iivari

Department of Information Processing Science, University of Oulu, P.O. BOX 3000, 90014
Oulu, Finland
mikko.rajanen@oulu.fi, netta.iivari@oulu.fi

Abstract. Usability is an important quality characteristic of software (SW) products and systems. Usability cost-benefit analysis models outline the potential benefits and costs of usability. This paper contrasts usability cost-benefit analysis literature with an empirical case in industrial setting, in which usability cost-benefit considerations (along with other usability activities) resulted in usability becoming a curse word. An interpretive case study was carried out in a SW development organization. Empirical analysis reveals that clearly divergent meanings and motives were attached to usability and its cost-benefit analysis in the organization. Increased sales and reduced development costs were strongly emphasized as benefits of better usability. However, very surprising meanings were attached to them both. Furthermore, the increased development costs associated with better usability were the main failure factor of the whole usability improvement effort. Implications both for theory and practice are discussed.

1 Introduction

This paper contrasts usability cost-benefit analysis literature with an empirical case in industrial setting, in which usability cost-benefit considerations (along with other usability activities) resulted in usability becoming a curse word. An interpretive case study [20] has been carried out in a software (SW) development organization. Empirical analysis reveals that clearly divergent meanings and motives have been attached to usability and its cost-benefit analysis in the organization.

Usability is defined as one of the main SW product and system quality attributes in the international standard ISO 9126. Usability refers to the capability of the product to be understood by, learned, used by and attractive to the user, when used under specified conditions [18]. Another widely referred to definition of usability is in standard ISO 9241-11, where usability is defined as: "the extent to which a product can be used by specified users to achieve specified goals with effectiveness, efficiency and satisfaction in a specified context of use" (see e.g. in [17]).

Usability has many potential benefits for development organizations, such as increased productivity and customer satisfaction. But even today there are quite few product development organizations reportedly having incorporated usability activities in their product development process. Bringing usability activities into the product development life cycle has been a challenge since the beginning of usability activities over fifty years ago [25]. One reason for this is that the benefits of better usability are

C. Baranauskas et al. (Eds.): INTERACT 2007, LNCS 4663, Part II, pp. 511–524, 2007.

not easily identified or calculated. Usability engineering has been competing for resources against other project groups, who do have objective cost-benefit data available for management review [19].

In the literature offering recommendations on how to introduce 'usability' into the development organizations, however, business perspective is emphasized. It is argued that one should take care that usability contributes to the business success of the development organizations [7], [13], [21], [22], [27]. Generally, usability is postulated as an important competitive edge in maturing SW markets [15], [24], [28]. However, it is also emphasized that one should ascertain that usability makes sense from the business perspective and is related to the achievement of key business goals [7], [13]. It is especially important to show the benefits achieved [21], [22], [27]. However, consideration of cost-benefit tradeoffs is also recommended [22], [24], [31]. Resources should be well planned and budgeted [3], [22], [24] and one should assure that usability does not increase development costs and time [7], [24].

We have carried out a detailed analysis of literature offering advice on usability cost-benefit analysis. Based on the literature review, an analytical framework for the empirical analysis has been developed and utilized in making sense of the empirical data derived from one case organization, into which usability cost-benefit analysis was introduced along with other usability activities. Existing literature made us also sensitive to the fact that very divergent meanings can be attached to usability in practice, the studies showing that it has been used only as a buzzword or as mere slogan without any proper understanding of it [1], [9], [16], [30]. Due to the assumed importance of the usability cost-benefit analysis, but also keeping in mind the risk that this term and its analyses may be used and interpreted in a multitude of different (and even conflicting) ways, this case study examines the process of meanings negotiation related to usability and its cost-benefit analysis in one case organization.

The paper is organized as follows. The next section reviews literature on usability cost-benefit analysis as a theoretical basis of our empirical analysis. The third section presents the case involved in this study and the procedures of data gathering and analysis. The following section outlines the results of our empirical examination. The final section summarizes and discloses the central themes and observations of the paper, outlines the limitations of this study, and suggests paths for future work.

2 Usability Cost-Benefit Analysis

There are surprisingly few published models for analyzing the costs and benefits of usability in development organizations. Most of the usability cost-benefit models analyzed in this paper were selected from the book Cost-Justifying Usability, by Bias and Mayhew [5]. This book was published in 1994, but it is still the best source of different usability cost-benefit models. The second edition of the book was published 2005, but it did not change the usability cost-benefit models [6]. The analyzed models from Cost-Justifying Usability were selected into this report, because they succeed in representing the variety of different views for usability cost-benefit analysis. In addition, Donahue's [11] usability cost-benefit article was included, since it is the latest published article on analyzing usability costs and benefits. Furthermore, Bevan [4] has published a usability cost-benefit analysis model in TRUMP-report. The model was included also for this analysis, because it has a slightly different viewpoint related to different business benefits of usability. The model estimates the potential usability benefits in four different product life cycles, while the other analyzed models do not deal as clearly with usability benefits in relation to the product life cycles.

There are many published models for calculating usability benefits, and as many ways of identifying the benefits. A business benefit is a positive return that the development organization expects to obtain as a result of an investment. There has been some discussion in publications about the potential business benefits of usability, but most of them are focused on specific case studies of usability benefits, or on the overall aspects of usability cost-benefit analysis [26].

The costs of better usability, on the other hand, can be categorized into three groups: *one-time costs*, *recurring costs* and *redesign costs*. One-time costs or initial costs cover, for example, the costs of establishing a laboratory for usability testing. Therefore, the cost is a one-time investment for usability. Recurring costs are, for example, the salary costs of the usability professionals employed in the usability testing laboratory. Therefore, the recurring costs are needed to actually do the usability activities. Redesign costs cover the costs of redesigning the prototypes based, for example, on the usability test results. Therefore, redesign costs apply only when prototypes are built and tested and there is an identified need for the redesign. These costs usually affect the product development project directly, whereas the one-time costs and recurring costs affect usually the usability team.

Next, we discuss in more detail these usability costs and benefits in relation to the published usability cost-benefit models.

2.1 Existing Usability Cost-Benefit Analysis Models

Ehrlich and Rohn [12] analyze the potential benefits of better usability from the viewpoint of vendor company, corporate customer and end user. They state that by incorporating usability activities into product development project both the company itself and its customers gain benefits from certain areas. When compared to other usability cost-benefit models analyzed in this paper, Ehrlich and Rohn present the most comprehensive discussion about different aspects of usability cost-benefits.

Ehrlich and Rohn do not clearly present an overall formula for calculating the value of usability benefits. However, according to them, the vendor company can identify benefits from three areas:

1. Increased sales
2. Reduced support costs
3. Reduced development costs

In some cases the link between better usability and increased sales can be found, but usually it can be difficult to relate the impact of better usability directly to increased sales. One way to identify the impact of usability to sales is to analyze how important role does usability have in buying decision. The cost of product support can be surprisingly high, if there is a usability problem in important product feature and the product has lots of users. Better usability has direct impact to the need of product support and, therefore, great savings can be made through less need for support. By focusing on better product usability and using usability techniques, the vendor company can cut development time and costs.

The corporate customer can expect benefits, when more usable product reduces time the end users need training. In addition to official training, there are also hidden costs of peer-support. End users often seek help from their expert colleagues, who therefore suffer in productivity. It is estimated that this kind of hidden support cost for every PC is between $6.000 and $15.000 every year [8]. End users are the final recipients of more usable product. According to Ehrlich and Rohn, increased usability can result in higher productivity, reduced learning time and greater work satisfaction for the end users. The end-users can benefit from higher productivity, when the most frequent tasks take less time.

According to Ehrlich & Rohn, the costs of usability can be divided into initial costs and sustaining costs. They identify one-time costs and provide some example calculations of one-time costs of usability. Ehrlich & Rohn also identify and provide some example calculations and further discussion of recurring costs.

Bevan [4] estimates the potential benefits of better usability to the organization during development, sales, use and support. The vendor can gain benefits in development, sales and support. Customer can benefit in use and support. When the system is developed for in-house use, the organization can identify benefits in development, use and support. In each category, there are a number of possible individual benefits where savings or increased revenue can be identified. The total amount of benefits from better usability can be calculated by adding all identified individual benefits together. Bevan discusses mainly usability benefits through increased sales, less need for training and increased productivity. Benefits through decreased development time are identified, but they are not discussed in detail.

Bevan does not identify one-time costs of better usability at all. Bevan identifies the recurring costs of usability, but does not provide example calculations or further discussion about calculating the recurring costs.

Karat [19] is approaching the usability benefits through cost-benefit calculation of human factors work. This viewpoint is different from the other analyzed usability cost-benefit models. There are some examples of identified potential benefits. The benefits are identified as:

1. Increased sales
2. Increased user productivity
3. Decreased personnel cost through smaller staff turnover

The development organization can gain benefits when better usability gives competitive edge and therefore increases product sales. Customer organization can gain benefits when end user productivity is increased through reduced task time and when better usability reduces staff turnover. Karat describes a usability cost-benefit analysis of three steps. In the first step, all expected costs and benefits are identified and quantified. In the second step, the costs and benefits are categorized as tangible and intangible. The intangible costs and benefits are not easily measured, so they are moved into a separate list. The third step is to determine financial value for all tangible costs and benefits. Karat also links the usability cost-benefit analysis into business cases.

Business cases provide an objective and explicit basis for making organizational investment decisions [19].

Karat identifies one-time costs, recurring costs and prototype redesign cost of usability, but he does not provide further documentation or example calculations.

Mayhew and Mantei [23] argue that cost-benefit analysis of usability is best made by focusing the attention on the benefits that are of most interest to the audience of the analysis. The relevant benefit categories for the target audience are then selected and benefits are estimated. Examples of relevant benefit categories are given for vendor company and internal development organization. Vendor company can benefit from:

1. Increased sales
2. Decreased customer support
3. Making fewer changes in late design life cycle
4. Reduced cost of providing training

The benefits for internal development organization can be estimated from categories of increased user productivity, decreased user errors, decreased training costs, making fewer changes in late design life cycle and decreased user support. To estimate each benefit, a unit of measurement is chosen for the benefit. Then an assumption is made concerning the magnitude of the benefit for each unit of measurement. The number of units then multiplies estimated benefit per unit.

According to Mayhew & Mantei the calculation of the costs of better usability is fairly straightforward, if the necessary usability tasks are identified. They identify one-time costs and provide some example calculations of one-time costs. Mayhew & Mantei also identify and provide some example calculations and further discussion of the recurring costs of usability. They also identify the prototype related redesign costs and provide some example calculations of this cost factor, but there is no further documentation about calculating the redesign costs.

Donahue's [11] usability cost-benefit analysis model is based on the model of Mayhew & Mantei. In this model, the costs and benefits of better usability are analyzed through costs for development organization and benefits for customer organization. According to Donahue, the most important aspect of usability cost-benefit analysis is calculating the savings in the development costs.

Donahue identifies one-time costs and provides some example calculations of one-time costs of usability. He also identifies recurring costs, but does not provide example calculations or further discussion about calculating the recurring costs.

2.2 Analytic Framework for Empirical Analysis

Table 1 summarizes the costs and benefits of usability outlined by the usability cost-benefit analysis models presented above. Our focus in the empirical analysis will be on the development context, because the empirical data has been gathered solely from that context. However, also the benefits to be achieved through better usability in the use context (including both the customers making the buying decisions and the end users) are summarized in the table 1. This is because we assumed that in the development context, one should acknowledge the benefits achievable in the use context, while motivating the usability activities in the development context.

Table 1. Analytic framework for empirical analysis of usability costs and benefits

	Development context	Use context
Benefits	Increased sales	Reduced training time
	Reduced support costs	Increased productivity
	Reduced development costs	Increased (customer, user) satisfaction
	Reduced training costs	
		Reduced staff turn over
Costs	One-time costs	-
	Recurring costs	
	Redesign costs	

In addition, we acknowledge that the benefits can be separated into tangible and intangible benefits [19]. However, advice for the cost-benefit analysis is offered only related to the tangible benefits. Furthermore, a noteworthy observation is that the models mostly assume that the benefits should and can be quantifiable. In all, our empirical analysis will be based on the assumed usability costs and benefits listed in table 1, acknowledging also the distinctions between tangible/intangible and quantifiable/non-quantifiable benefits mentioned above.

3   Research Method

This is an interpretive case study on 'usability cost-benefit analysis' in a SW development organization. Generally, in interpretive case studies the goal is to understand and to make sense of the world, not to explain in the predictive sense. In the focus are the meanings attached to the phenomenon studied. The researchers try to capture the native's point of view, to produce 'thick descriptions', and to gain thorough understandings of particular cases. Theories are used only as sensitizing devices. [10], [20].

The case organization involved in this study is a small-to-medium sized SW development company developing large scale business-to-business information systems (IS) and SW intensive products targeted at international markets. The customer organizations have their own customers, who are an important end user group of the company's products. In addition, inside the customer organization, there are different kinds of end users, who mostly are different persons than the ones who make the buying decisions. Related to the most of the company's products, the end users do not have technical background nor much training related to the use of the products.

Access to the case organization was gained through a research project that aimed at introducing usability activities into SW development organizations. The case organization participated in the research project for two years. Prior to that, the organization had very limited background in usability activities. The only activities that had been carried out in the organization were few usability tests and heuristic evaluations carried out as student work. In the company, an in-house improvement project 'Usability' was launched. The improvement work was initiated by a process assessment, in which the current state of the usability activities in the organization was evaluated. Afterwards, many different kinds of usability activities were experimented with in the organization, including customer visits, usability requirements definition workshops, paper prototyping, usability testing and the development of a user interface (UI) style guide. Usability cost-benefit analysis was discussed in several meetings, but no formal cost-benefit analysis was carried out.

The research material was gathered during two year's time. The material was collected while conducting the process assessment in the organization, and while supporting the Usability project. The process assessment consisted of interviews of 20 people working in different units of the organization. The assessment produced a large amount of research material, including assessment reports, interview transcripts and field notes kept by the researchers. In addition, the researchers had regularly meetings with the Usability project team and with the personnel of certain functional units of the organization. Memos from the meetings and all e-mail correspondence with the personnel have been saved for the purposes of the research. The research team also continued keeping field notes after all joint events. Furthermore, the key personnel of the Usability project were interviewed several times during the project.

Regarding data analysis, we utilized the analytic framework developed for empirical analysis (see section 2.2) as a sensitizing device. We searched for meanings attached usability and its cost-benefit analysis in the research material focusing especially on meanings attached to the usability costs and benefits - both from the viewpoint of the development and the use context – expressed in the case organization.

4 Empirical Findings

In this section we describe our empirical findings related to meanings attached to the usability costs and benefits expressed by the personnel of the case organization. The section reveals that regarding usability benefits, increased sales and reduced development costs were strongly emphasized, but also that very surprising meanings were attached to them both. Reduced training and support costs, on the other hand, were only mentioned. From the viewpoint of the use context, increased customer satisfaction was acknowledged. However, regarding usability costs, the costs associated with usability during the development were the main failure factor of the whole usability improvement effort. Next these issues will be discussed in more detail.

4.1 Usability Benefits as Increased Sales and Decreased Development Costs

Increase in sales, achievable through usability, was a very important motivating factor for the company to participate in the research project:

"The company is expecting some concrete advantages (from the improvement effort) to appear. (...) The product should be more usable, and there should appear clear savings in money and increase in sales." (Interview, usability specialist)

A noteworthy observation is that 'concrete advantages' and 'clear savings in money and increase in sales' were highlighted as fast as after one years joint effort.

'Increased sales' was assumed to be achieved through using usability as a tool to convince the customer in sales and marketing:

"ISO standard [17] aroused unexpected enthusiasm. Ed (a project manager) figures out appropriate slogans (dealing with usability) and t-shirts (with the slogans) for the company. He was delighted of the possibility to slash the demands of customers with the help of this authoritative standard. It is a good tool in the sales and marketing." (Field notes)

"Eric (a development manager) noticed that if the company can appeal to the standard [17] and affirm the customer that the usability capability of the organization is on a high level, the company could prove that the customer is the one who is wrong. (…) "We design our products according to the principles of this standard, so we are the ones who are right"." (Field notes)

"Customers do not know what is good for them. The company has to convince the customers that the company knows better. One way to do that is to appeal to the fact that the company participates in the university project dealing with usability issues. This might give authority to the company in relation to the customer. "(Field notes)

The marketing was eagerly expecting that their: "marketing demos with high usability will sell themselves and conquer the world" (Field notes). Improvement of the image of the company was emphasized: "Improvement of our company's image is one of the main reasons why we participate in this project" (Interview, usability specialist). Previously, the company had also acquired a quality system that was promoted in the sales and marketing, even though the quality system was not actually implemented in the development (Field notes). Therefore, there seems even to be a history of this type of 'convincing of the customer'. In all, one can conclude that usability was seen by the management as a tool for improving the image of the company and as a tool for controlling the demands made by the customers.

The reduced support and training costs were only mentioned in the company. The main functions for the customer support were "to hold the hand of the customers so that they feel better" and to "act as a bug report filter between customers and development team" (Field notes). Usability benefits were not assumed to realize significantly in the customer support. The possible benefits of better usability through reduced training costs was not seen as a very important factor either, since the company wanted to train only a limited number of contact persons, who, in turn, trained some of the end user groups whatever way they wanted to do that (Field notes).

The reduced development costs, on the other hand, were a significant selling point of usability improvement inside the organization. As already has been highlighted, the company clearly stated that they needed usability for keeping the customers away from the development process:

"Eric (a development manager) told me the basic reasons why we would participate. We need to be more convincing in the eyes of the customer. That way we could dictate some things, for example UI issues. The project would offer facts which could enable us to do that." (Interview, usability specialist)

The project managers were longing for a weapon against customers:

"Usability will be an advertising gimmick and sales argument. A powerful weapon against the customers, shortening the development time and a source of authority that allows us to write the specs as we see best – and the best way is the old way like we have always done these things." (Field notes).

"According to Ed (a project manager) usability is a nice slogan in the marketing and helpful when too demanding customer must be tamed. Usability is still not everything. Ed says that they really do not need any more new wishes or opinions from the users. Too much user-centered design and user involvement with several differing users' voices does not sound very inspiring." (Field notes)

The above citation reveals that the reduced development costs were associated with 'keeping the customer out of the development' instead of 'getting the requirements right and for that reason getting rid of late changes' that typically has been outlined as the factor reducing the development costs. This can be connected to the company's use of specification documents to make the customer to 'say yes':

"Susan (a developer) tests the system. She has noticed some usability problems during the tests and communicated them to the development. In the tests one is not supposed to evaluate usability. And noticed usability problems may still be ignored, if the system functions the way described in the specification. The customer has already said yes." (Field notes)

Therefore, in this company the goal is to make the customer to sign the specification document, after which the customers should not be involved with the development at all. The customers are expected to pay for each 'late change' separately after signing the specification document.

The possible benefits of better usability for the use context were not discussed much in the case organization. Generally speaking, the management, sales and development were not very interested in the benefits of better usability to the customer and the end users, but instead they maintained that "the system should look very nice and usable for the paying customer" (Field notes). In addition, "if the interests of end users and customer are conflicting, the customer wins" (Field notes).

Increased customer satisfaction was mentioned as a potential benefit of usability. Customer satisfaction had also been followed up, but not systematically. Related to the efforts of following up customer satisfaction, however, it was required that "increased customer satisfaction should have a positive effect on company's profit" (Field notes). This observation may be related to the company's noteworthy hurry to gain also clear financial indications of the benefits of usability, mentioned earlier.

4.2 Usability Costs as Increased Development Costs

A big problem in the case organization was that the developers questioned the practicality of usability activities. For instance Rick, a developer manager, continuously questioned the usefulness of the usability activities:

"Rick suspects whether the specification produced by the UI team through paper prototyping is finished. He doubts whether the exceptions and all the requirements are taken into account. He supposes that the specification is yet not completed." (Field notes)

"Rick again suspects the suitability of user-centered design. Last time he raised doubts about whether the requirement specifications (produced by a UI team) are complete: have all exceptions and requirements been taken into account? Now he argues that paper prototyping seems to have too many loops and users; when can you stop?" (Field notes)

In this company, "staying on the schedule" was considered as the main issue in the development project. "It would be good, if the development time was shortened through usability activities, but by no means can the usability work hinder the development work and delay the schedule." (Field notes)

The developers and their managers suspected that the usability activities increase the development time instead of reducing it. In addition, they viewed usability activities, altogether, as useless:

"Of the cooperation Pete (a developer) mentions that as a result something concrete and visible needs to appear. Usability activities have not resulted in that so far." (Field notes)

Financial reasons eventually led the organization to even abandon usability improvement altogether:

"When we were making the budget for this year, the question was: why spend resources on this (usability)? It costs money when people participate in this; they spend time on that. What can you get out of this? (...) This type of questioning exists and it is good, because it all comes down to money and resources. We have limited resources and must have clear arguments." (Interview, development manager)

"When compared to the costs one can raise a question that what has been received? The company has spent much more money on UI design than what was planned. (...) Eric (a development manager) says the company has moved backwards: in the beginning this (usability improvement effort) was a big thing, but now the situation is that soon nothing is done. Eric asks Rick (a development manager): has usability become a curse word?" (Field notes)

"According to Eric, Rick has decided that no user-centered design activities will be carried out in the new product development project. (...) Due to the bad reputation it currently has, the term usability will not be mentioned for a while" (Field notes)

Therefore, the costs of usability (in the sense of developers' perception of increased development costs, even though UI design costs would have realized in any case) seem to have resulted in usability becoming a curse word. Especially the recurring usability costs and the redesign costs that realized during the paper prototyping seem to have had such a serious effect on the whole usability improvement effort.

It can be argued that by introducing the concept of usability cost-benefit analysis, the costs of usability were made to appear very clearly, but the possible benefits remained too vague to really have an effect. The usability activities appeared as too costly and time consuming to the management, even though the actual UI design and redesign tasks, time and costs would have realized to a certain extent in any case (since the company's products and systems all have a UI).

The benefits of better usability were not given enough time to become visible, because the usability improvement effort was halted so quickly. The promises of future benefits through better usability were not enough to convince the management to continue the usability activities in the case organization.

5 Concluding Discussion

This paper contrasted usability cost-benefit analysis literature with an empirical case in industrial setting, in which usability cost-benefit considerations (along with other

Table 2. Empirical results in relation to the analytical framework on usability cost-benefits

Usability Cost-Benefits	Empirical findings
Benefits for the development context	- Increased sales through use of usability as a tool in sales and marketing, as a tool for convincing the customer, resulting in marketing demos that sell themselves and conquer the world
	- Reduced development costs through usability keeping the customers out of the development
Benefits for the use context **Costs for the development context**	- Increased customer satisfaction that, however, needs to have a positive, visible effect on company's profit - Increased (recurring and redesign related) development costs (actually UI design costs that would have realized in any case), usability activities condemned as ineffective, labor intensive and time consuming

usability activities) resulted in usability becoming a curse word. Table 2 summarizes our empirical results in relation to the analytical framework that was developed based on our literature review on usability cost-benefit analysis models (see table 1).

In all, our empirical analysis revealed that divergent meanings and motives were attached to usability and its cost-benefit analysis in the case organization. Increased sales and reduced development costs were strongly emphasized as benefits of better usability. However, very surprising meanings were attached to them both. Reduced training and support costs, on the other hand, were only mentioned. From the viewpoint of the use context, increased customer satisfaction was acknowledged. However, the increased development costs associated with better usability were the main failure factor of the whole usability improvement effort.

Next we discuss the implications of the empirical results in relation to the existing usability cost-benefit analysis literature. First of all, we emphasize that usability cost-benefit analysis models need to recognize more clearly that it will take time that the usability benefits are realized, and the costs will be evident much earlier. In all, time is an important issue for the development projects. The project managers may be hesitant to introduce any usability activities to their project, because they fear that those activities only consume more time, and the promised savings in the development time through less need for redesign are quite vague. The costs of usability activities are very much tangible and quantifiable, but the possible benefits are quite intangible and usually not easy to quantify reliably. Also, the cost of better usability is to be paid early in the development project, whereas the promised benefits of better usability may or may not be achieved in the distant future.

Altogether, the usability cost-benefit analysis models seem to highlight issues that are either too insignificant, too vague or solely aim at serving business needs neglecting the interests of the end user. In our empirical case, it can be argued that the usability cost-benefit models did not succeed in raising the right issues to convince the management to continue the usability improvement effort. The potential benefits of usability already acknowledged in the case organization seemed to be not enough for the management. In addition, some of the possible benefits of better usability that the usability cost-benefit models identify were considered as insignificant. As mentioned, reduced training and support costs were ignored in the case organization. In addition, the managers pointed out that even more insignificant issues are highlighted in these models. For example, in one of the project workshops, after a researcher presentation arguing that savings in printing costs of product manual should be counted also as a benefit from better usability, a manager from another participating company made a very critical comment that "This is peanuts. We should not spend any time discussing this issue. When I am handling project costing several millions, why should I care about saving few hundreds through having to print fewer pages for the product manual?" (Field notes). Having to print fewer pages for the product manual was raised as a possible benefit through better usability by many usability cost-benefit analysis models, but the managers in the workshop considered calculating and even discussing this benefit just a waste of time.

Regarding neglecting the interests of the user, our case shows that the management, sales and development were only interested in the paying customers and did not show interest in the end users. It can be argued that the usability cost-benefit models did not raise the right benefits so that the management, sales and development would have paid more interest to the users. One could even argue that the usability cost-benefit considerations might have directed the attention solely to the paying customer and to the finances of the development organization, which, of course, also need to be considered, but which should not result in total neglect of the end user interests.

Therefore, the empirical results outlined in this paper are next contrasted with the conference theme 'social responsibility', arguing for socially responsible HCI. Actually, the results achieved within this study can be argued of being very alarming from this viewpoint. The management goals of 'taming the customer' and 'improving the image of the company' by appealing to usability can be criticized of being overtly capitalist, and even as 'misuses of usability', since in this situation one does not necessarily develop usability at all, but only uses it to convince and in the worst case to hoax the customer. The management goal of 'taming the customers' with the help of usability might even be viewed as a way of 'silencing the users', instead of 'giving them a voice' [2]. This can also be interpreted as a form of technological colonialism [2], only dressed in the gown of 'usability'. In the case, the users and the customers can be argued of being 'colonized' by appealing to usability for the sake of management goals of the development organization. It can be argued that this kind of 'misuse of usability' runs against the noble principles of HCI tradition, where the purpose is to understand and appreciate particularly the end users and to provide design solutions with good usability to serve them the best way possible.

Altogether, according to Spinuzzi [29], this type of capitalist orientation can be viewed as the 'realization of Scandinavians worst fears'. He refers to the Scandinavian IS research tradition (e.g. [14]) that has advocated workplace democracy and union involvement in the development of computer systems. The tradition relied on the notion of conflict between capital and labor, and positioned itself strongly on the side of the labor against the 'oppressors'. One could argue that also 'usability people' (and usability cost-benefit analysis models) should be positioned on the side of 'the user', not 'the manager', i.e. they should aim at ensuring that the usability efforts are beneficial especially for the user, even though hopefully also for the other stakeholder groups. In all, regarding research on usability cost-benefit analysis, we argue that the researchers should carefully consider the different kinds of interpretations of usability costs and benefits, and particularly the different kinds of uses of their analysis revealed in this paper. In addition, we argue that the research community should take some responsibility of these uses and interpretations, or at least consider how to advocate more 'appropriate' uses and interpretations.

Regarding limitations of this study, the results are based on the analysis of only one case. Clearly more empirical research, employing a larger amount of cases, is needed to understand this phenomenon in depth. However, by focusing on only one case we were able to analyze this particular case and the interpretations of usability and its costs and benefits emerged inside the organization in great detail. In addition, future research is needed related to usability-cost benefit analysis, particularly when carried out in professional manner, which was not the case in this case organization.

References

1. Artman, H.: Procurer usability requirements negotiations in contract development. In: Bertelsen, O.W., Bødker, S., Kuutti, K. (eds.) Proc. 2nd Nordic Conference on Human-Computer Interaction, pp. 61–70. ACM Press, New York (2002)
2. Asaro, P.: Transforming Society by Transforming Technology: the science and politics of participatory design. Accounting, Management and Information Technologies 10(4), 257–290 (2000)
3. Aucella, A.: Ensuring Success with Usability Engineering. Interactions (May + June 19–22, 1997)
4. Bevan, N.: Cost Benefit Analysis version 1.1. Trial Usability Maturity Process. Serco Usability Services (2000)
5. Bias, R., Mayhew, D.: Cost-Justifying Usability. Academic Press, Boston (1994)
6. Bias, R., Mayhew, D.: Cost-Justifying Usability, Second edn., An Update for the Internet Age. Academic Press, Boston (2005)
7. Bloomer, S., Croft, R.: Pitching Usability to Your Organization. Interactions (November + December 18-26, 1997)
8. Bulkeley, W.: Study finds hidden costs of computing. The Wall Street Journal, B4 (November 2, 1992)
9. Catarci, T., Matarazzo, G., Raiss, G.: Driving usability into the public administration: the Italian experience. International Journal of Human-Computer Studies 57, 121–138 (2002)
10. Denzin, N.K., Lincoln, Y.S.: Introduction: The Discipline and Practice of Qualitative Research. In: Denzin, N., Lincoln, Y. (eds.) Handbook of Qualitative Research, 2nd edn., Sage Publications Inc, Thousand Oaks (2000)
11. Donahue, G.: Usability and the Bottom Line. IEEE Software 18(1), 31–37 (2001)
12. Ehrlich, K., Rohn, J.: Cost Justification of Usability Engineering: A Vendor's Perspective. In: Bias, R., Mayhew, D. (eds.) Cost-Justifying Usability, pp. 73–110. Academic Press, London (1994)
13. Fellenz, C.B.: Introducing Usability into Smaller Organizations. Interactions 4(5), 29–33 (1997)
14. Greenbaum, J., Kyng, M.(eds.): Design at Work. Cooperative Design of Computer Systems. Lawrence Erlbaum Associates, New Jersey (1991)
15. Grudin, J.: Systematic Sources of Suboptimal Interface Design in Large Product Development Organizations. Human-Computer Interaction 6(2), 147–196 (1991)

16. Iivari, N.: Discourses on 'culture' and 'usability work' in software product development. Acta Universitatis Ouluensis, Series A, Scientiae rerum naturalium 457 (2006)
17. ISO 13407. Human-centered design processes for interactive systems. International standard (1999)
18. ISO/IEC 9126-1. Software Engineering, Product quality, Part 1: Quality model. International Standard (2001)
19. Karat, C.-M.: A Business Case Approach to Usability Cost Justification. In: Bias, R., Mayhew, D. (eds.) Cost-Justifying Usability, pp. 45–70. Academic Press, London (1994)
20. Klein, H.K., Myers, M.D.: A Set of Principles for Conducting and Evaluating Interpretive Field Studies in Information Systems. MIS Quarterly 23(1), 67–94 (1999)
21. Mayhew, D.: Strategic Development of Usability Engineering Function. Interactions 6(5), 27–34 (1999)
22. Mayhew, D.: The usability engineering lifecycle: a practitioner's handbook for user interface design. Morgan Kaufmann Publishers, San Francisco (1999)
23. Mayhew, D., Mantei, M.: A Basic Framework for Cost-Justifying Usability Engineering. In: Bias, R., Mayhew, D. (eds.) Cost-Justifying Usability, pp. 9–43. Academic Press, London (1994)
24. Nielsen, J.: Usability engineering. Academic Press, Boston (1993)
25. Ohnemus, K.: Incorporating Human Factors in the System Development Life Cycle: Marketing and Management Approaches. In: IPCC96, pp. 46–53. IEEE, Los Alamitos (1996)
26. Rajanen, M.: Different Approaches to Usability Cost-Benefit Analysis. In: Remenyi, D., Brown, A. (eds.) Proc. ECITE 2006, pp. 391–397. Academic Press, Reading (2006)
27. Rosenbaum, S., Rohn, J.A., Humburg, J.: A Toolkit for Strategic Usability: Results from Workshops, Panels, and Surveys. In: Turner, T., Szwillus, G., Czerwinski, M., Paterno, F., Pemberton, S. (eds.) Proc. CHI 2000, pp. 337–344. ACM, New York (2000)
28. Rosson, M., Carroll, J.: Usability Engineering: Scenario-based Development of Human-Computer Interaction. Morgan-Kaufman, San Francisco (2002)
29. Spinuzzi, C.: A Scandinavian Challenge, a US Response: Methodological Assumptions in Scandinavian and US Prototyping Approaches. In: Haramundanis, K., Priestley, M. (eds.) Proc. 20th Annual International Conference on Computer Documentation, pp. 208–215. ACM, New York (2002)
30. Tudor, L.: Human Factors: Does Your Management Hear You? Interactions 5(1), 16–24 (1998)
31. Vredenburg, K., Mao, J., Smith, P.W., Casey, T.: A survey of user-centered design practice. In: Wixon, D. (ed.) Proc. of CHI'02, pp. 471–478. ACM, New York (2002)

DREAM & TEAM: A Tool and a Notation Supporting Exploration of Options and Traceability of Choices for Safety Critical Interactive Systems

Xavier Lacaze and Philippe Palanque

LIIHS – IRIT, Université Paul Sabatier
118 route de Narbonne, 31062 Toulouse Cedex 4
{lacaze, palanque}@irit.fr
http://liihs.irit.fr/palanque

Abstract. Justification of choices made throughout the design process of systems is a recurrent desire and quite often a formal request from certification authorities in the safety critical domain. However, even though some work has already been done in the early phases of the development processes, justifying choices in the later phases such as detailed design or implementation remain a cumbersome activity left (without any support) in the hands of the developers. This paper presents a notation called TEAM (Traceability, Exploration and Analysis Model) and its associated tool called DREAM (Design Rationale Environment for Argumentation and Modelling). The paper presents first the notation and its specificities with respect to other Design Rationale notations. Both the notation and the tools are presented on a case study showing how they can support design of interaction techniques for Air Traffic Control workstations. We also present the rationale that we have gathered while designing the graphical representation of the notation.

1 Introduction

Traceability of choices is a critical aspect of the development processes in the field of safety critical systems. Some standards, and especially in the field of safety critical systems, such as DO 178 B [21]) defines the guidelines for development of aviation software. This standard explicitly requires the use of methods and techniques for systematically exploring design options and for increasing traceability of design decisions. DO 178 B is a document describing a design process, however, even though it is widely used in the aeronautical domain, the design rationale part remains superficially addressed without any guidance for the designers or developer on how to reach the objectives. Similarly, the ESARR (Eurocontrol Safety Regulatory Requirement) on Software in Air Traffic Management Systems [6] explicitly requires traceability to be addressed in respect of all software requirements (pp. 11 edition 0.2).

While traceability has been a recurring concern in the field of HCI since the late 80's (reaching a climax in 1996 with the book survey [17]) there is still no mature enough notation and tool to engineer traceability i.e. to support the exploration of options and the traceability of choices made throughout the development process.

This paper presents such a notation called TEAM and its associated tool called DREAM. The notation extends QOC notation [15] in a way to be especially suited for

C. Baranauskas et al. (Eds.): INTERACT 2007, LNCS 4663, Part II, pp. 525 – 540, 2007.

the traceability of interactive systems. The tool supports the edition and the exploita-tion of models. Visualization techniques have been embedded to support specifically the tasks associated to models exploitation.

Section 2 describes previous work in the field of design rationale and more pre-cisely work dealing with interactive systems. Last part of this section introduces some criteria used to compare this previous work and to rationalize the need for additional work in order to support interactive system designers' activities. Section 3 presents the DREAM-TEAM approach i.e. both the notation and the tool. The description of the notation TEAM is based on QOC and has an emphasis on extensions that have been proposed and the rationale for their addition. Then the DREAM tool is rapidly pre-sented. The tool is available for download on the web at the following address: http://liihs.irit.fr/dream. Last section (section 4) presents the actual use of DREAM-TEAM approach on a case study in the filed of interactive Air Traffic Management workstations. This case study applies the approach to interaction technique design for clearances' (orders given to the pilots in the approach phase) input.

2 Related Work

This section presents related work on design rationale. It positions the work described in the paper with respect to the current state of the art in the field. It is structured around two aspects: notations for modelling and storing information and tools that support the edition and retrieval of information stored in models. In order to fit the number of pages limitations we have gathered screenshots of the tools in one single figure: **Fig. 1**. These tools are presented in detail in the following sections.

2.1 IBIS - gIBIS

gIBIS [4] (*Graphical IBIS*) is a tool supporting design activities. Main objective of gIBIS is to capture design rationale emerging during these activities. gIBIS supports IBIS (*Issue-Based Information System*) notation [10]. A snapshot is provided on area 2 (bottom left corner) of **Fig. 1**.

IBIS notation is the first notation that explicitly relates design activities and design rationale. IBIS main goal is to capture decisions that are made and so with an histori-cal perspective (i.e. how and why designers have taken this decision). IBIS breaks down design into *Issues*. An *Issue* could be related to *Answer, Statements*, or *Posi-tions*. These three elements are linked with one or more *Arguments* (positive or nega-tive). A network, called *issue map*, represents dependencies between *Issues*. Issues are connected together by four kinds of dependencies: *more general than, similar to, temporal successor of, logical successor of*. The main drawback of this notation lays in the *arguments*. *Arguments* support or deny one solution. Each solution has pro and cons arguments, but there is no way to compare solutions. gIBIS does not provide any support for handling large diagrams such as nesting, duplication of issues, … This is not a problem when small diagrams are edited, but when it come to real size applica-tions, not supporting scalability may lead to inconsistent diagram.

gIBIS extends IBIS notation by adding two kinds of nodes in order to improve flexibility:

(1) *external*, allows integrating other electronic documents (pictures, videos, mail, text etc.);

(2) *other*, this node include all thinks users can not associate to other nodes. And two links are added, one for generalised a *position* and one in order to specialise a *position*.

gIBIS users are supposed to focus on three points: to capture design history, to support several kinds of conversation media (mail, news, etc.), to search information into diagrams, and navigate on diagrams. **Fig. 1** (area 2) provides a snapshot of the gIBIS environment. On the left part, a diagram is displayed with both detailed and global view. Top right corner displays textual representation of the diagram. The set of buttons provides functions for diagram edition (add node, add link, delete, etc.) while the right corner displays additional textual information about currently selected node.

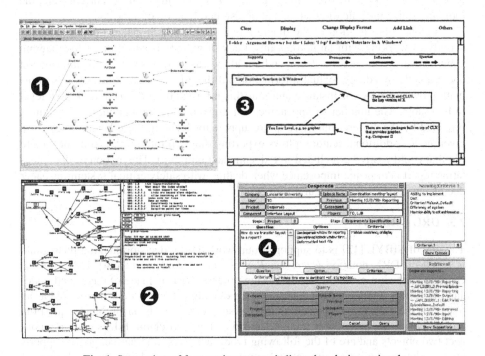

Fig. 1. Screenshot of four environments dedicated to design rationale

gIBIS was evaluated by a one year study [5]. From this study it is claimed that most users understood usefulness of design rationale thanks to the tool. This was not the case during the learning stage of the notation without tool support. However, the study has also shown that the tool required sequential editing of diagrams i.e. first *issue* then *position* and *argument*. It is not allowed, for instance, to enter *arguments* without having first edited *issue* and *position*. However, due to this constraint, gIBIS diagrams are always syntactically correct.

2.2 IBIS - Compendium

Compendium [3] is based on IBIS notation too. Compendium is a follow up of Quest-Map and improves it by allowing the integration of Excel™ and Word™ files into diagrams. Compendium features a graphical interface and has been used in several projects both academic and industrial. Authors are not satisfied about the tool and they have shown that users did not use the tool in the expected/right way. They used it to keep history of ideas, solutions, and as shared memory. They did not use it as a tool to capture rationale during the design phases as they were supposed to.

A snapshot of the environment is proposed on **Fig. 1** (area 1). Each node is associated with an icon. Issues are displayed as a question mark, positions as a light bulb, positive arguments as green plus, and negative arguments as red minus. Users have to be logged on the system in order to use it. This feature allows Compendium to store data about who made modification and when they were made. In its current state, the tool only stores the date of creation and of last modification of nodes.

No global visualisation of the diagram is available which makes cumbersome the activity of working with large diagrams. Lack of global visualisation of the diagram slows down the navigation. Compendium allows users to provide more information about a node by adding textual information but there is no mean to access this information by searching for instance and thus this information remains at a too low level to be usable. The number of appearances of a given node throughout the diagram is provided by the system, but there is no support for locating the other instances of a given node. Additional feature allows exporting diagram into html, textual or picture file that could easily be included in a documentation report. This notion of documentation report is of prime importance when dealing with safety critical systems as paper documents can be used as legal documents.

2.3 DRL - SIBYL

The aim of SIBYL [12] is to support group work during decision making phases and is based on DRL notation (*Decision Representation Language*) [14]. DRL aims at capturing decision made during the design process. DRL is made of edges and nodes and thus offers a graphical representation for diagrams. Each node is considered as an object of the following type: alternative, goal (i.e. the decision problem), question, group, viewpoint, procedure, status (decided or not) and claim. Edges can only connect two objects and are of the following types: achieves (alternative, goal); supports (claim, claim); denies (claim, claim); presupposes (claim, claim); is a sub goal of (goal, goal); answers (claim, question); is an answering procedure for (procedure, question); is a result of (claim, procedure); tradeoffs(object, object, attribute); is a kind of (object, object); suggests (object, object).

DRL notation allows users to split a design problem into one or more sub problems. As for IBIS notation, each option is evaluated independently from the others. The resulting diagram is highly structured. Scalability is a also a main issue for this notation as diagrams grow up rapidly and feature a lot of edges crossings and this makes DRL a not easy to use notation (both in terms of reading and producing diagrams).

SIBYL (see area 3 of **Fig. 1**) supports DRL. SIBYL was built following Potts and Bruns model [20], [13]. This model can be seen as a set of guideline for building interactive system supporting a design rationale notation. SIBYL is implemented with a database where information is stored in and can be retrieved from. Even though a Graphical representation is provided there is no support for global visualisation.

2.4 QOC - Desperado

Desperado [19] is based on QOC notation. As the work presented in this paper builds upon QOC too, we present this notation in more detail than the previous ones. In this section we first introduce the notation and then we describe Desperado tool. Other tools have been proposed to support the edition of QOC diagrams as for instance [22] but Desperado is, from our point of view the more mature.

QOC (*Questions, Options, Criteria*), is a semi formal notation (see **Fig. 2**) meant to be is easy to use and to understand. Each actor, involved in the design process, could understand and use the notation whatever their background is.

A typical QOC diagram can be break down into three columns and links between items of columns. Each row represents a notation's item: questions, options, and criteria. For one question, several options are associated. Option represents a design solution for the question. An option is evaluated by several criteria, each criterion supports (strong link) or denies (doted line link) the option. A criterion can be used to evaluate several options and thus may appear several times in the diagram. Criteria permit to model qualitative comparison between options. When choices are made, designers have to select (according to criteria for instance) the option. The selected option (is framed (see for instance option3 in **Fig. 2**) and usually the selected option is the one that satisfies the larger number of criteria. In QOC, an option may lead to another question (as for instance question 2 in **Fig. 2**) thus explicitly showing links between diagrams. In addition, arguments can be attached to link between options and criteria in order to describe with further detail, either the content or the underlying rationale for the value assigned to the link. The explicit handling of criteria is one of the main advantages of QOC with respect to other design rationale notations.

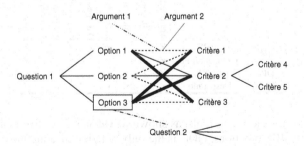

Fig. 2. An example of a QOC diagram

A snapshot of Desperado environment is provided in area 4 of **Fig. 1**. Desperado was built for storing and reusing design rationale data. Desperado is related with a data base storing all the information. Edition of models is only sequential and is done by means of form filling following four steps: First step (set up), users have to fill in context related information (question description, user name, design step, people related, etc.). The tool helps users by providing data from the database. In the second step, users fill in options, criteria, and provide an impact value of criteria to options. Some values may be prompted by Desperado according to the other values for the other options in the diagram. At step three, users index relevant electronic documents. Last step allows users to create new questions related to the one under consideration and thus refine the model into a sub-model. Users can also search (using keywords request), and modify previously edited diagrams.

Editing phase is constrained due to the imposed sequence data input. The tool does not make it possible to store pending questions, questions not yet resolved (after a question the user must edit options). There is no global representation of data, making it hard to handle large models event though this is a typical size for DR diagrams.

2.5 Comparative Analysis

In this section, we provide a comparative analysis of the notations and their environments tool plus notation. Comparison is made by criteria. Notations (first column in Table 1) are evaluated with respect to arguments (possibility to plug argument in the diagram), valuations (level of valuation), criterion and hierarchical (possibility to build nested diagram). The relation to criterion is ticked if the corresponding notation allows for a given criterion to be related to several options in order to provide a comparative analysis of options. Tools (second column in Table 1) are compared with the following criteria (last column in Table 1): database (link with a database or not), graphical displays (included direct manipulation), links with other electronic documents, and the implementation of specific features supporting the edition phase (such as undo/redo, etc.).

Table 1. Summary of evaluation of design rationale notations and tools

		Notations				Tools			
		Argument	Valuation	Criterion	Hierarchical	Data base	Graphical	Relation with documents	Edition
IBIS	gIBIS	✓	2	-	✓	-	✓	✓	-
	Compendium	✓	2	-	✓	✓	✓	✓	✓
DRL	SIBYL	✓	2	-	-	-	-	-	-
QOC	Desperado	✓	3	✓	✓	✓	-	-	-

Evaluation of notations and tools, as shown in Table 1 gives two main information about QOC and IBIS notations. QOC is the only notation meeting the criterion attribute. QOC also offers three levels of valuation between criteria and options. QOC satisfies all criteria we decided to evaluate but its related tool Desperado satisfies only one criterion. Concerning IBIS, gIBIS and Compendium are useful tools (they allow the edition of diagrams and information storage) but they embed the limitations of IBIS notation. Besides, none of the notations and tools defines clear relationships with

Human Computer Interaction concerns and they do not provide any support for dealing with specific information for the design of interactive system.

Following this comparative study and the requirements extracted from our projects in the field of safety critical interactive systems, we purpose hereafter to extend QOC notation in order to embed HCI components and empower the notation. We also designed a tool supporting this notation meeting most of the criteria presented above.

3 DREAM and TEAM Approach

TEAM (*Traceability, Exploration and Analysis Mode*)) & DREAM (*Design Rationale Environment for Argumentation and Modelling*) are a new approach dedicated to the support of systematic exploration of option and traceability of decision that are made throughout the development of safety critical interactive systems. As stated above TEAM is based on QOC notation [15], so, building on section 2, we first present all the extensions we designed from standard QOC and then how DREAM has been designed to support the edition and manipulation of TEAM diagrams.

3.1 Extensions

Currently we have embedded four extensions to 'standard' QOC diagrams in order to support the specific needs for interactive systems engineering: task model and scenarios, ergonomic criteria and usability factors, weights to criteria and factors and connection to software architecture models for interactive systems.

Tasks models extension [11] aims at integrating task models in QOC diagrams in order to be able (through scenarios extracted from the task models) to assess respective performance of the various options under consideration. As task analysis and modelling is at the core of User Centred Design [18], integration of task models must be embedded in the rationalisation process. Besides, the extraction of scenarios from task models provides precise and concrete information for assessing the relative efficiency and usability of different design options. In TEAM, task models are connected to options thus allowing representing the fact that an option is able to support the performance of a given task by the user.

Ergonomic criteria and usability factors extension has been introduced by Farenc and Palanque [7]. In the original QOC there is no way to store and thus to argue with respect to user and stakeholders requirements. However, it is clear that in User Centred Development, users play an important role in the decisions made. In this extensions user requirements are expressed as a set of factors. The factors correspond to high-level requirements such as learnability, safety, usability, etc., and some criteria may increase or decrease the satisfaction of a factor. A factor can be connected to one or several criterion. The early identification of factors has been based on McCall's classification [16] that is widely used in software engineering. The elements of the classification are the following: (1) quality factors (requirements expressed by the clients and/or users); (2) quality criteria (that can be measured for a given option according to a given scenario); (3) metrics: allow the actual valuation of a criterion.

According to studies done by Shum [23] QOC notation can transcribe exactly what users' want but a remaining issue is that criteria are at the same level i.e. it is not possible to say that a given criterion is more important than another one. Applying the notation in the field of safety critical interactive systems we have seen that such weighting of criteria is required as this is very often mentioned when decisions are taken. For this reason, we propose to associate to criterion and factor a weight describing their relative importance for stakeholders and users. The weight as defined in TEAM can have up to five valuations: starting from 1 (important) to 5 (optional). For the same reasons a weight is also associated to each criterion but for a given option. Thus in a given diagram a given criterion might be weighted as important while being weighted as optional in another diagram. Similarly, weights are associated to factors. The actual weight of a factor has an impact on the weight of the related criteria.

Arch model [0] is an extension of Seeheim model [8]. Arch breaks down an interactive system into five components: the domain specific component, the domain adaptor component, the dialogue component, the logical level interaction component, and the interaction toolkit component. Arch is both generic and precise enough to provide a framework for structuring design rationale diagrams. Our extension proposal is to relate each question to a component of the Arch model. As we are dealing with interactive systems design, we have decided to merge the domain specific component and the domain adaptor component into one called functional core. As the argumentation is often targeted to presentation (in the broad sense) and not towards one of the two presentation components of Arch, we have decided to integrate them. To summarise, each question can be attributed to one of the 3 following components: functional core, dialogue and presentation. It is also possible to not relate the question to any component of the arch model.

3.2 Tool Support DREAM

DREAM has been designed in order to support all the features of the TEAM notation presented above. It has been designed to support users' activities such as edition of TEAM diagrams (including storing related documents for argumentation), modification and visualization techniques for handling large diagrams. DREAM is available on the web and can be downloaded (together with some excerpts from case studies) at the following address: http://liihs.irit.fr/dream .

During edition phase (corresponding to the recording of information and the exploration of options), DREAM interaction tries to reduce syntax errors (with respect to TEAM syntax) as only authorised relations between two nodes are allowed. DREAM provides a feedback animation when a node is modified. When modification is made on a duplicated node, animation is provided on all entity of this node. This permits user to see the impact of the changes throughout the entire diagram.

DREAM also supports the decision phase (when design decisions are made by designers). 'Classical' QOC diagram can be inconsistent as it is possible to choose an option o1 (appearing in a set of option s1) for a question q1 and but to select a different one o2 (appearing in a different set of option s2 where o1 appears too) for another question q2. This kind of consistency in the choice phase is detected by DREAM and prompted to the user for modification.

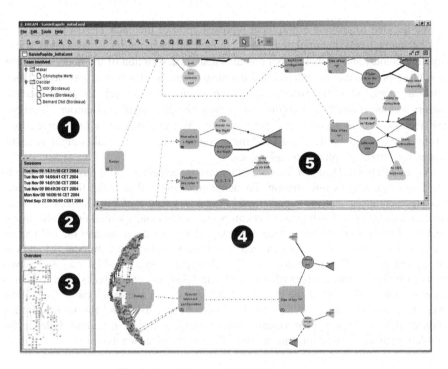

Fig. 3. User Interface of DREAM environment

Usually Design Rationale is seen an element or document only available at the end of the design process. As in User Centred Development the design process is iterative, it is required to support the edition and decision phases in an iterative manner too. We propose to capture each step of the edition of the diagram and to store information about the changes made, who made them and when. The same holds for the decision phase. To support these activities, DREAM tool features a session area (see area 1 and 2 of Figure 3). A session is made of a diagram (and all its related documents), a list of authors, and a date. We distinguish to types of authors involved in the design process. The makers: people who create and elaborate the diagram. The deciders: people who make decisions and give the global trends to follows. Deciders could be customer(s) and/or user(s). Decisions made by makers are mostly guided by deciders. DREAM permits to start new session or to start a new file from a selected session.

One of the critical characteristic of DREAM is that it embeds functionalities that are of great advantages with respect to manual edition of diagrams. One of these is related to the multiple appearances of nodes within a given diagram. In this section we already mentioned this aspect for options but it is also true for criteria, factors, tasks and scenarios. For instance the same factor can appear in several places. Changing the weight of such a factor has an impact on all the other instances of the factor and an animation feedback is provided when a modification is done, to help user to see the impact of the modification on the entire diagram.

We decided to provide a graphical representation of the each TEAM element that can be interactively manipulated. Each element of the notation is associated with a glyph, a colour, and a label. Label contains a short description of the node, a description more precise can be entered and documents can be attached to any node. Questions are depicted as red square, options as orange disc, criteria as green triangle, factors as blue triangle, and arguments as grey triangle. Glyph and colour, of criteria and factors, evolve according to their weight. A strong weight is represented by a strong glyph (bold border) and brightness colour; whereas a weak weight is represented by a fuzzy glyph and pastel colour.

As stated above, Design Rationale diagrams are expected to be large and containing a large quantity of information. To tackle this, DREAM provides three simultaneous representations that are represented in areas 3, 4 and 5 of **Fig. 3**. Area 5 is standard visualisation of the diagram that can be zoomed in and zoomed out. This view is dedicated to edition activities. Area 3 displays the entire diagram, and the red rectangle match with the current view in area 5. A third visualisation is bifocal [2] and can be seen in area 4. This view displays TEAM diagrams in a tree-like way and allows users to focus on detailed part of the tree (right hand part called focus) and to keep a context view of the rest of the tree (left hand part called context+focus). They allow users to focus on one node (a factor for instance) and to see all the nodes that are connected to it. This type of visualization is really useful as it counter balance the problem of allowing multiple appearance of the same node in a diagram.

4   An Air Traffic Control Case Study

This section presents the use of TEAM and DREAM on a case study. This case study comes from the Air Traffic Management domain and deals with interaction design issues on an Air Traffic Control workstation.

4.1   Context

The DREAM/TEAM approach has been applied to the entire case study and is one of the 3 case studies we developed so far. One of the main objective for this case study were the following:

- Every information concerning design process could be store by means of the TEAM notation;
- Extensions are used and useful with respect to 'classical' QOC;
- DREAM tool supports the various activities of the several kinds of users involved in the design process.

The case study has been developed with colleagues at the CENA (French Centre for Studies on Air Traffic Management) and is based on an interactive application designed and developed by them. The context is the one of 'approach' air traffic controllers i.e. controllers in charge of aircraft approaching an airport. The aircrafts are handed over to them by so called 'enroute' air traffic controllers and they are supposed (after preparing the aircrafts route appropriately) to transfer them to the 'tower' controllers in charge of take-off, landing and taxiing.

The approach air traffic controller can be in charge of a significant number of air-crafts and might have to issue a lot of clearances[1] in a very short period of time. This activity is different from the one of the other types of controllers for whom time scale is much longer.

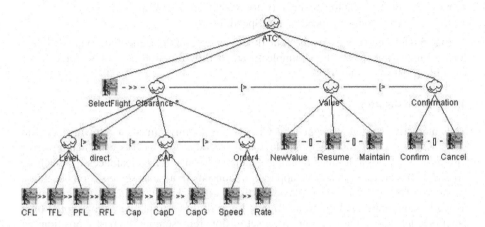

Fig. 4. Task model describing ATC activity

Figure 4 presents (using the CTT notation [24]) a task model of an 'approach' air traffic controller. This task model is only partial but conveys all the information relevant to the case study. The task is divided in four high level sub-tasks: select a flight, select clearance (level, cap (i.e. heading), speed, rate, etc.), select value and confirm or cancel. After selecting the aircraft, the ATC selects the type of clearance to be issued. The selection of the type of clearance is made by pressing at least once on the keys named "level", "cap", "direct" and "speed". The clearance value is typed-in using the keyboard and can be either a new value (i.e. a number), a confirmation "maintain" or a correction "resume" the previous value. A graphical feedback is provided when the value is validated.

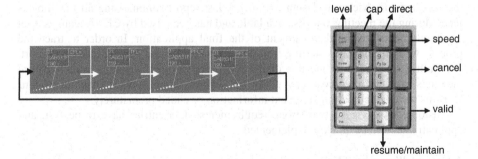

Fig. 5. Left hand part: cyclic access to level menu. Right hand part functions related to keys.

---

[1] A clearance is the name given to the orders sent by the controller to the pilot. This can be changing heading, flight level, speed, …

Ten kinds of clearances are identified, only four buttons are available. Functions are classified by themes and statically associated to keys (see **Fig. 5**):

- Key "num lock" corresponds to level menu (CFL, TFL, PFL, RFL);
- Key "/" corresponds to direct menu;
- Key "*" corresponds to cap menu (Cap, Right Cap, Left Cap) ;
- Key "-" corresponds to speed menu (Speed, Rate).

Fig. 5 (right part) presents the four functions accessible sequentially via key "num lock". Menus are cyclic, for example to reach PFL function user press three times (modulo four) key "num lock".

4.2 Rationalisation

The interactive system designed by CENA was mainly aimed at allowing ATC to issue clearances as rapidly as possible. Other (secondary) concerns were making error rate as low as possible and avoiding syntactically incorrect clearances as much as possible. The current interactive application consists in a radar screen, a mouse and a keyboard. The radar screen displays all flights controlled by the air traffic controller as well as incoming and outgoing flights. Each flight is graphically represented by a label (see left hand side of Figure 5), a set of dots representing the past 5 positions of the aircraft and speed vector (a straight line) providing information about both speed (line length) and direction (line direction). The flight label contains the following information flight id, plane id and altitude level.

The design team at CENA followed a user centred design [18] and iterative approach. After some information gathering, they implemented a first prototype. This version evolved during several meetings involving users and designers. After each meeting minutes were prepared and distributed. Those meeting, held on a regular basis, offered the opportunity to users to comment and practice the various prototypes. The process ended after the tenth meeting.

In order to validate the DREAM/TEAM approach we used the tool and the notation to model all the information contained in the minutes. The information gathered was ranging from graphical design sketches (representing graphical appearance of objects), automata (describing the interaction technique) as well as decisions about the retained and discarded design options. A last report summarising all the choices made during the meeting was also available and has been used by CENA team as a set of requirements for the development of the final application. In order to trace the process we built diagrams starting from these ten reports and the summarizing report. We built a first diagram and this diagram evolved with information extracted from meetings in a chronological way. Only six sessions appear in the diagram as four sessions were not containing relevant information or ended prematurely.

Customers/users gave two strong requirements: data entries have to be fast, and application had to be quickly implemented.

4.3 Modelling with TEAM

For space reasons we do not present the entire models resulting from the design rationale activity. A more complete one can be found in [25] this section the modelling process itself but we describe the output of the process. Task models and scenarios were not used in the design process by CENA and this is the reason why do not appear on the diagram. Four criteria were identified and are duplicated (i.e. "fast", "honesty", "user's automatism", and "efficient quickly"). They are connected to most of the options. The resulting diagram is displayed on **Fig. 6** and contains 203 nodes (41 questions, 55 options, 21 criteria, 6 factors, and 20 arguments). The point here is not to describe individually each node but to present salient information that provides insights about the process, the notation and the tool.

Left hand side of Fig. 6 presents a subset of the entire diagram resulting from the modelling process while right hand side emphasises one frame extracted from the diagram that is discussed hereafter.

The five rounded rectangles highlight one couple criterion/factor. This couple appears five times in the diagram. The criterion is "performance" meaning that performance can be assessed in several places in the diagram for several options. The factor is "fast" and models a customer/user requirement that interaction is required to be fast.

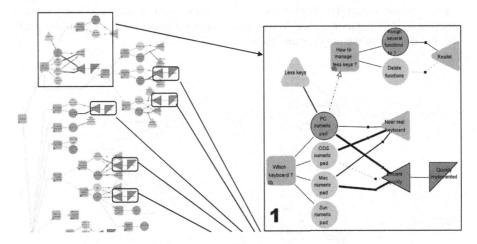

Fig. 6. Excerpt of the entire diagram of the case study

Frame (enlarged on the right hand side of Fig. 6) deals with the question of choice of keyboard, options considered are PC numeric pad, ODS numeric pad (keyboard already available on ATC workstations), Macintosh numeric pad, and Sun numeric pad. Options are valuated (expected Sun num pad option) by two criteria: "near real keyboard" and "efficient quickly". Intuitively, we would suppose that designers would select ODS numeric pad option but in fact they chose PC numeric pad instead. One of the main reasons for this choice lies in the other factor "easy to implement" and this get a strong weight. Besides, as modelled, key arrangement of the PC numeric pad is closer to the ODS one keyboard. However, as shown in frame number one this design choice raised a new question: "how to manage fewer keys?" i.e. how to have as few keys as possible for entering clearances.

Graphical visualisation supports the analysis of diagrams in order to detect questions poorly investigated or design choices under discussion. Indeed, it is easy to spot (even on a large diagram) a question related to only one option and (2) options are not related to any criterion.

During the six meeting providing relevant data, diagrams evolved. Some parts changed often as, for instance the part concerning syntax for input of clearances' values. DREAM versioning facilities provide an easy way to support this kind of activity.

4.4 Rationalising DREAM

Diagram is Fig. 7 shows the design rationale result about the design of the graphical representation of TEAM diagrams in DREAM. This design of this graphical representation has been done with Jean-Luc Vinot graphical designer. From left to right we can see the design questions (how to represent each node in TEAM) and then the set of options that have been envisaged. Criteria are related to the tasks of editing (e.g. easiness to distinguish the various types of nodes), some effort constraints (e.g. easiness to implement) and some perception considerations (e.g. reading by block, perceptive colour, perceptive brightness …). The main point of this task was to assess whether TEAM notation was able to capture such graphical rationale that is outside the initial scope of the notation and the tool.

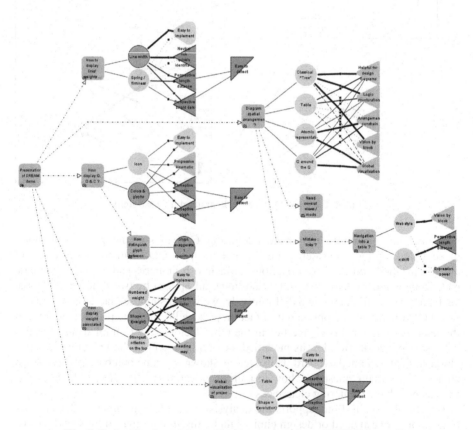

Fig. 7. Rationalisation of the graphical representation of DREAM notation

5 Conclusion

In this paper we have presented a notation (TEAM) and its case tool (DREAM) that are dedicated to the engineering of interactive systems. The approach presented here focuses on the design process and more precisely on the traceability and rationalisation. The notation is anchored in HCI research and provides explicit links to architecture (Arch), user centred development process (iterative prototyping), task analysis and modelling and scenarios and thus provides a generic framework for gathering these multiple information sources in a single model.

The approach builds on existing work in the field of design rationale integrating successful aspects and providing solutions to the identified limitations. The approach has been applied to several case studies including interaction techniques design, graphic design and software engineering side of interactive systems design.

Acknowledgement

We would like to thank members of the former CENA (Research Centre on Air Traffic Control in Toulouse) namely Christophe Mertz who developed the ATC system presented in this case study and Jean-Luc Vinot (graphic designer at CENA) who designed the graphical representation of TEAM and accepted to rationalise the process.

References

1. Bass, L., Little, R., Pellegrino, R., Reed, S., Seacord, R., Sheppard, S., Szezur, M.: The Arch Model: Seeheim Revisited. In: User Interface Developpers' Workshop (1991)
2. Cava, R.A., Luzzardi, P.R.G., Freitas, C.M.D.S.: The Bifocal Tree: a Technique for the Visualization of Hierarchical Information Structures. In: IHC 2002 – 5th Workshop On Human Factors In Computer Systems, Fortaleza (2002)
3. Compendium is available at: http:www.compendiuminstitute.org/tools/compendium.htm
4. Conklin, J., Begeman, M.L.: GIBIS: A Hypertext Tool for Exploratory Policy Discussion. ACM Transactions on Office Information Systems 6(4), 303–331 (1988)
5. Conklin, J., Burgess-Yakemovic, K.C.: A Process-Oriented Approach to Design Rationale. In: [17], pp. 393–427 (1996)
6. ESARR 6. EUROCONTROL Safety Regulatory Requirement. Software in ATM Systems. Edition 1.0 (2003), http://www.eurocontrol.int/src/public/standard_page/esarr6.html
7. Farenc, C., Palanque, P.: Exploitation Des Notations De Design Rationale Pour Une Conception Justifiée Des Applications Interactives. IHM'99. 11ièmes Journées Sur L'Ingénierie Des Interfaces Homme-Machine (1999)
8. Green, M.: Report on Dialogue Specification Tools. User Interface Management Systems, pp. 9–20. Springer, Heidelberg (1985)
9. Johnson, C.W.: Using Design Rationale To Support Formal Methods In The Development of Human-Computer Interfaces. HCI Journal 11(4), 291–320 (1996)
10. Kunz, W., Rittel, H.: Issues As Elements of Information Systems. PhD, Univ. of California (1970)

11. Lacaze, X., Palanque, P., Navarre, D.: Evaluation de Performance et Modèles de Tâches Comme Support a la Conception Rationnelle des Systèmes Interactifs. 14eme Conférence Francophone sur L'Interaction Homme Machine. In: IHM 2002, pp. 17-24 (2002)
12. Lee, J.: SIBYL: A Tool for Managing Group Design Rationale. Computer Supported Cooperative Work, pp. 79–92. ACM Press, New York (1990)
13. Lee, J.: Extending the Potts and Bruns Model for Recording Design Rationale. In: Proceedings of the 13th International Conference on Software Engineering, pp. 114–125 (1991)
14. Lee, J., Laï.: What's in Design Rationale. In: [17], pp. 21–51 (1996)
15. MacLean, A., Young, R.M., Bellotti, V.M.E., Moran, T.P.: Questions, Options, Criteria: Elements of Design Space Analysis. In: [17] (1996)
16. McCall, J., Richards, P., Walters, G.: Factors in Software Quality. Rome Air Development Center (RADC), RADC-TR-77-369, vol. III (November 1977)
17. Moran, T.P., Carroll, J.M.(eds.): Design Rationale: Concepts, Techniques, and Use. Lawrence Erlbaum Associates, Mahwah (1996)
18. Norman, D.A., Draper, S.W.: User-Centred System Design: New Perspectives on Human Computer Interaction. Lawrence Erlbaum Associates, Hillsdale (1986)
19. Ormerod, T.C., Mariani, J., Ball, L.J., Lambell, N.: Desperado: Three-in-one indexing for innovative design: Interact -Seventh IFIP Conference on Human-Computer Interaction. IOS Press, London (1999)
20. Potts, C., Bruns, G.: Recording the Reasons for Design Decisions. In: Proceedings of the 10th International Conference on Software Engineering, pp. 418–427 (1988)
21. RTCA/DO-178B. Software Considerations in Airborne Systems and Equipment Certification (December 1, 1992), http://www.rtca.org/
22. Sage, M., Johnson, C.W.: Pragmatic Formal Design: A Case Study in Integrating Formal Methods into the HCI Development Cycle. In: DSVIS, pp. 134–155. Springer, Heidelberg (1998)
23. Shum, S.J.: Cognitive analysis of design rationale representation. PhD Thesis. York, UK: Department of Psychology, University of York (1991).
24. Paternò, F.: Model-Based Design and Evaluation of Interactive Application. Springer, Heidelberg (1999)
25. Lacaze, X., Palanque, P., Barboni, E., Bastide, R., Navarre, D.: From DREAM to Realitiy: Specificities of Interactive Systems Development with respect to Rationale Management. In: Dutoit, A.H., McCall, R., Mistrik, I., Paech, B. (eds.) Rationale Management in Software Engineering, pp. 155–172. Springer, Heidelberg (2006)

A Glass Box Design: Making the Impact of Usability on Software Development Visible

Natalia Juristo[1], Ana Moreno[1], Maria-Isabel Sanchez-Segura[2],
and Maria Cecília Calani Baranauskas[3]

[1] School of Computing - Universidad Politécnica de Madrid, Spain
[2] Department of Computing - Universidad Carlos III de Madrid, Spain
[3] Institute of Computing – UNICAMP State University of Campinas, Brazil
{natalia, ammoreno}@fi.upm.es, misanche@inf.uc3m.es,
cecilia@ic.unicamp.br

Abstract. User-centered design is not just about building nice-looking and usable interfaces, and software development is not just about implementing functionality that supports user tasks. This paper aims to build a tighter fit between human-computer interaction and software engineering practices and research by addressing what software and usability engineering practitioners can learn from each other regarding the impact of usability on software development. More specifically we aim to support usability people in helping developers to elicit requirements that can incorporate usability functions into software development. The paper shows what type of impact usability has on software models and suggests how this impact can be dealt with at the requirements elicitation and specification stages of the development cycle.

Keywords: usability features, software development.,

1 Introduction and Motivation

User-centered design is not just about building nice-looking and usable user interfaces, and software development is not just about implementing functionality that supports user tasks. Belonging to different traditions and times, the disciplines of software engineering (SE) and human computer interaction (HCI) have evolved separately and developed their own methods to meet the needs of software application customers and users. Over the last twenty years, especially, several practices have been developed in both communities. This illustrates the human-centered perspective's influence on the software development lifecycle. Stakeholder involvement in the requirements elicitation process and evolutionary process models [39], which enable iterative construction of the application software to best meet the user requirements, and the widespread use of prototyping by the HCI community are examples of the approximation of both disciplines [31].

Even so, the closeness of the two disciplines has not facilitated their practitioners' work. One of the most significant problems is that there is little knowledge and communication about each others' jobs, even though they are supposed to work together and collaborate on developing software applications. Both communities use

C. Baranauskas et al. (Eds.): INTERACT 2007, LNCS 4663, Part II, pp. 541 – 554, 2007.

different vocabulary and sometimes the same word to represent different artifacts. The word "design", for example, can be understood and used differently in both communities: to express the software modeling phase (in SE), and the final look and feel of the product (in HCI).

The boundaries between SE and HCI and attempts at bridging gaps between the two disciplines by fusing the efforts of the two communities come up against plenty of challenges. Seffah [37] discusses the major obstacles and related myths as viewed by the two communities. He argues that some widespread expressions, such as "friendliness of the user interface", and "user interface" *per se*, are some of the underlying obstacles to more usable interactive systems. In his view, such terms give the impression that the user-centered approach and usability methods are only for "decorating a thin component sitting on top of the software or the "real" system". The behavior of some practitioners in both communities illustrates this dichotomy that isolates the user interface from the remaining system. Some software engineers consider themselves the "real" designers of the software system, leaving the task of making the UI more "user friendly" to the usability people. On the other hand, some usability professionals and interaction designers believe that it is their job just to design and test the interface with users, leaving the task of implementing the system functionality that supports the user tasks to the software engineers.

Two separate processes – one for the overall system development process and another for the user-centered process – for building an interactive system are certainly not manageable. It would not appear to be possible to control and synchronize software development and user-centered design separately. Also, efficiency would fall and costs would increase because of the overlapping functions between the two processes. Milewski [31] argues that, despite improvements in SE-HCI interactions, problems of communication and efficiency still remain and deserve further investigation. Seffah [36] proposes that software and usability engineers should learn from each other to facilitate and encourage the convergence of practices in both communities. Therefore we need to investigate and to promote the mutual understanding of the activities and responsibilities of the two communities in the construction of usable systems.

We argue that by making the impact usability has on software development visible to usability people, they will be better prepared to help developers and analysts to elicit the requirements necessary to develop the software. To do this, the HCI people must have an "insider" view of the software to be able to see how to best mediate between users and developers and ensure that usability issues will be properly dealt with in the software design during the whole development cycle. This paper aims to shed light on how usability recommendations relate to software models and suggests an approach to deal with this as of the SE requirements stage.

The paper is organized as follows. The next section discusses the concept of usability as a quality requirement for software and, as such, the suggested interdependencies with other software-related concepts. It also discusses the roles the two communities have to play to integrate their practices and build usable interactive systems. Section 3 gives an example to illustrate the implications of considering a usability feature in the software model of a real application. Section 4 proposes a way to guide developers and usability engineers through the process of eliciting and specifying requirements to deal with usability features at design time. Section 5 sets out our conclusions.

2 Usability as a Quality Attribute for Software

Software quality has been traditionally associated with the satisfaction of specified requirements that are primarily functional. This perception of quality was broadened as of ISO/IEC 9126 [20], which defines quality from a user perspective as functionality, reliability, usability, efficiency, maintainability and portability. Thus, the concept of usability that in the HCI field tradition has been associated with the "usefulness" of software and represented by its learnability, efficiency of use, memorability, few and noncatastrophic errors and subjective satisfaction [32], [38], gains a formal status as a quality attribute for software.

Quality in use has a broader sense, although some ergonomic standards (e.g. [21] and [22]) take the expression to be a synonym of usability. Bevan [6] explains the ISO/IEC 14598-1[23] concept of quality in use as the combined effect of the system's quality characteristics, and the way they are experienced by the end user. In particular, it depends on the circumstances in which a system is used, including factors such as the tasks, equipment (hardware, software and materials), and the physical and social environment. As discussed in Bevan [5], quality in use depends not only on software usability, but also on other software quality attributes: the appropriateness of the provided functionality for a given task, the performance that users can achieve using the system, and system reliability.

For the past two decades software usability has been perceived from the SE perspective as related to the presentation of information to the user [37],[16]. This underlying belief has led software engineers to treat usability primarily by separating the presentation portion from the system functionality, as recommended by generally accepted design strategies (for example, MVC or PAC [10]). This separation makes it easier to modify the user interface in the hope of improving its usability, without affecting the rest of the application. Consequently, usability, unlike other software quality attributes, has been considered late in the development process.

Nevertheless, some authors have recently shown that usability has implications beyond the user interface *per se*. Perry and Wolf have claimed that usability issues place static and dynamic constraints on the software components [33]. Bass et al. [2] and Bass and John [3] used a bottom-up approach based on fieldwork observation to describe a set of scenarios representing software usability issues that have an effect on the software architecture. The STATUS project [25],[26] decomposed usability into features and studied which features have an impact on software architecture. The implications of usability features for software design materialize as the creation of special items (components, responsibilities, interactions, classes, methods, etc.) that affect both the presentation and application layers of the software system architecture. Therefore, addressing usability features at the end of the construction process leads to major rework. To avoid this, it has been suggested that software usability should be addressed proactively at architectural time instead of retroactively after testing [4],[8],[16],[27].

While the SE community developed its own set of methods and tools to manage the software development lifecycle and covering usability concerns, the HCI community has developed a variety of user-centered approaches to software design over the last decades. Although many developers recognize the importance of user-centered design (UCD) for achieving usability, the methods and techniques are not the everyday practice for software developers for many reasons, some of which have already been mentioned in this paper. Seffah and Metzker [37] also point out that UCD techniques are usually regarded as being uncoupled from the mainstream software development lifecycles, and propose educating software and usability professionals to work together as a way of filling the gap between software and usability engineering. The authors argue that a sound understanding of HCI and SE culture and practices will help practitioners to communicate and upgrade methodologies. They also suggest the need to consider a possible cause-and-effect relationship between the internal software quality attributes and the UI usability factors. For example, for a system that must provide continuous feedback, developers should consider this point when designing time-consuming system functionalities [36].

Faulkner [14] also analyzes the need for integration between HCI and SE practices. Faulkner explains this integration in terms of their role in the context of the computer science curriculum. She claims that usability practitioners lack essential SE skills. This is why they find it so difficult to influence developers' activities and attitudes. At the same time, software developers receive only rudimentary training in usability and user-centered approaches to design, despite the fact that between 50% and 80% of all source code is concerned with the user interface [7],[11]. Along similar lines, other authors [18], [15] acknowledge the importance, for all software practitioners, not only of being acquainted with a variety of usability methods, but also of being able to determine which method is best suited for a particular situation in a software project. We argue that this is important the other way round too: usability practitioners should also be able to visualize and understand what impact usability features are likely to have on software models. This way they will be able to understand the implications they have and be able to communicate better with developers and mediate in the requirements elicitation process.

In this paper we propose a "glass box" approach to software design showing that usability recommendations have an impact and therefore should have features represented in software models. These are recommendations involving building certain functionalities into the software to improve user-system interaction. For example, features like cancel an ongoing task [9], undo a task [38],[42],[30] receive feedback on what is going on in the system [19],[38],[41] or adapt the software functionalities to the user profile [35], [42]. In general terms we advocate bringing usability into the software development process earlier, at requirements time, as is being done with other quality attributes [1]: "The earlier key quality attribute requirements are identified and prioritized, the more likely it is that the essential quality attributes will be built into the system. It is more cost-effective to reason about quality attribute tradeoffs early in the lifecycle than later in the lifecycle when modifications are often difficult, impractical, or even impossible".

3 The Impact of Usability Recommendations on Software Design

Both HCI [24] and SE [17] deal with usability as a non-functional requirement. Usability requirements specify user effectiveness, efficiency or satisfaction levels that the system should achieve. These specifications are then used by the usability people at the evaluation stage: "Task A should be performed by a novice user in less than X minutes", or "End user satisfaction with the application should be higher than Z on a 1-to-5 scale". Dealing with usability as a non-functional requirement is useful for evaluation purposes, but it is not appropriate for developing usable software.

Usability recommendations have an impact on software design [28]. Suppose that we want to build the cancel functionality for specific commands into an application. The recommendations mention "provide a way to instantly cancel a time-consuming operation, with no side-effects" [41] or "if the time to finish the processing of the command will be more than 10 seconds, along to the feedback information, provide a cancel option to interrupt the processing and go back to the previous state"[32]. To satisfy such requirements the software system must at least: gather information (data modifications, resource usage, etc.) that allow the system to recover the status prior to a command execution; stop command execution; estimate the time to cancel and inform the user of progress in cancellation; restore the system to the status before the cancelled command, etc. This means that, apart from the changes that have to be made to the UI presentation to add the cancel button, specific software components must be built into the software design to deal with these responsibilities. Building the cancel usability feature into a finished software system is not a minor change; it takes a substantial amount of software design rework. Therefore, it should be dealt with well in advance like any other software system functionality. The same applies to other usability recommendations that represent specific functionalities to be incorporated into a software system. We have termed these recommendations functional usability features (FUF), as most of these heuristics/rules/principles make recommendations on functionalities that the software should incorporate.

3.1 Functional Usability Features (FUFs)

The usability literature has provided an extensive set of guidelines to help developers to build usable software. Each author has named these guidelines differently: design heuristics [32], principles of usability [4],[38], usability guidelines [19], etc. Although all these recommendations share the same goal of improving software system usability, they are stated at different levels. For example, there are very abstract guidelines, like "prevent errors" [32] or "support internal locus of control" [38],[19], and others that provide more definite usability solutions, such as "make the user actions easily reversible" [19] or "provide clearly marked exits" [32].

To identify a preliminary list of functional usability features we took the usability features with strong design implications (according to the STATUS project [25],[26] and Bass et al. [2],[3]). Table 1 shows the list of FUFs. The usability features in Table 1 are not intended to be an exhaustive list; they are a starting point for identifying usability features with an impact on software system functionality. They are a good example of usability features that have to be considered at the software requirements stage.

If the usability-related functionalities described in Table 1 are properly described in the software requirements specification, developers are more likely to build them into the system.

Table 1. A Preliminary List of Functional Usability Features

Usability Features	Usability benefits
Feedback	Nielsen [32], Constantine & Lockwood [12], Shneiderman [38], Hix & Hartson [19]
Undo / Cancel	Nielsen [32], Hix & Hartson [19], Shneiderman [38], Constantine & Lockwood [12]
User input errors prevention/correction	Shneiderman [38], Hix & Hartson [19], Constantine& Lockwood [12]
Wizard	Constantine& Lockwood [12]
User profile	Hix & Hartson [19]
Help	Nielsen [32], Constantine& Lockwood [12]
Commands aggregation	Nielsen [32], Constantine& Lockwood [12], Hix [19]
Shortcuts (key and tasks)	Nielsen [32], Constantine& Lockwood [12], Shneiderman [38], Hix & Hartson [19]
Reuse information	Constantine & Lockwood [12]

Properly specifying functional usability features is not that simple. For example, Nielsen's feedback heuristic "The system should always keep users informed about what is going on through appropriate feedback within reasonable time" [32] does not provide the amount of information that a software developer needs to satisfactorily specify the feedback functionality, build the software design model and implement it adequately.

To illustrate what information is missing let us look at the complexity and diversity of the feedback functionality. There are four possible types of feedback: Interaction Feedback to inform users that the system has heard their request; Progress Feedback for tasks that take some time to finish; System Status Display to inform users about any change in the system status, and Warnings to inform users about irreversible actions. Additionally, each feedback type has its own peculiarities. For example, a developer needs many details to build a system that provides a satisfactory System Status Feedback: what states to report, what information to display for each state; how prominent the information should be in each case (for example, should the application keep control of the system while reporting, or should the system let the user work on other tasks while status reporting), etc.

Therefore, a lot more information than just a description of the usability feature must be incorporated in the software requirements specification document for developers to properly build the feedback feature into a software system. This information needs to be discussed with and elicited from the different stakeholders, and requirements elicitation, analysis and specification is a process where both developers and usability engineers have a role to play.

3.2 Making the Relationship Between FUFs and Software Design Visible

This section discusses an example illustrating the incorporation of one FUF for a system developed to manage on-line table bookings for a restaurant chain. The FUF we will look at deals with one particular kind of feedback, System Status Feedback (to report the system status to users) [41],[13].

Figure 1 illustrates part of the UML [29] class model for this system, including the classes involved in the restaurant table booking process only. The original classes designed without considering system status feedback are shown on a white background in the diagram and the classes derived from the later inclusion of this feature on a grey background. Let us first analyze this diagram without taking into account the system status feedback. The Interface class represents the part of the bookings terminal with which the user interacts to book a table at the restaurant over the Internet. The Restaurants-Manager and Reservations-Manager are two classes specialized in dealing with restaurants and bookings, respectively. They have been added to make the system more maintainable by separating the management processes so that they can be modified more efficiently in the future. The Reservations class accommodates the information related to each booking that is made at the restaurant, whereas the restaurant is represented by the Restaurant class and each of the tables at this restaurant that are not taken are identified by the Table class.

The System Status Feedback Usability Feature involves the system notifying the user of any change of state that is likely to be of interest. HCI experts recommend that the notification should be more or less striking for the user depending on how important the change is. The status changes that the client considered important referred to failures during the performance of certain system operations owing either to runtime faults, insufficient resources or problems with devices or external resources (specifically Internet). This means that the system should have the following specific responsibilities to provide this usability feature:

R1: The software should be able to listen to active commands, because they can provide information about the system status. If this information is useful to the user, the system should be able to pass this information on as, when and where needed.

R2: As the system may fail, the software should be able to ascertain the state of active commands, because users should be informed if the command is not working due to outside circumstances. The system should be equipped with a mechanism by means of which it can check whether a given command is being executed and, if the command fails, inform users that the command is not operational.

R3: The software should be able to listen to or query external resources, like networks or databases, about their status and inform the user if a resource is not working properly.

R4: The software should be able to check the status of the internal system resources and alert users in advance to save their work, i.e. if the system is running short of a given resource and is likely to have to shut down.

The grey boxes in Figure 1 show the changes that had to be made to the design model for the software to be able to deal with these responsibilities. They include three new classes, five new methods, and four new associations. Their description follows:

Three new classes:

Internal-Resource-Checker, responsible for changes and for determining failures due to internal system resources like memory, etc. It deals with responsibilities *R1*, *R2* and *R4*.

External-Resource-Checker, responsible for changes and determining failures due to external system resources like networks, databases, etc. It deals with responsibility *R3*.

Status-Feedbacker, responsible for providing the client with information stating the grounds for both changes and system failures in the best possible format and using the most appropriate heuristic in each case. It deals with all four responsibilities.

Five new methods:

ExternalResourcesAvailable determines whether the external resources are available.

CheckSystemResources determines whether the system has the resources it needs to execute the booking operation for the restaurant.

AreYouAlive finds out whether the active command is still running correctly.

IAmAlive, enables the Reservations-Manager to tell the system that it is still running, i.e. that it is alive.

Feedback tells the user of any changes or failures identified in the system while the table is being booked at the restaurant.

Four new associations between:

Reservations-Manager&StatusFeedbacker enables the ReservationsManager class to tell the StatusFeedbacker about changes or system failures that are relevant for the user and about which the user is to be informed.

Internal-Resource-Checker&Status-Feedbacker and *External-Resource-Checker&Status-Feedbacker* can tell the Status-Feedbacker class that a change or failure has occurred.

Reservations-Manager&Internal-Resources-Checker enables the Internal-Resources-Checker to check that the reservation process is still active and working properly.

If an external resource, in this case the network, failed, the *External-Resources-Checker* would take charge of detecting this state of affairs (as no *ExternalResourceAvailable* message would be received). It would then alert the user through the *Status-Feedbacker*. If the shaded classes were omitted from this diagram, the system would not be able to detect the network failure. Note that a skilful software developer could have implemented this operation with a time-out in anticipation of a possible network failure. In this case, however, the potential usability of the application would depend on the developer's skill, with no guarantee of it working properly. Explicitly incorporating the components for this usability feature in the software design models provides assurance that these components will be codified by the programmer and, therefore, the usability feature will be included in the final system.

The above example illustrates what impact the inclusion of the System Status Feedback feature has on software design (and therefore on later software products and code). Other designers could have come up with different, albeit equally valid, designs to satisfy the above-mentioned responsibilities. For example, a less reusable

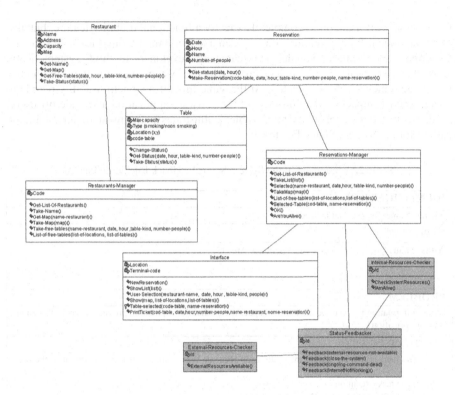

Fig. 1. Class Diagram for restaurant management with System Status Feedback feature

class model might not have included new classes for this type of feedback but have added any new methods needed to existing classes. In any case, the incorporation of this usability feature to the system can be said to have a significant impact on software design.

Note that this example only shows the effect of this usability feature for a specific functionality (table booking). This effect is multiplied if this feature is added to the other system functionalities and even more so if we consider all the other FUFs.

4 Guiding the Elicitation and Specification of Functional Usability Features

As we have shown in the last section, usability features, like any other quality attribute, have an impact on software design. Consequently, they should be considered as of the early stages of software development.

Usability elicitation patterns (USEP) were developed for each usability mechanism identified and are available[1] as a result of the STATUS project and later research. The USEP can be viewed not only as a support for software developers to extract all

---

[1] At http://is.ls.fi.upm.es/research/usability/usability-elicitation -patterns

the necessary information to completely specify a functional usability feature, but also as an instrument for communication between and a common ground for both software developers and usability people. This can help developers to think systematically about the effect of usability mechanisms across the system, assisting them to identify what requirements will be affected. At the same time, it may help usability people to understand its impact on the "insides" of the software application and trade off users' needs against developers concerns. Table 2 illustrates a fragment of an elicitation pattern for the System Status Feedback.

Table 2. A Fragment of the System Status Feedback Elicitation Pattern

IDENTIFICATION
Name: Name: System Status Feedback
Family: Feedback
Alias: Status Display [7], Modelling Feedback Area [2]

PROBLEM
Which information needs to be elicited and specified so that the application provides users with system status information?

CONTEXT
When changes that are important to the user occur or When failures that are important to the user occur: - During task execution - Because there are not enough system resources - Because external resources are not working properly. Examples of status feedback can be found in status bars on windows applications; train, bus or airline schedule systems; VCR displays; etc

SOLUTION	
Usability Mechanism Elicitation Guide	
HCI Rationale	Issues to be discussed with stakeholders
1. HCI experts argue that the user wants to be notified when a change of status occurs [7] 2.... 3...	Changes in the system status can be triggered by user-requested or other actions or when there is a problem with an external resource or another system resource. 1.1 Does the user want the system to provide notification of **system statuses**? If so, which ones? 1.2 Does the user want the system to provide notification of system **failures** (they represent any operation that the system is unable to complete, but they are not failures caused by incorrect entries by the user)? If so, which ones? 1.3 Does the user want the system to provide notification if there are not **enough resources** to execute the ongoing commands? If so, which resources? 1.4 Does the user want the system to provide notification if there is a problem with an **external resource** or device with which the system interacts? If so, which ones? 2.1 ... 2.2 ... 3.1 ...

Table 2. (*continued*)

Usability Mechanism Specification Guide
The following information will need to be instantiated in the requirements document. - The system statuses that should be reported are X, XI, XII. The information to be shown in the status area is..... The highlighted information is ...... The obtrusive information is.... - The software system will need to provide feedback about failures I, II, III occurring in tasks A, B, C, respectively. The information related to failures I, II, etc.... must be shown in status area.... The information related to failures III, IV, etc, must be shown in highlighted format. The information related to failures V, VI, etc , must be shown in obtrusive format. - The software system provides feedback about resources D, E, F when failures IV, I and VI, respectively, occur. The information to be presented about those resources is O, P, Q. The information related to failures I, II, etc....must be shown in the status area..... The information related to failures III, IV, etc, must be shown in highlighted format. The information related to failures V, VI, etc, must be shown in obtrusive format. - The software system will need to provide feedback about the external resources G, J, K, when failures VII, VIII and IX, respectively, occur. The information to be presented about those resources is R, S, T. The information related to failures I, II, etc....must be shown in the status area..... The information related to failures III, IV, etc, must be shown in highlighted format. The information related to failures V, VI, etc, must be shown in obtrusive format.

This system is an attempt at an innovative solution for reserving restaurant tables using a reservation support terminal located at street level and connected to Internet.

When a customer accesses a reservation support terminal, the terminal asks the user the name of the restaurant, the date and the time at which he or she would like to book a table. Through a central reservations office, which has information on the status of all the tables in the restaurant chain, the terminal checks whether there is a vacant table at the chosen restaurant at the elected time. If there is, the central reservations office, with the aid of the chosen restaurant, first sends a plan of the restaurant and then the vacant tables with their respective positions on the plan. This way the reservation support terminal can reconstruct the restaurant plan indicating which tables are vacant.

The user selects a table and enters the number of people for which the table is to be booked. The reservation support terminal communicates this information to the central reservations office, which then checks with the restaurant that everything is still in order. If everything is OK, the terminal asks the user to enter the name under which the table is to be booked. The user enters the name, and the terminal communicates this information to the central reservations office. The central reservations office books the table and issues a ticket specifying the date, time, table number and the name under which the table has been booked. *This confirms the reservation (status).*

If there are no vacant tables at the time specified by the user, the reservation support terminal informs the customer, giving the user the option of asking the system to list the restaurants that have vacancies on the day and at the time of his/her choice.

System operationality should be such as to take into account possible system and network (Internet) crashes. The user should be given a warning if the system is not working because of an item that is vital for function execution being blocked (internal resources). Additionally, the user will be warned obtrusively if the system is unable to access the network in the course of table booking due to a network crash, as the user should not be allowed to continue with the reservation if a connectivity failure (external resources) prevents the customer's request from being satisfied.

Fig. 2. Fragment of a requirement modified with FUF

The *identification* part of the USEP gives an understanding of the generics of the usability mechanism to be addressed, and the *problem* and *context* to which it applies. The *solution* part contains two elements: the *usability mechanism elicitation guide* and the *usability mechanism specification guide*. The usability mechanism elicitation guide provides knowledge for eliciting information about the usability mechanism. It lists the issues that stakeholders should discuss to properly define how the usability mechanism needs to be considered along with the corresponding HCI rationale (i.e. the HCI recommendation used to derive the respective issues). Usability engineers could help developers to understand the HCI rationales in the guide and to mediate the discussion of the related issues with stakeholders. They may also extend and adapt the information when necessary for specific situations.

The elicited usability information can be specified following the usability mechanism specification guide. This guide is a prompt for the developer to modify each requirement affected by the incorporation of each mechanism. Figure 3 shows a fragment of a requirement for the restaurant booking application, modified to include all the usability mechanisms that affect it. The parts added as a result of using the respective USEPs are highlighted using bold face and italics.

Modifying a requirement to include certain usability mechanisms involves adding the details describing how to apply these mechanisms to this functionality. The remaining development phases are undertaken as always, and the new usability functionality is integrated into the development process.

5 Conclusions

Although belonging to different traditions and times, the disciplines of software engineering (SE) and human computer interaction (HCI) share the same goal of meeting the needs of application software customers and users. Even so, the boundaries between SE and HCI and attempts at bridging gaps between the two disciplines by fusing the efforts of both communities come up against plenty of challenges. The literature suggests that the main obstacles are problems of communication and efficiency, and that software and usability engineers have little knowledge of each others' jobs.

This paper aimed to facilitate and encourage the convergence of practices in both communities by first showing that usability does have an impact on software models and second proposing a pattern-based way of dealing with usability features with particular functional implications at requirements time. Usability features are more difficult to specify than it would seem; a lot of details need to be explicitly discussed with stakeholders and need the expertise of both usability engineers and software developers. Although the functional usability features addressed by USEPs are not sufficient to make software usable, they do represent the features with the biggest impact on functionality. The potential benefits of USEPs have been investigated in real projects developed as part of an SE Master program since 2003. Different analyses of final system usability performed have shown how useful the elicitation patterns are for building more usable software.

In summary, the proposed approach encourages a mutual understanding of the activities and responsibilities between the two communities with a view to the construction of usable systems. By making the implications of functional usability features in software models visible, better prepared usability engineers will be able to mediate between users and developers at requirements elicitation and specification time and to ensure that usability issues will be properly dealt with during the whole development cycle.

Acknowledgments. We thank CNPq (476381/2004-5) and the Cátedra Ibero-Americana Unicamp-Santander Banespa for supporting one of the authors.

References

1. Barbacci, M., Ellison, R., Lattanze, A., Stafford, J.A., Weinstock, C.B., Wood, W.G.: Quality Attribute Workshop, 3rd ed. CMU/SEI-2003-TR-016, Software Engineering Institute (2003)
2. Bass, L., John, B., Kates, J.: Achieving Usability through Software Architecture. Technical Report. CMU/SEI-2001-TR-005, Software Engineering Institute, CMU (2001)
3. Bass, L., John, B.: Linking Usability to software architecture patterns through general scenarios. The Journal of Systems and Software 66(3), 187–197 (2003)
4. Bass, L., John, B., Juristo, N., Sanchez, M.I.: Usability Supporting Architectural Patterns. In: Tutorial International Conference on Software Engineering (2004)
5. Bevan, N.: Quality and usability: A new framework. In: van Veenendaal, E., McMullan, J. (eds.) Achieving software product quality, The Netherlands, pp. 25–34 (1997)
6. Bevan, N.: Quality in Use for All. In: User interfaces for all. In: Stephanidis, C. (ed.) Lawrence Erlbaum, Mahwah (1999)
7. Bias, R.G., Mayhew, D.J.: Cost-Justifying Usability. Elsevier, Amsterdam (2005)
8. Bosch, J., Juristo, N.: Designing Software Architectures for Usability. In: Tutorial International Conference on Software Engineering (2003)
9. Brighton.: Usability Pattern Collection (2003), www.cmis.brighton.ac.uk/research/patterns/
10. Buschmann, F., Meuneir, R., Rohnert, H., Sommerland, P., Stal, M.: Pattern-Oriented Software Architecture, A System of Patterns. J. Wiley and Sons, Chichester (1996)
11. Chirstel, M. G., Kang, K.C.: Issues in Requirements Elicitation. Technical Report CMU/SEI-92-TR-012, Software Engineering Institute, CMU (1992)
12. Constantine, L., Lockwood, L.: Software for Use: A Practical Guide to the Models and Methods of Usage-Centered Design. Addison-Wesley, Reading (1999)
13. Coram, T., Lee, L.: Experiences: A Pattern Language for User Interface Design (1996), http://www.maplefish.com/todd/papers/experiences/Experiences.html
14. Faulkner, X., Culwin, F.: Enter the Usability Engineer: Integrating HCI and Software Engineering. ITICSE ACM, pp. 61–64 (2000)
15. Ferré, X., Juristo, N., Moreno, A.: Which, When and How Usability Techniques and Activities Should be Integrated. In: Seffah, A., Gulliksen, J., Desmarais, M.C. (eds.) Human-Centered Software Engineering - Integrating Usability in the Software Development Lifecycle. Human-Computer Interaction Series, vol. 8, Kluwer, Dordrecht (2005)
16. Folmer, E., van Group, J., Bosch, J.: Architecting for usability: a survey. Journal of Systems and Software 70(1-2), 61–78 (2004)
17. Guide to the Software Engineering Body of Knowledge. version (2004), http://www.swebok.org
18. Holzinger, A.: Usability Engineering Methods for Software Developers. Communications of the ACM 48(1), 71–74 (2005)
19. Hix, D., Hartson, H.R.: Developing User Interfaces: Ensuring Usability through Product and Process. J. Wiley and Sons, Chichester (1993)
20. ISO/IEC FCD 9126-1 Software product quality - Part 1: Quality model (1998)
21. ISO 9241-11 Ergonomic requirements for office work with visual display terminals (1998)

22. ISO 13407 User-centred design process for interactive systems (1999)
23. ISO/IEC 14598-1 Information Technology - Evaluation of Software Products Part 1 General guide (1998)
24. Jokela, T.: Guiding Designers to the World of Usability: Determining Usability Requirements through Teamwork. In: Seffah, A., Gulliksen, J., Desmarais, M. (eds.) Human-Centered Software Engineering, Kluwer, Dordrecht (2005)
25. Juristo, N., Moreno, A., Sánchez, M.: Architectural Sensitive Usability Patterns. ICSE Workshop Bridging the Gaps between Usability and Software Development (2003)
26. Juristo, N., Moreno, A., Sánchez, M.: Techniques and Patterns for Architecture-Level Usability Improvements. Deliv. 3.4 STATUS project (May 2003), http://www.ls.fi.upm. es/status
27. Juristo, N., Moreno, A., Sánchez, M.: Clarifying the Relationship between Software Architecture and Usability. In: 16th International Conference on Software Engineering and Knowledge Engineering (2004)
28. Juristo, N., Moreno, A., Sánchez, M.: Analysing the impact of usability on software design. Journal of System and Software. Accepted for publication (2007)
29. Unified Modeling Language (UML). Version 2.0. OMG Object Management Group Visited January 2007 (2007), http://www.omg.org/technology/documents/formal/uml.htm
30. Laasko, S.A.: User Interface Designing Patterns. Visited October 2004 (2003), http://www.cs.helsinki.fi/u/salaakso/patterns/index_tree.html
31. Milewski, A.E.: Software Engineers and HCI Practitioners Learning to Work Together: A Preliminary Look at Expectations. In: Proceedings of the 17th Conference on Software Engineering Education and Training CSEET '04, IEEE, Los Alamitos (2004)
32. Nielsen, J.: Usability Engineering. John Wiley & Sons, Chichester (1993)
33. Perry, D., Wolf, A.: Foundations for the Study of Software Architecture. ACM Software Engineering Notes 17(4), 40–52 (1992)
34. QUISTM Questionnaire For User Interaction Satisfaction, http://lap.umd.edu/QUIS/
35. Rubinstein, R., Hersh, H.: The Human Factor. Digital Press, Bedford, MA (1984)
36. Seffah, A., Djouab, R., Antunes, H.: Comparing and Reconciling Usability-Centered and Use Case-Driven Requirements Engineering Processes, pp. 132–139. IEEE, Los Alamitos (2001)
37. Seffah, A., Metzker, E.: The Obstacles and Myths of Usability and Software Engineering. Communications of the ACM 47(12), 71–76 (2004)
38. Shneiderman, B.: Designing the User Interface: Strategies for Effective Human-Computer Interaction. Addison-Wesley, Reading (1998)
39. Sommerville, I.: Software Engineering, 7th edn. Pearson Education (2004)
40. Tidwell, J.: Common Ground: A Pattern Language for Human-Computer Interface Design (1999), http://www.mit.edu/%7Ejtidwell/interaction_patterns.html
41. Tidwell, J.: Designing Interfaces. Patterns for Effective Interaction Design. O'Reilliy, USA (2005)
42. Welie, M.: Amsterdam Collection of Patterns in User Interface Design (2003), http://www.welie.com/

Are Engineers Condemned to Design?
A Survey on Software Engineering and UI Design in Switzerland

Ljiljana Vukelja[1], Lothar Müller[1], and Klaus Opwis[2]

[1] University of Applied Sciences Rapperswil, Switzerland
{lvukelja, lmueller}@hsr.ch
[2] University of Basel, Switzerland
klaus.opwis@unibas.ch

Abstract. In this paper we present the results of a descriptive online survey conducted among Swiss software developers regarding their engineering practices with a special focus on the design and development of user interfaces. This enables an insight into the everyday life of a software engineer and can lead usability practitioners, project managers and clients to a better level of cooperation in designing user interfaces through understanding how software engineers work. While software is developed and tested in a professional way, several problem areas were detected: firstly, software engineers frequently develop user interfaces alone, without the help of Human-Computer Interaction (HCI) professionals. Secondly, they have a limited knowledge of HCI. Thirdly, whilst they have contact to end users, they do not make use of this for user interface design. Finally, usability tests are rare and seldom result in big changes.

Keywords: Software engineering, user interface design, user-centered design, survey.

1 Introduction

Today, user-centered methods in software engineering are well developed and a wide range of literature on this subject has been produced (see e.g. [5-7, 11, 14, 18]. Nevertheless there are complaints about the usability of the products. As illustrated by Nelson et al. [21] poor usability leads to low levels of satisfaction amongst users. What then are the reasons for the apparent low quality of products? On one hand, the user-centered methods might not be good enough; on the other they might not be practiced correctly or even at all. We will, however, leave the discussion of the quality of the methods to other research, and instead will look into the practice of software engineering in Switzerland.

Most previous surveys have concentrated either on software engineering [9] or on Human-Computer Interaction practice [13, 16, 27], but rarely have they examined the relationship between the two. Jerome and Kazman [15] investigated this relationship by asking software (SW) engineers *and* HCI practitioners separately about each other,

C. Baranauskas et al. (Eds.): INTERACT 2007, LNCS 4663, Part II, pp. 555–568, 2007.

reaching the conclusion that there are misunderstandings between the two groups. In our study we will concentrate *only* on the SW engineers and look at their everyday practice. We will describe what they do and how they do it, focusing in particular on the design and the development of user interfaces (UI).

The paper begins with a description of the parameters of our survey and a presentation of the results attained. This is followed by a detailed discussion. Finally, in concluding we will also consider possible further research.

2   Survey

Two key questions underpin the survey:
- *Which* software development methods are used?
- *Who* designs and develops user interfaces and how?

2.1   Method

We conducted a descriptive online survey among SW professionals in Switzerland during March and April 2006. The recipients were addressed through mailing lists and over personal contacts and were asked to fill in an online form. The demographics of addressed mailing lists and personal contacts are comparable, since we used general mailing lists of Swiss SW engineers and similar personal contacts. To avoid bias specialized mailing lists were excluded. Our target group was technically experienced and uses the Internet extensively, justifying an online survey [4]. No financial incentives were offered to those who took part though they were informed that they were contributing to a research project [28]. In order to increase the response rate we sent the survey as a personally addressed email invitation to our own contacts, since emails sent from a known sender are less likely to be tagged as spam [28]. Mailing list recipients were not addressed personally, but we assumed that members would have confidence in the quality of the mailing lists.

2.2   Basic Population and Sample

In 2003 in Switzerland there were 13,597 companies working in the area of computing services. These companies employed an average size of 4.9 employees [3]. This is equal to a total of some 67,174 employees in the area of information technology.

We emailed 1,874 addresses: 74 from personal contacts and 1,800 addresses selected from three mailing lists. Our target group was SW developers (and not HCI experts) in Switzerland, because we wanted to know how *SW developers* work. We received 134 completed forms.

Even though we addressed recipients belonging to general mailing lists on SW engineering there is possibly a correlation between participation and the questions posed in the survey (self-selection bias). It is possible that only those interested in UI design chose to answer. By asking the participants to refer to their current or last project, we tried to avoid the problem of reporting the "general" feeling about how SW is or should be developed.

Due to the anonymity, it is not known whether some participants referred to the same project, so the number of projects covered may be less than 134. Only a systematic sample could avoid this.

2.3 Questions

The survey contained 25 questions and took an average of 30 minutes to complete. Firstly, we asked for information about the project participants were working on, their company, and the participants' activities within the project. The next section of questions addressed SW engineering methods and asked participants to describe the actual development process. This was followed by questions concerning requirements definition, change management, and testing habits. The next questions dealt with UI design and contact with end users. Finally, we asked the participants about their knowledge in the area of user-centered design.

In total the survey consisted of 13 open-ended questions where participants were asked to answer by writing free text, 3 yes/no questions and 7 questions where more than one answer could be ticked. The vast majority of questions were open-ended, the aim being to let respondents say what they wanted, rather than limiting them to a pre-selected (and possibly biased) choice of answers. We then categorized the responses for further analysis. Perhaps not surprisingly on account of the open-ended nature of some of the questions participants did not always answer these questions. The final two questions asked firstly, whether the participant was interested in the results of the survey and secondly, whether he or she would be willing to take part in an interview on the subject. Following a positive response the participant's identity was requested.

A copy of the survey questions can be attained from the authors.

3   Results

In this section, we will examine the results of the survey. The numbers in **boldface** are those emphasised in the text.

Note that the sample size of every question is different because, as alluded to above, not all of our 134 respondents answered all of the questions.

3.1 Respondents

The initial questions in the survey concerned the company where the participants work and the project in which they are involved. Table 1 displays the types of companies classified according to [1]. A company of micro size has less than 10 employees, a small company has 10 - 50, a medium one 50 - 250, and a large one more than 250 employees. We defined the size of the SW development department (last column in Table 1) to be ten times less in size than that of the overall company. Thus, a small SW development department has less than 5 employees, a medium one has 5 - 25, and a large department employs more than 25 people. It can be seen that more than 42% of SW development departments are big. Our sample consists mostly of large companies and large SW development departments. This matches well with the countrywide distribution [2].

From our analysis 44.4% of respondents work on a proprietary product, 41.4% on a one-time project for external customers and 18.0% on a one-time project for internal customers. This suggests that a big portion of SW development is being conducted externally by specialized and professional providers.

Table 1. Company types

Size	# of companies		# of SW development departments
	this survey	country average	
Micro	21 (22.6%)	842,657 (26.3%)	
Small	18 (19.4%)	680,728 (21.2%)	22 (25.9%)
Medium	22 (23.7%)	619,863 (19.3%)	27 (31.8%)
Large	32 (34.4%)	1,063,437 (33.2%)	36 (**42.4%**)
Total	93 (100%)	3,206,685 (100%)	85 (100%)

Table 2 shows the primary role of the participants along with other activities that participants undertake. In terms of activities the respondents were able to choose one or more answers from a predefined list, whereas for the primary role they were asked to explicitly name their role in free text. According to the responses received 70.1% conduct tasks of a developer. As their primary role 38.5% gave an answer of "developer", and 39.3% said they were "project managers". This confirms that we reached the main target of our study: the SW engineers.

Table 2. Tasks carried out by respondents

Job	Primary role	Activities
Developer	47 (**38.5%**)	94 (**70.1%**)
Project manager (PM)	48 (**39.3%**)	64 (47.8%)
Software architect	8 (6.6%)	74 (55.2%)
Application tester	-	41 (30.6%)
Customer	-	7 (5.2%)
Requirements engineer (REn)	-	52 (38.8%)
Usability engineer (UEn)	3 (2.5%)	25 (18.7%)
Consultant	3 (2.5%)	-
Other	13 (10.7%)	-

An average team (see Fig. 1) consists of 7.8 people: 4.2 are developers, 0.5 have a profession dealing with the UI (REn, UEn).

89.6% of teams have no requirements engineer and 85.7% of teams have no UI engineer. Note that in cases where no requirements engineer is present there still might be a UI engineer and vice versa. If we consider requirements engineers and UI engineers to be experts in HCI then from Table 3 it is apparent that 77.9% of SW teams work entirely without HCI professionals. In addition, we examined the data to

Awareness Solutions for Informal Communication Negotiation Support at Work

Agnieszka Matysiak Szóstek

Industrial Design, Eindhoven University of Technology, Den Dolech 2,
5600MB Eindhoven, The Netherlands
a.matysiak@tue.nl

Abstract: The goal of our project is to design and evaluate an awareness system that supports handling interruptions for both interruption actors: interruptees and interruptors.

Introduction

Informal communication between coworkers is considered as an optimal way to exchange rapid feedback, share local context and reference common depictions [2]. But it comes at a cost: interruptions. If interruptions occur at wrong moments they cause loss of concentration, anxiety and time pressure [1]. However, once initiated at right times they serve as natural breaks and provide content for expressive interaction between colleagues. Current solutions supporting handling interruptions assume the interruptee's availability to be the best predictor of an appropriate interruption moment [2]. Yet, interruptors seem not to fully adhere to those availability indications as the proposed systems fail to help them convey their communicative needs. Also interruptees seem to experience social responsibility and they often reevaluate their availability according to the actual needs of their interruptors [4].

Information Needs in Negotiating Interruptions

A key challenge in designing awareness systems supporting handling interruptions lies in provision of means for expressing information needs that reach beyond simple availability indications. Participants in our studies reported needs that would help them to increase efficiency in interruption negotiation, which can be grouped in three groups: those related to social proximity between the actors, those defining the nature of the interruption subject and those determining the anticipated interruption duration. In order to determine whether our classification is accurate we have constructed two Technology Probes out of two interconnected devices: one standing in one's office and another located in front of one's door. At any time of the day the office occupant could indicate his/her communicative status on the *office probe* and the interruptor his/her information needs on the *corridor probe*. The evaluation of the probes showed that despite the probe straightforwardness and the simplicity of the proposed interaction a possibility of sharing relevant information needs was highly valued by both interruptors and interruptees.

C. Baranauskas et al. (Eds.): INTERACT 2007, LNCS 4663, Part II, pp. 569–570, 2007.

Social and System Influence on Interruption Behaviour

As the next step we set out to verify in what way different system and social behaviours influence interruptions. We have conducted an experiment testing the *system condition*, which offered a manual or an automatic approach to handling interruptions and the *social condition*, which identified two relationships: the *Team* representing people sharing a common goal and the *Group* representing those who did not share a goal but assumed social reciprocation. The results show that actors who share a common goal behave in a more sensitive manner when handling interruptions than those who do not share it. The choice between the manual and automatic system behaviour seems to depend on moment–to–moment activities of both actors rather than their social relationship. Participants in both roles and in both social conditions liked the possibility to select system behaviour to fit their current task.

Future Work and Conclusions

Through this research we aim to i) extend the current knowledge about information needs essential for successful interruption negotiation ii) contribute an awareness system supporting negotiating interruptions that in its expressiveness reaches beyond availability indications and iii) produce guidelines informing the design of a future systems supporting informal communication at work.

The following step in our study is to design and evaluate an awareness system that addresses previously collected information needs and interruption handling strategies. In our design we want to consider two situations, in which the intent for initiating interruption is produced: a moment when the interruptor forms a plan to go and interrupt, while still remaining at his/her own workplace and a moment when the interruptor takes an opportunistic decision to interrupt when either passing by the interruptee's office or remaining at the same office that the interruptee is present in. In both cases the interruptor needs to be provided with the interruptee's status indication and must have an opportunity to present some of the interruption characteristics.

References

[1] Adamczyk, P.D., Bailey, B.P.: If not now, when?: the effects of interruption at different moments within task execution. In: CHI, ACM Press, New York (2004)
[2] Fogarty, J., Hudson, S., Atkeson, C., Avrahami, D., Forlizzi, J., Kiesler, S., Lee, J., Yang, J.: Predicting human interruptability with sensors. ACM Transactions (2005)
[3] Nardi, B., Whittaker, S.: The place of face-to-face communication in distributed work, Distributed Work. MIT Press, Cambridge (2001)
[4] Wiberg, M., Whittaker, S.: Managing availability: supporting lightweight negotiations to handle interruptions. ACM Transactions 1 (2005)

Sensemaking and Knowledge Building in System Development

Elina Eriksson

Uppsala University, Dept. of IT/HCI, PO Box 337, SE-75105 Uppsala, Sweden
Elina.Eriksson@it.uu.se

One major goal of research within the HCI (Human-Computer Interaction) community is to develop or refine theories and methods that can be used in practice, in the system development process. However usability methods are not always with ease adopted in the system development process or in organizations [1,2].

In my research, I have so far concentrated on system developers and their role in user centered system design since they will affect the usability of the resulting IT-system by making design decisions late in the system development process. In order to better consider the user and the usage of the system, the system developers need to adopt new methods.

Field methods are one type of methods in order to collect data about the user and the context of system usage. However the methods can seem to be time consuming and produce large amounts of data. On CHI'2002 four panelists offered their view of the practice and challenge of making field methods a part of the product development process. One conclusion was that in order to adopt field methods it is important to address the designers' needs [3].

Previous research on field studies in practice has much focused on adapting and streamlining the field studies to the limited time scale of systems development [4,5].

However time is not the only aspect that hinders system developers to adopt new methods, preceding attitudes and values might also play an important part of the adoption. Hence the developers must appreciate the methods and see them as useful and appropriate for their work [6]. If the system developers are negative the methods will not be used.

My concern is to understand how system developers make sense of HCI-methods and particularly field studies. How do the system developers perceive the methods and what do they think is the advantages and disadvantages with the methods? Do the system developers regard the methods as useful and helpful in their work and in what way?

The research question is:

How do system developers make sense of HCI-methods and particularly field studies?

In my research my over-arching method is action research, described in Rasmussen [7]. Action research aims at doing a change in practice at the same time as research is performed. The methods I have used are qualitative, collecting data about the people, the system and the context. Examples of methods used are semi-structured interviews, field studies and participatory observations.

C. Baranauskas et al. (Eds.): INTERACT 2007, LNCS 4663, Part II, pp. 571–572, 2007.
© IFIP International Federation for Information Processing 2007

Since my research is interpretative and qualitative, the criteria of evaluation used within the conventional research paradigm, is not applicable. Instead this research follows the quality criteria given by Klein and Myers [8]. They present seven principles that an interpretative researcher should consider during the whole research process. The principles cannot be applied in a mechanistic way, rather as a researcher I must reflect on how my research relates to these principles, to which extent and apply those principles that are appropriate.

I am a part of an action research project that our research group is doing in collaboration with three public authorities in Sweden. The research goal is to understand how an organization understands user centered system design, implements the methods, and make use of them. We are also interested in understanding what are the obstacles and beneficial factors of the implementation process. The project goal of the organization is to get better systems for their case handlers and by this better work and more healthy workers.

My results will give a deeper understanding of the problem of implementing user centered system design methods in organizations, and particularly how system developer perceive, understand an make sense of usability methods such as field studies. Furthermore, my work in the action research project will also affect the organizations in which the research is performed. Not only by us introducing user centered methods, but also by our presence, asking questions and giving advice which will affect how the people in the organization reflect on what they are doing which leads to a change in the organizational knowledge.

References

1. Boivie, I.: A Fine Balance: Addressing Usability and Users Needs in the Development of IT Systems for the Workplace. Acta Universitatis Upsaliensis, Uppsala 85 (2005)
2. Boivie, I., Aborg, C., Persson, J., Löfberg, M., Boivie, I., Blomkvist, S., Persson, J.: Why usability gets lost or usability in in-house software development. Interacting with Computers 15(4), 623–639 (2003)
3. Wixon, D.R., Ramey, J., Holtzblatt, K., Beyer, H., Hackos, J.A., Rosenbaum, S., Page, C., Laakso, S.A., Laakso, K.P.: Usability in Practice: Field Methods Evolution and Revolution. In: Conference on Human Factors in Computing Systems, CHI 2002, pp. 880–884 (2002)
4. Kujala, S., Kauppinen, M., Nakari, P., Rekola, S.: Field Studies in Practice: Making it Happen. In: Proceedings of INTERACT 2003, Zürich, pp. 359–366 (2003)
5. Millen, D.R.: Rapid Ethnography: Time Deepening Strategies for HCI Field Research. In: Proc. Designing Interactive Systems, DIS 2000, pp. 280–286. New York (2000)
6. Riemenschneider, C.K., Hardgrave, B.C., Davis, F.D.: Explaining Software Developer Acceptance of Methodologies: a Comparison of Five Theoretical Models. IEEE Transactions on Software Engineering 28(12), 1135–1145 (2002)
7. Lauge, Baungaard.: Rasmussen: Action Research—Scandinavian Experiences. AI & Society 18(1), 21–43 (2004)
8. Klein, H., Myers, M.: A Set of Principles for Conducting and Evaluating Interpretive Field Studies in Information Systems. MIS Quarterly 23, 67–94 (1999)

Just Email It to Me! Why Things Get
Lost in Shared File Repositories

Emilee J. Rader

University of Michigan, School of Information
1075 Beal Ave., Ann Arbor MI, 48109
ejrader@umich.edu
Dissertation Advisor:
Judith Olson jsolson@umich.edu

Abstract. Shared file repositories are a type of information technology application used by workgroups to store and share files online. Their use in organizations is becoming more frequent; however, repository users are not always able to effectively find and access information, especially when files in the repository have been created and maintained by others. Through field studies involving current users of shared file repositories, I will document and analyze the scope and consequences of the problem. In addition, I will test hypotheses about possible remedies through a series of experiments exploring the effects of common ground on folder hierarchy and naming structure, and the ability of users to find and access files.

Keywords: Shared file repositories, social computing, information management, common ground.

1 Introduction

Much of an organization's information is represented in the form of documents, such as reports, memos, meeting minutes, email messages, etc. Ineffective document management incurs costs such as "lost work time, ineffective access to information, duplication of effort, failure to share information, and information overload" [6]. Many different kinds of workgroups including research labs, corporate teams, and software developers use central online repositories for storing information. These repositories are maintained by many organizations, "for their potential value in the day-to-day operations of the organization" [8]. They are essential for document sharing, and can be greatly beneficial for organizational efficiency, communicating organizational goals, and also for learning and innovation. They can contain "mission critical information" such that if it were lost there would be serious consequences [2].

Despite the importance of the information stored within them, shared file repositories generally do not have explicit rules or structures for organization and searching, like a library catalog does. Instead, they tend to accumulate content over time and become more and more disorganized, such that users have difficulty finding the files they need. The research described below examines situations in which users are not able to effectively find and access information in shared file repositories, and suggests possible remedies for these problems.

C. Baranauskas et al. (Eds.): INTERACT 2007, LNCS 4663, Part II, pp. 573–576, 2007.

2 Shared File Repositories

Shared file repositories are online storage spaces used by workgroups for storing, organizing, and sharing documents and other files, and their use is increasing. A shared file repository is more complex than just an "aggregate of every individual's contribution" [7], and maintaining it is a collaborative activity. This makes repositories different from other ways shared work files are commonly stored, such as in email mailboxes, on personal computers, or posted to internal company websites. People differ in the ways in which they structure their personal file repositories, as has been observed in many personal information management studies; for example, [1]. Individual goals and strategies for managing information could affect the choices users make when storing or seeking files in a shared file repository. A repository user is generally familiar with his fellow group members, and with projects and joint work activities they are engaged in together. However, he can expect to be familiar with only some of the files stored in a shared file repository, and he may or may not have been involved with creating the hierarchy and naming structure, or with storing and moving files around in the repository. This creates a situation different from both searching the web and one's personal information, where a user might be trying to find files with which she is unfamiliar, or looking for familiar files stored in unfamiliar places. This can be frustrating enough that users seeking information circumvent shared file repositories altogether, opting to request files from others via email instead – thus the title of my dissertation.

3 Common Ground

The functionality available in most shared file repositories is essentially identical to personal information management software, with additional capabilities allowing multiple people to interact with them simultaneously. However, the communication and collaboration inherent to group work lead to problems not accounted for in the design of personal information management tools, nor addressed in the personal information management literature. For example, previous research has demonstrated that if two random users were to create a name for the same file, it is unlikely that they would choose identical words [4]. Fortunately, users of shared file repositories are not necessarily random pairs of people who are unknown to each other. In the best case, they share a work context and even have some knowledge about each other's preferences and personal styles. So, while there is naturally a great deal of variability in people's choices when storing files in a shared file repository, their knowledge about each other and their shared context – their common ground – might mitigate the problem somewhat, if it were somehow brought to bear.

Common ground [3] is the mutual knowledge, beliefs and assumptions that people share about each other. It is inferred based on joint membership in cultural communities and through shared perceptual experiences, and accumulates via conversation. As conversation progresses, people introduce ideas and vocabulary that become part of their common ground, and can subsequently be referred to without the overhead of having to re-introduce them. There is much experimental evidence to support the idea that common ground affects language use. Speakers tailor their utterances for listeners, with performance implications. In addition, people create labels for their own use that are different from those created for an unknown future person [5]. People tailor what they say to whomever is the intended recipient; it is reasonable to think that common ground might indeed affect the names information producers create for files they store in a shared file repository.

4 Proposed Research

In my dissertation, I build on the current understanding of personal information management tasks and tools by examining similar tasks in group situations having multiple participants and stakeholders. CTools (ctools.umich.edu) is an example of software used at the University of Michigan that includes shared file repository functionality. I conducted a pilot study with faculty, staff and students using CTools to support ongoing collaborative projects, in which I collected data through interviews and server event log analysis.

Through this continuing field study, I will obtain a more detailed understanding of the problems users encounter under real work conditions when using a shared file repository, including how decisions are made about what to share via a repository, how files should be named, and where they should be stored. I will also document the scope and consequences of the problems users have with finding and accessing files. The field study will include additional semi-structured interviews, content analysis of the structure, naming conventions, and information contained within shared file repositories, and further analysis of usage log data providing information about user behavior and structural changes to the repositories over time. In addition, I will test hypotheses about possible remedies through a series of experiments exploring the effects of common ground, made salient by various feedback and incentive mechanisms, on choices made by users when storing, organizing, and seeking files using shared file repositories.

I am also studying the properties and usage of a different kind of online application for sharing information, the popular social bookmarking and tagging website, del.icio.us (http://del.icio.us). This system provides the capability for users to bookmark web pages and associate user-generated metadata, or tags, with them. Through this project I am able to study an application used by millions of people, and gain valuable insight into design alternatives to the traditional hierarchical file-and-folder structure for storing information.

Shared file repositories are typically not considered to be communications technologies in the same way email and instant messaging are. Yet these applications support asynchronous interactions and information exchanges between workgroup members. Through choices about which files are stored in close proximity, who is given access, and via metadata such as file author and usage frequency, repositories can communicate information to others about which activities are more important, how projects are related, and even the power relationships within the workgroup. This research will provide a better understanding of social interactions mediated by shared file repositories in workgroup settings, as well as suggesting technological and social interventions that can be used to inform the design and development of future applications.

References

1. Berlin, L.M., Jeffries, R., O'Day, V.L., Paepcke, A., Wharton, C.: Where did you put it? Review of Information Science and Technology. In: The American Society for Information Science and Technology, Medford, NJ, vol. 37, pp. 3–50 (2002)
2. Blair, D.C., Kimbrough, S.O.: Exemplary documents: a foundation for information retrieval design. Information Processing and Management 38, 363–379 (2002)
3. Clark, H.H.: Common Ground. Using Language. Cambridge University Press, Cambridge (1996)
4. Furnas, G.W., Landauer, T.K., Gomez, L.M., Dumais, S.T.: The vocabulary problem in human-system communication. Commun. ACM 30(11), 964–971 (1987)
5. Fussell, S.R., Krauss, R.M.: The effects of intended audience on message production and comprehension: Reference in a common ground framework. Journal of Experimental Social Psychology 25(3), 203–219 (1989)
6. Gordon, M.D.: It's 10 a.m. do you know where your documents are? The nature and scope of information retrieval problems in business. Information Processing & Management 33(1), 107–122 (1997)
7. Jian, G., Jeffres, L.: Understanding Employees' Willingness to Contribute to Shared Electronic Databases: A Three Dimensional Framework. Communication Research 33(4), 242–261 (2006)
8. Trigg, R.H., Blomberg, J., Suchman, L.: Moving document collections online: The evolution of a shared repository. In: Kyng, M., Bodker, S., Schmidt, K. (eds.) Proc. Sixth European Conference on Computer-Supported Cooperative Work, pp. 331–350. Kluwer Academic Publishers, Copenhagen, Denmark (1999)

Crossmodal Interaction: Using Audio or Tactile Displays in Mobile Devices

Eve Hoggan

Multimodal Interaction Group | GIST, University of Glasgow, UK, G12 8QQ
eve@dcs.gla.ac.uk

Abstract. Mobile device users can be in a variety of different situations where visual, audio, or tactile feedback is not appropriate. This research aims to investigate the design of auditory/tactile crossmodal icons which can provide an alternative form of output using the most appropriate modality to communicate information. The results of this research will aid designers of mobile displays in creating effective crossmodal cues which require minimal training and provide alternative presentation modalities through which information may be presented if the context requires.

1 Introduction

Providing non-visual information to mobile users is an important area of research. We spend a great deal of our lives using mobile devices. Whether it is in a bag or we are at a noisy party, we still want to be able to interact with our device. In these situations, visual feedback is not always appropriate. However, although a user's eyes may be busy focusing on their primary task, many activities do not otherwise restrict users from attending to information using their other senses.

Manufacturers already include basic audio and vibrotactile features in products like mobile phones. Unfortunately, when the device is in a bag or pocket, tactile feedback can go unnoticed. If a user is listening to music, audio feedback can be ineffective. Thus, mobile applications could benefit from providing alternative presentation modalities depending on the situation. As the context changes, so should the feedback modality. This research exploits existing features of mobile devices by making information available to both the auditory and tactile senses so that the user can receive the information in the most suitable way.

2 Crossmodal Auditory and Tactile Interaction

This research investigates the design of crossmodal auditory and tactile feedback using crossmodal icons [4]. Crossmodal icons can be automatically instantiated as an Earcon [1] or Tacton [2], such that the resultant cues are equivalent and can be compared as such; enabling mobile devices to output the same information interchangeably via different modalities.

C. Baranauskas et al. (Eds.): INTERACT 2007, LNCS 4663, Part II, pp. 577–579, 2007.

The crossmodal parameters used in auditory and tactile icons to encode the same information are the amodal attributes available in those two senses e.g. intensity, rate, rhythmic structure, texture and spatial location. The first stage in this research was to identify the different crossmodal parameters which could be used as feedback and what sort of information could be encoded in such parameters.

2.1   Crossmodal Parameter Experiments and Application of Parameters

Three experiments investigating possible parameters and mappings have been conducted so far to determine which audio or tactile parameters can be considered as amodal and can map the same information between modalities. This is difficult because some of the most effective parameters available in the audio domain do not have direct mappings to the tactile domain and *vice versa*. So far, the experiments have investigated rhythms with texture and spatial location as potential parameters in both stationary and mobile environments [3, 4]. Results show that mapping audio with differing timbres or amplitude modulation to tactile amplitude modulation can create crossmodal roughness and 3D audio spatial locations can be mapped to tactile body positions on the waist with 72% accuracy when the user is mobile.

A complete set of crossmodal icons have now been created which use a combination of these parameters to encode information across the modalities. The experiment underway at present is investigating whether, if a user is trained to understand 3 dimensional alerts in one modality, they can then identify them in the other. The results for overall crossmodal Earcon recognition when trained with crossmodal Tactons show an average recognition rate of 85.1% while the results for overall crossmodal Tacton recognition when trained with crossmodal Earcons show rates of 75%. Early results are positive and indicate that once trained in one modality users can then understand the crossmodal cues in the other modality.

3   Future Work

Now that we have a complete set of 3 dimensional crossmodal icons we intend to address several research questions. What types of applications would benefit from crossmodal icons? Can crossmodal feedback aid users in mobile touchscreen interaction, navigation and collaborative tasks? What methods can be used to teach users to understand crossmodal alerts? What habits do mobile users develop? If users are given a choice of modalities, which combination do they choose to use, in what applications and in what situations? In order to answer these questions our research will involve integrating and evaluating crossmodal icons in several mobile applications which allow for the varying physical and social environments within which such devices are used.

Our research has shown that feedback can be created which exploits users' abilities to transfer knowledge from one modality to another By taking this into account and designing applications with adaptive crossmodal feedback, users will have the ability to interact with their devices even when their situation and surroundings change.

References

1. Blattner, M.M., Sumikawa, D.A., Greenberg, R.M.: Earcons and Icons: Their Structure and Common Design Principles. Human Computer Interaction 4(1), 11–44 (1989)
2. Brown, L.M., Brewster, S.A., Purchase, H.C.: A First Investigation into the Effectiveness of Tactons. In: Proc WorldHaptics 2005, pp. 167–176. IEEE, Los Alamitos (2005)
3. Hoggan, E., Brewster, S.: Crossmodal Icons for Information Display. In: Proc CHI '06 Extended Abstracts, pp. 857–862. ACM Press, New York (2006)
4. Hoggan, E., Brewster, S.A.: Crossmodal Spatial Location: Initial Experiments. In: Proc NordiCHI, Norway, pp. 469–472. ACM, New York (2006)

The Impacts of Hyperlinks and Writer Information on the Credibility of Stories on a Participatory Journalism Web Site

Kirsten A. Johnson

Drexel University, 3141 Chestnut St., Philadelphia, Pa., 19104
kaj27@drexel.edu

Abstract. Credibility in mainstream media continues to wane, giving rise to new forms of journalism supported by the Internet. One of these new forms of journalism is participatory journalism. This is a form of journalism in which content is produced by ordinary citizens, usually on web sites. One of the most popular participatory journalism web sites at this time is ohmynews.com. Like mainstream media, this site, as well as ones like it, have credibility obstacles to overcome. This paper outlines a proposed study in which the researcher will test whether or not the presence of information about a writer and sources used to write a story on a participatory journalism web site affects the perceived credibility of the story.

Keywords: Participatory journalism, Citizen journalism, weblogs, blogs, computer mediated communication, CMC, credibility

Research Area: Participatory journalism, blogging, user created content, computer mediated communication.

Brief Description of Research Topic: Participatory journalism and markers of credibility. Does providing information about the writer of a story and sources used to write the story affect its credibility?

1 Introduction

This proposed study seeks to understand the relationship between information and credibility. Credibility is one of the key components upon which journalism is built. Once credibility is compromised it can be detrimental to a news organization. One of the ways traditional media try to lend a measure of credibility to their information is by adhering to a filter-then-publish model. This means that the information that comes into a newsroom is edited prior to being released to a mass audience. Conversely, participatory journalism web sites tend to operate under a publish-then-filter model, where information is released to the mass audience and then it is edited. In some cases people with journalism experience are employed as editors, whereas in other cases, visitors to the site can act as editors. The missing layer of editorial oversight may cause credibility problems for these sites [1].

A study [2] on which elements help and hurt the perceived credibility of web sites shows that including markers of expertise can help boost the perceived credibility of

C. Baranauskas et al. (Eds.): INTERACT 2007, LNCS 4663, Part II, pp. 580–585, 2007.

the site. The authors of the study suggest web sites can convey expertise through listing information about the author, as well as citations of, and references to, the author's work. The authors of the study also point out that they believe many sites miss the chance to convey this expertise to those who visit their sites.

Building upon this study, perhaps participatory journalism sites can improve perceived credibility by providing information about those who write on the sites, as well as allowing visitors to their sites to verify information easily through the use of hyperlinks embedded in the story.

While there have been many studies done on traditional media and credibility perceptions, there haven't yet been any credibility studies done that pertain exclusively to participatory journalism. In fact, scholarly literature on participatory journalism is scant, so this study seeks to add to this body of literature, as well as build on previous studies in the areas of web credibility and trust.

1.1 Antecedents to Participatory Journalism

The idea of allowing ordinary citizens to have a voice in news coverage is not a new one. The civic, or public journalism movement, allows the concerns of citizens to help shape the news agenda [3, 4, 5]. The presidential election in 1988 is often cited as the time civic journalism emerged. During this time journalists raised concerns that the election news being covered wasn't news that was of interest to citizens, and that journalists hadn't remembered the public in their coverage [5]. The rise of civic journalism was spurred by declining newspaper readership and increased competition in the delivery of news, particularly 24 hour news stations like CNN [3].

Tom Curley, President and CEO of the Associated Press [6], notes that the Internet has played a large role in altering the news landscape and giving a boost to the civic journalism movement.

Consumers will want to use the two-way nature of the Internet to become active participants themselves in the exchange of news and ideas. The news, as 'lecture,' is giving way to the news as a "conversation." (para. 40)

Gill [7] argues that this idea of news as "conversation" has helped give rise to participatory journalism web sites, because participatory journalism expands two-way communication between readers and media. Interaction often is encouraged between journalists and readers. Blogging is another way to encourage interaction between writers and readers because it provides different viewpoints on shared experiences [7]. It can also be used as a tool for journalists to help "serve as a collective databank used to jog the faulty memories of those who write or report for major media" [7], p. 2.

Weblogs, also known as blogs, pre-date the creation of participatory journalism sites. Some argue that blogs can be considered a form of participatory journalism if they include journalistic news content [7, 8].

1.2 Participatory Journalism

Participatory journalism, also referred to as "grassroots journalism" and "citizen journalism," is the idea that news content is produced by ordinary citizens with no formal journalism training [9]. In their paper titled *We Media: How Audiences are*

Shaping the Future of News and Information, Shayne Bowman and Chris Willis [9] use the following working definition of participatory journalism:

> The act of a citizen, or group of citizens, playing an active role in the process of collecting, reporting, analyzing and disseminating news and information. The intent of this participation is to provide independent, reliable, accurate, wide-ranging and relevant information that a democracy requires. (p. 9)

Media futurists predict that by the year 2021 citizens will produce 50% of the news peer to peer [9]. Despite worries about citizen journalism weakening traditional journalism, some traditional media outlets have embraced reports by citizen journalists. Coverage of large-scale disasters by citizens, beginning in 2004, when a tsunami hit South Asia, helped fuel the participatory journalism movement. Shortly after the event, tourists took more than 20,000 tsunami pictures and posted them to Flickr.com. The London bombings on July 7, 2005 allowed citizens to become involved in media coverage. Video shot from citizens' camera phones was used in the BBC's coverage of the bombings that evening. The BBC reports citizens sent more than 20,000 e-mails, 1,000 pictures, and 20 videos within the first 24 hours following the bombing [10].

Hurricane Katrina in 2005 spurred major traditional media sources to solicit pictures, stories, and video from their audience. Although major news organizations like CNN, MSNBC, and *The New York Times* received a lot of material from citizens, little of it was used [11].

Arguably the most well-known and popular participatory journalism web site in the world is ohmynews.com, founded by Oh Yeon Ho of South Korea in February 2000. Ohmynews.com has more than 42,000 registered citizen journalists and 95 full-time staff [12]. Editors review and post hundreds of articles a day written by the citizen journalists. The most carefully edited articles are located prominently on the page. The articles that have not been edited yet are featured less prominently on the page [13]. From February 2005 through July 2005 ohmynews.com had anywhere from about 3 million to about 18 million page views per day [14].

As trust in traditional media continues to wane, more people are going online to get their news. About 50 million Americans get their news from the Internet in a typical day [15].

2   Research Questions

The lack of research on markers that lead to higher levels of perceived credibility of participatory journalism web sites has led to this study's three main research questions.

RQ 1: To what extent does providing information about a writer's background and providing a picture of the writer on a participatory journalism site affect the perceived credibility of the story?

Previous studies [2, 16, 17] show that providing information about the author of online information as well as a picture may enhance the credibility of the site. The researcher believes that this finding can be extended to individual stories on a participatory journalism web site. The researcher hypothesizes that providing both information about the writer's background and providing a picture of the writer will enhance the credibility of stories found on the participatory journalism site ohmynews.com. In this study, "information about a writer's background" is defined as information about the life and previous activities of the author of a news article on the ohmynews.com web site. "Perceived credibility" in this study will be assessed as it has been in a number of previous studies, by measuring the following: believability, accuracy, trustworthiness, bias, and completeness [18, 19, 20, 21, 22].

RQ 2: To what extent do hyperlinks that allow users to verify information contained in a story on a participatory journalism site affect the perceived credibility of the story?

Hyperlinks can be important in helping users form judgments about online credibility [16, 23]. The researcher hypothesizes that stories on the participatory journalism web site ohmynews.com that contain hyperlinks will be rated by participants as more credible than stories that do not contain hyperlinks.

RQ3: To what extent does providing information about a writer's background, a picture of the writer, and hyperlinks that allow users to verify information contained in a story on a participatory journalism site affect the perceived credibility of the story?

Research Question 3 seeks to examine the interaction of all the factors. The researcher hypothesizes that the stories on the participatory journalism site ohmynews.com that contain all of these pieces of information (writer information, a picture, and hyperlinks) will be rated by participants as more credible than stories that don't contain all of the above information.

2.1 Procedures

The study will include 120 participants. These participants will be undergraduate students at Elizabethtown College, who are at least 18 years of age. The entire study will be done online. The participants will be divided into four groups. One group will see only the stories, one group will see the stories and the writer information, one group will see the stories and the hyperlinks, and one group will see the story, the writer information and the hyperlinks. Each group will read the same three stories (one hard news story, one feature story, and one sports story). After reading each story they will fill out a questionnaire, about the credibility of the story they just read.

In addition to collecting information from participants using questionnaires, information will also be collected using a commercially available tracking software program. This will allow the researcher to collect information concerning how long participants took to read each story, and which hyperlinks participants clicked on, if any, in each story.

2.2 Analysis

The results from the questionnaires filled out by all of the groups will be analyzed to determine whether or not the perceived credibility of the story changed when the following variables: the presence of information about the writer, hyperlinks, and both the information about the writer and the hyperlinks were introduced. The independent variables in the study are the information about the writer and the hyperlinks, and conversely the absence of that information. The dependent variable will be the change in perceived credibility between the 4 groups. The change in credibility will be calculated using a one-way ANOVA at the .05 significance level.

3 Expected Contributions

This study will add to the small, but growing body of literature on participatory journalism. To date, there have not been any studies that have examined markers of credibility on participatory journalism sites, so this would be the first. This study will also help those creating participatory journalism sites understand how to make their sites more credible to users. User created content is becoming more prevalent on the web, and studies aimed at examining this phenomenon will be needed to understand this new generation of content creators. This study is just the first, of many possible studies, that will look at this growing trend of online content creation.

References

1. Gilster, P.: Digital Literacy. John Wiley & Sons, New York (1997)
2. Fogg, B.J., Marshall, J., Laraki, O., Varma, C., Fang, N., Paul, J., et al.: What Makes Websites Credible? A Report on a Large Quantitative Study. In: Proceedings of the Conference on Human Factors in Computing Systems CHI 2001 (March 31-April 5, 2001)
3. Eksterowicz, A.J., Roberts, R., Clark, A.: Public Journalism and Public Knowledge. Press/Politics 3(2), 74–95 (1998)
4. Grimes, C.: Whither the Civic Journalism Bandwagon? Press/Politics 2(3), 125–130 (1997)
5. Rosen, J.: What Are Journalists For? Yale University Press, New Haven (1999)
6. Curley, T.: Text of Opening Keynote by Tom Curley, http://journalist.org/2004conference/archives/000079.php
7. Gill, K.E.: How Can We Measure the Influence of the Blogosphere? In: Paper presented at WWW2004, New York (May 17-24, 2004)
8. Blood, R.: Weblogs and Journalism: Do They Connect? Nieman Reports 57(3), 61–63 (2003)
9. Bowman, S., Willis, C.: We Media: How Audiences are Shaping the Future of News and Information (2003), http://www.hypergene.net/wemedia/weblog.php
10. Sambrook, R.: Citizen Journalism and the BBC. Nieman Reports 59(4), 13–16 (2005)
11. Bowman, S., Willis, C.: The Future Is Here, But Do News Media Companies See It? Nieman Reports 59(4), 6–10 (2005)
12. Ihlwan, M., Hall, K.: OhmyNews: Voices from the Street. Business Week Online, http://www.businessweek.com/magazine/content/06_20/b3984072.htm?campaig _id=search
13. Schroeder, C.M.: Is This the Future of Journalism? (2004), http://www.msnbc.msn.com/id/5240584/site/newsweek/
14. Alexa Internet, Inc., (2006), http://www.alexa.com/data/details/related_links?q=&url=english.ohmynews.com
15. Horrigan, J.B.: Online News (2006), http://www.pewinternet.org/ppf/r/178/report_ display.asp

16. Fogg, B.J.: Stanford Guidelines for Web Credibility (2002), http://www.webcredibility.org/guidelines
17. Fogg, B.J., Marshall, J.: Web Credibility Research: A Method for Online Experiments and Early Study Results. In: Paper presented at the Conference on Human Factors in Computing Systems CHI 2001, Seattle, WA (March 31-April 5, 2001)
18. Flanagin, A.J., Metzger, M.J.: The Perceived Credibility of Personal Web Page Information As Influenced by the Sex of the Source. Computers in Human Behavior 19, 683–701 (2003)
19. Gaziano, C., McGrath, K.: Measuring the Concept of Credibility. Journalism Quarterly 63, 451–462 (1986)
20. Johnson, T.J., Kaye, B.K.: Wag the Blog: How Reliance on Traditional Media and the Internet Influence Credibility Perceptions of Weblogs Among Blog Users. Journalism and Mass Communication Quarterly 81(3), 622–642 (2004)
21. Meyer, P.: Defining and Measuring Credibility of Newspapers: Developing an Index. Journalism Quarterly 65, 567–574 (1988)
22. Newhagen, J., Nass, C.: Differential Criteria for Evaluating Credibility of Newspapers and TV News. Journalism Quarterly 66, 277–284 (1989)
23. Stewart, K.J., Zhang, Y.: Effects of Hypertext Links on Trust Transfer. In: Paper presented at the ICEC 2003, Pittsburgh, PA (2003)

Understanding the Evolution of Users' Personal Information Management Practices

Manas Tungare

Dept. of Computer Science and Center for Human Computer Interaction
Virginia Tech
Blacksburg, VA, USA
manas@vt.edu

Abstract. Information is being disseminated much faster than we can assimilate it, leading to information overload. In addition to desktop computers, users use a vast array of other devices to manage their information, which leads to information fragmentation. It has not yet been studied how users adapt their information management practices in response to the introduction of new devices into their personal information ecosystem. As part of my doctoral research, I plan to study this evolution, which is important for the design of next-generation devices and to establish future research directions in personal information management.

1 Introduction

One of the biggest challenges of our time is to create mechanisms to effectively consolidate and control the management of personal information. We have developed amazing capabilities to record, store, and transmit massive quantities of information with minimal effort; however this has relegated us to part-time workers and part-time librarians of our own personal information. In spite of the ease of recording, creating, receiving, storing, and accumulating digital materials, managing and using them sensibly is difficult [1]. With time, the amount of information generated by humans can only increase, while human attentional resources have remained constant [2], thus presenting an alarming future for information workers whose job requires them to stay informed. *Information overload* is defined as occurring when the information processing demands on an individual's time to perform interactions and internal calculations exceed the supply or capacity of time available for such processing [3]. Even worse than information overload is *information fragmentation*, the condition of having a user's data in different formats, distributed across multiple locations, manipulated by different applications, and residing in a generally disconnected manner (e.g. [4]).

To study the problems caused by information overload, information fragmentation and multiple devices, we need appropriate terminology, concepts, and principles. As reviewed in my prior work [5], I have characterized this collection of devices as a *personal information ecosystem* and drawn parallels with biological systems as a way of

C. Baranauskas et al. (Eds.): INTERACT 2007, LNCS 4663, Part II, pp. 586–591, 2007.

understanding the devices that participate in the ecosystem, the relationships among them, the type of user activities that the ecosystem supports, and the equilibrium that must be maintained. We use this ecosystem as a framework with which to study the problem in more detail. Based on our previous work, we have observed that personal information management (PIM) practices evolve rather slowly, much like evolution in biological ecosystems.

As part of my doctoral research, I seek to study how personal information management strategies evolve over an extended period of time and the impact of changes in life patterns on these practices. In one set of studies, I plan to explore how the availability of information management devices (computer, PDA, MP3 player, etc.) affects information management practices: in particular, how new information management practices develop to make use of the newly introduced devices. The second set of studies will examine how changes in work environment influence personal information management practices. Overall, I am interested in exploring the internal and external factors that change the equilibrium of the personal information ecosystem.

2   The Problem

Personal Information [6] includes (1) the information a person keeps for personal use (e.g. files), (2) information about a person but kept by and under the control of others (e.g. health information), (3) information experienced by a person but outside the person's control (e.g. books or Web sites browsed), and (4) information directed to a person (e.g. email). The unique situational aspect of the working environment [7] makes it difficult to study PIM as compared to general information storage and retrieval (ISAR) systems [7].

2.1   Previous Studies in PIM

Many of the studies that have been conducted in the area of Personal Information Management (details in [8]) are limited to how we manage information on a particular device (e.g. desktop), or how we manage a particular type of information (e.g. bookmarks or emails). They have looked at a single snapshot of organizational behavior, not a continuous or long-term inspection of user behavior. The *evolution* of a user's information practices as she progresses from one work context to another, or from one role to another, has not been studied in detail.

2.2   PIM with Multiple Devices

One of the major causes of information fragmentation is that we no longer are restricted to a single device, or a single source of information; most of our information is scattered across multiple devices, such as desktop computers at the office, laptops at home, portable digital assistants (PDAs) on the road, and of course, cellphones. We are not aware of any study so far that has explicitly considered the presence of multiple devices in a user's personal information ecosystem, or examined how they affect a user's information management practices.

3   Research to Date

We reviewed the information fragmentation problem in [9], including its many visible symptoms, primary causes, and philosophical underpinnings. Understanding the need for users to be able to access all of their data, across devices, across collections, and with minimal fragmentation, we designed and developed the Syncables framework [10], which lets applications migrate their task information seamlessly across multiple platforms. Information need not be saved to a file first, and the framework provides a unified addressing scheme for each unit of data stored (e.g. a calendar event, a person's contact information, a file, or a piece of context data such as the current cursor position inside a word processor). Applications can thus directly address data created or manipulated in other applications, and create deep links between data items. These are similar in concept to the information trails proposed by Vannevar Bush in his seminal 1945 paper [11].

We asked users about their information management practices related to different collections, (e.g. files, music, research papers) [12]. Based on the varied responses, it was clear that in spite of useful tools that address the management of information and methods recommended by experts, PIM is still highly individualized. In [5], we discussed some of the design issues in PIM systems for multiple devices and proposed a characterization of a user's many devices in terms of a biological ecosystem.

4   Proposed Research Design

I plan to study how personal information management strategies evolve over an extended period of time and the impact that changes in life patterns have in these practices. Overall, we are interested in exploring which internal and external factors change the equilibrium of the personal information ecosystem. The ecosystem evolves with new processes, new interdependencies between components, and new flow amongst components.

4.1   Exploring Internal/External Factors

We hypothesize that the distinction between filer/piler behavior and several other PIM practices is one that might be initially influenced by personal traits of the users. However, we have observed how users' practices change over time and how some practices are different for the different types of media [12]. For the studies proposed, we plan to:

- conduct basic cognitive tests on the participants (field dependent/independent, assessed using the embedded figure test [13], and a memory test [14]).
- conduct a survey to assess the participants' information management practices. The survey is intended to determine which of the already established 'bins' of PIM practices (e.g. filer, piler, spring cleaner, etc.) do users classify themselves into. (like in [15]).
- conduct the same survey at the end of the subject participation, to assess how their information management practices changed over time.

We want to learn if there is correlation between internal factors (personal traits) and PIM practices. Furthermore, by repeating the survey at the end of the study, we will identify if the practices changed over the time of the study. The studies themselves (see following sections) will provide insight as to what might prompt the change.

4.2   Natural Transitions in Life: Work Environment Change

The effect that a change in work environment has on information management practices has not been studied before. We plan to track several participants as they change work environments to try to answer the following research questions: how do the new information flows at the new work environment influence or prompt changes in information management practices? How is equilibrium maintained and do new practices help the ecosystem reach equilibrium? How much resistance does a user have to changes? What is the relationship between the participant's internal factors and the external factors as it relates to these changes?

4.3   Understanding Long-Term Changes in Users' Workflows

Based on our initial observations [12], and on several findings from the literature, we know that introduction of new devices lead to changes in PIM strategies. What we do not know is how these changes take place. We believe that the changes follow a generic strategy: users first acknowledge they have a problem, then explore different strategies and tools, trying to find a balance between the use of new tools while reducing the change in existing practices (i.e., trying to maintain the equilibrium of their ecosystem). This is followed by trying out an approach, that might not be the one they settle with; there is a period of transition where a hybrid of both, old and new systems is used. Finally, there is a successful deployment of the new strategy, resulting in PIM practices that are either more effective than before, or as good as before but without the failures.

With this study, we hope to address the following research questions: how do the new devices affect what users do? What interrelationships develop between devices? How are pairs of devices are used together (symbiosis)? What types of failures are caused by the use of new technology? How long does it take to adopt new workflows (i.e., ecosystem reach equilibrium)? How is information fragmented over the different devices? Does this cause problems for the participant? How does the participant cope with this fragmentation?

4.4   Participants

We will recruit students transitioning from undergraduate to graduate school, MS students transitioning from graduate school to industry, PhD students transitioning from graduate school to a professional career, and professionals joining a company in the Corporate Research Center at Virginia Tech. We will recruit 2 for each of the above categories, for a total of 8 participants. In the case of the students, we will contact them before the change in job environment to conduct an initial data gathering and interview. For the professionals, we plan to contact them through their companies before they move to the area.

We plan to supply devices to a user (laptop, PDA, MP3 player) and capture data about the user's interaction with them to study the management of different collections: music, video, files, photos, etc. Interviews with individual participants on a weekly basis and monthly focus groups will help understand the users' stories better.

5   Goals and Key Contributions

I expect that these proposed studies will contribute significantly to the state-of-the-art in PIM research and in the development of tools for PIM tasks. In particular,

- the findings from our experiments will help us understand the relationships among various internal and external factors that influence an individual's PIM strategies,
- understanding these factors will help enrich the Personal Information Ecosystems model to guide further studies and experiments in PIM,
- the enriched model will be useful to designers of next-generation PIM systems to create tools that fit well into users' personal information ecosystems, and
- these studies will help companies and universities make natural life transitions easier for new members (students or employees) from a personal information management point of view.

Acknowledgments

I would like to thank my advisor, Dr. Manuel Pérez-Quiñones, for insightful discussions and his valuable guidance at each step of the way. Prof. Steve Harrison and Pardha S. Pyla participated in many brainstorming sessions which directly or indirectly influenced the current research.

References

1. Czerwinski, M., Gage, D.W., Gemmell, J., Marshall, C.C., Pérez-Quiñones, M.A., Skeels, M.M., Catarci, T.: Digital memories in an era of ubiquitous computing and abundant storage. Commun. ACM 49(1), 44–50 (2006)
2. Levy, D.M.: To grow in wisdom: Vannevar Bush, Information Overload, and the Life of Leisure. In: JCDL '05. Proceedings of the 5th ACM/IEEE-CS joint conference on Digital libraries, pp. 281–286. ACM Press, New York (2005)
3. Schick, A.G., Gordon, L.A., Haka, S.: Information overload: A temporal approach. Accounting, Organizations and Society 15(3), 199–220 (1990)
4. Bergman, O., Beyth-Marom, R., Nachmias, R.: The project fragmentation problem in personal information management. In: CHI '06. Proceedings of the SIGCHI conference on Human Factors in computing systems, pp. 271–274. ACM Press, New York (2006)
5. Tungare, M., Pyla, P.S., Pérez-Quiñones, M., Harrison, S.: Personal information ecosystems and implications for design. Technical Report cs/0612081, ACM Computing Research Repository (2006)
6. Jones, W., Teevan, J.: Personal Information Management. University of Washington Press, Seattle, Washington (2007)

7. Barreau, D.K.: Context as a factor in personal information management systems. J. Am. Soc. Inf. Sci. 46(5), 327–339 (1995)
8. Teevan, J., Capra, R., Pérez-Quiñones, M.: 3. In: How people find information, University of Washington Press, Seattle, Washington 17 (2007)
9. Tungare, M., Pyla, P.S., Sampat, M., Perez-Quinones, M.: Defragmenting information using the syncables framework. In: Proceedings of the 2nd Invitational Workshop on Personal Information Management at SIGIR 2006 (2006)
10. Tungare, M., Pyla, P.S., Sampat, M., Pérez-Quiñones, M.: Syncables: A framework to support seamless data migration across multiple platforms. In: IEEE International Conference on Portable Information Devices (IEEE Portable) (2007)
11. Bush, V.: As we may think. The Atlantic Monthly (1945)
12. Pérez-Quiñones, M., Tungare, M., Pyla, P.S., Kurdziolek, M.: A special topics course on personal information management. Technical Report TR 06-26, Virginia Tech Dept. of Computer Science, Blacksburg, VA (2006)
13. Witkin, M., Oltman, P., Raskin, E., Karp, S.: Group Embedded Figures Test Manual. Mind Garden, Inc, Redwood City (1971)
14. Crawford, J.R., Smith, G., Maylor, E.A., Sala, S.D., Logie, R.H.: The prospective and retrospective memory questionnaire (prmq): Normative data and latent structure in a large non-clinical sample. Memory 11(3), 261–275 (2003)
15. Malone, T.W.: How do people organize their desks?: Implications for the design of office information systems. ACM Trans. Inf. Syst. 1(1), 99–112 (1983)

Multimodal Interaction in a Ubiquitous Environment

Mayuree Srikulwong

Department of Computer Science, University of Bath, Claverton Down,
Bath, BA2 7AY, United Kingdom
M.Srikulwong@bath.ac.uk

Abstract. Result of my literature review shows the important characteristics of three distinct modalities and the factors influencing interaction in a ubiquitous computing context. Research aim is to develop the principles for the design of multimodal interactive systems in a ubiquitous environment.

Keywords: Multimodality, Multimodal Interaction, Ubiquitous Computing.

1 Introduction

A ubiquitous environment has different characteristics from traditional networked computing. Firstly, it has a high level of mobility and users are dynamic. Secondly, the architectural space may contain both fixed and mobile devices. Thirdly, interaction can be ad-hoc among peer nodes. These characteristics cause new problems and challenge us to find the most appropriate forms of interaction. Such new structures of interaction should be natural and its interface should be seamless. Multimodality can be used as a bridging concept between naturalistic behavior and engagement with the system.

Multimodality refers to multiple paths of communication employed by users to carry input and output. Its variations offer choices for interaction which should appropriately help, support and extend the way users communicate and perform activities in different situations. Much of past multimodality research has aimed to solve information representation focusing on the usage of visual and audio sensory channels. A recent study [1] suggests that only 1% of multi-sensory research is on haptic sense. Unlike visual perception, haptic is bidirectional, i.e. can be used as both input and output to the systems. If we use human body as a whole for interaction design, we will benefit from its characteristics which are depth, height, breadth, and body posture. Applications may be designed for free movement and interactions can be naturally controlled by haptics and gesture.

2 Related Research

Brewster et al. [2] added sound into interaction action to overcome the limitation of mobile phones' screen size. Cao et al. [3] used time multiplexing crossmodal cues, i.e. vibration and sound, to enhance privacy in public spaces. O'Neill et al. [4]

C. Baranauskas et al. (Eds.): INTERACT 2007, LNCS 4663, Part II, pp. 592–597, 2007.

proposed a novel interaction technique, called Directional Stroke Recognition (DSR), which is solely based on the direction of gesture. Nesbitt [5] has given guidelines for multimodal and tactile displays of abstract data in the virtual environment.

Although these works and guidelines are ones of the significant pieces of work in multimodality and ubiquitous computing areas, they are not unified. We still have little understanding of the relationship between these two research areas. Much of the previous multimodality research has focused on the use of visual and audio channels and the use of alternative sensory channels to enhance the usage of the visual channel. The fact that much of past research has omitted the use of haptic interaction means that opportunities to improve the level of system usability were lost. Hence, these guidelines are inadequate to be used as principles for the design of multimodal interactive systems in a ubiquitous environment.

3 Problem Statements and Research Question

3.1 Problem Statements

Firstly, there is a lack of understanding of the relationship between the concept of multimodality and ubiquitous computing. Secondly, there are no established principles regarding multimodal interaction in a ubiquitous environment. Thirdly, only visual and audio channels of human senses have been comprehensively studied.

3.2 Research Question

Consequently, my aim is to study the addition of haptic communicative channel into the multimodal interaction model. My research attempts to develop principles for the design of multimodal interactive systems for a ubiquitous environment. My contribution to the ubiquitous computing field of study is to answer the following research question:

How haptic interaction can be appropriately added into a multimodal interaction model for a ubiquitous environment in order to make the interaction transparent with a better level of efficiency and effectiveness?

In term of efficiency, I will focus on usability, specifically, on learnability. Once a user learns how to use the system and obtain skill, then the interaction between such users and the systems become transparent. This transparency, then, is achieved when the user has shifted their focus of interaction from the technologies to the tasks.

In term of effectiveness, my focal point is on cognitive awareness. The users achieve a state of consciousness via the available feedback data, perceiving it and subjecting it to further cognitive processing. In some safety-critical situations, e.g. aviation systems, awareness breakdown can lead to disaster. As a result, interaction design for such systems should include the notification of the undesirable state changes. This information should be *effective* in such visually cluttered environment to catch the users' attention, leading to higher levels of perception and awareness.

The main point here regards clear, explicit and informative system feedback. Systems which omit the use of haptic channel miss an opportunity to improve the level of learnability and cognitive awareness. Haptic input and output could be used as an alternative as well as in combination with the other busy perceptive channels to reduce learning time on task, and make the interaction become transparent more rapidly and to help increasing the users' cognitive awareness of current activity.

Subsequently, my investigation will be based on the following hypotheses:

Hypothesis 1: The inclusion of semantically rich haptic communication in visual/audio interaction will significantly decrease the number of breakdowns, as users will shift their focus from the technology to the tasks.

Hypothesis 2: The inclusion of semantically rich haptic notifications about a system's change will significantly reduce the number of breakdowns, as users will be more aware of the current state of the system.

3.3 Approach and Methodology

The dissertation consists of two major segments: literature review and experiments. The result of preliminary study in the following section is based on the former. The outcome of my research, the principles for multimodal interactive system design, will be based on both. Then, such principles will be used as a tool to design an instance of multimodal interactive system and be evaluated through data collected from system testing.

In order to develop these principles, further empirical studies and a number of experiments have to be carried out. Some projects would be initially run in a controlled environment to obtain understanding of characteristics, impacts and limitations of different modalities. Subsequently, some projects will be selected and evaluated in the field in order to draw out the relationships between the already-understood modalities' characteristics[1] and those[1] of ubiquitous computing. Results from field tests are expected to provide rich and contextual information to complement those from the controlled experiments.

4 Proposed Work

4.1 Preliminary Results

The initial study has focused on finding factors and characteristics of components existing in a ubiquitous interaction space. The results of my literature review are presented as factors of the taxonomy of multimodal interaction design for a ubiquitous environment in table 1 – 4 and figure 1.

The taxonomy consists of eight factors which are information, usage modes, modality, user contexts, user type, degree of publicness, level of mobility and level of user control factors. This preliminary review provides an overview picture of what factors influencing the design of multimodal interactive systems in a ubiquitous setting.

---

[1] See 4.1 Preliminary Results.

Table 1. Information factor

Information Type	Data Structure
Meta Data	Linear
Objects	Circular
Attributes	Tree
Notification	Graph
	Object-oriented
	Relational

Table 2. Usage mode factor

Usage Mode
Alternate
Synergy
Exclusive
Concurrent

Table 3. Modality factor

Modality	Interactivity type	Interaction activity	Differential property
Visual	Abstract Signal, Icon, Textual, Graphic, 3D, Animation	See, Look, Explore, Navigate	Size, Color, Texture, Orientation, Shape
Audio	Abstract Sound, Natural Sounds, Speech	Listen, Navigate	Frequency, Wave Length, Period, Amplitude, Velocity, Speed
Haptic	Abstract mechanical pattern, Natural pattern	Touch, Feel	Resistance, Capacitance, Position, Velocity, Acceleration, Force, Torque, Pressure, Types of grasp, Temperature of contacting body part, roughness, vibration pattern, hardness, stiffness, weight

Table 4. User context factor

User Context
User preference
User intent
User Previous experience
User needs and desire
User physical status

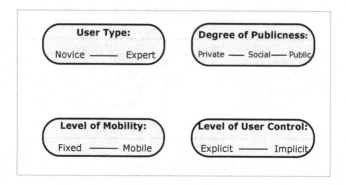

Fig. 1. User type, Degree of publicness, Level of device mobility and Level of user control factors

4.2 Future Steps

The following steps are to perform a series of empirical studies and experiments in order to find relationships amongst the factors in the taxonomy. In other words, how so we combine multiple sensory channels and find a balance between them? In which situation could we use different channels? What are the users' available communicative channels in different situations? How would the multimodal interactive systems *look, sound* and *feel*?

A first set of experiments will be to test different combinations of modalities for two types of applications, an interpersonal communication application and an aviation control system.

The first application is to add a channel, i.e. haptic, to convey communicative meaning for interpersonal communication in a ubiquitous context. The chosen scenario is the communication between people at home with a fixed device, i.e. picture frame equipped with a set of pre-stored images with related tag information, and family members on the move with their GPS enabled mobile devices. The main objective of this experiment is to investigate the users' understanding of haptic meaning.

The second application is to manipulate modalities in a visually-cluttered environment, i.e. an aircraft cockpit wherein interaction is safety-critical [6]. The chosen scenario is an aircraft descent scenario with interventions from the autopilot. The main objectives of this experiment are: to investigate the pilot's attention drawn from rapidly changing cockpit (multimodal) interface by the autopilot and to discover the best perceptible modality for improving the overall safety for this environment.

For each testing, both quantitative and qualitative data will be collected. Quantitative data (e.g. time taken, number of errors and number of reported observations) will be gathered automatically by the application and analysed in relation to learnability and awareness. Qualitative data will be collected through video recording, post-session interviews and questionnaires to validate the quantitative results and to capture user preference and acceptance.

Further sets of experimental projects include the applications which have different degrees of publicness and levels of user control[2] in order to examine the attributes of each factor in the taxonomy and relationships amongst them.

5 Conclusion

Preliminary results of my study are based on a literature review. Future work includes the development of experiments and the validation of the hypotheses. The principles produced will be used to support system designers in making decisions about the usage of three modalities (i.e. visual, audio, and haptic) in a ubiquitous computing context.

Acknowledgments. I would like to thank my supervisor, Dr.Eamonn O'Neill, for guidance and support and to HCI@Bath for comments.

References

1. Aziz, F.A., Nicholas, L.: Simulated Lifting with Visual Feedback BCS-HCI2006, vol. 2, London (2006)
2. Brewster, S.: Overcoming the Lack of Screen Space on Mobile Computers. Personal Ubiquitous Computing 6, 188–205 (2002)
3. Cao, H., Olivier, P., Jackson, D., Armstrong, A., Huang, L.: Enhancing privacy in public spaces through crossmodal displays (2005)
4. O'Neill, E., Kaenampornpan, M., Kostakos, V., Warr, A., Woodgate, D.: Can we do without GUIs? Gesture and speech interaction with a patient information system. In: Personal and Ubiquitous Computing, Springer, Heidelberg (2005)
5. Nesbitt, K.V.: A Framework to Support the Designers of Haptic, Visual and Auditory Displays. In: GOTHI 2005, Canada (2005)
6. Hourizi, R., Johnson, P.: Towards an explanatory, predictive account of awareness. Computers & Graphics 27, 859–872 (2003)

---

[2] See Figure 1.

Interaction and Visualization Techniques for Programming

Mikkel Rønne Jakobsen

Dept. of Computing, University of Copenhagen
Copenhagen, Denmark
mikkelrj@diku.dk

Abstract. Programmers spend much of their time investigating the source code of a program, which often involves navigating and understanding delocalized code fragments. This Ph.D. project explores the use of information visualizations that are designed to support programmers in these activities. I use controlled experiments to provide precise measurements of the usability of visualizations and detailed insight into users' interaction with visualizations. Also, case studies are used to understand how professional programmers use visualizations in realistic work activity. Overall, this research will contribute empirically founded insight into the design and use of visualizations in programming.

Application

My Ph.D. thesis has the working title "Interaction and Visualization Techniques for Programming". My scholarship is running from June 1st 2006 until May 31st 2009. This paper describes the research problems that form the basis of the thesis and outlines the dissertation research. I have also submitted a short paper to Interact 2007 called "Transient Visualizations".

My advisor is associate professor Kasper Hornbæk (kash@diku.dk), Department of Computing, University of Copenhagen.

The research area for this project is human computer interaction and information visualization. The research topic is empirical studies of the use of information visualizations to support programming.

Introduction

Programming is a complex human activity. Programmers are often required to develop correct source code from a general description of how the program should work. Programmers spend much of their time reading and understanding existing code, which typically requires navigation between delocalized fragments of code. As the source code grows in size and complexity, navigating and understanding the source code becomes mentally demanding.

Information visualization concerns the use of interactive visual representations of data to support problem solving. Use of information visualization to support

C. Baranauskas et al. (Eds.): INTERACT 2007, LNCS 4663, Part II, pp. 598–603, 2007.

programming has received considerable attention from the research community [e.g., 9,12]. Relatively few studies, however, have examined the effects of using visualizations in programming. Further empirical studies are needed to understand better how users interact with tools in modern programming environments and how visualization techniques can enhance these interactions.

The complexity of activities performed by programmers that are engaged in challenging tasks has implications for both design and evaluation of visualizations. First, it is complicated to design usable visualizations that support the diversity of activities that goes on in programming. Second, it is difficult to make realistic studies that yield generalizable results. For example, source code editing is rarely considered in design and evaluation of visualization techniques, even though writing and editing source code is an integral part of programming. Thus, techniques that have a documented positive effect on program understanding may prove impractical for programming work in general. Furthermore, empirical research is often limited to studying participants performing simple tasks, often with insufficient experience with the programming tools that are used. Thus, further research is needed to found a broad and deep empirical insight into the use of visualization in programming tools.

An overall hypothesis for this Ph.D. project is that information visualizations can support navigation and understanding of source code. To investigate this claim, visualizations are designed and evaluated. An important aim of this research is to combine visualizations with tools in modern programming environments to support the complex and varied work of professional programmers.

Related Work

Recent studies of professional programmers performing maintenance tasks indicate that navigating and understanding source code can be difficult and time consuming [1,10,11]. Ko et al. [10] studied 10 expert Java programmers performing maintenance tasks in a modern programming environment and found that participants spent up to 35% of their time navigating between dependencies in the code. Latoza et al. [11] reported from an observational study of 7 professional programmers that the biggest usability problem involved getting lost while navigating around the source code. Specifically, reading and understanding code fragments that are located in different parts of a source code file requires programmers to scroll or jump between locations in the file [1]. Also, the files containing code fragments related to a task may be located in different parts of the hierarchy of source code. Navigating between code fragments in source code comprised of thousands of files requires considerable efforts of the user. These findings indicate a potential for improving programming tools to better support navigation and understanding of source code.

Furnas's fisheye views [6] present an approach to supporting navigation and understanding of source code. In fisheye views, all source code lines are assigned a degree of interest based on their a priori importance and their relation to the line in focus. Lines with a degree of interest below some threshold are removed from the view. The resulting view provides both focus details and context information. Combining a fisheye views with a source code editor may help programmers navigate and understand the source code: it may improve understanding, and reduce the need to navigate, because lines of source code that are useful given the programmer's focus of attention are shown in the view; it may allow programmers to navigate faster, because target information is shown in the fisheye view.

Intuitively, visualizations that represent hierarchical data structures by visual enclosure seem useful for representing hierarchically organized source code. Two-dimensional representations of the entire source code provide programmers with an overview that may potentially support navigation between delocalized source code. Earlier research of two-dimensional representations of source code has focused on other aspects. For example, SeeSys applies space-filling techniques to visualize statistics in code that is hierarchically divided into subsystems, directories and files [2]. Thumbnail views of source code arranged in two-dimensional space may facilitate the forming of a spatial memory of the source code to support navigation [4]. Evaluations may prove such two-dimensional arrangements of source code useful. However, scaling such arrangements of thumbnails to show large amounts of source code in its entirety may be difficult. In contrast, space-filling techniques such as Treemaps can scale to very large amounts of data [5].

Research Method and Contributions

This research project mainly contributes empirically founded insight into the use of visualizations in programming. My research aims to strengthen the empirical literature on information visualization. For researchers, important areas of further work are pointed out. For designers, my work may provide advice about how information visualizations can be combined with modern programming environments.

I use elements from different empirical research methods. Controlled experiments are conducted to provide precise measurements of usability of visualizations and to describe users' interaction with interfaces that contain visualizations. Case studies are used to provide evidence about the benefits of visualizations used by professional programmers doing normal work in their own environment. Combining different methods can potentially increase the validity and trustworthiness of the outcome [8].

Prior Research

Fisheye Views of Source Code

My first research contribution published at CHI 2006 reported an experimental study of a fisheye view of source code [7]. The design that was evaluated combined a fisheye view with a source code editor by dividing the editor window into two areas: the focus area comprised the editable part of the view and the context area contained mainly readable context information. Semantic relations between parts of the source code were included in the calculation of the degree of interest. The fisheye view was fully integrated with the Eclipse development environment.

The experiment compared the usability of the fisheye view with a common, linear presentation of source code. Sixteen participants performed tasks significantly faster with the fisheye view, although results varied dependent on the task type. The participants generally preferred the fisheye view and analysis of participants' interaction with the fisheye view showed effective use of the context information to complete tasks. Results indicated that semantically related information is important, while source code displayed because of a high a priori degree of interest is less useful. Limitations of the experiment call for follow-up studies. First, participants in the experiment were given relatively short practice time with the fisheye view and were thus not confident in using the fisheye view. Second, realism of the programming environment was reduced because the tools available to the participants in the experiment were limited. Third, the study investigated only simple programming activity. Questions raised include (1) what types of information to include, (2) how to effectively use display space, and (3) how to improve interaction in the fisheye view to facilitate both investigation and editing of source code.

Transient Visualizations

As mentioned above, a fisheye view was found to support participants in task involving navigation and understanding. However, some participants expressed concern that the fisheye view could be inappropriate for writing and editing code because they want a large view of source code for those tasks [7]. One idea is to allow users to call up the fisheye view on demand.

In general, transient use of information visualization close to the user's focus of attention presents an approach to support specific contexts of use without permanently changing the user interface. Using transient visualizations to facilitate infrequent and unpredictable contexts of use, the original permanent view can be dedicated to information used in frequent contexts of use. For example, information needed for navigating to dependencies in the code could effectively be shown on demand in a transient fisheye view of source code. Experimental studies are planned as part of this project to investigate the usefulness of transient visualizations, in particular with regard to programming.

To obtain empirical evidence about the usefulness of transient visualizations, I conducted an experiment. Twenty participants performed search and navigation tasks using map interfaces. One interface contains an overview permanently fixed in the upper-right corner of the detail window. In another interface, users can temporary call up an overview at the mouse cursor position. Results show clear preference for the interface with the transient overview. However, no overall difference between the two interfaces was found for task completion times and accuracy.

Future Research

Fisheye Views of Source Code

Currently, I plan a controlled experiment to compare interfaces that use transient and permanent fisheye views of source code. Fig. 1 shows part of the interface that uses the transient fisheye view of source code. The experiment combines a study of participants performing maintenance tasks, with measurement of usability in repeated trials involving navigation and understanding tasks. The experiment aims to uncover whether transient fisheye views can be used for navigating and understanding source code efficiently, without compromising on a large view of code for reading and editing. Additionally, participants will get adequate training to be proficient with the interface prior to measurements of usability.

Next, I am planning a case study to investigate how professional programmers use fisheye views in real work. The study aims to observe participants and collect quantitative information about their use of fisheye views of source code. Establishing a protocol of programming work will enable detailed analysis of interaction patterns in the use of fisheye views compared with a traditional, linear view of source code. A prerequisite for the study to yield useful results is a stable and usable interface that programmers will use in their work.

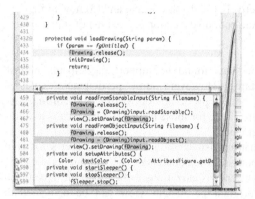

Fig. 1. Detail screenshot of a transient fisheye view of source code that uses popup windows above and below the editor window to show program lines related to the user's focus

Fig. 2. Preliminary design of a map visualization of Java source code using a treemap approach

Transient Visualizations
Results from the ongoing experiments with transient visualizations that are part of this project will be consolidated to provide an empirical basis for discussing the benefits and limitations of transient visualizations.

Map Visualizations of Source Code
Two-dimensional map visualizations are investigated with the aim of supporting understanding and navigation of source code. Fig. 2 shows a preliminary design of such a map, which represents the entire source code of a Java program. Map visualizations may utilize spatial cognition to provide programmers with an overview of the entire source code. One use of such a map is to highlight those delocalized code fragments that are being investigated in a maintenance task, for example by highlighting code that has been read or edited. Other possible uses include visualizing dependencies in the source code to support understanding or visualizing results of a search in source code to help programmers find and navigate relevant code.

An initial study is planned to uncover important factors in the design of the visual representations in maps. For example, the spatial layout of the source code representation must be stable to facilitate spatial cognition. Also, appropriate information residue or landmarks are needed to find information for navigating in the source code. User studies of participants performing tasks that target search and spatial memory are needed to investigate whether maps of source code can support the forming of spatial memory. I plan controlled experiments to compare the use of maps to conventional tools, and case studies to examine how programmers will adopt map visualizations in their programming work practices in the long term.

References

1. de Alwis, B., Murphy, G.C.: Using Visual Momentum to Explain Disorientation in the Eclipse IDE. In: Proc. VL/HCC, pp. 51–54 (2006)
2. Baker, M.J., Eick, S.G.: Space-filling software visualization. Journal of Visual Languages and Computing 6(2), 119–133 (1995)
3. Bederson, B.B., Shneiderman, B., Wattenberg, M.: Ordered and quantum treemaps: Making effective use of 2d space to display hierarchies. ACM Trans. Graph., 21(4), 833–854 (2002)
4. DeLine, R., Czerwinski, M., Meyers, B., Venolia, G., Drucker, S., Robertson, G.: Code thumbnails: Using spatial memory to navigate source code. In: Proc. VLHCC, pp. 11–18 (2006)
5. Fekete, J.-D., Plaisant, C.: Interactive Information Visualization of a Million Items. In: Proceedings of InfoVis'02, p. 117 (2002)
6. Furnas, G.W.: The FISHEYE view: A new look at structured files. Technical Report #81-11221-9 (1981)
7. Jakobsen, M.R., Hornbæk, K.: Evaluating a fisheye view of source code. In: ACM CHI Conference, pp. 377–386 (2006)
8. McGrath, J.E.: Methodology Matters: Doing Research in the Behavioural and Social Sciences. In: Baecker, R.M., et al. (eds.) Readings in Human-Computer Interaction, Morgan Kaufmann Publishers, San Francisco (1995)
9. Price, B.A., Small, I.S., Baecker, R.M.: A Taxonomy of Software Visualization. In: Proceedings of the 25th Hawaii Int. Conf. on System Sciences, pp. 597–606 (1992)
10. Ko, A.J., Aung, H., Myers, B.A.: Eliciting design requirements for maintenance-oriented ides. In: Proc. ICSE, pp. 126–135 (2005)
11. LaToza, T.D., Venolia, G., DeLine, R.: Maintaining mental models: a study of developer work habits. In: Proc. ICSE, pp. 492–501 (2006)
12. Storey, M.-A.: SHriMP views: an interactive environment for exploring multiple hierarchical views of a Java program. In: ICSE 2001 Workshop on Software Visualization (2001)

Visually Exploring Large Social Networks

Nathalie Henry

INRIA Futurs/LRI & University of Sydney
Bat. 490 University Paris-Sud, 91405 Orsay, France
J12, University of Sydney, NSW 2006, Australia
nathalie.henry@lri.fr
http://insitu.lri.fr/~nhenry

This PhD is a cotutelle co-advised by:

- Dr. Jean-Daniel Fekete [1], INRIA Futurs, France
- Pr. Peter Eades[2], National ICT Australia & University of Sydney, Australia.

Research Area and Topic. Information Visualization and Human Computer Interaction. This PhD focuses on visualization and interaction to navigate, explore and present large social networks.

1   Introduction

Vast new datasets are available for social scientists to analyze with the increasing use of internet technologies. Email clients, instant messenger and chat; photo sharing and peer-to-peer file exchange; open-source programming platforms and online editable encyclopedias such as wikipedia—all give social scientists ready-to-analyze data about how people communicate and collaborate.

This data avalanche raises new challenges these datasets are *far larger* than those they traditionally analyzed. (For example, the English version alone of Wikipedia contains 1.7 million articles). Also, they frequently contain *richer* information such as the history of each item: who contributed, when, for how much, and they *evolve through time* (the network structure changes as articles are added, transformed or removed).

The stakes of social network analysis are rising : intelligence agencies struggle to discover terrorist networks or epidemiologists to detect and contain outbreaks of diseases such as avian influenza and SARS.

Analysts require effective tools for handling these large, rich and dynamic social networks, to perform reliable yet flexible analysis at many levels, from overviews of the whole to a detailed analysis of important sections. The goal of this PhD is to provide them with visual interactive tools to support both their exploration process and the communication of their findings.

---

[1] jean-daniel.fekete@inria.fr
[2] peter.eades@nicta.com.au

C. Baranauskas et al. (Eds.): INTERACT 2007, LNCS 4663, Part II, pp. 604–610, 2007.

2   Related Work

Social networks are composed of actors (people or groups) linked by relationships (for example kinship, communication or collaboration). As social networks are graphs, their analysis is closely related to the exploration of graphs in general. There are many programs designed to support network analysis. The International Network for Social Network Analysis repository lists more than 50 different programs, and 10 new ones were introduced at last year's Infovis conference (30% of the articles). I classify these systems in two categories.

Menu-based systems and programming packages provide a wide range of functionalities to analyze and visualize social networks. Popular systems such as UCINet[1] and R[2] offer many features for statistical analysis, and common graph software and packages such as Pajek[3] and JUNG[3] also provide a broad range of algorithms to create visual representations of a network. However, mastering all the functionalities of these systems requires a considerable effort for novice users, as they require knowledge of how the algorithms work and how to combine or sequence them. Guess [4] is designed to support a more exploratory process. It provides a simple script language for manipulating the visualizations. However, even it remains inaccessible for many novice users, as it is unclear that social scientists will invest time learning it.

Visual exploration systems have emerged recently. They provide interactions to navigate and manipulate networks, which makes them accessible to novice users. Following Ben Shneiderman's mantra [5]: "Overview first, zoom and filter, then details-on-demand", they provide users with dynamic queries [6] (operations with a direct feedback on the representation).

Systems such as SocialAction[7] start the analysis with a node-link diagram of the full graph. For large and dense graphs, however, node overlap and edge crossing quickly makes these representations unreadable. Users must filter or aggregate nodes to get a readable visualization. SocialAction's strongest feature is its ranking of possible operations the user can perform at each step, providing guidance for the exploration process.

Since providing a readable representation of the whole network is challenging, several systems completely gave up on providing an overview. For example, Vizster[8] and TreePlus[9] concentrate on displaying and navigating in only a small part of a network centered on a specific actor. This "ego-centered" strategy lets users have a readable representation on the screen at all times. Other systems take other radical approaches. PivotGraph [10] starts the exploration from a high-level aggregated network. The user visualizes nodes' categories and their relationships, and then interacts with the visualization to explore lower levels. Finally, NetLens[11] completely gave up the graph representation. It uses simple visualizations such as histograms to explore the graph by its attributes, filtering them back and forth to answer questions.

---

[3] JUNG http://jung.sourceforge.net

3   Approach

This PhD follows statistician John Tukey's concept of Exploratory Data Analysis [12]: the primary purpose of visualizing and exploring is to raise questions and gather insights about a large quantity of data. Unlike most statistical work, which evaluates *a priori* questions according to a model, exploration by information visualization has the potential to start analysis without assumptions, or open new perspectives on a previously-analyzed dataset. For these purposes, overviews of the whole network are crucial.

While traditional node-link diagrams are user-friendly, readability suffers for large and dense networks. These factors often make it impossible to use them to visualize the entire network. We have sought alternatives to these representations. I believe adjacency matrix representations (Figure 1a) have a vast potential to investigate large and dense graphs. Ghoniem et al. published a study[13] comparing readability of both representations for several basic tasks of exploration. Results show that matrices outperform node-link diagrams for most of these tasks, especially when the network becomes dense. Figure 1b shows an example of the better readability of matrices for dense networks.

Social networks vary from very sparse (genealogy trees) to very dense (tables of goods exchange) including a locally dense category (small world networks). My approach is to take advantage of both representations, improving them, combining and merging them to handle many different cases.

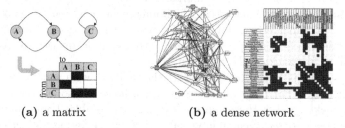

(a) a matrix   (b) a dense network

Fig. 1. Matrix and node-link representations

4   Contributions

The major contribution of this PhD is a visual and interactive system to help social scientists analyze large networks. My expected contributions are:

- Use participatory design techniques to determine social science analysts' needs and requirements for an interactive exploration system;
- Assessment of matrix-based representation readability as well as their improvement in general (ordering of their rows and columns) and on specific tasks important for social networks analysis (path-related tasks);
- Create novel visualizations designed for locally dense networks (small-world networks) as well as associated interaction techniques;
- Combine existing and novel visual representations into a system oriented toward interactive exploration.

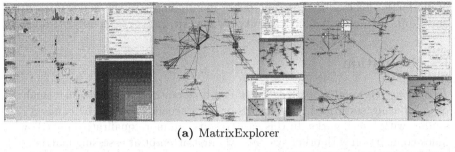

(a) MatrixExplorer

(b) Zoom on MatLink   (c) Zoom on NodeTrix

Fig. 2. MatrixExplorer, MatLink and NodeTrix

MatrixExplorer: an Exploration System[14, 15]. From a serie of interviews followed by a participatory design workshop, I collected a set of requirements for visually exploring social networks. One of the major outcome was the need for multiple representations of a same network and tools to help analysts find a consensus on their findings. From this study, I designed MatrixExplorer, a system combining matrices and node-link diagrams (Figure 2a). When users apply dynamic queries on one representation, they can observe the results on the other as well. Matrices are generally used to manipulate the network (filtering, ordering, clustering) and node-link diagrams to visualize the resulting one (smaller and sparser) and finally communicate findings. I observed that ordering rows and columns of matrices was crucial to better understand them. Thus, I developed an ordering algorithm based on heurisitics for the traveling salesman problem.

MatLink: Improving Matrix Representations[16]. Ordering a matrix helps identifying communities and central actors, both important tasks for analysis. However, matrices still suffer of a weakness for path-related tasks (how many actors connect A to B?). I designed an interactive solution to solve that major disadvantage of matrices: MatLink (Figure 2b). The principle is to overlay a linear node-link diagram on the matrix headers as well as display interactively the shortest path between selected actors. Currently, I am working on integrating MatLink into ZAME[17], a multiscale matrix explorer. MatLink can provide visual cues on what is not directly visible on the screen, and thus aid navigation.

NodeTrix: a Hybrid Representation[18]. A large category of social networks are globally sparse but locally dense. In this case, the structure is readable with a node-link diagram, but dense sub-parts are not. To solve that problem, I created a hybrid representation : NodeTrix , a node-link diagram visualizing dense sub-parts as matrices (Figure 2c). To smoothly manipulate NodeTrix, I designed a set of interaction techniques based on direct manipulation of the nodes using drag-and-drop. A video is available at http://insitu.lri.fr/~nhenry/nodetrix/.

5   Evaluation

Evaluating representations readability can be quantitatively done on a small set of tasks using controlled experiments or on a broader context by running case studies with benchmarks. In this case, results are more qualitative but allows a quick comparison with other systems. My first attempt at assessing matrix readability was a controlled experiment[19]. It partly failed because of the difficulty to operationnalize the exploratory process and to objectively compare subjects' interpretations and findings. To solve that problem, I worked with researchers from HCIL on defining a task taxonomy for graphs [20]. The second experiment I performed was much more focused, using five tasks and a technique I developped to generate representative datasets[^4]. It ended with significant results showing that MatLink improved matrices[16]. However, it is hard to generalized these results to the global process of exploration. To validate NodeTrix in a more realistic context, I chose to perform a case study using benchmarks.

Evaluating a visual exploration system is much more complicated as the process to control is long and difficult to operationnalize [21], which exclude controlled experiment. I chose to validate MatrixExplorer *a priori*, by implying users before and during its design. I am currently running a case study, describing how MatrixExplorer is used to explore a large quantity of data and what visualizations are created. Future evaluation would include a longitudinal study. These studies requires effort from both the system creator and the users in term of time and implication. However, they provide rich feedback and materials to analyze the exploration process and improve greatly the tool.

6   Directions for Future Research

At this stage, I can extend my PhD in many directions, I will only present the four I am interested in.

1. *Creating novel visualizations and interaction techniques.* This would especially be usefull to reorganize the high number of controls required to manipulate a network. I can imagine integrating them directly in the visualizations or design smart interaction techniques to replace them.
2. *Guiding the exploration.* Allowing analysts to visualize their previous analysis, annotating it and providing some indicators to guiding the next steps of the exploration would help them in their work and help us to understand the exploration process.
3. *Releasing a stable system.* This is mandatory to run a longitudinal study. I would integrate and instrument all prototypes to log users' actions.

[^4]: http://www.infovis-wiki.net/index.php/Social_Network_Generation

4. *Providing support for collaboration and communication.* This extension would help analysts to work together and to present their findings.

I briefly presented my research work on visual and interactive exploration of social networks. I am looking forward to the Doctoral Consortium to gather feedback on my research work and discuss the future direction of my PhD.

References

[1] Borgatti, S., Everett, M., Freeman, L.: UCINET V user's guide. Analytic Technologies, Natick, MA (1999)

[2] R Development Core Team: R: A Language and Environment for Statistical Computing. R Foundation for Statistical Computing, Vienna, Austria (2006) ISBN: 3-900051-07-0.

[3] Nooy, W., Mrvar, A., Batagelj, V.: Exploratory Social Network Analysis with Pajek. Structural Analysis in the Social Sciences. Cambridge Univ. Press, Cambridge (2005)

[4] Adar, E.: Guess: a language and interface for graph exploration. In: CHI '06. Proceedings of the SIGCHI conference on Human Factors in computing systems, Montréal, Québec, Canada, pp. 791–800. ACM Press, New York, NY, USA (2006)

[5] Shneiderman, B.: The Eyes Have It: A Task by Data Taxonomy for Information Visualization. Visual Languages, 336–343 (1996)

[6] Ahlberg, C., Williamson, C., Shneiderman, B.: Dynamic queries for information exploration: An implementation and evaluation. In: Proceedings of the ACM CHI'92: Human Factors in Computing Systems, pp. 619–626 (1992)

[7] Perer, A., Shneiderman, B.: Balancing Systematic and Flexible Exploration of Social Networks. IEEE TVCG (Infovis'06 proceedings) 12(5), 693–700 (2006)

[8] Heer, J., Boyd, D.: Vizster: Visualizing Online Social Networks. In: Proceedings of the IEEE Symposium on Information Visualization, p. 5. IEEE Computer Society Press, Los Alamitos (2005)

[9] Lee, B., Parr, C.S., Plaisant, C., Bederson, B.B., Veksler, V.D., Gray, W.D., Kotfila, C.: Treeplus: Interactive exploration of networks with enhanced tree layouts. IEEE TVCG (Infovis'06 proceedings) 12(6), 1414–1426 (2006)

[10] Wattenberg, M.: Visual exploration of multivariate graphs. In: Proceedings of the CHI conference, Montréal, Québec, Canada, pp. 811–819. ACM Press, New York (2006)

[11] Kang, H., Plaisant, C., Lee, B., Bederson, B.B.: Netlens: Iterative exploration of content-actor network data. In: Proc. of IEEE VAST, pp. 91–98 (2006)

[12] Tukey, J.: Exploratory Data Analysis. Addison-Wesley, Reading (1977)

[13] Ghoniem, M., Fekete, J.D., Castagliola, P.: On the readability of graphs using node-link and matrix-based representations: a controlled experiment and statistical analysis. Information Visualization 4(2), 114–135 (2005)

[14] Henry, N., Fekete, J.D.: Matrixexplorer: Un systéme pour l'analyse exploratoire de réseaux sociaux. In: Proceedings of IHM2006, International Conference Proceedings Series, pp. 67–74 (2006)

[15] Henry, N., Fekete, J.D.: MatrixExplorer: a Dual-Representation System to Explore Social Networks. IEEE TVCG (Infovis'06 proceedings) 12(5), 677–684 (2006)

[16] Henry, N., Fekete, J.D.: Matlink: Enhanced matrix visualization for analyzing social networks. In: Proceedings of Interact (to be published, 2007)

[17] Fekete, J.D., Elmqvist, N.: Do, T.N., Goodell, H., Henry, N.: Navigating wikipedia with the zoomable adjacency matrix explorer. INRIA Tech. Report (April 2007)

[18] Henry, N., Fekete, J.D., McGuffin, M.: Nodetrix: Hybrid representation for analyzing social networks. IEEE TVCG (Infovis'07 proceedings).

[19] Henry, N., Fekete, J.D.: Evaluating visual table data understanding. In: BEyond time and errors: novel evaLuation methods for Information Visualization (BELIV'06), Venice, Italy, ACM Press, New York (2006)

[20] Plaisant, C., Lee, B., Parr, C.S., Fekete, J.D., Henry, N.: Task taxonomy for graph visualization. In: BELIV'06 workshop, Venice, Italy, pp. 82–86. ACM Press, New York (2006)

[21] Plaisant, C.: The challenge of information visualization evaluation. In: Proceedings of the AVI Conference, Gallipoli, Italy, pp. 109–116. ACM Press, New York (2004)

Cultural Usability: The Effects of Culture on Usability Testing

Qingxin Shi

Department of Informatics, Copenhagen Business School, Denmark
qs.inf@cbs.dk

Abstract. Culture has already played an important role in the global market. It not only affects products, but also impacts on usability evaluation methods. This project aims to examine in the established thinking aloud usability evaluation method (TA UEM), how does the evaluator build a supportive relationship and communicate effectively with the user in order to find relevant usability problems in culturally localized applications. It includes three parts, pilot study, field study and experiments, to get both qualitative data and quantitative data. From this project, we hope to find an effective way to structure our TA UEM methodology to capture or be sensitive towards the mental models and ways of thinking in different cultural groups.

Keywords: Thinking Aloud Usability Testing, Culture, Localization, Evaluator Effect.

1 Basic Information of the PhD Research

Dissertation advisor: Torkil Clemmensen, tc.inf@cbs.dk; Kan Zhang, zhangk@psych.ac.cn
The research area or sub-area of my work: The research area of my work is usability, and the sub-area is cross-cultural usability evaluation method.
Universal resource locator (URL): www.cbs.dk/staff/shi and http:// culturalusability.cbs.dk/
Brief description of research topic: It's to investigate the cultural effects on thinking aloud usability testing, focusing on relationship and communication between evaluators and users from same and different cultures.

2 Introduction

With the advent of globalization and IT revolution, we can no longer overlook the aspect of culture in the design of user interfaces and products. In order to capture global markets, the products and software must be tested in target cultures to make sure that they are acceptable and suitable for people's cultural characteristics. But some previous studies have found that culture not only influences the products or interface design, but also the design methods used in building interfaces [1]. The PhD project will examine the cultural effects on thinking aloud usability testing.

Thinking aloud usability testing method has been extensively applied in industry to evaluate a system's prototypes of different levels of fidelity [2]. The primary goal of a

C. Baranauskas et al. (Eds.): INTERACT 2007, LNCS 4663, pp. 611–616, 2007.

usability test is to find a list of usability problems from evaluators' observations and analysis of users' verbal and non-verbal behavior; thus, the relationship between the evaluator and user is very important for finding accurate usability problems. Tamler [3] suggested establishing a trusting and supportive relationship in order to make the users honestly disclose their thoughts and feelings.

During usability testing, representative users are required to complete pre-established tasks by using the system. This measurement is largely related to specific users and specific tasks. However, people differ across regional, linguistic and country boundaries; therefore, if the evaluator and user have different cultural backgrounds, they may be strongly influenced by their local cultural perspective, perception and cognition, so the interaction and communication between them may be different from those who are from the same culture. Since usability testing involves human-human interaction, the evaluator and user's cultural background must be considered, or else there may be a misunderstanding between them. Therefore, how to build an effective relationship in the usability test has become a key issue in cross-cultural usability testing.

Although the thinking aloud usability test is generally thought to be an effective and successful technique [4], practitioners do not conform to the theoretical basis of the thinking aloud method in the industrial area which was described by Ericsson and Simon [5]. Therefore, Boren and Ramey [5] proposed speech communication theory as a theoretical basis for thinking aloud in usability testing, focusing on evaluator-test user communication. In my PhD project, I also want to examine how the two thinking aloud approaches are used in cross cultural usability testing. From our pilot study, we found that it might be better to follow Ericsson and Simon's approach to do the thinking aloud for foreign evaluators, since they may not be certain what the critical issue is that needs to be probed. In order not to influence the users and get more accurate information, the better way is to interrupt them less and avoid false leading. On the other hand, it might be better to follow the communication approach proposed by Boren and Ramey for native evaluators. Although we have such hypotheses, it is not confirmed by previous researches. This research will try to find what is the effective approach applied in the local and foreign culture in order to find the critical and accurate usability problems of the culturally localized application.

2.1 Research Question

In the established thinking aloud usability evaluation method (TA UEM), how does the evaluator build a supportive relationship and communicate effectively with the user in order to find relevant usability problems in culturally localized applications?

The research question is divided into three sub-questions:

1. Do users produce different thinking aloud protocols when they are with a native or foreign evaluator during the usability test?
2. How are the two thinking aloud approaches (Ericsson and Simon's approach and Boren and Ramey's approach) applied in cross-cultural usability testing? What is the effective approach for local evaluator and what is the effective approach for foreign evaluator?
3. How do we structure our TA UEM methodology to capture or be sensitive towards the mental models and ways of thinking in different cultural groups?

3 Culture Theory

The PhD project will be primarily based on Nisbett's culture theory [6, 7]. His theory focuses on the cognition and perception differences; for example, people from western countries and eastern countries will be different in causal attribution, categorization, and attention to the context vs. salient object [8]. This theory is more relevant to usability testing because thinking aloud usability evaluation methodology asks users to work on typical tasks and to verbalize their task performance and thought process [9]. The whole process involves users' cognition and perception characteristics. The results of the usability test, i.e., usability problems, which are found by the evaluators, are also involved in the evaluators' cognition and perception of the whole test process. When cultural differences exist between the evaluator and test user, some usability problems might be masked, instead of being uncovered.

In my study, temporarily, I define culture as an integrated pattern of local practice knowledge, cognition, and behavior, which is both a result and process of interacting with the environment and society. This project involves three countries: Denmark, India and China. Because Denmark is a western country, and it can also represent the type of society for which usability testing methodology was developed. China is a typical eastern country and India is a multicultural and multilingual country.

4 Main Factors in Cross-Cultural Usability Testing

4.1 Evaluator and User's Cultural Background

Cultural background needs to be considered since users from different cultures may not be influenced to the same degree when they are with a foreign evaluator. Northern European culture is a typical task-focus culture [10], which means that users in those countries may not be influenced when the evaluator is from another country since they pay more attention to the task, not the evaluator. While East Asian culture and Indian culture are socio-emotional relational orientation cultures[10], users in these countries may be influenced more when they are with a foreign evaluator, since the users' effort and attention are directed towards the interpersonal climate of the situation. For example, a study done by Vatrapu and Pérez-Quiñones [1] shows that Indian users who were with a foreign evaluator did not talk as freely as those who were with a local evaluator when testing a localized website. But this may not be the case for Danish users. In our future study, we will use foreign evaluators in India, China and Denmark to see whether the effect degree is the same in different cultures.

4.2 The Application/Software/Interface Being Tested

The requirement of an evaluator's cultural background is also related to the application or product which is tested in the target culture. There are two approaches to design products for international markets: globalization and localization [11]. "Globalization seeks to make products general enough to work everywhere and localization seeks to create custom versions for each locale" [11,p.158]. If testing a localized application which adapts specific cultural elements for a specific target culture, the results of the usability test may be more related to the evaluator and user's cultural background. Since usually the purpose of doing usability testing in different culture is to see whether this application is accepted by the target culture, which is the localization process, in the PhD research, I still use culturally localized application/software.

4.3 Evaluator Effect

The influence of culture on usability testing may also be derived from another factor called Evaluator Effect: the total number of usability problems found will depend upon the knowledge and experience of the evaluator and the number of evaluators [4]. The evaluator effect indicates that even in one culture, evaluators with different experience will find different usability problems. The effect may be much more significant when the evaluators are from two different cultures, since they do not even have the same cultural background. Even though they are both very qualified and professional, their cognitive process and knowledge cannot be the same, which may be a strong impact factor on cross cultural usability testing.

In a cross-cultural usability test, how can we minimize the evaluator effect which is derived from culture? It is very hard to change the foreign evaluator's cognitive process, but it may be much easier to increase his/her knowledge related to the culturally localized application. The foreign evaluator does not need to master all the target cultural knowledge, because it is impossible. But he can get some important information just related to this application. Maybe he/she needs to know the background, using habits and some related culture features of the application in the target culture, which will be very helpful for them to understand and communicate with the users in the usability test.

5 Methodology

In my PhD project, I will do both field study and experiments to collect both quantitative and qualitative data. Before the field study, we did pilot studies of experiments to collect data in lab conditions in Denmark, India and China, in order to get a general idea of the communication and relation models in the three countries. Then we did field study in order to examine in the industrial area, how the evaluators do the test and the relation and communication between evaluator and test user in the three countries. Next, I will design some experiments to create a comparable condition to explore the effective relation and communication pattern between foreign/local evaluator and test user.

5.1 Field Study

We conduct field observation in order to find the cultural difference in usability testing in Denmark, India and China. We have finished the field study in India and China and also did one study in Denmark. Maybe we will have one or two more field studies in Denmark. In the field studies which we have done, we went to the companies which did the usability test, and observed their tests.

Until now, we have observed one company in Denmark, one in India and five companies in China. In each company, we did field observation with video cameras of thinking aloud usability test sessions and afterwards interviewed the evaluators, test users and the usability department manager to get more deep information. We used three observer/interviewers: a Dane, an Indian and a Chinese. I will analyze the data in my PhD thesis.

5.2 Experiments

Since methods of experimental design and data analysis contribute more general enterprise of science [12], I will do a series of experiments in Denmark, China and India to figure out such issues:

1. Get a general knowledge of thinking aloud usability testing in Denmark, India and China, and a general knowledge of thinking aloud usability testing facilitated by local and foreign evaluator.
2. Examine the two thinking aloud approaches used in cross-cultural usability testing.
3. Investigate whether training could act as the effective way to structure our TA UEM methodology to capture or be sensitive towards the mental models and ways of thinking in different cultural group.

Application: Culturally localized application.
Variables:

1. Culture: Denmark, India and China.
2. The evaluator and user from the same culture or from different culture.
3. The thinking aloud approach (Boren and Ramey or Ericsson and Simon's approach) that the evaluator follows.
4. The related cultural knowledge that the local and foreign evaluator mastered about the application.
5. Foreign evaluators being trained or not with the target cultural knowledge related to the culturally localized application.

Dependent variables: The number and type of usability problems found by evaluators (severe vs. non-severe usability problems, and shared vs. unique usability problems), suggestions, positive comments, negative comments and culturally related comments which are made by the users.

6 Conclusion

This project aims to investigate the cultural influence on usability testing from an empirical and theoretical viewpoint. Using foreign evaluator may be much more convenient and less costly in some situation. For example, a Chinese company hopes to extend their products in Denmark. It may be more effective to get feedback to the designers and less costly if using their own usability professionals to do the test in Denmark instead of employing a Danish usability professional. Considering the cross-cultural cost-benefit analyses, it is worth to do the research of how to use a foreign evaluator conducts the usability test in the target country. From my PhD research, I hope to design a new and more effective thinking aloud usability test with less cultural bias for the global market. Besides, this study can also contribute to further understanding of how the two thinking aloud approaches applied in cross-cultural usability testing.

References

1. Vatrapu, R., Pérez-Quiñones, M.A.: Culture and Usability Evaluation: The Effects of Culture in Structured Interviews. Journal of Usability Studies 1(4), 156–170 (2006)
2. Law, E.L.-C., Hvanneberg, E.T.: Analysis of Combinatorial User Effects in International Usability Tests. In: CHI 2004, Vienna, Austria (2004)
3. Tamler, H.: High-tech versus high-touch: The limits of automation in diagnostic usability testing, http://www.htamler.com/papers/techtouch/
4. Clemmensen, T., Goyal, S.: Cross cultural usability testing. Working paper, Copenhagen Business School, Department of Informatics, HCI research group, 2005-006, p. 20 (2005)
5. Boren, M.T., Ramey, J.: Thinking aloud: Reconciling theory and practice. IEEE Transactions on Professional Communication 43(3), 261–278 (2000)
6. Nisbett, R.E.: Cognition and Perception East and West. In: 28th International Congress of Psychology in Beijing (2004)
7. Nisbett, R.E., Norenzayan, A.: Cultural and Cognition. In: Medin, D.L. (ed.) Stevens' Handbook of Experimental Psychology, 3rd edn. (2002)
8. Nisbett, R.E., Masuda, T.: Cultural and point of view. PNAS 2003 100(19), 11163–11170 (2003)
9. Ramey, J., et al.: Does Think Aloud Work? How Do We Know? In: CHI 2006 (April 22-27, 2006)
10. Sanchez-Burks, J., Nisbett, R.E., Ybarra, O.: Cultural Styles, Relational Schemas and Prejudice Against Outgroups. University of Michigan (2000)
11. Horton, W.: Graphics: The not quite universal language, in Usability and Internationalization of Information Technology. In: Aykin, N. (ed.) pp. 157–188. Lawrence Erlbaum, Mahwah (2005)
12. Maxwell, S.E., Delaney, H.D.: Designing Experiments and Analyzing Data, A Model Comparison Perspective, 2nd edn. Lawrence Erlbaum Associates, Mahwah, New Jersey (2004)

Consistency on Multi-device Design

Rodrigo de Oliveira and Heloísa Vieira da Rocha

University of Campinas, Institute of Computing, Campinas SP 13081-970, Brazil
oliveira@ic.unicamp.br, heloisa@ic.unicamp.br

Abstract. We propose consistency priorities to support multi-device interface design minimizing the user's cognitive effort while performing the same task on different interfaces. The methodology is being evaluated through a framework that generates Pocket PC interfaces from desktop web pages. Initial results point to the acceptance of the approach.

Research sub-areas: design methods, mobile computing, web design.

1 Introduction

Mobile devices introduced a great challenge for Human Computer Interaction: to develop multi-device interfaces for today's applications. Some have tried device oriented designs with linear transformations, creating mobile interfaces from scratch, like Avantgo (www.avantgo.com) and Usable Net (www.usablenet.com); others looked for dynamic and automatic adaptations, but still focusing on the device [1,4,9]. These and other related approaches were well received, but the generated interfaces are different from the original in some aspects that complicate interaction with more than one device to perform the same task, especially when refinding and/or comparing information [8,10]. Many works addressed consistency and continuity problems focusing on user interface generation [5,6] and task migration [12], but their guidelines are generally not sufficiently concrete for an automatic interface framework. A recent proposal [11] solves the multi-device design problem by passing the control of every appliance to a handheld interface generated automatically. Despite the valued ideas, many device specific interaction types [13] important to each context of use can be lost on the process, besides the need to carry a mobile device to control everything.

We propose consistency priorities for multi-device interface design that aims to improve usability and the user's experience when performing similar tasks on different devices. Some prototypes were implemented for automatic desktop web page adaptation to handhelds, such as Pocket PCs and smartphones. Initial evaluations point to the acceptance of this approach. Formal user evaluations will be conducted to check these first impressions.

2 Constructing the Proposal

In order to highlight the problem and start a discussion over the main assumptions of this proposal, we are going to borrow an example from Sharp et al. [13] and adapt it to a multi-device context.

C. Baranauskas et al. (Eds.): INTERACT 2007, LNCS 4663, Part II, pp. 617–623, 2007.
© IFIP International Federation for Information Processing 2007

Consider a person that had no contact with whatever interactive product to heat things. Now suppose we present him/her the stove with the task: *"Heat this bottle of water the fast you can"*. The process of understanding how things work uses inductive inference based reasoning. Individuals draw conclusions about objects or events on the basis of previous observations of similar objects or events. On this example, the person has no experience with any related product, so the first minutes will be just for exploration. After a while, the individual will eventually understand how the stove works and accomplish the task, improving his/her mental model with information like *"the more I turn this knob to the right, the more this flame becomes warm"*, *"the more this flame becomes warm, the faster the water heats"*, etc. Now suppose we present him/her a thermostat and another task analogous to the previous: *"Heat this room the fast you can"*. Both tasks are basically the same and so the individual will take the decision inductively, turning the thermostat knob most to the right. Although the applications had the same purpose (to heat things), their operation was inconsistent to the expected, thought the thermostat always heats the room in a constant speed, no matter how much the knob is turned to the right. The user could learn this new concept, but on a multi-device context with constant product refinement and maintenance, many usability attributes would be in risk, such as memorability, security, efficiency and others. Next subsection presents our proposal of consistency priorities to avoid ambiguous scenarios like this.

2.1 Stating the Hypothesis

Pyla et al. [12] argue that consistency needs to be better defined if it is to be the overriding factor in the design of multiple user interfaces. In fact, there isn't a consensus about what consistency really is and how it can be applied [11].

We think about consistency on the user's side. Individuals mentally draw conclusions about objects or events on the basis of previous observations of similar objects or events. These internal constructions that can be manipulated enabling predictions are called mental model [3]. Figure 1 sketches the user's mental model update cycle while executing tasks.

In order to help users form an accurate and useful mental model of a system while interacting with any of its interfaces, we suggest applying consistency on multi-device contexts using the following priorities:

1. *Task Perception* - the same control mechanisms to execute a task and their disposal on the interface. If these requirements cannot be followed with good usability on devices with different control attributes (e.g. size, weight, material, etc.) and properties (e.g. fluidity, flexibility, opacity, etc.), perception should be mapped to each device's interaction type maintaining usability.
2. *Task Execution* - the same actions flow to execute a task. If the control mechanisms available on a given interface had to be adapted for the others by the task perception priority, the actions flow should be maintained on a

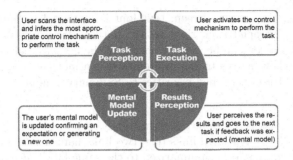

Fig. 1. User's mental model update cycle. Task perception and execution are the key processes to build a consistent mental model for decision making.

logical perspective. Although this may repass bad design decisions and lose opportunity to improve usability on each interface independently, user's decision making is supported under a consistent multi-device context, providing ease of learning/remembering and safety of use. Next priority improves efficiency.

3. *Task Personalization* - the ability to change task perception and execution according to the users' preferences. The goal is to achieve the best design for any user which is the configuration that user expects. This can be related to the *personally consistent design* concept [11], but with an active position for the user. As a result, efficiency and ease of expert use is provided to avoid the downsides of consistency [7].

It's important to understand the correct application of these consistency priorities as they can be easily misunderstood. For example, if an individual wants to check an account balance through an ATM machine, a tablet PC and a telephone, there is no possibility to perceive and perform the task in the same way. If the mentioned devices are important to the end user, adaptation to the contrasting interaction types is a price they are willing to pay. In fact, that's part of the *task personalization* priority. So the focus is to provide the same task perception and execution under a logical perspective, be it through words typed, written or said. This is in accordance with Nichols' work [11] about benefitting from user's experience, but opens space for the rich interaction types of the actual appliances in a consistent way.

3   Towards an Empirical Validation

3.1   Proposing the Methodology

On this section, we are going to take an application designed for multi-device access and improve it using our proposal. The application chosen is the Summary Thumbnail [8], a prototype designed to automatically adapt desktop web pages for handhelds. Here's how it works: the original web page is shrunken to fit horizontally on the smaller screen, text font is increased to improve legibility and letters are cropped from right to left until sentences fit on the available space. Complete texts can be read by accessing the *detailed view* through a click on the page, which moves to the original desktop interface with full scrolling. After applying the consistency priorities to Summary Thumbnail, we identified two issues:

1. *Ambiguous task perception:* the right-to-left cropping generates ambiguities, especially for navigational links (e.g. two links named *"delete account"* and *"delete client"* could be summarized to the same label *"delete"*);
2. *Different and ambiguous task execution:* the new concepts of *thumbnail view* and *detailed view* along with their access procedures, resulting interaction fear (i.e. after clicking a link, there is no way to predict if it will visit it or move to the detailed view) and context loss on the original desktop interface with full scrolling.

The first problem could be solved by applying simple lexical analysis like the one given by Buyukkokten et al. [2], which will also maintain efficiency on runtime web page transformations. Additionally, we point a few restrictions:

- *Long texts summarization*: reducing long texts is time consuming and results tend to be questionable. The right-to-left cropping approach might be better;
- *Navigational links summarization*: anchors, buttons, hyperlinks and other access structures are the only interface objects to be considered for a more refined text summarization as their corresponding actions may be critical and shouldn't be misunderstood. Thought they are usually short sentences, the TF/IDF (term frequency / inverse document frequency) technique [2] could be enough when applied together with stem dictionaries. Additionally, it should be extended to use domain orientation. Different dictionary files could be generated remotely from database collections, each one containing information of term occurrences in each particular domain, and used by the interface adapter according to the web page being summarized.

The Summary Thumbnail's second problem is more complicated as the detailed view is a whole new concept that doesn't exist on the original task model but is fundamental to the approach. However, as it seems to demand a low learning curve to understand its operation, we decided to maintain it, but with a smaller cognitive effort on the transition to and from the thumbnail view. Next section explains how it was implemented on the first prototypes.

3.2   Constructing and Evaluating the Prototypes

On the first prototype generation (see Figure 2a), we used focus-plus-context to provide a faster detailed view over the thumbnail. Full texts and normal sized images are presented inside a *hint* window whenever users point to the corresponding object on the page. They can even confirm the full text to stay on page and this information is stored for future accesses (task personalization).

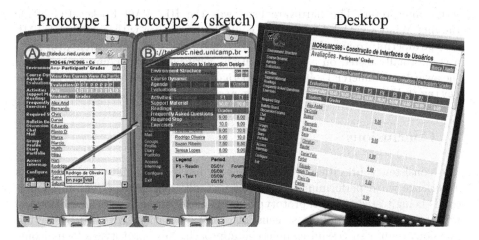

Fig. 2. Prototypes detailed view: **(a)** First generation: interface is shrunk, texts are summarized (right-to-left cropping) and fonts are increased. When the user points to summarized text, detailed view appears over the thumbnail without losing context (full text can be displayed on the thumbnail using the *on page* button and this information is stored for future accesses). If the user points to any link, an additional button is provided on the detailed view to visit it. **(b)** Second generation: TF/IDF [2] and stem dictionaries are used for better summarizations. The detailed view uses focus-plus-context technique with a low opacity level to improve context view.

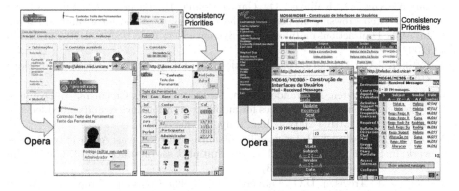

Fig. 3. Comparison between interfaces generated with the Consistency Priorities and Opera *Fit to Screen*. The first was much better evaluated on informal tests.

As the hint detailed view loses format attributes useful on iconic systems, we are developing the next prototype generation with the Direct Migration [10] (no transformation applied to the page) inside the hint window with a lower opacity value to improve context view (see Figure 2b).

Currently, the automatic interface adaptation doesn't require additional Internet traffic and takes less than two seconds to adapt a web page using the browser script interpreter. The hardware used was the HP iPAQ Pocket PC h2400 running Windows Mobile 2003 but could be any other with a CSS, DHTML and JavaScript compatible browser. Recently, the first generation prototype was informally tested on a few institutions with much better impressions than the awarded commercial solution by Opera (`www.opera.com/products/mobile/reviews`). Figure 3 compares screens generated by both approaches.

4 Conclusions

The consistency priorities proposal aims to improve usability and the user's experience when performing similar tasks on different devices. The methodology is being tested through prototypes designed to automatically adapt desktop web interfaces for handheld screens. Informal evaluations revealed better impressions than a successful commercial approach. Next prototypes focus iconic interfaces and evaluations will be taken to verify the advantages of this proposal.

References

1. Berti, S., Correani, F., Mori, G., Paternó, F., Santoro, C.: Teresa: a transformation-based environment for designing and developing multi-device interfaces. In: Proc. CHI 2004 Extended Abstracts, Vienna, Austria, pp. 793–794 (April 2004)
2. Buyukkokten, O., Kaljuvee, O., Garcia-Molina, H., Paepcke, A., Winograd, T.: Efficient web browsing on handheld devices using page and form summarization. In: ACM Transactions on Information Systems, New York, USA, vol. 20, pp. 82–115 (2002)
3. Craik, K.J.W.: The nature of explanation. Cambridge University Press, Cambridge (1943)
4. Coninx, K., Luyten, K., Vandervelpen, C., Bergh, J.V.D., Creemers, B.: Dygimes: dynamically generating interfaces for mobile computing devices and embedded systems. In: Proc. MHCI 2003, Udine, Italy, pp. 256–270.
5. Denis, C., Karsenty, L.: Inter-usability of multi-device systems: A conceptual framework. In: Seffah, A., Javahery, H. (eds.) Multiple User Interfaces, pp. 373–385. John Wiley & Sons, Chichester (2003)
6. Florins, M., Trevisan, D.G., Vanderdonckt, J.: The Continuity Property in Mixed Reality and Multiplatform Systems: A Comparative Study. In: CADUI 2004, Funchal, Portugal, pp. 323–334 (2004)
7. Grudin, J.: The case against user interface consistency. CACM 32(10), 1164–1173 (1989)
8. Lam, H., Baudisch, P.: Summary thumbnails: readable overviews for small screen web browsers. In: Proceedings of CHI 2005, Portland, OR, pp. 681–690 (2005)
9. Lin, J.: Using design patterns and layers to support the early-stage design and prototyping of cross-device user interfaces. Doctoral Thesis, p. 557. University of California, Berkeley, California (2005)
10. Mackay, B., Watters, C., Duffy, J.: Web page transformation when switching devices. In: Proc. of the Mobile HCI 2004, Glasgow, Scotland, pp. 228–239 (2004)

11. Nichols, J.: Automatically generating high-quality user interfaces for appliances. Doctoral Thesis. Pittsburg, Pennsylvania: Carnegie Mellon University, p. 322 (2006)
12. Pyla, P., Tungare, M., Pérez-Quiñones, M.: Multiple User Interfaces: Why consistency is not everything, and seamless task migration is key. In: Proceedings of the CHI 2006 Workshop on The Many Faces of Consistency in Cross-Platform Design (2006)
13. Sharp, H., Rogers, Y., Preece, J.: Interaction design: beyond human-computer interaction, 2nd edn., p. 800. Wiley & Sons, Chichester (2007)

A Critical Analysis of the Semiotic Engineering Evaluation Methods

Silvia Amelia Bim

Departamento de Informática – PUC-Rio. Rua Marques de São Vicente, 225 RDC. CEP 22453-900. Rio de Janeiro – RJ. Brazil.
sabim@inf.puc-rio.br
http://www.inf.puc-rio.br/~sabim

Abstract. Semiotic Engineering is a semiotic theory of HCI that views human-computer interaction as a contingent process of designer-to-user metacommunication. The theory currently has two evaluation methods, Communicability Evaluation and Semiotic Inspection. The aim of our research is to do a critical analysis of both methods in order to align them with each other, especially in ontological and epistemic terms, and to position them more clearly in the Semiotic Engineering territory.

Keywords: Semiotic Engineering, Evaluation Methods, Communicability Evaluation Method, Semiotic Inspection Method.

1 Introduction

Semiotic Engineering [1] is a semiotic theory of HCI which takes a metacommunication perspective on human-computer interaction [2]. A system's interface, along with the interaction patterns enabled by it, is characterized as a message sent from the system's designer to the system's user through the system's interface. Metacommunication stems from the fact that this message communicates how and what for users can themselves communicate with the system.

Semiotic Engineering defines "communicability" as the central quality of interest for the theory. Formally, "communicability is the distinctive quality of interactive computer-based systems that communicate efficiently and effectively to users their underlying design intent and interactive principles" [5]. In this research we are dealing with two evaluation methods proposed in association with Semiotic Engineering: the Communicability Evaluation Method (CEM) and the Semiotic Inspection Method (SIM). CEM and SIM are both qualitative and interpretive methods [3]. CEM focuses on the *reception* of the message sent by the designer to the user based on empirical evidence. SIM, on its turn, focuses on the *emission* of the metacommunication message, by analyzing the internal consistency and cohesiveness of the communicative strategies encoded in a system's interface, as well as its external consistency with a statement of the design intent. It is thus an analytical method.

C. Baranauskas et al. (Eds.): INTERACT 2007, LNCS 4663, Part II, pp. 624–625, 2007.

2 Research Hypothesis, Expected Contributions and Methods

Our research hypothesis is that, although they have some clear distinctions not only in perspective but also in terms of produced results, CEM and SIM have important relations with one another to the extent that SIM may, in some contexts of evaluation, be carried out as a step of CEM. However, because both methods characterize the same phenomenon, communicability, but are themselves in different stages of maturity (CEM was formulated in 2000, and SIM in 2006), it is important to align them with each other and to position them as clearly as possible in the Semiotic Engineering territory. Our hypothesis here is that such strict theoretical framing will allow us to obtain (by using CEM and SIM to evaluate interactive software) solid evidence of how this theory can effectively contribute with new insights for HCI.

We expect that our research results will contribute to strengthen the scientific quality of Semiotic Engineering, by promoting the feedback loop between theory and practice. Additionally, a clearer definition of CEM and SIM can certainly improve the way how they are taught, learned, and professionally practiced, which are more pragmatic contributions of this research.

In order to achieve our expected contributions, a qualitative research [4] will be conducted in three parts. The first part consists of a qualitative study through in-depth interviews with open-ended questions [6], aiming at understanding the experience of different groups with the methods, and the meanings assigned by groups and individuals to their experience. The second part consists of a number of experiments with the methods themselves. They will be used in various types of contexts in order to help us identify ease and difficulty in applying them. The third part of the research consists of a critical analysis and comparison of results obtained in the first and second parts.

Acknowledgments. Silvia Amelia Bim and Clarisse Sieckenius de Souza thank CNPq for research grants for carrying out this research.

References

1. de Souza, C.S.: The Semiotic Engineering of Human-Computer Interaction. The MIT Press, Cambridge (2005)
2. de Souza, C.S., Leitão, C.F., da Prates, R.O., da Silva, E.J.: The Semiotic Inspection Method. In: Proceedings of IHC-2006, SBC, Natal, RN (2006)
3. Denzin, N.K., Lincoln, Y.S.: The landscape of qualitative research: Theories and issues. Publications, Thousand Oaks, CA (2003)
4. Denzin, N.K, Lincoln, Y.S.: Handbook of Qualitative Research, 2nd edn. Sage Publications, Thousand Oaks (2000)
5. Prates, R.O., de Souza, C.S., Barbosa, S.D.J.: A method for evaluating the communicability of user interfaces. ACM Interactions 7(1), 31–38 (2000)
6. Seidman, I.: Interviewing as Qualitative Research: a guide for researchers in Education and the Social Sciences. Teachers College Press, New York (1998)

Why Gender Matters in CMC?
Supporting Remote Trust and Performance in Diverse
Gender Composition Groups Via IM

Xiaoning Sun

Drexel University, College of IST, 3141 Chestnut Street Philadelphia PA 19104, USA
xiaoning.sun@ischool.drexel.edu

Abstract. An important yet largely unexplored area in HCI is how gender affects trust development and performance in virtual settings. This proposed study aims to investigate whether providing social chat activities to collaborators in a social dilemma game before they collaborate via remote text chat can support trust development and performance among remote team members. This study will provide an understanding of how communication media as well as initial social activities affect male, female and mixed gender pairs' trust development and performance in a virtual environment from a simulated longitudinal perspective. Ultimately, the results of this study may provide insights into ways of improving performance of teams made up of diverse individuals in real world virtual collaborations.

1 Introduction and Research Questions

In recent years HCI researchers have made significant progress in understanding how different communication media influence people's trust perceptions and task performance in virtual environments. In this research little attention has been paid to the effects of gender differences in communication in virtual environments. However, there is good reason to investigate the role of gender, given research in the discipline of communication studies that has shown gender effects in face-to-face and virtual communications. This research aims to bring the gender factor into computer-mediated communication (CMC) from an HCI perspective, responding to central concerns of efficiency, effectiveness, and user perceptions. The primary objective of this research is to explore gender differences in synchronous computer-mediated communication with and without initial social activities. In particular, I ask whether initial social activities affect trust development and performance of male, female and mixed gender pairs in a social dilemma game.

The primary research questions are 1) How does gender influence people's trust development over multi-trials of a competitive task via the IM System? 2) How effectively does pre-task activity, i.e. social chat, help different gender pairings achieve higher levels of trust and better performance over multi-trials of a competitive task? 3) Is there a larger benefit of pre-task activity for males than for females in doing a task which involves conflicts of interest? If the answer is YES, do males achieve the same level of trust as females? 4) Qualitatively, how do different gender pairings use language to communicate via the IM System and how does their language affect trust?

C. Baranauskas et al. (Eds.): INTERACT 2007, LNCS 4663, pp. 626–627, 2007.

2 Research Plan

Following up on a previous study which I conducted from Fall 2005 to Spring 2006 [1], using many of the same procedures, my dissertation study will still focus on trust and performance with different gender pairings, but from a simulated longitudinal perspective. Specifically, it aims to answer the question: How can males improve their low initial trust in low-end technologies [1], such as IM?

A 3x2 between subjects design will be used: gender pairing (male/male vs. male/female vs. female/female), and pre-task interaction (interaction vs. no interaction). All participants will use the IM System to do an investment game. The pairs will be strangers and the gender of the partners will be revealed by the experimenter immediately before pairs perform their task. In terms of the pre-task interaction, pairs in this condition will have a 10-minute getting acquainted session, using IM to introduce themselves and get to know each other before they begin the trust game.

For the data analysis, I will largely be doing quantitative analysis on trust and performance based on the post-questionnaire and the various quantitative measures of behavior (cooperative behavior, investment payoff, number of defections). Also, I plan to do qualitative work based on the communications of pairs' discussion during the task. The goal of the qualitative work is to determine whether male, female and mixed gender pairs use different patterns of language. This will enhance understanding of how language helps build trust.

3 Significance to HCI

This study covers three areas of research, communications, gender and trust, and may impact society in several ways. First, the results will provide possible ways of establishing higher levels of trust among remote workers who have to communicate via low-end media, i.e., IM, especially for teams made up of solo males who perceive lower levels of initial interpersonal trust [1]. Second, this research will contribute to the literature of the effects of group gender composition on performance outcomes. To date, there is only a small body of literature that deals with this issue in HCI. Third, the discourse analysis of conversation style in IM will provide understanding of communication patterns in different gender groups. Indeed, as the work place becomes more diverse in term of gender culture and business becomes more global, team leaders need to become even better at interacting with diverse team members and more flexible in adjusting their own styles to different group compositions.

Reference

1. Sun, X., Zhang, Q., Wiedenbeck, S., Chintakovid, T.: Gender Differences in Trust Perception when Using IM and Video. In: Proc. of CHI2006, ACM Press, New York (2006)

PeerCare: Challenging the Monitoring Approach to Eldercare

Yann Riche

INRIA/LRI, Univ. Paris-Sud, France – Univ. of Queensland, Australia
yann.riche@lri.fr

This Ph.D. is jointly advised by Wendy Mackay (INRIA) and Stephen Viller (Univ. of Queensland). It takes place in the Human Computer Interaction and Computer Mediated Communications research areas, and focuses on the design and evaluation of communcation appliances for seniors to better "age in place".

1 Introduction

Recent projections show that by 2050, 34% of the European population will be aged 65 or more. Institutions are seeking alternatives to existing care solutions, focusing essentially on providing support for the elderly to stay at home. To date, most of the related research has been focused towards monitoring technologies to overcome this issue. While these systems are a mean to help the caregiver, they only indirectly help the elderly. Moreover, using automatons as caregivers presents many problems [1], including stigmatization of dependance. In contrast, studies like Giles et al.'s [2] emphasize the role of social networks well-being of elderly. Therefore, alternatives are needed for independent people with no critical health concerns who are willing to be proactive about their health and to maintain high social connectedness. My project adopts this approach by seeking ways of supporting informal care behaviours to help the elderly "age in place". My primary focus is to explore how communication appliances can play a significant role in this regard. My work also seeks to validate designs and concepts by conducting user-centered and participatory design processes, and by validating them using in situ, longtudinal deployments. Communication appliances, introduced in the interLiving project [3], are defined as a "[. . .]simple-to-use, single-function devices that let people communicate, passively or actively, via some medium, with one or more remotely-located friends or family" [4]. My project seeks to benefit from the existing social networks of elderly and use communication appliances to strenghthen their role in elderly's well aging.

2 Research Methodology

Communication appliances is a fairly new concept and I believe it has a vast potential to help seniors age in place. The goal of this PhD is to explore this potential and provide seniors with prototypes and devices they will use. For

C. Baranauskas et al. (Eds.): INTERACT 2007, LNCS 4663, Part II, pp. 628–630, 2007.
© IFIP International Federation for Information Processing 2007

this purpose, my research methodology is to **Use participatory design and user-centered design techniques** to better understand elderly people's needs and how communication appliances can be smoothly integrated to their environment, **Implement a technology probe** to study the communication in situ and bring the design process into their environment, and **Design, prototype and deploy** several communication appliances with seniors to support their communication.

3 PeerCare

To understand the role of communication for seniors living at home, I conducted a user study with women aged between 62 and 88, living in private flat or in sheltered housing. The major outcome of this study was the important role of seniors' relationships with each other in their well being. The concept of *Peer-Care*, central line in this PhD, is defined as senior to senior relationships in which people provide informal reciprocal care to one another. This opposes the current monitoring approaches where the relationship is unilateral. The particularity of PeerCare behaviors is that it exists between people sharing a common interest in having someone care for them. The intensity, frequency and type of care may vary over time, but the flow of care is overly maintained and bilateral.

Several major questions are raised for the design, development and evaluation of technology to support PeerCare: How to overcome technical problems to deploy the technology in situ? How to approach, motivate and imply users in the design? How to objectively evaluate the benefit of a communication appliance? These questions raises fondamental issues concerning the approach to integrate research technologies in a home environment, recrute users and evaluate communications/ambient devices. To answer the first question, I have designed and implemented markerClock [5], a device designed to study the benefit of communication appliances for elderly. To explore the second question, I have a conducted a participatory design process looking at communication devices for elderly in general and PeerCare in particular. To provide answers to the third question related to the evaluation of communication appliances and their benefits, I will deploy and evaluate markerClock in elderly people's homes.

References

[1] Haigh, K.Z., Yanco, H.A.: Automation as caregiver: A survey of issues and technologies. In: AAAI Workshop Automation as Caregiver, pp. 39–53 (2002)
[2] Giles, L., Glonek, G., Luszcz, M., Andrews, G.: Effects of social networks on 10 year survival in very old Australians: The Australian longitudinal study of aging. Journal of Epidemiology and Community Health 59, 574–579 (2005)
[3] Hutchinson, H., Mackay, W., Westerlund, B., Bederson, B.B., Druin, A., Plaisant, C., Beaudouin-Lafon, M., Conversy, S., Evans, H., Hansen, H., Roussel, N., Eiderback, B.: Technology probes: inspiring design for and with families. In: Conf. on Human factors in Computing Systems, Ft. Lauderdale, USA, pp. 17–24. ACM Press, New York (2003)

[4] Mackay, W., Riche, Y., Labrune, J.-B.: Communication appliances: Shared awareness for intimate social networks. In: ACM SIGCHI 2005 Workshop on Awareness Systems: Known results, theory, concepts and future challenges, Portland, OR, US, ACM Press, New York (2005)

[5] Riche, Y., Mackay, W.: Markerclock: A communicating augmented clock for elderly [short paper under review]. In: Baranauskas, C., Palanque, P., Abascal, J., Barbosa, S.D.J. (eds.) Interact 2007. LNCS, vol. 4663, Springer, Heidelberg (2007)

HCI Brazilian Community – After 10 Years

Raquel Oliveira Prates[1,2]

[1] Departamento de Ciência da Computação – UFMG,
Av. Antônio Carlos, 6627, Prédio do ICEx, sala 4010, Belo Horizonte - MG
rprates@dcc.ufmg.br
[2] Chair of the Special Interest Group in Human-Computer Interacton (CEIHC)
Brazilian Computer Society (SBC)

Abstract. The Brazilian HCI community first started organizing itself in 1997 and after 10 years has grown and consolidated itself nationally and internationally.

Keywords: Brazil, HCI community, Brazilian Computer Society, SBC, CEIHC, Brazil-CHI, BR-CHI, SIGCHI, IFIP.

Research in HCI in Brazil started in the end of 80´s and beginning the 90´s. At that time there were a few researchers who were interested in the discipline. By the end of 90´s, although some of these researchers had been doing work on HCI for a decade, there was no HCI community in Brazil. In 1997, after some Ph.D. students participated in CHI 2007 they thought it would be interesting to find out who was working with HCI in Brazil. With the support of Professor Clarisse de Souza they started the efforts in that direction. The first step was to create a website containing the information on people (mainly professors and grad students) working in the field and their work.

In that same year at CHI, Richard Anderson who was SIGCHI Chair for Local Chapters at the time encouraged the group to create a Brazilian Local Chapter. The Brazilian Local Chapter (or BR-CHI) was created as a prospective chapter [1]. BR-CHI allowed us to exchange experiences with different HCI communities worldwide that were facing or had faced similar challenges as the ones ahead of us trying to consolidate the Brazilian HCI community. Also it played an important role as the first formal HCI organization in which people working or interested in the field in Brazil could get in touch with or become a member of.

The following year, 1998, the first HCI event (IHC) was organized in Brazil as a 3 day workshop organized within the Brazilian Symposium on Software Engineering. The workshop was successful and became an annual event for the Brazilian HCI community. In its 5th edition in 2002 the event became a Symposium. That same year was created the Special Interest Group in Human-Computer Interaction (CEIHC) in the Brazilian Computer Society (SBC) [2]. The HCI community was growing and consolidating itself within Brazil as well as internationally. In 1999, the Brazilian Computer Society designated the first representative for the Brazilian HCI community to participate in IFIP-TC13. In 2000, Br-CHI became a SIGCHI chartered chapter and in 2001, CHI organized a Development Consortium on HCI in Latin America. During this consortium the idea of having a Latin-American HCI conference was discussed.

C. Baranauskas et al. (Eds.): INTERACT 2007, LNCS 4663, Part II, pp. 631–632, 2007.
© IFIP International Federation for Information Processing 2007

In IHC 2002, the idea became a plan, and IHC started to alternate every other year with the Latin-American Conference in HCI (CLIHC). The first edition of CLIHC was held in Rio de Janeiro in 2003, the 2nd in Mexico in 2005, and its 3rd edition will be organized as part of INTERACT 2007. In 2006, for the first time IHC proceedings have been published in ACM/DL. Finally, in 2007, the Brazilian HCI community is honored to be hosting INTERACT, in its first edition south of the equator.

The Brazilian HCI community has come a long way from having a directory of people interested in HCI in 1997 to hosting INTERACT 2007. In these 10 years some of the relevant achievements the Brazilian HCI community has accomplished are:

- A consolidated event (IHC) that brings together the Brazilian HCI community;
- Participation of members of the Brazilian HCI community in organizing and program committees of relevant international HCI events;
- Representatives in relevant scientific societies in Brazil (SBC) and internationally (SIGCHI/ACM, IFIP);
- Relevant publications of results of HCI research in Brazil in a number of international events and journals;
- Participation of members of the Brazilian HCI community in editorial boards of relevant HCI journals;
- Publication of a book about an HCI theory developed in Brazil aimed at the international HCI community by MIT Press [3];
- Publication of educational material on HCI in Portuguese as books or chapters of Brazilian computing books, and translation of a well known and recommended book to Portuguese [4];
- Recommendation of HCI as a mandatory course to Computer Science and Information System curricula by SBC;
- Initial recommendation and discussion on a program for an HCI course at undergrad level, and possibilities for grad level courses;
- An increasing number of HCI professors and researchers in Universities, as well as professionals in industry;

We hope that experience of the Brazilian HCI community can be used by other HCI communities to get started, consolidated or have an active role scientifically. One important ingredient that has been essential to our community to succeed has been the dedication and willingness to participate and make it happen of all its members.

References

1. BrCHI – SIGCHI/ACM Brazil CHI Local Chapter, available at: http://ead.unifor.br/brchi/
2. CEIHC – Comissão Especial de IHC da SBC (HCI Special Interest Group in the Brazilian Computer Society. available at: http:// www.sbc.org.br/ihc
3. de Souza, C.S.: The Semiotic Engineering of Human-Computer Interaction. The MIT Press, Cambridge (2005)
4. Preece, J., Rogers, Y., Sharp, H.: Design de Interação: Além da Interação Homem-Computador. Bookman, Porto Alegre (2005)

uiGarden, - An Online HCI Society in Two Languages

Christina Li

uiGarden.net
Christina.li@uigarden.net

Abstract. uiGarden, - a bilingual webzine, gives an opportunity between practitioners and researches working in user experience designer field from the Chinese and English speaking part of the world to exchange opinions and gain further knowledge within the field.

Keywords: Online HCI Society, bilingual webzine, China.

1 Background

China is predicted to become the biggest market leader and an economical giant in the foreseeable future. This is the reason why the world is focusing its attention and investments in China. A steady flow of Chinese nationals are still leaving China parallel to this. Domestic ventures in the West deal with customers who have Chinese backgrounds from China. It is due to these two factors that there is a major increase in demand for usability.

The experience of different cultures coming into contact with each other can be a positive influence in this modern life we are in. This involves intercultural exchanges, hence the term 'melting pot', as well as bewilderment, misunderstandings and miscommunication. Design professionals, whether from the West or from China, are encountering new challenges when creating usable and enjoyable user experience for their consumers. The demand of a place where user experience designers can easily exchange ideas and opinions is there. The benefit of gaining inside knowledge in the development and views of the other nation is huge.

uiGarden has started to meet this need. It was created from the teams' passion desire for user-centred design. These groups of practitioners and researchers, with professional technology and experience from the West and China, have committed themselves to act as a 'bridge' for the Western and Chinese HCI community. We understand the necessity for a free flow of exchange between the Western and Eastern usability practitioners. We plan for uiGarden to serve as an open platform, a possible opinion for fast and free information exchanges between professional people, who may not have met otherwise. uiGarden is unique in that it offers opportunity to discuss, explore and potentially resolve some of these differences. It can act as a catalyst to highlight the diversity of the websites between the West and the East.

2 The Webzine

The aim of the team is to offer fast and abundant exchange of information between the Western and Chinese design communities as well as to build a society that will

C. Baranauskas et al. (Eds.): INTERACT 2007, LNCS 4663, Part II, pp. 633–634, 2007.

eventually benefit both sides. The creation of uiGarden signifies a new phase in the way the West and East communicates.

For Western practitioners, the idea is to provide a space to communicate and exchange views between professionals. The website also serves as a portal in the user interface design industry in the Far East, allowing an insight into this increasingly vital market.

For Chinese practitioners, the site provides access to the latest developments in the West which includes Chinese translated articles from top Western experts and providing discussion boards for a closer look at each featured article.

The main contents are divided by categories including Opinion, Methods, Case studies and Reviews and Interviews with attention on: exploring theories and concepts that reflect current industrial practice, forecasts articles that refer to the challenges faced by our discipline, articles reflecting to the teaching of user-centred techniques and methodologies, case studies from projects showing the application of user-centred techniques from two communities, reviews of books, conferences, sites, software, tools and interactive projects , and interviews with leading experts in the field giving their point of view to professional issues.

Articles in this edition are in both Chinese and English. Discussion boards are available at the end of each article to allow readers to communicate with the author. Discussion threads are also translated into the other language enabling readers from the other community to also discuss the article with the author.

Apart from the direct discussion regarding the articles with their authors, we also offer forums in both languages for general discussions, focuses on a wide range of topics, therefore not limiting the discussion on just one article. Popular topics will also be translated in order for participants to know what the most discussed about issues are by their peers in the other community.

3 The Outcome

The aim of uiGarden is to facilitate information exchange and communication between the Western and Chinese user experience design communities. UiGarden was launched in January 2005 and it has achieved more than 550,000 page views since. In March 2007, the site has had more than 24,000 page views in total alone which averages over 500 unique visitors every day. This number is increasing at a fast rate with visitors coming from all over the world, of which 60% are from China and 40% from the rest of the world (data is for March 2007). uiGarden appears as a link to many well-known design and usability websites including HCI Bibliography, jnd.org, informationdesign.org, ixdg.org amongst many others. It has currently (April 2007) more than 2,000 subscribers by email, RSS and to its forums.

There is still much to learn from the project. It is our belief that Western designers will gain more ideas, when designing for global products, as more effective communication exists between the West and East. On the other side, learning usability theories and methods without the language barrier will also allow more people in China to understand and accept the concept, which will allow the Chinese usability and design industries to compete with the world.

The AIPO Society: Present and Future Trends

María Paula González[1,2], Toni Granollers[2], Cesar A. Collazos[3], and Julio Abascal[4]

[1] CONICET (National Council of Scientific and Technical Research) and
Department of Computer Science & Eng. – Universidad Nacional del Sur, Argentina
mpg@cs.uns.edu.ar
[2] GRIHO Research Group – Universitat de Lleida, Spain
{mpg,tonig}@diei.udl.cat
[3] Department of Systems - Universidad del Cauca. FIET-Sector Tulcan, Popayán, Colombia
ccollazo@unicauca.edu.co
[4] Informatika Fakultatea. University of the Basque Country, Spain
julio.abascal@si.ehu.es

Abstract. This paper presents an overview of the international *Asociación Interacción Persona-Ordenador* (AIPO), a growing society related to HCI and focused on the Spanish-speaking community. AIPO is aimed to support HCI related activities both in the academia and the industry, connecting hundreds of millions of potential members.

1 Looking to the Present: The AIPO Scope and Main Activities

Since 1999 the *Asociación Interacción Persona Ordenador* (AIPO)[1] has covered a wide spectrum of activities to promote HCI in the Spanish-speaking community.[2] Indeed, AIPO is a multidisciplinary society oriented towards people whose cultural background is primarily associated with the Spanish language and culture, regardless of ethnic and geographical differences. The AIPO society is open to everyone belonging to the above community. Their members are mainly university researchers specialized in HCI, doctoral students focused on HCI, and HCI-related professionals coming from the industry.

In the last decade, main AIPO activities were articulated through three axis: enhancing HCI education, promoting the integration of the industry and the academia in common projects around HCI, and studing an appropriate translation of international ideal values and standards associated with usability to the Spanish-speaking context of use. To enhance HCI education, AIPO has focused on analysing the state of the art of HCI proposals in Spanish-speaking universities[1]. Besides, a series of HCI-related academic events were sponsored, such as the 5th, 6th and 7th editions of the *Congreso Internacional de Interacción Persona Ordenador* (International Conference on HCI) held in 2004, 2005 and 2006 respectively; and the *I Jornadas de Trabajo sobre Enseñanza de CHI* (1st. Symposium on CHI Education) in 2005. A series of HCI-related books were published [2,3,4,5,6]. With respect to

---

[1] See www.aipo.es (webpage of the Asociación Interacción Persona Ordenador - AIPO).
[2] Note that this community is formed by inhabitants of Spain and all Spanish-speaking countries in North, Central and South America, including almost 35 million people living in the USA with Spanish-related origins.

C. Baranauskas et al. (Eds.): INTERACT 2007, LNCS 4663, Part II, pp. 635–636, 2007.
© Springer-Verlag Berlin Heidelberg 2007

the integration of the industry and the academia in common projects around HCI, relevant people from the Spanish industry were included in the AIPO board. AIPO also collaborated with a exhibition stand at the industrial *Internet Global Congress* (IGC) in 2006. Concerning the appropriate translation of international ideal values and standards associated with usability, AIPO sponsored the project *Iniciativa UsabAIPO* (started in 2004 and still underway), which involved the participation of more than 15 university research groups specialized in HCI. The usability of official webs in the context of the Latin-America academia was tested, and some ideal values, metrics, heuristics and Cognitive Walktroughs were proposed [7,8,9].

2 Looking to the Future: The AIPO Challenges and Trends

During next years, a central trend in AIPO is related to reinforce the participation of members coming from Latin American countries. As an example, the Colombian branch of AIPO was created in 2007. Besides, a Master in HCI sponsored by AIPO will be started next academic year 2007-2008 at Universitat de Lleida (Spain). Their contents were elaborated following the Bolonia Process[3] on the basis of the consensus between HCI researchers and professionals coming from the industry, including members of the AIPO board. Different AIPO members (belonging to different universities) are expected to participate as professors in this new Master program.

Acknowledgments. Project ADACO (TIN2004-08000-C03-03)

References

[1] Granollers, T.: HCI in Spanish speaking countries. IFIP TC 13 Seminar Trends in HCI. Spain (2007)
[2] La Interacción Persona Ordenador, Abascal, J., et al. (eds). AIPO, (Copyright 2001-2006), electronic book available at http://griho.udl.es/ipo/libroe.html ISBN 84-607-2255
[3] Granollers, T., Lorés, J., Cañas, J.J.(eds.): Diseño de Sistemas Interactivos Centrados en el Usuario. Ed. UOC (2005), ISBN 84-9788-320-9
[4] Lorés, J., Granollers, T.: La Ingeniería de la Usabilidad y de la Accesibilidad aplicada al diseño y desarrollo de sitios web. Universitat de Lleida, (2004)
[5] Navarro, R., Lorés, J.: HCI related papers of Interacción'04. Springer, Heidelberg (2005) ISBN 1-4020-4204-3
[6] Presente y Futuro de la Docencia e Inv. en Interacción Persona-Ordenador. Redondo, M., Bravo, C., Lorés, J. (eds.) Linces Artes Gráf. (2005), ISBN 84-689-2758-9
[7] González, M.P., Lorés, J., Granollers, T.: Assessing Usability Problems in Latin-American Academic Webpages with Cognitive Walkthroughs and Datamining Techniques. In: HCII'07, Beijing, China. LNCS, Springer, Heidelberg (2007)
[8] González, M. P., Lorés, J., Pascual, A., Granollers, T.: Evaluación Heurística de Sitios Web Académicos Latinoamericanos dentro de la Iniciativa UsabAIPO. In: Proc. INTERACCION'06, pp. 145–157 (2006) ISBN 84-690-1613
[9] Lorés, J., González, M. P., Pacual, A.: Primera fase de análisis del Proyecto UsabAIPO. In: Paraninfo, Th. (ed.) Proc.INTERACCIÓN'05, pp. 217-221, (2005) ISBN 84-9732-436-6

---

[3] See http://ec.europa.eu/education/policies/educ/bologna/bologna_en.html

A Multimodal Medical Sculptor

Roberto S. da Rosa Junior, Marcus A.C. Farias, Daniela G. Trevisan,
Luciana P. Nedel, and Carla M.D.S. Freitas

Instituto de Informática, Universidade Federal do Rio Grande do Sul
Campus do Vale - Bloco IV - Prédio 43425 Av. Bento Gonçalves, 9500
91501-970   Porto Alegre - RS - Brazil
{rsjunior, macfarias, dtrevisan, nedel, carla}@inf.ufrgs.br

Abstract. This work introduces the design of a multimodal application allowing
the user to sculpt 3D medical data. We are considering interaction modalities
such as blowing and gesture to segment the 3D data visualized. Besides we present a multimodal platform for the rapid development of multimodal interactive
systems as a central tool for an iterative user-centered design process.

Keywords: multimodal interaction, medical application, 3D interaction, Open-
Interface.

1 Introduction

The growing interest in multimodal interface design is inspired largely by the goal of
supporting more transparent, flexible, efficient, and powerfully expressive means of
human-computer interaction. Multimodal interfaces are expected to be easier to learn
and use, and are preferred by users for many applications. Such systems also have the
potential to function in a more robust and stable manner than unimodal recognition
systems involving a single recognition-based technology, such as speech, pen, or
vision [1].

Likewise, the ratio of users' multimodal interaction increased significantly as the
tasks became more difficult. Analysis of users' task-critical errors and response laten-
cies across task difficulty levels increased systematically and significantly as well,
corroborating the manipulation of cognitive processing load [1]. For these reasons in
this work we have applied multimodal interaction to medical applications. Tasks
requiring manual segmentation of occluded organs (such as liver segmentation) is a
difficulty and loaded task. In this case the whole user interaction focus might be
placed on the task space. It means that using the same interaction paradigm and providing interaction techniques that avoid changes in the user interaction focus could
facilitate and increase the task performance. In next sections this work introduces the
design of a multimodal application allowing the user to sculpt 3D medical data. We
are considering interaction modalities such as blowing and gesture to segment the 3D
data visualized. Besides we present a multimodal platform for the rapid development
of multimodal interactive systems as a central tool for an iterative user-centered
design process.

C. Baranauskas et al. (Eds.): INTERACT 2007, LNCS 4663, Part II, pp. 637–640, 2007.

2 System Overview

To develop a multimodal system is necessary to have interaction modalities and mechanisms for modalities fusion. An interaction modality can be defined as the composition of a language plus a device. For instance <blowing + microphone> and <gesturing in the physical space + webcam>. Mechanisms for modalitites fusion inform the manner these modalities will be combined. For instance some fusion mechanisms such as redundancy, equivalence, complementary and assignment are described in [2]. In our implementation the two interaction modalities are complementary i.e. the user should blow in the microphone and move the marker in front of the webcam to inform the multimodal command *erase + position* to the 3D medical sculptor (see Figure 1). However the gesture modality alone is capable to produce the movement of the selected virtual hand metaphor in the medical viewer.

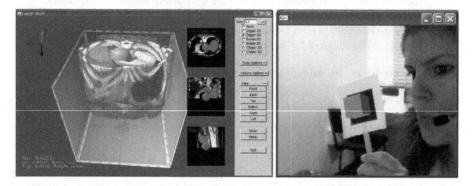

Fig. 1. Interaction components of the multimodal medical sculptor

2.1 OpenInterface

OpenInterface[1] is an open source platform for the rapid development of multimodal interactive systems as a central tool for an iterative user-centered design process. It is a component-based architecture allowing the integration of heterogeneous native interaction components as well as the connection between components to develop new multimodal application. Each component is registered into OpenInterface Platform using the Component Interface Description Language (CIDL described in XML). The registered components properties are used to compose the execution pipeline of the multimodal application. This execution pipeline is sent to the OpenInterface Kernel (C/C++) to run the application.

2.2 Interaction Components

To develop our multimodal medical sculptor we integrated into the OpenInterface platform three components for interaction: one component for noise detection, one for gesture detection and one for medical visualization (i.e. the sculptor) described as following.

---

[1] http://www.openinterface.org

Medical Sculptor Component

This component provides a set of tools for volume sculpting. These tools were described by [4] and had used three-dimensional geometries associated to the metaphor of the virtual hand [3]. The virtual hand is represented as different cursors and its formats reproduce in three dimensions the performance areas on the volume 3D. The sculpting tools are Rubber 3D, Digger 3D and Clipper 3D.

The Eraser 3D tool eliminates voxels inside a virtual cylinder. The virtual cylinder consists of an infinite line and a circular region around this line. This region is calculated using a projection plane, a 2D point P on this plane and the radius r of the tool (Figure 2a). The selection of a voxel for elimination is done by first projecting its center into the projection plane. For each projected center, a distance d to P is computed. Every voxel with $d < r$ is removed.

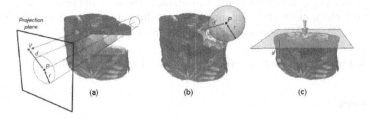

Fig. 2. (a) Eraser 3D (b) Digger 3D (c) Clipper 3D

Another tool, the Digger 3D (Figure 2b) eliminates voxels in the interior of a virtual sphere. The region is defined using a 3D point P and a ray r specified by the user. The selection of a voxel for removal is done calculating the Euclidean 3D distance d of its center to P. The voxel is removed if $d < r$. The Clipper 3D tool (Figure 2c) eliminates voxels situated above of a plane defined by the user. The selection of a voxel for removal is made by calculating the minimal distance of its center to the clipping plane. The distance is calculated by the dot product of the voxel coordinates and the plane coefficients. Voxel is eliminated in case the distance is negative.

Additionally to 2D and 3D mouse interactions described in [4] we added new multimodal interaction. Now we can move the cursor position with gesture interactions and apply the tools using noise detection.

Noise Detector Component

The NoiseDetector component provides a single command that can be activated using a microphone. The technique is simple and doesn't require much processing. The component takes small sound buffers from the microphone and when it detects a sufficient noise, it calls a callback function passing *true* (otherwise, it passes *false*). In this implementation, it passes *true* when more than 40% of the samples (absolute value) are greater than 0.8 (their maximum value is 1.0). The best way to generate such noise is by blowing directly into the microphone. Each time the noise is detected a single event is sent to the medical viewer resulting the erase interaction at the position indicated by the gesture detector component.

Gesture Detector Component

The Gesture Detector component uses the ARToolkit[2] library to capture the 3D user position in the physical space. We are using a webcam while the user is moving a printed marker in the physical space to control the 3D medical viewer. Each time this component detects the marker in the video image its position is sent to the medical viewer component resulting the translation (x, y, z axis) operation of the selected virtual hand metaphor.

3 Conclusion and Future Works

We presented in this work a multimodal medical sculptor including three interaction components: gestures detector, noise detector and the medical viewer and sculptor. The OpenInterface platform was used to connect these components. Next step will take account the multimodal user interaction evaluation compared to the interaction modes using 2D and 3D mouse as described in previous work [4].

Acknowledgments. The authors would like to thank CNPq - Brazil.

References

1. Oviatt, S.L.: Multimodal interfaces. In: Jacko, J., Sears, A. (eds.) The Human-Computer Interaction Handbook: Fundamentals, Evolving Technologies and Emerging Applications, ch.14, pp. 286–304. Lawrence Erlbaum Assoc, Mahwah (2003)
2. Bouchet, J., Nigay, L., Ganille, T.: ICARE software components for rapidly developing multimodal interfaces. In: Proceedings of the 6th international conference on Multimodal interfaces ICMI 2004, pp. 251–258. ACM Press, New York (2004)
3. Bowman, D.A., Hodges, L.F.: Formalizing the design, evaluation, and application of interaction techniques for immersive virtual environments. Journal of Visual Languages and Computing 10(1), 37–53 (1999)
4. Huff, R., Dietrich, C.A., Nedel, L.P., Freitas, C.M.D.S., Olabarriaga, S.D.: Erasing, Digging and Clipping in Volumetric Datasets with One or Two Hands. VRCIA 2006. In: pp. 271–278 (2006)

---

[2] http://sourceforge.net/projects/artoolkit/

I-Candies: Supporting Semi-formal Communication in a Coffee Corner

Khairun Fachry[1,*], Ingrid Mulder[2], Henk Eertink[2], and Hans Zandbelt[2]

[1] User System Interaction
Eindhoven University of Technology
Eindhoven, NL
Archives and Information Science, University of Amsterdam, Amsterdam, NL
k.n.fachry@uva.nl
[2] Telematica Instituut
Brouwerijstraat 1, Enschede, NL
{ingrid.mulder, henk.eertink, hans.zandbelt}@telin.nl

Abstract. This paper describes the development of a multi-user interactive display in the coffee corner that makes the office workers aware of events happening within the company aiming to stimulate social interaction. New input devices, i-Candies (fake candies integrated with RFID tags) are used as multi-user input devices for explicit interactions with the display. The interactive display and i-Candies have been deployed and tested within the office environment.

Keywords: Design, Tangible User Interface, Context-aware System.

1 Introduction

In today's knowledge-intensive world, knowledge workers face more and more complex information. However, much can be achieved by presenting the right information at the right place for the knowledge workers. In this paper, we describe a service that presents information of interest to knowledge workers in a coffee corner, while they are having breaks. As a first step in a user-centered design process, we observed knowledge workers in order to understand their behaviors in an office coffee corner. The observations confirmed that the office workers tend to perform informal and semi-formal communication while they are in the coffee corner. It is in keeping with the finding of Whittaker et al. [10] that a shared physical environment promotes informal social communication. From those findings, we designed a multi-user interactive display in the coffee corner that makes the office workers aware of events that are happening within the company and of general events and news. Furthermore, Agamanolis [1] found that half the battle in designing an interactive situated or public display is designing how the display will invite that interaction. In keeping with Churchill et al. [3] users need constant encouragement and demonstration to interact with the interactive public display. This project aims to entice office workers' curiosity by: on the one hand, re-using and

---

* Corresponding Author.

C. Baranauskas et al. (Eds.): INTERACT 2007, LNCS 4663, Part II, pp. 641–644, 2007.

automatically refreshing company-related information, and on the other hand by introducing a new way of interaction input device, the i-Candies.

2 A Sweet Dish for the Coffee Corner

In order to attract office workers an ideal company awareness system should show daily updated information. Both company-specific content that reuses existing information and content of general interest were combined. Consequently, the system remained interesting and useful for the employees. In this way, we enticed the office workers to check for new content on the display. On this display, the following categories of information were presented:

1. *Company Announcements* are taken from the internal knowledge management system.
2. *Latest Publications* presents the most recent publications of the company.
3. *Where are Our Colleagues* presents the location of their colleagues.
4. *What is Happening in the World* presents the international news.
5. *How is the weather?* presents the weather forecast.

From the observation study, we learned that input devices should be easy to use and fun to use. Taken these requirements into account, a sweet dish inspired us to symbolize the social interaction of drinking coffee resulting in the design of i-Candies in combination with an i-Bowl as input devices. The i-Candies have been designed in the form of colorful candies to make the interaction playful and interesting. The metaphors of the i-Candies and the i-Bowl match the environment of the coffee corner, as there are cups and tea bags around the table. More importantly, the physical form of the I-Candies raises curiosity of the office worker. The i-Candies were made of foam and were integrated with RFID tags. The i-Bowl is a small bowl that with an integrated RFID reader. Pictures of all i-Candies are presented on the display as navigational cues. The user chooses the content she wants to see by placing an i-Candy on the i-Bowl. The display then presents the requested information, updates its screen and presents the next possible presentation. All i-Candies are on the table which enables users to easily choose and pick i-Candies and stimulates the involvement of multiple users. Still, one i-Candy can be placed inside the i-Bowl, which facilitates a social way for interaction allowing a group of people interaction with the system simultaneously.

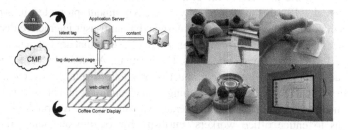

Fig. 1. The system architecture and making of the i-Candies

The prototype has been implemented as a web-based application running on the coffee corner display. The context information needed by the coffee corner system is provided by the the RFID identification. The RFID identification is facilitated by the CMF [8]. CMF provides the attributes location, time, and RFID tag number and stores them in a database of the application server. New content is provided if a new RFID tag is detected, using a polling mechanism. It will detect the tag number and retrieves the page associates with the tag number.

In keeping with Mark Weiser's vision of ubiquitous computing where a world in which computational services can be naturally and "invisibly" integrated into our physical environment [9], the i-Candies and the i-Bowl are used to illustrate how everyday objects related to drinking coffee can be part of a context-aware coffee environment. Computers usually have very well-defined input interfaces i.e. mouse and keyboard. In the current project, we therefore, focused on making this input interface "blended" in the environment and more playful for the users. The interaction tags of candies is a part of the evolving line of tangible interface work [2, 6], which determined to investigate interactive techniques for input devices. Candies are something that is consumed during informal meetings could make people feel sweet and rejuvenated during the coffee break. The nature of a candy as something that is sweet is being replicated to human feelings. In our system, the displayed information comprises interesting news and company information that make people think and smile. Also the candies are being shared by people as the nature of the information that is presented in the coffee corner. The information that the i-Candies control has been studied before. The Notification Collage [5] portrays items posted by users within a workgroup by creating a collage, rather than a single item at a time. Placing one i-Candy at a time presents a single item which provides content that is more easily digestible for the users. Furthermore, work on designing technology-rich spaces to attract user interaction and enhance human-to-human sociability has been a promising research. The GROUPCAST [7] and Intellibadge systems [4] are applications that present information in a large display in a shared area. In the current project we elaborated upon these ideas by combining information with 'sweet' input devices and providing ways to make the passersby curious about the system.

3   Discussion and Conclusions

To evaluate the experience of the office workers while interacting with the system, we tested the system in a real office coffee corner. Based on user interviews as well as raw usage data, it can be concluded that the system entices people to interact with it. Interview results also indicated that the users like the metaphor and the game-like interaction of the candies. More importantly, users like the continuously updated content. The content made them more aware of their surrounding activities in an easier and faster way. Furthermore, the system usage was logged to count the number of i-Candies placed on the i-Bowl. Even though, after some time, the users get used to the i-Candies, usage of the system did not decrease drastically. This might be due to the dynamic content of the system. Occasional heavy usage of the system was due to guests visiting the company. As first-time users, their curiosity to try out the system was much higher than the frequent users of the system. Another interesting result is that even after the evaluation period, the system is still in use in the office. The users gave positive feedback and proposed many ideas of applications that the company awareness system could be tapped into. Interestingly, by showing the recently published articles in the coffee corner, colleagues were encouraged to archive their work in line with administrative rules without feeling compelled to do. Another not trivial result of the i-Candies was that it influenced the interaction among the research engineers in a positive way. Mainly because of the fact that our prototype derived upon existing ideas, and relies upon existing work done by colleagues on context-aware systems, our implementation in the available coffee corner was established in many related projects and therefore also influenced many colleagues' work. The positive effect of playing with the system was that they get more insight in their contributions and their perspectives, and consequently, results in constructive collaborative design. A striking example is that it quickened the debugging process, and definitely contributed to good working relationships among the involved designers.

References

1. Agamanolis, S.: Designing Displays for Human Connectedness. In: O'Hara, K., Perry, M., Churchill, E., Russell, D. (eds.) Public and situated displays: Social and interactional aspects of shared display technologies, Kluwer, Dordrecht (2003)
2. Camarata, K., Do, E.Y.-L., Johnson, B.D., and Gross, M.D.: Navigational blocks: Navigating information space with tangible media. In: Proceedings of the International Conference on Intelligent User Interfaces. San Francisco, USA, January 2002, pp. 31–38 (2002)
3. Churchill, E.F., Nelson, L., Denoue, L., Helfman, J., Murphy, P.: Interactive systems in public places: Sharing multimedia content with interactive public displays: A case study. In: Proceedings of the 2004 Conference on Designing Interactive Systems (DIS2004), Cambridge, MA, pp. 7–16 (August 2004)
4. Cox, D., Kindratenko, V., Pointer, D.: IntelliBadge™: Towards Providing Location-Aware Value-Added Services at Academic Conferences. In: Dey, A.K., Schmidt, A., McCarthy, J.F. (eds.) UbiComp 2003. LNCS, vol. 2864, pp. 264–280. Springer, Heidelberg (2003)
5. Greenberg, S., Rounding, M.: The Notification Collage. In: Proceedings of CHI 2001, pp. 514–521. ACM Press, New York (2001)
6. Ishii, H., Mazalek, A., Lee, J.: Bottles as a Minimal Interface to Access Digital Information. In: Extended Abstracts of CHI 2001, pp. 187–188 (2001)
7. McCarthy, J.F., Costa, T.J., Liongosari, E.S.: UNICAST, OUTCAST & GROUPCAST: Three Steps toward Ubiquitous Peripheral Displays. In: Abowd, G.D., Brumitt, B., Shafer, S. (eds.) Ubicomp 2001: Ubiquitous Computing. LNCS, vol. 2201, pp. 332–345. Springer, Heidelberg (2001)
8. van Sinderen, M.J., van Halteren, A.T., Wegdam, M., Meeuwissen, H.B., Eertink, E.H.: Supporting context-aware mobile applications: an infrastructure approach. IEEE Communications Magazine 44(9), 96–104
9. Weiser, M.: The Computer for the 21st Century, in Scientific American 265(3), 94–104 (1991)
10. Whittaker, S., Frohlich, D., Daly-Jones, O.: Informal communication: What is it like and how might we support it? In: Proceedings of CHI 1994 (1994)

Multi-modal Search Interaction: Helping Users Make Connections Between Conceptual and Spatial Maps

Christian Beck and Craig Birchler

School of Informatics 901 East 10th St.
Indiana University, Bloomington, IN 47408
{cmbeck, cbirchle}@indiana.edu

Abstract. In this paper we describe an interface for searching and conceptualizing related information. We describe a specific application of this interface for searching traditional artists in the state of Indiana. The interface employs multimodal interaction by allowing the user to search for artists using a map of the state of Indiana alongside a conceptual hierarchical map of crafts and subcrafts. The two interfaces work in parallel with each other so that as a user interacts with one interface, it affects what is displayed on the opposing map. The goal of this application is twofold. One goal is to provide users with a better and simpler means for searching a specific set of information using only relevant and related data. The second goal is to provide companies, organizations or institutions with an interface that will allow them to provide clients or targeted users with a more effective way to search their database.

Keywords: Conceptual map, spatial map, interactive searching.

1 Introduction

We have developed an interface that seeks to help users make more meaningful connections between data while also providing a logical means for conceptualizing data. We have created an interface for businesses or organizations to input data into an application that populates this interface dynamically. Here however, we describe the interaction with the interface. We begin by outlining a small sample of conceptual and spatial networks already in use. We then illustrate the problem we intend on solving with our interface.

1.2 Examples

Visual Thesaurus. Plumb's Visual Thesaurus (www.visualthesaurus.com) is a conceptual network that links words based on the connections that link them together. The interface is a joy to use and effectively allows the user to understand more meaningful links between words based on different meanings. However, this application only works for datasets of connected entities based on likeness (in this case, similar words). It is not optimal for conceptualizing other hierarchical or spatial concepts.

Google Maps. Google Earth (earth.google.com) is an interface that allows for easy spatial visualization of basic data. However, while a user may filter data shown on the

C. Baranauskas et al. (Eds.): INTERACT 2007, LNCS 4663, Part II, pp. 645–648, 2007.

map, it is a one-way relationship. A user can filter data on the map using different parameters but not vice-versa.

Gapminder.org. This site provides a unique and powerful tool for viewing data using multiple attributes. A user can view countries in terms of GDP, time, location and population size. However, whereas we are concerned with conveying a relationship between multiple representations, gapminder.org *integrates all representations into a single interface. Additionally, the data is represented for the sake of representation, not for a specific goal such as trying to find a country to visit, for example.*

1.2 Problem

The examples we have described all succeed more or less in their goals but they only work to a certain extent. We are proposing an interface that can build on examples such as these in order to explore how conceptual maps can be used as searching devices rather than simply for representation and visualization. Our interface provides communication between two conceptual maps in order to allow a user both to conceptualize related data and to create a more meaningful and effective search.

2 Interface

Our interface is open to appropriation towards any number of instances that involve the representation of multiple conceptual networks. Here we describe one instance of use for a folklore group that seeks to allow users to search and view their database of traditional folk artists in the state of Indiana. The interface couples a spatial network with a conceptual, hierarchical network. The spatial network highlights counties and cities based on whether they contain folk artists. Each artist will be contained in a county. The county represents the number of artists by becoming a darker color. If a user clicks on a county, the artists will then be laid out according to city. Opposite the map, a conceptual network constructs a hierarchical structure of crafts that are represented by the artists.

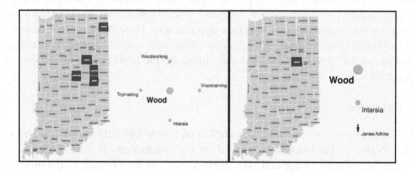

Fig. 1. On the left, a user has refocused on the parent craft 'wood'. Counties with data associated with the network remain highlighted on the map. On the right, a single relevant county remains based upon the user's selection of the sub-craft 'intarsia' from the parent craft of 'wood'. A single data node, 'James Adkins', is present in the network. Data is represented contingent upon the scale of the opposing side.

The database includes hundreds of sub-crafts that are divided into around twenty parent crafts. For example, a typical craft is glass with a sub-craft of glass-blowing. The system is open to allow for infinite levels but for our particular client's need, in this application we have included two. Once a user clicks on a sub-craft, the craft network is then populated with artists in that area. While a user refines the scales by clicking on counties or crafts, the manipulated network will affect the other as shown below.

The pair of images in fig. 1 shows what happens when a user searches based upon the hierarchical network of crafts. In this instance the user selects the craft 'wood' then the sub-craft 'intarsia'. On the left, this action filters down the counties on the map to show only those that have people associated with the four sub-crafts within 'wood'. In the right image of fig. 1, the available sub-crafts have reduced to 'intarsia' based upon the user's selection. In this case there is only one person shown as a node off of 'intarsia'. Accordingly, only one county is represented. From this, it is clear which county James Adkins resides.

The interface also utilizes the ability for the user to search for craft artists on the map instead of the craft network. In this instance the user could zoom into the map by clicking on a region of Indiana which would then change the parent crafts visible on the network. The highlighted counties would remain unchanged, however the scale would affect the craft network to show only crafts present in that region. Incidentally, the user could select a craft as seen in fig.1 and the network would then filter counties in that specified region. The interface gives two methods for searching through craft artists while each affects visible data on the opposite side. As a result, the user can better understand the nature of the data, make more meaningful connections between how crafts and geography are related, and search in a way that better represents the nature of the data (e.g. spatially and hierarchically).

3 Conclusion

We have described what we feel to be an innovative contribution to HCI-design by presenting a multi-modal, interactive search interface. Existing applications such as Plumb's Visual Thesaurus and Google Earth are innovative and entertaining towards their own goals. However, we have proposed an interface that can build upon the one-way filtering and single data representation. The core component of our interface lies in the power it gives the user to view a set of data in multiple representations. We hope to have accomplished this by creating not only an interaction between the interface and the user but between the different data representations themselves. In doing so we feel this interface provides a more intuitive interaction rather than one that restricts the user by conforming their interpretation to only what the interface provides. For example, our multi-modal interfaces allow users to not only ask questions like, "Where are wood craftspeople in the state of Indiana?" but to be able to follow up with questions such as, "Who practices woodcarving in Hamilton County?" We have attempted to create an interface that will model itself upon how the user conceptualizes data rather than the undesirable alternative of forcing meaning and conception onto the user [1].

3.1 Future Work

While we believe to have described an innovative contribution to the field of HCI, we have yet to empirically prove our concept. The effectiveness of our application will be determined in two areas: usability studies and user experience. First, usability studies will be developed in tandem with future development of the network visualization. As stated, we are open to development of the application based upon a wide variety of data types, each with their own organizational and user needs. In this instance we have modeled hierarchical and spatial representations. While maps are a commonly understood means of spatial visualization, we do not claim that a wheel of nodes is necessarily best to represent hierarchies. In fact, currently we are creating new methods of representation for the craft network by clustering groups of crafts, and using font-size to convey information density much like tag clouds. Visualization of the data must be contingent upon a combination of the type of data being represented, the basic desires of the organization compiling the data, and the users expected to benefit from it. Multiple variations of data types will need to be categorized so as to aid in development and testing of corresponding visualizations.

Second, we hope to determine effectiveness in terms of the user's ability to develop new connections not readily apparent between types of data visualization. A proof of concept has been derived and, through study of individual development of knowledge based upon the multi-modal interface, we hope to develop supporting data which proves our claims. Knowledge will be measured as a comparison of understanding between using unidirectional and multidirectional interface styles. From these tests we hope to further refine our prototype so that it can be expanded and appropriated for usage in other areas.

Acknowledgments. Thanks to Jeff Bardzell for giving us guidance throughout our development of this application, to Jon Kay for his collaboration on behalf of the Traditional Artists of Indiana (TAI), and Dave Roedl for his coding help.

Reference

1. Krippendorf, K.: The Semantic Turn. Taylor and Francis Group, London (2006)

Podcast Generator and Pluriversiradio: An Educational Interactive Experience

Alberto Betella and Marco Lazzari

University of Bergamo, Faculty of Educational sciences, Piazzale Sant'Agostino, 2
I-24124 Bergamo Italy
marco.lazzari@unibg.it

Abstract. This paper presents an open source podcast publishing application which has been implemented to create an educational podcasting service at the University of Bergamo (Italy) and has subsequently been adopted by several universities and other podcasters in Italy and abroad.

Keywords: educational podcasting, free software, open source, podcast publishing, distance education, distance learning, mobile learning.

1 Introduction

The use of podcasting is spreading throughout the education sector due to the increasing popularity of mobile media players. Podcasting is becoming an interesting and attractive way for distributing educational materials [1, 2], and several schools and universities have set up podcasting services [3, 4]. This paper presents an open source software, Podcast Generator (PG), which comprises a set of web based tools, that allow users to upload audio or video media files via a web form along with information (e.g. description, keywords) and create a podcast feed. PG was developed to implement Pluriversiradio, a podcasting service at the University of Bergamo.[1]

The first version of PG was designed in September 2005, when podcasting was still an unknown technology to the majority of the internet users. In the design process we considered to start improving some existing podcast-publishing applications. Our research did not produce successful results; besides a plug-in which needed a full installation of the Wordpress[2] blog software to work, we found two scripts which could be adopted to comply our aim The first one, PodAdmin,[3] consisted of a simple interface which allowed to upload mp3 files and created a basic XML feed, but lacked important functionalities such as file renaming on upload in case of duplicated files. The second one was a php script[4] which allowed to create a RSS feed reading a folder on a server where the user had previously uploaded mp3 files, but some major features such as password protection were not available. Moreover, we contacted Apple to receive more information about iTunes U, the educational podcasting platform adopted by some universities in the USA, but they replied that the service was not available at that time outside the USA and Canada.

---

[1] Web site: http://www.pluriversiradio.it - Feed: http://www.pluriversiradio.it/feed.xml
[2] http://wordpress.org/
[3] http://podadmin.sourceforge.net/
[4] http://www.ontology.com/canton/projects/podcasting-script.php

C. Baranauskas et al. (Eds.): INTERACT 2007, LNCS 4663, Part II, pp. 649–652, 2007.
© IFIP International Federation for Information Processing 2007

Therefore, we started designing our own application and released it under free GNU/GPL license in order to share our work with the open source community. Our main goal was creating an easy to use, yet powerful, web based software to allow any user, even without programming experience and knowledge, to create a podcasting service in a few steps and automatically generate a w3c-compliant XML feed. To achieve this goal the script had to feature an easy setup process and an interactive interface to let the user communicate with the server in a transparent way. The practical implementation of PG started on February 2006: the software was written in PHP and was officially released on Sourceforge.net, the world's largest open source software development web site, on April 2006. Pluriversiradio, which is based on PG, has been used during the second semester of the year 2005-2006 for courses on multimedia communication at the University of Bergamo; after those first experiments, other lecturers began recording podcasts for their students. Quantitative and qualitative analyses of exam results and satisfaction surveys highlight that involving students in producing podcasts had positive effects on learning [5].

2 Features

Podcast Generator features an automatic setup wizard which allows to install the script on an http server in a very short time and without any technical knowledge of PHP; after a guided setup the user is able to handle the administration (uploading, editing, deleting episodes) without further configuration. PG supports 21 media file types (mp3, ogg, m4v, mov, etc.) and web mp3 streaming, and generates XML feeds, meeting the w3c standards and supporting iTunes-specific tags; it provides a password protected administration interface to manage episodes and customize the script and builds dynamic 'All Podcasts' and 'Recent Podcasts' web pages.

PG is especially suitable for podcasters who do not have technical knowledge but wish to use podcasting in their classes. It is also suitable for experienced podcasters who want to save time and avoid the risk of syntax errors when dealing with the RSS feed. The setup wizard and the whole program interface are available in twelve languages[5] and several volunteers are working on other translations.

3 Architecture

The software architecture works on different key levels we assume as "modules". These modules operate on the server-side and are processed by the PHP engine which generates the web page for the client.

3.1 Module 1: Database

Podcast Generator and Pluriversiradio are based either on a flat CSV file and on a MySQL database to store episodes data and information. We oriented our choice to maintain the CSV feature in order to keep low server requirements to run the

---

[5] Catalan, Chinese, Danish, Dutch, English, French, German, Italian, Japanese, Portuguese, Romanian, Russian.

program: in order to install PG, just a server with PHP support is needed and no MySQL is required. On uploading or editing every episode, a description file containing data provided by the user (such as title, description, keywords, etc.) is generated and associated to the uploaded media file. On the other hand, Pluriversiradio features a MySQL database to store episodes data and operate complex search aimed at reducing the number of downloads and saving bandwidth.

3.2 Module 2: Web-Based Interface and User Interaction

The web based administration interface of Podcast Generator does not require the user to have any technical knowledge. It is based on HTML and Javascript, so that the browser can validate some input fields before they are sent to the server. The interface also features a colored output which displays in green every successful action and in red any possible errors, so that users are given an immediate visual message. In case of server-related problems, PG will output some server configuration parameters (e.g. 'max_upload_size') which can help to understand the problem.

The use of a combination of HTML and Javascript allows to simplify the interface and display just the essential dialog boxes, showing the optional fields on demand: the user is required to fill just two fields (title and short description) in the file upload form; anyway it is possible to check 'add extra information' and a set of new options will appear on the web page: a long description, an image, keywords and author's data can be provided. This implies a targeted user experience towards what really is needed, avoiding displaying several forms to be filled in order to upload a single episode. Fields in the administration interface offer hints to help users understand the function of every choice and show guidelines to the data required. The interaction is easy and users are given access to the PHP engine through a simple back-end layer.

3.3 Module 3: PHP Engine

Podcast Generator's PHP engine processes users' input and creates dynamic web pages showing the recent podcasts, an archive containing a list of all episodes and a detailed 'permalink' page for each audio or video file. It also generates the XML podcast feed and re-creates it automatically on new uploads or modifications through the administration interface. The PHP engine performs multiple internal controls that check input text and correct it automatically. For instance, if the user uploads files containing non-valid characters, they will not be rejected but automatically corrected (e.g. spaces are replaced by underscores).

3.4 Module 4: Security

The administration interface is secured by a password; the user and password feature is handled by sessions, a PHP native feature, that assigns a unique session ID to the user and allows to preserve certain data across subsequent accesses. This licenses the user to maintain the identity and avoids multiple password requests during the same session. The software also performs multiple controls on variables passed through the GET method in the pages URLs. Every variable is double-checked and in case of file inclusion into the web page, an effective existence control is performed in order to avoid cross site scripting attacks.

4 Current Results

Podcast Generator has been downloaded more than 14,000 times from Sourceforge servers in its first year and is currently used by at least 500 podcasting services, such as the Department of Neurological Sciences of the University of Bari (Italy), the universities of Aarhus (Denmark), Delaware (USA), Central Queensland (Australia) and Caen Basse-Normandie (France).[6]

The quick diffusion of PG is due to its efficiency, ease of use and installation: the open source nature of the program allowed the cooperation of a set of kind users, who translated the whole software. Moreover, the Dutch foundation Kennisnet Ict op School used PG for publishing a screencast series about podcasting with open source and promoted the use of our software in schools: for this purpose they have also developed a video podcast that shows the installation procedure of PG.[7]

References

1. Brittain, S., Glowacki, P., Van Ittersum, J., Johnson, L.: Podcasting Lectures. EDUCAUSE Quarterly 3, 24–31 (2006)
2. Cambell, G.: There's Something in the Air: Podcasting in Education. EDUCAUSE Review 40(6), 32–47 (2005)
3. Frydenberg, M.: Principles and Pedagogy: the Two P's of Podcasting in the Information Technology Classroom. In: Proc. of the 23rd Annual Conf. for Information Systems Educators ISECON 2006, Dallas, TX (2006)
4. Malan, D.: Podcasting Computer Science E-1. In: Proc. of the 38th ACM Technical Symp. on Computer Science Education SIGCSE '07, Covington, KY (2007)
5. Lazzari, M.: Podcasting in the Classroom: Involving Students in Creating Podcasted Lessons. In: Proc. of the Conf. HCI Educators HCIEd 2007, Aveiro, Portugal (2007)

---

[6] http://www.neuroscienze.uniba.it/; http://www.media.au.dk/podcast/;
http://admissions.udel.edu/uwired/; http://streaming.cqu.edu.au/podcast/;
http://www.ingenium.unicaen.fr/podcastgen/
[7] http://files.ictopschool.net/podos/mp4/09.mp4

A New Performance Measure Taking into Account the Mental Load in Mobile Text Entry Tasks

Franck Poirier and Hamed H. Sad

Université de Bretagne-Sud
VALORIA - Centre de recherche – 56000 Vannes-France
`franck.poirier, sad@univ-ubs.fr`

Abstract. Text entry research has received a lot of attention in recent years because of the need for more effective and usable entry methods on mobile devices. Technical limitations such as screen size have led to the design of entry interfaces that mentally load the user in order to obtain better performances. Current evaluation methodologies of these interfaces focus on text entry speed and error rate but don't pay enough attention to the mental load. In this paper, we concentrate on the evaluation of the load's effect on text entry process and we present a comparative evaluation of three mobile text entry methods with and without the application of a secondary task. We also define a performance measure that takes into account the mental load characteristic for a given text entry interface.

Keywords: Mobile text entry, mental load, evaluation, secondary task.

1 Introduction

Mobile text entry process can be viewed as the integration of two sub-processes. The first is the text creation in which an idea should be translated into words and sentences in a particular language. The second is the process of converting these words and sentences to an electronic form using a text entry technique with minimal resources (small screen, tiny soft keyboard...). In mobile context, these two sub-processes are always executed concurrently, which causes an increase in the mental load compared to the desktop interaction context. Moreover, in the mobile environment, the user may be on the move while executing the two processes, which also increases the load.

In the literature of human-computer interaction (HCI) many words and expressions have been used to describe "How busy is the operator?". In interface design, the term *"cognitive load"* is used. But, in this domain, this word is more general and indicates one or more of the following three components: perceptual load, central processing and motor load [3]. In this paper, we use the term *"mental load"* to indicate the amount of resources used for the perceptual and central processing activities, where memory operations and decision-making are involved.

2 Mental Load in Mobile Text Entry

A review of mobile text entry methods shows that, for their evaluation, the motor

C. Baranauskas et al. (Eds.): INTERACT 2007, LNCS 4663, Part II, pp. 653–656, 2007.
© IFIP International Federation for Information Processing 2007

activities required for the interaction have received the most attention [4], [6]. Most of the evaluations of text entry methods are based on the entry speed expressed in Words per Minute (WPM). The mental load corresponding to a particular entry technique affects the entry speed and also the error rate, but these quantities do not totally reflect this load.

Comparisons of different text entry methods based only on motor components of the user-interaction are not sufficient. The mental operations associated with different methods may be very dissimilar, so the evaluation should take into account the mental load. For example, using a menu augmented soft keyboard [2] for suggesting the next character after each keypress, increases the speed, but also the cognitive load while typing. This increase cannot be reflected by the theoretical input rate based on motor movement computing. The mental load can be measured by the application of a secondary task [1]. The degradation of performance after using the secondary task reflects the difficulty of operating the tested technique.

In this work, we chose as secondary task the digit monitoring task. While operating the entry technique, the user should monitor voiced digits regularly separated in time, but randomly in order. The time period between two numbers is the factor that controls the level of difficulty. The user should respond to the repetition of two identical consecutive digits. This task requires auditory perception, working memory, and decision making. This will constitute a simple central executive task.

We think that the digit monitoring task is clearly a secondary task in relation to the text entry operation. Humans are usually capable of interacting with a visual based task like an entry method while manipulating auditory secondary task.

3 Experimental Work

We compared three text entry methods. The first one was Phraze-It (www. prevalentdevices.com/) where a letter is entered by exactly two keystrokes (fig.1-a). The second method was 4-Key EdgeWrite (4KEW) [5] where the entry of a character is done by 2 to 7 keystrokes on four keys in a specific sequence (fig. 1-b). The third method, UniGlyph (fig. 1-c), developed in our lab, is based on a 3-key ambiguous keyboard where letter association with keys is based on graphic information.

We decided to apply the secondary task test for comparing these three methods. The subjects, 5 Master students, had already completed 5 sessions on the three methods. So, we assumed that the mental load caused by learning is lowered enough, and the application of the random digits monitoring secondary task gives us information about the mental load associated only with the method operation.

We carried out one new session for each participant, with the addition of the digit monitoring secondary task. We have presented the necessary instructions on the

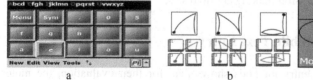
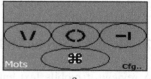

a   b   c

Fig. 1. The Phraze-it Keyboard (a), the 4KEW Keyboard (b) and the UniGlyph Keyboard (c)

secondary task to each user before she/he began. The time period between two consecutively voiced numbers was set to 1.75 second. This period allowed the user to interact with entry and in the same time to be able to monitor the secondary task.

Results

The result of secondary task application is shown in table 1 where the intersection of a participant and a text input method is the percentage secondary task missing rate. It is defined as the ratio of the number of detected repetitions to the total number of repetitions in percentage. A repetition is detected if the subject responded to it before the voicing of the following number. There is no significant difference between UniGlyph and 4KEW ("Average missing rate" row of table 1). There is more evident difference in performance degradation in WPM and accuracy. Phraze-It gives the lowest charge and the lowest percentage performance degradation.

Table 1. Secondary task missing rate percentage, WPM degradation and error rate increase. The error rate is the ratio of the correctly entered characters to the total number of characters.

Method / Participant	UniGlyph	Phraze_It	4 Key EdgeWrite
Participant 1	25	9,76	16
Participant 2	14,85	16,98	19,67
Participant 3	20	20	20
Participant 4	35	27	30
Participant 5	57	31	53
Average missing rate	30,75	20,94	27,73
Mean WPM degradation (%)	-41,84	-21,39	-24,8
Mean Error increase (%)	43,1	2,72	10,55

Analyses

First, it is clear that the application of the random number monitoring task leads to a remarkable performance degradation in the primary task. This indicates that the working memory subcomponent tapped by the secondary task is involved in the performance of the primary task and validates the applicability of our choice for the secondary task. The random number monitoring task seems to be suitable to discriminate between different methods based on the mental operating load.

We define a Performance Measure (PM) that takes into account the efficiency and the mental load characteristics for a given interface:

$$PM = (ES*EA)(1-MLWF*STMR*DIS*DIA)$$

where:

~ ES: Entry Speed expressed in words per minute (wpm),
~ EA: Entry Accuracy is (1- error rate), between 0 (error free) and 1

~ MLWF: Mental Load Weighting Factor determines the importance of mental load effect in the evaluation (>0),

~ STMR: Secondary Task Missing Rate between 0 (all repetitions were detected) to 1(all repetitions were missed),

~ DIS: Degradation In Entry Speed as a result of secondary task application.

~ DIA: Degradation In Accuracy as a result of secondary task application

The greater the performance measure is, the lower the user is cognitively loaded and more efficient is the text entry method.

The calculated values of PM for UniGlyph, Phrase-It, 4KEW are respectively 11.2, 9.0, 5.3, respectively, at MLWF=2 and 6.3, 8.8, 4.3 at MLWF=20. For small values of MLWF (MLWF =2), i.e. we are interested in the performance rather than the mental charge effect, it is found that UniGlyph is the best method. For greater values of MLWF (MLWF=20), i.e. the mental load effect is the more important, Phrase-It is the more suitable method. As all the variables change with practice, the performance measure should be determined at the same level of experience for all tested methods.

4 Conclusion

In this paper we argue the necessity of evaluating the operating mental load involved in mobile text entering by the secondary task technique. This approach allows a more complete evaluation and fair comparison of different entry methods. We propose to identify the mental load, at a certain amount of practice, by applying the digit monitoring secondary task. We defined a performance measure in order to rank mobile text entry methods according to the efficiency and the level of mental load.

References

1. Hegarty, M., Shah, P., Miyake, A.: Constraints on using the dual-task methodology to specify the degree of central executive involvement in cognitive tasks. Memory & Cognition 28(3), 376–385 (2000)
2. Isokoski, P.: Performance of menu-augmented soft keyboards. In: Proceedings of the SIGCHI conference on Human factors in computing systems (2004)
3. John, B.E., Kieras, D.E.: Using GOMS for user interface design and evaluation: which technique? ACM Trans. Comput.-Hum. Interaction 3(4), 287–319 (1996)
4. Soukoreff, R.W., MacKenzie, I.S.: Theoretical upper and lower bounds on typing speed using a stylus and soft keyboard. Behaviour & Information Technology 14 (1995)
5. Wobbrock, J., Myers, B., Rothrock, B.: Few-key text entry revisited: mnemonic gestures on four keys. In: Proceedings of the SIGCHI conference on Human Factors in computing systems (2006)
6. Zhai, S., Hunter, M., Smith, B.A.: The metropolis keyboard - an exploration of quantitative techniques for virtual keyboard design. In: Proceedings of the 13th annual ACM symposium on User interface software and technology (2000)

Collabohab: A Technology Probe into Peer Involvement in Cardiac Rehabilitation

Julie Maitland

University of Glasgow, 17 Lilybank Gardens, Glasgow G12 8QQ, UK
jules@dcs.gla.ac.uk

Abstract. Mobile and ubiquitous systems designed to promote an increase in physical activity by harnessing social influence have so far had variable success. Taking a cardiac rehabilitation program as a specific health domain, in which physical inactivity is one of several targeted behaviours, the research described in this paper aims to elicit understanding of peer-involvement in health-related behavioural change and explore the potential for effective technological support. This paper introduces the technology probe Collabohab and discusses the accompanying methodological approach being adopted to establish insight into the important but so far little understood phenomenon of social support within health-related behavioural change.

Keywords: health, cardiac rehabilitation, social support, technology probe.

1   Introduction

Physical inactivity is a widespread problem. The World Health Organisation estimates that 60% of the worldwide population does not achieve the minimum recommended level of activity [1]. Over recent years the problem of physical inactivity has received much interest from computer scientists in both the academic and commercial domain. The ever-increasing ability of pervasive technology to detect the nature of an individual's movements lends itself well to the established behavioural change technique (BCT) of self-monitoring [2], and has led to the development of many physical activity promoting applications [3-5]. The evolution of single-user activity promotion systems into multi-user equivalents seems to be a natural progression in this area of research, as the inclusion of social support promises to increase the likelihood of increased and prolonged physical activity. However, previous studies of multi-user activity promotion systems, including our own, have generated diverse and sometimes conflicting results [3-6]. In response to these findings we have decided to explore the potential of social support within activity promotion systems further. Unlike the previous work already mentioned, in which the systems were designed for and evaluated with relatively fit and healthy individuals, we focus on individuals who have a vested interest in increasing their daily activity levels: individuals enrolled on a cardiac rehabilitation program.

The planned study aims to investigate peer involvement in an existing cardiac rehabilitation program while exploring the potential for supportive technological

C. Baranauskas et al. (Eds.): INTERACT 2007, LNCS 4663, Part II, pp. 657–660, 2007.

interventions—systems that support *appropriate* peer-involvement in rehabilitation programs. By designing and deploying a technology probe into a rehabilitation program we aim to determine the information needs of rehabilitation participants and their peers, and to discover what level of involvement they feel is appropriate. By discovering how, when, why and with whom rehab participants wish to share information, steps can be taken towards developing technological means of supporting the different levels and dimensions of peer involvement and social support.

This paper will begin by providing a brief overview of the role of social support within health and behavioural change applications. We will then describe the methodological approach being taken in this work and introduce the technology probe, Collabohab, which has been designed for the purpose of the planned study.

2 Background

Social support is widely acknowledged as having a positive relationship with many health related outcomes [7-9], and within rehabilitation social support is considered a resource for behavioural change [2]. Despite such wide acknowledgement, understanding of the underlying mechanisms and dynamics of social support is lacking. Efforts being made in the fields of mobile and ubiquitous computing (Ubicomp) to effectively harness social influence within health-related behavioural change applications have so far had variable success.

In a short term trial of a system that shared daily step counts and goal progress between friends, Consolvo et al [3] found that the trial group who shared their data were significantly more successful at achieving their goals than the control group who did not share their data with anyone. In contrast, a similar system that shared physical activity and nutritional intake was found to be no more effective than the single-user equivalent [4]. A longer-term trial of a step count-based game also found that the group who shared data and played as a team were no more successful than those who played alone [5]. There are many differences between the systems (manner of data capture and presentation) and their respective trials (duration and conditions), but an important difference to highlight is that it was only during the trial of the first system, in which social networks were found to be significant, were the people who shared data aware of and familiar with each other before the trial. This seems to suggest that existing peer groups benefit most from the inclusion of social support in such activity promotion applications.

Through our pilot-study of Shakra, a mobile phone-based application that detects the amount of time a person spends walking and shares that information between friends, we found that participants responded positively to the application and enjoyed looking at each others' daily activity levels [6]. Different groups of friends used it in different ways: one group used it as a game; constantly competing to beat each other's accumulated activity totals. The second group displayed less competitive tendencies, instead setting each other's activity levels within the context of the person undertaking the activity. The younger member of the group viewed one of her friends as a positive role-model, and so would set her own daily goals in relation to the activity total of her role-model; she would not compete with her friend but aimed instead to remain within a set amount of her friend's total minutes. The final group was not particularly interested in how much activity each other had accumulated but enjoyed the sense of awareness that the tool provided of each other when they were apart. Our study highlights the diverse nature of peer groups, and along with the findings discussed earlier, emphasises the need for a greater understanding of how, when, why and with whom people would like to share health behaviour-related information about themselves.

3 Collabohab

The aim of this work is to explore, in depth, the issues and factors of social support that are important to the cardiac rehab participants and explore the potential for use of mobile and communications technology in this domain. The study will focus on patterns of interaction exist between rehab participants, their rehabilitation physiotherapists and nurses, and specific members of their friends and family. A technology probe, called Collabohab, will be deployed into the lives of such peer groups for the duration of the rehabilitation program. Unlike Hutchinson et al's [10] technology probes, the physicality of Collabohab is not particularly provocative. However, in the same way that Gaver et al [11] advocate the use of low-tech everyday media, it is suggested that presenting novel and exploratory uses of commodity technology will also serve as a catalyst for interesting and informative responses.

Collabohab is a mobile-phone based multimedia rehabilitation journal that allows participants to share their experiences with their peer group. The mobile phone will allow the rehabilitation participants to monitor their behavioural and physiological risk factors (as currently written on a record card). Using the same activity inference techniques as Shakra [6], the amount of time that the carrier spends walking is monitored by the phone. The remaining behavioural (smoking, diet and alcohol intake) and physiological data (cholesterol, blood pressure, pulse and weight) can be manually entered by the rehab participant or nurse using the phone or a web-interface. Photographic, audio and video 'memoirs' can be captured and uploaded from the phone to the journal. A basic temporal representation of the participants' data will be accessible on the phone, and a web page will provide full visualisation of their journal entries and allow them to annotate their data. Only rehab participants will be given a phone. Using a web browser, rehab professionals and peers will be able to view the journal of the participant they know, for whom they can also leave messages. Rehabilitation participants will also be able to view and contribute to each other's journals.

Analysis of Collabohab's logs will help reconstruct patterns of use and interaction over the 10 week rehabilitation period. This quantitative data will be augmented with information gathered during in-depth interviews with all of the study participants performed at the beginning, mid-point and on completion of the rehabilitation program. Having been asked to capture 'things' relating to their rehab experience (e.g. people, places, events, etc); the multimedia memoirs will serve as a resource for discussion during the interviews. It is hoped that by taking this mixed quantative/qualitative approach we will learn not only about what interactions occurred through and around the probe, but about why those interactions happened. Is sharing data in this manner just another case of 'Big Brother' for the rehab participant or is it a valuable source of one dimension of social support: feeling cared for? The study will also generate important feedback on the usability and suitability of Collabohab as a supportive technology. Learning about Collabohab's failures and successes will guide the design of the next generation of supportive collaborative rehabilitation technology.

4   Contribution to HCI

Two goals drive this research: we want to (1) generate insight into the social dynamics that surround behavioural change within a rehabilitation program and (2) investigate ways in which technology can be used to support and exploit these dynamics. While Shakra [6] marks preliminary and exploratory steps in this area, the study described in this paper aims to satisfy the first goal while continuing advances towards the second.

As interest in the HCI community surrounding the application of technology to health-related behavioural change increases, the need to ground such applications with knowledge of their intended domain grows. This work will contribute to the body of knowledge surrounding social influence within behavioural change applications and provide guidelines for the development of such systems within cardiac rehabilitation programs.

References

1. WHO, World Health Organisation (2006), http://www.who.org
2. McLean, N., et al.: Family involvement in weight control, weight maintenance and weight-loss interventions: a systematic review of randomized control trials. International Journal of Obesity 27, 987–1005 (2003)
3. Consolvo, S., et al.: Design Requirements for Technologies that Encourage Physical Activity. In: CHI. 2006, Montreal
4. Gasser, R., et al.: Persuasiveness of a Mobile Lifestyle Coaching Application using Social Facilitation. In: IJsselsteijn, W., de Kort, Y., Midden, C., Eggen, B., van den Hoven, E. (eds.) PERSUASIVE 2006. LNCS, vol. 3962, Springer, Heidelberg (2006)
5. Lin, J.J., et al.: Fish'n'Steps: Encouraging Physical Activity with an Interactive Computer Game. In: Dourish, P., Friday, A. (eds.) UbiComp 2006. LNCS, vol. 4206, Springer, Heidelberg (2006)
6. Maitland, J., et al.: Increasing the Awareness of Daily Activity Levels with Pervasive Computing. In: Pervasive Computing Technologies for Healthcare, IEEE, Austria (2006)
7. Haughton McNeill, L., Kreuter, M., W., Subramanian, S., V.: Social Environment and Physical activity: A review of concepts and evidence. Social Science & Medicine 63(4), 1011–1022 (2006)
8. Arthur, H.M.: Depression, isolation, social support, and cardiovascular disease in older adults. Journal of Cardiovascular Nursing 21(55), 52–57 (2006)
9. Berkman, L., Glass, T.: Social integration, social support, and health. In: Berkman, L., Kawachi, I. (eds.) Social Epidemiology, Oxford University Press, New York (2000)
10. Hutchinson, H., et al.: Technology Probes: Inspiring Design for and with Families. In: CHI. 2003 (2003)
11. Gaver, B., Dunne, T., Pacenti, E.: Design: Cultural probes. interactions 6(1), 21–29 (1999)

Envisioning Probe Kit: Creativity and Storytelling to Capture the Inner Thoughts of People

Patrizia Andronico[1], Patrizia Marti[2], and Maurizio Martinelli[1]

[1] Istituto di Informatica e Telematica del CNR
Via G. Moruzzi, 1, Pisa, Italy
{patrizia.andronico, maurizio.martinelli}@iit.cnr.it
[2] Dipartimento di Science della Comunicazione, Università di Siena
Via Roma 56, 53100 Siena, Italy
marti@unisi.it

Abstract. During the last few years the interest in Information and Communications Technologies (ICT) fields has spread towards wireless and mobile devices which can support activities in everyday life. Designing for play, learning and awareness is becoming more and more a factual aspects of research willing to meet users' needs. In such a broaden range of possible applications for the new ubiquitous and pervasive technologies, classical HCI methods for revealing efficiency and effectiveness of an innovative product are no more adequate. Taking into consideration human experience during the interaction with ICT devices needs a more creative and multidisciplinary design approach. This work was developed within a European project called MobileMAN[1] whose aim was to develop a self-organizing and infrastructure-less network with the potentiality of the well-known MANET (Mobile Ad hoc NETwork) paradigm. Our goal in the MobileMAN project was to investigate with potential end users, the possible applications useful for everyday activities that could work with this emerging technology. We then tried to adopt a more creative and multidisciplinary approach, inspired by the "Probe Kit" developed at the Royal College of London.

Keywords: ubiquitous computing, probe kit, creativity, storytelling, UCD, Cultural Psychology.

1 Mobile Ad Hoc NETworks

A MANET is a wireless network without any type of infrastructure, autonomous and suitable enough for creating a communication link between people who are sharing an activity or are meeting up casually. This kind of network is rather spontaneous and generally temporary in time. Users can collaborate each others until they stay in the same place where the network is been formed; when they go away from this point, in

---

[1] MobileMAN (http://cnd.iit.cnr.it/mobileMAN), has been studied and developed within a European research activity funded by the European Community in the "Information Society Technologies (IST)" program as a *Future Emerging Technology* project. The project started in October 2002 and terminated in December 2005.

C. Baranauskas et al. (Eds.): INTERACT 2007, LNCS 4663, Part II, pp. 661–664, 2007.
© Springer-Verlag Berlin Heidelberg 2007

fact, connections are not still available and people will no longer communicate. A MANET is quite useful in a citizen network environment, just because any single node can act as router switch, bridge or server, being free of infrastructure constraints. Such a characteristic should decrease communication expenses while increasing societal communication abilities. Concepts like mobility and ubiquitous computing are becoming essential in the new nomadic societies: information and services need to be accessible from anywhere and in anytime.

Disaster recovery or military situations are the most common applications developed through mobile wireless ad hoc networks. Only recently the interest is moving towards civilian applications, such as data sharing during a meeting, on-the-road safety, aged assistance, and even monitoring of savage animals to study habits and movements [1]. MobileMAN project has reserved a special attention on the implication of ICT to improve the quality of life and social cohesion, as envisioned in [2].

2 Theoretical Framework and Experimental Set Up

For the definition of the experimental phase, we took into consideration the theoretical framework known as Cultural Psychology, considering two of the most important contributors of the discipline: Lev Vygotsky and Jerome Bruner. While the Vygotsky's work is mainly concentrated on the creativity activities inside any person, Bruner has concentrated his studies on the importance of storytelling in the creation of the self. Creativity for Vygotsky is in the society itself: each person learns anything and internalizes it from the social context, from which they can then produce some new creative idea [3]. Story creation (fictional stories) and storytelling in general, seem to help children in building around their own personal vision of the world [4].

Usually considered in pedagogical and educational areas, recently several researchers recovered and recognized Vygotsky and Bruner studies as important resources for the design of new methodological approach in the modern Information and Communication Society. As pointed out in [5], "Social, historical and cultural dimensions of cognition are receiving increasing attention, and their relevance in developing collaboration technologies is widely recognized".

For the experiment we designed and set up the "Envisioning Probe Kit". We propose the kit as a set of activities to be carried out by a group of 18 persons, constituted by student of the Engineering Faculty of the University of Pisa. We chose this particular group of student because they have already participated to other more technical experiment in the MobileMAN project and for this reason they had a strong expertise in Ad hoc Networks issues. This common ground could be useful for a better comprehension of the purpose of the experiment, but not at all necessary to deal with the Probe kit.

The aim of the probe kit was to involve users in the design process from the beginning, collecting information about their private life and providing designers with a deeper knowledge of people daily habits and activities. Gathering data from people in such a way it is quite difficult to be analyzed due to the ambiguity they took in that reflect ambiguities in real life, in speech, in images, and in most of our activities. In the context of data collected with the probe kit, ambiguity is seen as an opportunity for designers to be inspired mainly for technological applications not related to work context. In our time most of the new technologies affect everyday lives in situation like play, learning or awareness, and people more and more are asking for applications for fun or their spare times.

3 The Envisioning Probe Kit Activities

The Envisioning Probe was formed by activities from the original probe (such as taking picture, making a collage, commenting pre-stamped postcards), and activities we add on purpose for this particular occasion. Specifically we create a group blog where any participant could write personal stories, or inventing some, or only commenting stories written by the others. We opted for a blog because in the recent years is becoming a very important tool, not only as a personal diary, as it was in the original intention, but also as collaborative web pages, so easy to update. In this way we wanted to explore the collaboration between the single participants of the experiment as well as trying to capture the inner thought of each ones, who could be free to write whatever they wanted without being recognized because of a nickname chose in advance. We add also an activity, called "e-card", in which participants should comment and forward to others cards we previously sent them by email. With the e-cards we wanted to compare the use of electronic mail for sending card in relation with the traditional postcard.

At the first meeting with the group, we illustrated the activities of the kit and gave them the folder with all the tools they needed for the experiment, as shown in table 1.

Table 1. Activities of the Envisioning Probe Kit

Activities	Action to be performed	Aim	Results
Traditional postcard	Each kit had a set of 5 postcards pre-stamped and with a fixed address, prepared with a photo and a comment. The participants had to comment the postcard, if they wanted to, and pass to another person that should do the same. The last person had to post the postcard by a fixed date.	Investigate the collaboration between people as well as the multi-hop of the passing postcards. Explore the comment participants left on the card.	48% of the postcards returned to us with some comments. 47% of the comments were made by a single person, while 53% were the multi-hop activity with more than one comment.
Photos	Each kit had a list of 20 items participants should explore by taking a picture and sending to us by email.	Personal reflection on everyday topics explored with a visual mode of communication.	13 persons out of 18 sent us the photos required, often not completing the entire set.
Collage	Each kit had just a theme that any participant could explore with any possible technique used in a collage.	Personal reflection on the theme proposed and research of the images, text, and whatever they needed to complete the task.	Only 4 person out of 18 complete the collage.
Blog	Personal and collaborative blog lasted for two weeks.	Personal reflection. Investigate on the ability of inventing stories, or interacting with the other posts, using one of the most innovative tools for communicating online.	13 person out of 18 write on the blog.
e-cards	5 e-cards were sent to each participant that should comment and send to other, similar to the activity with the traditional postcard.	Compare this activity with the email, with the traditional sending of postcards.	None of the e-cards were returned.

Each activity had a different time to be performed, and the entire experiment lasted for about two months. All the participants had a different implication in each activity, maybe due to their personal ability in completing the tasks. In any case during the experiment the atmosphere within the group was quite enthusiastic and collaborative.

4 Conclusion and Future Works

The amount of data we collected in such a way took with them a lot of ambiguity related to the personal and inner thoughts of the participants. Ambiguity arises from Conceptual Art movement of the 60s where the attention was mainly on ideas rather than on form. While technologies are increasingly adopted outside the work place, ambiguity seems to reach a great interest for design in HCI fields.

Analyzing such a set of data, and particularly, crossing the possible interpretations, it was a big work for designers, not yet completed. Firstly we started redistributing some of the data returned from the entire kit according to four maps related to: public and private spaces, activities in everyday lives, relationships, technological and not technological tools. The maps helped us in reflecting better on the possible scenario that could match the desiderata we found in the responses of the experiment, and the requirements of the MobileMAN technology.

For the future we would like to create some mock-up from the scenarios and test them again with potential end users.

References

1. Pelusi, L., Passarella, A., Conti, M.: Beyond MANETs: dissertation on Opportunistic Networking, Tech. Report 2006/01, Computer Networks Department, IIT – CNR, Maggio (2006), http://bruno1.iit.cnr.it/ bruno/techreport.html
2. Ducatel, K., Bogdanowicz, M., Scapolo, F., Leijten, J., Burgelman, J.-C.: Scenario for Ambient Intelligence in 2010. European Commission Community Research Finall Report, Seville, (2001), http://www.cordis.lu/ist/istag.htm
3. Vygotsky, L.S.: Mind in society: The development of higher psychological processes. In: Cole, M., John-Steiner, V., Scribner, S., Souberman, E. (eds.) Harvard University Press, Cambridge (1978)
4. Bruner, J.S.: The culture of education. Harvard University Press, Cambridge (1996)
5. Tuomi, I.: Vygotsky in a TeamRoom: an exploratory study on collective conceptformation in electronic environments, System Sciences (1998)

Initial Development of a PDA Mobility Aid for Visually Impaired People

David McGookin[1], Maya Gibbs[1], Annu-Maaria Nivala[2], and Stephen Brewster[1]

[1] Department of Computing Science, University of Glasgow, Glasgow G12 8QQ, UK
{mcgookdk,stephen}@dcs.gla.ac.uk
[2] Finnish Geodetic Institute, Geodeetinrinne 2, P.O. Box 15, Finland
annu-maaria.nivala@fgi.fi

Abstract. We discuss requirements surrounding a mobile navigation system for visually impaired people. We describe an initial prototype based on a PDA using GPS location tracking. This prototype has so far failed to provide reliable location detection, due to the use of GPS in built up environments. We discuss how our system may improve detection by switching between a range of different location tracking technologies. However, we conclude that there may still be times when these technologies fail, and more work is needed on how to support the user in such circumstances.

1 Introduction

When navigating an environment, visually impaired people are presented with a number of problems. Hazard avoidance such as street furniture and uneven surfaces can be overcome with the use of a white cane or guide dog. However "macro-navigation", finding directions from A to B [1], presents more problems. Many local government organisations provide mobility officers who can help a visually impaired person navigate the environment, and help with learning (or re-learning) locations. However, such services are limited, and not of use for people visiting other towns or places when on business or holidays. A way to overcome these problems would be the use of a mobile navigation device, which would help to guide a visually impaired person around an environment. Several such systems have been proposed, but few evaluated. The most notable was MoBIC developed by Petrie *et al.* [1]. Further research has been carried out since then, but mostly on different tracking systems and alternate interfaces to display information to the user [2]. Whilst these are important, in the last few years the growth in availability and power of mobile devices, as well as increasing mobile availability of the internet, has increased the potential functionality of mobile navigation systems for the visually impaired. We believe it is therefore appropriate to investigate mobile navigation systems on low cost mobile devices. In this paper we present our initial requirements capture and prototype system, as well as issues for future design decisions.

C. Baranauskas et al. (Eds.): INTERACT 2007, LNCS 4663, Part II, pp. 665–668, 2007.

2   Issues Surrounding Navigation

To further understand the problems of navigation for visually impaired people, and determine requirements for our system, we carried out a semi-structured interview with a middle aged, blind individual who worked as a transcription officer for the Royal National Institute of the Blind (RNIB) in the UK. The interview covered navigation in the world and how this was accomplished.

An emphasis on macro rather than micro navigation was emphasised. The use of a white cane to detect immediate obstacles was successful, but the ability to navigate to and from unfamiliar locations was more difficult. As the participant noted, *"I certainly wouldn't turn up at, say, Aberdeen* (**railway**) *station and expect to navigate my way somewhere. Even if it is only within 200 yards."*. The participant also noted than in addition to just directions from A to B, information about temporary impediments to navigation would be useful. These seem to fall somewhat between micro and macro navigation, being things which would be detectable with a white cane aid, but would be beneficial to avoid all together. For example, when a pavement (sidewalk) is being resurfaced and pedestrians are diverted through a sectioned off area of the road. Additionally, he noted that it would be useful to select routes on more that simply shortest distance, with other factors such as avoiding traffic or steep inclines being preferred. The participant felt that people *"don't generally like looking out of place, or sounding out of place"*, so the system should not draw attention to the user. Therefore speech input was felt to be inappropriate, but speech output was preferred as walking using headphones *"doesn't look too out of place these days"*.

The requirements identified here are broadly in line with those identified by Strothotte *et al.* [3] as part of to MoBIC project, highlighting that users still have the same basic needs although technology has moved on in the last decade.

3   Prototype Overview

Based on the requirements identified, we designed and implemented an initial prototype to provide route navigation abilities. Once the initial capabilities have been implemented and evaluated, we will be able to implement more of the features identified during our requirements capture.

Our initial system runs as an application on a Dell Axim Pocket PC, and retrieves location information using the global positioning system (GPS) via a TomTom Bluetooth GPS receiver. At the moment the application automatically detects the user's location and then calculates a route to a destination based on selection from a list. We store data in files formatted in Geographic Mark-up Language which is a standard XML compliant format developed for cartographic information. Once loaded into our system the map is held as a weighted graph (each road segment is assigned a "weight" dependent on its length), and the route to the user's destination is calculated using a shortest path algorithm. That is to say that the application calculates the route with the lowest sum total of weights. Whilst in our initial system weightings are strictly geographic distances, we can easily change the weightings to reflect different navigation priorities, such as avoiding particularly steep or busy roads. In the future we may be able to interface the system, through wireless networks, to local council works notifications to bias against areas where road works or other construction is occurring, thereby addressing some of the issues identified in our interview.

As was requested in the requirements phase, synthetic speech was used to provide all feedback from the system. Once the user has selected a destination, the system informs what direction to walk in, and then when to turn left or right at appropriate intersections. The user can also request the system provides the current location. Output is played through a single ear piece or, if the user prefers, the PDA's in-built speaker.

To simplify user input we have applied a simple menu based interface. A back, forward and select button are presented on the PDA screen and can be felt by the user via a raised paper control panel overlaying the touch screen. This allows controls to be shaped differently and therefore be easier to identify than using the inbuilt buttons on the PDA, or using the keypad of a smart phone device. However we must still identify how well this interface will scale when more functions are added.

4   Initial Evaluations

So far we have not carried out any field trials of our system using visually impaired people. We have however carried out technical evaluations to establish the quality of information available from our system, and a short user evaluation of the interface. Whilst users found the interface straightforward to navigate, the location detection of our system has been less successful. Our system, in a desire to use "off the shelf" location tracking, uses standard GPS. In our tests this has proven to be an inadequate technology to support the navigation tasks, with many occasions where the system failed to correctly detect its position and inform the user when to change direction. That GPS is poor in built up environments is a known problem (our test area was on a hill surrounded by tall buildings), and many others have proposed using differential GPS [2] which uses an additional ground transmitter to improve location. However these systems still require line of sight with GPS satellites, otherwise incorrect locations will be determined. For example, the MoBIC system was evaluated in an area with open spaces [1]. However many towns and cities do not always afford such open space. Other systems propose that the environment be augmented with radio frequency identification (RFID) tags to more easily detect location [4], but these must be available across the whole area to be useful. Another technology, not yet applied to visually impaired navigation, is Skyhook Technology's Loki system (www.skyhookwireless.com). This uses an updated map of available Wi-Fi access points to determine the location of the user. However accurate location detection is currently only available in a limited number of locations. There is not currently a single technology that can always be relied upon to deliver accurate positioning.

5 Future Work

Whilst it may be possible to use different technology to determine the user's location, these different technologies produce that information with differing degrees of fidelity. When comparing the position of multiple technologies there may be conflicts between their reported positions, or in some cases, no position at all. Whilst we will seek to improve the accuracy of detecting the user's location by using different, and perhaps multiple technologies, we also need to determine what should happen when an accurate position cannot be determined. The variable coverage of location based technologies is currently being studied in visual scenarios as seamful design [5]. Here the breaks in technologies, the seams, rather than being hidden from the user, are made more obvious, allowing awareness of problems before they occur. For example, our navigation system may monitor areas of poor signal strength and notify the user when it detects that it is at the boundary of that area. Further investigation into the exposition of seams in such non-visual applications may help to overcome many of the problems of currently tracking the position of the user.

6 Conclusions

Mobile navigation presents a significant problem for visually impaired people. From our requirements capture we can identify several issues that could be overcome with the constructive use of technology. However, from our initial prototype system, there are several problems in the use of tracking technology that can easily cause the user's location to be mistakenly detected. Whilst we believe that the position tracking of our system can be improved, there remains no one technique that can guarantee correct location, and any system will, at times, lose the position of the user. We propose that further research, on how best to make the user aware of failings in tracking technology in non-visual scenarios would significantly improve the quality of mobile navigation solutions.

References

1. Petrie, H., Johnson, V., Furner, S., Strothotte, T.: Design lifecycles and wearable computers for users with disabilities. In: Proceedings of the first international workshop of Human Computer Interaction with mobile devices, Glasgow, UK, GIST, vol. 1 (1998)
2. Loomis, J.M., Klatzky, R.L., Colledge, R.G.: Navigating without vision: Basic and applied research. Optometry & Vision Science 78(5), 282–289 (2001)
3. Strothotte, T., Petrie, H., Johnson, V., Reichert, L.: Mobic: User needs and preliminary design for mobility aid for blind and elderly travellers. In: Placencia Porrero, I., Puig de la Bellacasa, R. (eds.) The European Context for Assistive Technology, pp. 384–352. IOS Press, Amsterdam (1995)
4. Coroama, V.: Experiences from the design of a ubiquitous computing system for the blind. In: CHI 2006, Montreal, Canada, vol. 2, pp. 664–669. ACM Press, New York (2006)
5. Chalmers, M., Dieberger, A., Höök, K., Rudström, À.: Social navigation and seamful design. Cognitive Studies 11(3), 1–11 (2004)

Voice Interfaces in Art – An Experimentation with Web Open Standards as a Model to Increase Web Accessibility and Digital Inclusion

Martha Carrer Cruz Gabriel

University of Sao Paulo, University Anhembi Morumbi, R. Ibaragui Nissui 115 #1204,
04116-200 São Paulo, SP, Brazil
martha@martha.com.br

Abstract. The web has been largely mute and deaf but since the beginning of the 21st century this scenario is changing with the possibility of using intelligent voice interfaces on web systems. In this paper we present the *Voice Mosaic* – a system that allows voice interactions on the web through the telephone. Its voice interface uses speech recognition and synthesis solutions developed with VoiceXML, an open-standard in voice technologies adopted by the W3C. *Voice Mosaic* is an artwork that allows people to get in touch with the possibility of talking to the web, intending to cause awareness about it. Since the technology used in *Voice Mosaic* can be used to improve accessibility (for visual impaired people) and digital inclusion (since the telephone is one of the cheapest devices in the world), dissolving borders and amplifying the pervasiveness, we believe that the concepts presented here can be useful to other developers.

Keywords: voice, web, interface, hybridization, telephone, accessibility, digital inclusion.

1 Introduction

Voice interfaces are a fascinating subject. The human dream of talking to computers in a natural way is not new. Science fiction books and movies that live in our imagination present several examples of this aspiration, as old television and movie series like "Star Trek," where the Enterprise's staff talk to the ship systems and androids like commander DATA; "Lost in Space," where Will Robinson had in his robot a very loyal and confident friend; the conversations and human interactions with the robots C3PO and R2-D2 in "Star Wars"; "Blade Runner" and its androids and voice driven interfaces; among others [3].

Until recently, talking to computers was in the realm of fiction – the web has been largely mute and deaf. However in the beginning of the 21st century talking to computers has become possible and easy due the enormous advances in speech synthesis and voice recognition technologies as well as the open standards adopted by the W3C (such as VoiceXML). The accuracy level reached by voice technologies now has allowed us to use them widely on the web.

C. Baranauskas et al. (Eds.): INTERACT 2007, LNCS 4663, Part II, pp. 669–672, 2007.
© IFIP International Federation for Information Processing 2007

The potential of using voice interfaces is explosive. From speech-only applications integrated to the whole web, to multi-modal applications combining aural and visual abilities into web browsers, voice interfaces add to the flavor of the web a fundamental spice, which is surely going to impact it.

Tim Berners-Lee said at SpeechTEK 2004, NY- "Speech technology is an important ingredient for the Web to realize its full potential." In fact, voice interfaces on the web bring undeniable resources for several areas, as convenience for mobile users, v-commerce, natural interactions, and usability. Beyond the more obvious utilizations for voice interfaces, the ability to talk to the web also provides an important way to improve web-accessibility – not only by multi-modal applications, but also through speech-only ones. Besides that, speech-only applications liberate users from any client computer device to access the internet – in this case, all they need is any telephone in any place in the world. In this sense, since the telephone is one of the cheapest devices in the world, voice interfaces can help improving digital inclusion. This is the alliance of the widest computing network with the most pervasive communication device on Earth – internet & telephone.

However, talking to computers adds "ears" and "mouths" to the Internet organism, changing the way we interact with it, bringing new possibilities and new challenges as well. We must face the increasing complexity that voice interfaces bring to the web while we also open new channels for digital inclusion, provide more accessibility and increase mobility through voice. All these things affect the human role inside the high-tech social structure we live in, at once causing excitement and fear.

In this context, in 2004, it was created the *Voice Mosaic* – a web-art work that allows voice interactions on the web through the telephone, causing border dissolution between Internet and telephone. As said once by Hendrik Willem Van Loon [1], "*The arts are an even better barometer of what is happening in our world than the stock market or the debates in congress.*" and we believe that artworks help people to understand and experience the new emergent techno-social world that surround us, where convergence and hybridization have become ubiquitous and easy, and "to talk to computers or the web" is going to become common.

Since the technologies used in *Voice Mosaic* can be used in other kinds of voice applications on the web, improving accessibility and digital inclusion, we will present next the work and its main aspects, regarding either the art concept or the technological implications. This artwork received several awards and was also presented at SIGGRAPH Art Gallery 2006, in Boston, MA (USA).

2 Voice Mosaic

The *Voice Mosaic* is a web-art application that combines speech and image, building a visual mosaic on the web with the chosen colors and recorded voices of people who interact with it from any place in the globe. The voice interface, developed with open-standards in speech synthesis and voice recognition technologies (VoiceXML), works through phone calls from any telephone – mobile or not. To participate in English, call in US: (800) 289-5570 or (407) 386-2174 / PIN number: 9991421055 (to participate in Portuguese, call in Brazil: (11) 2122-0203 / application code: 1155723602). The mosaic is accessed on the web at www.voicemosaic.com.br.

The application was developed in 2004, in three languages – Portuguese, English and Spanish - in order to encourage global participation. The phone calls form the mosaic on the web, and it happens spontaneously, therefore the mosaic changes as time goes on and its ongoing aesthetics and final result are unpredictable.

In this context, the work causes time-space collapse, and maps in one screen the participations that comes from several different geographical places, in different languages, and different times. Furthermore, using the search field, one can easily locate his/her participation by searching his/her own phone number. Also, one can locate all tiles in the mosaic within the same telephone area, which means to map geographical participations in the visual work.

The work puts together several dualities that do not oppose each other, but complete each other: speech / image, simple / complex, old / new, low-tech / high-tech, time / space, individual / community, passive / active, expected / uncertain, among others, in order to cause reflection and awareness about talking to the web, media convergence and hybridization between the telephone and the web.

2.1 Interfaces and Technology

The work has two interfaces – the voice interface accessed by phone and the web interface. As the web interface uses common and well known technologies – html, data base and Flash --, we will focus here on the voice interface, which is the core of the system.

The voice interface works via phone (mobile or not) interacting with the web. It is developed with VoiceXML, a structured language that offers support to build dialogs. When accessed by phone, the interface uses a Voice Gateway which allows voice recognition and speech synthesis during the conversation.

During the interaction by phone the person talks to the interface, choosing a color and recording a free speech message.

There are seven options available for choosing the color. This number, seven, is due the limit of information that a person can hold in the short-term memory. According to Miller [2] and explained in Zakia [4], "There is a limit to the amount of unrelated information a person can hold in short-term memory (STM), from five to nine items, averaging seven. (...) Since we are limited in the amount of information we can retain correctly in STM, one should be cautious with the amount of information included in a multimedia program if it is going to have some memorable impact".

The free speech message is limited to 15 seconds because of the web interface where it will be listened – recorded files longer than 15 sec. would generate WAV files larger than 100kb, which is the maximum file size to allow a comfortable user experience while clicking and listening to the mosaic tiles without waiting too long to start playing.

The voice interface was designed using both pre-recorded human voice (in the welcome message) and synthesized text-to-speech voices to instruct the user, in order to cause the experimentation of the differences and similarities between them. Also, it is used touch tone and speech tone interactions in order to put side by side voice recognition (human-like feature) and touch recognition (machine-like feature) intending to cause reflection about the two ways of interacting by phone – talking and dialing.

In order to allow data visualization either by tracking or by locating the interactions in the visual mosaic, the voice interface records the Caller ID phone number. Due that we can know where the interactions come from in the globe and also locate all the interactions from within a specific area code. This reveals the space collapse in the mosaic on the web.

The phone calls, through the voice interface, are the way the data (and people) enter the *Voice Mosaic* on the web. No data enters the work via its web interface, which is used only for purposes of data visualization, interpretation and reflection.

3 Conclusion

The web and telephone have been the realm for the state of the art in voice technologies.

Voice Mosaic is on the web, and it has received voice participation for more than two years now, summing up about 800 tiles. Although we could realize that people do not know much about the technology they are experiencing in the work, they use it easily and get excited about "talking to the web" and becoming immediately a permanent tile there. We also realized that technical people (IT, engineers, etc.) were more resistant to first experiment with the work than lay people. The kind of messages people create is also interesting – they range from recorded music and people singing to love declarations and creative use of the voice.

From now on we think that it will be possible to provide wider and deeper experimentation with voice interfaces due to the available technologies integrating the web and telephone. We expect it will probably allow us all to break frontiers and go further in human accessibility and digital inclusion developments.

An interactive poster was created based on this paper intending to show the concepts involved in *Voice Mosaic's* development and also to present the conclusion of this work, encouraging the audience to experiment the voice interface via phone and the web interface in order to check the results.

References

1. Loon, H.W.V.: The Arts (1937)
2. Miller, G.: The Magical Number Seven, Plus or Minus Two: Some Limits on our Capacity for Processing Information. Psychological Review 63, 81–97 (1956)
3. Perkowitz, S.: Digital People: From Bionic Humans to Androids. Joseph Henry Press, Washington (2004)
4. Zakia, R.: Perception and Imaging. Focal Press (1997)

Evangelizing Usability to 700 People: Strategies for Building a User-Centered Organizational Culture

Filipe Levi, Paulo Melo, Ubirajara de Lucena,
Cynthia Belleza, and José Arcoverde

CESAR – Recife Center for Advanced Studies and Systems
Rua Bione 220, Bairro do Recife, Recife, Brazil
{filipe.levi, paulo.melo, ubirajara.junior, cynthia.belleza,
mabuse}@cesar.org.br

Abstract. For the last three years, CESAR's user experience team has endeavored to build a user-centered organizational culture. In this report, we present some succeeding empirical strategies for evangelizing usability, in the hope that professionals in similar contexts might benefit from them.

Keywords: Usability evangelism, user-centered culture, ICT organizations.

1 Introduction

CESAR is a world-class private R&D institution that creates innovative products, processes and services using information and communication technologies.[1] Although recently awarded as the most innovative Brazilian research institute[2] and the best software services company in Brazil,[3] CESAR grew out of a traditional faculty of Informatics and kept a strict technology-centered mind for a long time.

For the last three years, the company has maintained a user experience team assembling professionals from Design, Cognitive Psychology, and Computer Science. Our first job was to design the concept of and execute a *usability factory* [1] for the Central Bank of Brazil, promoting the social inclusion of young disadvantaged adults in the technology industry. Since then, we have been working in a wide range of domains, from web and desktop systems to mobile games, interactive TV, transportation and kiosks. Some of our clients include Samsung, Siemens, and Dell.

2 Some Strategies

Changing an organizational culture is neither simple nor rapid, and usability practitioners must exercise perseverance in an everyday effort. From our own experience, the following strategies have proven successful:

---

[1] More about CESAR at http://www.cesar.org.br
[2] The 2004 FINEP award for *Most Innovative Research Institute in Brazil.*
[3] The 2005 Info200 magazine award for *Best Software Services Company.*

C. Baranauskas et al. (Eds.): INTERACT 2007, LNCS 4663, Part II, pp. 673–674, 2007.
© IFIP International Federation for Information Processing 2007

- Combine bottom-up and top-down evangelism. Make partners among colleagues and managers as well. Demonstrate the value of usability to the entire company.
- Talk to people about usability using their business or technical language. For instance, project managers might be interested in time and budget to perform usability techniques, while marketers might want to know about the benefits of a usable product to potential customers.
- Do not try to replace well-established things – such as processes, activities and roles. Instead, start by integrating new ones and demonstrating their value. More profitable practices will naturally replace old ones.
- Plan your steps and be patient. Consistent changes often happen gradually, not at once. Every little achievement has the potential to open bigger opportunities for you to do a better job.
- Collect metrics of your work continually. It helps a lot when you are given a chance to demonstrate the return of investment in usability or to estimate resources for user-centered activities within a project.
- If possible, work in teams or talk to other usability practitioners at your company. Discussions enrich your opinions and improve your decision-making skills.
- Work close to the engineering people, not apart from them. Be careful not to give the impression of being an isolated group of inaccessible specialists.
- Extend your professional network. Establish partnership with other companies and share experiences with usability professionals from your ecosystem.

3 Main Achievements and New Challenges

CESAR is now completing the full integration of usability with its institutional software development process, what specialists argue to be the goal of late-stage evangelism efforts in a company [2]. The process – which adopts an iterative and incremental development approach – has just included some user-centered methods: *user research*, *rapid prototyping*, *usability consultancy*, and *user testing*, during the phases of, respectively, requirements, analysis & design, coding and testing.

Our next goal is to include field studies with users starting at the pre-sale phase of our software development process. We have noticed that most of our clients do not know enough about the real problems faced by their users and come to CESAR asking for solutions which might not actually address those problems. We are also engaged in applying qualitative methods during the maintenance phase, after our products have been released, in order to continually improve the user experience.

References

1. Levi, F., Melo, P., Lucena, U.: Accessibility Implementation Planning for Large Governmental Websites: a Case Study. In: Proceedings of the 4th Latin American Web Congress, Cholula, Mexico, pp. 113–118 (2006)
2. Nielsen, J.: Jakob Nielsen's Alertbox: Evangelizing Usability: Change Your Strategy at the Halfway Point (2005), http://www.useit.com/alertbox/20050328.html

HxI : An Australian Initiative in ICT-Augmented Human Interactivity

Christian Müller-Tomfelde[1,2], Belinda Kellar[1], and Peter Eades[1]

[1] HxI Initiative – [braccetto] Project
[2] CSIRO ICT Centre
{firstname.lastname}@hxi.org.au

Abstract. The nature of global business today means people often need to work as part of geographically dispersed teams. As such, organisations around the globe are looking to improve the way employees collaborate and share knowledge, even if they are collaborating across large distances. The complexity of dealing with distributed knowledge workers is heightened by the increasing struggle by individuals to extract and make sense of the huge amounts of data that needs to be processed in order to extract meaningful insights within their work context. The HxI Initiative is a new national initiative in Australia, which is driven by these overarching business drivers. Research is planned and conducted to improve the ability of humans to interact with information, their colleagues and their environments in the modern organization.

Overview

The HxI Intiative was established in 2006 by three of Australia's publicly funded research organisations – Commonwealth Scientific Research Organisation (CSIRO), Defence Science Technology Organisation (DSTO) and National ICT Australia (NICTA) as a new national initiative in ICT-Augmented Human Interactivity. The initiative is distributed across Australia, with key sites in Sydney and Adelaide (see also [1]).

The term 'HxI' describes the trend towards ubiquity and human experience in information communications technology (ICT) environments. Specifically, the "x" in the term 'HxI' represents research from a number of disciplines that collectively enhance "the factor of human interactivity". In this way, the HxI Initiative's research is focused on augmenting the ability of humans to interact with information, with each other, and with their environments through the effective application of ICT [3]. This includes research into the development of innovative interaction technologies; novel interactive visualisation approaches, ubiquitous computing environments, and integrated telepresence for cooperative work.

The aims of the HxI Initiative include not only the development of world-class scientific and industrial outcomes in the field, but at a strategic level the development of human capital in this multi-disciplinary field. This includes developing strategies to build Australia's presence in the field of human interactivity; reducing fragmentation

C. Baranauskas et al. (Eds.): INTERACT 2007, LNCS 4663, Part II, pp. 675–676, 2007.

across related research disciplines and building human capital through targeted recruitment and research training in the HxI field.

Foundational Project [braccetto]

The [braccetto] project is the first and foundational project of the HxI Initiative. The project is the largest HCI related project ever undertaken in Australia. It began in late 2006.

The [braccetto] project is exploring how the effective application of ICT in mixed presence groupware can help geographically distributed teams collaborate more effectively [2]. Specifically, the project is developing new methods for supporting simultaneous work between multiple people at multiple sites, using software tools tightly coupled to high-quality, multi-party telepresence technology. The project will design and evaluate tools and models of distributed teamwork. The eventual aim is to improve criteria such as productivity, performance and team effectiveness between remote co-workers.

The project is investigating a range of novel mixed presence groupware capabilities, including the development of a research and transitioning platform called [braccetto] TeamNets. [braccetto] TeamNets is a family of hardware and software elements that can be rapidly composed into a range of distributed collaboration systems. It includes the use of high quality audio and video communication, synchronous application sharing over a distance and rapidly configurable, adaptable and synchronised operating environments [2, 3]. A real-world domain experiment in the national security field, was undertaken in November 2006 and results from this study and underlying research into awareness and mixed-presence groupware is providing stimuli to the development of new models and systems for distributed intense collaboration environments. Further large scale experiments are planned.

Future research to be addressed by the [braccetto] project includes: combining remote awareness cues (communicative gestures, direction of attention) with a generic groupware platform for arbitrary applications; conducting large-scale formative evaluations of a combined high quality telepresence, groupware and ubiquitous computing system; and assessing situation awareness and workspace awareness in mixed presence groupware applications for geographically dispersed teams.

References

1. HxI Initiative (accessed 24, February 2007) (2007), http://www.hxi.org.au/
2. Schremmer, C., Krumm-Heller, A., Vernik, R., Epps, J.: Design Discussion of the [braccetto] Research Platform: Supporting Distributed Intensely Collaborating Creative Teams of Teams. In: Proc. HCI International 2007 (2007)
3. Vernik, R., Kellar, B., Epps, J., Schremmer, C.: HxI: A National Research Initiative in ICT-Augmented Human Interactivity. Internal Report (accessed April 18, 2007) (2006), http:/www.hxi.org.au/images/stories/documents/ verniket_al_oct06.pdf

Introducing HCI in Corporate IT Department in a Large Company in Brazil

Andre Vinicius Fontes Dantas[1], Carlos Freud Alves Batista[1], Cassiano Ebert[1],
Maíra Greco de Paula[1,2], and Simone Diniz Junqueira Barbosa[2]

[1] Petrobras/TI/SERV-TI/DS, Rua da Assembléia, 100, Centro, RJ, Brasil
[2] Informatics Dept., PUC-Rio, Rua Marquês de São Vicente, 225, Gávea, RJ, Brasil
`{andrevinicius, carlos.freud, cassiano.ebert,`
`maira.greco.STK}@petrobras.com.br, simone@inf.puc-rio.br`

Abstract. This paper describes the introduction of human-computer interaction activities in the Corporate IT Department in a large energy company in Brazil. It is certified by ISO 9001:2000, and thus has a set of norms that IT employees must follow during the software development process. We discuss the introduction of HCI activities into these norms.

Keywords: software development process norms, human-computer interaction.

1 Introduction

This paper describes the introduction of human-computer interaction (HCI) activities in the Corporate Information Technology (IT) Department in a large energy company in Brazil, which develops software for the company employees. It is certified by ISO 9001:2000, and thus has a set of norms that IT employees must follow during the software development process. For instance, there are norms for the development of applications following certain methodologies, and for software inspection and testing.

Due to the great diversity of users and system domains, we have decided to create a norm regarding the application of HCI concepts during the software development process. To develop this norm, a software engineering–usability technical group was formed with IT employees from various software development regions who had interest or experience in HCI. Before writing the norm, the group members participated in a tutorial on HCI, given by an R&D HCI laboratory[1]. This tutorial presented an overview of HCI concepts and design and evaluation activities. Also, the group members analyzed the software development standards in the company and then proposed an HCI application norm for the corporate IT.

2 The Development Process and the HCI Application Norm

The software development process in our company is composed of the following activities: 0) request from a business area; 1) process definition; 2) requirements analysis; 3) software design (logical and physical); 4) software construction, making

---

[1] SERG at PUC-Rio: http://www.serg.inf.puc-rio.br

C. Baranauskas et al. (Eds.): INTERACT 2007, LNCS 4663, Part II, pp. 677–679, 2007.

use of available frameworks and components; 5) software testing; 6) software validation with the client; and 7) deployment. There are standards guiding each activity and the construction of each artifact in the software development process. Also, inspection activities occur in parallel with the design and construction stages.

The HCI norm introduced new activities and artifacts in this process (Table 1) [1]. We highlight here the user interface (UI) model, which is composed of a) wireframes; b) the associated requirements; c) a description of each screen and UI element, indicating which ones are mandatory or optional, the default values, and data format, when applicable; d) relationships or dependencies between the UI elements; and e) a navigation map between the various screens. In its first version, the norm is applicable only to web applications. Usability inspection activities were introduced in two stages: during software design, of both UI model and prototype (if available); and after the software construction, of the final product. Some activities were defined as optional due to the lack of maturity and available professionals to carry them out.

Table 1. Usability-related activities introduced by the norm

Sw Dev Stage	HCI-related activity	Type
Requirements analysis	UI requirements elicitation questionnaire	Optional
Software design	UI model or	Mandatory
	UI prototype construction	
Software design	UI model/prototype inspection	Mandatory
Software construction	Final product's UI inspection	Mandatory
Software testing	Usability testing	Optional

2.1 Pilot Project

The user interface of a business-critical system was redesigned according to the new HCI norm, and presented to the higher IT management. The result was very positive, and everyone agreed with having a usability-related norm. Therefore, the technical group gained management support, which is crucial in a large company with IT departments distributed in various regions. Some developers and graphical designers commented that they liked the UI model very much, in that they didn't need to make decisions about HCI when doing their work.

2.2 Training and Deployment of the HCI Norm

Several employees were trained, including project leaders, analysts, developers, inspectors and testers. The inspectors showed some resistance, because they now have additional artifacts to inspect, besides all the software design artifacts traditionally used. We expect the changes in the organizational culture to be gradual, and will keep monitoring the professionals' attitudes towards the norm to make the necessary adjustments in the HCI-related activities or roles that perform them. The technical group is now monitoring the norm's application in the various regional departments, and is also extending the norm to include user interfaces for websites and portals, desktop application, Lotus Notes® applications, and mobile devices.

Acknowledgments. We thank all the members of the usability technical group in our company for their work in the usability standards and norms described here.

References

1. Solutions Development Area at PETROBRAS Corporate IT Department, Usability Guidelines for the Construction of Web User Interfaces, TI-IT-1T1-00123 (2006)

São Paulo State e-gov: LabIHC and e-Poupatempo´s Experience

Renato Facis, Carlos Alberto Neves Torres, and Jair Barreto de Vasconcelos

PRODESP – Information Technology Company of São Paulo State
Agueda Gonçalves Street, 240 - Taboão da Serra, São Paulo, Brasil
{rfacis, ctorres, jvasconcelos}@sp.gov.br
http://www.prodesp.sp.gov.br/labihc
http://www.poupatempo.sp.gov.br/e_poupatempo/index.htm

Abstract. This document describes the experience of São Paulo state government in its initiatives to develop an e-gov standard, focusing on the importance of centralization of access efforts from the citizen's perspective and the role of human-computer interaction and social and digital inclusion in this process.

Keywords: Electronic government (e-gov), social inclusion, digital inclusion, human-computer interaction (HCI), usability, accessibility.

As technology advances and e-gov guidelines develop fast, São Paulo state departments are more and more offering their services on the Web. Under this scenario in 2002 the São Paulo state government – through Casa Civil Strategic Information System Coordination and Prodesp´s Poupatempo Superintendence – identified the need to transfer to the web the citizen services standards previously only provided at Poupatempo Service Centers in a face-to-face mode. The aim was to reach excellence levels for digital environmental.

Hence "e-poupatempo" was born with the mission to guarantee the citizen's access to public e-services and to propose continuous service improvements based on such demand. Along the lines of social and digital inclusion, service rooms were provided where the citizens, supported by staff, could access e-services such as police incident registration, vehicle license plate registration query and payment, issuance of water / energy / telephone bills in case original ones are not available, among others.

These rooms also function as observatories of service usage and population profile. All occurrences are registered on-line and the usage variables are collected, adding up to 1.5 million occurrences since 2002. Some variables such as service identification, interaction duration and request for help are always collected, while specific campaigns are developed to identify more particular interaction obstacles, such as problems in text interpretation, font size, colors, filling up of certain forms, and so on.

"LabIHC" (Laboratory for Human-Computer Interaction) was created in 2003 to assess usability and accessibility of government sites, providing information to continuously improve government web site services, always focusing on the citizen. In this laboratory real tests are performed with the public service users; human-computer interface problems are hence identified based on usability and accessibility

C. Baranauskas et al. (Eds.): INTERACT 2007, LNCS 4663, Part II, pp. 680–681, 2007.

heuristics. The results are supplied to the governmental entities responsible for the web sites. Till this date the LabIHC results were:

- 23 web sites/electronic public services reviewed
- 50% of the occurrences identified were corrected by the responsible entities, even though they were not mandatory or punitive.

LabIHC also takes advantage of direct interface of the e-room with the citizen to do research and collect data about the web site usage. In 2004 a survey with more than 150.000 samples was prepared of the social and demographic profile and the difficulties faced by the citizen in his interaction with public web sites. The outcome was the development of the typical São Paulo state e-gov user profiles. Along the line of citizen focus, research correlating citizen expectations and preferences regarding the São Paulo e-gov was developed to guide subsequent initiatives. A concrete example of a problem identified through the e-poupatempo rooms was the difficulty citizens faced when filling out an electronic police registration form. In most cases the activity could not by completed without staff support. Based on this fact a detailed inspection was carried out by LabIHC with real citizen experiments and the registration form was revised subsequent to collaboration with Public Safety Department.

A set of rules and web interface standards were created based on the accumulated experience in order to standardize and guarantee the quality of the São Paulo state e-gov in its interaction with the citizen. Six manuals were issued via CC-9 resolution of the São Paulo state Casa Civil and are available to all governmental web developers.

Regarding accessibility, LabIHC also did qualitative research to learn about the e-gov expectations and demands from the special needs citizens, supporting initiatives in that direction.

E-poupatempo and LabIHC established successful partnerships with private companies. Intel sponsored LabIHC and Guarulhos e-poupatempo service room. Similarly AMD sponsored the e-poupatempo service room in Itaquera, São Paulo, making evident the interest of the private sector in technology and digital inclusion projects, as well as the governmental capability to execute these partnerships in a clear form at low cost and with good results.

Academic alliances are also remarkable in the history of LabIHC. LTS (Software Technology Laboratory from Polytechnic School - USP supported the installation of LabIHC and handed over the full methodology on usability, accessibility and HCI used in the tests since 2003.

In worldwide terms, e-poupatempo is part of the e-goia project (part of @LIS program – Alliance for Information Society), a cooperation initiative to accelerate the development of e-gov in Latin America and to strengthen the partnerships with European Community and the Latin American governments. In this project an integration database solution prototype was built – if an ID is stolen, for example, the citizen can register his loss on line and is promptly offered to get a new ID (by filling out his current data) and advised of the ID pick-up schedule at a Poupatempo address. At the same time the old document is cancelled.

As a consequence of this project, Inlets (International Laboratories Network for e-gov Services and Technology) was created to provide knowledge and expertise exchange among e-gov laboratories. LabIHC is one of the Brazilian participants in this initiative that gathers laboratories from 5 Europe and South American countries.

The Challenges of Creating Connections and Raising Awareness: Experience from UCLIC

Ann Blandford, Rachel Benedyk, Nadia Berthouze, Anna Cox, and John Dowell

UCL Interaction Centre, University College London, Remax House, 31-32 Alfred Place, London, WC1E 7DP, U.K
A.Blandford@ucl.ac.uk

Abstract. With current disciplinary structures and academic priorities, Human–Computer Interaction faces ongoing challenges: is it a discipline in its own right, or simply a sub-discipline of computer science, psychology or design? Is it a science or engineering discipline? Should it concern itself with developing theory or improving practice? UCLIC aims to find appropriate middle ways on such questions: it conducts scientifically-based HCI research with a view to improving practice, and thus have an impact on society. It is based in the disciplines of Psychology and Computer Science and promotes participation across the disciplines. Research and teaching cover cognitive, affective, physical, social and technical aspects of interactive system design and use.

Keywords: human error; digital libraries; design practice; formal models; affect; cognition; social and organisational impacts of technology.

1 Introduction

UCL Interaction Centre (UCLIC) was established in 2001, as an interdisciplinary group spanning Computer Science and Psychology. It succeeded the Ergonomics Unit, which had once been based in Engineering and latterly in Psychology, and it inherited an established Masters course in HCI with Ergonomics. Since its formation, it has faced challenges, some of which are inherent to the discipline and others of which are specific to UCLIC's situation. We outline some of these challenges here.

2 Selected Challenges

One obvious challenge is that of creating connections across disciplines. UCLIC is staffed by academics from both Psychology and Computer Science. This 'dual belonging' is essential to the work of UCLIC for maintaining effective dialogues with specialist peers and ensuring awareness of relevant research developments in the contributing disciplines. Nevertheless, it poses challenges of sustaining those effective dialogues, finding the points of common interest and developing shared understanding. For example, where UCLIC researchers work on applied problems such as interactive search [3] and human error [5], they can draw on the work of colleagues in Psychology on attention [4], but the applied problems are often of less immediate interest to the theoreticians.

C. Baranauskas et al. (Eds.): INTERACT 2007, LNCS 4663, Part II, pp. 682–683, 2007.
© IFIP International Federation for Information Processing 2007

As well as connections with the contributing disciplines, there is a challenge to create connections more directly between them. One strand of research is exploring how findings from psychology and other social sciences can be expressed in forms that can readily inform computer system design and, conversely, how the need for a better understanding of system users can create new research agendas in cognition, emotion and interaction (i.e. developing theory that is appropriately framed for informing practice).

As well as the challenge of creating connections with the contributing disciplines, there is that of creating connections with applied disciplines such as health informatics, clinical psychology and information studies, where the roles are typically reversed: HCI can provide useful established theory and methods on how to design effective systems for applied purposes, and the challenge is to find the cases where the domains of application provoke the development of new theory. For example, Attfield et al [1] relate empirical findings about writers' use of information systems to design theory. Similarly, Berthouze is investigating how technology capable of recognizing affective states from body language [2] can help chronic pain patients and their clinicians in dealing with the affective experience of pain.

Finally, we highlight the challenge of raising awareness in the broader practitioner and user community. In a recent interview, a Human Factors practitioner told us that his remit was to "give the customer what they ask for, not, you should note, what they need." This illustrates that general awareness is low – of the discipline, of the issues we address and of the factors that contribute to a positive interactive experience. Students enrolling on our Masters course in HCI with Ergonomics often tell us that they recently discovered that HCI exists as a discipline, with a body of knowledge and a set of skills to be learnt, and they are excited and delighted to have made this discovery. Educating students is an important part of our remit for facilitating HCI awareness and practice. However, improving public awareness clearly remains a challenge, for both UCLIC and the broader HCI community.

References

1. Attfield, S., Blandford, A., Dowell, J.: Information seeking in the context of writing: a design psychology interpretation of the problematic situation. Journal of Documentation 59(4), 430–453 (2003)
2. Bianchi-Berthouze, N., Kleinsmith, A.: A categorical approach to affective gesture recognition. Connection Science 15(4), 259–269 (2003)
3. Cox, A.L., Silva, M.: The role of mouse movements in interactive search. In: Proc. Cognitive Science Conference 2006, pp. 1156–1161 (2006)
4. Lavie, N., Hirst, A., de Fockert, J.W., Viding, E.: Load theory of selective attention and cognitive control. Journal of Experimental Psychology: General 133, 339–354 (2004)
5. Li, S.Y.W., Cox, A.L., Blandford, A., Cairns, P., Young, R.M., Abeles, A.: Further investigations into post-completion error: the effects of interruption position and duration. In: Proc. Cognitive Science Conference 2006, pp. 471–476 (2006)

Usability, from a Bigger Picture

Mercedes Sanchez and José Luis Adán Gil

Mercedes Sanchez Usabilidade, R. Alfenas, 56 - Granja Viana, CEP 06351-165
Carapicuiba/SP, Brasil
falecom@mercedessanchez.com.br

Abstract. This paper presents the strategy of Mercedes Sanchez Usabilidade, a Brazilian consultancy firm, to spread the usability concept among consumers and companies in a way that no other company has ever done in Brazil. The strategy made usability news in the media and it is benefiting consumers, companies and professionals of user experience all over the country.

Keywords: usability, communication strategy, blog, Brazil.

1 Introduction

The usability concept is not familiar to Brazilians, as well as inside the companies. Many consumers tend to think it is their fault if they cannot use something, especially if it is related to computers and technology. They blame neither the product nor the company, instead they feel guilty. So, if consumer does not complain about designs that are not friendly, why would the companies worry about it?

In view of this fact, the Brazilian consultancy firm Mercedes Sanchez Usabilidade decided to focus on an extensive action of making usability known. The objective was to bring the concept closer to the daily reality of consumers and companies.

The strategy was to create and bring out a way for people to express themselves about products, services and sites that are not user friendly and, therefore, catch the attention of the companies. The blog *Tá Difícil* ("This is difficult") was put together for this purpose.

Mercedes Sanchez Usabilidade has been offering services related to User Experience since 2003 and is partner with usability companies from Europe and USA, conducting usability studies on web sites and mobile phones in Brazil, as part of global studies.

2 Sowing the Seeds

Mercedes Sanchez Usabilidade took the 2006 World Usability Day challenge seriously – by disclosing the usability concept and by encouraging people to protest against things that are difficult to use – and on November 14th, 2006 the blog "*Tá Difícil*" ("This is difficult") - www.tadificil.com.br – was launched, inspired by the American website "This is Broken".

C. Baranauskas et al. (Eds.): INTERACT 2007, LNCS 4663, Part II, pp. 684–685, 2007.
© IFIP International Federation for Information Processing 2007

"Tá Difícil..." became a discussion forum for consumers who face difficulties in using, from sites, systems and electronic products up to the doors and faucets. It is entirely fed by the users, who send pictures, texts and videos. By disclosing a problem, this generates comments of others who have already had the same or a similar problem. Little by little, it shows the consumers that if there is something that is difficult to use, it is not their fault and that they should complain about it.

There are some dramatic posts, such as the one from a 59-year-old gentleman who purchased a DVD recorder to *"convert my tapes from VHS to DVD, so that my grandchildren could know a little bit about my life story"* and who could not record anything because of difficulties in understanding how the gadget works. Another consumer spent 2 years fighting with an electronic dictionary, whose installation program leads the user to an error and requires that the installation CD be inserted every time the dictionary is used.

There are also posts from telecommunication company clients who feel outraged for being forced to navigate through the depths of the sites just to find a telephone number or an e-mail address.

3 The First Harvests

These and other stories, enriched with comments and tips from the readers of the blog, caught the eye of the media. The Usability subject, not only the blog, made the news on major Brazilian TV networks, radio stations, newspapers and magazines.

The companies started reacting in a very positive and even surprising manner at times, such as Philips Brasil, who added a link to *"Tá Difícil"* to the company's blog called *"SimplesCidade"*. Tales Rocha, Philips' Internet manager, said *"Tá Difícil is complementary to the company's blog and it is worth recommending it."*

The difficulties to access the online help reported by users of Submarino, a big e-commerce site, were dealt with by the company and this was communicated by the blog. The same happened with Banco Santander, who anticipated an improvement on the internet-banking menu, based on a complaint posted on *Tá Difícil*.

4 Conclusion

The usability concept is becoming closer to those thousands of users who have accessed the blog, those millions of people who watched it on TV, as well as those companies who are positioning themselves and are promoting improvements in their sites and products.

Mercedes Sanchez Usabilidade, through *Tá Difícil*, are doing their part in bringing about the Usability concept and in making people and companies aware of the need of making this world an easier place to live in.

User Experience Research at Tech Mahindra

Sanjay Tripathi

User Interaction Design Group, Tech Mahindra Limited
Sharda Centre, Pune- 411005 India
stripathi@techmahindra.com

Abstract. In this overview we describe how user experience research and design has been established in Tech Mahindra Ltd. (TechM), and how it is organised to support both short term development programs and long term research. While focusing on research activities at TechM, the challenges of assessing real user experience issues critical to business success, user experience measurement methodology and future research focus are discussed in this paper.

Keywords: Social computing, user experience metrics, index of integration, Telecom, Interaction design, HCI.

1 Introduction

Tech Mahindra Limited (TechM) is the global leader in providing end-to-end IT services and solutions to the Telecom industry. Over 25,000 professionals service clients across various telecom segments, from multiple offshore development centres across cities in India, UK and sales offices across America, Europe and Asia-Pacific.

TechM recognised six years ago, the key role User Experience plays in ensuring the customer satisfaction for its clients' services and products, and started building the capability in the domain of User Experience Design and Usability Engineering.

Advancements in the technology that has led to proliferation of access devices, pervasive presence of Internet, and the changing lifestyle of users have increased the complexity of developing the User Experience solutions.

The Service Delivery at TechM therefore is based on the philosophy of integration of user centred approach, customers' business imperatives and software engineering practices. The Research in this domain is carried out to support this philosophy. Our Research Group is distributed across locations, based on the demands of universal usability and local cultural influences on diversified user base of TechM's clients.

2 User Experience Design at Tech Mahindra

The TechM's User Interaction Design Group (UIDG) provides Usability and User Experience Design services to global customers. The group has deep theoretical knowledge combined with vast hands-on exposure in end-to-end User Experience solutions. The unique combination of capabilities and the multidisciplinary background

C. Baranauskas et al. (Eds.): INTERACT 2007, LNCS 4663, Part II, pp. 686–687, 2007.

of UIDG enable us to formulate a comprehensive approach taking into account the key dimensions of design, usability, technology and management.

At TechM, we follow a time tested methodology – UESDM. User Experience Solution Design Methodology process is unique and has evolved over the years with exposure to multiple assignments. UESDM is an iterative and methodical approach. It takes into consideration end user needs, business goals and usability best practices to successfully deliver end-to-end User Experience solutions.

3   Recent Success

Our team of experts has improved the ease of use of over 100 applications by offering the end-to-end design solutions, understanding the varied end user needs, diverse domains, overcoming the business challenges and technology constraints.

Research and capability division of UIDG at TechM started exploring new possibility of redefining users experience and its relevance for the business customers. It was often asked by our customers to provide better insight of users while they use their sites. We found that reports from web analytics (WA) tools alone are not adequate to provide insights in User Experience aspects. We have been successful in extending the capability of WA tool while incorporating User Experience attributes to the clickstream data generated by them.

We have also been successful in developing new User Experience Metrics (UXM) and its Index of Integration (IOI) in a collaborative research with Indian Institute of Technology.

UXM is an empirical inspection based User Experience on a scale of 0-100. The purpose of this metrics is to predict the quality of User Experience of a product early in a quantitative manner and without the help of user-based evaluation methods. This proved as effective measurement technique which is capable to predict the 'quality' of User Experience of a product.

IOI is an empirical process metric that represents the best possible integration of HCI activities in the software development. IOI helps to evaluate the impact of various HCI design activities on User Experience quality of the resulting product in a given domain.

4   Vision for Future

The field of Human Computer Interaction design being multi disciplinary and re-search oriented, TechM's UIDG has strong focus on the research activities. Keeping this perspective in mind, UIDG has already started working in the areas of Web 2.0, Rich Internet Application (RIA) and Web Analytics as immediate focus areas. Mobile user experience, alternative interaction style, alternative interfaces, and integrated social interaction etc. are the vision for future where we are aimed to bring our experience and expertise.

User System Interaction Program

Panos Markopoulos, Maddy Janse, Sanjin Pajo, Paula Deisz, Annemieke van Ruiten, Vanessa Sawirjo, and Albertine Visser

Technical University Eindhoven,
Den Dolech 2, 5612 EZ, Eindhoven, The Netherlands
{P.Markopoulos, M.D.Janse, S.P.Pajo, P.Deisz, A.M.V.Ruiten,
V.M.Sawirjo, A.Visser}@tue.nl

Abstract. The User System Interaction program (USI) is a post-master program at the Technical University Eindhoven (TU/e), the Netherlands. The program is designed to provide students with skills and capabilities for conceptualizing, designing, implementing and evaluating new products, services and applications. The students, working in multidisciplinary and multicultural teams, exploit new technologies for the benefit of users in the domain of communication and information technology.

Keywords: User-System Interaction, Human-Computer Interaction, research, design, education, professional development.

1 Introduction

The User System Interaction program (USI), started in 1998, is one of ten two-year full-time Technological Design programs coordinated by the Stan Ackermans Institute (SAI). SAI is a joint venture of the three technological universities of the Netherlands: Eindhoven University of Technology, Delft University of Technology and University of Twente. The SAI design programs have been developed to address the needs of industry for people who are capable of working in the multidisciplinary world of design and who are up to date with the latest design methods and technological developments. The SAI design programs are co-financed by the Dutch Government and by industry. Selected applicants of any of these programs receive a fixed-term employment contract as research assistants and are paid by the University. Graduates are awarded the title "Professional Doctorate in Engineering" (PDEng) and will be registered as a Technological Designer in the Dutch register kept by the Royal Institution of Engineers in the Netherlands (KIVI NIRIA).

Eligible students have a Master's degree in the engineering or behavioral sciences (MSc or MA), i.e., computer science, business engineering, mathematics, psychology and cognitive sciences or industrial design. They come from different countries all around the world. The program accepts about 20 applicants per year. Overall acceptance rate is about 30%. Each USI cohort is composed of a balanced group of students of multidisciplinary and multicultural background. The target composition is 50% engineering, 50% behavioral sciences, 50% Dutch citizenship and 50% non-Dutch citizenship.

C. Baranauskas et al. (Eds.): INTERACT 2007, LNCS 4663, Part II, pp. 688–689, 2007.
© IFIP International Federation for Information Processing 2007

2 Educational Program

The program starts with fourteen months of taught modules each lasting one or two weeks. Taught modules are clustered in five clusters: Understanding the User Experience, User Centered Design Processes, Software Engineering, Interaction Technologies and User research methodology. Lecturers in the USI program include internationally renowned experts from different universities and industries.

In the last part of the regular curriculum, students work in small project teams on design cases, in which they apply their knowledge and skills to concrete problems from projects outside the USI program. This design case covers a complete transition from a user requirements analysis, to design, prototype and evaluation. Design cases typically have a problem owner outside the USI program; in many cases industrial R&D departments. The majority of design cases result in publications and presentations at professional conferences and workshops.

Another component of the USI program constitutes the professional development program which provides the students with the necessary skills to function in their future professional environments. These courses address, for example, the training of presentation skills, project management, time management, working together in a multi-cultural environment and self-assessment.

3 Industrial Program

In the second part of the program, students work for nine months as professionals hired out to industry. Projects include interactive applications for consumer electronics, mobile communications, healthcare professionals or health applications for the home, automotive cockpit automation, etc. The projects are defined and conducted at the R&D departments of industrial organizations or applied research institutes. They are supervised by coaches from the host organization and the University.

4 USI Career Perspective

USI graduates often become part of multidisciplinary design teams within industry, business services or government institutions. Examples of positions held by USI graduates are usability engineer, usability consultant, human factors engineer, information architect and customer insight specialist.

For more information, on the program please consult the course website http://usi.tm.tue.nl.

Human Centric E-Learning and the Challenge of Cultural Localization

Albert Badre[1], Stefano Levialdi[2], Jim Foley[1], John Thomas[3], Carol Strohecker[4],
Antonella De Angeli[6], Preetha Ram[5], Ashwin Ram[1], and Jaime Sanchez[7]

[1] Georgia Institute of Technology
[2] Dipartimento di Informatica, Universita' di Roma "La Sapienza"
[3] IBM T.J. Watson Research
[4] University of North Carolina
[5] Emory University
[6] University of Manchester
[7] Universidad de Chile
badre@cc.gatech.edu

1 Introduction

The cutting edge of designing for the user experience today is found in the arena of designing for the user's cultural context {1}, {2}, {3}. This is primarily true because of global expansion of the Internet and Web usage. Brick and mortar businesses have learned to adapt their products to be culturally sensitive. For example, car manufacturers build the same basic platform with different styling and amenities depending on where the vehicle will be sold. To convey an appealing image to potential buyers and readers, publishers translating popular works into many languages usually have different covers designed for different countries: for this reason they aim towards the perception of an object and of its functions. We often differ in the way we experience the world around us. Our experiences differ relative to our primary language, educational practices, work habits, and what makes for an enjoyable experience, whether in what and how we like to play, what sounds that we appreciate, or colors that appeal to us {4}, {5}.

2 E-Learning and the Culture Sensitive Human Centric Challenge

The increasing interest in on-line learning leads us to seek answers to questions about how to provide virtual learning environments that enhance the learning experience, and at the same time address the needs of the culturally sensitive global learning context of the World Wide Web. More specifically, we look for solutions to questions about making the virtual learning context user compatible, learner effective, and totally accessible (universally usable).

Human-centric e-learning design means designing for the user experience in a specific learning context. Designing for context means constructing suitable learning environments grounded in the learner's learning ecology, be it a classic instructor-led classroom environment, learner-led customized setting, collaborative learning, or knowledge-based tutorials. We know that providing the right context plays a crucial role in learning {6}. Students who learn and then recall material in the same environment

C. Baranauskas et al. (Eds.): INTERACT 2007, LNCS 4663, Part II, pp. 690–691, 2007.
© Springer-Verlag Berlin Heidelberg 2007

with specific contextual cues will perform better than those made to recall in a different environment. Embedded in any context are cultural cues and clues that guide the process of observation and interpretation. The challenge for the interactive e-learning designer is to provide e-learning content and tools that invoke the unique cultural cues of multiple localized, and potentially conflicting contexts, while at the same time allowing for a common virtual learning environment, where virtual learners are having shared content and experience.

The fundamental challenge for the panel is for each panelist to put forward their vision for the future of human-centric virtual learning environments and virtual learning communities. The panel will explore the issue of what "human-centric" in the e-learning environment means, and how to resolve the issue of the seeming conflict between shared learning experience and the need to be culturally sensitive.

More specifically, the panel will be asked to consider the following questions:

1) What makes a virtual learning environment human-centric, and what are the requirements to make such an environment compelling and in high demand by potential participants?

2) Should the emphasis of learner-centered or user-centered, be more on the "learner" or the "user"? Is there a conflict to be resolved between "learner culture" and "user culture"?

3) How do we take cultural usability into account? While e-learning is by practice global, it has to be culturally sensitive to learner's unique environment. How do we reconcile the need for cultural localization with the requirement for universally consistent e-learning content?

4) Describe your vision of an e-learning environment (existing or imaginary) that meets what you consider to be human-centric requirements and culturally sensitive?

5) What are the implications of the growing virtual social networks, for human-centric and culturally sensitive e-learning?

References

1. Badre, A.N.: Shaping Web Usability: Interaction Design in Context, pp. 213–227. Addison Wesley, Boston (2002)
2. Marcus, A., Gould, E.W.: Cultural Dimensions and Global Web User-Interface Design: What? So What? Now What? In: 6th Conference on Human Factors and the Web in Austin, Texas (June 19, 2000)
3. De Angeli, A., Athavankar, U.A., Joshi, A., Coventry, L., Johnson, G.I.: Introducing ATM's in India: A contextual enquiry. Interacting with Computers special issue. Global human-computer systems 16(1), 29–44 (2004)
4. Marcus, A.: International and Intercultural User-Interface Design. In: Stephanidis, C. (ed.) User Interfaces for All, Lawrence Erlbaum, New York (2000)
5. Hofstede, G.: Cultures and Organizations: Software of the Mind. McGraw-Hill, New York (1997)
6. Godden, D., Baddeley, A.: Context-dependent memory in two natural environments. British Journal of Psychology 81, 465–46 (1975)

Meta-design and Social Creativity:
Making All Voices Heard

Gerhard Fischer (Panel Coordinator)

Center for Lifelong Learning and Design
University of Colorado, Boulder
gerhard@colorado.edu

Summary Statement. This panel will explore the two innovative and interrelated HCI themes *"meta-design"* (design for designer) and *"social creativity"* (transcending the individual human mind). It will focus on the contribution of these two themes to *socially-responsible interaction* by bringing together researchers from *different* backgrounds to explore the *controversial* issues associated with this objective.

Meta-design defines and creates socio-technical environments as living entities by extending existing design methodologies to allow users to become co-designers. It creates conditions to facilitate social creativity by supporting users as active contributors who can transcend the functionality and content of existing systems.

Much human creativity arises from activities that take place in a social context in which interaction with other people and the artifacts that embody group knowledge are important contributors to the process. Creativity happens not inside a person's head, but in the interaction between a person's thoughts and a socio-cultural context. *Social creativity* shifts from the idea of a tool—or set of tools—to the notion of a socio-technical environment in which all stakeholders have a voice. To sow the seeds of a more creative society, it is necessary to promote research methods and identify the unique challenges in developing assessment methods for creativity research.

Social creativity needs the "synergy of many," and this kind of synergy is facilitated by meta-design. However, a tension exists between creativity and organization [Florida, 2002]. A defining characteristic of social creativity is that it transcends individual creativity and thus requires some form of organization thereby possibly stifling creativity.

Relationship of the Panel to the Conference Theme "Socially Responsible Interaction". Meta-design and social creativity contribute to socially responsible design [CPSR, 2007] in the following dimensions:

- *Democratizing innovation:* meta-design allows owners of problems to engage in activities as a process of creating new possibilities and new artifacts, eliminating the constraint that users are restricted to what is given to them [von Hippel, 2005].
- *Making all voices heard:* Complex design problems seldom fall within the boundaries of one specific domain; they require the participation and contributions of different stakeholders with various backgrounds [Schön et al., 1999].

C. Baranauskas et al. (Eds.): INTERACT 2007, LNCS 4663, Part II, pp. 692–693, 2007.
© IFIP International Federation for Information Processing 2007

- *Changing professional practice:* Meta-design contributes to the creation of convivial tools which give each person the greatest opportunity to enrich the environment with the fruits of his or her vision [Illich, 1973].
- *Revolutionizing the creation of systems*: Open source software systems and collaborative content creation harness the possibilities of Web 2.0 architectures [Benkler, 2006; Tapscott & Williams, 2006].

Controversial Issues and Open Questions:

- Can an emphasis on meta-design and creativity lead to *economic growth* and *social transformation* and help communities benefit from *local knowledge* and engage their members in more meaningful and rewarding activities?
- Will meta-design and social creativity lead to *new divisions of labor*?
- What are the strengths and weaknesses of available meta-design environments and creativity tools? When are they most needed, and why?
- How can we *assess* and *evaluate* meta-design and social creativity?
- While meta-design as well as creativity tools are critical so as to democratize access, they may not be sufficient to promote active participation. What kinds of socio-cultural-political conditions need to be in place to effectuate the kinds of social relations conducive to active participations?

Participants:

- *Gerhard Fischer* (primary contact), University of Colorado, Boulder, USA, gerhard@colorado.edu; *unique perspective*: social creativity
- *Jennifer J. Preece,* College of Information Studies, □ University of Maryland, preece@umd.edu; *unique perspective:* communities
- *Piero Mussio,* University of Milan, Italy; *unique perspective*: meta-design
- *John Thomas;* IBM Yorktown Heights, USA; *unique perspective*: socially-responsible interaction
- *Rogerio dePaula:* Intel Sao Paulo, Brasil; *unique perspective*: computer use in underdeveloped countries and digital divide
- *Ben Shneiderman:* University of Maryland, USA; ben@cs.umd.edu; *unique perspective*: creativity support tools

References

1. Benkler, Y.: The Wealth of Networks: How Social Production Transforms Markets and Freedom. Yale University Press, New Haven (2006)
2. CPSR Computer Professionals for Social Responsibility (2007), available at http://www. cpsr.org/
3. Florida, R.: The Rise of the Creative Class and How It's Transforming Work, Leisure, Community and Everyday Life. Basic Books, New York (2002)
4. Illich, I.: Tools for Conviviality. Harper and Row, New York (1973)
5. Schön, D.A., Sanyal, B., Mitchell, W.J.: High Technology and Low-Incoming Communities. MIT Press, Cambridge (1999)
6. Tapscott, D., Williams, A.D.: Wikinomics: How Mass Collaboration Changes Everything, Portofolio. Penguin Group, New York (2006)
7. von Hippel, E.: Democratizing Innovation. MIT Press, Cambridge (2005)

Socially Responsible Design in the Context of International Development

A. Dearden, L. Dunckley, M. Best, S. Dray, A. Light, and J. Thomas

1 Introduction

Human beings evolved for many millennia; during most of that time, our major social contacts were within small, tightly knit groups who shared a common language, culture and physical context. Now, we find ourselves to be a part of a global community. Though we still have very different cultures, languages, perspectives, and physical contexts, we also share a planet with limited and shrinking resources and we share many interactions in our intellectual, technological and economic spheres. Potentially, technology offers many benefits to the many peoples of the world. Yet, there is also potential for damaging the diversity in the ecology of ideas and cultures that may be indispensable for humankind to survive the next millennium. More immediately, technology developed without sufficient understanding and involvement of those to be most affected by it will probably fail at best and in the worst cases, not only fail to provide anticipated benefits but produce negative side-effects. One such side-effect may well be making future technological usage more difficult.

While User-Centered Design and Participatory Design are important techniques within a cultural context in order to provide solutions that are useful, usable and acceptable, these approaches are particularly vital when there is a large discrepancy between the background knowledge and assumptions of end users and designers. In such cases, not only is it useful, it is, indeed, necessary to gain a deeper and broader understanding of people, users, contexts, and tasks. However, this understanding will always be filtered, and can all-to-easily be distorted and obscured by the unconscious cultural lenses of people from so-called "developed" countries when they are the developers of technology. Further complicating the problem, methods such as ethnography and participative design may have to be significantly modified or even replaced by entirely new and locally invented methods more appropriate to the specifics of situation, locale and/or culture.

There are great challenges involved in attempting to provide a socially responsible design process in the context of international development. However, these situations also provide potential benefits beyond those of development in less challenging circumstances. Since these circumstances are so novel, they also provide a potential breeding ground for new insights and methods of general applicability to HCI.

Most previous innovations were developed within the confines of one cultural context (although often spread to other cultures). Largely unexplored is the territory of creativity possible when the perspectives, strengths, and knowledge of multiple disparate cultures are brought to bear simultaneously. It is entirely possible to use ICT to strengthen and maintain local cultures rather than to accelerate a global lack of diversity. The panel authors listed above are organizing and running a workshop on this topic at CHI 2007 where over fifty participants from around the globe, including

C. Baranauskas et al. (Eds.): INTERACT 2007, LNCS 4663, Part II, pp. 694–695, 2007.
© IFIP International Federation for Information Processing 2007

participants from both so-called "developed" and "developing" countries, will be sharing their experiences and lessons learned in the area of user-centered design and international development ("UCD4D"). Based on our experiences at this workshop, we will make a final determination on the composition of the panel presenters at INTERACT in order to provide the broadest possible range of perspectives.

2 Participants

Dr. Michael Best, a computer scientist by training with graduate degrees from the MIT Media Lab, he is an Assistant Professor at the Sam Nunn School of International Affairs at Georgia Tech University. Dr. Susan Dray, an experienced consultant in HCI with extensive experience in the area of international development. Professor Lynne Dunckley, Director of Research at the Institute for Information Technology at TVU in the UK. Dr. John Thomas, Research Staff Member at IBM's T. J. Watson Research Center has been interested in cross-cultural issues in HCI since organizing workshops in this area in 1992 and 1993.

We also plan to include four international participants based on a CHI workshop on this topic; ideally, one each from South America, Africa, Asia and Indonesia. Panel participants will share the specifics of their experiences of combining user centered design for international development as well as various perspectives on guidelines, methodologies and general patterns that may be applicable for international development. We will also discuss what future steps and linkages we feel are necessary for UCD4D to influence processes more deeply. Ultimately, our goal is to involve interested INTERACT participants in this process.

3 Position Statements

Michael Best asks: Does the Internet empower communities in central Ghana or the Mekong Delta of Vietnam? I look at the broad issues of whether the Internet is useful for economic or social development or whether it exacerbates political divisions.

Susan Dray will discuss experiences doing international user research in a number of so-called "developing" countries, sharing insights about how to capitalize on cross-cultural research teams, as well as how to modify research methods to better "fit" across cultures.

Lynne Dunckley will discuss her experiences in researching usability methods in different cultural contexts and her current involvement in the development of ICT applications in sub-Saharan Africa.

John Thomas (main contact: jcthomas@us.ibm.com) will serve as moderator and provide a perspective on the interaction of cultures based on patterns of learning from The Walking People, a transcribed oral history of a branch of the Iroquois. In the multi-millennia long migration as recounted in this work by Paula Underwood, the group continually meets and interacts with cultures vastly different from their own. During all this time, they not only deal with immediate survival but constantly strive to learn general patterns of learning.

Sharing Perspectives on Community-Centered Design and International Development

M. Best[1], A. Dearden[2], S. Dray[3], A. Light[2], J.C. Thomas[4], Celeste Buckhalter[1], Daniel Greenblatt[1], Shanks Krishnan[1], and Nithya Sambasivan[1]

[1] Georgia Institute of Technology
[2] Sheffield Hallam University
[3] Dray and Associates
[4] IBM T J Watson Research
mikeb@cc.gatech.edu, a.m.dearden@shu.ac.uk, susan.dray@dray.com,
annl@dcs.qmul.ac.uk, jcthomas@us.ibm.com

Abstract. Our work with communities in developing countries suggests that HCI practice is a long way from maturity in these contexts. With this SIG, we are seeking to build on a CHI2007 workshop that brought together 50 people to share experience and plan a more integrated approach to the challenges of supporting international development with ICT. We would like to engage a wider cross-section of the community in considering the demands of researching and delivering meaningful design for countries with very different needs from those in the Global North. Our focus will be on issues of development and participation and the impact of differing values in our work.

1 Introduction

INTERACT 2007 has taken as its theme Socially Responsible Interaction, with an emphasis on universal usability. This SIG, in working to raise awareness of the diversity and impact of cultural and economic conditions around the world, takes universality as its theme and looks at how improving access and participation depends on flexibility and customization in design methods and outcomes. It seeks to gather people interested in how the design of technology can serve communities at different stages of development and with differing value systems, rather than treating them merely as groups of new consumers, or overlooking this unit of social organization.

Researchers and designers will increasingly find themselves on projects that require cross-cultural work in countries labelled as 'developing', as global commercial interests look to open up new markets. However, it is possible to go beyond this interest in other cultures to adopt a more directly engaged approach. This is not to dismiss the importance to individuals of becoming consumers of the new technologies and systems that are currently only available to the industrialized North, especially in situations where access to technology has previously not been a priority or an affordable reality. But a more engaged approach prioritizes working in communities, producing culturally-specific, meaningful, needs-led design for the particular context.

We argue that taking a socially responsible view requires us to go beyond ensuring that technology is usable by everyone, to explore how technologies can emancipate

C. Baranauskas et al. (Eds.): INTERACT 2007, LNCS 4663, Part II, pp. 696–697, 2007.
© IFIP International Federation for Information Processing 2007

and to consider which technologies to prioritize – to community-centered design. This raises a critical question of who makes these decisions and whose values are reflected in implementation.

The organizers of this SIG ran a workshop on the theme of "User-Centered Design and International Development" at CHI 2007 and are now building on the enthusiasm of participants to go beyond discussing means of conducting and employing HCI research, to consider impact at a community level. We are excited to be collaborating with researchers and practitioners from around the world, including Benin, India, China, Malaysia, Sierra Leone and South Africa, and continuing the development of this network by facilitating this SIG.

2 Who Should Attend

This SIG is for two groups of attendees – those with some experience of working in this field who want to compare and share practice, and others with little or no experience, who are interested in learning more. We believe that the ensuing discussions will offer everyone a chance to benefit, by making space to contemplate what UCD means for communities, rather than developers and commercial interests. Since every country has its own developing cultures as well as vulnerable and excluded groups, the approaches we are exploring have something to feed back into mainstream design practice, though we see this primarily as a chance to move the particular challenges of international development onto the agenda. We do not anticipate that all the learning will take place within the SIG, but hope to use it to seed international interest and to channel it into a community of practice(s).

Note: The organisers of this SIG have liaised with those organising the SIG on "Embedding HCI in Developing Countries: localizing content, institutionalizing education and practice". The two SIGs share a common background. But this SIG focuses on development, participation and values. The other SIG focuses upon localization of methods, capacity building, education and institutional support.

3 Format of Discussions

After an introduction, we anticipate addressing several issues, with the underlying theme of what constitutes community and development informing our discussions:

1. Whose values should guide us and how are these reflected in our work?
2. What does participation mean in these contexts?
3. How can we learn together, rather than assume that knowledge flows one-way?
4. What should be the agenda to come?

The duration of a SIG will not allow for detailed sharing or debate; therefore, we see this as an important beginning to ongoing dialogue.

We hope to be able to summarize our findings and to integrate them with the findings from the CHI Workshop. In addition, we hope to be able to continue to expand the group of people interested in this area and to develop sustainable networks of linkages for collaboration and support that are truly worldwide.

Embedding HCI in Developing Countries: Localizing Content, Institutionalizing Education and Practice

Andy Smith[1], Anirudha Joshi[2], Zhengjie Liu[3], Liam Bannon[4],
Jan Gulliksen[5], and Cecilia Baranauskas[6]

[1] Thames Valley University United Kingdom
andy.smith@tvu.ac.uk
[2] Industrial Design Centre, IIT Bombay, Mumbai, India
anirudha@iitb.ac.in
[3] Sino-European Usability Center, Dalian Maritime University
liuzhj@dlmu.edu.cn
[4] Interaction Design Centre, University of Limerick, Ireland
liam.bannon@ul.ie
[5] Uppsala University, Sweden
jan.gulliksen@it.uu.se
[6] Institute of Computing, Unicamp, Brazil
cecilia@ic.unicamp.br

Abstract. This SIG will facilitate a debate concerning how best to support the development of indigenous HCI in developing countries, both as part of education and training systems and within industrial practice.

1 Background

There are signs of a new world economic and political order, where countries like Brazil, China, India and South Africa are emerging key players. There is also a developing awareness of their increased economic and political "muscle", especially as they begin to develop bilateral and multilateral agreements among themselves, increasing their strategic importance on the world stage. Some of these countries have rapidly developing IT industries supporting local (domestic) and / or global (off-shoring) software development. In contrast to previous approaches, some are beginning to appreciate that a human-centred design approach to the development and use of ICT is critical both to maximize trade in local and global markets, and also in the socially-responsible development of their individual information societies.

In this SIG we will seek to explore how indigenous approaches to the human-centred ICT should shape the socially-responsible development of information societies in developing countries. The human-centred approach that we refer to here is of key importance in major segments of the ICT industry, in software applications for business and industry, in consumer markets, and in areas of health and defence. Successful growth of the ICT sectors in these countries, focusing on both internal and external markets, will be dependent on paying increased attention to human, social and cultural factors.

The number of usability professionals is growing significantly in those developing countries that have a significant ICT industry. Through a wide range of engagements

C. Baranauskas et al. (Eds.): INTERACT 2007, LNCS 4663, Part II, pp. 698–699, 2007.
© IFIP International Federation for Information Processing 2007

with usability practitioners it is clear to the organisers that there is a considerable appetite to learn about Western HCI case studies in the expectation that these can be implemented locally. However there are two problems to overcome. Firstly a richer, more nuanced, understanding of HCI is necessary in order for the most effective tools or techniques to be successfully selected and implemented – this implies a much broader 'education in HCI' rather than just 'training in tools'. We need to be able to judge the appropriateness of particular tools for particular tasks, and this requires HCI education, not simply training in techniques. Secondly the cultural and organisational differences between countries mean that HCI tools and techniques that have been developed in Western countries may not be effective in developing countries. What is required is the localisation of methods to meet local requirements.

2 Aims

We seek to discuss the building of effective localised HCI in developing countries by addressing issues such as:

- The extent to which the discipline of HCI is changed in different countries;
    - does software offshoring skew the tools and techniques adopted?
    - is culture significant in changing processes and how do we identify these?
- How do we gain national / institutional support for HCI;
    - so that HCI can feature in university curricular?
    - and so that professional accreditation can be developed?
- How do we promote best practice in industry,
    - both for global (offshoring) and local (domestic) systems development?

Note: The organisers of this SIG have liaised with those organising another SIG (Sharing Perspectives on Community-Centered Design and International Development). Whilst the two SIGs share a common background, the SIG described here focuses on localization of methods, capacity building, education and institutional support. The other SIG focuses in development, participation and values.

3 Organisers

Andy Smith has project managed two EC funded projects (Indo European Systems Usability Partnership – IESUP – and Sino European Systems Usability Network – SESUN) supporting HCI and usability in India and China. Liam Bannon has acted as a partner in both the IESUP and SESUN projects and manages other research projects in global software development. Jan Gulliksen has acted as a partner in both IESUP and SESUN and is Chair of IFIP WG 13.2 Methodology for User Centred Systems Design. Anirudha Joshi is based at the Industrial Design Centre and Indian Institute for technology Bombay, India and has been involved in IESUP and many local Indian HCI projects. Zhengjie Liu is Head of the Sino European Usability Center in Dalian, China and is the Chinese partner is SESUN. Cecilia Baranauskas is Associate Professor at the Institute of Computing – Unicamp, Brazil.

Collaborative Behavior and Supporting Technologies

Jonathan Grudin[1] and Steven Poltrock[2]

[1] Microsoft Research, Redmond, Washington, USA
[2] Boeing Phantom Works, Seattle, Washington, USA
jgrudin@microsoft.com, steven.poltrock@boeing.com

Abstract: Collaboration technologies are emerging rapidly to support groups, organizations, and society. This half-day course includes lectures, video illustrations, and case studies that cover experiences, current possibilities, and future trends, focusing on areas of rapid change. How might organizations use weblogs? Why has digital video taken so long to take hold, and what is happening now? What is the promise and practice with workflow management?

Keywords: collaboration technology, CSCW, adoption, emerging technologies.

1 Collaboration Technologies

In this half-day tutorial we focus on behavioral aspects affecting successful technology adoption, focusing on emerging and rapidly evolving collaboration technologies. We survey the current state of research and application, and identify specific trends and general issues that are central to design and use. Most INTERACT participants are aware of Computer Supported Cooperative Work research and collaboration technology, but the area is growing rapidly, with fundamental contributions coming from many directions.

2 Design and Evaluation Challenges

Successfully overcoming technical hurdles does not guarantee success. We briefly review behavioral, social, and organizational phenomena that undermine technically impressive applications, and some methods to address the challenges.

3 Research and Application

Our survey is structured around collaboration activities, which in turn are structured by human organizational entities such as teams, projects, companies, and communities. In this tutorial we focus on collaboration requirements addressed by technologies to support teams or groups, organizations, and communities.

3.1 Supporting Groups

Support for small groups and teams became a major focus of research and development when local area networks became widespread. Research into group

C. Baranauskas et al. (Eds.): INTERACT 2007, LNCS 4663, Part II, pp. 700–701, 2007.
© IFIP International Federation for Information Processing 2007

behavior has identified a range of group modes, functions, and task types, each presenting opportunities and challenges for technology support.

3.2 Supporting Organizations

In organizations, asynchronous sharing of work objects and coordination (workflow management) are key issues. Building on progress in group support, significant advances in enterprise-wide technology use are appearing.

3.3 Supporting Communities

Social spaces and interaction technologies appear (and disappear) with remarkable rapidity and force. Even ephemeral use often serves purposes and provides lessons.

4 The Future of Digitally Mediated Interaction

Our conviction is that the pace of technology impact is picking up. New technologies have complex effects that can be liberating and constraining, and that facilitate intended and unintended sharing of information. We note the potential of these technologies, and decisions that we must make as individuals and as members of organizations and society as to how they will be used.

Further Reading

Poltrock, S.E., Grudin, J.: Videoconferencing: Recent experiences and reassessment. In: Proc. HICSS 2005, IEEE Digital Library, Los Alamitos (2005)

Grudin, J.: Enterprise knowledge management and emerging technologies. In: Proc. HICSS 2006, IEEE Digital Library, Los Alamitos (2006)

Efimova, L., Grudin, J.: Crossing boundaries: A case study of employee blogging. In: Proc. HICSS 2006, IEEE Digital Library, Los Alamitos (2007)

Poltrock, S.E.: unpublished manuscript. Workflow in knowledge work: The promises and the perils.

Designing Multi-device User Interfaces: How to Adapt to the Changing Device

Fabio Paternò

ISTI-CNR, Via Moruzi. 1,
56124 Pisa, Italy
Fabio.Paterno@isti.cnr.it

Abstract. Nowadays, everyday life is becoming a multi-platform environment where people are surrounded by different types of devices through which they can connect to networks in different ways. Most of them are mobile personal devices carried by users moving freely about different environments populated by various other devices. Such environments raise many issues for designers and developers, such as the possibility of obtaining user interfaces able to adapt to the interaction resources of the available devices. The main learning objective is to gain knowledge and skills in methods and tools for the design of multi-device interfaces that can support designers and developers to address a number of issues raised by ubiquitous computing.

Keywords: Multi-device interfaces, Model-based design, Ubiquitous Environments

1 Tutorial Content

The tutorial starts with an introduction to multi-device interfaces, their importance and the issues that they raise in order to address adaptation to the changing interaction resources. Particular attention is dedicated to explaining how the device choice has an influence on the possible tasks to accomplish and how the structure of such tasks can vary in terms of possible secondary tasks, tasks' temporal relations, and content requires depending on the device.

Next, the tutorial provides an overview concerning results that can be obtained through model-based approaches when multi-device interfaces, even using different modalities, are considered, and will link up the discussion to projects currently underway. Indeed, as Myers, Hudson, and Pausch [1] indicated, while discussing the future of user interface tools, the wide platform variability encourages a return to the study of some techniques for device-independent user interface specification, so that developers can describe the input and output needs of their applications, so that vendors can describe the input and output capabilities of their devices, and so that users can specify their preferences. Then, the system might choose appropriate interaction techniques taking all of these into account. The basic idea is that instead of having separate applications for each device that exchange only basic data, there is some abstract description and then an environment that is able to suggest a design for a specific device that adapts to its features and possible contexts of use. Thus, a key

C. Baranauskas et al. (Eds.): INTERACT 2007, LNCS 4663, Part II, pp. 702–703, 2007.

aspect is to be able to have different views on interactive systems, each view associated with a different abstraction level. With the support of tools, XML-based languages and transformations, it is possible to move from one level to another and convert a description for one interaction platform to another for a different one.

Then, the tutorial shows how these concepts can be incorporated in authoring environments for multi-device interfaces and discuss how to address a variety of platforms with different modalities (such as graphical and vocal interfaces, digital TV, tilt-based interaction, ...). Examples of such tools will be discussed, along with a demo of one of them (Multimodal TERESA [2]), which is publicly available and developed by the instructor's group.

The second unit of the tutorial is dedicated to run-time support for multi-device environments. Issues and solutions for automatic transformation from desktop interfaces to different platforms will be first discussed, showing how presentation, navigation and content can be transformed and the usability issues to address in this process. The tutorial provides examples of results that can be obtained by tools provided by main software companies such as Google, Nokia, Microsoft, Opera along with research results from various groups (including the instructor's group).

Then, the tutorial moves on to discuss how mobile users can be supported in multi-device environments. To this end, distributed and migratory interfaces are introduced. Migratory interfaces are interfaces that can transfer among different devices, and thus allow the users to continue their tasks. This definition highlights important concepts: task performance continuity, device adaptation and interface usability. The diversity in features of the devices involved in migration, such as different screen size, interaction capabilities, processing and power supply, can make a user interface developed for a desktop unsuitable for a PDA and vice versa. For example, an interface layout designed for a desktop platform does not fit in the smaller screen of a PDA, or a graphic interface running on a desktop system must be transformed to a voice interface when the application migrates to a car. Thus, an interface cannot migrate as is from one device to another (except in case of homogenous devices), and needs intelligent engines in order to adapt it to the different features of the target platform taking into account usability principles. Task performance continuity means that when migration occurs users do not have to restart the application on the new device, but they can continue their task from the same point where they left off, without having to re-enter the same data and go through the same long series of interactions to get to the presentation they were accessing on the previous device. Lastly, a research agenda for the field is introduced and discussed.

References

1. Myers, B., Hudson, S., Pausch, R.: Past, Present, Future of User Interface Tools. Transactions on Computer-Human Interaction, ACM 7(1), 3–28 (2000)
2. Mori, G., Paternò, F., Santoro, C.: CTTE: Support for Developing and Analysing Task Models for Interactive System Design. In: IEEE Transactions on Software Engineering, vol. 28(8), pp. 797–813. IEEE Press, Los Alamitos (2002)

HCI Themes for the Future: Collaborative Design, Social Creativity, and Meta-design

Gerhard Fischer

Center for Lifelong Learning and Design University of Colorado, Boulder
gerhard@colorado.edu

Abstract. The participants will be acquainted with HCI themes for the future. These themes will be instantiated with new conceptual frameworks and illustrated with innovative systems. The presentation will be linked as much as possible to the concerns and experiences of the participants. The objective of the tutorial is to provide the participants with opportunities to think differently about the future challenges facing HCI research and practice and to illustrate with concrete examples how these challenges can be addressed.

The tutorial will focus on three major themes: (1) *design*, specifically collaborative design and an assessment of different design methodologies (including: user-centered design, learner-centered design, and participatory design); (2) *social creativity* which is required because complex design problems transcend the unaided, individual human mind; and (3) *meta-design* which creates environments involving users as active contributors rather than as passive consumers.

The themes of the tutorial will be illustrated with specific theoretical frameworks and innovative systems developed by the presenter and his colleagues and other research groups working on these topics. The relevance of these themes has been demonstrated by their impact on research, education, and design practices in companies, educational institutions, and research organizations with which we have collaborated.

Summary of Contents

The tutorial will discuss in depth fundamental problems facing HCI in the future. It will present conceptual frameworks, innovative systems, examples of new practices, and assessment efforts instantiating this vision. Evidence will be provided that system development is difficult not because of the complexity of technical problems, but because of the social interaction between different stakeholders as they learn to create, develop, and express their ideas and visions. It will introduce meta-design as a framework to create open systems in which users can modify and evolve the systems to fit their specific needs that could not be anticipated by the system developers at design time.

The tutorial will be centered on the specific, but integrated themes of *"Collaborative Design, Social Creativity, and Meta-Design"* representing a coherent vision for the future of HCI based on extensive research by the presenter and his colleagues at the University of Colorado, Boulder as well as in collaborations with other researchers and research centers around the world. It will explore major aspects about:

C. Baranauskas et al. (Eds.): INTERACT 2007, LNCS 4663, Part II, pp. 704–705, 2007.
© IFIP International Federation for Information Processing 2007

1. *design* and *collaborative design* [Benkler, 2006; Simon, 1996]: (1) *the importance of domain knowledge in design:* domains are not natural, God-given entities, but they are part of the "sciences of the artificial" [Fischer, 1994]; and (2) *the critical importance of evolutionary models in design:* evolution is required by the fact that design often has to proceed without final goals and therefore has to cope with fluctuating and conflicting requirements. The *seeding, evolutionary growth, reseeding process model* will be presented which is able to cope with fluctuating and conflicting requirements.

2. *social creativity: transcending the unaided individual human mind:* the power of the unaided individual mind is highly overrated [Arias et al., 2000; Norman, 1993]. Although creative individuals are often thought of as working in isolation, much of our intelligence and creativity results from interaction and collaboration with other individuals [Shneiderman, 2002] [Csikszentmihalyi, 1996].

3. *meta-design: empowering users to act as informed participants:* meta-design [Fischer & Giaccardi, 2006; Fischer et al., 2004] characterizes objectives, techniques, and processes for creating new media and environments that allow the owners of problems to act as designers contributing and benefiting from the creativity of all participants.

References

1. Arias, E.G., Eden, H., Fischer, G., Gorman, A., Scharff, E.: Transcending the Individual Human Mind: Creating Shared Understanding through Collaborative Design. ACM Transactions on Computer Human-Interaction 7(1), 84–113 (2000)
2. Benkler, Y.: The Wealth of Networks: How Social Production Transforms Markets and Freedom. Yale University Press, New Haven (2006)
3. Csikszentmihalyi, M.: Creativity — Flow and the Psychology of Discovery and Invention. HarperCollins Publishers, New York (1996)
4. Fischer, G.: Domain-Oriented Design Environments. Automated Software Engineering 1(2), 177–203 (1994)
5. Fischer, G., Giaccardi, E.: Meta-Design: A Framework for the Future of End User Development. In: Lieberman, H., Paterno, F., Wulf, V. (eds.) End User Development: Empowering people to flexibly employ advanced information and communication technology, pp. 427–458. Kluwer Academic Publishers, Dordrecht, The Netherlands (2006)
6. Fischer, G., Giaccardi, E., Ye, Y., Sutcliffe, A.G., Mehandjiev, N.: Meta-Design: A Manifesto for End-User Development. Communication of the ACM 47(9), 33–37 (2004)
7. Norman, D.A.: Things That Make Us Smart. Addison-Wesley Publishing Company, Reading (1993)
8. Shneiderman, B.: Leonardo's Laptop — Human Needs and the New Computing Technologies. MIT Press, Cambridge (2002)
9. Simon, H.A.: The Sciences of the Artificial. The MIT Press, Cambridge (1996)

How to Combine Requirements and Interaction Design Through Usage Scenarios

Hermann Kaindl

Vienna University of Technology
Gußhausstr. 27-29, A-1040 Vienna, Austria
kaindl@ict.tuwien.ac.at

Abstract. When the requirements and the interaction design of a system are separated, they will most likely not fit together, and the resulting system will be less than optimal. Even if all the real needs are covered in the requirements and also implemented, errors may be induced by human-computer interaction through a bad interaction design and its resulting user interface. Such a system may even not be used at all. Alternatively, a great user interface of a system with features that are not required will not be very useful as well.

Therefore, we argue for combined requirements engineering and interaction design, primarily based on usage scenarios. However, scenario-based approaches vary especially with regard to their use, e.g., employing abstract use cases or integrating scenarios with functions and goals in a systematic design process. So, the key issue to be addressed is how to combine different approaches, e.g., in scenario-based development, so that the interaction design as well as the development of the user interface and of the software internally result in an overall useful and useable system. In particular, scenarios are very helpful for purposes of usability as well.

Keywords: Interaction design, usage scenarios, requirements engineering, user interfaces, usability.

1 Purpose

This tutorial is targeted towards people who are supposed to work on the interaction design or the requirements in systems development, e.g., interaction designers, user interface developers, Web designers, requirements engineers, or project managers. Whatever the roles of the tutorial participants actually are in their daily work, they should get a better understanding of "other" viewpoints and tasks and, in particular, a common approach. The overall purpose of this tutorial is to teach how requirements engineering and interaction design relate and how they can be usefully combined. This can be important for creating better interactive systems in the future.

2 Key Learning Outcomes

In this tutorial, participants learn about combined (concurrent and intertwined) requirements engineering and interaction design. In particular, participants understand

C. Baranauskas et al. (Eds.): INTERACT 2007, LNCS 4663, Part II, pp. 706–707, 2007.
© IFIP International Federation for Information Processing 2007

how scenarios and use cases can be utilized both for requirements engineering and interaction design, though with different emphasis on the level of detail. They also understand the additional need to specify the functional requirements for the system to be built, even in the context of object-oriented (OO) development. Overall, they gain a better understanding of early systems design.

3 CV of the Presenter

Hermann Kaindl joined the Institute of Computer Technology at the Vienna University of Technology in Vienna, Austria, in early 2003 as a full professor. Prior to moving to academia, he was a senior consultant with the division of program and systems engineering at Siemens AG Austria. There he has gained more than 24 years of industrial experience in software development and human-computer interaction. He has published four books and more than ninety papers in refereed journals, books and conference proceedings. He is a senior member of the IEEE and a member of the ACM and INCOSE, and he is on the executive board of the Austrian Society for Artificial Intelligence.

References

1. Kaindl, H.: A Practical Approach to Combining Requirements Definition and Object-Oriented Analysis. Annals of Software Engineering 3, 319–343 (1997)
2. Kaindl, H.: A Design Process Based on a Model Combining Scenarios with Goals and Functions. IEEE Transactions on Systems, Man, and Cybernetics (SMC) Part A 30, 537–551 (2000)
3. Kaindl, H.: Adoption of Requirements Engineering: Conditions for Success. In: Proceedings of the Fifth IEEE International Symposium on Requirements Engineering (RE'01), invited State-of the-Practice Talk, Toronto, Canada, August, pp. 156–163. IEEE, Los Alamitos (2001)
4. Kaindl, H.: Is Object-oriented Requirements Engineering of Interest? Requirements Engineering 10, 81–84 (2005)
5. Kaindl, H.: A Scenario-Based Approach for Requirements Engineering: Experience in a Telecommunication Software Development Project. Systems Engineering 8, 197–210 (2005)
6. Kaindl, H., Jezek, R.: From Usage Scenarios to User Interface Elements in a Few Steps. In: Proceedings of the Fourth International Conference on Computer-Aided Design of User Interfaces (CADUI'2002), Valenciennes, France, May, pp. 91–102. Kluwer Academic Publishers, Dordrecht, The Netherlands (2002)
7. Kaindl, H., Kramer, S., Kacsich, R.: A Case Study of Decomposing Functional Requirements. In: Proceedings of the Third International Conference on Requirements Engineering (ICRE '98), Colorado Springs, CO, April, pp. 156–163. IEEE, Los Alamitos (1998)
8. Kaindl, H., Kramer, S., Hailing, M.: An Interactive Guide Through a Defined Modelling Process. In: People and Computers XV, Joint Proceedings of HCI 2001 and IHM 2001, Lille, France, September, pp. 107–124. Springer, London, England (2001)

Introducing HCI into an Organization: Making a Convincing Case for Usability

Gitte Lindgaard

Carleton University
Ottawa, Ontario K1S 5B6
Canada
gitte_lindgaard@carleton.ca

1 Extended Abstract

The influence of a usability team in a particular organization and its products depends partly on the organizational structure and culture and partly on the skill set in the usability team itself. Once management decides to embrace usability, the integration of a usability team should therefore be considered very carefully in light of the existing organizational structure and culture [1,5] without, of course, neglecting consideration of the skills required to ensure the long-term benefits of usability to the organization's products.

Strategically, the three most typical usability funding models found in organizations are (a) the core corporate model, (b) a 'taxation' system, or (c) a project-by-project model. In the core corporate funding model, management has recognized the benefits and value of HCI, and the services of the usability team are freely available for project teams. In such cases, the success of the usability team of enhancing the organization's products depends partly on the degree to which usability is integrated into the organization's product development procedures and partly on the ability of the team to deliver useful and usable results in a timely fashion. To the extent that usability is already integrated into the development process and thus presumably accepted especially by development and marketing, the usability team can concentrate entirely on providing services as defined in the development process. If, however, usability is not already firmly integrated into the development process, tension is likely to exist between usability- and project teams. In that case, usability team members typically play the dual role of constantly advocating, or 'selling', the benefits of usability to each project in a piecemeal bottom-up manner as well as delivering actual usability services. These teams are often forced to identify opportunities for collecting data with which to demonstrate the value of usability. Teams funded corporately are the least vulnerable as long as organizational re-structure does not force them into either a 'taxation' model or a project-by-project model of funding.

In the 'taxation' system model the usability team is not funded corporately. Instead, each department pays a 'tax', a levy that contributes to the team's existence. To the extent that usability is well integrated into the organization's development process, this model can work well since the paying departments have already embraced and understood the necessity of including usability into their products. If, however, the usability team is not perceived to perform well, it risks being eliminated.

C. Baranauskas et al. (Eds.): INTERACT 2007, LNCS 4663, Part II, pp. 708–709, 2007.
© IFIP International Federation for Information Processing 2007

Likewise, if usability is not already integral to the development process, the usability team's situation resembles that of the core corporate model in the sense that much of its work becomes piecemeal attempts to convince the rest of the organization of the value of usability. The same is true for usability teams that receive no corporate funding or a tax levy; they are the most vulnerable of all in the sense that their existence depends entirely on the degree to which they are successful at convincing individual project leaders to pay for their services. Typically, such teams are able only to perform usability tests, at least in their early days. This bottom-up introduction of usability is typical for most organizations new to usability. The relative merits, risks, and disadvantages associated with each of these models are discussed in this tutorial, aiming to give participants an opportunity to identify the model that strategically might best fit their own organization.

Regardless of the funding model adopted, usability teams must deliver more than lists of raw usability problems: problems must be translated into solutions, and the solutions must be achievable in a time- and cost-effective manner. Depending on the organization's readiness to embrace usability, the usability practitioner may also need to shape their messages so as to demonstrate the value of usability to different departments. For example, for senior management the usability message is best translated into dollars saved or dollars made [2,3,4]; for the training department, time saved in developing and administering training courses is important; for customer services, a measure of improved ease of use will be convincing. Several tools and techniques are introduced aiming to assist usability teams to select suitable tasks capable of generating appropriate data for different audiences in their efforts to demonstrate the value and cost-effectiveness of usability [6,7]. Some of the techniques discussed are applicable at the requirements analysis stage; others in the design phase and some are tied to evaluation in the pre- or post-deployment phases [4]. Practical hands-on exercises will be provided throughout this tutorial.

References

1. Hofstede, G.: Culture's Consequences: International Differences in Work Related Values. Sage Publications, Beverley Hills (1980)
2. Humburg, J., Rosenbaum, S.: Corporate strategy and usability research: a new partnership. In: Proceedings CHI'97, pp. 115–116. ACM Press, New York (1997)
3. Lindgaard, G.: Deconstructing silos: The business value of usability in the 21st Century. In: Proceedings17th. IFIP (International Federation for Information Processing) World Computer Congress, Montreal, August 25-30, pp. 3–22 (2002)
4. Lindgaard, G.: Usability testing and system evaluation: A guide for designing useful computer systems. Chapman & Hall, London (1994)
5. Schein, E.H.: Organizational Culture and Leadership, 3rd edn. Jossey-Bass, San Francisco (2004)
6. Souza, R.: Get ROI from design. The Forrester Report (June 2001)
7. Ulwick, A.W.: Turn customer input into innovation. Harvard Business Review, 91–97 (2002)

Software Usability Metrics and Methods

Patricia A. Chalmers

Air Force Research Laboratory
U.S. Joint Forces Command
Patricia.Chalmers@jfcom.mil

Keywords: usability, metrics, usability metrics, methods, usability methods, stakeholders, usability stakeholders, return on investment, ROI, evaluation, usability evaluation, usability test, usability experiment, usability consultation, usability evaluation, tracking technology

1 Introduction

Potential customers usually want to know how they will benefit if they hire a usability professional, and they may want numbers to measure those benefits, or calculate a return on investment. However, many professionals become confused when customers ask them to measure the usability of a software application, software program, web site, or other software product. In order to clarify the process of measuring usability, this tutorial first offers a definition of software usability metrics, gives examples of usability metrics, and reviews reasons for usability metrics. Next, the tutorial steps through the process of deciding what metrics and methods to use as well as when, where, and how to use them.

2 Definition of Metrics

For the purpose of this tutorial, we define software usability metrics as measures, in numerical terms, to assess software usability impacts on customers, potential customers, and other stakeholders.

3 Examples of Metrics

Some examples of usability metrics include the following: 1) Percentage of sales increases after software improvements compared to before software improvements, 2) Number of minutes it takes users to find information in a data repository, 3) Scores on tests and reports on surveys following an on-line training program, 4) Number of errors, fatal errors, and/or successes in accomplishing tasks, 5) Cost of budget and schedule overruns as a result of having to recode unusable software.

4 Purpose of Using Metrics

Reasons for applying metrics to software usability include, but are not limited to, the following: 1) To assist stakeholders in understanding the need for software usability,

C. Baranauskas et al. (Eds.): INTERACT 2007, LNCS 4663, Part II, pp. 710–711, 2007.
© IFIP International Federation for Information Processing 2007

2) To calculate a return on investment for potential customers, 3) To easily visualize usability findings (for example, via graphs, pie charts, and bar charts), and 4) To convey to stakeholders the results of usability tests, consultations, and experiments.

5 Analysis to Determine Metrics, and Methods to Yield Metrics

When analyzing the situation for a usability project usability professionals determine "what," "when," "where," and "how" they will use metrics and the prerequisites to incorporate those metrics. That is, what will be measured, when will it be measured, where will it be measured, and how will it be measured. To determine the answers to these questions professionals involve all stakeholders to ensure the metrics will meet stakeholder needs and goals. For example, if stakeholders want decreased time to perform a task, the metrics should include time on task. If stakeholders want their end users to experience certain emotions, metrics need to measure those emotions. If stakeholders want end users to remember on-line training, you will need to measure user recall. When designing the methods to yield metrics, professionals discuss the tests, experiments, and consultations necessary to provide the metrics their stakeholders need. The tutor discusses the use of subjective and objective metrics, principles of good test and experimental design, the environment to gather metrics (lab experiment, field study, tracking technologies), and reviews basic indicators of usability.

6 Implementation of Method to Determine Metrics

When implementing a usability test, experiment, or consultation, attendees are encouraged to measure iteratively (formative, interim, and summative evaluations), to be consistent when interacting with study participants, to gain and maintain participant support, and to incorporate solid research ethics.

7 Evaluation of Metrics and Methods

In evaluating their metrics, the attendees are encouraged to ask themselves: 1) Were my metrics appropriate? 2) Do I need additional metrics? 3) Do I need a different test, experiment, or consultation design? 4) If this project is part of an empirical study, should I report my findings? 5) How should I report my findings?

Clearance. Clearance Number AFRL 07-0029. Distribution A: Approved for public release; distribution unlimited.

Understanding Users In Context: An In-Depth Introduction to Fieldwork for User Centered Design

Susan M. Dray and David A. Siegel

Dray & Associates, Inc., 2007 Kenwood Parkway, Minneapolis, Minnesota 55405 USA
{firstname.lastname}@dray.com

Abstract. There is increased awareness of the need for design to be driven by deep understanding of users, their activity patterns, processes, needs and external influences--understanding that can only be gained by studying user behavior in the user's context. This requires that practitioners know how to plan and carry out observational studies of users, which in turn is a new skill for many. In addition, fieldwork is bigger than any one methodology. Therefore, in this tutorial, we will take a fresh and deeper look at fundamental principles, teaches a range of techniques, and examines important issues on which methods differ.

Keywords: Fieldwork, ethnography, user research, naturalistic observation, contextual inquiry, artifact walkthough, naturalistic usability evaluation.

1 Introduction

Observational research differs from other ways of gathering user data and complements other user-centered design (UCD) methods. For instance, deep understanding of challenges in users' work patterns can help identify user requirements for new tools, or may spark entirely new product concepts. Information about the context of use that is gained from these studies can inform specific design decisions including mental models and affordances of new products. The usage context and dynamics of use can both contribute to building of robust scenarios both to design to and to test against.

Doing useful and valid field research depends on how you approach the inherent challenges of such research. Examples include dealing with the inherent ambiguity of qualitative data from field studies; risks of anecdotal evidence; balancing observation and inquiry; sampling bias; reducing the risks of premature closure, identifying and controlling (to the extent possible) reactive effects and demand characteristics.

Planning the field research is a critical first step in assuring its validity.

Establishing a focus is a crucial step in preparing for field research. A focus determines what will be salient for the researcher, and helps guide the researcher in prioritizing the many avenues that can be pursued during the data gathering in the field. Defining the focus is probably the most critical step in determining how you set up the study and whether you will actually bring back useful and relevant information.

C. Baranauskas et al. (Eds.): INTERACT 2007, LNCS 4663, Part II, pp. 712–713, 2007.
© IFIP International Federation for Information Processing 2007

2 Four Data Gathering Techniques

2.1 Naturalistic Observation

Naturalistic observation is best adapted to situations where the opportunity for real time interaction with users in the process of their work is limited. It can also be useful in early, exploratory phases of research. Because of the lack of real-time interaction with users, however, it presents challenges for making sense of your observations.

2.2 Contextual Inquiry

Contextual Inquiry, in contrast, depends upon interaction with users in real time. Unlike a conventional interview, contextual inquiry is very non-linear. Opportunities to probe deeply versus opportunities to broaden the exploration arise unpredictably. There are specific inquiry techniques help the researcher not only to elicit samples of behavior and explore contextual dependencies, but also to balance depth with breadth.

2.3 Artifact Walkthrough

The actual interview techniques of Artifact Walkthrough can resemble those of Contextual Inquiry. However, Artifact Walkthroughs apply these techniques in situations where it is difficult to observe the process of interest. For example, the process may be intermittent and difficult to capture in real time, or it might be inappropriate to interrupt it. Artifact Walkthroughs allow for exploration of these processes retrospectively but ground the information in concrete evidence of behavior. Therefore they do not rely on simple recall. They also provide openings into wider exploration of the user's process. As with actual behavioral observation, they often bring out aspects of the process that the researcher would not have thought to ask about and the user would have thought to mention

2.4 Naturalistic Usability Evaluation

Naturalistic usability evaluation encompasses a range of techniques for evaluating the user's interaction with technology in the user's natural context, based on the user's own goals and materials. They therefore focus on tasks that are meaningful to this user or that incorporate the user's own content more easily than laboratory evaluations. They also allow you to study both usability and utility conjointly and to explore both discovery and task performance.

Usability Design: A New Rational Unified Process Discipline

Magnus Lif[1] and Bengt Göransson[2]

[1] Guide Redina, Smedsgränd 9, SE-753 20, Uppsala, Sweden
[2] IT-Arkitekterna, Stora Torget 4, SE-753 20, Uppsala, Sweden
Magnus.Lif@guide.se, Bengt.Goransson@it-arkitekterna.se

Abstract. A new discipline, Usability Design, is introduced as an extension to Rational Unified Process (RUP). The aim is to make RUP more user-centred. The discipline springs out of best practices for user-centred design and contains activities that have been carefully tested. Five new roles are introduced to take responsibility for the different activities. An example is given to show the content of the workflow, the workflow details and the activities. The Usability Design discipline help projects to focus on usability and the users throughout the system development lifecycle. In the tutorial the participants will learn how to work with the new discipline within the RUP framework. It will contain practical examples and there will be room for discussions based on the participants own experience.

Use-Centered Systems Design, Usability, Systems Development, Software Engineering, Rational Unified Process

1 Background

The Rational Unified Process is a software engineering process [3] that significantly has contributed to the software development practice. Today, it is widely used and has contributed to creating a more unified view on software development. However, from a usability point of view the RUP has several drawbacks. Problems with the use of the process have been observed in several projects [2]. It does not provide the support needed to produce a usable system. In a study by Gulliksen, Göransson, Boivie, Blomkvist, Persson & Cajander [1] the outcome of a project was compared with a list of principles for user-centred design. It shows how a project using RUP with clear intentions to apply a UCD approach ran into several problems that made it difficult to pursue with that approach.

The conclusion from this is that the RUP and use cases as such are not ideal for user-centred design. But, to manage having an impact in practice we have decided to relate our development process to a the RUP based approach, since this is one of the most widely used processes in the large, in-house development organisations we typically work with.

2 The Usability Design Discipline

In this tutorial we will introduce a new discipline, Usability Design (for short: UD discipline), extending the RUP. Our aim with the UD discipline is to complement the

C. Baranauskas et al. (Eds.): INTERACT 2007, LNCS 4663, Part II, pp. 714–715, 2007.
© Springer-Verlag Berlin Heidelberg 2007

RUP to make it more suitable for systems development where usability is acknowledged to be important. The way to do this is to apply a more user-centred approach to the process. Most of the analysis, design and evaluation work is performed during the inception phase and the early phases of elaboration. During the construction and transition phases there is less work done in the UD discipline. It mainly includes monitoring and making ad hoc design decisions. The actual coding of the GUI is not part of the UD discipline. The proposed discipline is drawn from our previous research and published literature.

2.1 Roles

The new roles suggested in the UD discipline are:

- Usability Designer.
- Field Study Specialist.
- Interaction Designer.
- Graphic Designer.
- Usability Evaluation Specialist.

2.2 The Workflow

The workflow includes the user-centred activites performed in each iteration of the UD discipline.
The activities are:

- Usability design plan.
- Conduct user studies.
- Perform competitor analysis.
- Conceptual design.
- Interaction design.
- Detailed design.
- Develop user assistance.
- Monitor usability work.
- Usability evaluation.

References

[1] Gulliksen, J., Göransson, B., Boivie, I., Blomkvist, S., Persson, J., Cajander, Å.: Key Principles For User Centred Systems Design. In: Special Section Designing It For Healthy Work, In Behaviour & Information Technology, November–December 2003, vol. 22(6), pp. 397–409, Taylor & Francis (2003)
[2] Gulliksen, J., Göransson, B., Lif, M.: A User-Centered Approach To Object-Oriented User Interface Design. In: Van Harmelen, M. (ed.) Designing Interactive Systems: Object Modeling And User Interface Design, Addison-Wesley, Reading (2001)
[3] Kruchten, P.: The Rational Unified Process—An Introduction. Addison Wesley Longman Inc., Reading, Mass., Usa (1998)

A Comparison of Navigation Techniques Across Different Types of Off-Screen Navigation Tasks

Grant Partridge[1], Mahtab Nezhadasl[1], Pourang Irani[1], and Carl Gutwin[2]

[1] University of Manitoba
Computer Science
{umpartr3, umnezhad, irani}@cs.umanitoba.ca
[2] University of Saskatchewan
Computer Science
gutwin@cs.usask.ca

Abstract. In many systems such as PDAs, users access data through a limited viewport. This means that users have to frequently navigate to regions that are off-screen to view important content. Many techniques exist for moving to off-screen regions; However, none of these have been evaluated across a range of different types of off-screen tasks. In this video, we demonstrate the effectiveness of several major off-screen navigation techniques across a variety of tasks. We also include two newly developed techniques – WinHop and Multiscale Zoom – that were based on complementary features of existing systems. Our results suggest that integrating complementary properties from different approaches can significantly improve performance on a wide range of off-screen navigation tasks.

1 Introduction

In many ubiquitous environments, the *workspace* can be much larger than the user's *viewport*. To perform retrieval and inspection tasks in these systems, users spend a substantial amount of time and effort navigating to locations that are outside the viewing space [6], commonly referred to as *off-screen locations*. Researchers have developed a variety of different navigation techniques to improve the performance of working with large workspaces on small devices. These navigation techniques include scrolling, zooming or panning. Such techniques are very common and are heavily embedded in map browsers such as Google Maps™. However, the performance of these navigation techniques have been explored with only a limited range of tasks [3,4,5,6].

Evaluating the performance of different techniques on a limited range of tasks has successfully demonstrated the performance benefits of different navigation systems in particular situations. However such an approach does not provide much information about what would be the best technique in a real-world setting. Therefore very little is known about how different techniques perform across a wider range of tasks. This knowledge is crucially important for software designers, who must choose techniques that can adequately support a range of user activities, rather than just a few tasks.

C. Baranauskas et al. (Eds.): INTERACT 2007, LNCS 4663, Part II, pp. 716–721, 2007.

In this video, we present the results of a study that explores the effectiveness of different off-screen navigation techniques across a variety of common tasks within a particularly common environment – a map browser with specific landmarks as semantic icons.

2 Related Literature

A number of existing navigation techniques can be used to interact with off-screen content. These techniques can be organized into three groups: time-multiplexing, space-multiplexing, and proxy-based techniques.

Time-Multiplexing Navigation: Time-multiplexing techniques allow users to interact with different regions of the workspace at different times – as a result, different views of the workspace are available in a serial fashion. Scrolling, panning, and zooming are the three most common techniques in this group. However, each of these techniques are clearly deficient for performing certain common tasks. Scrolling requires considerable effort for most location tasks. Panning can work well for small shifts in view, but degrades with larger workspaces. Unlike scrolling or panning, zooming allows users to view off-screen content in a non-linear fashion; that is, distant objects can be inspected before those that are nearby). However, to find a particular off-screen object from a set of candidates, the user may have to perform multiple zoom operations [3,6].

Space-Multiplexing Navigation: Space-multiplexing techniques allow users to concurrently view different regions of the workspace. The main method of showing multiple regions is to divide the viewport into two or more windows; as a result, these techniques utilize more display space than time-multiplexing techniques. Common space-multiplexing techniques include overview+detail systems (which typically consist of an overview inset within a detailed view) [2], focus+context views [4], and portals [7].

Proxy-Based Techniques: The emergence of large screens has led to a class of techniques known as proxy-based navigation techniques that bring representations of distant objects closer to the user's interaction space [1]. These forms of interaction have shown significant savings in the time required to select distant objects in comparison to conventional techniques. However, since these systems are relatively new and have been designed for mostly large screens, very little is known about the effectiveness of such techniques.

While all three classes of techniques have been studied to some extent, the focus has been upon examination of performance concerning very specific user tasks, so little is known about how they perform on a wider range of tasks. Even less is known about performance of such techniques in small-screen environments.

3 Off-Screen Navigation Tasks

Numerous taxonomies could be constructed to categorize the wide variety tasks involving off-screen objects in 2D workspaces. One useful distinction involves a classification of tasks as either spatially relative, involving relationships between two or more objects, or spatially absolute, involving relationships between an object and the workspace.

Spatially Relative Tasks

Spatially relative tasks require people to determine and understand spatial relationships between objects in the workspace. The relationship between the objects and the workspace itself is not required to complete the task. Users were asked to complete the following spatially relative tasks:

Proximity between Objects. Participants were asked to find the four-star hotel that was closest to a metro station. The system randomly placed 3 metro-hotel pairs on the map. One pair was always clearly closer together than the others.

Proximity from Reference. Participants were asked to find the closest four-star hotel to the centre of the map. The system randomly placed three targets; one of these was clearly closer upon inspection.

Cluster. Participants were presented with a set of targets (e.g., a four * hotel, a four * restaurant, and a metro station), and were asked to find a cluster of exactly these targets. The system randomly placed three clusters, of which only one contained the correct targets.

Spatially Absolute Tasks

Unlike spatially relative tasks, spatially absolute tasks involve determining the relationship of an object to the workspace that contains the item. The participants were required to complete the following tasks:

Existence. Participants were asked to determine if there was a four-star hotel icon on the map. There was a 50% chance of the target being present.

Location. Lines were added to the map to divide it into a 3×3 grid. Participants were asked to determine which section of the map contained the four-star hotel.

Object Count. Participants were asked to count the number of four-star hotels on the map. The system randomly placed 2-6 targets for each trial.

4 Two New Off-Screen Navigation Techniques

In a preliminary study, we compared performance of three main techniques – Hop, Zoom and DragMag – across the various types of off-screen tasks. We found that for absolute tasks, Hop was best and Zoom was worst, and for relative tasks, the opposite ordering occurred. The limitations and strengths of the techniques for absolute and relative tasks provided guidelines for designing two new off-screen navigation techniques: WinHop and Multiscale Zoom. Both these techniques inherited elements from prior navigation systems to form a hybrid with a purpose of greater effectiveness upon a wider range of tasks.

WinHop

WinHop is an extension of Hop, and so shares that technique's basic characteristics. Like Hop, proxies are made by sweeping a laser beam and intersecting it with various halos representing off-screen objects. However, instead of directly teleporting the user to an off-screen region as is the case in Hop, WinHop introduces a space-multiplexing inset window to let users explore the distant region without actually leaving their current location. When the user taps a proxy, a secondary viewport 'grows' out of the proxy; this new window teleports to the off-screen location, but nothing changes in the main view. The user may pan and zoom in the portal: panning by dragging the cursor; and zooming by moving a slider at the side of the portal window (Figure 1).

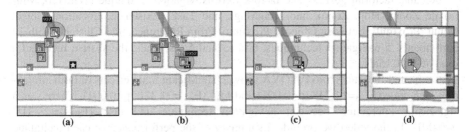

| (a) | (b) | (c) | (d) |

Fig. 1. The appearance of the WinHop window and translation from proxy to off-screen object. Clicking on a proxy (a), shifts the proxy to the center (b) and then opens a portal into the off-screen region around the object represented by the proxy (c & d).

Multiscale Zoom

The main problem with Zoom is that users cannot see sufficient details in the zoomed-out view. Multiscale Zoom addresses this problem by incorporating full-detail object representations that are fundamental to proxy techniques. The technique works by using different zoom functions for different elements in the workspace. In particular, object data has a greater endpoint, so that when the user zooms out to the overview, objects are not reduced in scale as much as the rest of the map. The end result is that objects remain above the threshold of visibility and readability

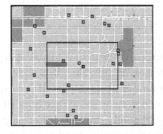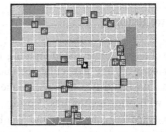

Fig. 2. Overview (zoomed-out view) with conventional Zoom (left), and with Multiscale Zoom (right). In multi-scale zoom the objects maintain their original size.

in the overview. Multiscale Zoom still preserves spatial relationships between targets (almost as well as regular Zoom), but also ensures that object details will be visible (Figure 2).

5 Results of the Study

We carried out an experiment to determine whether the two new hybrid techniques support a wider range of tasks. Twelve participants (8 male and 4 female) were involved. We compared WinHop and Multiscale Zoom to Zoom, Hop and DragMag. The study used the six tasks described earlier. The design consisted of a 5×6 within-participants factorial design. The factors were Navigation technique (WinHop, Multiscale Zoom, Hop, Zoom, and DragMag), and Task (Existence, Location, Object Count, Proximity Between Objects, Proximity From Reference, and Cluster). With 12 participants, 5 navigation techniques, 6 tasks and 5 test trials, the system recorded a total of 1800 trials.

A repeated-measures 5×6 ANOVA showed significant main effects of both *navigation technique* ($F_{5,55}$=14.738, p<0.001) and *task* ($F_{4,44}$=31.326, p<0.001). There was a significant interaction between navigation technique and task ($F_{20,220}$=23.315, p<0.001). In the video we provide a summary of the performance of each technique with respect to each of the tasks as shown in figure 3 below. Each circle represents the relative strength of a technique for a category of tasks.

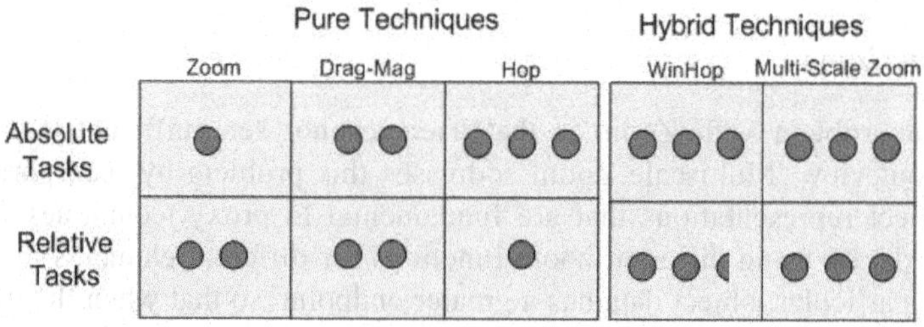

Fig. 3. The circles show the relative strength of each technique for the two different classes of tasks

6 Conclusion

Many techniques exist for navigating to off-screen content in a visual spatial workspace. However, any particular technique may not be suitable for a wide variety of tasks. We designed two new techniques based on our observations of how users performed with prior techniques. Results of our experiment show that both of the new techniques (Multiscale Zoom and WinHop) significantly improved user performance, particularly on tasks that are poorly supported by the primitive techniques. In practical terms, designers cannot expect to produce a technique that fits all different possible off-screen navigation tasks. Similarly, we cannot expect users to switch between techniques to execute different types of tasks. At best, we can produce new techniques that are effective on many common tasks and select the most appropriate for a given application.

References

1. Baudisch, P., Cutrell, E., Robbins, D., Czerwinski, M., Tandler, P., Bederson, B., Zierlinger, A.: Drag-and-pop and drag-and-pick: techniques for accessing remote screen content on touch- and pen-operated systems. In: Proc. Interact 2003, pp. 57–64 (2003)
2. Baudisch, P., Good, N., Bellotti, V., Schraedley, P.: Keeping things in context: a comparative evaluation of focus plus context screens, overviews, and zooming. In: Proc. CHI 2002, pp. 259–266 (2002)
3. Cockburn, A., Savage, J.: Comparing Speed-Dependent Automatic Zooming with Traditional Scroll, Pan and Zoom Methods. In: Proc. CHI 2003, pp. 87–102 (2003)
4. Gutwin, C., Fedak, C.: Interacting with big interfaces on small screens: a comparison of fisheye, zoom, and panning. In: Proc. Graphics Interface 2004, pp. 145–152 (2004)
5. Igarashi, T., Hinckley, K.: Speed-dependent automatic zooming for browsing large documents. In: Proc. UIST 2000, pp. 139–148 (2000)
6. Irani, P., Gutwin, C., Yang, X.: Improving selection of off-screen targets with hopping. In: Proc. CHI'06, pp. 299–308 (2006)
7. Ware, C., Lewis, M.: The DragMag image magnifier. In: Proc. CHI 1995, pp. 407–408 (1995)

Iztmo:
A New and Intuitive Way to Connect People

Danielle Gandarillas, Gil Guigon, and Ilana Paterman

Escola Superior de Desenho Industrial,
Universidade do Estado do Rio de Janeiro, Brazil
http://www.esdi.uerj.br

Abstract. Iztmo is a conceptual project of an electronic percussion instrument that works under a network environment to establish communication among multiple users. A new language is then created, based on rhythm, and enriched by each person's cultural background with the main purpose of being in harmony. Iztmo emits up to five sounds, divided in different ways of interaction: the user can strike it, rattle it, and scrape it. Some might play well, some might have no rhythm. But everybody will learn sharing this experience. A self-standing video was made to explain the concept and to demonstrate how the experience works.

Keywords: Interaction design - tangible media - conceptual design - digital device - communication - connection - music - experience.

1 Introduction

How to use new technologies to promote the exchange of cultural diversity, but preserving it, by making people from all over the world communicate through an intuitive, universal language? In one of the most instinctive ways of expression, we've come to an answer.

Iztmo is a device that promotes people with different backgrounds to become in harmony. Through the language of percussion rhythm, they can exchange their musical influences, teaching and learning, or even create codes to explore Iztmo's communication possibilities.

The process is simple: just turn your Iztmo on, and you are connected, by random, to up to five other users in the world. If the room you enter is too noisy, or too slow, you push a single button, and you'll be visiting other rooms which are being created in real time. These rooms, kindly called Izt-rooms, work like virtual drum circles, where everybody lets the rhythm run free, getting into a same pace.

2 Interaction

Like a percussion instrument, Iztmo is easy and intuitive to play. There are three actions you can do, in a total of five different sounds: striking (top, bottom, lateral), rattling and scraping.

C. Baranauskas et al. (Eds.): INTERACT 2007, LNCS 4663, Part II, pp. 722–725, 2007.

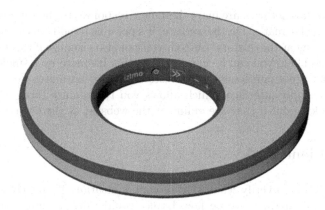

Fig. 1. Iztmo's device

Iztmo works along with a website, that enables functions not supported by the device: you can, for instance, configure the sounds of your device, and record and edit your musical experiences in a history of interactions. The decision to transfer additional features to a website, instead of increasing the device's functionality, is logic: we're dealing with an instrument, being necessary to give as much freedom as possible for the user. The device, then, has only the essential buttons to be connected and play.

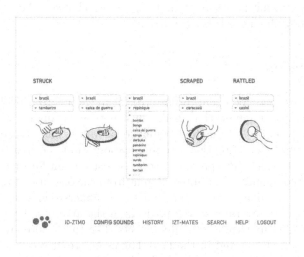

Fig. 2. Iztmo's website: the page to configure sounds

Since Iztmo introduces a new way to communicate, users need new identities. The ID-ztmo is a personal combination of sounds, i.e., a customized riff, that works as a name. You can be recognized in a room by playing your ID-ztmo; you can also be connected to a specific person by playing this person's ID-ztmo.

Users you interact with are more than mere responses to the sounds you make. They are your Izt-mates. On the website, it's possible to add a user you've played with, by looking at the 'history' button; you can also visualize if this user's device is turned on. Then, you can be connected to this Izt-mate by a single click, and continue that great jam session from yesterday. Your Izt-mates can be managed in an user-friendly interface, which allows you to organize them as you want, besides checking out if they are online at the website, at the device, or both.

3   Experience

It was necessary to verify what kind of communication, if any, could be established through rhythm. To see how Iztmo would work, several usability tests were made; since it's a conceptual product, we had to find a way to simulate Iztmo's conceptual aspects without counting with a real prototype.

Volunteers were called to sit in chairs organized in a circle. But there is a detail on that: they couldn't see each other, since the chairs were turned to the circle's exterior. In front of each volunteer, there was a table and, over it, a pot lid, a fork, and a matchbox. They were asked to use these objects to create sounds, as well as the own table, in the way they wanted, in one single rule: not to have any visual contact with the others.

The result was more than satisfactory; some of the volunteers could easily find a rhythm in common; some couldn't, but, after a while, they were all playing together, improvising new sounds and suggesting changes. And, what is more important: they all enjoyed the experience.

4   Conclusion

Iztmo does not exist. As a conceptual project, its goal is to provoke alternative ways to develop communication media in a networked digital world. Besides, conceptual approaches lead us to re-think social values and everyday habits.

A new language, with no visual communication, would be created with Iztmo. Feelings could be easily interpreted by sounds: a strong hit for rage, for example. It is a level of communication quite different from the ones used in digital media, for it does not need any representation to be understood (such as words or images). There are several research projects in the area of collaborative music, but they differ from Iztmo in many aspects, like in the presence of a visual language [1], [3], [4], [5] and in the fact that users are at a same real place [1], [2], [4]. The real presence of users is, again, a form of visual communication. Besides, Iztmo is a portable device.

This project was developed for Microsoft Research Design Expo 2004, which had the theme Connecting People to People, from friends to strangers. Connecting people with different cultures through a universal language, in a way to promote harmony between them, is Iztmo's premise. During the process, we have found out that some public events promote people's connection through music: drum circles, for example. Such manifestations reveal the human need of being part of public rituals, especially in big cities.

There are different levels of human needs that an interaction designer should be aware of. The more we realize which are these different levels, the better digital technologies will be applied to innovative, richer experiences.

References

1. Blaine, T., Perkis, T.: The Jam-O-Drum interactive music system: a study in interaction design. In: Proceedings of the conference on Designing interactive systems (DIS '00), ACM Press, New York (2000)
2. Oshima, C., Nishimoto, K., Suzuki, M.: Family ensemble: a collaborative musical edutainment system for children and parents. In: Proceedings of the 12th annual ACM international conference on Multimedia, New York, NY, USA (2004)
3. Gurevich, M.: JamSpace: designing a collaborative networked music space for novices. In: Proceedings of the 2006 conference on New interfaces for musical expression, Paris, France (2006)
4. Patten, J., Recht, B., Ishii, H.: Interaction techniques for musical performance with tabletop tangible interfaces. In: Proceedings of the 2006 ACM SIGCHI international conference on Advances in computer entertainment technology, Hollywood, California (2006)
5. Mueller, F.F., Agamanolis, S.: Pervasive gaming: Sports over a distance. Computers in Entertainment (CIE) 3(3) (2005)

Shortcuts:
A Visualization of Interactive Processes

Ilana Paterman

Escola Superior de Desenho Industrial,
Universidade do Estado do Rio de Janeiro, Brazil
http://www.esdi.uerj.br

Abstract. Shortcuts is a critical design contribution to suggest us to think about interactive processes, regarding immediateness and automation promoted by digital technologies. A video illustrates this theoretical approach, enabling the visualization of simple interactions of everyday life. The video shows several ordinary interactions, which are, little by little, graphically represented by their duration associated with body movement. The goal is to promote the awareness of physical interaction, duration and sensorial perception when creating new products and technologies.

Keywords: Interaction design, digital technologies, inteface design, tangibility, movement, subjectivity, visualization.

1   Introduction

If we wish to listen to music, we can use a small and delicate object that, plugged in our ears, allows us to have instantaneous access to thousands of different songs. If we wish to chat right now with a relative who is far away, we can take our mobile out of the pocket and, in a matter of seconds, this relative will take his phone out of his pocket too.

Physical interaction processes (what happens between wish and result) nearly vanish. The hurry is so that people get irritated if they have to make an extra click to complete a phone call. These processes don't get the chance of being pleasurable, because those who created them looked for their end, I mean, for results that could appear in the blink of an eye.

Such contemporary phenomena are being widely discussed lately, in books, movies, newspapers articles and even among internet users. Movements to criticize digital immediateness are getting attention but, unfortunately, these people are seen as luddites, or anti-technologic.

The goal of this critical design study [1], is to suggest an extra thinking about interactive processes. As metaphors of paths, these processes appear to us like choices. For a wish, we can take several different ways to achieve a result; some are long and demand time and attention; others are short, which we can call shortcuts. It takes more effort to cook in a traditional syle, instead of using a microwave; however, it is a much more engaging experience, and it becomes a pleasant moment of everyday life.

C. Baranauskas et al. (Eds.): INTERACT 2007, LNCS 4663, Part II, pp. 726–729, 2007.

2   Real Time, Real Space

In this video, four examples of ordinary interaction processes are chosen to illustrate this metaphor of shortcuts. A man selects a vinyl record to play; in the next scene, he is selecting an album in an iPod. A woman appears cooking next to a stove: then, this same woman puts some food in a microwave. A letter is waiting for its receiver in a mail box; the situation repeats, but in a digital context. Last, someone is looking for a picture in a drawer; this same person is, in the next scene, looking for a picure in a computer's folder. They appear in two different 'parallel realities', represented by two possible objects we can interact with: one understood as a long way, and another as a shortcut. Three of them are in communication media field, which are the focus of this study. Text, sound and image appear being accessed, each in two in different ways, by a same user; the scenes communicate a series of elements, intrinsic to the processes. These elements are both objective (duration, number of objects, dimensions and textures of objects, user's body movement) and subjective (joy, involvement, pleasure).

The presence of shortcuts pervades all moments in everyday life. When we have to accomplish trivial tasks, we tend to choose shorter and more practical ways to conclude them in the less time and effort possible. Besides situations with communication media, another example was added to the video: cooking. It is a pleasant process, one of the few that a lot of people agree that demand time and energy; we can interfere directly, reaching all mankind's five senses. It serves as a good example to suggest that values, such as duration, movement and sensorial perception, can be applied in other kinds of daily interaction. Especially those related to digital products, as they will soon face a time of deep changes.

In a near future, virtual information will be present in material objects and in real places. Interaction will, then, abandon a state of interface accessed through screens and buttons. The physical world will serve as support of information. Several technologies were already prepared for this reality, like the RFID (Radio Frequency Identity) and the NFT (Near Field Technology). Everyware, term created by Adam Greenfield, represents well what this new age of virtualiy means.

Hopefully, things won't have screens, nor keyboards. With the internet of things and places, we have to redesign the interactions with things and places. Therefore, the observation and analysis of everyday trivial movements, handles and gestures, with simple material objects, can give us hints to apply intuitive and spontaneous interactions to complex technologic demands.

Some progress has already been made in the direction of finding new human-computer interfaces. Current mobiles, PDAs and mp3-players are getting elements adapted to their contexts. However, they're still far behind the ideal. Studies areas, called, for example, tangible media at MIT Media Lab, and physical computing at the Interactive Telecommunications Program of NYU, have the goal of combining the world of objects to the world of information: physical interfaces are developed for digital data manipulation.

Fig. 1. The 'long way' interaction: duration, movement and sensorial perception are a strong part of the process

Fig. 2. The shortcut: simple actions for immediate results

3   Conclusion

The future of technology seems to be in the interaction with real things, and not in the immersion of a user in a virtual ambience, isolated, with no direct interference of the world around him. There are recent design projects that predict this tendency, for they consider users' experience in the real world – intuitive gestures for natural interfaces that don't need any explanatory manual to be used. Several articles in critical design are good examples [2], [3], to prove the importance and urgency of this subject. Besides, these works can guide research-through-design projects, serving as a basis to new paradigms in interaction design.

"A sensitively designed everyware will take careful note of the qualities our experiences derive from being situated in real space and time. The more we learn, the more we recognize that such cues are more than mere niceties – that they are, in fact, critical to the way we make sense of our interactions with one another." [4]

Real space and time: based on this statement, this video suggests that interactive processes can be visualized, by materializing traces of physical movement during the time these processes take. These traces become saturated in color as time goes by. In the end, all visualizations are put together: one image for the 'long ways', and another for the shortcuts. The last scene is a comparison of these two groups of traces, and reveals that we might miss something if we take shortcuts all the time.

Acknowledgments. I would like to thank the reviewers for their helpful comments and critics on this project, and suggestions of related academic work in the interaction design field. It has been my first try on presenting ideas outside the design school I've recently graduated. I also thank my supervisor, Prof. Silvia Steinberg, and my relatives and friends who worked as actors and composers for the video.

References

1. Dunne, A., Raby. F.: Design Noir: The Secret Life of Electronic Objects. Birkhser, Basel, Switzerland (2001)
2. Halln, L., Redstr, J.: Slow Technology Designing for Reflection, Personal and Ubiquitous Computing, vol. 5(3). ACM Press, New York (2001)
3. Hoven, E., van den Frens, J., Aliakseyeu, D., Martens, J.B., Overbeeke, K., Peters, P.: The expressive character of interaction: Design research & tangible interaction. In: Proceedings of the 1st international conference on Tangible and embedded interaction TEI, ACM Press, New York (2007)
4. Greenfield, A.: Everyware – the dawning age of ubiquitous computing. New Riders, Berkeley 74 (2005)

Author Index

Lecture Notes in Computer Science

Sublibrary 3: Information Systems and Application, incl. Internet/Web and HCI

For information about Vols. 1–4254
please contact your bookseller or Springer

Vol. 4505: G. Dong, X. Lin, W. Wang, Y. Yang, J.X. Yu (Eds.), Advances in Data and Web Management. XXII, 896 pages. 2007.

Vol. 4504: J. Huang, R. Kowalczyk, Z. Maamar, D. Martin, I. Müller, S. Stoutenburg, K.P. Sycara (Eds.), Service-Oriented Computing: Agents, Semantics, and Engineering. X, 175 pages. 2007.

Vol. 4500: N.A. Streitz, A. Kameas, I. Mavrommati (Eds.), The Disappearing Computer. XVIII, 304 pages. 2007.

Vol. 4495: J. Krogstie, A. Opdahl, G. Sindre (Eds.), Advanced Information Systems Engineering. XVI, 606 pages. 2007.

Vol. 4480: A. LaMarca, M. Langheinrich, K.N. Truong (Eds.), Pervasive Computing. XIII, 369 pages. 2007.

Vol. 4471: P. Cesar, K. Chorianopoulos, J.F. Jensen (Eds.), Interactive TV: A Shared Experience. XIII, 236 pages. 2007.

Vol. 4469: K.-c. Hui, Z. Pan, R.C.-k. Chung, C.C.L. Wang, X. Jin, S. Göbel, E.C.-L. Li (Eds.), Technologies for E-Learning and Digital Entertainment. XVIII, 974 pages. 2007.

Vol. 4443: R. Kotagiri, P.R. Krishna, M. Mohania, E. Nantajeewarawat (Eds.), Advances in Databases: Concepts, Systems and Applications. XXI, 1126 pages. 2007.

Vol. 4439: W. Abramowicz (Ed.), Business Information Systems. XV, 654 pages. 2007.

Vol. 4430: C.C. Yang, D. Zeng, M. Chau, K. Chang, Q. Yang, X. Cheng, J. Wang, F.-Y. Wang, H. Chen (Eds.), Intelligence and Security Informatics. XII, 330 pages. 2007.

Vol. 4425: G. Amati, C. Carpineto, G. Romano (Eds.), Advances in Information Retrieval. XIX, 759 pages. 2007.

Vol. 4412: F. Stajano, H.J. Kim, J.-S. Chae, S.-D. Kim (Eds.), Ubiquitous Convergence Technology. XI, 302 pages. 2007.

Vol. 4402: W. Shen, J. Luo, Z. Lin, J.-P.A. Barthès, Q. Hao (Eds.), Computer Supported Cooperative Work in Design III. XV, 763 pages. 2007.

Vol. 4398: S. Marchand-Maillet, E. Bruno, A. Nürnberger, M. Detyniecki (Eds.), Adaptive Multimedia Retrieval: User, Context, and Feedback. XI, 269 pages. 2007.

Vol. 4397: C. Stephanidis, M. Pieper (Eds.), Universal Access in Ambient Intelligence Environments. XV, 467 pages. 2007.

Vol. 4380: S. Spaccapietra, P. Atzeni, F. Fages, M.-S. Hacid, M. Kifer, J. Mylopoulos, B. Pernici, P. Shvaiko, J. Trujillo, I. Zaihrayeu (Eds.), Journal on Data Semantics VIII. XV, 219 pages. 2007.

Vol. 4365: C. Bussler, M. Castellanos, U. Dayal, S. Navathe (Eds.), Business Intelligence for the Real-Time Enterprises. IX, 157 pages. 2007.

Vol. 4353: T. Schwentick, D. Suciu (Eds.), Database Theory – ICDT 2007. XI, 419 pages. 2006.

Vol. 4352: T.-J. Cham, J. Cai, C. Dorai, D. Rajan, T.-S. Chua, L.-T. Chia (Eds.), Advances in Multimedia Modeling, Part II. XVIII, 743 pages. 2006.

Vol. 4351: T.-J. Cham, J. Cai, C. Dorai, D. Rajan, T.-S. Chua, L.-T. Chia (Eds.), Advances in Multimedia Modeling, Part I. XIX, 797 pages. 2006.

Vol. 4328: D. Penkler, M. Reitenspiess, F. Tam (Eds.), Service Availability. X, 289 pages. 2006.

Vol. 4321: P. Brusilovsky, A. Kobsa, W. Nejdl (Eds.), The Adaptive Web. XII, 763 pages. 2007.

Vol. 4317: S.K. Madria, K.T. Claypool, R. Kannan, P. Uppuluri, M.M. Gore (Eds.), Distributed Computing and Internet Technology. XIX, 466 pages. 2006.

Vol. 4312: S. Sugimoto, J. Hunter, A. Rauber, A. Morishima (Eds.), Digital Libraries: Achievements, Challenges and Opportunities. XVIII, 571 pages. 2006.

Vol. 4306: Y. Avrithis, Y. Kompatsiaris, S. Staab, N.E. O'Connor (Eds.), Semantic Multimedia. XII, 241 pages. 2006.

Vol. 4302: J. Domingo-Ferrer, L. Franconi (Eds.), Privacy in Statistical Databases. XI, 383 pages. 2006.

Vol. 4299: S. Renals, S. Bengio, J.G. Fiscus (Eds.), Machine Learning for Multimodal Interaction. XII, 470 pages. 2006.

Vol. 4295: J.D. Carswell, T. Tezuka (Eds.), Web and Wireless Geographical Information Systems. XI, 269 pages. 2006.

Vol. 4286: P.G. Spirakis, M. Mavronicolas, S.C. Kontogiannis (Eds.), Internet and Network Economics. XI, 401 pages. 2006.

Vol. 4282: Z. Pan, A. Cheok, M. Haller, R.W.H. Lau, H. Saito, R. Liang (Eds.), Advances in Artificial Reality and Tele-Existence. XXIII, 1347 pages. 2006.

Vol. 4278: R. Meersman, Z. Tari, P. Herrero (Eds.), On the Move to Meaningful Internet Systems 2006: OTM 2006 Workshops, Part II. XLV, 1004 pages. 2006.

Vol. 4277: R. Meersman, Z. Tari, P. Herrero (Eds.), On the Move to Meaningful Internet Systems 2006: OTM 2006 Workshops, Part I. XLV, 1009 pages. 2006.

Vol. 4276: R. Meersman, Z. Tari (Eds.), On the Move to Meaningful Internet Systems 2006: CoopIS, DOA, GADA, and ODBASE, Part II. XXXII, 752 pages. 2006.

Vol. 4275: R. Meersman, Z. Tari (Eds.), On the Move to Meaningful Internet Systems 2006: CoopIS, DOA, GADA, and ODBASE, Part I. XXXI, 1115 pages. 2006.

Vol. 4273: I. Cruz, S. Decker, D. Allemang, C. Preist, D. Schwabe, P. Mika, M. Uschold, L. Aroyo (Eds.), The Semantic Web - ISWC 2006. XXIV, 1001 pages. 2006.

Vol. 4270: H. Zha, Z. Pan, H. Thwaites, A.C. Addison, M. Forte (Eds.), Interactive Technologies and Sociotechnical Systems. XVI, 547 pages. 2006.

Vol. 4261: Y.-t. Zhuang, S.-Q. Yang, Y. Rui, Q. He (Eds.), Advances in Multimedia Information Processing - PCM 2006. XXII, 1040 pages. 2006.

Vol. 4256: L. Feng, G. Wang, C. Zeng, R. Huang (Eds.), Web Information Systems – WISE 2006 Workshops. XIV, 320 pages. 2006.

Vol. 4255: K. Aberer, Z. Peng, E.A. Rundensteiner, Y. Zhang, X. Li (Eds.), Web Information Systems – WISE 2006. XIV, 563 pages. 2006.